Counseling Strategies for Children and Families Impacted by Incarceration

Kenya Johns
Geneva College, USA

A volume in the Advances in Psychology, Mental Health, and Behavioral Studies (APMHBS) Book Series

IGI Global
PUBLISHER of TIMELY KNOWLEDGE

Published in the United States of America by
IGI Global
Medical Information Science Reference (an imprint of IGI Global)
701 E. Chocolate Avenue
Hershey PA, USA 17033
Tel: 717-533-8845
Fax: 717-533-8661
E-mail: cust@igi-global.com
Web site: http://www.igi-global.com

Library of Congress Cataloging-in-Publication Data

Names: Johns, Kenya, 1991- editor.
Title: Counseling strategies for children and families impacted by incarceration / Kenya Johns, editor.
Description: Hershey, PA : Information Science Reference, [2022] | Includes bibliographical references and index. | Summary: "This book focuses on providing in-depth information and background regarding the growing group of children and families impacted by incarceration, offering a resource and information regarding how to best understand and support those impacted by incarceration"-- Provided by publisher.
Identifiers: LCCN 2021045741 (print) | LCCN 2021045742 (ebook) | ISBN 9781799892090 (hardcover) | ISBN 9781799892106 (paperback) | ISBN 9781799892113 (ebook)
Subjects: LCSH: Children of prisoners--Counseling of--United States. | Children of prisoners--Education--United States. | Prisoners' families--Services for--United States. | School-to-prison pipeline--United States.
Classification: LCC HV8886.U5 C68 2022 (print) | LCC HV8886.U5 (ebook) | DDC 362.82/950973--dc23
LC record available at https://lccn.loc.gov/2021045741
LC ebook record available at https://lccn.loc.gov/2021045742

This book is published in the IGI Global book series Advances in Psychology, Mental Health, and Behavioral Studies (APMHBS) (ISSN: 2475-6660; eISSN: 2475-6679)

British Cataloguing in Publication Data
A Cataloguing in Publication record for this book is available from the British Library.

Advances in Psychology, Mental Health, and Behavioral Studies (APMHBS) Book Series

Harish C. Chandan
Argosy University, USA
Bryan Christiansen
Southern New Hampshire University, USA

ISSN:2475-6660
EISSN:2475-6679

Mission

The complexity of the human mind has puzzled researchers and physicians for centuries. While widely studied, the brain still remains largely misunderstood.

The **Advances in Psychology, Mental Health, and Behavioral Studies (APMHBS)** book series presents comprehensive research publications focusing on topics relating to the human psyche, cognition, psychiatric care, mental and developmental disorders, as well as human behavior and interaction. Featuring diverse and innovative research, publications within APMHBS are ideally designed for use by mental health professionals, academicians, researchers, and upper-level students.

Coverage

- Cognition
- Psychiatry
- Human Behavior
- Personality Disorders
- Counseling & Therapy
- Trauma & Stress
- Developmental Disorders
- Human Interaction
- Mental Health & Disorders
- Anxiety

IGI Global is currently accepting manuscripts for publication within this series. To submit a proposal for a volume in this series, please contact our Acquisition Editors at Acquisitions@igi-global.com or visit: http://www.igi-global.com/publish/.

The Advances in Psychology, Mental Health, and Behavioral Studies (APMHBS) Book Series (ISSN 2475-6660) is published by IGI Global, 701 E. Chocolate Avenue, Hershey, PA 17033-1240, USA, www.igi-global.com. This series is composed of titles available for purchase individually; each title is edited to be contextually exclusive from any other title within the series. For pricing and ordering information please visit http://www.igi-global.com/book-series/advances-psychology-mental-health-behavioral/110200. Postmaster: Send all address changes to above address.

Titles in this Series

For a list of additional titles in this series, please visit: www.igi-global.com/book-series

The Reproduction and Maintenance of Inequalities in Interpersonal Relationships
Tyler Ross Flockhart (Viterbo University, USA) Abigail Reiter (University of North Carolina, Pembroke, USA) and Matthew R. Hassett (University of North Carolina, Pembrke, USA)
Information Science Reference • © 2022 • 325pp • H/C (ISBN: 9781668441282) • US $215.00

Applying Mind Genomics to Social Sciences
Howard Moskowitz (Moskowitz Jacobs, Inc., USA) Arthur Kover (Fordham Business Schools, USA) and Petraq Papajorgji (European University of Tirana, Albania)
Information Science Reference • © 2022 • 281pp • H/C (ISBN: 9781799884095) • US $215.00

Developing, Delivering, and Sustaining School Counseling Practices Through a Culturally Affirming Lens
Sarah N. Brant-Rajahn (Messiah University, USA) Eva M. Gibson (Austin Peay State University, USA) and Mariama Cook Sandifer (Columbus State University, USA)
Information Science Reference • © 2022 • 383pp • H/C (ISBN: 9781799895145) • US $215.00

The Impact of the COVID-19 Pandemic on Child, Adolescent, and Adult Development
Nava R. Silton (Marymount Manhattan College, USA)
Information Science Reference • © 2022 • 262pp • H/C (ISBN: 9781668434840) • US $195.00

Stabilization Approaches in Mental Health Care
Peter Leslie King (Australian DBT Institute, Australia)
Medical Information Science Reference • © 2022 • 320pp • H/C (ISBN: 9781799882282) • US $360.00

Handbook of Research on Neurocognitive Development of Executive Functions and Implications for Intervention
Francisco Alcantud-Marín (University of Valencia, Spain) María Fernanda López-Ramón (University of Valencia, Spain) Esperanza Navarro-Pardo (University of Valencia, Spain) Veronica Moreno-Campos (University of Valencia, Spain) and Yurena Alonso-Esteban (University of Valencia, Spain)
Medical Information Science Reference • © 2022 • 494pp • H/C (ISBN: 9781799890751) • US $380.00

Mental Health and Wellness in Healthcare Workers Identifying Risks, Prevention, and Treatment
Clint A. Bowers (University of Central Florida, USA) Deborah C. Beidel (University of Central Florida, USA) Madeline R. Marks (University of Maryland, USA) Kristin Horan (University of Central Florida, USA) and Janis Cannon-Bowers (Cannon-Bowers Consulting, USA)
Medical Information Science Reference • © 2022 • 393pp • H/C (ISBN: 9781799888130) • US $325.00

IGI Global
PUBLISHER of TIMELY KNOWLEDGE

701 East Chocolate Avenue, Hershey, PA 17033, USA
Tel: 717-533-8845 x100 • Fax: 717-533-8661
E-Mail: cust@igi-global.com • www.igi-global.com

Table of Contents

Section 4
The Re-Entry Process

Detailed Table of Contents

By clearly identifying these variables, future intervention strategies can hopefully be developed to be more effective and efficient.

Externalizing behaviors and trauma-related symptoms were supported by Slocum et al. (2022) found that childhood experiences of physical and sexual abuse increased the likelihood of violence. The interconnectedness of ACEs and substance abuse is further supported by observations that physical victimization mediates the relationship between violence and substance abuse. These mediators (i.e., explanatory variables) provide reasonable, research-based explanations for the relationship between ACEs.

ACEs, Children, and Substance Use

As previously identified, substance use exposure concurrently affects those using the substance and the children exposed to the substance use and whose guardians have become incarcerated (*see Figure 1*). Unfortunately, the trend of children being exposed to substance use has not improved. Research indicates that throughout the 21st century, the number of children exposed to parental alcohol and drug abuse has continued to increase (Finkelhor, 2020). A study by Henry (2020) surveyed incarcerated adults who reported early experiences of familial incarceration and parental substance use as the most prevalent patterns of ACEs, with a sizable portion of individuals also meeting the criteria for alcohol or substance use disorders within the year prior to their incarceration.

A recent study evaluated the presence of ACEs and their impact on maladaptive behavior in children. Researchers found the odds of a preschooler being suspended or expelled increased by 80% for each increase in ACE exposure (Zeng et al., 2019). The top three ACEs that increase these odds are exposure to substance abuse, domestic violence, and mental illness. In a slightly older population, Craig et al. (2019) reported that within the context of youth who engage in moderate to high substance use, exposure to ACEs increases the probability of reoffending. As seen throughout the discussions in this chapter, there is a cyclical nature of ACEs exposure where both the offender and children of the offender are affected, particularly as it relates to substance use.

Criminogenic risk factors, both mediating and moderating, are keys to providing insight into understanding the long-term impacts of ACEs and substance use. Adolescent populations with a history of exposure to ACEs who report little to no substance use are significantly less likely to offend than those who report substance use, findings which remain consistent across race/ethnic and gender lines. Therefore, working with clients through an addiction model and substance use prevention focus could have not only provided holistic support to individuals and reduced ACEs but also lowered risks for incarceration.

GENDER DIFFERENCES, ACES, AND SUBSTANCE USE

A look at the country with the highest incarcerated population, the United States, reveals different trends for incarceration between genders. According to the US Bureau of Justice Statistics, in 2020, approximately 1.2 million residents in the US were incarcerated in state or federal prison facilities, serving sentences of 1-year or longer (Carson, 2021). Of these inmates, 83k was serving time in women's facilities. An additional 222k were serving less than 1-year terms in local prison populations (The Sentencing Project, 2020). From 2000 to 2019, the number of incarcerated women increased by 35%, whereas the number of incarcerated men decreased by 30%.

While percentages of incarcerated women continue to increase, prison infrastructure remains unchanged. For example, carceral spaces (i.e., structures of imprisonment) were originally created to accommodate male inmates, with an infrastructure favorable to the masculine ideal of power and authority (Anderson et al., 2019; Jewkes, 2021). Assessments and qualitative interviews with incarcerated women by Jewkes (2021) illustrated women's feelings of being controlled and disempowered by practices like their experiences prior to incarceration. Given the added layer that women enter the prison system with higher pre-incarceration trauma, physical and mental considerations, and stronger parental and household connections, the same incarceration model does not seem to fit. The ongoing experience of male-dominated intrusion in private areas, including showers and locked cells, left women feeling vulnerable. This system fosters oppressive and invasive reminders of unequal societal experiences for women.

According to the CDC (2021), ACEs affect all populations; however, different populations experience adversity to varying degrees. A comparative examination of ACEs categories of abuse (emotional, physical, or sexual); household challenges (violence against the maternal caregiver, substance abuse, mental illness, or imprisoned household member, or parental separation or divorce); and neglect (emotional or physical), revealed vast differences in adversity experienced before the age of 18 in men and women. For example, in terms of an overall number, women were more likely to report having four or more ACEs almost 50% more frequently than men (CDC, 2021). Women were also more likely to experience higher degrees of emotional and sexual abuse, whereas men were more likely to experience higher degrees of physical abuse (Felitti et al., 1998; Wolff et al., 2020). Physical abuse was the highest ACEs percentage reported by men, while substance abuse in the home was the highest ACEs percentage reported by women (CDC, 2021). It is important to remember that any adverse experience in childhood increases the propensity for problems across the lifespan. In this, gender does not sway the outcome. As the number of ACEs rises, men and women equally show an increased risk of depressed and anxious moods, hopelessness, relationship struggles, self-regulation difficulties, aggression, and substance use (Wolff et al., 2020).

Researchers have further explored the impact of ACEs on later substance use and incarceration of men and women and found significant correlations (Bowles et al., 2012; Guarino et al., 2012). The neuro-immune network hypothesis proposed by Nusslock and Miller (2016) posits that ACEs cause inflammation that dulls threat and response pathways in the brain, which can lead to harmful compensatory behaviors. This research uncovered that the most frequently used compensatory behavior in incarcerated women was substance use, particularly alcohol and opioid consumption, which is believed to be a practice of self-medicating to alleviate physical or emotional pain. Male inmates were more prone to rely on substance use for pleasure in social settings (Boppre & Boyer, 2019; Jones et al., 2020; Langan & Pelissier, 2001), leading to more frequent displays of public acts of aggression (Harer & Langan, 2001). Because women are more secretive about their substance use, it is often more difficult to uncover and therefore treat.

Cyclical patterns emerge in the research surrounding incarcerated female populations and the number of ACEs. Consider an example of this cycle: a young girl who lives with a single mom is exposed to emotional abuse in her home environment. Her mother started using prescription drugs as band-aids to the emotional pain. By the age of 18, the girl, in turn, is regularly binge drinking to numb the adversity encountered in her childhood, eventually graduating to misusing prescription opioids. This case study illustrates an all too familiar path for women who enter the prison system.

As demonstrated in the example, drug use and drug-related offenses are the leading contributing factors for women in the prison system. The repeating nature of substance use disorder often results in higher sentencing rates for women in the areas of trafficking as well as drug-related supporting offenses

Foreword

As I often do, I like to reflect on my experience as a long-time law enforcement professional and I can't help but to think about how much current cultural and social events have affected my rationalization of my overall impact and effectiveness. From my first assignment as a Security Policeman in the United States Air Force, to my duties as a patrol officer, and then to my appointment as chief of police, I fully committed my life and my purpose to exemplify what I believed to be the true meaning of "protect and serve". And so now, as a retired law enforcement officer who teaches Criminal Justice courses related to Mass Incarceration and Reentry Programs I, along with many other of my contemporaries, look back to the time when we were the willing and able foot soldiers of the so called "War on Drugs". Many of us ask, "What exactly did we gain by repeatedly locking up low level drug addicts whom often times needed mental health and drug treatment?"

As a nation, with highest incarceration rate of any other country in the entire world[1], I believe it has been way past time for us to seriously reevaluate how we define and how we dispense criminal justice; because as long as we continually deny that politics, racial bias and social status are an unfortunate aspect of our criminal justice system, our national legacy of being the "land of the free and home of the brave" will be forever tainted. This book aims to better understand and address the implications of incarceration.

Sincerely,

Charles "Mick" Jones
Chief of Police, United States Airforce, USA (retired)

ENDNOTE

1 Retrieved June 1, 2022. Equal Justice Initiative. https://eji.org/news/united-states-still-has-highest-incarceration-rate-world/

Preface

Early on in my career as a clinician it became evident that I would work closely with those that came from marginalized communities. Oftentimes these same clients were being incarcerated while in treatment. As my career evolved, I began to work more directly with those that were either incarcerated, had a family member incarcerated or was on the verge of being incarcerated. As a clinician, I often seek to be the most informed and up to date on the resources and realities that my clients and community was experiencing. Time after time I would look for resources regarding incarceration and to my dismay there would not be many. The few statistics and data would emerge but no real resources that help clinicians and those in the helping profession actually help. Thus, after writing on the topic of incarceration on several platforms, it became apparent that no resources would emerge and that we would have to create our own to better understand and be prepared to address incarceration.

Although incarceration is prevalent in the United States of America, the truth is that incarceration is a universal concern. All countries throughout the world are impacted by incarceration and there is a growing cost to incarceration. The cost is both societal and financial. As this book will cover, incarceration not only impacts those that are being incarcerated, but it also impacts their families, their communities and the overall fabric of all of our systems within society. With more than 10 million people being incarcerated around the world, the impact of incarceration can be felt in all communities, transcending all economic, geographic, religious, and racial subdivides.

There are several different types and definitions of incarceration, for this book, incarceration is referring to the confinement or imprisonment of an individual. As we delve further into this book, several types of incarceration will be discussed and described. In addition, this book will begin to cover the various areas in which incarceration affects our systems, thus the textbook will look at incarceration from various systemic perspectives.

This textbook is aimed at a wide range of individuals because incarceration has rippling impacts. *Counseling Strategies for Children and Families Impacted by Incarceration* focuses on providing in-depth information and background regarding the growing group of children and families impacted by incarceration. There is a lack of resources and information regarding how to best understand and support those impacted by incarceration. This book aims to help all groups: counselors, social workers, educators, community advocates, public figures, and social justice advocates. As the number of people impacted by incarceration increases, it is important that we acknowledge the issues and address the concerns faced by these professionals and the helping professionals. Incarceration impact on youth, impact on families, societal impacts on incarceration, social justice focuses on incarceration, school counseling resources, social work implications, counseling implication, community engagement, resiliency, trauma, testimonials, justice system implications. There is a lack of resources and publications regarding the effects on incarceration, this publication is important because of the positive impact it will have on the professionals that work with families impacted by incarceration and the most vulnerable populations impacted by incarceration. This will help provide support and further understanding. This is a pivotal time to create a book like this as the need for resources increase and the lack of them are currently present.

OVERVIEW

Counseling Strategies for Children and Families Impacted by Incarceration consists of 15 chapters that are separated into four distinct sections. Section 1 is the History of Incarceration, and the chapters can be described as:

Chapter 1, "Understanding the Intersection of Adverse Childhood Experiences and Incarceration: Background, Research, and Recommendations," focuses on providing a basic understanding of how Adverse Childhood Experiences (ACEs) impact the risk of being incarcerated within their lifetime. Research has shown that there is a correlation between the presence of ACEs and the rate of incarceration and recidivism. This chapter provides context and resources for professionals working with the re-entry population to better support them and reduce recidivism or reincarceration.

Chapter 2, "The History of Incarceration of African Americans/Blacks in the United States," is an overview of the history of incarceration within the African American/Black community. This chapter provides a foundational understanding on the complex relationship between incarceration and the most incarcerated group of individuals in the world, African Americans/Blacks. This chapter is an overview of how this group has been impacted and ways to decrease the mass incarceration of this group.

Chapter 3, "The Role Addiction Plays in America: What Focusing on the Wrong Issues Has Done," provides a basic introduction to addiction. This chapter serves as understanding the intersection of addiction and incarceration. This chapter focuses on understanding the implications addictions has on all populations including both children and adults.

Chapter 4, "Substance Abuse and Its Intersecting Factors: Treatment While Incarcerated," focuses primarily on the impacts treatment while incarceration can provide someone living with a substance use disorder. This chapter will provide the reader the opportunity to develop a glimpse of the treatment opportunities for those impacted by incarceration. Also, this chapter provides a further analysis of the implications that not having treatment has on recovery and the risk of reincarceration.

Section 2 of the textbook focuses on the effects of incarceration on the relationship between the parent and child. The chapters in this section can be described as:

Chapter 5, "Understanding Parental Incarceration and Its Effects on Children's Mental Health," focuses primarily on the connection and disruption the incarceration has on the mental and physical health of children impacted by incarceration. This chapter begins the section on the implications of incarceration on children.

Chapter 6, "Supporting the Parent-Child Bond," focuses on addressing the effects that incarceration has on the parent-child bond. This chapter will address the barriers present while a parent is incarcerated and provides strategies to best support families impacted by incarceration. This chapter is aimed at general solutions and options for all personnel that works with people impacted by incarceration that have children.

Chapter 7, "Foster Care Youth With an Incarcerated Parent," focuses on addressing the under researched area of foster children that are placed in foster care due to their primary guardian being incarcerated. There is a growing gap of youth being permanently displaced from biological parents and biological family members that impact the child's social, emotional and physical well-being. This chapter is focused on addressing the data on this dynamic while also providing supports and resources for social service agencies.

Section 3 of this textbook focuses on developing strategies of support while an individual or family member is incarcerated. The chapters are described as:

Chapter 8, "Counseling Strategies to Disrupt the School-Prison Nexus," focuses specifically on providing insight for professionals to understand the role that they may play in incarceration. This chapter provides insight into the challenges that providers face and supports providers with resources to be support students and reduce incarceration and recidivism. This chapter provides opportunities for provides to develop better strategies for mitigating the systemic barriers to support and incarceration.

Chapter 9, "School Supports for Students Impacted by Incarceration," is geared towards schools and school personnel to develop techniques and skills to directly support students that have been impacted by incarceration. This chapter is designed as a model for schools and school counselors to become aware of the stressors and implications that students are experiencing within the school.

Chapter 10, "Change the School-to-Prison Pipeline to Success Through School Counseling: Prevent Students' Incarceration and Support Students With Incarcerated Family Member," aims to provide support on how to decrease the rate of incarceration for youth. This chapter will provide support for school counselors, school professionals and professionals that work with students in a variety of school settings. This chapter addresses the growing rate of juvenile incarceration and the trauma associated with experiencing incarceration either directly or indirectly. Finally, this chapter provides concrete ways on how to develop advocacy strategies and provide support for professionals, school systems, social service agencies, juvenile detention centers and students.

Chapter 11, "Mitigating Juvenile Incarceration in Nigeria Through the Lens of Counseling," takes a wider view to better understand and support mitigation efforts in Nigeria. This chapter provides its reader the opportunity to better understand incarceration from the current pursuits for Nigerians.

Chapter 12, "Trauma-Engaged and Culturally Responsive Schools: Changing the School-to-Prison Pipeline," addresses the growing need for trauma informed treatment with juveniles and adolescents. This chapter directly describes the benefits of utilizing a trauma-engaged and culturally responsive approach to help minimize the growing school-to-prison pipeline with adolescents. Using these evidence-based approaches and resources provides support and techniques to best support and engage with juveniles.

The fourth and final section of the book focuses on the barriers and supports after a person is released from incarceration. The chapters are described as:

Chapter 13, "Parental Incarceration and Family Reunification," provides an in-depth analysis of the family dynamics during incarceration. This chapter examines the parallel processes that the family and the individual experiencing incarceration are working on. This chapter is an in-depth analysis that practitioners in the field can use to learn about resources, develop skills and provide support for their clients and their families during the reunification process.

Chapter 14, "Returning Home: The Re-Entry Process," is the conclusion of the book. This chapter focuses on addressing the realities of those that are in the re-entry process from incarceration. Although everyone has a different re-entry process, there are commonalities that emerge from the data. This chapter begins the process of addressing the needs of re-entry and the impact that it has on the incarcerated individual and their relationships with their families. This chapter focuses on the difficulties of reentry and provides strategies to best support individuals on their journey.

Chapter 15, "Collateral Consequences: Incarceration, Communities, and Reintegration," completes the book by addressing the concerns and community supports after being released from incarceration. The primary purpose of this chapter is to provide a beginning understanding and analysis of the resources available to those impacted by incarceration. Finally, this chapter aims at discussing ways to decrease recidivism.

In conclusion, *Counseling Strategies for Children and Families Impacted by Incarceration* provides a much-needed resource when working with those impacted by incarceration. There was a lack of available resources for counselors, social workers and those in the social services field that adequately identify and provide support to help enhance their skills and knowledge based. This book provides those in the profession an introductory to the complexities of incarceration. If we are committed to changing and doing better, we must equip those on the front lines with the best tools and support to adequately do their part and if not now, when?

Kenya Johns
Geneva College, USA

Acknowledgment

I would like to take the time to acknowledge that this work has truly been a labor of love and commitment that not even a global pandemic could stop. I first want to thank God for the opportunity to get this much needed work to those that work alongside those impacted by incarceration. This work would not be where it is without the support and commitment to this work without my amazing husband, Ian Johns, and my daughters, Milan & Makena, I appreciate you, I love you and I thank you because every day you make me better and grateful to do this thing called life with you. I would like to thank my mentor and friend, Dr. Natasha Barnes for her commitment to good quality work. I would like to thank all of the authors and contributors to this work, your work is going to help change the world and for that, I thank you.

I would like to acknowledge my mother, Debra Coleman, the person that instilled in me that our circumstances do not determine our worth, because of you, I will continue to always fight for those that deserve to be heard even when no one else wants to listen. To my siblings and family, thank you for always being my models and motivation to make sure that all stories and all people are represented.

Finally, I want to acknowledge all of those that have been impacted by incarceration. Incarceration hurts all of us. To all of you, your experiences, your thoughts, your beliefs and your potential are seen and is the motivation behind this work. May this textbook begin to change those experiences that you had and move us closer to justice and best practices for incarceration and a better quality of life that is truly equitable.

Editorial Advisory Board

Section 1

Understanding the Role of Incarceration

Chapter 1
Understanding the Intersection of Adverse Childhood Experiences and Incarceration:
Background, Research, and Recommendations

Tabitha Buchanan Schlatter
https://orcid.org/0000-0003-0617-8179
Tennessee Tech University, USA

Christina D. Dukes
Tennessee Tech University, USA

Stephanie P. Karlosky
https://orcid.org/0000-0002-6017-063X
Tennessee Tech University, USA

Tony Michael
Tennessee Tech University, USA

Katherine Hermann Turner
Tennessee Tech University, USA

Corrin N. Brown
Tennessee Tech University, USA

ABSTRACT

Extensive research has examined the role and effects of adverse childhood experiences (ACEs) throughout the lifespan. High associations are evident between ACEs and incarceration, as incarceration in the household affects children, and incarcerated individuals frequently have a high number of ACEs. Variables such as substance use, physical and mental health, gender differences, and risk factors for reoffending also have indicated a connection with ACEs and incarceration. While research findings have highlighted ACEs influence on health and wellness, current studies are beginning to examine the variables of resiliency, protective factors, and intervention strategies and their role in mitigating ACEs. The purpose of this chapter is to examine ACEs, the subsequent connections to incarceration and substance use, and the mitigating effects of resiliency and positive childhood experiences with incarcerations and families.

DOI: 10.4018/978-1-7998-9209-0.ch001

INTRODUCTION

The following chapter provides a focused review of Adverse Childhood Experiences (ACEs) related to the topic of incarceration. In the first half of the chapter, the authors take the perspective that relationships exist between ACEs and multiple other variables, including incarceration, risks associated with reoffending, physical and mental health, and school-related academic and behavioral problems. Special attention is given to substance use and gender differences, and the nature of their connection to ACEs.

The second half of the chapter reports on a collection of protective factors and targeted approaches for building resilience in youth. The ability of Positive Childhood Experiences (PCEs) to compensate for the negative effects of ACEs on health, including adult mental health, is explored. The thrust of this portion of the chapter is about approaches and strategies for strengthening resilience and protective factors in order to lessen the odds of incarceration for those who have exposure to multiple ACEs. Several clinical interventions and detailed school-based, trauma-sensitive interventions are examined along with a compelling case for school-based trauma-informed care.

The chapter aims to meet the following objectives:

1. To report specific relationships between ACEs and incarceration consistently documented in the substantive body of ACEs research.
2. To report the findings of other related constructs (substance use, physical and mental health, gender differences, risk factors for reoffending) that also share a connection with ACEs and incarceration.
3. To present a collection of determinants of resiliency, protective factors, and intervention strategies for use with families impacted by incarceration.

BACKGROUND

What Are ACEs?

The term ACEs originated from research by the Center for Disease Control (CDC) and Kaiser Permanente published in 1998 (Graf et al., 2021). Their findings were the result of two large-scale data collection waves from 1995 to 1997, with an ongoing longitudinal study of data collection targeting various health factors of the original participants. Analysis of the CDC Kaiser-Permanente study uncovered the socio-behavioral factors centered on three key categories of adversity that affected children: abuse (psychological, physical, and sexual), neglect (emotional and physical), and household dysfunction (substance abuse, parental separation/divorce, mental illness, maternal abuse, and criminal behavior). Since this original publication, researchers have continued to evaluate the phenomena and better understand how these early adverse experiences impact health and well-being in later life (CDC, 2021).

Researchers have found the influence on an individual varies depending on the extent and prevalence of ACEs exposure (Liu et al., 2021). For example, increased exposure to ACEs is connected to mental duress, smoking, and sleep disturbances (Zarse et al., 2019).

Why Are ACEs Important?

To understand the importance of ACEs, one must consider the sensitivity of a child as they develop biologically, psychologically, and socially from early childhood through adolescence. One area of increased understanding is the human brain, which develops significantly throughout childhood and adolescence. The presence of ACEs increases neurological vulnerability to significant, life-long impacts, including addiction (Zarse et al., 2019; Dube et al., 2002; 2003). Researchers have supported this notion by identifying significant links between exposure to ACEs and the development of neurological circuits which influence one's emotions, behaviors, and attention (e.g., Hambrick et al., 2019). These impacts related to increased ACEs exposure may have life-long repercussions on one's development.

The volume of studies linking ACEs to a range of nocuous physical and mental health outcomes has been substantial. Researchers have connected early experiences of household dysfunction (i.e., drug use, domestic violence) to increased risk for all subtypes of childhood maltreatment (i.e., neglect, physical abuse; Clemens et al., 2019). The most prevalent experience of childhood maltreatment reported was verbal abuse, followed by physical abuse, emotional neglect, sexual abuse, and physical neglect. In other noteworthy research, the relationships between childhood adversity, substance use, compromised physical and mental health, and incarceration are highlighted (Eaves et al., 2020; Fleming et al., 2020; Giano et al., 2021; Gjelsvik et al., 2014; Graf et al., 2021; Tang et al., 2021).

What Is the Relationship Between ACEs and Incarceration?

Since the majority of contacts with the justice system and incarcerations begin with committing a crime, one must consider the relationship between ACEs and criminal behavior. Researchers who specialize in crime, criminologists, have sought to understand the concept of age-crime curves. These curves are based on observations that criminogenic behavior peaks in adolescence and wanes as individuals advance in age (Shulman et al., 2013). While the observations have been debated, most of the identified criminogenic risk factors have received general acceptance by researchers.

Studies on the age-crime curves continue to find that exposure to criminogenic risk factors begins in early childhood and peaks in late adolescence. Greater exposure to ACEs has varying degrees of impact on the presence of specific criminogenic risk factors. Two of these factors, enhanced by the presence of ACEs, include psychosis and antisocial behavior, both of which have been found to precipitate engagement in aggressive behaviors (Schilling et al., 2007). Antisocial behavior refers to a pattern of socially irresponsible, exploitative, and guiltless behavior that sharply deviates from social norms (Black, 2015; Costa et al., 2020). As it is commonly known, such behaviors and patterns are descriptive of criminal behavior and consistent with justice system involvement, including incarceration. In a study by Felitti et al. (1998), conditions such as drug abuse, spousal violence, and criminal activity in the household may co-occur with specific forms of abuse that involve children. Also, children's exposure to incarcerated caregivers is an identified adverse experience with evidence of long-term mental health impacts. Childhood exposure to parental incarceration is linked to poor health-related quality of life (i.e., poor physical and mental health outcomes) as compared to individuals who did not have this experience (Gjelsvik et al., 2014).

Throughout the authors' research, a pattern became apparent (*see Image 1);* because children reside in households where there is dysfunction, also referred to as exposure to ACEs, there are greater odds that those children will experience maltreatment. This type of pattern between the factors suggests a chicken-egg connection or a perpetuating cyclic relationship between the factors.

Figure 1. The cycle of ACEs, substance use, incarceration, and ACEs

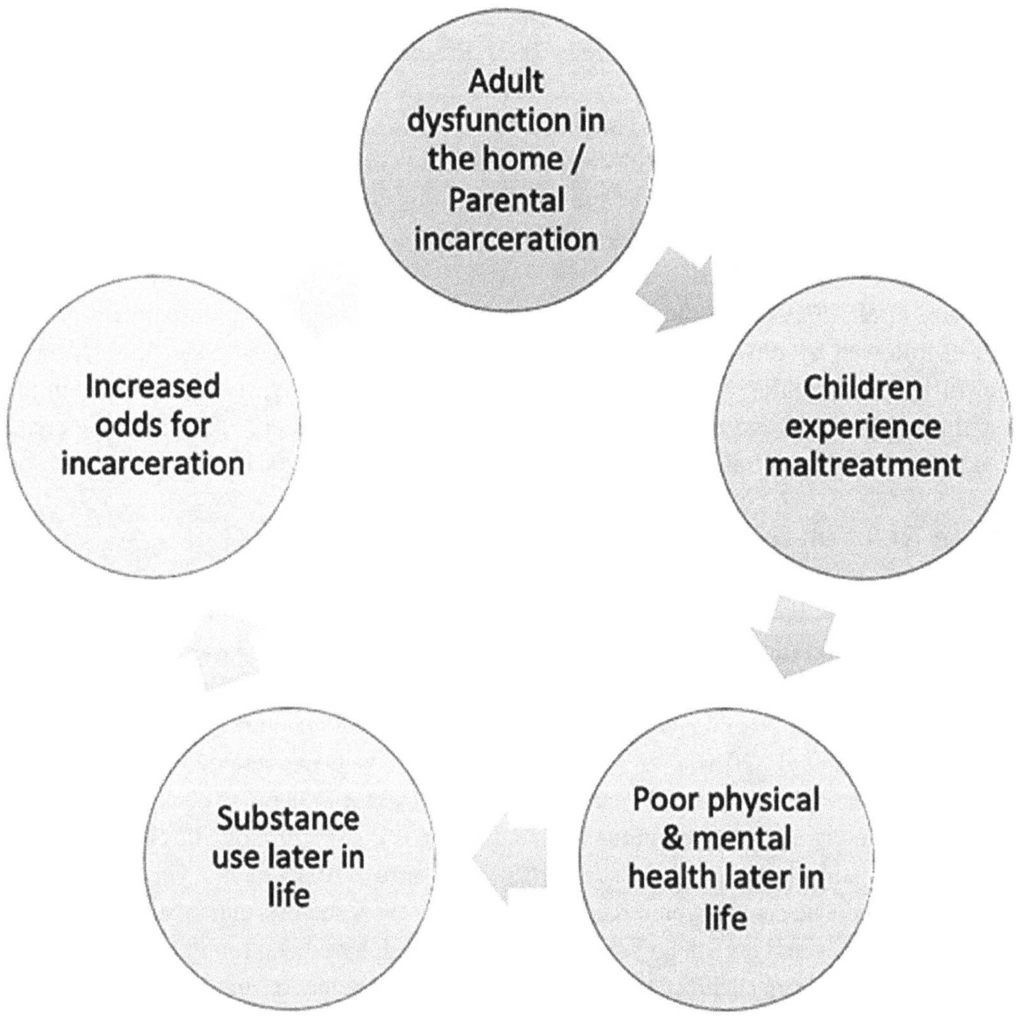

MAIN FOCUS OF THE CHAPTER

The primary focus of the chapter is to examine trends and correlations between ACEs and incarceration as well as several other related factors. This will be accomplished through the exploration of empirical literature published on the topic.

ACES AND INCARCERATION

Incarcerated populations have decreased steadily since 2008; however, 2019 brought a dramatic shift in incarcerated populations. Between 2019 and 2020, the US prison population decreased nationwide in all jurisdictions apart from Alaska. Incidences of violent and property crimes declined, and legislation was signed to shorten sentences resulting in lower arrest rates and higher release rates. As a result, the incarcerated population decreased by 19%, from 1000 per 100,000 in 2008 to 810 per 100,000 in 2020 (Gramlich, 2021). However, the most significant decline may be attributed to the pandemic as inmate deaths rose, admissions decreased, and releases were expedited to lower the risk of exposure to COVID-19 as well as to offset understaffed institutions (Minton et al., 2021).

Currently, a substantial body of research focuses on the connection between exposure to ACEs and adult incarceration. Understanding this relationship and the effects of both variables upon one another can create a more holistic understanding of incarcerated individuals and potentially provide keys to aid preventative interventions. One study of the male offender population in Wales provides some valuable data. In this research, the authors found that 45.5% of those incarcerated reported having four or more ACEs (Ford et al., 2019). Among the four or more ACEs identified, incidents of household dysfunction were ranked, with parental separation being the most prevalent, followed by witnessing domestic violence, familial incarceration, familial substance use, and living with someone with a mental illness. These finds support those of other scholars that have observed that ACE exposure is positively correlated with the risk of offending (Swopes et al., 2013).

A collection of research reviewed by Graf et al. (2021) similarly demonstrated a positive relationship between ACEs and involvement with the justice system. In this study, incarceration had adverse effects on the physical and mental health outcomes resulting in a compounded detrimental effect on individuals. In addition to the negative impact on individuals, the Graf et al. (2021) study also reported that incarceration has a broader negative fallout for communities. At this level, incarceration contributes to the destabilization of families, the impedance of opportunities for employment, and serves as an indicator of present and future poor community health overall.

Another notable finding that was cited in the sizeable review by Graf et al. (2021) was a study by Fagan and Novak (2018) in which the positive correlation between ACEs and justice system contact was separated along socioeconomic and racial lines. The trauma-crime relationship was significant for Black participants but not for White participants. One confounding variable in the study was thought to have been the over-policing of economically disadvantaged areas, which would account for the overrepresentation of Black participants having justice system contact.

ACES, INCARCERATION, AND SUBSTANCE USE

One specific ACE, substance use, has been shown to have a high prevalence in incarcerated populations. This ACE has been found to be a potential precursor to incarceration, as many inmates are serving time for substance-related offenses. Similarly, it has been found to impact future generations and the community. The presence of ACEs alone increases the potential for substance abuse as well as the likelihood of engaging in criminal activities (e.g., Slocum et al., 2022). Higher exposure to ACEs increases the prevalence of substance abuse, as seen in prison studies. The previously mentioned study of males in a Wales prison found that those who reported having exposure to four or more ACEs were two times more likely to have been convicted of drug offenses (Ford et al., 2019). Therefore, substance use may be a key area for intervention in the prevention of incarceration.

The correlation between childhood adversity, substance use, and incarceration is highlighted by Eaves et al. (2020), who collected ACEs data from 96 survey participants being detained in a county jail. The analysis found that respondents who reported substance use in the period of 30 days prior to incarceration had, on average, a higher number of ACEs. Specific connections between substances and ACEs were uncovered, including a correlation between methamphetamine use and individuals who lived with someone who had been incarcerated and with coerced sexual touching. Opiate use was related to having lived with depressed, mentally ill, or suicidal individuals, with anyone who engaged in misuse of prescription medications or illicit use of street drugs or having been touched sexually by an adult. Binge drinking was significantly related to having lived with someone who was a problem drinker or alcoholic.

Other studies found significant relationships, which support the research discussed. For instance, binge drinking in men is significantly correlated to sexual abuse and parental incarceration (Giano et al., 2021). In another study, lifetime stimulant use disorder and amphetamine-type stimulants (ATS) or cocaine use disorder were found in individuals with four or more ACEs (Tang et al., 2021). This study also reported the four most common ACEs as parental substance use, parental divorce or separation, sexual abuse, and witnessing domestic violence. The relationship between the specific substance abuse and the pattern of ACEs could provide a valuable understanding of the connection between these two phenomena.

To further examine the relationships between household incarceration and other ACEs, researchers used structural equation modeling (SEM) to create a path analysis that quantified the strength of those relationships and overall model fit (Fleming et al., 2020). More specifically, household incarceration was found to have a direct path to adult incarceration, low income, and substance use, but not mental health impairment. The combined direct and indirect paths illustrated that substance use accounted for 7% of the variance in the path model, while the impact of household incarceration on substance use was linked by both direct and indirect paths.

Another study by Grummitt et al. (2021) further refined the understanding of the relationship between these variables by identifying mediators and moderators between ACEs and substance use. Mediators are defined as variables that may provide explanations for the relationship, and moderators are defined as the factors that influence the strength of the relationship. The authors conducted a systematic review of 50 studies using a socio-ecological perspective to categorize variables into four main levels: 1) individual, 2) interpersonal, 3) community, and 4) public policy/culture. No mediators or moderators were found at the fourth level, public policy/culture.

On the individual level, Grummitt et al. (2021) report the most significant mediators were externalizing behaviors, anger, trauma-related symptoms, and reasoning for self-medicating usage of substances. On the interpersonal level, the authors report maternal connection and peer relationships as the more significant mediators. On the community level, they report the more evident mediators identified in the research are academic achievement and school mobility.

When exploring moderator variables (i.e., variables that demonstrate a stronger connection between substance use and ACEs), Grummitt et al. (2021) found that on the individual level, moderators were depressive symptoms, future orientation, and religiosity. On the interpersonal level, moderators were identified as family cohesion and quality of relationships, and on the community level moderators were social cohesion and neighborhood trust. Categorizing variables into these levels allowed researchers to better understand the specific factors influencing substance use in those who have experienced ACEs.

such as theft of property (Carson, 2021; Langan & Pelissier, 2001). Due to the war on drugs campaign and enhanced sentencing programs, women charged with drug offenses often receive more punitive sentencing than those charged with more violent offenses (Jones et al., 2021; Petersilia, 2011; The Sentencing Project, 2020). This is not to say women are not susceptible to committing violent offenses.

A closer look at violent offense patterns reveals clues to differing motivators in men as well as women. Though women may be convicted of a violent offense, in comparison, men are ten times more likely to be convicted of violent offenses, including homicide, sexual assault, and robbery (Carson, 2021). Research shows that men tend to direct their acts of aggression toward individuals outside of their family/friend circle (Greenfeld & Snell, 1999; Harer & Langan, 2001), whereas women tend to direct their aggression toward family members or partners. In addition, women who were charged with homicide were reported to be under the influence of a substance in 40% of the convictions (Greenfield & Snell, 1999), linking female inmates back to the cyclical pattern explored earlier.

Another behavioral distinction occurred between genders while serving their violent offense sentences. Violent tendencies in male inmates remained consistent (i.e., individuals who were violent prior to incarceration remained violent after incarceration); however, the same pattern did not transfer to females who showed a reduction in violence after incarceration (Harer & Langan, 2001). Violent tendencies in female inmate populations decreased to nonexistent when family and partner contact decreased. This shift in behavior could be related to a reduction in exposure to earlier pervasive threats in the household.

Given the connection between incarcerations and substance use and the differences between genders, it is worthwhile to consider the prevalence of substance use comparisons *(see Table 1)*

Table 1. Prevalence of lifetime substance use by percentages

Substance	Women	Men
Cocaine	2.7%	4.9%
Methamphetamine	1.5%	2.7%
Heroin	1.0%	2.3%
Injection Drug Use	1.1%	2.1%
Alcohol	31.9%	26.4%
Binge Drinking	14.6%	12.7%
Prescription Opioid Misuse	16.1%	12.4%

Source: Jones et al., 2020

Substance use prevalence between genders remains consistent in adults aged 18 and older, except for binge drinking percentages which decreased significantly in women; therefore, binge drinking percentages in men rank higher (Giano et al., 2021).

In summary, the cyclical trauma from childhood adversity to compensatory behaviors to punitive sentencing to re-traumatization in the prison system marks a clear pathway to incarceration for women. Rehabilitative processes that worked for men showed decreased success rates for women due to the difference in causes and motivators of violent and nonviolent offenses. In addition, women have unique mental and physical health considerations that need to be addressed in the incarceration system.

RESILIENCY FACTORS AND ACTIONABLE ALTERNATIVES

In comparison to the substantial exploration detailing the health dangers of cumulative ACEs, historically, empirical ACEs research centered on protective factors is sparse (Kia-Keating et al., 2011). Children who report significant adverse experiences are frequently raised in unsafe, insecure, and unstable conditions. As a result, these children may be exposed to prolonged toxic stress and/or acute trauma. These maladaptive experiences can hinder progression through the lifespan and across numerous wellness and health domains (Anda et al., 2006; Dube et al., 2001; Felitti et al., 1998). Nevertheless, it appears not all individuals who are threatened with hardships are at an equivalent danger of maladaptive developmental trajectories regardless of the psychological and physiological harm extended by ACEs (Masten, 2001). This variability in developmental trajectories is understood to be based on resiliency factors (Cicchetti, 2010; Luthar et al., 2000). Understanding resiliency factors is essential to ACEs research, as the variables can offer aspects of intervention with the capability to mitigate children from the maladaptive effects.

What Is Resilience?

According to Masten (2014), resilience is "the capacity of a dynamic system to adapt successfully to disturbances that threaten system function, viability, or development" (p. 6). Luthar et al. (2000) also referenced that resilience requires both exposures to severe adversity and positive adaptation despite this threat to development. Based upon these frameworks, resilience can be viewed as a multifaceted adaptation system to adversity. Resilience has also been conceptualized as a process and not a possession. This conceptualization of resilience as a process (in comparison to a possession) has transformed over time (Masten & Barnes, 2018; Wright & Masten, 2005). This means that resilience is not a pre-established or fixed trait that one can have, own, or acquire (Luthar et al., 2000). By contrast, resilience extends over the course of time when an individual attends or shows the process of functioning well in the face of adversity.

Building Resilience Through Positive Childhood Experiences

While ACEs have a significant impact on an individual's well-being, recent research has started to focus on the impact of positive childhood experiences (PCEs; Bethell et al., 2019) on children and adults. Using a sample of 6,188 adults at Johns Hopkins, Bethell and colleagues examined whether any PCEs could mitigate against the health effects of traumatic ones. The researchers' conceptualization was based on the premise that a percentage of kids with a high number of ACEs appear to grow to have ordinary development and adept adult emotional health. In doing so, the investigators sought to distinguish factors that generated a degree of resiliency in individuals that positively contributed to them despite ACEs. The study determined there are seven PCEs that can be statistically linked to good emotional and mental health in adults. The seven PCEs ask respondents to report how often or how much as a child they:

1. felt able to talk to your family about feelings.
2. felt your family stood by you during difficult times.
3. enjoyed participating in community traditions.
4. felt a sense of belonging in high school.
5. felt supported by friends.

6. had at least two non-parent adults who took genuine interest in you.
7. and felt safe and protected by an adult in your home.

By evaluating individuals who indicated high numbers of PCEs with those who referenced low or no PCEs, Bethell and colleagues' (2019) study revealed that people communicating more PCEs demonstrated 72% lower levels of adult depression and/or poor mental health and were 3.5 times more likely to get the social and emotional support they need as an adult. In doing so, the researchers discovered a dose-response association between PCEs and adult mental and relationship health with adults who had experienced ACEs, regardless of how many ACEs they had. A dose-response association means the more PCEs a child gets, the better their adult mental health is likely to be. Likewise, additional research had indicated that when parents were able to share ideas and talk about things that matter with their child, the child had a 1,200 percent greater chance of flourishing compared to those who did not have this type of communication (Bethell et al., 2019). These findings suggest the significance of PCEs, as an individual is less likely to experience the hardships and deficits of ACEs. On the other hand, if a person has no PCEs and one or two ACEs, the repercussions of the ACEs are more likely to emerge. Children with PCEs become adults who can seek social and emotional support. The effects of the PCEs study have helped encourage research and interventions in the direction of increasing PCEs to build resilience in children who have experienced trauma.

Resilience and Incarceration Research Findings

Considering the importance of PCEs, recent findings on incarceration, offenders, and resilience may provide insight into critical areas for helping professionals. For instance, by evaluating both the number of rearrests and reconvictions, Baglivio and Wolff (2020) found a high number of ACEs corresponded with greater reoffending, and a high number of PCEs were related to less recidivism. Baglivio and Wolff's results indicated youth with four or more ACEs who have six or more PCEs, the reconviction was 23% lower and rearrest 22% lower in comparison to those juveniles with four or more ACEs and less than six PCEs. This included controlling several demographic and criminal history variables.

Clements-Nolle and Waddington (2019) examined the association among ACEs, PCEs, internal resiliency, psychological distress, and external youth assets in 429 juvenile male and female offenders. Their results revealed that 52.8% reported four or more ACEs. Participants with four to five ACEs and six to eight ACEs were at increased risk for psychological distress. High internal resilience, family communication, school connectedness, and peer role models were associated with a reduction in psychological distress in the presence of high ACEs exposure. In the interaction models, having a high number of ACEs remained strongly associated with increased psychological distress. However, internal resilience and school connectedness significantly moderated the relationship between high ACEs exposure and psychological distress. These findings suggest that when considered with adequate interventions, supports, and other PCEs-adjacent experiences, people may profit from the associated learned resiliency. Furthermore, juveniles who experienced psychological trauma demonstrated the most benefit from specific protective programs and policies by exhibiting overall adaptability and confidence in their problem-solving abilities. Clements-Nolle and Waddington's (2019) results differ from the notion of learned helplessness (i.e., the concept when individuals consider their situation inescapable and expected), which has been highly associated with ACEs factors and latent effects in adulthood. These findings suggest that social programs and policies designed regarding specific risk factors concerning ACEs may lessen encounters with the criminal justice system.

Crouch, Smith, and Andersen (2022) examined caregiver incarceration, PCEs, and school success. Their results indicated that youth who had experienced household incarceration had a greater probability of repeating a grade than youth not exposed. Similarly, youth who encountered household incarceration had a smaller probability of living in a supportive neighborhood than youth without exposure. Their findings indicated that although many youths of incarcerated caregivers do experience PCEs and have school success, the children are at noticeably smaller amounts in contrast to their peers with non-incarcerated caregivers. The researchers questioned whether PCEs offer usefulness in policy interventions as they expand on existing community-level assets (e.g., mentoring programs that are created to increase protective factors).

A study commissioned by the Scottish Government (2018) explored childhood resiliency, strategies to reduce crime, and the use of trauma-informed approaches by professional staff who encounter youth exposed to adversity. The researchers acknowledged the following protective factors against offending behavior—this included neighborhood support, effective parenting, prosocial behavior, and attitudes, among others. The researchers also proposed that effective care begins when a broader perspective is taken. Common examples involved interventions prioritizing family and community-level support.

In prior research (Davis & Shlafer, 2017), where experiences of parental incarceration are linked to later offending behavior or histories of substance use, the recognition of building effective bonds with caregivers was warranted as a critical factor in reducing maladjustment across the lifespan. Implementing strategies that best align with these practices can help counteract the harmful effects of ACEs. Recidivism remains a core concern for those addressing the need to promote effective rehabilitation and healing from past trauma, which could influence levels of maladjustment and behaviors associated with later substance use (Petersilia, 2011).

SOLUTIONS AND RECOMMENDATIONS

Intervention Strategies for Families Impacted by Incarceration

Clinical Interventions

Interventions at any point in the incarceration cycle have the propensity to inspire rehabilitation and hope. Specific to children who live in a home with an incarcerated parent, Crouch et al. (2022) recommended PCEs interventions based on Healthy Outcome Positive Experiences (HOPE) established by the National Survey of Children's Health, which includes mental health counseling, teacher training, and family/parent support programs that encourage open communication and social support in the school and community to nurture a positive and safe environment for the child.

On the side of the incarcerated parent, Petersilia (2011) warns that better reentry programs that include more diverse job opportunities and provide transitional resources as well as rehabilitative and work programs while serving sentences offer inmates greater success. Likewise, in a system specifically designed for male inmates, Jewkes et al. (2020) encouraged prison facilities to tailor carceral spaces to better fit the unique nature of rehabilitative needs of female inmates through the empowerment of personal spaces, development of therapeutic support, and strengthening of self-identity. In addition, providing supportive resources to the remaining parent in the home while the incarcerated parent serves their sentence would help create an intervention in the ACEs cycle. With the higher percentages of prison populations consisting of male inmates, the most likely parent in the home would be the mother, who is also typically the first to sacrifice employment and other sustaining resources when families face struggles, as demonstrated on a national scale during the COVID-19 quarantine (Carli, 2020). Finding ways to better balance roles in marital partnerships and maintain advancement opportunities, equal and uninterrupted pay, and longevity benefits for women in the workforce would better stabilize families when a disruption occurs (Carli, 2020; Forste & Fox, 2012; Yavorsky et al., 2020).

When planning services, the role of a provider is first to develop a clear understanding of the individual's circumstances, resources, and needs while collaboratively assembling a service plan. The same protocol would be appropriate for assisting families that are struggling with the incarceration of a parent or other household member (and identified ACE). When considering interventions for families of incarcerated adults, the complexity of the family is a factor to be contemplated. The family complexity of incarcerated adults takes into consideration multi-partner fertility (MPF). MPF is described as having children with multiple partners. Researchers reported that MPF had been determined to be a risk factor for weaker family relationships (Dyer et al., 2018). They described an intervention using genograms to map the family complexity of incarcerated fathers based on the assumption that better defined families result in better planned interventions. They concluded that understanding the complexities of the family life of the incarcerated person will inform interventions for supporting healthy relationships as well as improving the chances of successful reintegration of the incarcerated person.

Research regarding the relationship between ACEs and physical and mental health outcomes and incarceration is robust for youthful populations. In an extensive review of literature about ACEs and justice system involvement, Graf et al. (2021) reported that multiple studies appraise the number of incarcerated youths that meet the criteria for posttraumatic stress disorder to be between 25% and 30%. The findings of this study are expressly important to pediatric providers who are positioned to have contact with individuals when they are young, at the time of exposure to ACEs, and later, at the point of contact with the justice system. As few other occupations have such potential for intervention with this at-risk group in the early stages, working to educate these medical service providers can have a longstanding impact. Training programs and continuing education programming for pediatric providers should give focus to the opportunity for positive, even preventive, impact on this demographic.

School/Education Based Interventions

A study reported on a dual strategy of combining early childhood education and home visits as an intervention for families impacted by incarceration. The researchers used a longitudinal research methodology to investigate whether the two-pronged intervention influenced the odds of boys being arrested. The results showed a positive correlation between the intervention and the rates of arrest for boys. The arrest rate was reduced by 4% for each month the boys received both interventions (Petitclerc et al., 2022). The results of this study align with the results of other studies, as reported by Petitclerc, that indicated early childhood education and home visits together could have a positive impact by lessening children's involvement with the justice system years later. However, the successful outcomes of this dual approach were not readily apparent until the children had matured. The mechanism of success for this approach was that it influenced multiple early risk factors such as cognitive and behavioral development of children, quality of parental engagement, and economic independence. The early impact on children's cognitive and behavioral abilities carried forward contributes to school success, motivation regarding school, and parental participation in matters related to children's education.

Children often experience several adversities simultaneously that are related to their parent's incarceration. When the incarcerated parent was the primary wage earner prior to incarceration, the family often can experience a loss of financial stability. This loss can have a domino effect resulting in other losses such as not being able to stay in their same residence, which can sometimes mean a loss of friends, changing schools, and day-to-day needs being unmet. The remaining caregiver frequently experiences increased stress affecting the relationship. Also, during this time, children may have encounters with social service agencies and the criminal justice system, which can be confusing experiences (Brown, 2018).

By understanding the lived experience of a child dealing with a parent's incarceration, school counselors can provide trauma-sensitive care and advocacy for the student. Further empathic understanding of children's needs can be helpful to the school counselor in developing tailored interventions for affected children. For example, in the table below are four basic questions from a child's perspective that reflect their needs, as well as two additional questions that are seldom spoken but are the essence of the other questions and reflect the most basic needs of children.

Table 2. Children's needs discerned through questions

Spoken Questions	Child's Needs	Recommended Response
"Where are you?"	To understand the location of the parent in their absence	Tell them the TRUTH* because once they learn the truth, distrust develops, and it harms relationships.
"Why are you there?"	To be able to make sense of the parent's absence	Tell them the TRUTH* because a family secret is a heavy burden. An apology can also be helpful.
"When are you coming home?"	To alleviate the anxiety that comes from uncertainty	Tell them the TRUTH* and use concrete language (two summers, 5 birthdays) because it is easier than vague answers, (a long time).
"Are you okay?"	To be reassured that the incarcerated parent is safe and can manage the difficult circumstances	Tell them the TRUTH* and balance it with reassurance that the parent would rather be with the child. *"I am ok in some ways (food, bed) and not ok because this is not a good place to be, and I am away from you."*
Unspoken Questions	**Child's Needs**	**Core Issue & Response**
"Do you love me?"	To feel loved	A child asked repeatedly for an expensive item. After the parent is arrested for selling drugs, the child might assume it was to be able to purchase the desired item. Response should reaffirm parent's love for the child."
"Do you blame me?"	To not feel responsible	A child who has been angry at the parent might assume the arrest was because of their negative thoughts about the parent. Response should reassure it is in no way the child's fault."

Source: Brook et al. (2013)

*Refers to the age-appropriate truth, which is factual but omits details that the child is unable to process. Too much detail creates further questions and heightens anxiety.

The information contained in the table can be useful for school counselors as a guide to individual counseling sessions with children impacted by incarceration, to develop content for a group plan for use in small group counseling sessions, and to use as a consultation tool when working with the parent remaining in the home with the child.

Additional school-based interventions include connecting the student with mentors as a source of a positive role model, bringing awareness to other educators about the implications of parental incarceration, challenging stigma by advocating for students who are being unfairly judged because their parent is incarcerated, providing support to the other caregiver by listening without judging and helping them to help their student, and when permissible, involve the incarcerated parent in the child's education (Brown, 2018). School counselors often have access to specialized materials (books, videos) to which the student can relate and realize that others also experience similar problems. Another example of an intervention that can be used by caregivers and professionals is simply being present and supportive of the child or family member as they learn to cope with stigma and grief due to their parent's absence.

Trauma-Informed Schools

The accumulation of stressors requires students to make significant adjustments, and when added together, these can have a traumatic impact on the child. In those cases, while school can sometimes be the most predictable environment for the child, experiencing trauma often interferes with the child's ability to learn and focus on school. School-based intervention has to do with a school's outlook on trauma. Because trauma has a significant impact on behavior, learning, and relationships, it is reasonable to expect untreated trauma would result in a host of school-related problems. In fact, studies on ACEs have reported troublesome impacts from toxic stress in school-aged children. The sources of toxic stress are identified in a study by Shonkoff and Garner (2012) as poverty, discrimination, and maltreatment that are linked to later problems in learning, behavior, and physical and mental health. The more ACEs, the more significant the disruption in child development (Baez et al., 2019).

Developmental concerns and delays are most readily noticed in the school setting because of the academic, social, and behavioral problems that emerge when specific expectations are placed on school-age children. Baez et al. (2019) reported on a school-based, trauma-informed intervention model that was based on a partnership between a community mental health provider of children's services and two urban, low-income middle schools. Provided as context for the intervention, both schools had similar demographics with less than 2% white, only 20% English proficiency, and high rates of students having special needs. The students in each school experienced multiple stressors, including high poverty rates, low educational achievement, high unemployment, high rates of chronic absenteeism, and double the amount of violence and incarceration in other neighborhoods.

The intervention paired social-emotional learning (SEL), which was in place as a universal approach, with trauma-informed care (TIC) as an integrated approach to address the needs of students struggling with trauma. The intervention consisted of three tiers, including schoolwide support (tier 1), group counseling (tier 2), and individual counseling and case management (tier 3). Students received services from each of the three tiers based on their assessed needs according to a modified ACEs survey instrument. The results of the study show strong support for the implementation of universal, schoolwide trauma screening. Those students who struggle in the areas of attendance, social skills, and behavior stand to benefit from the extra care and support they will receive when the reasons for their problems are known by educators and mental health professionals.

Counselor Competency in Advocacy

This recommendation is related to the identity of counselors and that they are skilled professionals who possess multiple competencies that would be tremendously beneficial to families impacted by incarceration. Advocacy is one such competency, and when used with communication skills that are familiar to counselors and with diplomacy and respect, advocacy has the potential to do much good for many. An example of how advocacy can be used in relation to the topic of incarceration is by school counselors. They should take up their role as advocates for children of incarcerated parents. Because of the stigma and social inequality, it becomes a social justice issue for which school counselors are in a unique position to champion the cause for the benefit of students who often bear the burden alone (Brown, 2018).

Counselors working with individuals are required to demonstrate competency in many areas. Those working with incarcerated populations, or those impacted by incarceration, may be expected to have more advanced skills in promoting individuals' understanding and access to community-based resources, enhanced awareness of systemic and environmental variables that impact lifespan development, and proficiency in providing evidence-based strategies for both prevention and intervention. Counselors are fundamentally driven to enhance individuals' lives and their ability to lead a healthy life; however, this drive must operate within the counselor's scope of practice. As such, it is recommended that counselors working with populations impacted by incarceration maintain a repertoire of resources to make available to clients. Prior to providing this list to clients, counselors may guide the individual in conducting a personal needs assessment. After exploring the individual's needs, the counselor may present the individual with the list for skill practice such as obtaining resources, identifying needs versus wants, and how to find needed resources.

FUTURE RESEARCH DIRECTIONS

One area in which further study is needed is the development and use of screening tools and interventions for students who struggle with high levels of trauma. The Baez et al. study (2019) suggests putting trauma screening tools and practical examples of interventions into a Toolkit as a standard for trauma-informed care in schools.

The authors see potentially significant benefits to creating a similar compilation of tools and organizing them into a Toolkit for the workplace. Such a Toolkit could be useful for Human Resource departments or Employee Assistance Program (EAP) providers and subsequently, increase wellness in the workplace. This could, in turn, facilitate employee productivity and engagement, which would be a positive outcome for both employee and employer.

Crouch et al. (2022) also recognized the need for PCEs research to measure the dose-response countereffects of ACEs, especially in the incarceration cycle. Brinkley-Rubenstein et al. (2018) further warned to carefully monitor interventions in the criminal justice system to avoid outcome interference in existing recovery programs that might lead to relapse and more punitive sentences.

CONCLUSION

As seen throughout the discussions in this chapter, research trends show a growing awareness of the impact of early experiences on the lifelong trajectory of an individual. Adverse experiences, commonly known as ACEs, which have not been mitigated by resiliency factors, have been found to be influential on an individual's behaviors and potentiality. Exposure to substance use is one ACE that has been revealed to have a strong impact on incarceration, recidivism, and perpetuating multigenerational criminal activity. With increased awareness of the impact of ACEs, an emphasis on early intervention, implementation of supportive therapies, and exposure to positive childhood experiences PCEs, individuals with a history of ACEs can experience a change in trajectory toward improved physical and mental health and an enhanced quality of life.

ACKNOWLEDGMENT

The authors would like to thank Mark Loftis, PhD for his advice and assistance with this chapter. It is because of his encouragement, mentoring, and open door that this project has come to fruition.

This research received no specific grant from any funding agency in the public, commercial, or not-for-profit sectors. Views expressed in this paper are those of the authors and do not necessarily represent the policies or opinions of Tennessee Technological University.

REFERENCES

Anda, R. F., Felitti, V. J., Bremner, J. D., Walker, J. D., Whitfield, C. H., Perry, B. D., Dube, S. R., & Giles, W. H. (2006). The enduring effects of abuse and related adverse experiences in childhood. *European Archives of Psychiatry and Clinical Neuroscience*, *256*(3), 174–186. doi:10.100700406-005-0624-4 PMID:16311898

Anderson, J. D., Pitner, R. O., & Wooten, N. R. (2019). A gender-specific model of trauma and victimization in incarcerated women. *Journal of Human Behavior in the Social Environment*. Advance online publication. doi:10.1080/10911359.2019.1673272

Báez, J. C., Renshaw, K. J., Bachman, L. M., Kim, D., Smith, V. D., & Stafford, R. E. (2019). Understanding the necessity of trauma-informed care in community schools: A mixed-methods program evaluation. *Children & Schools*, *41*(2), 101–110. Advance online publication. doi:10.1093/cs/cdz007

Baglivio, M. T., & Wolff, K. T. (2021). Positive childhood experiences (PCE): Cumulative resiliency in the face of adverse childhood experiences. *Youth Violence and Juvenile Justice*, *19*(2), 139–162. doi:10.1177/1541204020972487

Bethell, C., Jones, J., Gombojav, N., Linkenbach, J., & Sege, R. (2019). Positive childhood experiences and adult mental and relational health in a statewide sample: Associations across adverse childhood experiences levels. *JAMA Pediatrics*, *173*(11), e193007. Advance online publication. doi:10.1001/jamapediatrics.2019.3007 PMID:31498386

Black, D. W. (2015). The natural history of antisocial personality disorder. *Canadian Journal of Psychiatry, 60*(7), 309–314. doi:10.1177/070674371506000703 PMID:26175389

Boppre, B., & Boyer, C. (2021). "The traps started during my childhood": The role of substance abuse in women's responses to adverse childhood experiences (ACEs). *Journal of Aggression, Maltreatment & Trauma, 30*(4), 429–449. doi:10.1080/10926771.2019.1651808

Bowles, M. A., DeHart, D., & Webb, J. R. (2012). Family influences on female offenders's substance use: The role of adverse childhood events among incarcerated women. *Journal of Family Violence, 27*(7), 681–686. doi:10.100710896-012-9450-4

Brinkley-Rubinstein, L., Zaller, N., Martino, S., Cloud, D. H., McCauley, E., Heise, A., & Seal, D. (2018). Criminal justice continuum for opioid users at risk of overdose. *Addictive Behaviors, 86*, 104–110. doi:10.1016/j.addbeh.2018.02.024 PMID:29544869

Brooks, M., Gaynes, E., Krupat, T., & Lemaster-Schipani, D. (2013). Stronger together: Volume I, experiences of children of incarcerated parents. The Osborne Association.

Brown, E. (2018). *Imprisoned parents, challenged children.* ASCA SC. https://www.ascaschoolcounselordigital.org/ascaschoolcounselor/january_february_2018/MobilePagedArticle.action?articleId=1329904#articleId1329904

Brown, S., Fite, P. J., DiPierro, M., & Bortolato, M. (2017). Links between stressful life events and proactive and reactive functions of aggression. *Journal of Aggression, Maltreatment & Trauma, 6*(6), 691–699. doi:10.1080/10926771.2017.1322658 PMID:31223229

Brown, S. L., Wanamaker, K. A., Greiner, L., Scott, T., & Skilling, T. A. (2021). Complex trauma and criminogenic needs in a youth justice sample: A gender-informed latent profile analysis. *Criminal Justice and Behavior, 48*(2), 175–194. doi:10.1177/0093854820964513

Carli, L. L. (2020). Women, gender equality and COVID-19. *Gender in Management, 35*(7/8), 647–655. doi:10.1108/GM-07-2020-023

Carson, E. A. (2021, December). *Prisoners in 2020 – Statistical Tables* (NCJ 302776). US Department of Justice, Office of Justice Programs, Bureau of Justice Statistics. https://bjs.ojp.gov/library/publications/prisoners-2020-statistical-tables

Center for Disease Control. (2021, April 6). *About the CDC-Kaiser ACE Study.* https://www.cdc.gov/violenceprevention/aces/about.html

Cicchetti, D. (2010). Resilience under conditions of extreme stress: a multilevel perspective. *World Psychiatry, 9*(3), 145. doi:10.1186/1471-2458-13-3

Clemens, V., Berthold, O., Witt, A., Sachser, C., Brähler, E., Plener, P. L., Strauß, B., & Fegert, J. M. (2019). Child maltreatment is mediating long-term consequences of household dysfunction in a population representative sample. *European Psychiatry, 58*, 10–18. doi:10.1016/j.eurpsy.2019.01.018 PMID:30743239

Clements-Nolle, K., & Waddington, R. (2019). Adverse childhood experiences and psychological distress in juvenile offenders: The protective influence of resilience and youth assets. *The Journal of Adolescent Health, 64*(1), 49–55. doi:10.1016/j.jadohealth.2018.09.025 PMID:30579436

Costa Duriguetto, G., & Araujo, R. (2020). Psychopathology and criminality. *International Journal of Psychiatry Research, 3*(3), 1–7. doi:10.33425/2641-4317.1063

Craig, J. M., Intravia, J., Wolff, K. T., & Baglivio, M. T. (2019). What can help? Examining levels of substance (non)use as a protective factor in the effect of ACEs on crime. *Youth Violence and Juvenile Justice, 17*(1), 42–61. doi:10.1177/1541204017728998

Craig, J. M., Piquero, A. R., Farrington, D. P., & Ttofi, M. M. (2017). A little early risk goes a long bad way: Adverse childhood experiences and life-course offending in the Cambridge study. *Journal of Criminal Justice, 53*, 34–45. doi:10.1016/j.jcrimjus.2017.09.005

Crouch, E., Smith, H. P., & Andersen, T. S. (2022). An examination of caregiver incarceration, positive childhood experiences, and school success. *Children and Youth Services Review, 133*, 106345. doi:10.1016/j.childyouth.2021.106345

Currie, J., & Tekin, E. (2006). *Does Child Abuse Cause Crime?* National Bureau of Economic Research. doi:10.3386/w12171

Davis, L., & Shlafer, R. J. (2017). Mental health of adolescents with currently and formerly incarcerated parents. *Journal of Adolescence, 54*(1), 120–134. doi:10.1016/j.adolescence.2016.10.006 PMID:28011442

Dube, S. R., Anda, R. F., Felitti, V. J., Croft, J. B., Edwards, V. J., & Giles, W. H. (2001). Growing up with parental alcohol abuse: Exposure to childhood abuse, neglect, and household dysfunction. *Child Abuse & Neglect, 25*(12), 1627–1640. doi:10.1016/S0145-2134(01)00293-9 PMID:11814159

Dube, S. R., Anda, R. F., Felitti, V. J., Edwards, V. J., & Croft, J. B. (2002). Adverse childhood experiences and personal alcohol abuse as an adult. *Addictive Behaviors, 27*(5), 713–725. doi:10.1016/S0306-4603(01)00204-0 PMID:12201379

Dube, S. R., Felitti, V. J., Dong, M., Chapman, D. P., Giles, W. H., & Anda, R. F. (2003). Childhood abuse, neglect, and household dysfunction and the risk of illicit drug use: The adverse childhood experiences study. *Pediatrics, 111*(3), 564–572. doi:10.1542/peds.111.3.564 PMID:12612237

Dyer, W. J., Day, R. D., & Wiley, A. R. (2018). Jailed fathers and family complexity. *Social Work Research, 42*(3), 210–222. doi:10.1093wrvy015

Eaves, E., Camplain, R., Lininger, M., & Trotter, I. I. R. (2020). Adverse childhood experiences in relation to drug and alcohol use in 30 days prior to incarceration in a county jail. *International Journal of Prisoner Health*. Advance online publication. doi:10.1108/IJPH-06-2020-0038 PMID:34745314

Erwin, B. A., Newman, E., McMackin, R. A., Morrissey, C., & Kaloupek, D. G. (2000). PTSD, malevolent environment, and criminality among criminally involved male adolescents. *Criminal Justice and Behavior, 27*(2), 196–215. doi:10.1177/0093854800027002004

Fagan, A. A., & Novak, A. (2018). Adverse childhood experiences and adolescent delinquency in a high-risk sample: A comparison of white and black youth. *Youth Violence and Juvenile Justice, 16*(4), 395–417. doi:10.1177/1541204017735568

Felitti, V. J., Anda, R. F., Nordenberg, D., Williamson, D. F., Spitz, A. M., Edwards, V., & Marks, J. S. (1998). Relationship of childhood abuse and household dysfunction to many of the leading causes of death in adults: The adverse childhood experiences (ACE) study. *American Journal of Preventive Medicine*, *14*(4), 245–258. doi:10.1016/S0749-3797(98)00017-8 PMID:9635069

Finkelhor, D. (2020). Trends in adverse childhood experiences (ACEs) in the United States. *Child Abuse & Neglect*, *108*, 104641. Advance online publication. doi:10.1016/j.chiabu.2020.104641 PMID:32739600

Fleming, C. M., & Nurius, P. S. (2020). Incarceration and adversity histories: Modeling life course pathways affecting behavioral health. *The American Journal of Orthopsychiatry*, *90*(3), 312–323. doi:10.1037/ort0000436 PMID:31829646

Ford, K., Barton, E., Newbury, A., Hughes, K., Bezeczky, Z., Roderick, J., & Bellis, M. (2019). Understanding the prevalence of adverse childhood experiences (ACEs) in a male offender population in Wales: The prisoner ACE survey. *Public Health Wales*. https://research.bangor.ac.uk/portal/files/23356885/PHW_Prisoner_ACE_Survey_Report_E.pdf

Forste, R., & Fox, K. (2012). Household labor, gender roles, and family satisfaction: A cross-national comparison. *Journal of Comparative Family Studies*, *43*(5), 613–631. doi:10.3138/jcfs.43.5.613

Giano, Z., O'Neil, A., & Hubach, R. (2021). The effects of individual and dual ACE domains on binge drinking: Comparisons by gender. *Substance Use & Misuse*, *56*(11), 1–9. doi:10.1080/10826084.2021.1949604 PMID:34279181

Gjelsvik, A., Dumont, D. M., Nunn, A., & Rosen, D. L. (2014). Adverse childhood events: Incarceration of household members and health-related quality of life in adulthood. *Journal of Health Care for the Poor and Underserved*, *25*(3), 1169–1182. doi:10.1353/hpu.2014.0112 PMID:25130232

Graf, G. H. J., Chihuri, S., Blow, M., & Li, G. (2021). Adverse childhood experiences and justice system contact: A systematic review. *Pediatrics*, *147*(1), e2020021030. doi:10.1542/peds.2020-021030 PMID:33328338

Gramlich, J. (2021, August 16). *America's incarceration rate falls to lowest level since 1995*. PEW Research Center. https://www.pewresearch.org/fact-tank/2021/08/16/americas-incarceration-rate-lowest-since-1995/

Greenfield, L. A., & Snell, T. L. (1999). *Women offenders* (NCJ 175688). US Department of Justice, Office of Justice Programs, Bureau of Justice Statistics. https://bjs.ojp.gov/content/pub/pdf/wo.pdf

Grummitt, L., Kelly, E., Barrett, E., Keyes, K., & Newton, N. (2021). Targets for intervention to prevent substance use in young people exposed to childhood adversity: A systematic review. *PLoS One*, *16*(6), e0252815. Advance online publication. doi:10.1371/journal.pone.0252815 PMID:34097711

Guarino, H., Mateu-Gelabert, P., Quinn, K., Sirikantraporn, S., Ruggles, K. V., Syckes, C., Goodbody, E., Jessell, L., & Friedman, S. R. (2021). Adverse childhood experiences predict early initiation of opioid use behaviors. *Frontiers in Sociology*, *6*, 620395. Advance online publication. doi:10.3389/fsoc.2021.620395 PMID:34055961

Hambrick, E. P., Brawner, T. W., & Perry, B. D. (2019). Timing of early-life stress and the development of brain-related capacities. *Frontiers in Behavioral Neuroscience*, *13*, 183. Advance online publication. doi:10.3389/fnbeh.2019.00183 PMID:31447660

Harer, M. D., & Langan, N. P. (2001). Gender differences in predictors of prison violence: Assessing the predictive validity of a risk classification system. *Crime and Delinquency*, *47*(4), 513–536. doi:10.1177/0011128701047004002

Henry, B. F. (2020). Typologies of adversity in childhood & adulthood as determinants of mental health & substance use disorders of adults incarcerated in US prisons. *Child Abuse & Neglect*, *99*, 104251. Advance online publication. doi:10.1016/j.chiabu.2019.104251 PMID:31726246

Jewkes, Y., & Laws, B. (2021). Liminality revisited: Mapping the emotional adaptations of women in carceral spaces. *Punishment & Society*, *23*(3), 394–412. doi:10.1177/1462474520959623

Jones, C. M., Clayton, H. B., Deputy, N. P., Roehler, D. R., Ko, J. Y., Esser, M. B., ... Hertz, M. F. (2020). Prescription opioid misuse and use of alcohol and other substances among high school students—Youth Risk Behavior Survey, United States, 2019. *MMWR Supplements*, *69*(1), 38. doi:10.15585/mmwr.su6901a5

Kia-Keating, M., Dowdy, E., Morgan, M. L., & Noam, G. G. (2011). Protecting and promoting: An integrative conceptual model for healthy development of adolescents. *The Journal of Adolescent Health*, *48*(3), 220–228. doi:10.1016/j.jadohealth.2010.08.006

Langan, N. P., & Pelissier, B. M. (2001). Gender differences among prisoners in drug treatment. *Journal of Substance Abuse*, *13*(3), 291–301. doi:10.10160899-3289(01)00083-9

Liu, J., Abdin, E., Vaingankar, J. A., Lim, M. S. M., Verma, S., Tang, C., . . . Subramaniam, M. (2021). Positive mental health framework of transdiagnostic protective factors in elucidating the association between adverse childhood experiences and severe mental disorders. *Australian & New Zealand Journal of Psychiatry*. https://doi.org/00048674211053568

Luthar, S., Cicchetti, D., & Becker, B. (2000). The construct of resilience: A critical evaluation and guidelines for future work. *Child Development*, *71*, 543–562.

Masten, A. S. (2001). Ordinary magic: Resilience processes in development. *The American Psychologist*, *56*(3), 227.

Masten, A. S. (2014). Global perspectives on resilience in children and youth. *Child Development*, *85*(1), 6–20.

Masten, A. S., & Barnes, A. J. (2018). Resilience in children: Developmental perspectives. *Children*, *5*(7), 98.

Minton, T. D., Zeng, Z., & Maruschak, L. M. (2021). *Impact of COVID-19 on the local jail population, January-June 2020*. US Department of Justice, Office of Justice Programs, Bureau of Justice Statistics. https://copafs.org/wp-content/uploads/2021/09/icljpjj20.pdf

Nusslock, R., & Miller, G. E. (2016). Early-life adversity and physical and emotional health across the lifespan: A neuroimmune network hypothesis. *Biological Psychiatry*, *80*(1), 23–32. doi:10.1016/j.biopsych.2015.05.017

Petersilia, J. (2011, October). Beyond the prison bubble. *National Institute of Justice Journal*, *268*. https://nij.ojp.gov/topics/articles/beyond-prison-bubble

Petitclerc, A., & Brooks-Gunn, J. (2022). Home visiting and early childhood education for reducing justice system involvement. *Prevention Science*, 1–14. doi:10.100711121-022-01363-7 PMID:35267178

Schilling, E. A., Aseltine, R. H. Jr, & Gore, S. (2007). Adverse childhood experiences and mental health in young adults: A longitudinal survey. *BMC Public Health*, *7*(1), 1–10. doi:10.1186/1471-2458-7-30 PMID:17343754

Shonkoff, J. P., Garner, A. P., Siegel, B. S., Dobbins, M. I., Earls, M. F., Garner, A. S., McGuinn, L., Pascoe, J., & Wood, D. L. (2012). The lifelong effects of early childhood adversity and toxic stress. *Pediatrics*, *129*(1), e232–e246. doi:10.1542/peds.2011-2663 PMID:22201156

Shulman, E. P., Steinberg, L. D., & Piquero, A. R. (2013). The age-crime curve in adolescence and early adulthood is not due to age differences in economic status. *Journal of Youth and Adolescence*, *42*(6), 848–860. doi:10.100710964-013-9950-4 PMID:23595417

Slocum, L. A., Medel, J., Doherty, E. E., & Simpson, S. S. (2022). Unpacking the Criminogenic Aspects of Stress Over the Life Course: The Joint Effects of Proximal Strain and Childhood Abuse on Violence and Substance Use in a High-Risk Sample of Women. *Journal of Research in Crime and Delinquency*. Advance online publication. doi:10.1177/00224278211068188

Swopes, R. M., Simonet, D. V., Jaffe, A. E., Tett, R. P., & Davis, J. L. (2013). Adverse childhood experiences, posttraumatic stress disorder symptoms, and emotional intelligence in partner aggression. *Violence and Victims*, *28*(3), 513–530. doi:10.1891/0886-6708.VV-D-12-00026 PMID:23862313

Tang, S., Jones, C. M., Wisdom, A., Lin, H. C., Bacon, S., & Houry, D. (2021). Adverse childhood experiences and stimulant use disorders among adults in the United States. *Psychiatry Research*, *299*, 113870. doi:10.1016/j.psychres.2021.113870 PMID:33780857

The Scottish Government. (2018, May). *Understanding Childhood Adversity, Resilience, and Crime*. APS Group Scotland. https://www.gov.scot

The Sentencing Project. (2020, November). *Fact sheet: Incarcerated women and girls*. https://www.sentencingproject.org/wp-content/uploads/2016/02/Incarcerated-Women-and-Girls.pdf

Wolff, N., Aizpurua, E., Caravaca Sanchez, F., & Peng, D. (2020). Childhood abuse classes for incarcerated men and women: Are there unique gender patterns in abuse classes? *Journal of Interpersonal Violence*, *§§§*, 1–29. doi:0.1177/0886260520965974

Wright, M. O. D., & Masten, A. S. (2005). Resilience processes in development. In *Handbook of resilience in children* (pp. 17–37). Springer.

Yavorsky, J. E., Qian, Y., & Sargent, A. C. (2021). The gendered pandemic: The implications of COVID-19 for work and family. *Sociology Compass*, *15*. doi:10.1111oc4.12881

Zarse, E. M., Neff, M. R., Yoder, R., Hulvershorn, L., Chambers, J. E., & Chambers, R. A. (2019). The adverse childhood experiences questionnaire: Two decades of research on childhood trauma as a primary cause of adult mental illness, addiction, and medical diseases. *Cogent Medicine*, *6*(1), 1581447. doi:10.1080/2331205X.2019.1581447

Zeng, S., Corr, C. P., O'Grady, C., & Guan, Y. (2019). Adverse childhood experiences and preschool suspension expulsion: A population study. *Child Abuse & Neglect*, *97*, 104–149.

KEY TERMS AND DEFINITIONS

Age-Crime Curve: Developmental theory that observes an increase in criminal activity in adolescence and a decrease in criminal activity in adulthood.

Carceral Spaces: The prison environment experienced by incarcerated individuals.

Criminogenic Risk Factors: Problem areas in an offender's lifespan that may increase the chance of reoffending.

Learned Helplessness: A sense of powerlessness in one who has experienced repetitive adversity or trauma.

Learned Resiliency: The ability to bounce back in one who has experienced repetitive adversity or trauma.

Neuro-Immune Network Hypothesis: A heuristic framework first introduced by Nusslock and Miller in 2016 that explored the effect of stressors on the neural, cardiovascular, neuroendocrine, and immune functioning related to child development.

Positive Childhood Experiences (PCEs): Banked experiences in childhood that restore long-term positive outcomes by building trust, belonging, and relational connection.

Social-Emotional Learning (SEL): Social and emotional processes that establish positive health and wellbeing.

Toxic Stress: Repetitive stressors that may wear down the body's natural defenses causing lifelong mental and physical health problems.

Chapter 2
The History of Incarceration of African Americans/ Blacks in the United States

Valandra
https://orcid.org/0000-0002-6782-6400
University of Arkansas, USA

Tremaine Leslie
https://orcid.org/0000-0001-6235-9949
National Louis University, USA

ABSTRACT

The control, regulation, and policing of African American/Black people is a persistent feature of the history of White supremacist legislation, policies, and practices leading the construction of the era of mass incarceration. The mass incarceration of African American/Black families living in poverty in the United States has had a devastating impact on the lives of families and communities. The goal of this chapter is to examine the historical and contemporary legislative and policing practices resulting in the mass incarceration of African American/Black families. The authors also identify trends in incarceration rates to demonstrate the staggering reality that a significant portion of the African American/Black population in the United States lives locked up behind bars in federal and state prisons, or community supervisory conditions including probation and parole. The authors conclude by offering recommendations to minimize the incarceration of African Americans/Blacks and resources for clinicians to better support the community.

INTRODUCTION

The goal of this chapter is to chronicle the legacy of the disproportionate representation of African Americans/Blacks in the criminal justice system in the United States. The terms African American and Black are used interchangeably to define the ethnicity of individuals with ancestral origins in Africa and

DOI: 10.4018/978-1-7998-9209-0.ch002

direct family lineage in North America to the transatlantic slave trade or any person who self-identifies ethnically as African American and/or Black. The authors use the multi-systems life course (MSLC) (Murphy-Erby et al., 2010) perspective to examine the socio-historical, economic, and political contexts of African American incarceration beginning with the institution of Black enslavement and its evolution into modern-day mass incarceration. The Afrocentric Intergenerational Solidarity (AIS) (Waites, 2008, 2009) framework is used by the authors to contextualize African American family responses to incarceration through a lens of traditional African American generational cultural values. The authors chronicle the path of policing and social control of Black bodies through legislative policies and social practices by majority-White policymakers and organizations and reinforced with attention to interlocking educational, child welfare, and social systems. It is important to acknowledge that White supremacist ideology and values can be internalized and perpetuated by individuals in positions of power from any racial/ethnic background. The internalization of racism by people of color can be equally injurious to the lives of African American families (Speight, 2007).

The persistent systematic structure of policing and social control of Black people has led many scholars, civic leaders, and activists to argue that the enslavement of Black people in the United States did not end with the Emancipation Proclamation of 1865, but instead, evolved into a system of mass incarceration (Alexander, 2010; Stevenson, 2014). Including both the adult and juvenile criminal justice systems in which Black men, women, and children are disproportionately overrepresented, the authors document the historical evolution of policing policies and practices from slavery and the slave codes through Reconstruction, Jim Crow segregation, the Black migration from the south, and the industrial revolution. The authors examine the historical origins of contemporary methods of controlling Black bodies including incarceration, community supervision, probation, and parole with particular attention to the intersections of race, gender, class, and age in understanding the types of offenses African Americans are typically charged with and convicted of, and the sentencing practices and decision-making mechanisms that drive policies and practices within the adult, juvenile, child welfare, and school systems. The authors identify legislation and practices resulting in the disproportionate sentencing of Black children as adults and their confinement in adult prison systems and the role of child welfare as a pipeline to the juvenile justice system. Additionally, the authors demonstrate how overwhelmingly White public-school administrators, teachers, and decision-makers use harsh "Zero Tolerance" school policies and practices to routinely push Black children out of school and into the prison pipeline. Implications for policy, practice, and advocacy are discussed. The purpose of this chapter is to provide a tool to engage counselors in culturally responsive policy and practice and resources to reduce the risk factors that contribute to African American family incarceration. While African American families from diverse socioeconomic backgrounds experience incarceration, the chapter focuses primarily on the experiences of Black families living in poverty.

BACKGROUND

In *The 1619 Project*, authors Leslie Alexander and Michelle Alexander assert that "modern day policing, surveillance, and mass criminalization as well as white vigilante violence and 'know-your-place aggression,' are patterns of repression and control established during slavery and rooted in histories of white fear – not merely of Black crime or Black people but of Black liberation" (2021, p. 102). The interconnectedness of slavery, white fear, and mass Black incarceration is reflected in the Vera Institute (www.vera.org) special report *Reimagining Prison* on the history of race and prison in America as it is recognized that true reform of the prison system requires a critical examination and reckoning "with the ways in which prisons in this country are entwined with the legacy of slavery and generations of racial and social injustice" (Delaney, et al., 2018, n.p.). The template of White racist ideology that drives the current system of mass imprisonment of Black bodies in the United States has its origins in the 17th century repressive legislation and constitutions of the British colonies, known as slave codes, used by White colonial rulers to enslave, restrict the movement, and constrain the inalienable rights of Black men, women, and children in every way possible (Alexander & Alexander, 2021; Middleton, 2020). Slave codes were used to criminalize Black people getting married, reading, and writing, running away, owning a gun, socializing with Whites, and White slave patrols (Hadden, 2003) surveilled and curtailed Black people by any means necessary (Hinton & Cook, 2021). The Virginia Assembly codified slavery in 1705 designating Blacks as chattel property and instituted a separate judicial system for Blacks employing plantation police forces and slave patrols to monitor Black movement, congregating, and rebellion of enslaved as well as freed Black people (Middleton, 2020).

The period of 1865 – 1940 saw a massive surge in the arrests and incarceration of Black people as state governments caved into and perpetuated White fears and anxiety over newly freed Blacks and the loss of free labor in responding to the economic depression brought on by the Civil War (Garbenstein, 2018). After the emancipation of Black people in 1865, White legislators worked systemically and consistently with federal and state judicial and law enforcement systems in the north and south, to continually create and enact policies that legitimized the restriction, subordination, and disproportionate imprisonment of Black families (Delaney et al., 2018, Hinton & Cook, 2021). Middleton (2020) captured the depth and breadth of this regulation when he asserted that:

Rooted in the bigotry that undergirded American slavery, the codification of slave codes, northern black laws, and southern black codes in the colonies and later the states deeply shaped the lives of black people from the 17th through the 20th centuries [and] denied African Americans virtually every privilege and immunity the government gave to whites (p.2).

In 1865, passage of the 13th Amendment outlawed slavery except as punishment for a crime providing the loophole White lawmakers and courts needed to sign into law a series of rulings that essentially criminalized Black life setting the stage for the mass imprisonment of Black Americans through convict leasing, prison farms, and chain gangs designed to provide a cheap source of labor and continue White control and subordination of Black people (Delaney et al., 2018). In the 1870's Black Codes were passed in the south outlawing common behaviors including "walking without a purpose," "walking at night," "hunting on Sundays," or "settling on public or private land" and by 1871 Virginia's Supreme Court declared that an incarcerated person is "a slave of the state." By the 1870s 95% of people in the custody of the criminal justice system in southern states were Black. Maintaining criminal custody of Black bodies was critical to rebuilding the south after the war and enforcing the racial social order (Equal Justice Initiative, 2020). These laws were also designed to strip Black people of their rights to citizenship and their voting rights. Convict leasing ended by 1928 but was replaced by chain gangs and prison farms (Hinton & Cook, 2021). Additionally, White lynch mobs during the era of Jim Crow policed the activities of Black people and controlled their access to economic, social, and political resources maintaining a culture of white supremacy and domination (Anderson, 2016, Hinton & Cook, 2021).

The period of 1920 – 1970 characterized by rapid industrialization, urbanization, and the migration of Black Americans to the north saw an expansion of prison populations in the northern states as Black Americans increased competition for jobs, contributed to conditions of overcrowding and ignited the historical reflexive impulse of White anxiety and fear. Over six million Black Americans migrated from the south to northern cities between 1910 and 1970. Government campaigns branding Black citizens new to the region as "public enemies" supported criminal stereotypes, stoked fears, and contributed to a swell in incarceration and mandatory sentencing policies that disproportionately targeted Black citizens. Between 1926 and 1940, state prisons in the north increased by 67 percent (Delaney et al., 2018). White supremacist myths of Black inferiority and criminality persisted in the north contributing to roughly doubling racial disparities in prison populations in northern states affected by the Great Migration by the 1970s (Muller, 2012; Travis, Western, & Redburn, 2014). The 1960's "law and order" rhetoric of the Nixon presidential campaign and the "War on Crime" legislation resulting from President Lyndon Johnson's campaign linked race, crime, and political rhetoric further stoking the myth of Black criminality which led to the enactment of harsher, punitive, punishment-oriented policies to "crack down" on criminals (Hinton & Cook, 2021). Black citizens were disproportionately targeted as policing surveillance coincided with a national recession, high levels of unemployment among Black urban residents, social disorganization in urban cities, and increases in drugs and gangs (Delaney et al. 2018; Hinton & Cook, 2021). Between 1970 and 2008, the federal and state prison population increased from 196,441 to over 1.6 million people disproportionately impacting Black Americans who were imprisoned at a rate of six and half times higher than White men (Delaney et al., 2018).

Historical and Prevailing American Values and Ideologies

Social welfare scholars argue that Americans live in a value-laden and value-based society and values "are the major premises by which ideologies are formulated and are the basis for social welfare policies and practices" intended to support social treatment and control of specific populations (Day & Schiele, p.6). Day and Schiele (2013) maintain that major social, political, economic, and religious institutions are driven by nine basic dominant American social values and ideologies used by the White power structure for social treatment of White people and social control of people of color. The social control and criminalization of African American families through often intersecting value-laden social welfare policies and practices can also place Black families at greater risk for incarceration. The nine most basic dominant American values identified by Day and Schiele (2013) include:

1. *Christian charity values* – the obligation to distribute resources to the poor based on perceived "worthiness" or "deservedness." Individuals or groups perceived as "deserving" or "worthy" are helped by society whereas those perceived as "undeserving/unworthy" or "able-bodied" are met with social controls and means tested measures before goods or services are distributed. These values were reflected in campaigns like the War on Poverty efforts which, in urban Black communities, were conflated with increased police and law enforcement involvement in social welfare initiatives through the Safe Streets Act of 1968 (Hinton & Cook, 2021).
2. *Democratic egalitarianism and individualism* – the ideological myth that all citizens are equal before the law, and no one has privileges, and all rights are available to all citizens regardless of cultural characteristics. The ideal that with individual effort and personal motivation, not dependency, any American can achieve success. This myth negates the ways structural barriers related to race,

class, and gender disparities, for example, impede opportunities for African American families who disproportionately live with poverty and systemic racism. The myth of meritocracy – the idea that advancement is solely tied to ability and skills rather than unearned privileges based on social position.

3. *The Protestant work ethic and capitalism* – related to individualism and the Judeo-Christian values of charity, work for economic gain is the way to success and a sign of morality and a moral obligation, regardless of whether labor is exploited with low wages and/or poor work conditions. Conversely, poverty and public dependency are signs of immorality and contribute to stigmatizing stereotypes such as "welfare queens" – a demonizing derogatory framing of Black women recipients of public assistance who were presumed to misuse welfare payments. The term was popularized during the 1976 Reagan campaign to promote cutbacks in the allocation of federal funding of public assistance programs. The legacy of the "welfare queen" stereotype continues to shape public social welfare policy discourse and the accessibility of deserving resources in African American families.
4. *Social Darwinism* – the theory that individuals and groups are subject to the same laws of natural selection as plants and animals in that only the strongest and fittest will survive. Thus, state support of the poor is against the laws of "economic nature" and the lives of people who are "economically unfit" should not be saved by giving them public assistance. They are poor by choice, moral degenerates and therefore should perish. Over time, this belief has extended to other marginalized groups including people of color, lesbian, gay, bisexual, transgender, queer, intersex (lgbtqi+), elderly, immigrants, etc. and used to justify political and social conservatism and to discourage social, political, and economic interventions to address structural discriminatory practices and policies across all sectors of society.
5. *The New Puritanism* – enforces compliance with patriarchal and puritan values including chastity, particularly for women; honesty in dealing with others, abstinence from things defined by religion and custom as immoral and the sanctity of heterosexual marriage and family and patriarchal authority as well as the condemnation of communal living and homosexuality.
6. *Patriarchy* – a system in which power and authority are vested in men, whereas women and other powerless groups such as children, workers and enslaved persons are oppressed and often owned. Today it is a worldwide system of exploitation of women, transgender people, and some men (sexism), the poor (classism), Black, Indigenous, people of color (racism), and people and groups of developing countries (neocolonialism or imperialism).
7. *White Privilege* – a racialized hierarchy of power based on the set of benefits and advantages inherited by those categorized as "white" in the social process and structure of American society. The belief that European American norms and mores are universal and supreme to other cultural prescriptions and interpretations. While white privilege is based on race, it is appropriate to identify other forms of privilege (for example based on class, gender, sexuality, ability, etc.) in society. An ideology that a particular cultural characteristic inherently makes one entitled to a set of unearned benefits and advantages over others based on race.
8. *Marriage and the nuclear family* – the normalization and sanctioning of heterosexual marriage in which a man and woman are legally joined to create and maintain a family consisting exclusively of a husband, wife, and a few children. Patriarchy under grids expectations for marriage and family. Monogamy is both law and custom. African American single parent, extended, or intergenerational family structures have traditionally been framed as deviant or undesirable based on this ideology. For example, the infamous 1965 Moynihan Report by Daniel Patrick Moynihan, who served as

Assistant Secretary of Labor under President Lyndon B. Johnson, blamed poverty, and the decline in Black nuclear families on the rise in single-mother families instead of a lack of jobs. This victim-blaming report coincided with the beginning of the War on Poverty campaign. Ignoring the adverse economic and social effects of the criminal justice system's incarceration of Black men, Moynihan argued that increases in female-headed households in Black families created a matriarchal society that undermined the family responsibilities and role of Black men in caring for their families.

9. *The "American Ideal" and Otherness* – values about personal appearance that uphold and admire the slender, blue-eyed, blonde-haired, tall, able-bodied, young white middle-class look as the "ideal" standard of beauty and physical perfection. By extension, this ideal look is associated with intelligence, independence, assertiveness, strength, and normal, good, positive virtues. Conversely, those who do not fit this "ideal' look are "otherized" and stereotypes are used to objectify them as different, abnormal, bad, deficient, deviant, disabled, and in need of social control.

These nine American values and ideologies operate in tandem and independently in a White dominant economic, political, educational, and social welfare system to shape social welfare and legislative policies that continue the legacy of social control, hyper-policing, and restricting the lives of African Americans including placing them at greater risk for incarceration.

MAIN FOCUS OF THE CHAPTER

Scope and Prevalence of Mass Incarceration

According to the Equal Justice Initiative, (http://eji.org) the lives of Black people in the United States have been severely affected by the era of slavery, the era of racial terror from Reconstruction to the end of World War II, the era of Jim Crow and civil rights, and now the era of mass incarceration. The mass incarceration of Black men, women, and children living in poverty in the United States over the past 50 years has had a devastating impact on the lives of families and communities. The disproportionate representation of Black citizens in the criminal justice system is attributed to several intersecting factors including the war on drugs waged primarily in poor communities of color, and a criminal justice system that perpetuates race and class inequalities in law enforcement, sentencing policy, and disenfranchisement of offenders (Alexander, 2010). The long-standing effects of mass incarceration on family dynamics including parent-child attachment, the relationships between families and children and the availability and accessibility of economic and social resources are well documented in the literature.

The mass incarceration of Black American parents impacts the lives of their children as well. In 2016, about half of Black women in state prisons were mothers with minor children and 48% of Black men reported having a minor child. At the federal level 54% of Black women and 64% of Black men were parents with minor children (Maruschak, Bronson, & Alper, 2021). In 2007, 1 in 15 Black children had a parent in prison and Black children were 7.5 times more likely than Latinex and White children to have a parent in prison (The Sentencing Project, 2012). Contrary to the popular misperception, there is no empirical support for the assertion that children with incarcerated parents are at a greater risk for involvement in the criminal justice system than their peers (Mumola, 2000). The existence of numerous pre-incarceration variables (substance misuse, mental health, domestic violence, chronic poverty, etc.) limits making a causal relationship between parental incarceration and a greater risk of child involvement in crime and incarceration. Nevertheless, parental incarceration is now considered an adverse child experience (National Resource Center on Children & Families of the Incarcerated, 2014).

According to statistics from the Bureau of Justice (Carson, 2020), the total imprisonment rate fell 29% among Black adults from 2009 to 2019 making it the lowest rate in 30 years since 1989. Despite this downward trend, in 2018 Non-Latinex Blacks were 12.5% of the total United States population yet comprised 69% of adult arrestees for nonfatal violent crimes (33%) and serious nonfatal crimes (36%) based on data from the Federal Bureau of Investigations' Uniform Crime Reporting Program (Beck, 2021). At year-end 2019, Black male adults (2,203 per 100,000 black male U.S. residents) were incarcerated at a rate almost six times that of White male adults (385 per 100,000 White male U.S. residents) and nearly twice the rate of Latinex male adults (757 per 100,000 Latinex male U.S. residents) (Carson, 2020). African American men of all ages (2,724 inmates per 100,000) comprised 37% of male inmates in state and federal prisons with imprisonment rates four to ten times greater than White men and one to three times greater than rates for Latinex men. Black men ages 18 to 19 represented the largest disparity of any age group, with an incarceration rate 12 times greater than White males of the same age group in 2019 (Carson, 2020).

African American women of all ages (109 inmates per 100,000) comprised 22% of the female inmate population in state and federal prisons. Black women were imprisoned at rates two to four times greater than the incarceration rate of White women and one to two times greater than Latinex women (Carson, 2015). By year-end- 2019, the incarceration rate for Black women (83 per 100,000 Black female U.S. residents) was almost two times the rate of White women (48 per 100,000 White female U.S. residents) and less than one and a half times the rate of Latinex females (63 per 100,000 Latinex female U.S. residents) (Carson, 2020).

In 2014, an estimated 5 million adults were under community supervision on probation (3,864,100) or parole (856,900). Non-Latinex Blacks represented 30% of probationers and 39% of parolees relative to 54% non-Latinex White probationers and 43% parolees, and 13% Latinex or Latino probationers and 16% parolees. In 2014, drug offenses accounted for more than half (53%) of Black federal prisoner convictions while 25% served sentences related to weapons offenses including carrying, exhibiting, firing, possessing, or selling a weapon. Violent crimes (murder, homicide, robbery, aggravated assault, rape, etc.) represented less than 10% of Black federal prisoner convictions. For Black prisoners under state jurisdiction, 57% were convicted of violent crimes, and property (16%), drug (16%) or weapons (10.3%) offenses. The perpetual criminalization of Black citizens justified the expansion of the prison system and racial disparities in policies and practices at every stage of the incarceration process including arrests, sentencing, convictions, and placement (Hinton & Cook, 2021).

African American Children and Youth

In a 2008 policy brief Arya and Augarten reported "while African American youth do not commit more crime than White youth, they are overwhelmingly subjected to more punitive treatment including transfer to the adult courts and detention in adult jails." (p. 1). At 16% of the total number of adolescents in the United States, African American adolescents disproportionately account for 40% of all youth incarcerated in the United States, a 21% increase from 2010 when they represented 33% of the delinquency caseload. Trends in the juvenile justice system in 2010 indicated racial disparities across almost all types of offense. Case rates (cases per 1,000 juveniles ages 10 - 17) were substantially higher for Black youth than the rates for other youth for person (assault, homicide, murder), property (vandalism, theft, burglary,) and public order (disorderly conduct, curfew, loitering) offenses. Black youth accounted for the greatest overrepresentation for person offenses with Black females representing 41% of cases and Black males 40% in 2010. However, for drug offenses, Black females were underrepresented making up 14% of the juvenile population but only 11% of drug cases. Cases involving Black (59%) or American Indian (60%) were more likely to be petitioned for court than cases involving Asian (57%) or White (50%) youth representing racial disparity in the processing of cases. Once adjudicated delinquent, cases involving Black youth were more likely to result in a disposition of out-of-home placement than cases involving youth of other races, particularly in cases involving drug offenses in which black youth represented 27% of all adjudicated cases compared with Asian (17%), White (16%), and American Indian (16%) youth.

National relative rate index (RRI) data indicated that Black youth were arrested for delinquency offenses at a rate 3.3 times the rate for white youth, detained at a rate 1.4 times the rate of white youth, and were less likely than white youth to be diverted. These findings are consistent with previous research using the Disproportionate Minority Contact (DMC) approach to assess disparities and fairness in the juvenile justice system (Brinkley-Rubinstein, Craven, & McCormack, 2014; Richetelli, Hartstone, & Murphy, 2009; Soler & Gary, 2009). Research trends provide conclusive evidence that like African American adult experiences of mass incarceration, African American youth face racial disparities throughout major decision points in which they encounter the juvenile justice system. These decision points include arrests, referral to court, diversion, secure detention, case petitioning, delinquency adjudication, probation, confinement in a secure prison, and judicial waiver to adult criminal court (Arya & Augarten, 2008; Richetelli, et al., 2009; Sickmund & Puzzanchera, 2014). The extent of these disparities can and do vary among states.

Educational Racial Disparities - Impact on Incarceration

The United States department of Education reported that Black youth represent over 70% of all school-related arrests (United States Department of Education, 2012). Despite the 1954 Supreme Court landmark ruling in Brown v. Topeka Board of Education which overturned the Jim Crow White supremacist practice of "separate-but-equal doctrine," persistent in its reach and impact, this white racist ideology continues to structure the educational segregation of Black students, in effect, enacting what some scholars have coined as "The New Jim Crow in education". The New Jim Crow in education - the hyperregulation, displacement, monitoring, adultification, and commodification of Black youth in the public school system pushes Black children into the child welfare and juvenile justice system (Horsford, 2019). School policies and practices including school closings have resulted in the displacement of Black principals and teachers (Hill & Jones, 2021; White, 2016), leaving Black children exposed and vulnerable to White racial bias that places them disproportionately at risk for harsh school discipline resulting in school suspensions, expulsions, arrests, placement in the foster care and juvenile justice systems (Horsford, 2019; Monahan et al., 2014; Picower, 2009). During the 2011 – 2012 school year, Black children represented 16% of the total student population. However, White school officials suspended 32% of Black children in-school, suspended 33% of Black students out-of-school, 42% of Black students received more than one out-of-school suspension and 34% of Black children were expelled (Nance, 2016). Additionally, Black children were 27% of students referred to law enforcement and 31% of students White administrators subjected to arrests. During the previous school year, one in every six Black students in K-12 public schools were suspended at least once by White administrators while White students were suspended at a rate of one to every twenty. Disturbingly worse yet, African American preschool children made up 18% of enrollment during the 2011 -12 school year but accounted for 48% of preschool children who received more than one out-of-school suspension by White administrators (Nance, 2016).

So-called colorblind school policies and practices including the use of zero tolerance discipline, maximum security schools, and police resource officers in schools have the effect of pushing Black children out of the public school system and into the prison pipeline (Lhamon & Samuels, 2014; Losen & Martinez, 2013; Staats, 2014). Additionally, White school official's adultification (Epstein, Blake, & González, 2017) of Black children as older, more aggressive, and culpable than their White peers even when they exhibit the same developmental behaviors, expose Black children to disproportionately harsher discipline and treatment that includes criminalization, suspension, expulsion, referral to alternative schools, law enforcement, and juvenile detention more than White students (Intercultural Development Research Association, 2021). Black children and youth are also subjected to racially criminalizing stereotypes by White school officials resulting in dress code violations - framing clothing worn by Black boys as symbolic of gang activity and clothing worn by Black girls as sexually suggestive (Anderson et al., 2019). Black students also report higher rates of exposure to racial discrimination, placing them at greater risk for racial stress and trauma than their White peers (Saleem et al., 2020; Williams et al. 2018).

Child Welfare Racial Disparities – Impact on Incarceration

White racial bias has also been a long-standing feature of the child welfare system. About 15 – 20% of children entering the child welfare system have an incarcerated parent and Black children remain overrepresented in the child welfare system but not because they are at greater risk of parental abuse than children of other races or ethnicity but primarily due to racial bias (Child Welfare Information Gateway, 2021). African American children account for about 14% of the child population, but they represent 23% of the foster care population and racial disparities occur at nearly every major decision point in the child welfare system (Annie E. Casey Foundation, 2020; Children's Bureau, 2020). African American families are more likely to be reported by Whites for suspected maltreatment (Krase, 2013), are investigated at disproportionally higher rates by White workers than other families (Kim et al., 2017), and are at greater risk along with Indigenous families of being confirmed for maltreatment and placement within the foster care system (Yi et al., 2020).

Initially excluded from the developing foster care system in the 1800's, by 2000, Black children were the largest group of children in foster care and remain overrepresented (Billingsley & Giovannoni, 1972; Hogan & Siu, 1988; Roberts, 2012). Once in the child welfare system, Black families are also more likely than other families to receive disparate treatment - more time in foster care, less likely to reunify with their families, multiple placements, less services, higher rates of removal from their homes, and higher termination of parental rights (Garcia, et al., 2016; Lu et al., 2004; Maguire-Jack et al., 2020; U.S. Government Accountability office, 2007; Wideman et al., 2020).

Roberts (2012) argues that the foster care, social services, and criminal justice systems are intersecting structures of White power that function to monitor, regulate, and punish poor Black mothers and by extension their children "by keeping them under intense state supervision." Extensive research also recognizes the role of the foster care system as a pipeline to prison, in that "children living in or aging out of foster care are at high risk for being locked up in juvenile detention and adult prison" (Roberts, 2019, n.p). Multiple placements also increase a child's risk of juvenile detention involvement (Roberts, 2012).

SOLUTIONS AND RECOMMENDATIONS

Anti-Racist Practice Frameworks

Counseling practitioners can partner with African American families in ways that build on strengths and promote generational resilience while supporting families as they navigate the economic, financial, and sociocultural complexities associated with involvement in the criminal justice system. The use of culturally specific, multi-systems frameworks can facilitate this process offering counseling practitioners an integrated approach that involves both direct practice and social justice advocacy and policy efforts. Cross-cultural self-reflection and attendance to the worker's own cultural lens and social position can facilitate critical assessment of everyday racism or racial microaggressions (Sue et al., 2007) that African American families encounter when they come in contact with White service delivery systems.

Two useful practice frameworks available for understanding the complexity of the risk and protective factors affecting African America families' experiences with mass incarceration include the multi-systems life course (MSLC) perspective (Murphy-Erby et al., 2010) and the Afrocentric Intergenerational Solidarity (AIS) model (Waites, 2008). The MSLC perspective offers clinicians a practice assessment tool that considers the lived experiences and worldviews of communities of color and integrates four theories including ecological systems (Bronfenbrener, 1989), life course theory (Elder, 1995), symbolic interactionism (Blumer, 1969), and theories of social action and change (Murphy-Erby et al., 2010). The main components of each theory are outlined in Table 1:

Table 1. Main components of the MSLC perspective

Theory	Main Components
Ecological Systems	• Interrelated structural opportunities and limitations. • Economic, financial, educational, housing resources. • Federal and state laws, agency policies and practices. • Interrelated biological, socio-cultural, and physical contexts.
Life Course	• Historical social factors that shape life pathways and choices across generations. • The transitions individuals and families experience across the life course.
Symbolic Interactionism	• The implications of the meaning made of life experiences and assigned by others. • The symbols that reflect the meaning made of life experiences and assigned by others. • Beliefs about the perceptions of others. • Behaviors shaped by cultural symbols.
Social Change	• Social justice and social action efforts aimed at challenging systems of oppression and exclusion. • Strategies aimed to reduce power and privilege standpoints that perpetuate the status quo.

Using the MSLC perspective helps clinicians recognize:

1. How limited choices in the criminal justice system shape parental responsibilities, family and child relationships, dynamics, and contact.
2. How parental incarceration contributes to limitations in the availability of parent-child attachment and bonding processes necessary for healthy child development.

3. How social stigma, and socioeconomic barriers interact with legal conditions of incarceration, release, and reentry and shape behavior and parental options across the family life cycle.
4. How the timing of life events like incarceration may impact children and/or their parents differently due to their stage of development at the time the event occurs.
5. How the symbolism and meaning associated with given developmental tasks across the life course, such as child autonomy, may be compromised due to parental incarceration.
6. How the meaning families make of their lives can shape child and family resilience.
7. How historical disparities continue to affect the distribution of resources and the need for social change efforts.
8. How parental free will is constrained by powerful ideological and social forces, such as white supremacy, discrimination, and prejudice.

The Afrocentric Intergenerational Solidarity (AIS) perspective (Waites, 2008) is a culturally responsive strengths-based approach for understanding the usefulness of African centered value-based practices and the role of intergenerational relationships within African American families over time as sources of resilience and survival. As a practice approach the AIS perspective can assist clinicians identify and respond to the intergenerational dynamics of mass incarceration. The intergenerational solidarity (Bengtson & Roberts, 1991) framework can help clinicians assess the degree of social cohesion and conflict between generations. It provides a classification system of six domains of intergenerational cohesion or solidarity and/or conflict. Waites (2009) expanded the intergenerational solidarity framework by incorporating Afrocentric culturally relevant values including a holistic interdependent collective identity, respect for oral traditions, mutual aid and kinship, and a worldview that embraces emotional wisdom, reciprocity, and spirituality (Schiele, 2000). African American family history, traditions, extended family, kin and non-kin generational roles, shared values, and practices are privileged. The main components of the AIS perspective are outlined in Table 2:

Table 2. Main components of the AIS perspective

Domain	Main Competent
Affectional	• Expressed sentiments of closeness to or conflicts with extended family, kin, and non-kin members • Communication patterns used to express closeness/conflicts • Ways members share affection across generations • Emotional and generational ties present
Associational	• Who are identifiably significant family members • Type and frequency of contact between generations
Consensual	• Shared values and beliefs between generations • Important generational family history • Connections to cultural activities with African American communities
Functional	• Help-seeking and receiving traditions across generations • How family respond to members in need of assistance • Family members with resources • How patterns of support are demonstrated across generations
Normative	• Expected familial roles, responsibilities, and functions across generations • Family norms • How deviations from expectations are addressed
Structural	• Familial geographical proximity and migration patterns • Opportunities for cross-generational interactions • Barriers to cross-generational interactions

Using the AIS perspective helps clinicians recognize:

1. The structural, familial, and generational risk and protective factors that influence African American family exposure to incarceration.
2. Generational family strengths and limitations when developing prevention and intervention strategies.
3. How cultural values and beliefs support generational resilience and can provide counter narratives that challenge and dispel racist stereotypes, and myths stemming from White racist ideologies and domination.
4. Reciprocity - affirm that both client and practitioner have valuable wisdom, knowledge, and expertise from which to draw on in the working relationship.
5. The importance of honoring spirituality and emotional wisdom as sources of knowledge and resources.
6. The importance of honoring African American family help seeking values and traditions.

Cross Cultural Practice

Cross cultural practice with African American families experiencing incarceration requires practitioners to understand how their own cultural lens shapes their perceptions of the world and the clients with whom they work (Miley, O'Melia, & DuBois, 2013). The reflective cultural inventory exercise can help clinicians think about themselves as multicultural beings and raise awareness of how personal beliefs and values can influence cross-cultural interactions and how status, privilege, and power associated with cultural group membership can shape the nature of collaborative cross- cultural relationships in work with African American families experiencing incarceration. Attention to ones own cultural values, social position, and biases can aid in reducing racial microaggressions (Sue et al., 2007) that can act as barriers to clinical practice cross-cultural transactions when clinicians impose their cultural values and devalue and pathologize the lived experiences and worldview of African American clients. It is important to note that clinicians of any racial or ethnic background can internalize anti-Black racial biases and stereotypes of the larger society (Speight, 2007) and impose them in clinical work with African American families experiencing incarceration.

Step 1 – Cultural Inventory (Miley et al. 2013)

After answering the following questions, complete only the first column of the table below, defining your cultural identity.

Personal Identity

- What are your ethnic or cultural identities?
- Which cultural identities most influence the way you define yourself?
- How do you demonstrate your cultural identities?
- What values are associated with these cultural identities?
- Do you feel about these identities?
- Have you ever experienced discrimination (or felt devalued) based on your cultural identities?

- What privileges do your cultural identities afford you?

Spiritual Beliefs

- What are your spiritual beliefs and how were they formed?
- How important are spiritual beliefs in your daily life?
- How do these beliefs influence the way you perceive others who hold different beliefs and influence your choices and behaviors?

Knowledge of Others

- What other cultural groups are present in your community?
- What do you know about the beliefs, values, and customs of members of these other cultural groups?
- What is the source of this knowledge?
- Have your interactions with people from these cultures reinforced or altered this knowledge base?
- How do your cultural perspectives differ from those of your clients?
- What stereotypes or prejudices do you hold about other cultural groups?
- What is the source of your biases?
- What are you doing to increase your knowledge about people who are culturally different from you?

Cross-Cultural Skills

- Do you impose dominant norms or honor the integrity of your clients' culture?
- Are you currently involved in relationships or activities involving ongoing interactions with people from other cultures?
- What is your comfort level while interacting with people who are culturally different from you?
- Are you able to talk with people who are culturally different from you about differences?

Step 2 – Assessing Your Social Location Within the Socio-political Context of the USA

The next step of the cultural inventory is for counselors to assess dimensions of their own identity within the context of the socio-political values and ideologies that shape American society. For this step clinicians should reread the definitions of each of the nine basic dominant America values and ideologies and complete Table 3. When assessing whether a dimension of their identity or culture is privileged, clinicians should think about how aware they are of this cultural characteristic. Do they take it for granted in their daily life? Does it give them easy access to resources that they might not otherwise obtain so easily? Can they get by comfortably in life without giving it a second thought? If the answer is yes to these three questions, it's likely a privileged dimension of identity that will shape their perspective and life experiences differently than if it were not. When assessing whether a dimension of their identity or culture is devalued, clinicians should think about how aware they are of this cultural characteristic. Do they feel that they must defend, hide, minimize it regularly? Does it create barriers to accessing resources that others who do not share this characteristic may experience readily? Is the characteristic stigmatized by the wider society? If the answer is "yes" to these three questions, it is likely that this dimension of identity is devalued by the wider society. Think about how aspects of personal identity provide privilege or are devalued and then examine how each may affect their work with African American clients experiencing incarceration.

Table 3. Assessing your social location within the socio-political context of the USA

Multicultural Dimensions of Identity	Define Your Cultural Identity	Is this Dimension Privileged or Devalued? Yes, No, Sometimes
Race		
Ethnicity		
Gender		
Sexual Orientation		
Spiritual/Religious Orientation		
Ability/disability		
Socioeconomic Status		
Language		
Level of Education		
Age		
Culture		
Physical Appearance (height, weight, hair color/length, etc.-not including skin color		
Geographic location (urban, suburban, rural, inner city, etc.)		
Regional location (North, South, Midwest, East, etc.),		
Citizenship Status (legal resident, permanent residence, undocumented, temporary/work visa, etc.)		
Family Status		
Communication Style		
Political views		

Step 3 - Crime and Incarceration Inventory

As helping professionals, counselors must recognize their attitudes, beliefs, and perceptions of members of a specific group, or experiences about an issue or problem to provide unbiased, culturally responsive services. Below are some of the common attitudes and misconceptions of people involved in the criminal justice system. After reading each statement, respond to the questions that follow.

Common Attitudes, Beliefs, and Misconceptions

- People who engage in criminal behavior are immoral and unfit to raise children.
- Children exposed to criminal behavior grow up to be criminals.
- People who engage in criminal behavior should be: (1) punished, (2) given an opportunity for rehabilitation, (3) denied the right to vote.
- Only certain kinds of people engage in criminal behavior.
- Once a criminal always a criminal.
- Engaging in criminal behavior is a (1) choice, (2) biological, (3) social.
- Criminal-like tendencies can be passed to future generations.
- Criminals are bad for the neighborhood.
- Criminals are bad people who do bad things.
- Prison is no place for a child to visit.
- Children exposed to prison facilities are at-risk of engaging in delinquent behavior.
- Incarcerated adults become hardened criminals.
- Incarcerated adults are guilty of the crimes they are charged with committing.
- The criminal justice system is (1) impartial, (2) colorblind, (3) neutral
- In criminal justice, punishment should be more important than rehabilitation.
- It is a waste of time to try to rehabilitate some criminals.
- Criminals are incapable of (1) parenting, (2) rehabilitation.

Self-Reflective Questions and Assessment

1. Do you ascribe to any of the attitudes and beliefs outlined above or any others not listed?
2. What factors influence your beliefs and attitudes about crime and incarceration?
3. What is/are the source(s) of your knowledge about crime and incarceration?
4. How do you feel about the beliefs and attitudes you have about crime and incarceration?
5. How do your beliefs and attitudes about crime and incarceration shape your personal and professional choices and behaviors?
6. What are you doing to increase your knowledge about people who engage in criminal behavior and experience incarceration?
7. How do you think your attitudes and beliefs about people who engage in criminal behavior and experience incarceration will influence your work with Black incarcerated parents, youth, children, families?

After responding to the questions above, counselors should conduct an honest self-assessment of the gaps, barriers, and limitations of their ability to work effectively with African American families experiencing incarceration and take steps to actively remedy their challenges before engaging in clinical interventions or providing services.

Policy Advocacy and Activism

Macro-Level

Black Americans have an extensive history of responding to structural racism through civic and community organizing, civil rights policy advocacy, activism, and working with political and religious abolitionist and allies from diverse racial groups to challenge racial disparities in multiple sectors of society (Hinton & Cook 2021). The MSLC framework offers counseling practitioners a roadmap for using an integrated approach to practice across all levels (micro, mezzo, and macro). Counselors committed to equity and justice can partner with national civil rights and social justice organizations like the Equal Justice Initiative (www.eji.org) committed to ending mass incarceration and excessive punishment and the NAACP (https://www.naacp.org), dedicated to challenging racial and economic injustice. Organizations like the National Black Justice Coalition (www.nbjc.org) and the Black Lives Matter movement (http://blacklivesmatter.com) emphasize an intersectional approach to addressing systemic oppression and policy advocacy. Another grassroots organization with a mission to dismantle unjust criminalized systems that exploit and blame poor communities and communities of color is the Poor People's Campaign (www.poorpeoplescampaign.org). These are only a few of the national, regional, and grassroots organizations working to eliminate systems of oppression affecting the lives of Black people and other marginalized populations.

Addressing racial disparities within the school system requires a multi-pronged approach. The trauma-informed school movement (Overstreet & Chafouleas, 2016) offers school officials an opportunity to collaborate with community-based mental-health and behavioral service counseling practitioners, parents, and students to transform school culture, policies, practices, and programming to create a safe educational culture where racial equity can prevail for all students (Stevens, 2017). *The Huffpost* (2017) reported more than 23,000 out of 132,000 schools have embraced a trauma-informed school culture reducing suspensions by 85%, dropping expulsions by 40%, and many reported significant reductions in bullying, truancy, dropout rates, and tardiness (Stevens, 2021). Scholars also recommend removing resource (police) officers from schools and reducing the reliance on them as disciplinarians, and offering implicit bias training generally and specifically on adultification to reduce the targeting of Black girls and boys (Epstein et al, 2021; Nance, 2016). Counselors can urge the creation of an interdisciplinary taskforce consisting of legislators and agency policymakers and officials within the educational, juvenile justice, law enforcement and child welfare systems to work with the civic organizations identified above to examine policy reforms to reduce the racial disparities that exist across these systems.

Mezzo-Level

Clinicians can also act at an agency and community-level to address race-based barriers affecting the lives of African American communities experiencing incarceration. Counselors can routinely examine their own agency policies and practices to make sure they are anti-racist, facilitate racial equity, empower, and affirm the life experiences of racialized clients and are not alienating. Counselors can develop and promote anti-racist training for service providers, staff, and administrators as a beginning step toward creating an anti-racist work culture. Representation matters. Hire racially diverse counselors who look like the clients they serve and live in the same communities in which clients live. Demonstrate efforts to build bridges with communities and reduce tokenism. Partner with faith-based organizations within the community to provide services and invite clients to the table as part of decision-making and planning supports effective sustainable community-based practice.

FUTURE RESEARCH DIRECTIONS

The mass incarceration of African American/Black families in the U.S. can be understood within a historical context of struggle for racial freedom and justice that has continued for centuries. Understanding this context requires counselors to expand their knowledge and intervention skills beyond individual and family therapy. Counselors must be equipped to engage in policy advocacy and social activist work. This level of counseling requires skills in interdisciplinary knowledge and effective collaborative community-based skills. Essentially, the field of counseling education will need to expand its curriculum, pedagogy, philosophy and evolve in its framing of the "problem" beyond the individual client to a focus on the systems that impact the quality of life and freedoms of clients particularly African American families experiencing generational incarceration. Future research is needed to expand the field of counseling and its curriculum and training in preparing current and future counselors for integrative practice at community and societal levels of practice.

CONCLUSION

The legacy of white supremacy and structural racism is woven in the historic fabric of America and endemic in the policies and practices that shape our contemporary society. Structural racism has significantly shaped the experiences of African American families living with mass incarceration. The intersections of law enforcement, criminal justice, child welfare, education, and social services can manifest like a matrix of domination and oppression (Collins,1990) or serve as a transformative force for racial healing and change in the lives of African Americans experiencing incarceration. Counselors must see this history for what it is in all its manifestations and its evolution through centuries of policies and practices that have demonstrated a singular goal of maintaining white racial economic, political, and social power through the surveillance, restriction, regulation, and control of Black bodies en masse. It's time to set a new course of action.

REFERENCES

Agyepong, T. E. (2018). *The criminalization of Black children: Race, gender, and delinquency in Chicago's juvenile justice system, 1899-1945*. University of North Carolina Press. doi:10.5149/northcarolina/9781469636443.001.0001

Alexander, L., & Alexander, M. (2021). Fear. In N. Hannah-Jones, C. Roper, I. Silverman, & J. Silverstein (Eds.), A New Origin Story: The 1619 Project (pp.97–122). One World.

Alexander, M. (2010). *The new Jim Crow: Mass incarceration in the age of colorblindness*. The New Press.

Anderson, C. (2016). *White Rage: The Unspoken Truth of Our Racial Divide*. Bloomsbury.

Anderson, R. E., Saleem, F. T., & Huguley, J. P. (2019). Choosing to see the racial stress that afflicts our Black students. *Phi Delta Kappan: The Professional Journal for Educators*. https://kappanonline.org/racial-stress-black-students-anderson-saleem-huguley/

Annie E. Casey Foundation. (2020). *Children in poverty by race and ethnicity in the United States*. https://datacenter.kidscount.org/data/tables/44-children-in-poverty-by-race-and-ethnicity

Arya, N., & Augarten, I. (2008). Critical condition: African American youth in the justice system. *Race Ethnicity*, 1–49.

Beck, A. J. (2021). Race and ethnicity of violent crime offenders and arrestees, 2018. U.S. Department of Justice. Office of Justice Programs. Bureau of Justice Statistics.

Bengtson, V. L., & Roberts, R. E. I. (1991). Intergenerational solidarity in aging families: Anexample of formal theory construction. *Journal of Marriage and Family*, *53*(4), 856–870. doi:10.2307/352993

Billingsley, A., & Giovannoni, J. M. (1972). *Children of the storm: Black children and American child welfare*. Harcourt Brace Jovanovich.

Blumer, H. (1969). *Symbolic interactionism: Perspectives and method*. Prentice-Hall.

Brinkley-Rubinstein, L., Craven, K. L., & McCormack, M. M. (2014). Shifting perceptions of race and incarceration as adolescents age: Addressing disproportionate minority contact by understanding how social environment informs racial attitudes. *Child & Adolescent Social Work Journal*, *31*(1), 25–38. doi:10.100710560-013-0306-4

Bronfenbrener, U. (1989). Ecological systems theory. *Annals of Child Development*, *6*, 187–249.

Carson, E. A. (2020). *Prisoners in 2019*. U.S. Department of Justice. Office of Justice Programs. Bureau of Justice Statistics.

Child Welfare Information Gateway. (2021). *Child welfare practice to address racial disproportionality and disparity*. U.S. Department of Health and Human Services, Administration for Children and Families, Children's Bureau. https://www.childwelfare.gov/pubs/issue-briefs/racial-disproportionality/

Children's Bureau. (2020). *The AFCARS report: Preliminary FY 2019 estimates as of June 23, 2020 – No. 27*. U.S. Department of Health and Human Services, Administration for Children and Families. https://www.acf.hhs.gov/cb/resource/afcars-report-27

Collins, P. H. (1990). Black feminist thought in the matrix of domination. In Black feminist thought: Knowledge, Consciousness, and the Politics of Empowerment (pp. 221 – 238). Unwin Hyman.

Day, P. J., & Schiele, J. (2013). *A New History of Social Welfare* (7th ed.). Pearson.

Delaney, R., Subramanian, R., Shames, A., & Turner, N. (2018). *American History, Race, and Prison*. Vera Institute of Justice.

Elder, G. H. (1995). The life course paradigm: Social change and individual development. In P. Moen, G. H. Elder, & K. Luscher (Eds.), *Examining lives in context: Perspectives on the ecology of human development* (pp. 101–139). doi:10.1037/10176-003

Equal Justice Initiative. (2020). *Reconstruction in America: Racial violence after the civil war, 1865 – 1876*. Author.

Equal Justice Initiative. (2021). https://eji.org/criminal-justice-reform/

Garland, D. (2001). Introduction. In D. Garland (Ed.), Mass imprisonment: Social causes and consequences (pp. 1-3). Sage.

Grabenstein, H. (2018). *Inside Mississippi's notorious Parchman prison*. PBS NewsHour.

Hadden, S. E. (2001). *Slave patrols: Law and violence in Virginia and the Carolinas*. Harvard University Press.

Hill, A.J. & Jones, D.B. (2021). The effect of school closings on teacher labor market outcomes and teacher effectiveness. *Education Finance and Policy*, 1 – 25. . doi:10.1162/edfp_a_00317

Hinton, E., & Cook, D. (2021). The mass criminalization of Black Americans: A Historical overview. *Annual Review of Criminology*, *4*(1), 261–286. doi:10.1146/annurev-criminol-060520-033306

Hogan, P. T., & Siu, S. (1998). Minority children and the child welfare system: An historical perspective. *Social Work*, *33*(6), 493–498. doi:10.1093w/33.6.493

Honore-Collins, C. P. (2005). The impact of African American incarceration on African American children in the child welfare system. *Race, Gender, & Class*, *12*(3/4), 107–118.

Horsford, S. (2019). School Integration in the New Jim Crow: Opportunity or Oxymoron? *Educational Policy*, *33*(1), 257–275. doi:10.1177/0895904818810526

Intercultural Developmental Research Association. (2021). *Understanding and Addressing Racial Trauma and Supporting Black Students in Schools*. www.idra.org/wp-content/uploads/2021/02/Understanding-and-Addressing-Racial-Trauma-and Supporting-Black-Students-in-Schools-IDRA.pdf

Kaeble, D., Maruschak, L. M., & Bonczar, T. P. (2015). *Probation and parole in the United States, 2014*. U.S. Department of Justice. Office of Justice Programs. Bureau of Justice Statistics.

Kim, H., Wildeman, C., Jonson-Reid, M., & Drake, B. (2017). Lifetime prevalence of investigating child maltreatment among US children. *American Journal of Public Health*, *107*(2), 274–280. doi:10.2105/AJPH.2016.303545 PMID:27997240

Kohli, R., Johnson, R. N., & Perez, L. H. (2006). Naming racism: A conceptual look at internalized racism in US schools. *Chicano/Latino. Law Review*, 183–206.

Krase, K. S. (2013). Differences in racially disproportionate reporting of child maltreatment across report sources. *Journal of Public Child Welfare*, *7*(4), 351–369. doi:10.1080/15548732.2013.798763

Lhamon, C. E., & Samuels, J. (2014). *Dear colleague letter from the U.S. Department of Justice and the U.S. Department of Education*. https://www2.ed.gov/about/offices/list/ocr/letters/colleague-201401-title-vi.pdf

Losen, D. J., & Martinez, T. E. (2013). Out of school & off track: The overuse of suspensions in American middle and high schools. The Center for Civil Rights Remedies at the Civil Rights Project (UCLA).

Lu, Y. E., Landsverk, J., Ellis-Macleod, E., Newton, R., Ganger, W., & Johnson, I. (2004). Race, ethnicity, and case outcomes in child protective services. *Children and Youth Services Review*, *26*(5), 447–461. doi:10.1016/j.childyouth.2004.02.002

Maguire-Jack, K., Font, S. A., & Dillard, R. (2020). Child protective services decision-making: The role of children's race and county factors. *The American Journal of Orthopsychiatry*, *90*(1), 48–62. doi:10.1037/ort0000388 PMID:31081655

Maruschak, L. M., Bronson, J., & Alper, M. (2021). *Survey of prison inmates, 2016: Parents in prison and their minor children. U.S. Department of Justice. Office of Justice Programs.* Bureau of Justice Statistics.

Middleton, S. (2020). *Repressive legislation: Slave codes, northern Black laws, and southern Black codes.* Oxford Research Encyclopedias. American History., doi:10.1093/acrefore/9780199329175.013.634

Miley, K. K., O'Melia, M. W., & DuBois, B. L. (2022). *Generalist social work practice: An empowering approach* (9th ed.). Pearson.

Monahan, K. C., VanDerhei, S., Bechtold, J., & Cauffman, E. (2014). From the school yard to the squad car: School discipline, truancy, & arrest. *Youth & Adolescence*, *43*(7), 1110–1122. doi:10.100710964-014-0103-1 PMID:24526497

Morris, M. (2016). *Pushout: The criminalization of Black girls in schools*. The New Press.

Muller, C. (2012). Northward migration and the rise of racial disparity in American incarceration, 1880 – 1950. *American Journal of Sociology*, *118*(2), 281–326. doi:10.1086/666384

Mumola, C. J. (2000). Incarcerated parents and their children. US Department of Justice. Office of Justice Programs. Bureau of Justice Statistics.

Murphy-Erby, Y., Christy-McMullin, K., Stauss, K., & Schriver, J. (2010). Multi-systems life course: A new practice perspective and its application in advanced practice with racial and ethnic populations. *Journal of Human Behavior in the Social Environment*, *20*(5), 672–687. doi:10.1080/10911351003751868

Nance, P. (2016). Over-Disciplining students, racial bias, and the school-to-prison-pipeline. *University of Richmond Law Review. University of Richmond*, *50*, 1063–1074.

National Resource Center on Children & Families of the Incarcerated. (2014). *Children and families of the incarcerated fact sheet*. Rutgers University.

Picower, B. (2009). The Unexamined Whiteness of teaching: How White teachers maintain and enact dominant racial ideologies. *Race, Ethnicity and Education*, *12*(2), 197–215. doi:10.1080/13613320902995475

Richetelli, D. M., Hartstone, E. C., & Murphy, K. L. (2009). *A second reassessment of disproportionate minority contact in Connecticut's juvenile justice system*. The Office of Juvenile Justice Programs. U.S. Department of Justice to the state of Connecticut.

Roberts, D. (2012). Prison, foster care, and the systemic punishment of Black mothers. *UCLA Law Review. University of California, Los Angeles. School of Law*, *59*, 1474–1500.

Saleem, F. T., Anderson, R. T., & Williams, M. (2019). Addressing the "Myth" of racial trauma: Developmental and ecological considerations for youth of color. *Clinical Child and Family Psychology Review*, *23*(1), 1–14. doi:10.100710567-019-00304-1 PMID:31641920

Schiele, J. H. (2000). *Human services and the Afrocentric paradigm*. Haworth Press.

Sickmund, M., & Puzzanchera, C. (Eds.). (2014). *Juvenile offenders and victims: 2014 national report*. National Center for Juvenile Justice.

Soler, M., & Gary, L. M. (2009). *Disproportionate minority contact: Addressing disproportionate minority contact in juvenile justice*. Office of Juvenile Justice and Delinquency Prevention.

Speight, S. L. (2007). Internalized racism: One more piece of the puzzle. *The Counseling Psychologist*, *35*(1), 126–134. doi:10.1177/0011000006295119

Staats, C. (2014). *Implicit racial bias and school discipline disparities: Exploring the connection*. Kirwan Institute for the Study of Race and Ethnicity. Special Report. 1-20.

Sue, D. W., Capodilupo, C. M., Torino, G. C., Bucceri, J. M., Holder, A. M. B., Nadal, K. L., & Esquilin, M. (2007). Racial microaggressions in everyday life: Implications for clinical practice. *The American Psychologist*, *64*(4), 271–286. doi:10.1037/0003-066X.62.4.271 PMID:17516773

Travis, J., Western, B., & Redburn, S. (2014). *The growth in incarceration in the United States: Exploring causes and consequences*. The National Academics Press.

United States Department of Education. (2012). *Civil rights data collection*. United States Department of Education.

U.S. Government Accountability Office. (2007). *African American children in foster care: Additional HHS assistance needed to help states reduce the proportion in care* (GAO-07-816). https://www.gao.gov/products/GAO-07-816

Waites, C. (Ed.). (2008). *Social work practice with African Americans: An intergenerational perspective*. Routledge.

Waites, C. (2009). Building on strengths: Intergenerational practice with African American families. *Social Work*, *54*(3), 278–287. doi:10.1093w/54.3.278 PMID:19530575

White, T. (2016). Teach for America's paradoxical diversity initiative: Race, policy, and Black teacher displacement in urban schools. *Education Policy Analysis Archives*, *24*(16), 16. Advance online publication. doi:10.14507/epaa.24.2100

Wildeman, C., Edwards, F. R., & Wakefield, S. (2020). The cumulative prevalence of termination of parental rights for U.S. children 2000 – 2016. *Child Maltreatment*, *25*(1), 32–42. doi:10.1177/1077559519848499 PMID:31113210

Williams, M. T., Printz, D. M. B., & DeLapp, R. C. T. (2018). Assessing racial trauma with the trauma symptoms of discrimination scale. *Psychology of Violence*, *8*(6), 735–747. Advance online publication. doi:10.1037/vio0000212

Yi, Y., Edwards, F. R., & Wildeman, C. (2020). Cumulative prevalence of confirmed maltreatment and foster care placements for U.S. children by race/ethnicity, 2011 – 2016. *American Journal of Public Health, 110*(5), 704–709. doi:10.2105/AJPH.2019.305554 PMID:32191517

ADDITIONAL READING

Abrams, S. (2019). *Lead from the Outside: How to build your future and make real change*. Picador.

Asim, J. (2018). *We can't breathe: On black lives, white lies, and the art of survival*. Picador.

Crenshaw, K., Gotanda, N., Peller, G., & Thomas, K. (Eds.). (1995). *Critical race theory: The key writings that formed the movement*. The New Press.

Dillard, C. (2020). The weaponization of whiteness in schools. *Learning for Justice*, 65, https://www.learningforjustice.org/magazine/fall-2020/the-weaponization-of-whiteness-in-schools

Feagin, J. R. (2020). *The white racial frame: Centuries of racial framing and counter-framing* (3rd ed.). Routledge. doi:10.4324/9780429353246

Hartman, S. V. (1997). *Scenes of subjection: Terror, slavery, and self-making in nineteenth-century America*. Oxford University Press.

Jones-Rogers, S. E. (2019). *They were her property: White women as slave owners in the American South*. Yale University Press.

Miller, R. J. (2021). *Halfway Home: Race, Punishment, and the Afterlife of Mass Incarceration*. Little, Brown and Company.

Smith, C. (2021). *How the word is passed: A reckoning with the history of slavery across America*. Little, Brown, and Company.

Theoharis, J. (2018). *A more beautiful and terrible history: The uses and misuses of civil rights history*. Beacon Press.

KEY TERMS AND DEFINITIONS

Adultification: The perception that Black children are older, adult-like, less innocent, and more culpable than their White peers when they exhibit the same developmentally appropriate behaviors.

Anti-Racism: The active process of recognizing, acknowledging, and challenging white supremacist ideology by changing beliefs, policies, and practices to redistribute power and resources in racially equitable ways.

Disparity: The unequal distribution of and accessibility to resources across different groups.

Disproportionality: The overrepresentation or underrepresentation of a group relative to its representation in the total population.

Disproportionate Minority Contact (DMC): The Juvenile Justice and Delinquency Prevention Act (JJDPA) requires states to identify and address DMC at multiple decision points in processing juvenile cases, not just at the point of confinement.

Implicit Racial Bias: unintentional or unconscious prejudice toward someone based on their skin color, racial, or ethnic origin.

Matrix of Domination: A sociological paradigm coined by Dr. Patricia Hill-Collins to locate and explain lived experiences with interlocking forms of oppression based on various classification of identity (race, class, age, sexual orientation, gender, etc.) within the social contexts that produce them.

Racial Microaggressions: Intentional and unintentional everyday verbal, behavioral, or environmental humiliations that communicate negative racial slights, insults, assaults, invalidations of people categorized as nonwhite.

Racial Stress or Trauma: The negative effects of race-related distress. Symptoms may include anxiety, depression, anger, fear, sadness, helplessness, shame, hypervigilance, isolation, avoidance, etc.

Relative Rate Index (RRI): A tool designed to identify and measure disparities across the stages of processing cases in the juvenile justice system by comparing rates of juvenile justice contact experienced by different youth groups.

Structural Racism: The systemic ways policies and practices are developed, maintained, and perpetuated differentially to privilege and advance some groups favorably and disadvantage and disenfranchise other groups.

White Supremacy: The ideological belief in the inherent superiority of people categorized as White and the inherent inferiority of racial, ethnic groups categorized as nonwhite.

Chapter 3
The Role Addiction Plays in America:
What Focusing on the Wrong Issues Has Done

Lilia Farmanara Kneidel
Florida Atlantic University, USA

ABSTRACT

The purpose of this chapter is to address the impact addiction has throughout the United States among various aspects of society. This specifically includes a focus on individuals incarcerated because of the role addiction has had in their life and the role incarceration has on addiction. This chapter will also dive into the research behind who is more likely to end up with an addiction, how children and adolescents are affected by addiction, the effects of parental incarceration on children and adolescents, various treatment methods for addiction, and how addiction is portrayed in the media.

INTRODUCTION

When people think of individuals incarcerated for drug offenses, they normally limit their opinions to stereotypes such as drug dealers or drug addicts who were unlucky and got caught, placing them into correctional facilities in order to deter this behavior from happening again. However, the connection between addiction and incarceration has been increasing for several decades in the United States (U.S.). Recently, the National Institute on Drug Abuse (NIDA) (2020) released data on prison populations across the U.S., showing that most of the U.S. prison population (an estimated 65%) has an active substance use disorder (SUD). Another 20-25% were documented as being under the influence of drugs and or alcohol at the time of their crime, but not considered to have an active SUD. However, this 20-25% also includes individuals with a history of substance abuse, individuals who committed a crime for drug money or individuals who were incarcerated for a past drug or alcohol violation (Sack, 2014). Overall,

DOI: 10.4018/978-1-7998-9209-0.ch003

this leaves the U.S. with a shocking 85% rate of individuals incarcerated for a crime somehow related to substance use.

As drug use continues to rise in the U.S., it has become increasingly obvious that incarceration does not deter substance abuse. More than 300,000 people were held in state or federal prisons in the U.S. for drug-related crimes as recently as 2015, an approximate 12% increase since 1980, when this number was less than 25,000 (Carson & Anderson, 2016; Snell, 1995; The Pew Charitable Trusts, 2018). More so, while the number of individuals incarcerated for drug-related offenses has increased, so has their time spent behind bars. Federal prisons are managed by the federal government, housing those who have been found guilty of violating federal laws. This includes crimes which occur across state lines or against government agencies. State prisons are managed by state governments, for inmates who have been found guilty of violating state laws (Conaway & Strickler, 2018). Typically, those housed in federal prison spend more time incarcerated than those in state prison. Drug-related offenders housed in state prisons and released in 2009 had an average prison stay of 2.2 years, which jumped 36% since 1990 (The Pew Charitable Trusts, 2012, 2018). For federal drug-offenders, this number increased by 153% in a 24-year period (from 1988 to 2012), with an average of two to five years spent behind bars (The Pew Charitable Trusts, 2018). It is important to note that not all drug-related offenses occur by individuals suffering from an active SUD, but the statistics are important to consider regarding the abuse and/or trafficking of illegal substances as they each influence the other. Unfortunately, instead of focusing on treating addictions which keep drug trafficking in business, the U.S. have focused for decades on arresting drug traffickers and drug dealers, never facing the root of the problem. Incarcerating individuals with SUDs with the assumption that they will be deterred from returning to prison due to their drug habits is ignorant and consistently debunked in the literature. Upon completion of this chapter, readers will be able to understand not only evidence-based counseling techniques for individuals suffering from SUDs but explore the many facets of addiction and other effective methods to decrease drug abuse other than incarceration.

BACKGROUND

SUDs, as well as every other recognized mental illness, are defined by the American Psychiatric Association (2013) through the *Diagnostic and Statistical Manual of Mental Disorders (DSM-5)*. According to the *DSM-5* (American Psychiatric Association, 2013), substance-related disorders result from the use of 10 separate classes of drugs, including caffeine, cannabis, hallucinogens, inhalants, opioids, hypnotics/anxiolytics, stimulants, sedatives, tobacco, and other/unknown substances. In the use of any of these (or more than one) substances, a SUD is diagnosed by the appropriate health care professional when the recurrent use of one or more of these substances causes significant impairments, such as health problems or the inability to meet one's responsibilities (e.g., work, school, and home). The individual may also desire to end his/her substance use but is or has been unsuccessful at cutting down or controlling his/her substance use, as described by the Substance Abuse and Mental Health Services Administration (SAMHSA) (2012). SUDs may also be referred to as drug addictions or addictions. According to Powledge (1999), this disorder is a brain disease due to the altering of the biochemistry and anatomy of neurons within the brain, triggered by excessive drug use, thus altering how the brain even functions. Attempting to define drug addiction can be difficult because of the complexity of the illness. Volkow (2018), the current Director of the National Institute of Drug Abuse (NIDA), described drug addiction as an "intense, and, at times, uncontrollable drug craving, along with compulsive drug seeking and use that persist even in the face of devastating consequences" (p. 2). This definition includes a number of drugs including nicotine, alcohol, and illicit and prescription drugs.

TREATING THE WRONG PROBLEM

Treating Substance Use Disorders in Federal and State Prisons

It is often wondered how some end up more susceptible to developing an addiction than others. The term, "addictive personality is thrown around, but what does this statement mean exactly? Chandler et al. (2009) discussed how studies have revealed that addiction is a disorder of the brain with strong genetic ties, meaning that, if someone has a family history of addiction, he/she is at greater risk for ending up with an addiction. It is important for an individual to understand the risks intertwined with drug addiction, especially for those genetically predisposed. Risk factors and protective factors should be heavily studied in addicts as a means to determine whether they were genetically predisposed. Unfortunately, there remains a large disconnect between addiction research and the most effective treatments for addiction, especially for those dealing with addiction while working their way through the criminal justice system. Approximately 80-85% of prisoners could benefit from drug abuse treatment, but never receive it (Karberg & James, 2005; Mumola & Karberg, 2006). Adding salt to the wound, those with SUDs are at a higher risk for infectious diseases (e.g., hepatitis C and human immunodeficiency virus) and likely to have comorbid psychiatric disorders (Abram & Teplin, 1991; Chandler et al., 2004).

On paper, prison seems to be the perfect place for those with SUDs to "get clean," a slang term for someone whose body has become dependent on a substance (typically drugs/alcohol) and is in the process of withdrawing from drugs or alcohol. Instead, The National Center on Addiction and Substance Abuse (CASA) (2009) found in a study on inmates with SUDs that only 11% received treatment for their disorder at federal and state prisons or local jails. Approximately 1.9 cents of every dollar spent by federal and state governments throughout the U.S. go towards paying for prevention and treatment services for SUDs, while 95.6% goes towards paying the consequences for having a SUD (Sack, 2014). Providing treatment for SUDs is cost effective, at approximately $14.6 billion (NIDA, 2020; Volkow, 2018) compared to the cost of drug abuse ($193 billion), of which $113 billion covered costs associated with drug-related crimes. The most significant benefit to the economy in treating SUDs is the avoidance of crimes, as incarceration is extremely costly.

According to NIDA (2020), effective treatment methods for incarcerated people suffering from a SUD should be comprehensive, including some form of behavioral therapy along with educational services and medication (depending on the client). One form of behavioral therapy used to treat addiction is cognitive behavioral therapy (CBT). There is an abundance of research supporting the effectiveness of CBT in treating addiction (Carroll et al., 1994; Dutra et al., 2008; Magill & Ray, 2009; McHugh et al., 2010; Rawson et al., 2002). CBT can be implemented through individual or group counseling and helps patients modify their existing behaviors related to their addiction, helping to effectively manage their triggers and ultimately altering their drug habits (NIDA, 2020). Another form of behavioral therapy which is widely used to treat addiction (with success) is contingency management (CM) therapy, where client is provided with motivational incentive when they perform positive behaviors. CM is effective because it is grounded in operant learning theory, providing the client with a non-drug reinforcer (an incentive) for avoiding substance use. CM approaches are grounded in operant learning theory and involve the administration of a nondrug reinforcer (e.g., vouchers for goods) following demonstration of abstinence from substances. A large number of clinical studies support the effectiveness of CM with patients suffering from SUDs (Higgins et al., 2000; McHugh et al., 2010; Petry et al., 2000; Petry & Martin 2002; Sindelar et al., 2007; Stitzer & Petry, 2006).

Medication usage in treating addiction varies depending on a variety of factors, but may include methadone, buprenorphine, and naltrexone, to name a few (NIDA, 2020). A comprehensive treatment plan should also include services upon release from prison, such as employment and housing assistance, and continuous drug education (Gicquelais et al., 2019). Providing incarcerated individuals suffering from SUBs with a variety of treatments allows them an opportunity they may not be privileged enough to receive outside of jail or prison walls. Not treating a drug-abusing offender while he/she is incarcerated leaves out an excellent opportunity to not only improve public health and safety, but to also improve medical outcomes for individuals who otherwise would have never received it (Chandler et al., 2009; Knight & Farabee, 2004).

The History of the War on Drugs

In order to understand how the war on drugs has become what it is today, it is important to take a look back on its history. A single plant, known as the opium poppy, is the main ingredient in a number of drugs including heroin, morphine, and other opiates. The opium poppy was used in a variety of ways for centuries as both a recreational drug and a pain-relieving medicine. Friedrich Sertürner, a German scientist, isolated morphine from opium in 1803. It was used as a powerful painkiller, as the active narcotic ingredient in opium is, in its pure form, ten times stronger than opium (Corbett et al., 2006). Along with the invention of the hypodermic needle in 1853, morphine became extremely sought out, widely used as the main painkiller throughout the United States Civil War. This led to approximately 400,000 soldiers becoming addicted to the drug (Rosenblum et al., 2008). By the 1890s, heroin was used for medicinal use in place of morphine as cough syrup sold over the counter. Doctors prescribed it for everything from insomnia to hysteria and promoted its use in babies and young children suffering from a head cold. When the early 1900s emerged, heroin addiction in the U.S. and western Europe was at an all-time high (Pathan & Williams, 2012).

By the 1960s, drugs were viewed as something those who were rebelling against the government were involved in, as social upheaval and political dissent grew while the war continued. By June of 1971, President Richard Nixon declared a "war on drugs," heavily increasing the size and presence of federal drug control agencies and establishing harsher sentencing laws, such as mandatory sentences, along with no-knock warrants (Pathan & Williams, 2012). As marijuana became increasingly popular, especially among those who felt strongly against the war, Nixon temporarily placed marijuana into the Schedule One category for drugs (i.e., the most restrictive category). Decades later, this "war on drugs," which is still continuing today (with some changes), was and is still viewed as a huge failure by researchers and policymakers throughout the U.S., as the consequences for low-level drug offenses are still viewed as a criminal justice issue rather than what they actually are- a public health issue.

The Failure of the War on Drugs

Incarceration has proven to have negligible effect on public safety, as crime rate reductions have been attributed to causes other than incarceration for approximately 75% to 100% of reductions (Stemen, 2017). However, the U.S. continue to arrest individuals for drug possession at alarmingly high rates (triple the amount since 1980) despite evidence proving its lack of influence (Stauffer, 2016). This equates to about one arrest for drug possession every 25 seconds, while arrests for drug sales are still six times below the number arrested for possession (Stauffer, 2016). Instead of decreasing the rates of substance abuse, incarcerating those suffering from addiction has been shown to be linked to an increased likelihood of death due to drug overdose (Centers for Disease Control and Prevention, 2021). Individuals released from prison are approximately 13 times more likely to die within their first two weeks after release than the general population, typically from an overdose, leaving them at a 129% higher risk of dying from an overdose than the general public (Binswanger et al., 2007; Pearl, 2018). Since President Nixon's "war on drugs" in the 1970's, not only has the degree of drug use and SUDs not declined, but the commercial drug empires in both North and South America have only grown. New drugs have emerged and continue to take lives, as individuals with SUDs continue to line the pockets of drug empires, which is then used to build even larger realms to work from.

The Role of Race

Many illegal drugs were used for thousands of years both for medicinal and spiritual purposes, so the question remains: Why are certain drugs legal, but other drugs are not? Disturbingly, the answer does not surface from empirical research or scientific data related to the dangers behind the consumption of these substances, but from what kinds of people are associated with certain drugs (Drug Policy Alliance, 2021).To provide a few examples, the first anti-opium laws were established in the 1870s, fixated on the use by Chinese immigrants. In the early 1900s, the first anticocaine laws were born, linked directly to Black men in the South. In the 1910s and 1920s, the first antimarijuana laws were announced, associated with Mexican migrants and Mexican Americans in the Midwest and Southwest (Drug Policy Alliance, 2021). It was with these laws directly targeting minority groups, along with President Nixon's "war on drugs" declaration in the early 1970's, that minority communities (especially Black and Latino) remain the focus of extensively disproportionate drug enforcement and sentencing procedures and practices (Drug Policy Alliance, 2021).

According to the United States Census Bureau (2019), the U.S. are made up of the following racial categories: 60.1% White, 18.5% Hispanic or Latino, 13.1% Black or African American, 5.9% Asian American, 1.3% American Indian or Alaskan Native, and 0.3% Native Hawaiian or other Pacific Islander. The National Survey on Drug Use and Health (SAMHSA, 2018) reported the following details related to U.S. citizens with a SUB aged 12 or older by racial demographic in the U.S.: White, 7.7%, Hispanic or Latino, 7.1%, Black or African American, 6.9%, Asian American: 4.8%, American Indian or Alaskan Native, 10.1%, and Native Hawaiian and Other Pacific Islander: 9.3%. The disproportionate experience of Black Americans throughout our criminal justice system has played a significant role in discussions surrounding prison reform. The statistics make it abundantly clear: Black Americans are more likely to be incarcerated than White (Raphael, 2011). In 2007, a Black man was more than three times more likely to be incarcerated than a non-Hispanic White man with the same education level and age (Raphael, 2011). To specify further, statistics show that while Blacks and Whites sell and/or use illegal drugs at similar rates, Black people are 2.7 times more likely than White people to be arrested for a drug-related crime, and their sentences are typically 50% longer (Mitchell & Caudy, 2013; The Hamilton Project, 2015).

While White Americans (specifically, White men) suffer from the highest rates of opioid misuse and deaths from opioid overdose (approximately 35,000 in 2018 alone), White Americans, overall, also have fewer barriers to treatment than some other races in the U.S. (Pullen & Oser, 2014). As of 2014, approximately 92% of addiction treatment centers were located in urban areas (Pullen & Oser, 2014; SAMHSA, 2018), but the rates of addiction in rural areas has continued to climb. Other barriers to treatment other than location include poverty, no health insurance coverage, and difficulties understanding how to access treatment (Pullen & Oser, 2014).

Substance Abuse Among Families

The upsurge in the frequency of parental incarceration over the last 30 years is mainly because of the increases in not only drug arrests, but more severe consequences for drug-related offenses (Zhang et al., 2009). In 2007, approximately 60% of parents who were incarcerated had been charged with crimes directly related to drug offenses (mainly, drug possession). Two thirds of incarcerated parents serving time in state prisons were suffering from a SUD. Children of incarcerated parents are more likely to experience a host of social, emotional, and mental health concerns, including traumatic situations which occurred either before, during their parents' incarceration, or after their parents' release. This could be through a disruption to their environment (transient placements) or reduced quality of care (including a lack of contact with stable role models or adult figures), and a lack of financial security (Bennett et al., 2012; Dallaire, 2007; Glaze & Maruschak, 2008). These kinds of limitations for children with incarcerated parents leave them with higher risk factors including lower rates of academic achievement, an increased risk of substance abuse, and delinquency (Bennett et al., 2012; Dallaire, 2007; Davis & Shlafer, 2017; Jackson et al., 2018). According to a survey on youth behavior, Davis and Shlafer (2017) determined that past and present parental incarceration increased the likelihood of tobacco, alcohol, marijuana, prescription drugs, and substance abuse and dependence. Research also suggests (Biederman et al, 2000; Clark et al., 2005; Davis & Shlafer, 2017) that youth exposed to substance abuse by their parents are more likely to abuse substances themselves particularly when exposure occurs during the adolescent years. Thus, risk factors such as these leave youth with incarcerated parents at much higher risk for intergenerational cycles of substance use and abuse, and involvement with the criminal justice system, compared to those raised in households without these experiences (Davis & Shlafer, 2017).

There are four possible factors that show a possible connection between parental incarceration and adolescent substance use/abuse (Davis & Shlafer, 2017). The first suggests that children separated from their parents because of incarceration experience high levels of trauma because of it (Turney & Haskins, 2014). As the literature suggests, children with incarcerated parents (especially mothers) show symptoms of posttraumatic stress disorder, such as trouble sleeping, depression and anxiety, and struggling to concentrate. Without the proper supports, these children/adolescents are more likely to use drugs and alcohol to cope with these issues (Arditti, 2012). Another factor to consider is the strain put on the family system as a result of parental incarceration, as there may be a change in their environment due to the loss of income and a disruption to the roles of the family (Agnew, 1992; Foster & Hagan, 2009). This strain can alter a child's ability to adjust to new surroundings, increase antisocial type behaviors, leading to the possible use and abuse of drugs/alcohol (Agnew, 1992).

This unique population needs a high level of support from various areas (e.g., educators and mental health professionals) in order to reduce their risk factors, as children of incarcerated parents are also more likely to end up incarcerated at some point in their lives (Seymour & Hairston, 1998). In order to effectively serve this unique population, counselors who work with children of incarcerated parents are more likely to present services with higher rates of effectiveness when they understand the characteristics of these types of children, the policies (and lack thereof) in place for assisting children/families impacted by incarceration, and the experiences and emotions of children with (an) incarcerated parent(s) (Bennett et al., 2012). Programs outside of the criminal justice system that support families affected by incarceration (both during and after incarceration has occurred) should be evidence-based in order to be effective, in order to mitigate the harm associated with incarceration. Unfortunately, programs within prisons related to parenting skills are common, but rarely focus on how to meet the needs of their children while incarcerated (Murphey & Cooper, 2015). Much of what surrounds incarceration, whether from a child or parents' perspective, is trauma. There is trauma in the separation of the parent and child, a possible lack of sympathy and support from others, feelings of shame and guilt, feeling stigmatized, and more, all of which can lead to an impaired ability to cope with current and future stress and trauma (Justice Strategies, 2017).

The Influence of the Media on Addiction

Research has consistently reported similar results surrounding the influence that substance use in the media has on adolescents and young adults (Jackson et al., 2018). Now more than ever, substance use has become a normal part of television, movies, brand Web sites, and social networking sites. Although legal substances (e.g., alcohol and cigarettes) are not permitted for use by individuals under the age of 21, the tobacco and alcohol industries target youth and adolescents in their advertisements. Unfortunately, the majority of the education adolescents receive about substances comes from representations presented through the media. This leaves youth and adolescents that have not experienced substance use or SUDs (whether directly or indirectly) receiving key environmental influences by what is portrayed in the media (Gupta et al., 2016; Jernigan, Noel et al., 2017; Leonardi-Bee et al., 2016; Smith & Foxcroft, 2009; Stautz et al., 2016). Exposure via new media (i.e., social networking sites, and brand Web sites) has risen rapidly. Social norms and cognitions appear to at least partially account for the effects of portrayals on youth substance use (Jackson et al., 2018). Substances are represented throughout films, television, concert and sporting event sponsorships, and even video games. This is no accident, however; adolescents are high media consumers of media entertainment and highly influenced by influences from the various media sources to which they are exposed. Adolescents do not possess the same cognitive capacities that adults do, as the human brain does not even begin developing until age 25. This may help various media outlets to present their drug/alcohol products as attractive, as adolescents are not able to distinguish the experiences presented in advertisements from what actually occurs in real life (Jernigan, Padon et al., 2017; Meier, 2011). The animation, constant camera cuts, and loud music affect adolescents' executive control, making them more susceptible to these kinds of advertisements as well (Jernigan Padon et al., 2017; Meier, 2011).

SOLUTIONS AND RECOMMENDATIONS

If government agencies throughout the U.S. can work alongside mental health professionals to come to a mutual understanding on viewing SUDs as a mental health disorder rather than a crime, the U.S. will continue moving in the right direction. Trauma, along with symptoms of trauma, often surface when attempting to determine why a patient has ended up diagnosed with a SUD. Typically, trauma (and/or symptoms of trauma) are found very often as one of the cooccurring disorders with the most significant rates for patients also being treated for a SUD (Atkins, 2014; SAMHSA, 2014; Tkach, 2018). Individuals receiving treatment for a SUD are five times higher than the rest of the population to also be receiving treatment for posttraumatic stress disorder, leading medical professionals to understand that providing treatment for SUDs are likely to include a cooccurring trauma (Atkins, 2014; SAMHSA, 2014; Tkach, 2018).

CONCLUSION

Fortunately, the U.S. are not in the same position they were in the 1970s. States have begun providing access to drugs such as naloxone (commonly known as Narcan, its brand name), which is used to treat a narcotics overdose (NIDA, 2021). Furthermore, the criminal justice systems throughout many states are moving away from approaches that view drug use as criminal behavior and, instead, have begun to incorporate ideologies focused on reducing harm for drug users (McClellan et al., 2018). However, there is still progress to be made, as several debates have occurred surrounding the relationship between drug use and various crimes (e.g., robbery) and in what level the criminal justice system should be involved when determining not only an appropriate, but an effective method of rehabilitation for offenders suffering from drug abuse. Another form of treatment/rehabilitation that various states have adopted also include drug courts, the first of which was established in Miami, Florida, in 1989 (Chandler et al., 2009). Drug courts were created to provide a correlation between treatment and the legal process. Today, more than 3,500 drug courts exist across the U.S., approximately half of which are for adults (U.S. Department of Justice, 2021). Numerous states created alternatives to incarceration for first time drug offenders (including juveniles) that focus on treatment rather than punishment, and some states have created diversion programs to avert the expensive costs of incarcerating nonviolent drug offenders, focusing instead on treatment and rehabilitation (Chandler et al., 2009).

This research received no specific grant from any funding agency in the public, commercial, or not-for-profit sectors.

REFERENCES

Abram, K. M., & Teplin, L. A. (1991). Co-occurring disorders among mentally ill jail detainees: Implications for public policy. *The American Psychologist*, *46*(10), 1036–1045. doi:10.1037/0003-066X.46.10.1036 PMID:1746771

Agnew, R. (1992). Foundation for a general strain theory of crime and delinquency. *Criminology*, *30*(1), 47–87. doi:10.1111/j.1745-9125.1992.tb01093.x

American Psychiatric Association. (2013). *Diagnostic and statistical manual of mental disorders* (5th ed.). Author.

Arditti, J. (2012). Child trauma within the context of parental incarceration: A family process perspective. *Journal of Family Theory & Review*, *4*(3), 181–219. doi:10.1111/j.1756-2589.2012.00128.x

Atkins, C. (2014). *Co-occurring disorders: Integrated assessment and treatment of substance use and mental disorders*. PESI Publishing and Media.

Bennett, E., Lewis, M., & Hunsaker, E. (2012). Counseling kids with incarcerated caregivers. In *Proceedings of the ACA Conference* (*vol. 1*). VISTAS.

Biederman, J., Faraone, S. V., Monuteaux, M. C., & Feighner, J. A. (2000). Patterns of alcohol and drug use in adolescents can be predicted by parental substance use disorders. *American Academy of Pediatrics*, *106*(4), 792–797. doi:10.1542/peds.106.4.792 PMID:11015524

Binswanger, I. A., Stern, M. F., Deyo, R. A., Heagerty, P. J., Cheadle, A., Elmore, J. G., & Koepsell, T. D. (2007). Release from prison—A high risk of death for former inmates. *The New England Journal of Medicine*, *356*(2), 157–165. doi:10.1056/NEJMsa064115 PMID:17215533

Carroll, K. M., Rounsaville, B. J., Nich, C., Gordon, L. T., Wirtz, P. W., & Gawin, F. (1994). One-Year Follow-up of Psychotherapy and Pharmacotherapy for Cocaine Dependence. *Archives of General Psychiatry*, *51*(12), 989–997. doi:10.1001/archpsyc.1994.03950120061010 PMID:7979888

Carson, E. A., & Anderson, E. (2016). *Prisoners in 2015*. United States Department of Justice, Bureau of Justice Statistics. https://www.bjs.gov/content/pub/pdf/p15.pd

Center for Substance Abuse Treatment. (2012). *Managing chronic pain in adults with or in recovery from substance use disorders*. Substance Abuse and Mental Health Services Administration. https://www.ncbi.nlm.nih.gov/books/NBK92053/table/ch2.t5/

Centers for Disease Control and Prevention. (2021, March 3). *Drug overdose deaths: Drug overdose deaths remain high*. https://www.cdc.gov/drugoverdose/deaths/index.html

Chandler, R. K., Fletcher, B. W., & Volkow, N. D. (2009). Treating drug abuse and addiction in the criminal justice system: Improving public health and safety. *Journal of the American Medical Association*, *301*(2), 183–190. doi:10.1001/jama.2008.976 PMID:19141766

Chandler, R. K., Peters, R. H., Field, G., & Juliano-Bult, D. (2004). Challenges in Implementing evidence-based treatment practices for co-occurring disorders in the criminal justice system. *Behavioral Sciences & the Law*, *22*(4), 431–448. doi:10.1002/bsl.598 PMID:15282833

Clark, D. B., Cornelius, J. R., Kirisci, L., & Tarter, R. E. (2005). Childhood risk categories for adolescent substance involvement: A general liability typology. *Drug and Alcohol Dependence*, *77*(1), 13–21. doi:10.1016/j.drugalcdep.2004.06.008 PMID:15607837

Conaway, D., & Strickler, M. (2018, January 8). *What is the difference between state and federal prisons?* https://www.conawayandstrickler.com/blog/what_is_the_difference_between_state_and_federal_prisons/

Corbett, A. D., Henderson, G., McKnight, A. T., & Paterson, S. J. (2006). 75 years of opioid research: The exciting but vain quest for the Holy Grail. *British Journal of Pharmacology*, *147*(S1), 153–162. doi:10.1038j.bjp.0706435 PMID:16402099

Dallaire, D. H. (2007). Incarcerated mothers and fathers: A comparison of risks for children and families. *Family Relations*, *56*(5), 440–453. doi:10.1111/j.1741-3729.2007.00472.x

Davis, L., & Shlafer, R. J. (2017). Substance use among youth with currently and formerly incarcerated parents. *Smith College Studies in Social Work*, *87*(1), 43–58. doi:10.1080/00377317.2017.1246797 PMID:29170570

Drug Policy Alliance. (2021). *A brief history of the drug war*. https://drugpolicy.org/issues/brief-history-drug-war

Dutra, L., Stathopoulou, G., Basden, S. L., Leyro, T. M., Powers, M. B., & Otto, M. W. (2008). A Meta-Analytic Review of Psychosocial Interventions for Substance Use Disorders. *The American Journal of Psychiatry*, *165*(2), 179–187. doi:10.1176/appi.ajp.2007.06111851 PMID:18198270

Foster, H., & Hagan, J. (2009). The mass incarceration of parents in America: Issues of race/ethnicity, collateral damage to children, and prisoner reentry. *The Annals of the American Academy of Political and Social Science*, *623*(1), 179–194. doi:10.1177/0002716208331123

Gicquelais, R. E., Mezuk, B., Foxman, B., Thomas, L., & Bohnert, A. S. B. (2019). Justice involvement patterns, overdose experiences, and naloxone knowledge among men and women in criminal justice diversion addiction treatment. *Harm Reduction Journal*, *16*(1), 1–11. doi:10.118612954-019-0317-3 PMID:31311572

Glaze, L. E., & Maruschak, L. L. M. (2008). *Parents in prison and their minor children*. U.S. Department of Justice. https://www.ncjrs.gov/App/abstractdb/AbstractDBDetails.aspx?id=244893

Gupta, H., Pettigrew, S., Lam, T., & Tait, R. J. (2016). A systematic review of the impact of exposure to internet-based alcohol-related content on young people's alcohol use behaviours. *Alcohol (Fayetteville, N.Y.)*, *51*(6), 763–771. PMID:27522028

Higgins, S. T., Wong, C. J., Badger, G. J., Ogden, D. E., & Dantona, R. L. (2000). Contingent reinforcement increases cocaine abstinence during outpatient treatment and one year of follow-up. *Journal of Consulting and Clinical Psychology*, *68*(1), 64–72. doi:10.1037/0022-006X.68.1.64 PMID:10710841

Jackson, K. M., Janssen, T., & Gabrielli, J. (2018). Media/marketing influences on adolescent and young adult substance abuse. *Current Addiction Reports*, *5*(2), 146–157. doi:10.100740429-018-0199-6 PMID:30393590

Jernigan, D., Noel, J., Landon, J., Thornton, N., & Lobstein, T. (2017). Alcohol marketing and youth alcohol consumption: A systematic review of longitudinal studies published since 2008. *Addiction (Abingdon, England)*, *112*(1), 7–20. doi:10.1111/add.13591 PMID:27565582

Jernigan, D. H., Padon, A., Ross, C., & Borzekowski, D. (2017). Self-reported youth and adult exposure to alcohol marketing in traditional and digital media: Results of a pilot survey. *Alcoholism, Clinical and Experimental Research*, *41*(3), 618–625. doi:10.1111/acer.13331 PMID:28219114

Justice Strategies. (2017, June 14). *How can schools, teachers, and counselors help children impacted by incarceration?* [Blog post]. https://www.justicestrategies.org/coip/blog/2017/06/how-can-schools-teachers-and-counselors-help-children-impacted-incarceration

Karberg, J. C., & James, D. J. (2005). *Substance dependence, abuse, and treatment of jail inmates, 2002*. Bureau of Justice Statistics.

Knight, K., & Farabee, D. (2004). *Treating addicted offenders: A continuum of effective practices*. Civic Research Institute.

Leonardi-Bee, J., Nderi, M., & Britton, J. (2016). Smoking in movies and smoking initiation in adolescents: Systematic review and meta-analysis. *Addiction (Abingdon, England)*, *111*(10), 1750–1763. doi:10.1111/add.13418 PMID:27043456

Magill, M., & Ray, L. A. (2009). Cognitive-behavioral treatment with adult alcohol and illicit drug users: A meta-analysis of randomized controlled trials. *Journal of Studies on Alcohol and Drugs*, *70*(4), 516–527. doi:10.15288/jsad.2009.70.516 PMID:19515291

McClellan, C., Lambdin, B. H., Ali, M. M., Mutter, R., Davis, C. S., Wheeler, E., Pemberton, M., & Kral, A. H. (2018). Opioid-overdose laws association with opioid use and overdose mortality. *Journal of Addictive Behaviors*, *86*, 90–95. doi:10.1016/j.addbeh.2018.03.014 PMID:29610001

McHugh, R. K., Hearon, B. A., & Otto, M. W. (2010). Cognitive behavioral therapy for substance use disorders. *The Psychiatric Clinics of North America*, *33*(3), 511–525. doi:10.1016/j.psc.2010.04.012 PMID:20599130

Meier, P. S. (2011). Alcohol marketing research: The need for a new agenda. *Addiction (Abingdon, England)*, *106*(3), 466–471. doi:10.1111/j.1360-0443.2010.03160.x PMID:21299664

Mitchell, O., & Caudy, M. S. (2013). Examining racial disparities in drug arrests. *Justice Quarterly*, *32*(2), 288–313. https://perma.cc/T3XU-JZVF. doi:10.1080/07418825.2012.761721

Mumola, C. J., & Karberg, J. C. (2006). *Drug use and dependence, state and federal prisoners, 2004*. Bureau of Justice Statistics. doi:10.1037/e560272006-001

Murphey, D., & Cooper, P. M. (2015). *Parents behind bars*. Child Trends. http://www.childtrends.org/wp-content/uploads/2015/10/2015-42ParentsBehindBars.pdf

National Institute on Drug Abuse. (2020). *Criminal justice drug facts*. https://www.drugabuse.gov/publications/drugfacts/criminal-justice

Pathan, H., & Williams, J. (2012). Basic opioid pharmacology: An update. *British Journal of Pain*, *6*(1), 11–16. doi:10.1177/2049463712438493 PMID:26516461

Pearl, B. (2018, June 27). *Ending drug war numbers*. https://www.americanprogress.org/issues/criminaljustice/reports/2018/06/27/452819/ending-war-drugs-numbers/

Petry, N. M., & Martin, B. (2002). Low-cost contingency management for treating cocaine- and opioid-abusing methadone patients. *Journal of Consulting and Clinical Psychology*, *70*(2), 398–405. doi:10.1037/0022-006X.70.2.398 PMID:11952198

Petry, N. M., Martin, B., Cooney, J. L., & Kranzler, H. R. (2000). Give them prizes, and they will come: Contingency management for treatment of alcohol dependence. *Journal of Consulting and Clinical Psychology*, *68*(2), 250–257. doi:10.1037/0022-006X.68.2.250 PMID:10780125

Powledge, T. M. (1999). Addiction and the brain: The dopamine pathway is helping researchers find their way through the addiction maze. *Bioscience*, *49*(7), 513–519. doi:10.2307/1313471

Pullen, E., & Oser, C. (2014). Barriers to substance abuse treatment in rural and urban communities: Counselor perspectives. *Substance Use & Misuse*, *49*(7), 891–901. doi:10.3109/10826084.2014.891615 PMID:24611820

Raphael, S. (2011). Incarceration and prisoner reentry in the United States. *The Annals of the American Academy of Political and Social Science*, *635*(1), 192–215. doi:10.1177/0002716210393321

Rawson, R. A., Huber, A., McCann, M., Shoptaw, S., Farabee, D., Reiber, C., & Ling, W. (2002). Comparison of contingency management and cognitive-behavioral approaches during methadone maintenance treatment for cocaine dependence. *Archives of General Psychiatry*, *59*(9), 817–824. doi:10.1001/archpsyc.59.9.817 PMID:12215081

Rosenblum, A., Marsch, L. A., Joseph, H., & Portenoy, R. K. (2008). Opioids and the treatment of chronic pain: Controversies, current status, and future directions. *Experimental and Clinical Psychopharmacology*, *16*(5), 405–416. doi:10.1037/a0013628 PMID:18837637

Sack, D. (2014, August 14). We can't afford to ignore drug addiction in prison. *The Washington Post*. https://www.washingtonpost.com/news/to-your-health/wp/2014/08/14/we-cant-afford-to-ignore-drug-addiction-in-prison/?noredirect=on

Seymour, C., & Hairston, C. F. (Eds.). (1998). *Children with parents in prison: Child welfare policy, program, and practice issues*. Transaction.

Sindelar, J., Elbel, B., & Petry, N. M. (2007). What do we get for our money? Cost effectiveness of adding contingency management. *Addiction (Abingdon, England)*, *102*(2), 309–316. doi:10.1111/j.1360-0443.2006.01689.x PMID:17222286

Smith, L. A., & Foxcroft, D. R. (2009). The effect of alcohol advertising, marketing and portrayal on drinking behaviour in young people: Systematic review of prospective cohort studies. *BMC Public Health*, *9*(1), 1–11. doi:10.1186/1471-2458-9-51 PMID:19200352

Snell, T. L. (1995). *Correctional populations in the United States,1993*. Department of Justice. https://www.bjs.gov/content/pub/pdf/cpop93bk.pdf

Stauffer, B. (2016, October 12). *Interview: Why the U.S. should de-criminalize drug use*. https://www.hrw.org/news/2016/10/12/interview-why-us-should-decriminalize-drug-use

Stautz, K., Brown, K. G., King, S. E., Shemilt, I., & Marteau, T. M. (2016). Immediate effects of alcohol marketing communications and media portrayals on consumption and cognition: A systematic review and meta-analysis of experimental studies. *BMC Public Health*, *16*(1), 1–18. doi:10.118612889-016-3116-8 PMID:27278656

Stemen, D. (2017, July). *The prison paradox: More incarceration will not make us safer*. https://www.vera.org/publications/for-the-record-prison-paradox-incarceration-not-safer

Stitzer, M., & Petry, N. (2006). Contingency management for treatment of substance abuse. *Annual Review of Clinical Psychology*, *2*(1), 411–434. doi:10.1146/annurev.clinpsy.2.022305.095219 PMID:17716077

Substance Abuse and Mental Health Services Administration. (2014). *SAMHSA's concept of trauma and guidance for a trauma-informed approach*. Substance Abuse and Mental Health Services Administration.

Substance Abuse and Mental Health Services Administration. (2018). *2018 national survey of drug use and health (NSDUH) releases*. https://www.samhsa.gov/data/release/2018-national-survey-drug-use-and-health-nsduh-releases

The Hamilton Project. (2015). *Rates of drug use and sales, by race; rates of drug related criminal justice measures, by race*. https://www.hamiltonproject.org/charts/rates_of_drug_use_and_sales_by_race_rates_of_drug_related_criminal_justice

The National Center on Addiction and Substance Abuse. (2009). *From CASA's 2009 shoveling up II: The impact of substance abuse on federal, state and local budgets report*. https://www.ojp.gov/ncjrs/virtual-library/abstracts/shoveling-ii-impact-substance-abuse-federal-state-and-local-budgets

The Pew Charitable Trusts. (2012). *Time served: The high cost, low return of longer prison terms*. The Pew Charitable Trusts. https://www.pewtrusts.org/~/media/assets/2012/06/06/time_served_report.pdf

The Pew Charitable Trusts. (2015). *Federal drug sentencing laws bring high cost, low return*. https://www.pewtrusts.org/-/media/assets/2015/08/federal_drug_sentencing_laws_bring_high_cost_low_return.pdf

The Pew Charitable Trusts. (2018, March 8). *More imprisonment does not reduce state drug problems*. https://www.pewtrusts.org/en/research-and-analysis/issue briefs/2018/03/more-imprisonment-does-not-reduce-state-drug-problems

Tkach, M. J. (2018). A psychosocial linguistic exploration of the use of alcoholic as a social label of self-identity in AA and 12-step programs. *Alcoholism Treatment Quarterly*, *36*(1), 101–114. doi:10.1080/07347324.2017.1355221

Turney, K., & Haskins, A. R. (2014). Falling behind? Children's early grade retention after paternal incarceration. *Sociology of Education*, *87*(4), 241–258. doi:10.1177/0038040714547086

United States Census Bureau. (2019). *QuickFacts United States*. https://www.census.gov/quickfacts/fact/table/US/PST045219

U.S. Department of Justice. (2021). *Drug courts*. https://www.ojp.gov/pdffiles1/nij/238527.pdf

Volkow, N. D. (2018). Preface. In *Principles of drug addiction treatment: A research-based guide* (3rd ed.). National Institute on Drug Abuse. https://www.drugabuse.gov/publications/principles-drug-addiction-treatment-research-based-guide-third-edition/preface

Zhang, Y., Maxwell, C. D., & Vaughn, M. S. (2009). The impact of state sentencing policies on the U.S. prison population. *Journal of Criminal Justice*, *37*(2), 190–199. doi:10.1016/j.jcrimjus.2009.02.012

ADDITIONAL READING

Alleyne, V. (2007). Locked up means locked out. *Women & Therapy*, *29*(3-4), 181–194. doi:10.1300/J015v29n03_10

Bahr, S. J., Masters, A. L., & Taylor, B. M. (2012). What works in substance abuse treatment programs for offenders? *The Prison Journal*, *92*(2), 155–174. doi:10.1177/0032885512438836

Bronon, J., Stroop, J., Zimmer, S., & Berzofsky, M. (2017). *Drug use, dependence, and abuse among state prisoners and jail inmates, 2007–2009*. U.S. Department of Justice.

Inciardi, J. A., Martin, S. S., & Butzin, C. A. (2004). Five-year outcomes of therapeutic community treatment of drug-involved offenders after release from prison. *Crime and Delinquency*, *50*(1), 88–107. doi:10.1177/0011128703258874

Light, S. (2020). Incarceration and the failure of opioid addiction treatment in the United States. *Contemporary Sociology: A Journal of Reviews, 49*(6), 487-491. doi:10.1177/0094306120963120b

Pearson, F. S., & Lipton, D. S. (1999). A meta-analytic review of the effectiveness of corrections-based treatments for drug abuse. *The Prison Journal*, *79*(4), 384–410. doi:10.1177/0032885599079004003

Tsai, J., & Gu, X. (2019). Utilization of addiction treatment among U.S. adults with history of incarceration and substance use disorders. *Addiction Science & Clinical Practice*, *14*(9), 1–9. doi:10.118613722-019-0138-4 PMID:30836991

Volkow, N. D. (2021). Addiction should be treated, not penalized. *Neuropsychopharmacology*, *1-3*(12), 2048–2050. Advance online publication. doi:10.103841386-021-01087-2 PMID:34404909

Wolff, N., Huening, J., Shi, J., Frueh, B. C., Hoover, D. R., & McHugo, G. (2015). Implementation and effectiveness of integrated trauma and addiction treatment for incarcerated men. *Journal of Anxiety Disorders*, *30*, 66–80. doi:10.1016/j.janxdis.2014.10.009 PMID:25617774

KEY TERMS AND DEFINITIONS

Drug Addiction: A habitual and uncontrollable psychological and/or physical need for substances (i.e., heroine, nicotine, and cocaine).

Incarceration: Confinement to a jail or prison; to be confined to a single space.

Rehabilitation: The act of reestablishing an individual to living a healthy, normal life through various practices including therapy and/or medication(s).

Substance Use Disorder: The medical definition for an individual suffering from a drug definition.

Trauma: Experiencing an extremely disturbing or distressing situation.

Treatment: Medical care (physical or psychological) provided to an individual (sometimes referred to as the "patient") for an injury, infection, or illness.

War on Drugs: A government-led campaign or initiative aimed at ending illegal drug-use altogether, drastically increasing prison sentences for even minor drug offenses.

Chapter 4
Substance Abuse and Its Intersecting Factors:
Treatment While Incarcerated

Hannah Sunshine Bland
Spalding University, USA

ABSTRACT

This chapter will provide recent data on the state of incarceration within the United States of America and will demonstrate the need for a change in care to reduce recidivism and increase the overall mental health of those who are currently in prison. Included will be an overview of the relevance of drug and drug-related crimes within the American prison system, factors that influence the use and abuse of drugs, and how these crimes are treated within state and federal facilities. Alternative approaches and treatment options will be identified and discussed in relation to implementation and success rates within the prison system.

INTRODUCTION

Data complied by the U.S. Department of Justice indicates that at the end of 2020, 1,215,821 people were under the jurisdiction of state or federal correctional authorities (Carson, 2021). Additional data indicates that 549,100 inmates were confined midyear in local jails across the U.S. in 2020 (Minton & Zeng, 2021). An estimated 1,155,610 arrests occur per year for drug law violations in the U.S. (McVay, 2022). Of these arrests, 86.7% were for possession of a controlled substance; only 13.3% were for sale or manufacturing of a drug (McVay, 2022). 48% of federal prisoners are serving a sentence for a drug offense (Beatty & Snell, 2021). This data speaks to the reality that drug abuse is a significant problem within the United States. Rather than treating the drug abuse and the intersecting factors that impact abuse, we choose to penalize those who are struggling with addiction.

A multiplicity of factors impact the likelihood that one will abuse drugs or alcohol. Risk factors include a family history of addiction, having certain mental health disorders, peer pressure, lack of family involvement, early use, and taking a highly addictive drug (Mayo Clinic, 2017). Abuse, neglect,

DOI: 10.4018/978-1-7998-9209-0.ch004

and household dysfunction in childhood are also factors that influence drug use and abuse (Bath et al., 2021). The more risk factors one has, the more likely one is to begin using. Incarcerated individuals have significantly more risk factors when compared to non-incarcerated individuals. 97% of the prison population has at least one adverse childhood experience, with 78.1% having four or more (Compassion Prison Project, 2022). The most commonly identified adverse experiences were emotional abuse, physical abuse, emotional neglect, substance abuse, and parents living apart (Compassion Prison Project, 2022). 18% of state prisoners and 10% of federal prisoners spent at least part of their childhood living in foster care (Beatty & Snell, 2021). Of inmates who were newly admitted to a federal facility, 45% of them reported childhood trauma (Colman et al., 2016).

These concerns, though often prevalent during the trial and facility intake processes, go untreated. Special conditions may be placed upon inmates during sentencing as part of their release. More than three quarters of state prisoners and 94% of federal prisoners received at least one special condition (Beatty & Snell, 2021). The two most common conditions were the payment of court costs and the payment of fines; 64% of state prisoners and 84% of federal prisoners were required to repay court costs and an equal amount of 37% of inmates were required to pay fines (Beatty & Snell, 2021). Only 16% of state prisoners and 32% of federal prisoners were mandated to drug and alcohol treatment (Beatty & Snell, 2021). An even smaller portion of individuals were mandated to some form of psychiatric or psychological counseling, with only 8% of state prisoners and 7% of federal inmates being required as a special condition (Beatty & Snell, 2021). This focus on punitive measures, such as required financial obligations, is a misguided attempt to bring about a sense of change and responsibility within the prisoner. Special conditions fail to bring about real change as they ignore the deeper issues that led an individual to engage in criminal behavior, namely substance abuse and mental health problems.

Once sentenced, treatment options do not improve. The Federal Bureau of Prisoners currently classifies inmate need for mental health services on a four level system. Level one inmates do not require significant mental health care, while level four inmates require inpatient psychiatric care (Federal Bureau of Prisons, 2021). Despite many having a significant history of mental health treatment, both in-patient and out-patient, and 23% having been diagnosed with a mental illness while incarcerated, 96% of inmates were placed on level one care (Thompson & Eldridge, 2018; Federal Bureau of Prisons, 2021). Of the 146,253 inmates, only 5,180 were on level two care, 722 on level three care, and 464 or .3% on level four care (Federal Bureau of Prisons, 2021). Only 3% of inmates are classified as high enough to receive regular mental health treatment. In some federal facilities, regular mental health care has dropped by 86% since 2014 (Thompson & Eldridge, 2018). 63% of prisoners with a history of mental health illness do not receive treatment while incarcerated (National Alliance on Mental illness, 2022). 50% of inmates who were taking medication to manage their mental health conditions prior to incarceration were not able to continue their regimen once incarcerated (National Alliance on Mental Illness, 2022). Treatment specific to substance abuse is minimal as well. A decreasing number of inmates are participating in drug treatment programs in federal prisons, despite an increase in prisoners and prison crowding (Federal Bureau of Prisons, 2021). Only 10,465 inmates participated in residential drug treatment programs; an additional 13,570 participated in non-residential drug treatment programs (Federal Bureau of Prisons, 2021).

While it is clear from the aforementioned data that treatment for substance abuse and related mental health conditions are clearly lacking in prisons, it is also important to discuss recidivism rates in relation to substances. Recidivism is the return to criminal acts that result in re-arrest, reconviction, or return to prison (National Institute of Justice, 2022). The following chapter will clearly outline the factors related to substance abuse that impact incarceration and recidivism rates, will identify treatment modalities that have been identified as non-beneficial, and will provide treatment models that can be implemented within the justice system to improve the lives of prisoners and decrease recidivism rates.

BACKGROUND

Substance Use Disorders

The Diagnostic and Statistical Manual of Mental Disorders 5th Edition, often referred to as the DSM-5, is the leading text for defining and describing psychiatric disorders. Amongst these disorders are Substance Use Disorders, or SUDs (DSM-5, 2013). The defining feature of a substance use disorder is "a cluster of cognitive, behavioral, and physiological symptoms indicating that the individual continues using the substance despite significant substance related problems" (DSM-5, 2013, p. 483). Substance use disorders encompass 11 criterion and are further divided into four criteria groupings (DSM-5, 2013). The first grouping is focused on impaired control (DSM-5, 2013). Individuals with a substance use disorder will often misuse a substance by increasing the amount of use and/or the duration of use; this is seen frequently with the misuse of prescription drugs (Chiappini & Schifano, 2022). Individuals will also report a desire to decrease or discontinue use, but lack the ability to do so despite sincere effort (Sripada, 2022). Additionally, individuals spend a significant amount of time obtaining, using, or recovering from the effects of substances; in some cases, all daily activities are centered on the desired substance (DSM-5, 2013).

The second criteria grouping is focused on social impairment (DSM-5, 2013). Substance use can have a significant impact on one's ability to interact and function with others in the world. Interpersonal relationships can often be damaged including romantic, platonic, and professional ones (Adam & McNeely, 2020). Despite these continued interpersonal problems, individuals with a substance use disorder will continue to use. In many cases, individuals will withdraw from family and/or social events in order to continue using their chosen substance (Adam & McNeely, 2020). Obligations that once may have been of importance are no longer prioritized and impact all facets of the person's life, including work, home, and school (DSM-5, 2013).

Criteria grouping three is focused on symptoms related to risky use (DSM-5, 2013). Risky use is often related to one utilizing substances in a physically hazardous location, such as an abandoned building, location in which drugs are sold and utilized by others in active addiction, or other locations such as prisons and jails (Adam & McNeely, 2020). This criteria grouping also includes the continued use of a substance despite having knowledge that continued use is likely causing or worsening the existence of a physical or mental health problem (DSM-5, 2013). For example, high co-morbidity rates exist between substance abuse disorders and anxiety disorders, bipolar disorders, and psychotic disorders (NIDA, 2020). About half of people who experience a mental illness will also be diagnosed with a substance use disorder in their lifetime (NIDA, 2020). Approximately one in four people who have a serious mental illness also have a substance use disorder (NIDA, 2020). Physical health decline is also associated with substance use disorders. Those diagnosed with a substance use disorder are at a higher risk for cancer, sexually transmitted diseases, and heart disease (Hser &Schulte, 2014).

The final criteria grouping involves pharmacological criteria (DSM-5, 2013). Both tolerance and withdrawal are considered pharmacological and have a significant impact on one's ability to achieve and maintain sobriety. Tolerance is the need for an increased dose of the substance to achieve the desired impact; tolerance may also be marked by a decrease in effect when using the usual dose (DSM-5, 2013). Withdrawal begins after a decreased use of a substance and is defined as a "syndrome that occurs when blood or tissue concentrations of a substance decline in an individual who had maintained prolonged heavy use of the substance (DSM-5, 2013, p. 484). Withdrawal symptoms vary greatly depending on the substance(s) being consumed, but often include nausea or vomiting, muscle aches, sweating, and mood changes (DSM-5, 2013). In some extreme cases, seizures can occur during the withdrawal process; the likelihood of seizures occurring increase with each time a person relapses and re-enters the withdrawal process (Oxford Treatment Center, 2020).

Substance use disorders can vary greatly in terms of severity and are based on the number of criteria the individual meets. Severity can range from mild to severe; changes in severity can occur depending on the individual's current use (DSM-5, 2013). 8.4% of the general population has a substance use disorder (Lipari & VanHorn, 2017). In stark contrast, 53% of people in jails, 56% of people in state prisons, and 50% of people in federal prisons meet diagnostic criteria for a substance use disorder and have varying severity levels (Aminawung et al., 2019). It is important to understand not only what the criteria for a substance use disorder is, but also the intersecting factors that influence one to begin using substances in the first place. In particular, the next section will focus on intersecting factors that influence prisoners to utilize substances.

INTERSECTING FACTORS

When attempting to determine how one developed a substance use disorder, it is important to consider a multiplicity of factors that were occurring prior to diagnosis. These factors likely continue post diagnosis and continue to impact the person's ability to achieve and maintain sobriety. Common factors that impact those who are incarcerated include socioeconomic status, often referred to as SES, education level/employment history, peer/family pressure to utilize and/or sell substances, and general life stressors after release from prison (Mayo Clinic, 2017). Stressors post-release have a significant impact on relapse and recidivism rates (Beaty et al., 2014).

Socioeconomic Status

Socioeconomic status is defined by the American Psychological Association as "the social standing or class of an individual or group [and] is measured by a combination of education, income, and occupation" (American Psychological Association, 2022, *Socioeconomic status*). SES is divided into three main categories: high, middle, and low (American Psychological Association, 2022). Those who fall into a low SES category are more likely to experience a number of negative life outcomes and experiences. Those who were raised in low SES households have higher levels of emotional and behavioral difficulties, social problems, and delinquent behavior (Branje et al., 2015). Lower levels of SES, including those who live below the poverty line, are also associated with higher rates of mental health disorders such as anxiety and depression and serious mental illness (SAMHSA, 2016). One study found that opioid overdoses were more concentrated in areas that were socioeconomically disadvantaged (Cerda et al., 2019). Other studies have found unemployment and homelessness to be associated with a higher risk of overdose (Grinspoon, 2021).

Studies related specifically to SES and incarceration paint a grim picture. Incarcerated men are significantly more likely to be poor and live in poverty stricken neighborhoods. These same individuals were also more likely to have grown up in poverty and in neighborhoods with high unemployment (Barnhorst & Hayes, 2020). The rate of incarceration also varies drastically based on family income. Men that come from families with an average income below $14,000 per year are 20 times more likely to be incarcerated when compared to individuals with an average income in the top 10%. Individuals in the lowest income bracket, the bottom 1%, are 40 times more likely to be incarcerated. (Looney & Turner, 2018). Within one year of release, ex-prisoners continue to struggle with poverty and low SES. Based on tax records, 49% of ex-prisoners earn less than $500 per year and only 20% earn more than $15,000 (Looney & Turner, 2018). The median income is only $10,900 per year (Looney & Turner, 2018). The current median household income in the United States is $67,521.00 (Shrider, et al., 2021). This is significantly higher than the median income of an ex-prisoner. Poverty is at an all time high, with 37.2 million people in poverty (Shrider et atl., 2021). This is a marked increase from previous years and has seen an 11.4 percent increase in a single year. Though the increase in poverty rate as been in part due to the pandemic, other poverty factors, such as education, must be discussed.

Education

Educational status is a significant factor that is related to substance abuse, trauma, and incarceration. Multiple studies have been completed that discuss and support the idea that a lack of education significantly increases the likelihood one will end up incarcerated. High school drop outs are 3.5 times more likely to be arrested than high school graduates (Stipek, 2014). 62 percent of state prisoners have not completed high school (Beatty & Snell, 2021). 57 percent of federal prisoners have not received a high school diploma (Beatty & Snell, 2021). Only 11 percent of state prisoners had attended college for any length of time, with only four percent actually attaining a degree (Beatty & Snell, 2021). 14 percent of federal inmates had attended some college, with only 8 percent obtaining a college degree (Beatty & Snell, 2021). This is a drastic difference from current graduation rates, which shows that 88 percent of students in the 2018-2019 academic year graduated with a high school diploma. These rates vary based on state, with the lowest state graduation rate being 75 percent and the highest being 94 percent (Kerr, 2021).

To combat this, the majority of correctional facilities have educational programs in place. 95 percent of confinement facilities and 65 percent of community-based facilities offer some type of education program, such as a high school equivalency or GED program (Maruschak & Buehler, 2021). 54 percent of confinement facilities offer special education classes (Maruschak & Buehler, 2021). An additional 58 percent of confinement facilities and 18 percent of community-based facilities offer college courses (Maruschak & Buehler, 2021). Though these programs are in place, they often lack the technological resources and additional staff supports that prisoners need to succeed. Programs are often online and leave prisoners will little access to instructor support that is needed to secure a good grade. Due to this, and other issues, only six percent of prisoners nationwide are utilizing college education programs (Bender, 2018).

For prisoners that do utilize their incarceration period to obtain a GED or some form of education, job prospects and higher education opportunities do not increase once released. Of the 33 percent of formerly incarcerated individuals who have obtained a GED, 73 percent of them received their GED in prison (Couloute, 2018). On average, 27 percent of prisoners obtain a GED while incarcerated (Couloute, 2018). Less than ten percent of those who receive a GED while incarcerated will go on to complete any college coursework once released; of those, less than one percent will actually attain a college degree (Couloute, 2018). When it comes to completing college, approximately one in three people in the general population who hold a GED will complete (Couloute, 2018). Only one in 20 ex-prisoners with a prison obtained GED will complete college once released (Couloute, 2018).

This inability to attain higher education upon release is due to a number of factors. First, prisoners who are incarcerated in state or federal facilities are ineligible to receive federal aid (Federal Student Aid, 2021). Though they are able to file for aid directly prior to release, this requires them to have assistance to file for aid as well as assistance in applying to higher education institutions; prisoners will also need a home plan in order to provide information related to their home address and contact information (Federal Student Aid, 2021). Some individuals, despite release status, will never be able to apply for aid as certain crimes negate one's ability to ever apply for financial aid (Federal Student Aid, 2021). Second, many ex-prisoners do not apply for college admission once released due to fears that they will be discriminated against during the admission process. Though questions related to criminal history have been dropped from college applications since 2019, this does not prevent institutions from enquiring about criminal history (Rosenthal, 2018). Studies still show that criminal history negatively impacts one's likelihood of being accepted into a higher education institution (Couloute, 2018). Last, even if one does get accepted into a higher education institution, they may be banned from practicing within their chosen field. If not banned, they may be severely limited in their abilities and may not be able to obtain licensure needed to practice independently. For example, those will a criminal record may be banned from practicing law in at least 11 different states (Couloute, 2018). Helping professions, such as counseling, social work, and psychology may also bar individuals from obtaining a license to practice depending on one's criminal history. These limitations will significantly impact one's ability to obtain employment and to obtain increased financial security.

Employment History

Entangled within socioeconomic status and education is one's employment history. Only 11 percent of federal prisoners held employment in the four months prior to their incarceration (Carson et al., 2021). Females incarcerated were nine percent more likely to hold employment during that period than men (Carson et al., 2021). Those who had served for violent offenses were significantly less likely to hold employment prior to incarceration; those with property damage related crimes held the highest rate of employment prior to incarceration, with 14 percent employed in the four months prior to incarceration (Carson et al., 2021). Of those employed, the median earnings in the quarter prior to incarceration only totaled \$3,800.00, with women making up to \$1,100.00 less than their male counterparts (Carson et al., 2021). Additional studies show that only 49 percent of incarcerated men were employed two years prior to incarceration; the median earnings for those individuals was only \$6,250.00 and only 13 percent earned more than \$15,000.00 (Looney & Turner, 2018). This employment data is connected to one's educational attainment status; those without a GED are unlikely to be employed and, further, are less likely to be employed in a position that provides a wage that allows for financial security.

Employment history continues to play a role once an individual is released from incarceration. Individuals who are released from prison must be able to account for their lapse in employment during their incarceration period. This resume gap may deter employers in favor of those who have consistently been employed. Alternatively, individuals may choose to put employment held while incarcerated on their resume. This, however, immediately alerts a potential employer to their previous incarceration status. This results in poor outcomes for those attempting to gain employment after release. In the first year after release, only 55 percent of ex-prisoners report any income (Looney & Turner, 2018). Median earnings were only $10,090.00, with four percent of those employed earning less than $500.00 (Looney & Turner, 2018). Upon release, it takes an average of six months for a person to find employment; those in the lowest and highest age brackets took upwards of nine months to gain employment (Carson et al., 2021). Post-release, individuals experience an unemployment rate five times higher than the general population (Couloute & Kopf, 2018). In ex-prisoners aged 25-44, the unemployment rate is 27%, which is significantly higher than the 5.2% unemployment rate of their peers in the general population (Couloute & Kopf, 2018).

It is important to note that this data does not include illegal means of employment that one may engage in. With legal jobs lacking the necessary income to provide for themselves and potential family members, ex-prisoners may return to previous criminal behavior. High recidivism rates are seen amongst drug and drug related crimes, with 76.9 percent of state and 41.9 percent of federal drug traffickers being re-arrested within five years of release (United States Sentencing Commission, 2017). 68 percent of drug offenders recidivate within three years of being released (Belenkno et al., 2013). 41 percent of women who currently reside in urban jail settings worked both as sex workers and a care/service job prior to incarceration; 24 percent worked exclusively as sex workers (Kim, 2020). Despite negative outcomes on their mental and physical health, women recognized the need to continue their sex work to supplement their income (Kim, 2020). Having a history of prior prostitution is a significant predictor of future position arrests; 28% of women are rearrested for prostitution within 30 months (Koegler et al., 2019).

Stressors Post-Release

When looking at factors that impact substance abuse and incarceration, one must address the stress that is associated with release from incarceration. Though many who have not been incarcerated may view release as a freeing moment for ex-prisoners, that is often not the case. Release from incarceration brings about a new set of expectations and norms which must be followed. These are radically different from prison and can increase anxiety around the transition. Additional factors include family obligations, difficulties with returning to an old or entering a new environment, and requirements set by the parole board that must be followed. These will be discussed below.

Prison culture, sometimes referred to as prison code, is a set of values, norms, and beliefs generally followed by the prison population (Theerathitiwong, 2017). This code is vastly different from norms that one may find amongst the general population and creates a strong divide between prisoner and correctional employees. The average time served in a state prison is 2.6 years (Kaeble, 2018). For almost three years a prisoner is taught to follow and abide by these codes; these become ingrained and part of one's natural behavioral and thought patterns. When nearing release, prisoners are expected to make a sudden shift in cultural values to match that of the society they are returning to. Suddenly rules such as maintaining your honor at all costs (including through violent means) is no longer applicable (Theerathitiwong, 2017). Additional codes related to not trusting authority figures, such as correctional officers, probation officers, and the police can make for difficult interactions post-release. For those that are required to meet with probation officers, this value of mistrust may mean that ex-prisoners are not sharing vital information with probation officers and other authority figures. Substance abuse is often a common occurrence amongst the prison population, with various forms of drugs and alcohol being snuck in or made for consumption. An individual with a substance use disorder is likely to agree with this cultural norm and will find it difficult to shift their belief system towards one of sobriety upon release. Behaviors that were not only normal, but expected, while incarcerated will now result in re-arrest if acted upon in society.

Once released, individuals are often inundated with tasks and relationships that were left in disarray upon their incarceration. 684, 500 state and federal prisoners are the parent of at least one minor child; this is 47 percent of state and 58 percent of federal prisoners (Maruschak et al., 2021). State and federal prisoners have a combined total of 1,473,700 minor children (Maruschak et al., 2021). Of those incarcerated parents, 626,800 were men and 57,700 were women (Maruschak et al., 2021). Parents who have recently been released from prison will likely have a variety of tasks related to their parenthood. Many parents will need to work towards reunification with their children as approximately six percent of all kids in foster care, or 30,000 children, are in care as a direct result of parental incarceration (Council of States Governments Justice Center, 2011). If not in foster care, children may have been left with the non-incarcerated parent or a family member. Parents will then need to work out visitation, parental rights, and possible reunification with that family member and/or the court system.

Besides children, ex-prisoners will need to work on repairing relationships with spouses, significant others, family, and friends. 14 percent of prisoners are currently married and 19 percent report being divorced (Beatty & Snell, 2021). Many others are in a non-marital romantic relationship. Incarceration places significant strain on romantic relationships as relationships are often limited to short phone calls, infrequent visitations, and lack of privacy surrounding interactions. Additionally, the non-incarcerated individual takes on significant financial and emotional strain that is not easily repaired. Two out of three families had difficulty with meeting basic needs as a result of a family member's incarceration (DeVuono-Powell et al., 2015). An additional one in five families were unable to afford housing due to a family member's incarceration (DeVuono-Powell et al., 2015). Upon release, families continue to struggle as a criminal history makes it difficult to gain housing, employment, and public assistance. One in five ex-prisoners are denied assistance, such as food stamps, after release; a third of the individuals denied had children living in the home (DeVuono-Powell et al., 2015). 79% of families are denied housing due to the criminal status of the recently released individual and one in ten are evicted once their released love one attempts to move into the home (DeVuono-Powell et al., 2015). The inability to meet basic physiological and safety needs creates significant stress for not only the individual, but the entire family unit.

Environmental factors also play a significant role in the lives of those who are released from prison. Through the recovery process, individuals are often taught that they must radically change their environment in order to gain and maintain sobriety. Namely, they must change people, places, and things. For those with a substance use disorder who are exiting prison, this can be a difficult, if not impossible task. Many ex-prisoners are required return to the same disadvantaged neighborhoods or communities in which they were arrested as this is the only place in which they could get an approved home plan (Mennis et al., 2016). These are often high crime neighborhoods in which substance use and drug dealing are common. By placing ex-prisoners back into an environment that is disadvantaged, we are reducing the likelihood of success (Mennis et al, 2016). Returning to a neighborhood in which the individual knows who and where to gain illegal substances from, as well as where crime often occurs, we are reinforcing negative patterns that were learned prior to and during the incarceration period. The stress of maintaining sobriety is often too much to manage, and has a high potential to result in relapse.

Lastly, recently released individuals must maintain and comply with all of the recommendations made by the parole board and their parole officer; the exception to this would be if the individual is being discharged. Common conditions that must be met to maintain parole, thereby remaining out of prison, includes maintaining residence and employment, avoiding all criminal activity and any contact with past victims, remaining sober, completing drug screens as often as weekly, attending recovery meetings, and not leaving the designated geographic area without prior permission from the parole officer (Steiner, 2022). Additionally, parole officers will request parolees to meet them at designated times to check in (as often as weekly) and will drop by unannounced at their residence for home checks (Steiner, 2022). Ex-prisoners must find a way to balance all of the required meetings they must attend, while also maintaining employment and attending any mental health services, parenting services, or other meetings dictated to them.

Due to all of these varying stressors, inmates often see increases in depression, anxiety, and stress post-release. 30.8 percent of ex-prisoners saw an increase in depression symptoms three weeks after release (Berg et al., 2016). An additional 29.8 percent saw a significant increase in stress levels (Berg et al.). Release may be traumatic for many as, depending on how long one has been incarcerated, the world may be drastically different than remembered. Changes in technology, communities, and the growth of family and friends can all be catalysts for stress, depression, and anxiety. With all of these intersecting factors in mind, we must consider how these impact mental health, wellness, and substance abuse.

MENTAL HEALTH AND SUBSTANCE ABUSE

Substance use disorders and mental health disorders are often comorbid in nature, meaning two or more occur within an individual at the same time. Mental health disorders are greatly impacted by the intersecting factors addressed above and are of significant concern when we consider prisoners who struggle with co-occurring disorders. Trauma significantly reduces one's overall wellness and is a contributing factor to the development of a mental health disorder. Though the definition may vary depending upon the field of study, trauma is generally defined as an emotional response to an incident or series of incidents that are emotionally disturbing or life threatening in nature (American Psychological Association, 2022; Center for Health Care Strategies, 2021). These events have lasting adverse effects on an individual's ability to function in key areas including: mental, physical, social, emotional, and/or spiritual areas (Center for Health Care Strategies, 2021). While no all-inclusive list of traumatic events exists, as not all people will find the same things traumatic, some events that may be considered traumatic include: physical, sexual, or emotional abuse, neglect, living with a mentally ill or substance addicted family member, separation from a loved one, poverty, oppression, and violence within the individual's area of residence (Center for Health Care Strategies, 2021).

The Adverse Childhood Experiences Study, first conducted and published in 1998 explored the relationship between adverse childhood experiences and one's likelihood to experience negative mental, physical, and social outcomes as an adult (Felitti et al., 1998). This study, which has since been replicated and supported by numerous research studies, shows a connection between childhood trauma and negative life outcomes. Individuals who experienced four or more adverse experiences as a child were two times more likely to smoke, seven times more likely to consider themselves an alcoholic, ten times more likely to have injected street drugs, and were 12 times more likely to have attempted suicide (Felitti et al., 1998). Those who have four or more adverse childhood experiences are also 20 times more likely to experience incarceration during their lifetime (Young, 2017).

Prisoners who have four or more ACEs are more likely to have been diagnosed with a mental health disorder, to engage in self-harm before and while incarcerated, to make a suicide attempt before and during incarceration, and to identify as having a low mental well being (Ford et al., 2020). Childhood abuse with male prisoners has been connected to mental health difficulties, an increased risk for crime and recidivism, substance use problems, and behavioral issues (Goddard & Pooley, 2019). Up to 90 percent of female prisoners have experienced at least one form of abuse in their lives (Meyer, 2016). Female prisoners are at a greater risk for self-harm, poor emotional regulation, and PTSD symptoms (Howard & Karatzias, 2016). Additionally, female prisoners have high rates of diagnosable mental health disorders, with 84 percent meeting diagnostic criteria for one or more disorders; the most common disorders are major depression, posttraumatic stress disorder, personality disorders, and substance use disorders (Tye & Mullen, 2006). 82 percent of female prisoners met criteria for a substance use disorder (O'Donnell, 2013). Trauma and trauma associated behaviors are associated with an increased likelihood that one will be arrested and incarcerated in adulthood (Jaggi et al., 2016).

TREATMENT

With high comorbidity rates within the prisoner population, treatment must account for both substance use disorders and co-occurring mental health disorders. Current treatment regimens vary in facilities based on whether it is a jail or prison, available staffing, and community supports. Treatments may also vary based on whether the facility houses male, female, or mixed populations. Historically, the justice system has failed to provide adequate treatment options to meet the needs of those who are incarcerated. This failure has led to many harsh critiques and has resulted in some positive changes in the system. Though much is left to be done in order to ensure care is sufficient, the justice system is beginning to look it the right direction.

Currently, the Federal Bureau of prisons recognizes the importance of rehabilitative measures regarding substance use disorders. Federal prisons have four distinct ways in which they currently treat substance abuse amongst its population (Federal Bureau of Prisons, 2022). Psychoeducation measures are utilized during their Drug Abuse Education series (Federal Bureau of Prisons, 2022). This series consists of 30-40 hours of education provided to prisoners related to the detrimental consequences of drug use; this program also helps staff to identify prisoners who may need further treatment (Federal Bureau of Prisons, 2022). Federal facilities also offer a non-residential or a residential substance abuse treatment program. The non-residential program is a twelve-week course that utilizes cognitive behavioral therapy approaches in a group setting to help prisoners develop rational thinking, communication skills, and support in adjusting to incarceration (Federal Bureau of Prisons, 2022). The residential program, referred to as RDAP, is a nine-month program where prisoners undergo daily intensive treatment for their substance use (Federal Bureau of Prisons, 2022). Prisoners who attend they program live in a unit sperate from the general prison population, spend at least half of the day in treatment, and utilize the other half of the day for work or educational purposes (Federal Bureau of Prisons, 2022). Currently, the federal prisons have 79 active RDAP locations in 71 facilities (Federal Bureau of Prisons, 2022). Internal reports completed by the Federal Bureau of Prisons indicate that program completion outcomes include: reduce drug and alcohol relapse, reduce criminality and recidivism, reduced misconduct, an increase in education levels, increased employment opportunities upon returning to the community, and improved health and mental health symptoms and conditions (Santos, 2021). Last, a transitional program is offered that helps prisoners transition out of RDAP and into community settings (Federal Bureau of Prisons, 2022).

Many state run facilities have similar educational programs offered to prisoners based on need. The most notable substance abuse program currently being run within state facilities is the RSAT program. This program, named the Residential Substance Abuse Treatment program, is a grant funded program that is located is all of the nation's 56 states and territories (Harrison & Martin, 2003). The goal of the RSAT program is to "break the cycle of drugs and violence by reducing the demand for, use, and trafficking of illegal drugs" (U.S. Department of Justice, 2016, pg. 4). The RSAT program is 6-12 months in duration, provides separating housing distinct from the general prison population, and allocates a significant portion of the prisoner's day to substance abuse treatment (U.S. Department of Justice, 2016). In addition to residential treatment, some prisoners are offered medication assisted treatment prior to release to assist in the maintenance of their sobriety (Bureau of Justice Assistance, 2019). A total of 38 state facilities offer medication assisted treatment, MAT for short; per year an average of 356 out of 688 eligible prisoners utilize the MAT program (Bureau of Justice Assistance, 2019). 73 percent of prisons utilize Vivitrol, 14 percent utilize Suboxone, and 12 percent use Methadone (Bureau of Justice Assistance, 2019). Though success and data outcomes will vary for each state or territory, a recent Kentucky report indicated that of the surveyed released prisoners who completed the program, 61.6 percent had not been re-incarcerated, 87.8 percent were living in stable housing, 76.6 were employed, 58.8 percent did not have a positive drug test in the year since release, 67.5 percent attended some form of AA or 12-step program, and 67.2 percent of those who were referred to aftercare attend the appointment (Staton et al., 2019).

Some jail facilities also have RSAT programming in place, but are less common (Bureau of Justice Assistance, 2019). Jail facilities have an additional level of difficulty when attempting to determine appropriate treatment measures as they are receiving individuals directly from the community. Due to this, they are often processing individuals through intake who are active addicts and are currently intoxicated in some manner. Approximately 547,000 people are currently being held in local jails (Sawyer & Wagner, 2022). Of those, jail officials estimate that around 80 percent of them are utilizing opioids prior to entry (Westervelt, 2022). It is currently estimated that at least two thirds of the current jail population has a drug abuse or dependence problem (Westervelt, 2022). Currently, only 20 percent of jailed inmates receive any type of drug treatment; only one percent receive detoxification services (Bureau of Justice Assistance, 2022). Based on this data, only one in 79 people experiencing withdrawal in jail are receiving detoxification services. Those who do not receive services are required to detox without support, making the incarceration period substantially more difficult. Many people die while in jail due to their withdrawal; current data shows that from 2000 to 2019 deaths related to drug and alcohol intoxication increased 397 percent (Bureau of Justice Assistance, 2022).

Despite some form of substance abuse programming occurring at federal, state, and local levels, these have not been enough to disrupt the flow of chemically dependent prisoners. Critics of the current programming speak to the lack of programmatic oversight in residential programs, failure to endorse evidence-based drug and alcohol treatment, and a lack of consistency in enough qualified staff to adequately meet the needs of prisoners (Stainbrook et al., 2017; Bureau of Justice Assistance, 2022). Often, those who provide funding do not provide enough support to residential programs and leave much of the programming to the determination of on-site staff. This hands-off approach results in programs not following through on the original guidelines set forth in their funding contracts, thus prisoners do not get the needed treatment. Current concerns also speak to the lack of policy and protocol related to substance abuse in the correctional setting. Many facilities do not have clear communication and designated roles between officers, staff, medical staff, and mental health providers (if available) which results in untimely or inadequate responses to withdrawal symptoms or overdoses (Bureau of Justice Assistance, 2022).

Additional concerns include officers and staff who bring contraband into the facility for prisoners in exchange for money or sexual favors (Renaud, 2018).

Guidelines to improve substance abuse services have been established by several organizations. The National Commission on Correctional Health Care is an accreditation program that seeks to improve correctional health care (NCCHC, 2022). This organization recognizes the lack of adequate care in facilities and has set standards to ensure care for prisoners who have a substance use disorder. This is a 14-step process that covers a prisoner from entry to exit and utilizes best practices (NCCHC, 2022). As part of the process all inmates are to be screened upon entry for risk factors and symptoms of withdrawal; prisoners who screen positive will trigger the following response: evaluation on current use, assessment for comorbidity, a formal assessment for withdrawal, and, if female, will be given a pregnancy test (NCCHC, 2022). This process also accounts for those who are utilizing medication assisted treatment for sobriety and encourage facilities to allow the continuance of this treatment while incarcerated; prisoners should also be offered treatment prior to release and follow-up services (NCCHC, 2022). The organization also recognizes the importance of mental health treatment in conjunction with substance abuse treatment and includes the use of non-medication based therapies to aid in the recovery process (NCCHC, 2022). The full document can be found on the National Commission on Correctional Health Care's website. Implementation of this plan in correctional settings would begin the process of providing continuity of care, addressing the underlying mental health factors that impact substance abuse, and has the possibility of reducing recidivism rates as those leaving will be provided transitional services.

The Substance Abuse and Mental Health Services Administration has also provided a guide for correctional facilities to follow that would provide meaningful care. This guide has four overarching steps: assess, plan, identify, and coordinate (SAMHSA, 2017). These are broken down into ten key phases that assess clinical and social needs, develop individualized treatment plans, identify community providers, and coordinate care after release that will meet the needs of that specific prisoner (SAMHSA, 2017). Both of these guides seek to provide a format to facilities to follow that will allow for the most successful outcomes for both facilities and prisoners. Continuity of care, adequate staffing, properly trained staff, clear policy/protocol, the use of multiple treatment modalities, and aftercare planning are the main features of these plans.

In addition to providing substance abuse treatment as outlined above, facilities must begin to value mental health care for prisoners. As previously mentioned, the majority of prisoners do not qualify for mental health services and are unable to maintain their medication treatment regimen once incarcerated (Federal Bureau of Prisons, 2021). Mental health staff are also lacking in facilities, which leaves mentally ill individuals unable to receive care. In order to combat this, the correctional system must prioritize the hiring of mental health professionals and must work to train their non-mental health staff on mental health as it relates to the prison population. Current data shows that correctional officer training on mental health increases the safety and security of both officers and prisoners (Kois et al., 2019). Unfortunately, training requirements are not standardized across facilities; required yearly training hours in mental health range from only 1.5 hours to 80 hours (Kois et al., 2019). More frequent and intensive mental health training may be of great benefit to facilities.

It is also crucial that facilities begin to understand and implement a trauma-informed care approach with prisoners. Trauma-informed care is a shift in treatment approach in which we ask individuals "what happened to you" rather than "what is wrong with you" (Center for Health Care Strategies, 2021). This approach acknowledges that we must look at a person in a holistic manner; to understand an individual's current substance use or mental health disorder, we must first understand the experiences that led them to this point in their lives. By implementing this method, the justice system will begin to recognize the lasting impact of trauma, recognize the signs of trauma, integrate evidence-based knowledge into their programs and policies, and actively avoid engaging in behaviors that are re-traumatizing for prisoners (Center for Health Care Strategies, 2021). Thus far, trauma-informed approaches have shown to be beneficial in correctional. Data has shown an increase in positive prisoner responses to cognitive behavioral treatment that is centered on reducing criminal risk factors and treatment focused on substance abuse recovery (Miller & Najavits, 2012). One successful implementation of this approach is the Seeking Safety Program (Adams et al., 2017). More information about this program can be found on the Seeking Safety website.

CONCLUSION

Substance abuse amongst correctional settings is a significant problem that has grown in severity. Mental health issues have also become increasingly common amongst the prison population. These concerns are often related to traumatic events experienced prior to incarceration, such as abuse, neglect, or poverty. Without properly treating both substance abuse and mental health concerns, which are often co-occurring, we will continue to see high recidivism rates within the correctional system. Though some treatment options are currently available to prisoners such as educational programs, medication assisted treatment, and residential substance abuse treatment programs, these are not sufficient. The justice system must begin to seriously consider the implantation of highly respected programming to ensure quality and consistent care is provided to those in their care. Additionally, mental health treatment must be prioritized through the hiring of mental health staff and the implementation of trauma-informed care practices.

REFERENCES

Adam, A., & McNeely, J. (2020). *Substance use screening and risk assessment in adults*. Johns Hopkins University.

Adams, S., Houston-Kolnik, J., & Reichert, J. (2017). *Trauma-informed and evidence-based practices and programs to address trauma in correctional settings.* https://icjia.illinois.gov/researchhub/articles/trauma-informed-and-evidence-based-practices-and-programs-to-address-trauma-in-correctional-settings

American Psychiatric Association. (2013). *Diagnostic and statistical manual of mental disorders* (5th ed.). American Psychiatric Publishing.

American Psychological Association. (2022). *Trauma*. https://www.apa.org/topics/trauma#:~:text=Trauma%20is%20an%20emotional%20response,symptoms%20like%20headaches%20or%20nausea

American Psychological Association. (2022). *Socioeconomic status*. https://www.apa.org/topics/socioeconomic-status

Aminawung, J., Chamberlain, A., Fox, A., Nyamu, S., Shavit, S., & Wang, E. (2019). Illicit substance use after release from prison among formerly incarcerated primary care patients: A cross-sectional study. *Addiction Science & Clinical Practice*. https://ascpjournal.biomedcentral.com/articles/10.1186/s13722-019-0136-6

Bath, E., Brown, L., Conrad, S., Folk, J., Kemp, K., Marshall, B., Ramos, L., Rosen, B., & Tolou-Shams, M. (2021). The prospective impact of adverse childhood experiences on justice-involved youth's psychiatric symptoms and substance abuse. *Journal of Consulting and Clinical Psychology*, *89*(6), 483–498. doi:10.1037/ccp0000655 PMID:34264697

Beatty, L., & Snell, T. (2021). *U.S. department of justice profile of prison inmates 2016*. https://bjs.ojp.gov/content/pub/pdf/ppi16.pdf

Beaty, B., Binswanger, I., Calcaterra, S., Min, S., & Mueller, S. (2014). The association between social stressors and drug use/hazardous drinking among former prison inmates. *Journal of Substance Abuse Treatment*, *47*(1), 41–49. doi:10.1016/j.jsat.2014.02.002 PMID:24642070

Belenko, S., Hiller, M., & Hamilton, L. (2013). Treating substance use disorders in the criminal justice system. *Current Psychiatry Reports*, *15*(11), 414. doi:10.100711920-013-0414-z PMID:24132733

Bender, K. (2018). *Education opportunities in prison are key to reducing crime*. https://www.americanprogress.org/article/education-opportunities-prison-key-reducing-crime/

Berg, J., Roberts, M., Bock, B., Martin, R., Stein, L., Parker, D., McGovern, A., Shuford, S., & Clarke, J. (2016). Changes in depression and stress after release from a tobacco-free prison in the united states. *International Journal of Environmental Research and Public Health*, *13*(1). PMID:26771622

Branje, S., Keijsers, L., Loeber, R., Meeus, W., Pardini, D., & Rekker, R. (2015). Moving in and out of poverty: The within-individual association between socioeconomic status and juvenile delinquency. *PLoS One*, *10*(11). https://www.ncbi.nlm.nih.gov/pmc/articles/PMC4648521/#:~:text=Socioeconomic%20status%20(SES)%20is%20one,treated%20as%20a%20static%20characteristic PMID:26575271

Bureau of Justice Assistance. (2022). *Managing substance withdrawal in jails: A legal brief.* https://bja.ojp.gov/doc/managing-substance-withdrawal-in-jails.pdf

Carson, A. (2021). *U.S. department of justice prisoners in 2020-statistical tables*. https://bjs.ojp.gov/content/pub/pdf/p20st.pdf

Carson, A., Sandler, D., Bhaskar, R., Fernandez, L., & Porter, S. (2021). *Employment of persons released from federal prison in 2010*. https://bjs.ojp.gov/content/pub/pdf/eprfp10.pdf

Center for Health Care Strategies. (2021). *What is trauma?* https://www.traumainformedcare.chcs.org/what-is-trauma/

Cerda, M., Fink, K., Gaidus, A., Greunwald, P., Keyes, K., Martins, S., Pear, P., Ponicki, W., & Rivera-Aguirre, A. (2019). Urban-rural variation in the socioeconomic determinants of opioid overdose. *Drug and Alcohol Dependence*, *195*, 66–73. doi:10.1016/j.drugalcdep.2018.11.024 PMID:30592998

Chiappini, S., & Schifano, F. (2022). What about "pharming?" issues regarding the misuse of prescription and over the counter drugs. *Brain Sciences*, *10*(10), 736. doi:10.3390/brainsci10100736 PMID:33066476

Colman, I., Eljdupovic, G., Martin, M., & Mckenzie, K. (2016). Risk of violence by inmates with childhood trauma and mental health needs. *Law and Human Behavior, 39*(6), 614–623. PMID:26214301

Compassion Prison Project. (2022). *How common are adverse childhood experiences*. https://compassionprisonproject.org/childhood-trauma-statistics/

Couloute, L. (2018). *Getting back on course: Educational exclusion and attainment among formerly incarcerated people*. https://www.prisonpolicy.org/reports/education.html#:~:text=GEDs%20in%20prison&text=We%20found%20that%20of%20the,attained%20a%20GED%20while%20incarcerated

Couloute, L., & Kopf, D. (2018) *Out of prison & out of work: Unemployment among formerly incarcerated people*. https://www.prisonpolicy.org/reports/outofwork.html

DeVuono-Powell, S., Schweilder, C., Walters, A., & Zohrabi, A. (2015). *Who pays? The true cost of incarceration on families*. http://whopaysreport.org/executive-summary/pdf-executive-summary/

Eldridge, T., & Thompson, C. (2018). *Treatment denied: The mental health crisis in federal prisons*. https://www.themarshallproject.org/2018/11/21/treatment-denied-the-mental-health-crisis-in-federal-prisons

Federal Bureau of Prisons. (2021). *Federal bureau of prisons program fact sheet*. Author.

Federal Bureau of Prisons. (2022). *Substance abuse treatment*. https://www.bop.gov/inmates/custody_and_care/substance_abuse_treatment.jsp

Federal Student Aid. (2021). *Federal student adult for adults in correctional and juvenile justice facilities*. https://studentaid.gov/sites/default/files/aid-info-for-incarcerated-individuals.pdf

Felitti, V., Anda, R., Nordenberg, D., Williamson, D., Spitz, A., Edwards, V., Koss, M., & Marks, J. S. (1998). Relationship of childhood abuse and household dysfunction to many of the leading causes of death in adults the adverse childhood experiences (ACE) study. *American Journal of Preventive Medicine, 14*(4), 245–258. doi:10.1016/S0749-3797(98)00017-8 PMID:9635069

Ford, K., Bellis, M., Hughes, K., Barton, E., & Newbury, A. (2020). Adverse childhood experiences: A retrospective study to understand their associations with lifetime mental health diagnosis, self-harm or suicide attempt, and current low mental wellbeing in a male welsh prison population. *Health & Justice, 8*(1), 13. doi:10.118640352-020-00115-5 PMID:32533348

Goddard, T., & Pooley, J. (2019). The impact of childhood abuse on adult male prisoners: A systematic review. *Journal of Police and Criminal Psychology, 34*(2), 215–230. doi:10.100711896-018-9260-6

Grinspoon, P. (2021). *Poverty, homelessness, and stigma make addiction more deadly*. https://www.health.harvard.edu/blog/poverty-homelessness-and-social-stigma-make-addiction-more-deadly-202109282602

Howard, R., & Karatzias, T. (2016). From childhood trauma to self-harm: An investigation of theoretical pathways among female prisoners. *Clinical Psychology & Psychotherapy*. Advance online publication. doi:10.1002/cpp.2058 PMID:27878907

Hser, Y., & Schulte, M. (2014). Substance use and associated health conditions throughout the lifespan. *Public Health Reviews, 39*(2). https://www.ncbi.nlm.nih.gov/pmc/articles/PMC5373082/

Jaggi, L., Mezuk, B., Watkins, D., & Jackson, J. (2016). The relationship between trauma, arrest, and incarceration history among black americans: Findings from the national survey of American life. *Society and Mental Health*, *6*(3), 187–206. doi:10.1177/2156869316641730 PMID:27795871

Kaeble, D. (2018). *Time served in state prison 2016.* https://bjs.ojp.gov/content/pub/pdf/tssp16.pdf

Kerr, E. (2021). *See high school graduation rates by state.* https://www.usnews.com/education/best-high-schools/articles/see-high-school-graduation-rates-by-state#:~:text=The%20high%20school%20graduation%20rate,News%20Best%20High%20Schools%20rankings

Kim, S., & Peterson, C. (2020). The health effects of gendered and devalued work: Health outcomes of incarcerated women engaging in sex work and care/service work. *Health & Justice*, *8*(1), 23. doi:10.118640352-020-00124-4 PMID:33206239

Koegler, E., Preble, K., Cimino, A., Stevens, J., & Diehl, S. (2019). Examining recidivism in a prostitution diversion program. *International Journal of Offender Therapy and Comparative Criminology*. Advance online publication. doi:10.1177/0306624X19866115 PMID:31364427

Kois, L., Hill, K., Gonzales, L., Hunter, S., & Chauhan, P. (2019). Correctional officer mental health training: Analysis of 52 u.s. jurisdictions. *Criminal Justice Policy Review*, *31*(4), 555–572. doi:10.1177/0887403419849624

Lipari, R., & VanHorn, S. (2017). *Trends in substance use disorders among adults aged 18 or older.* https://www.samhsa.gov/data/sites/default/files/report_2790/ShortReport-2790.html

Looney, A., & Turner, N. (2018). *The Brookings Institution work and opportunity before and after incarceration.* https://www.brookings.edu/wp-content/uploads/2018/03/es_20180314_looneyincarceration_final.pdf

Maruschak, L., Bronson, J., & Alper, M. (2021) *Parents in prison and their minor children: Survey of Prison Inmates 2016.* https://bjs.ojp.gov/library/publications/parents-prison-and-their-minor-children-survey-prison-inmates-2016#:~:text=An%20estimated%20684%2C500%20state%20and,of%20federal%20prisoners%20(58%25)

Maruschak, L., & Buehler, E. (2021). *Census of state and federal adult correctional facilities.* https://bjs.ojp.gov/content/pub/pdf/csfacf19st.pdf

Mayo Clinic. (2017). *Drug addiction substance use disorder.* https://www.mayoclinic.org/diseases-conditions/drug-addiction/symptoms-causes/syc-20365112

McVay, D. (2022). *Drug policy facts arrests and the criminal legal system.* https://www.drugpolicyfacts.org/chapter/crime_arrests

Mennis, J., Stahler, G., & Mason, M. (2016). Risky substance use environments and addiction: A new frontier for environmental justice. *International Journal of Environmental Research and Public Health*, *13*(6), 607. Advance online publication. doi:10.3390/ijerph13060607 PMID:27322303

Meyer, S. (2016). *Women in prison: Histories of trauma and abuse highlight the need for specialized care.* https://theconversation.com/women-in-prison-histories-of-trauma-and-abuse-highlight-the-need-for-specialised-care-68668

Miller, N., & Najavits, L. (2012). Creating trauma-informed correctional care. *European Journal of Psychotraumatology*, *3*(1), 17246. doi:10.3402/ejpt.v3i0.17246 PMID:22893828

Minton, D., & Zeng, Z. (2021). *U.S. department of justice jail inmates in 2020- Statistical tables.* https://bjs.ojp.gov/content/pub/pdf/ji20st.pdf

National Alliance on Mental Illness. (2022). *Mental health treatment while incarcerated.* https://www.nami.org/Advocacy/Policy-Priorities/Improving-Health/Mental-Health-Treatment-While-Incarcerated

National Institute of Justice. (2022). *Recidivism.* https://nij.ojp.gov/topics/corrections/recidivism

National Institutes on Drug Abuse. (2020). *Common comorbidities with substance use disorders research report.* https://www.ncbi.nlm.nih.gov/books/NBK571451/

O'Donnell, D. (2013). *BJA policy brief.* https://bja.ojp.gov/sites/g/files/xyckuh186/files/Publications/WomensPathwaysToJail.pdf

Renaud, J. (2018). *Who's really bringing contraband into jails? Our 2018 survey confirms it's staff not visitors.* https://www.prisonpolicy.org/blog/2018/12/06/jail-contraband/

Rosenthal, A. (2018). *Common application bans the box.* https://ccresourcecenter.org/2018/08/09/common-application-bans-the-box/

Santos, M. (2021). *RDAP introduction.* https://prisonprofessors.com/rdap-introduction/

Sawyer, W., & Wagner, P. (2022). *Mass incarceration: The whole pie 2022.* https://www.prisonpolicy.org/reports/pie2022.html

Shrider, E., Kollar, M., Chen, F., & Semega, J. (2021). *Income and poverty in the united states.* https://www.census.gov/content/dam/Census/library/publications/2021/demo/p60-273.pdf

Sripada, C. (2022). Impaired control in addiction involves cognitive distortions and unreliable self-control not compulsive desires and overwhelmed self-control. *Behavioural Brain Research*, *418*, 113639. doi:10.1016/j.bbr.2021.113639 PMID:34710509

Stainbrook, K., Hanna, J., & Salomon, A. (2017). *The rsat study: The characteristics and components of funded treatment and aftercare services.* https://www.ojp.gov/pdffiles1/nij/grants/250715.pdf

Staton, M., Dickson, M., Tillson, M., & Winston, E. (2019). *Criminal Justice Kentucky Treatment Outcome Study.* https://corrections.ky.gov/Divisions/ask/Documents/CJKTOS%20FInal%20Report%202019.pdf

Steiner, M. (2022). *What is parole? How does parole work?* https://www.nolo.com/legal-encyclopedia/how-does-parole-work.html#:~:text=Parole%20Conditions&text=maintain%20employment%20and%20a%20residence,or%20alcohol%20recovery%20meetings%2C%20and

Substance Abuse and Mental Health Services Administration. (2017). *Implementation guide.* https://store.samhsa.gov/sites/default/files/d7/priv/sma16-4998.pdf

The Oxford Treatment Center. (2020). *The kindling effect: Alcohol withdrawal issues.* https://oxfordtreatment.com/substance-abuse/alcohol/kindling-effect/

Theerathitiwong, S. (2017). *The encyclopedia of corrections.* John Wiley & Sons.

Tye, C., & Mullen, P. (2006). Mental disorder in female prisoners. *The Australian and New Zealand Journal of Psychiatry*, *40*(3), 266–271. doi:10.1080/j.1440-1614.2006.01784.x PMID:16476155

United States Sentencing Commission. (2017). *Recidivism among federal drug trafficking offenders.* https://www.ussc.gov/research/research-reports/recidivism-among-federal-drug-trafficking-offenders

U.S. Department of Justice. (2016). *RSAT for state prisoners program.* https://bja.ojp.gov/sites/g/files/xyckuh186/files/media/document/BJA-2016-9023.pdf

Westervelt, E. (2019). *County jails struggle with a new role as america's prime centers for opioid detox.* https://www.npr.org/2019/04/24/716398909/county-jails-struggle-with-a-new-role-as-americas-prime-centers-for-opioid-detox

Young, D. (2017). *Transforming trauma seeking recovery for those in corrections.* https://www.pacesconnection.com/fileSendAction/fcType/0/fcOid/505446391196077409/filePointer/505446391196077421/fodoid/505446391196077416/Corrections%20Today%20Young%20Transforming%20Trauma%20CCP%20March%20April%202017.pdf

Section 2

Effects of Incarceration on the Relationship Between Parent and Child

Chapter 5
Understanding Parental Incarceration and Its Effects on Children's Mental Health

Sara Pickett
University of Cincinnati, USA

Jordan McCoy
University of Cincinnati, USA

ABSTRACT

While a deeper understanding of the effects of mass incarceration in the United States has gained recent traction and attention, it is less recognized that the children of those incarcerated are also greatly affected. There is a growing body of research that focuses on how parental incarceration affects the mental health of children. However, there is a critical need to further the conversation around how incarceration creates a trickledown effect of mental health issues. The goal of this chapter is to examine how and why mass incarceration has led to increased mental illnesses and disenfranchisement for sentenced individuals and their children. By discussing this complex system, further truths will be revealed, and important questions will be generated. The authors conclude with questions, and suggestions, in the hopes that this will lead to further research and action that have vast implications for the mental health community as it pertains to the discussed population.

INTRODUCTION

The current issue of mass incarceration in the United States has become a national crisis, and in many ways, a tragic norm within certain communities. According to the Bureau of Justice (Kaeble & Cowhig, 2018), in 2016 there were 6,613,500 people supervised in the United States adult correctional systems, or 2.7% of the total population of this country. Of this amount, 2,162,400 were incarcerated in jail or prison. This is a particularly alarming rate considering that this translates into one in every 37 adults being under supervision of the criminal justice system (NAACP, n.d.). In 2020, the number of people

DOI: 10.4018/978-1-7998-9209-0.ch005

incarcerated in jail or prison rose to nearly 2.3 million, and approximately 7 million people were under correctional supervision (Sawyer & Wagner, 2020). In the last forty years, overall incarceration in the United States has increased astronomically (The Sentencing Project, n.d.). Although these statistics might not initially appear striking or disproportionate to the larger population of the United States, they are considerably more profound when compared to other industrialized nations.

Research has shown that poverty, lack of education, mental health, and trauma, especially for people of color and the BIPOC community, are strong predictors of incarceration for adults (Massoglia, 2008). In turn, criminal behavior by a parent and incarceration of a parent have been linked to a decline in mental health in children and their own subsequent criminality (Arditti, 2012a; Wildeman and Western, 2010). Wildeman and Western (2010) write that "a number of studies show an association between parental incarceration and the criminality of children" (p. 168). In many ways, there is evidence to argue for the existence of a parent to child prison pipeline. In terms of available statistics, one in 12 children in the United States have experienced parental incarceration in some capacity. When this ratio is assigned a number, it is over 5.7 million children under the age of 18 who have had at least one parent incarcerated at some point during their lifetime (Gotsch, 2018).

Conducting research studies proving direct causal effects of parental incarceration on children's mental health are challenging. Arditti (2012b) writes how "it is unclear whether parental incarceration is the cause of family problems or a 'risk marker'-that is, a symptom of other family problems and social conditions" (p. 98). Turney and Goodsell (2018) argue that research looking at direct effects of parental incarceration on children would be not particularly feasible and potentially unethical as well. However, studies have shown strong associations between parental incarceration and negative outcomes for children due to several micro and macro level factors (Arditti, 2012b). As such, there is a profound need for further research that can shed light on how to combat intergenerational incarceration and its effects on the mental health of parent and child. In many ways, the well-being and mental health of future generations is at stake.

The goal of this chapter is to further add to the literature on this topic to increase awareness and promote real change for the studied population. The absence of further research will continue to limit understanding and the extent to which mental health interventions can be designed to ameliorate the fallout associated with parental incarceration. However, the authors of this chapter are not interested in research without action; such an approach would ultimately be unjust to the population discussed. Therefore, the expectation is that this chapter will elucidate how negatively impactful incarceration is on the mental health of offenders and their children by funneling a discussion that begins at the macro level and concludes with a discussion of the micro level issues related to this topic. It is expected that this chapter will have a positive impact not only by bringing awareness to this issue and adding to the available body of literature, but also by providing real innovative solutions to the problem. In turn, these solutions can be disseminated throughout a number of professions to maximize their influence and efficacy for both theoretical and practical purposes.

BACKGROUND

The Evolution of Mass Incarceration in the United States

The United States incarcerates more people than any other country in the world, and incarceration rates for both men and women have grown exponentially in this country over the last several decades. (Wagner & Sawyer, 2018; Western & Wildeman, 2009). Up until approximately the mid-1970s, the United States' incarceration rate was notably on par with other Western industrialized nations such as Germany and France (Whitman, 2003). However, while incarceration rates have had a relatively steady increase in the last few decades in many other industrialized nations, mass incarceration has now become an American phenomenon (Comfort et al., 2016). Although the United States currently holds approximately 5% of the overall population of the world, it contains nearly 21% of those who are incarcerated throughout the world (NAACP, n.d.). In 2011, Walmsley (2011) reported that the United States' incarceration rate was ten times higher than that of such countries as Denmark and Norway. According to the Prison Policy Initiative, the United States incarcerates 698 people for every 100,000 residents (Sawyer & Wagner, 2020). Put into further context, El Salvador, which has the second highest incarceration rate of another country, incarcerates 614 people to every 100,000 residents. There are 31 states within the United States that have higher incarceration rates per capita than the country of El Salvador (Sawyer & Wagner, 2020).

Changes in policing, policies, and an ever-increase conservative political climate on both sides of the aisle are credited as major contributors to the massive increase in the United States' incarcerated population (Mauer, 2001; Sykes & Pettit, 2014). President Reagan's inception of the War on Drugs in the 1980s saw a rapid rise in drug arrests and sentences (Wakefield, Lee, & Wildeman, 2016). From 1985 to 2000, two-thirds of the increase in incarcerated people was due primarily to drug offenses and sentences. Put more starkly, from 1980 to 2010 the number of people serving time for a drug offense(s) increased by 1,100% (Alexander, 2010). Furthermore, citing a spike in crime during the 1970s, the perceived lawlessness of the civil rights movement, and prison riots, many politicians pushed for, and ran on a platform of being tough on crime (Mauer, 2001). This would ultimately become a political catch phrase, a talking point, and a sound bite through the 1980s and 90s and would greatly influence public opinion on the necessity for more prisons. Since the 1970s, the concept of incarceration has transitioned from being seen as a place for rehabilitation to something that provides needed control of crime and criminals (Greene, 2002).

Additionally, increasingly aggressive police tactics, the 1994 Crime Bill, the "Three Strikes" law, and much harsher jail sentences for drug offenses and other non-violent crimes all contributed to a massive uptick in the amount of people incarcerated in the United States in the last four decades (Mauer, 2001; Wheelock & Hartmann, 2007; Sutton, 2013). However, as several prominent scholars such as Garland (2001) and Alexander (2011) have suggested, the birth of mass incarceration in the United States is really a story about racism and classism in this country. These scholars, along with many others, argue that the criminal justice system is a revised version of Jim Crow (Garland, 2001; Alexander, 2010). In essence, the argument is that mass incarceration in the United States is an alternative system of control aimed at replacing other racist laws and structures such as Jim Crow from the earlier part of the last century. Therefore, incarceration in this country should be viewed as an intentional system of confinement and control over large populations of marginalized people (Alexander, 2010). Unfortunately, incarcerating large numbers of marginalized adults does not exist in a vacuum-it has a significant trickle-down effect on other people and systems including communities, families, and children (Western & Wildeman, 2009).

Race and Class Disparities Amongst the Prison Population

In the introduction to his book *Mass Imprisonment: Social Causes and Consequence*, David Garland (2001) uses the phrase "mass imprisonment" to describe the overwhelming and extraordinarily high rates of incarceration that exists in the United States alone (Sykes & Pettit, 2014). Garland (2001), who was one of the first scholars to recognize and coin this term, explains the difference between imprisonment and mass imprisonment. While imprisonment is the confinement of separate and isolated offenders, mass imprisonment is a systematic and strategic move to incarcerate large groups of subjugated people (Garland, 2001). Within the United States, this mostly involves incarcerating poor people of color-although more specifically young Black males (Garland, 2001; Pettit & Western, 2004; Pettit, 2012). As scholar Angela J. Davis (2017) observes, this approach is not limited to incarceration; it pervades throughout the entire criminal justice system. Davis (2017) writes, "The criminal justice system polices black men at every step of the process" (p. 178). Therefore, one cannot talk about modern day incarceration in the United States without discussing the influence of race and class on those convicted and serving sentenced time. The influence of race and class on who is ultimately arrested, sentenced, and serves prison time has a profound impact on those who offend as well as their children, families, and communities (Sexton, 2016).

Despite steadily declining crime rates since the 1990s in the United States, current incarceration numbers remain exceptionally high, and prison rates show that a highly disproportionate number of marginalized people are incarcerated (Levitt, 2004; Travis & Western, 2017). Currently, 57.6% of the prison population in the United States is White while 38.5% is Black (Federal Bureau of Prisons, 2021). It must be considered, however, that Black Americans make up just 13.4% of the total population in the United States (United States Census Bureau, 2019). Overall, Black people are incarcerated at a rate that is five times higher than White people in this country (NAACP, n.d.). Furthermore, Black people make up 22% of police shootings that turn fatal and 35% of death penalty executions (Inman, 2020). In general, people of color, though more specifically Black males, are more likely to be suspected and arrested by the police, given harsher sentences by judges, and have much higher rates of recidivism (Reisig et al., 2007; Davis, 2017; Kizielewicz, 2018). In other words, many Black men who are convicted and serve sentenced time often return to jail or prison due to a variety of factors including many social inequalities.

Class disparities in incarceration rates are also evident in the numbers. High rates of incarcerated poor people are related to class biases from the public, police, judges, and prosecutors (Kopf, 2018). Poor people struggle to adequately defend themselves in court; good legal representative costs money, time, and access (Butler, 2013). Although education level is not always an indicator of socioeconomic status, it is commonly believed that the two factors have at least a correlative association. On average, those incarcerated at the state level have approximately a 10th grade level of education, and 70% did not graduate from high school or have their GED (Western & Pettit, 2010). Sykes and Pettit (2014) write that the "growth of incarceration has been concentrated among people with low levels of education" (p. 128). Unfortunately, when it comes to intersectionality and having two or more marginalized statuses, the chances of incarceration often increase. Being poor and Black are often seen socially and treated politically as a combination of identities worthy of the harshest treatment (Butler, 2013; Smiley & Fakunle, 2016). Black men who do not graduate from high school are more likely to be incarcerated than employed, and statically speaking, two- thirds of Black men without a college degree will be incarcerated in their lifetime (Butler, 2013).

MENTAL HEALTH AMONGST THE PRISON POPULATION

To move toward a deeper understanding of the effects of parental incarceration on children's mental health, the effects of incarcerations on offenders' mental health must first be understood and reviewed. It is important to note that studying the causal relationship between incarceration and mental health is difficult, though not impossible, due in part by the fact that individuals with mental health concerns prior to incarceration often have a higher risk of being incarcerated than those without preexisting mental health issues (World Health Organization, n.d.). Several studies have identified how a high percentage of incarcerated individuals have experienced what is known as a legacy of victimization and various types of traumatic events, including the trauma of racism, prior to serving time (Wolff et al., 2009; Williams, 2020). In turn, research has also shown that pre-incarceration trauma exposure is associated with increased likelihood of being arrested and incarcerated especially for Black Americans (Jaggi et al., 2016). During incarceration, it has been found that symptoms of depression and suicidality often worsen (Wildeman & Wang, 2017). Through a systematic review and meta-analysis, Piper and Berle (2019) found positive associations between experiencing Potentially Traumatic Events (PTEs) while incarcerated and developing PTSD symptoms.

Of the millions of people currently detained in state and federal prisons in the United States, approximately 23% of them have expressed experiencing some form of mental illness (Cox et al. 2017). Although certainly an issue since its creation, mental health and illnesses have only increased with mass incarceration. According to Prins (2011), causes for the increase in mental health concerns can be attributed to multiple factors, but deinstitutionalization and lack of community funding are two of the main identified reasons. In 2004, there were approximately 100,000 beds available in psychiatric hospitals and units in the United States (Torrey et al., 2010). When recognizing that there were nearly 300 million people in the United States in 2004, that left approximately one bed per 3,000 people (Torrey et al., 2010). Unfortunately, this issue and the burden of housing patients who would otherwise qualify for acute psychiatric services now frequently falls on prisons and jails. Furthermore, as the public continues to view offenders as those deserving punishment, lack of funding initiatives make it difficult for incarcerated individuals with mental health concerns to receive treatment that is proven to be more effective and cost efficient. Giliberti (2015) writes that "housing an inmate with mental illness in jail costs $31,000 annually, while community mental health services cost about $10,000" (para. 7).

Additionally, since the closing and reducing of many mental health facilities throughout the country, the United States has seen a significant increase in mental health patients who are homeless. This in turn has led to an increase in committed crimes and incarceration of folks who are mentally ill and without stable housing (Lamb & Bachrach, 2001). Unfortunately, these inmates, and others who struggle with mild to acute mental health concerns, often experience increased symptoms while incarcerated without the proper care and treatment. Correctional staff frequently respond to inmates' maladaptive behaviors with little regard for their mental health. Fellner et al., (2015) report that staff may leave inmates with "lacerations, second degree burns, deep bruises, and damaged internal organs (para. 2)" without any regard around how this kind of traumatic experience could lead to further decline in a person's mental health. Schappell et al. (2016) state that those with mental health concerns are more likely to be victimized while incarcerated which has the potential to further exacerbate mental health issues.

Current living conditions within jails and prisons are stark, dirty, often highly dangerous. While prisons' living conditions would be challenging for most people, they are especially challenging for those struggling with mental health issues (Ford, 2019). Furthermore, chronic stress is a common experience while incarcerated, and its effects lead to a variety of subsequent problems for prisoners. Massoglia (2008) discusses the overwhelming levels of stress often felt from the dramatic change in "life event" from the transition of being a non-incarcerated person to someone who is serving prison time. The shift into a potentially hopeless and less advantaged social position void of nearly all rights and privileges can create a considerable number of struggles and stress for many people (Haney, 2001). Additionally, incarceration often involves repeated and prolonged exposure to various external stressors. These can come in the form of real or imagined fear of violence, isolation, under exposure to positive stimuli, poor physical living conditions and access to healthy foods (Talik & Skowronski, 2017). Even something as basic as a lack of exposure to the outside results in many inmates having on average a higher vitamin D deficiency (Wildeman & Wang, 2017). This prolonged exposure to chronic stress in which an incarcerated person regularly exists in a heightened state of anxiety and awareness can have lasting negative mental and physical health effects (Haney, 2001).

With most incarcerated individuals identifying as male, there can be a tendency to be hypervigilant amongst the guards. Biases based on gender, race, and class that arise within the correctional setting due to working with men (even more specifically minority men) and their perceived threat to staff can lead to overtly aggressive behavior under the guise of law and order (Oliver, 2003). It is believed that this overt use of force by guards continues to increase in part due to "deficient mental health treatment in corrections facilities, inadequate policies to protect prisoners from unnecessary force, insufficient staff training and supervision, a lack of accountability for the misuse of force, and poor leadership" (Fellner et al., 2015, n.p). With prisons lack of appropriate training for staff and often inadequate mental health treatment, conditions continue to be unsafe and poorly managed for those offenders with mental health struggles.

While some prisons have designated areas for those diagnosed with mental health concerns, other facilities have no guidelines for housing those with such issues (ViceNews, 2015). With the lack of regulations, those with mental health diagnoses are often put into solitary confinement (Hagan et al., 2018). While some argue that this is out of protection from the general population, others see it as a form of punish and an extreme way to handle inmates with mental health struggles. Hagan et al. (2018) describe how inmates with mental illnesses, for instance, require protective custody in higher numbers, commit rule violations more frequently, are more likely to receive solitary confinement as a punishment, and tend to serve longer sentences in segregation than those without such problems.

Additionally, prison facilities are often understaffed and lack resources which in turn has resulted in the overuse of solitary confinement as a solution for mentally ill inmates. Haney (2003) notes that effects of solitary confinement "are analogous to the acute reactions suffered by torture and trauma victims, including post-traumatic stress disorder or PTSD" (p. 132). In 2015, then President Obama requested that solitary confinement and its procedures be investigated due to perceived overuse. The report revealed stark findings, and as such, the United States government decided to put mandates on solitary confinement sentences (United States Department of Justice Archives, 2017). These mandates included capping the allotted time spent in solitary confinement since it was determined that having stricter and shorter mandates for those placed in solitary confinement is imperative in order to reduce unnecessary mental health symptoms that frequently arise (United States Department of Justice Archives, 2017).

Effects of an Incarcerated Parent's Return Home

Upon their release from prison and return home, formerly incarcerated individuals often face a host of issues and struggles. Individuals with prior problems with addiction and mental health problems are more likely to be arrested and serve time in prison or jail than those who do not struggle with these issues (World Health Organization, n.d.). While in prison, it is unlikely that these issues are addressed or resolved, and therefore often offenders are released with these problems only heightened and exacerbated (Wallace et al., 2016). Furthermore, studies have found that many individuals released from prison suffer from what is known as post-incarceration syndrome. Symptoms of this condition are arguably a subcategory of PTSD (Liam & Kunst, 2013). These factors alone make reintegration difficult for many people. Additionally, most programs aimed at helping to assist in a person's reentry are often less than adequate, and usually do not focus on addressing mental health problems (World Health Organization, n.d.). Not surprisingly, studies such as Wallace et al. (2016) reveal that receiving familial support following a person's release from prison positively affects their mental health. There appears to also be a correlative relationship between having a lack of, or negative, familiar support and a decrease in a formerly incarcerated person's mental health during incarceration and after release.

Further exacerbating the issue of reentry is related to the disproportion number of incarcerated individuals who are poor, have low levels of completed education, and who are a racial minority (Alexander, 2012, Morenoff & Harding, 2014). Many people who fall under one, or all, of these categories live in urban areas of low SES, and as a result these communities must overwhelmingly support these folks after they are released from prison (Eason et al., 2017). This strain on the community involves trying to provide structural and emotional support, as well as physical, mental health, and economic resources for large numbers of recently released individuals. However, as Morenoff & Harding (2014) write, "Many former prisoners return to communities to live alongside other former prisoners, which carries implications for competition for scarce resources, criminal opportunities…" (p. 414). Besides these communal concerns, racial and class biases along with a decrease in opportunities due to lack of education and the stigma of having served prison time adds additional stressors for those reintegrating into society (Keene, Smoyer, & Blankenship, 2018). The struggle of learning potentially unfamiliar social norms and needing and wanting to provide monetarily for themselves and their families is coupled often with the inability to find and sustain meaningful work (Western et al., 2015; McKay et al., 2018). Some of these stressors are highly associated with a person's chances of recidivism (Perry, 2016). Along with the stigma of having a criminal record, incarceration often stifles a person's skill development and prevents work experience which makes finding employment often very difficult for a newly released person (McKay et al., 2018). Therefore, specifically men who have a history of serving time are 14% less likely than men who have never been involved in the penal system to contribute to their families (Wildeman & Western, 2010).

The experience of reentry for formerly incarcerated women is at times specific and especially challenging. Women in general are more likely than men to have a history of victimization, which includes long-term physical and sexual abuse that can cause severe mental health problems and drug addiction (Opsal & Foley, 2013). As Massoglia et al. (2014) explain, experiences with physical abuse, mental illness, and drug abuse are potential factors in a woman's incarceration. Therefore, women who are released from prison are more likely to have had victimization histories, a further decrease in mental and physical health while incarcerated, and as a result, many women have particularly difficult reentry experiences. Furthermore, women offenders who are released are less likely than men to receive emotional and financial support from their families, and more likely to end up homeless, which may resort to obtaining income from various illegal activities such as sex work (Freaudenburg et al., 2005; Opsal & Foley, 2013). Reuniting with their children is a main obstacle for women after serving time in prison especially if the children were put into foster care (Peniston, 2014, Shaw et al., 2015). Lastly, since poor women and women of color in the United States are disproportionately represented in arrests and sentenced time, they face even deeper levels of hardships upon release due to societal and systemic biases and stigmas (Opsal & Foley, 2013).

The profound impact and disruption of incarceration and the experienced traumatic stressors from this life event for both parent and child often results in a difficult transition when the parent returns home (Hairston, 2018). An already emotionally and physically strained and unfamiliar parent-child relationship can become even more challenging (McKay et al., 2018). Changes in a child's behavior, both due to normal patterns of maturation and potentially because of parental incarceration, can be difficult for the returning parent to navigate and understand. For the child, it can be triggering if the father especially struggles to reengage and reconnect; it can feel in many ways as if he is still playing out the role of the absent parent that may have existed before and during imprisonment (Peniston, 2014). Feelings of abandonment due to parental incarceration could result in the child continuing to use maladaptive coping skills previously established to manage these difficult feelings along with the new reality of their parent's presence and authority (Black, 2010). For most children, this is a supremely overwhelming and stressful juggling act of emotions. In general, much of the effects of incarceration on the parent and the experienced struggles in returning home are also felt directly and indirectly by the children.

PARENTAL INCARCERATION AND CHILDREN'S MENTAL HEALTH

According to Foster and Hagan (2012), a high percentage of people incarcerated in the United States are parents; in 2010, 52% of offenders at the state level and 63% of offenders at the federal level had minor children (Glaze & Maruschak, 2010). Therefore, with every parent incarcerated there is a child left to cope with this separation. Joyce Arditti (2005) discusses how Kenneth Doka's concept of disenfranchised grief can be aptly applied to children and families of incarcerated individuals. Disenfranchised grief is "defined as occurring when persons experience a loss that is not or cannot be openly acknowledged, publicly mourned, or socially supported" (Arditti, 2005, p. 253). Therefore, often the stigma of incarceration in general, and specifically of a parent serving sentenced time, results in socially invisible and invalidated feelings of loss, shame, and grief for the child (Arditti, 2005; Moore et al., 2016). Experiences of loss that often cannot be acknowledged or understood, as well as society viewing this loss as a safety necessity, have profound effects on children's mental, emotional, and physical well-being (Damron, 2010). It is important to consider, however, that if a parent is abusive and violent within the home, his or her imprisonment is potentially seen and experienced as a kind of relief for the child (Akesson et al., 2012; Foster & Hagan, 2012; Sykes & Pettit, 2014).

Other macro-level factors create what is known as chronic adversity and therefore exacerbates the effects of imprisonment on children (Thompson & Haskins, 2014). A disproportionately high percentage of incarcerated adults in the United States are poor and/or of a racial minority. When looking at Black children specifically, more than half of the parents who did not complete high school were also found to have been incarcerated at some point (Alexander, 2010; Butler, 2013). This is in comparison to White children where 14% of them had an incarcerated parent who did not graduate from high school (Sykes & Pettit, 2014). Recent studies have found that living in impoverished neighborhoods and being a racial minority can cause increased experiences of adversity and are strongly correlated with specific stressors and trauma (Wofford & Ohrt, 2018). In other words, chronic and persistently experienced social adversities related to SES and race in turn can create stressors and trauma specifically related to race and poverty (Odafe et al., 2017; Williams, 2020). For children of color living in poverty, their marginalized statues often place them in an oppressed and disadvantaged social position where there is limited access to a multitude of necessary resources, living conditions can be chaotic and unpredictable, and where there is often an increased threat of violence (Foster & Hagan, 2012; Thompson & Haskins, 2014; Wofford & Ohrt, 2018). Combining these factors with absence of a parent who is incarcerated results in many of these children struggling at nearly every level in their lives and development.

While it is difficult to determine causal effects of parental incarceration on the children "because incarceration is so highly correlated with other markers of disadvantage" (Sykes & Pettit, 2014, p. 128), various studies suggest that having an incarcerated parent has overtly negative effects for children. Instead of incarceration being simply a life event for the child, it appears to be more closely aligned to a traumatic stressor, which is defined as an exposure to a situation, or event, that causes prolonged and pervasive symptoms of distress (Foster & Hagan, 2012; Carlson et al., 2013). Furthermore, Aditti (2012a) argues that parental incarceration qualifies as an adverse childhood experience (ACE), which can cause a series of mental health problems and impairments. Like Arditti, Korgaonkar et al. (2013) discuss how early life trauma (ELT), which is categorized as exposure to traumatic stressors during childhood and adolescence, can severely affect children's emotional brain circuits and subsequently lead to mental health problems in the future. This theory runs counter to the previously held thought that children were only peripherally affected by trauma exposure (Alisic et al., 2011). Instead, current studies on child trauma theory align with Korgaonker et al. by stating that experiencing a traumatic event such as a natural disaster, unexpected death of a loved one, or parental incarceration has the potential to create biological and psychological long-term impairment for the child (Alisic et al., 2011; Thompson & Haskins, 2014). These experiences, in turn, are considered precursors and causes for many high-risk behaviors and mental health illnesses beginning in childhood (Arditti, 2012a). It has been found that experiences of childhood trauma are strong predictors for mental health problems for many juvenile offenders (Hoeve et al., 2015).

For a child with an incarcerated parent, the experienced trauma and stressors are caused by several different factors. These stressors are not only coming from the emotional and physical loss, or feelings of shame, grief, and sadness, but also due to seeing a decline in their imprisoned parent's mental and physical health (Massoglia, et al., 2014; Wildeman & Wang, 2017), long and costly trips for short prison visits (Wildeman & Western, 2010), and the creation of the prison widow (Arditti, 2005). The term prison widow refers to the often-female parent who takes on the role of being head of a single-parent household, and who must carry the financial and emotional burden while the husband or male partner serves time (Arditti, 2005; Comfort et al., 2016; McKay et al., 2018). Unfortunately, such women and their children can experience ostracization from the community and directly, or indirectly, blamed for their partner's crimes (Arditti, 2005; Wildeman & Wang, 2017). These potentially overwhelming demands on the non-incarcerated adult can lead to isolation, depression, and parental neglect, and thus creating further difficulties for the child (McKay et al., 2018; Wildeman & Wang, 2017).

Although many children with an incarcerated parent meet the criteria for one or more DSM-5 trauma diagnosis, the effects of traumatic stress on these children can manifest in a variety behaviors and mental health symptoms. Children may exhibit externalizing behaviors such as hyperactivity or inability to focus at home and school, aggression, and/or a disregard for rules and authority figures (Akesson et al.,

2012). Children can also demonstrate internalizing behaviors which include depression, anxiety, and/or being socially withdrawn or isolated (Wildeman & Western, 2010; Akesson et al., 2012). Such difficult behaviors can cause increased stress in the home between the available parent or guardian(s), which can result in further relational strain (Damron, 2010). Foster and Hagan (2012) found that children with incarcerated mothers were approximately two times more likely to exhibit symptoms of depression (in comparison to paternal incarceration). One study that examined the effects of maternal incarceration on 36 children found that symptoms of PTSD were displayed in 1/3 of the participants (Arditti, 2012b). Despite mothers being incarcerated at much lower rates than fathers, it is evident that the effects maternal incarceration on children can be considerable (Foster & Hagan, 2012; Turney & Wildeman, 2015).

As the rate of female incarceration increases in this country, so does the likelihood of child homelessness, inconsistent housing, and/or placement into foster care for the affected children (Cho, 2010; Wildeman & Western, 2010). An incarcerated mother means potentially removing the only viable parent or guardian, and thus creating a scenario in which many children are more likely to be placed into the foster care system (The Sentencing Project, 2012). Children with incarcerated mothers are five times more likely to be placed in foster care than children with incarcerated fathers (Dewan, 2018). In 2009, the United States Government Accounting Office reported that 14,000 children were receiving non-primary home care and services due to parental incarceration (Shaw, Bright, & Sharpe, 2015). In general, poor children and children of color are disproportionately represented in the foster care system (Knott & Donovan, 2010). Black children are two times more likely than White children to be placed in a foster home (Juvenile Law Center, 2018). Studies indicate that Black and Latino children placed in foster care are less likely to be reunified with their parent once released from prison and have a smaller chance of being adopted out of foster care (Shaw et al., 2015). Furthermore, up to a quarter of children who have spent time in foster care will find themselves serving time in a juvenile justice facility (Juvenile Law Center, 2018).

There is ample evidence to indicate the existence of a parent to child prison pipeline. Studies have repeatedly demonstrated strong associations and correlations between parental incarceration and negative effects on the child's well-being, which include developing various behavior problems, a lack of academic focus, and mental health issues (Sykes & Pettit, 2014; Wildeman & Western, 2010). Some of these behaviors, such as being outwardly aggressive, hyperactive, dismissive of rules and violating social norms, can lead to diagnoses such as attention deficit disorder (ADHD), oppositional defiant disorder (ODD), or conduct disorder (Erford et al., 2015; Wofford & Ohrt, 2018). Children, especially young boys of color, who are diagnosed with one of these disorders are often disciplined more frequently and harshly by parents and teachers than their White peers (McNeil et al., 2002; Balingit, 2018; Low, 2018). Increased instances of discipline and the severity of punishment in school toward these children, along with other potential stressors from having an incarcerated parent, have been shown to lead to higher dropout rates from high school (Lee et al., 2011). Studies have also indicated that dropping out of high school can be a major predictor for juvenile and subsequent adult incarceration (Dillon, 2009; Ewert et al., 2013).

SOLUTIONS AND RECOMMENDATIONS

The goal of this chapter has been to understand how and why mass incarceration in the United States is in many ways an intergenerational crisis especially within the Black and other marginalized communities, and how mental health plays a central role in this issue. Understanding the macro to micro level factors is the first step toward change and solutions. The question is how can mental health professionals use this information to provide effective treatment for children who experience parental incarceration to combat the plethora of negative effects? The authors of this chapter believe that treating and addressing a variety of disorders and presenting symptoms in these children will help in the here-and-now as well as prevent future generations from being incarcerated themselves. Therefore, further questions that need to be asked such as what effective treatments have been used so far, and where does the treatment need to go in order to combat this major mental health issue?

The available research on mental health treatment and incarceration is strongly focused on treating incarcerated individuals, or those who previously served time in prison or jail. There is still a limited amount of research on how to treat children who have experienced parental incarceration despite the growing number of incarcerated individuals who are parents (Sykes & Pettit, 2014). Of the available research, it is suggested that mental health professionals become more aware of the specificities and particular needs pertinent to these children. It is imperative that mental health professionals become well-informed and well-training in affective treatment interventions for ADHD, conduct disorder, oppositional defiant disorder, and depression since these diagnoses have been found to be significantly higher for children with incarcerated parents (Phillips et al., 2002; Herrera, 2018). Additionally, mental health professionals working with children who have experienced parental incarceration must be educated on how societal risk factors (low SES, being a racial minority, limited education) and family risk factors (single-parent home, neglect, inconsistent and fluctuating caregivers) effect children's lives, attachment, and well-being (Phillips & O'Brien, 2012; Buntin & Ayanian, 2017). It would be additionally advantageous to know how these various risk factors affect their parents' mental health and communities.

Arditti (2005) advocates for an ecological approach for families affected by incarceration. Mental health professional implementing an ecological treatment model could better understand reasons and meaning behind feelings and behaviors through a multi-level contextual analysis (Conyne & Cook, 2004). The nuanced effects of incarceration can be seen and understood more thoroughly through this lens, and thus creating more validation, sympathy, and solutions as opposed blame and shame for children and their incarcerated parents. Additionally, Phillips and O'Brien (2012) provided some tangible treatment interventions for children of incarcerated parents following the completion of a pilot study in which they utilized interventions believed to be more sensitive and relevant for children experiencing parental incarceration. Their suggestions include mental health professionals specifically addressing the child's feelings around their parent's incarceration as well as any subsequent changes in their behavior and home life as a result of this traumatic life stressor. Furthermore, the possible lack of materials items including food and consistent shelter (i.e., physical safety) need to be addressed as part of the treatment plan (Phillips & O'Brien, 2012).

Mental health professionals treating children with incarcerated parents must also gain an understanding and seek out various protective factors (resources at school and within the community, meaningful relationships, etc.), along with promoting family counseling when necessary and appropriate (Golden, 2009; Zabern & Bouteyre, 2017). Davis and Shlafer (2017) argue that a strong and healthy parent-child relationship from either or both parents (whether incarcerated or not) is a protective factor for children potentially developing mental health problems. However, the more adversity a child faces, the less salient this protective factor becomes (Davis & Shlafer, 2017). The entire mental health community should be informed and committed to helping children with incarcerated parents since these kids often content with daily chronic adversity, trauma, and on-going stressors as well as an increased chance of incarceration themselves. While it would be impossible for one single group to solve this issue alone, the work of committed mental health professionals can make a lasting impact and potentially begin to end of the cycle of intergenerational incarceration.

FUTURE RESEARCH DIRECTIONS

Mass incarceration in the United States has reached epic proportions that have caused major lasting effects on offenders as well as their children, partners, and communities. This is an intergenerational crisis, especially within the Black community, and in many ways, it is a major mental health issue (Wildeman & Western, 2010). Although an awareness and understanding of these effects have remained either silent or peripherally present throughout society, and at times within the mental health community, mental health researchers and professionals have begun addressing the negative effects and impact of incarceration through direct treatment service and research. However, to further address and dismantle this systemic issue and expand the mental health community as a whole, greater advocacy, leadership, and research are needed on a number of additional levels.

Advocating for the mental health needs of this population means understanding that this is a social justice issue. The rights of poor people, people of color, BIPOC community, and those who struggle with chronic mental health problems are being compromised daily through mass imprisonment and its effects (Alexander, 2010). Therefore, whether it is through direct mental health service, research studies, published articles, or changes at the policy level, there must be "a philosophy of counseling that emphasizes cultural responsiveness and systemic intervention" (Gladding, 2011, p. 495). As Courtland Lee explains, mental health professionals should see themselves as change agents who advocate for those who are disenfranchised, and face challenges that the mental health profession can and should address (Gladding, 2011). Being a strong mental health social justice advocate through a variety of means will not only help the effected population, but it will help strengthen, legitimize, and advance the mental health profession (Decker, Manis, & Paylo, 2015). Further rooting the profession in multiculturalism and diversity through needed evidence-based research studies, peer reviewed articles, and teaching on the mental health needs of this population will leave a lasting professional and social impact.

Overall, there remain gaps in the literature on understanding how to best treat children who suffer from mental illnesses partially due to parental incarceration. There is, therefore, a critical need to further determine the impact of parental incarceration on children and how best to treat these effects in a mental health setting through meaningful research and data. Research is important and can provide some much-needed answers. Research, however, has been cited as being at times oppressively structured toward upholding the dominant master narrative (Dillard, 2020). Therefore, focused academic research around this topic is minimally important and impactful if it does not ultimately amount to direct services and subsequent change for those facing the identified challenges directly. As such, research in the field of mental health and parental incarceration should serve as an action-oriented platform that helps empower and give voice to those previously silenced. The potentiality for research to create meaningful action and real change is incredibly exciting especially as it pertains to incarceration where marginalized Americans have been disproportionately affected and silenced. Engaging in further research on incarceration, children, mental health has the potential to slowly dismantle a system of structural racism and classism within specific communities that holds a legacy of historical and inherited trauma (Alexander, 2010; Kelly et al., 2020). Therefore, the implications for future research are immense; furthering the research around this topic is not only a rallying cry for liberation, but also a genuine form of advocacy in action.

CONCLUSION

As trained mental health professionals, the authors of this chapter firmly believe in the importance and necessity of understanding the multiplicity of how and why things develop to find solutions to the identified issue(s). This is certainly true when discussing mass incarceration in the United States. Garland (1990) writes, "We need to realize that in the penal realm-as in all social experience-specific events or developments usually have a plurality of causes which interact to shape their final form" (p. 280). In the case of incarceration and mental health, this task may at times seem daunting and difficult due to its layers of complexities. However, it is precisely because there are a tremendous amount of people who suffer mentally and emotionally at the hands of mass incarceration in the United States that doing nothing is not an option. In fact, the authors would argue that it is in the unraveling through understanding of these various layers and causes that the act of dismantling a racially and economically discriminatory system starts, and mental health healing begins for the effected population.

SUMMARY

This chapter discusses the history of mass incarceration in the United States and its negative effects on prisoners to more fully elucidate how children and their mental health are additionally affected by this issue. The authors utilize the available literature to explain how and why children are affected by an incarcerated parent and advocating and presenting solutions to this intergenerational crisis. This chapter is particularly committed to outlining how poor communities of color have been generationally devastated by mass incarceration. In seeing the linkages between parental incarceration and children's mental health decline, the authors believe the mental health community will lead the charge in addressing this problem for marginalized communities through research, advocacy, and direct service.

CASE STUDY

Ryan C. was a Black male teenager who lived in Cincinnati, OH. He attended both special education and regular education classes in high school. He had an IEP, an assigned support staff member available at school, a therapist, and a school counselor. He was diagnosed with ADHD and several learning disabilities and took a number of medications daily. Ryan lived with his mother and stepfather both of whom were emotionally and physically abusive toward him. Child protective services had been called many times with little to no changes every time. Ryan lived below the poverty line.

Ryan's father was incarcerated for several felonies. His father was expected to serve at least a decade in prison, and Ryan had limited contact with him. Due to issues related to money, Ryan was never able to visit his father in prison. As Ryan transitioned from a pre-teen to a teenager, he spoke less of his father and became more outwardly aggressive in school and home. Ryan would have what he described as "episodes" where he would scream and yell to the point of the police being called to his house. Ryan could be polite, kind, and gentle, but once he was triggered, his anger would often overtake his mood and behaviors. Despite these adversities, and potentially undiagnosed mental health disorders, Ryan's determination and his team of loving practitioners resulted in him graduating from high school on-time.

At the ceremony, Ryan saw his mother cry, which was reportedly the only time he had ever seen her cry in front of him.

ACKNOWLEDGMENT

This research was supported by the University of Cincinnati and the 2021 Dean's Dissertation Completion Fellowship.

REFERENCES

Akesson, B., Smyth, J., Mandell, D., Doan, T., Donina, K., & Hoven, C. (2012). Parental involvement with the criminal justice system and the effects on their children: A collaborative model for researching vulnerable families. *Social Work in Public Health*, *27*(1-2), 148–164. doi:10.1080/19371918.2012.629898 PMID:22239383

Alexander, M. (2010). *The New Jim Crow: Mass Incarceration in the Age of Colorblindness*. New Press.

Alisic, E., Jongman, M., van Wesel, F., & Kleber, R. (2011). Building child trauma theory from longitudinal studies: A meta-analysis. *Clinical Psychology Review*, *31*(5), 736–747. doi:10.1016/j.cpr.2011.03.001 PMID:21501581

Arditti, J. A. (2005). Families and incarceration: An ecological approach. *Families in Society*, *86*(2), 251–260. doi:10.1606/1044-3894.2460

Arditti, J. A. (2012a). Child trauma within the context of parental incarceration: A family process perspective. *Journal of Family Theory & Review*, *4*(3), 181–219. doi:10.1111/j.1756-2589.2012.00128.x

Arditti, J. A. (2012b). *Parental Incarceration and the Family: Psychological and Social Effects of Imprisonment on Children, Parents, and Caregivers*. New York University Press.

Balingit, M. (2018). Racial disparities in school discipline are growing, federal data show. *The Washington Post*. https://www.washingtonpost.com/local/education/racial-disparities-in-school-discipline-are-growing-federal-data-shows/2018/04/24/67b5d2b8-47e4-11e8-827e-190efaf1f1ee_story.html?noredirect=on&utm_term=.303a447ba026

Black, C. (2010). Understanding the pain of abandonment. *Psychology Today*. https://www.psychologytoday.com/us/blog/the-many-faces-addiction/201006/understanding-the-pain-abandonment

Buntin, M., & Ayanian, J. (2017). Social risk factors and equity in medicare payment. *The New England Journal of Medicine*, *376*(6), 507–510. doi:10.1056/NEJMp1700081 PMID:28177864

Butler, P. (2013). Poor people lose: Gideon and the critique of rights. *The Yale Law Journal*, *122*(8), 2176–2204.

Carlson, E., Smith, S., & Dalenberg, C. (2013). Can sudden, severe emotional loss be a traumatic stressor? *Journal of Trauma & Dissociation*, *14*(5), 519–528. doi:10.1080/15299732.2013.773475 PMID:24060034

Cho, R. (2010). Maternal incarceration and children's adolescent outcomes: Timing and Dosage. *The Social Service Review*, *84*(2), 257–282. doi:10.1086/653456

Comfort, M., McKay, T., Landwehr, J., Kennedy, E., Lindquist, C., & Bir, A. (2016). The cost of incarceration for families of prisoners. *International Review of the Red Cross*, *98*(903), 783–798. doi:10.1017/S1816383117000704

Conyne, C., & Cook, E. (Eds.). (2004). *Ecological counseling: An innovative approach to conceptualizing person-environment interaction*. American Counseling Association.

Cox, R. M., Skirius, M. S., Lenz, A. S., James, R. K., & Packard, C. (2017). The effects of repeated exposure to the ARRAY program with offenders with mental illness. *Journal of Addictions & Offender Counseling, 38*(2), 98-114. doi:10.1002/jaoc.12033

Damron, N. (2010). *Poverty fact sheet: Life beyond bars: Children with an incarcerated parent.* Institute for Research on Poverty. https://www.irp.wisc.edu/publications/factsheets/pdfs/Factsheet7-Incarceration.pdf

Davis, A. J. (2017). The prosecution of black men. In A. Davis (Ed.), Policing the black man: Arrest, prosecution, and imprisonment (pp. 178-208). First Vintage.

Davis, L., & Shlafer, R. (2016). Mental health of adolescents with currently and formerly incarcerated parents. *Journal of Adolescence*, *54*(1), 120–134. doi:10.1016/j.adolescence.2016.10.006 PMID:28011442

Decker, K., Manis, A., & Paylo, M. (2015). Infusing social justice advocacy into counselor education: Strategies and recommendations. *The Journal of Counselor Preparation and Supervisor*, *8*(3). Advance online publication. doi:10.7729/83.1092

Dewan, S. (2018). Family separation: It's a problem for U.S. citizens, too. *The New York Times.* https://www.nytimes.com/2018/06/22/us/family-separation-americans-prison-jail.html

Dillard, N. (2020). Designing research to dismantle oppression. Utilizing critical narrative analysis and critical participatory action research in research on mothering and work and beyond. *Journal of International Women's Studies*, *21*(7), 1–9.

Dillon, S. (2009). Study finds high rate of imprisonment among dropouts. *The New York Times.* https://www.nytimes.com/2009/10/09/education/09dropout.html

Eason, J., Zucker, D., & Wildeman, C. (2017). Mass imprisonment across the rural-urban interface. *The Annals of the American Academy of Political and Social Science*, *671*(1), 202–216. doi:10.1177/0002716217705357

Erford, B., Bardhoshi, G., Ross, M., Gunther, C., & Duncan, K. (2015). Meta-analysis of counseling outcomes for youth with conduct disorder. *Journal of Counseling and Development*, *95*(1), 35–44. doi:10.1002/jcad.12115

Ewert, S., Sykes, B., & Pettit, B. (2013). The degree of disadvantage: Incarceration and inequality in education. *The Annals of the American Academy of Political and Social Science*, *651*(1), 24–43. doi:10.1177/0002716213503100

Federal Bureau of Prisons. (2021). *Inmate race* [chart]. https://www.bop.gov/about/statistics/statistics_inmate_race.jsp

Fellner, J., Parker, A., & Rau Barriga, S. (2015). *Callous and cruel: Use of force against inmates with mental disabilities in U.S. jails and prisons.* https://www.hrw.org/report/2015/05/12/callous-and-cruel/use-force-against-inmates-mental-disabilities-us-jails-and#page

Ford, M. (5, April 2019). The everyday brutality of American's prison. *The New Republic.* https://newrepublic.com/article/153473/everyday-brutality-americas-prisons

Foster, H., & Hagan, J. (2013). Maternal and paternal imprisonment in the stress process. *Social Science Research, 42*(3), 650–669. doi:10.1016/j.ssresearch.2013.01.008 PMID:23521986

Freudenberg, N., Daniels, J., Crum, M., Perkins, T., & Richie, B. (2005). Coming home from jail: The social and health consequences of community reentry for women, male adolescents, and their families and communities. *American Journal of Public Health, 95*(10), 11725–11736. doi:10.2105/AJPH.2004.056325 PMID:16186451

Garland, D. (1990). *Punishment and modern society: A study in social theory.* Oxford University Press. doi:10.7208/chicago/9780226922508.001.0001

Garland, D. (2001). The meaning of mass imprisonment. In D. Garland (Ed.), *Mass imprisonment: Social cause and consequences* (pp. 1–2). Sage. doi:10.4135/9781446221228.n1

Giliberti, M. (2015). *It's outrageous: Jails and prisons are no place to treat mental illness; just ask Paton Blough.* https://stepuptogether.org/updates/its-outrageous-jails-and-prisons-are-no-

Gladding, S. T. (2011). Courtland Lee: A global advocate for counseling. *Journal of Counseling and Development, 89*, 493–499.

Glaze, L., & Maruschak, L. (2010). *Bureau of justice statistics special report: Parents in prison and their minor children.* U.S. Department of Justice. https://bjs.ojp.gov/content/pub/pdf/pptmc.pdf

Golden, L. (2009). Counseling children: Working with families. *Counseling and Human Development, 41*(6), 1–10.

Gotsch, K. (2018, April 24). Families of mass incarceration. *The Sentencing Project.* https://www.sentencingproject.org/publications/6148/

Greene, J. (2002). *Getting Tough on Crime: The History and Political Context of Sentencing Reform Developments Leading to the Passage of the 1994 Crime Act.* https://www.justicestrategies.org/sites/default/files/Judy/GettingToughOnCrime.pdf

Hagan, B. O., Wang, E. A., Aminawung, J. A., Albizu-Garcia, C. E., Zaller, N., Nyamu, S., Shavit, S., Deluca, J., Fox, A. D., & Transitions Clinic Network. (2018). History of solitary confinement is associated with post-traumatic stress disorder symptoms among individuals recently released from prison. *Journal of Urban Health, 95*(2), 141-148. doi:10.1007/s11524-017-0138-1

Hairston, C. (2018). Family relationships during incarceration and when fathers return home. *Journal of Offender Rehabilitation, 57*(2), 67–68.

Haney, C. (2001). *The psychological impact of incarceration: Implications for post-prison adjustment.* https://aspe.hhs.gov/basic-report/psychological-impact-incarceration-implications-post-prison-adjustment

Haney, C. (2003). Mental health issues in long-term solitary and "Supermax" confinement. *Crime and Delinquency, 49*(1), 124–156. https://doi.org/10.1177/0011128702239239

Herrera, M. (2017). *A child's mental health and antisocial behavior: A close look at effects of parent incarceration based on timing.* https://pqdtopen.proquest.com/doc/1970070524.html?FMT=AI

Hoeve, M., Colins, O., Mulder, E., Loeber, R., Stams, G., & Vermeiren, R. (2015). Trauma and mental health problems in adolescent males. *Criminal Justice and Behavior, 42*(7), 685–702.

Inman, S. (2020). *Racial disparities in criminal justice: How lawyers can help.* American Bar Association. https://www.americanbar.org/groups/young_lawyers/publications/after-the-bar/public- service/racial-disparities-criminal-justice-how-lawyers-can-help/

Jaggi, L., Mezuk, B., Watkins, D., & Jackson, J. (2016). The relationship between trauma, arrest, and incarceration history among black Americans: Findings from the national survey of American life. *Society and Mental Health, 6*(3), 187–206.

Juvenile Law Center. (2018). *What is the foster care-to-prison pipeline?* https://jlc.org/news/what-foster-care-prison-pipeline

Kaeble, D., & Cowhig, M. (2018). *Correctional populations in the United States, 2016.* U.S. Department of Justice. https://www.bjs.gov/content/pub/pdf/cpus16.pdf

Keene, D., Smoyer, A., & Blankenship, K. (2018). Stigma, housing and identity after prison. *The Sociological Review, 66*(4), 799–815. doi:10.1177/0038026118777447

Kelly, S., Jeremie-Brink, G., Chambers, A., & Smith-Bynum, M. (2020). The Black Lives Matter movement: A call to action for couple and family therapists. *Family Process, 59*(4), 1374–1388.

Kizielewicz, C. (2018). Black men have higher rates of recidivism despite lower risk factors. *Eurek Alert!* https://www.eurekalert.org/pub_releases/2018-10/cajr-bmh101818.php

Knott, T., & Donovan, K. (2010). Disproportionate representation of African-American children in foster care: Secondary analysis of the National Child Abuse and Neglect Data System, 2005. *Children and Youth Services Review, 32*(5), 679–684. doi.org/10.1016/j.childyouth.2010.01.003

Kopt, D. (2018). New data clearly illustrate the poverty-to-prison pipeline. *Quartz.* https://qz.com/1233966/new-data-clearly-illustrate-the-poverty-to-prison-pipeline/

Korgaonkar, M., Antees, C., Williams, L., Gatt, J., Bryant, R., Cohen, R., Paul, R., O'Hara, R., & Grieve, S. (2013). Early exposure to traumatic stressors impairs emotional brain circuitry. *PLOS ONE, 8*(9), 1-8. doi:.org/ doi:10.1371/journal.pone.0075524

Lamb, H. R., & Bachrach, L. L. (2001). Some perspectives on deinstitutionalization. *Psychiatric Services, 52*(8), 1039–1045. doi:10.1176/appi.ps.52.8.1039

Lee, T., Cornell, D., Gregory, A., & Fan, X. (2011). High suspension schools and dropout rates for black and white students. *Education & Treatment of Children*, *34*(2), 167–192. doi:10.1353/etc.2011.0014

Levitt, S. (2004). Understanding why crime fell in the 1990s: Four factors that explain the decline and six that do not. *The Journal of Economic Perspectives*, *18*(1), 163–190.

Liam, M., & Kunst, M. (2013). Is there a recognizable post-incarceration syndrome among released "lifers"? *International Journal of Law and Psychiatry*, *36*(3-4), 333–337.

Low, K. (16, February 2018). Understanding punishment and oppositional behavior. *Verywellmind.* https://www.verywellmind.com/punishment-and-oppositional-behavior-20730

Massoglia, M. (2008). Incarceration, health, and racial disparities in health. *Law & Society Review*, *42*(2), 275–306. doi:10.1111/j.1540-5893.2008.00342.x

Massoglia, M., Pare, P., Schnittker, J., & Gagnon, A. (2014). The relationship between incarceration and premature adult mortality: Gender specific evidence. *Social Science Research*, *46*, 142–154. doi:10.1016/j.ssresearch.2014.03.002

Mauer, M. (2001). The meaning of mass imprisonment. In D. Garland (Ed.), *Mass imprisonment: Social cause and consequences* (pp. 1–2). Sage.

McKay, T., Comfort, M., Grove, L., Bir, A., & Lindquist, C. (2018). Whose punishment, whose crime? Understanding parenting and partnership in a time of mass incarceration. *Journal of Offender Rehabilitation*, *57*(2), 69–82. doi:10.1080/10509674.2017.1294640

McKay, T., Landwehr, J., Lindquist, C., Feinberg, R., Comfort, M., Cohen, J., & Bir, A. (2018). Intimate partner violence in couples navigating incarceration and reentry. *Journal of Offender Rehabilitation*, *57*(5), 273–293.

McNeil, C., Capage, L., & Bennett, G. (2002). Cultural issues in the treatment of young African American children diagnosed with disruptive behavior disorders. *Journal of Pediatric Psychology*, *27*(4), 339–350. doi.org/10.1093/jpepsy/27.4.339

Moore, K., Stuewig, J., & Tangney, J. (2014). The effects of stigma on criminal offenders' functioning: A longitudinal mediational model. *Defiant Behavior*, *37*(2), 196-218. doi:10.1080/01639625.2014.1004035

Morenoff, J., & Harding, D. (2014). Incarceration, prisoner reentry, and communities. *Annual Review of Sociology*, *40*, 411–429. doi:10.1146/annurev-soc-071811-145511

NAACP. (n.d.). *Criminal justice fact sheet.* https://www.naacp.org/criminal-justice-fact-sheet/

Odafe, M., Salami, T., & Walker, R. (2017). Race-related stress and hopelessness in the community-based African American adults: Moderating role of social support. *Cultural Diversity & Ethnic Minority Psychology*, *23*(4), 561–569. doi.org/10.1037/cdp0000167

Oliver, M. B. (2003). African American men as "criminal and dangerous": Implications of media portrayals of crime on the "criminalization" of African American men. *Journal of African American Studies*, *7*(2), 3–18.

Opsal, T., & Foley, A. (2013). Making it on the outside: Understanding barriers to women's post-incarceration reintegration. *Sociology Compass*, *7*(4), 265–277. doi:10.1111oc4.12026

Peniston, D. (2014). *Incarceration and Father-Absence: An Exploration of Fatherhood after Prison.* https://search.proquest.com/openview/d412d35c2e69a374307aafc59825e88f/1.pdf?pq-origsite=gscholar&cbl=18750&diss=y

Perry, S. (2016). *Coming Home: Challenges Related to Reentry and Recidivism for Previously Incarcerated New Mother.* Retrieved from https://scholarworks.wm.edu/cgi/viewcontent.cgi?article=1960&context=honorstheses

Pettit, B. (2012). *Invisible men: Mass incarceration and the myth of black progress*. Russell Sage Foundation.

Pettit, B., & Western, B. (2004). Mass imprisonment and the life course: Race and class inequality in U.S. incarceration. *American Sociological Review*, *69*(2), 151–169. doi:10.1177/000312240406900201

Phillips, S., Burns, B., Wagner, R., Kramer, T., & Robbins, J. (2002). Parental incarceration among adolescents receiving mental health services. *Journal of Child and Family Studies*, *11*(4), 385–399. doi-org.proxy.libraries.uc.edu/10.1023/A:1020975106679

Phillips, S., & O'Brien, P. (2012). Learning from the ground up: Responding to children affected by parental incarceration. *Social Work in Public Health*, *27*, 29–44. doi:10.1080/19371918.2012.629914

Piper, A., & Berle, D. (2019). The association between trauma experienced during incarceration and PTSD outcomes: A systematic review and meta-analysis. *Journal of Forensic Psychiatry & Psychology*, *30*(5), 854–875.

Prins, S. J. (2011). Does transinstitutionalization explain the overrepresentation of people with serious mental illnesses in the criminal justice system? *Community Mental Health Journal*, *47*, 716–722. https://doi.org/10.1007/s10597-011-9420-y

Reisig, M., Bales, W., Hay, C., & Wang, X. (2007). The effect of racial inequality on black male recidivism. *Justice Quarterly*, *24*(3), 408–434.

Sawyer, W., & Wagner, P. (2020). *Mass incarceration: The whole pie 2020.* Prison Policy Initiative. https://www.prisonpolicy.org/reports/pie2020.html

Schappell, A., Docherty, M., & Boxer, P. (2016). Violence and victimization during incarceration: Relations to psychosocial adjustment during reentry to the community. *Violence and Victims*, *31*(2), 361-378. http://dx.doi.org.uc.idm.oclc.org/10.1891/0886-6708.VV-D-13-00188

Sexton, T. (2016). Incarceration as a family affair: Thinking beyond the individual. *Couples and Family Psychology: Research and Practice*, *5*(2), 61–64.

Shaw, T., Bright, C., & Sharpe, T. (2015). Child welfare outcomes for youth in care as a result of parental death or incarceration. *Child Abuse and Neglect*, *42*, 112-120. doi:org/ doi:10.1016/j.chiabu.2015.01.002

Smiley, C. J., & Fakunle, D. (2016). From "brute" to "thug:" The demonization and criminalization of unarmed Black male victims in America. *Journal of Human Behavior in the Social Environment*, *26*(3-4), 350–366.

Sutton, J. R. (2013). Symbol and substance: Effects of California's three strikes law on felony sentencing. *Law & Society Review*, *47*(1), 37–72.

Sykes, B. L., & Pettit, B. (2014). Mass incarceration, family complexity, and the reproduction of childhood disadvantage. *The Annals of the American Academy of Political and Social Science*, *654*(1), 127–149. doi:10.1177/0002716214526345

Talik, E., & Skowronski, B. (2017). The sense of quality of life and religious strategies of coping with stress in prison inmates. *Journal of Religion and Health*, *57*(3), 915–937. doi:10.100710943-017-0455-4

The Sentencing Project. (n.d.). *Criminal justice facts.* https://www.sentencingproject.org/criminal-justice-facts/

The Sentencing Project. (2012). *Parents in prison.* https://www.sentencingproject.org/wp-content/uploads/2016/01/Parents-in-Prison.pdf

Thompson, R., & Haskins, R. (2014). Early stress gets under the skin: Promising initiatives to help children facing chronic adversity. *The Future of Children*, *24*(1), 1–8.

Torrey, F. E., Kennard, A. D., Eslinger, D., Lamb, R., & Pavle, J. (2010). *More mentally ill persons are in jails and prisons than hospitals: A survey of the states.* https://knox.oh.networkofcare.org/library/final_jails_v_hospitals_study.pdf

Travis, J., & Western, B. (2017). Poverty, violence, and black incarceration. In A. Davis (Ed.), Policing the black man: Arrest, prosecution, and imprisonment (pp. 294-321). First Vintage.

Turney, K., & Goodsell, R. (2018). Parental incarceration and children's wellbeing. *The Future of Children*, *28*(1), 147–164.

Turney, K., & Wildeman, C. (2015). Detrimental for some? Heterogeneous effects of maternal incarceration on child wellbeing. *Criminology & Public Policy*, *14*(1), 125–156. doi-org.proxy.libraries.uc.edu/10.1111/1745-9133.12109

United States Census Bureau. (2019). *Quick facts: United States* [Census Data]. https://www.census.gov/quickfacts/fact/table/US/IPE120219

United States Department of Justice Archives. (2017). *Report and recommendations concerning the use of restrictive housing.* https://www.justice.gov/archives/dag/report-and-recommendations-concerning-use-restrictive-housing

ViceNews. (2015). *Institutionalized: Mental health behind bars* [Video]. YouTube. www.youtube.com/watch?v=-fQ50a-m92Y

Wagner, P., & Sawyer, W. (2018). *Mass incarceration: The whole pie 2018.* Prison Policy Initiative. https://www.prisonpolicy.org/factsheets/pie2018_allimages.pdf

Wakefield, S., Lee, H., & Wildeman, C. (2016). Tough on crime, tough on families? Criminal justice and family life in American. *The Annals of the American Academy of Political and Social Science*, *665*(1), 8–21. doi.org/10.1177/0002716216637048

Wallace, D., Fahmy, C., Cotton, L., Jimmons, C., McKay, R., Stoffer, S., & Syed, S. (2016). Examining the role of familial support during prison and after release on post-incarceration mental health. *International Journal of Offender and Comparative Criminology*, *60*(1), 3–20. doi:10.1177/0306624X14548023

Walmsley, R. (2011). *World prison population list* (9th ed.). International Centre for Prison Studies. https://www.prisonstudies.org/sites/default/files/resources/downloads/wppl_9.pdf

Western, B., Braga, A., Davis, J., & Sirois, C. (2015). Stress and hardship after prison. *American Journal of Sociology*, *120*(5), 1512–1547. doi:10.1086/681301

Western, B., & Pettit, B. (2010). Incarceration and social inequality. *Daedalus*, *139*(3), 8–19. doi.org/10.1162/DAED_a_00019

Western, B., & Wildeman, C. (2009). The black family and mass incarceration. *Annals*, *621*, 221–242.

Wheelock, D., & Hartmann, D. (2007). Midnight basketball and the 1994 crime bill debates: The operation of a racial code. *The Sociological Quarterly*, *48*(2), 315–342. doi:10.1111/j.1533-8525.2007.00080.x

Whitman, J. (2003). Harsh Justice: Criminal Punishment and the Widening Divide Between America and Europe. Oxford.

Wildeman, C., & Wang, E. (2017). Mass incarceration, public health, and widening inequality in the USA. *Lancet*, *389*, 1464–1474. doi:10.1016/S0140-6736(17)30259-3

Wildeman, C., & Western, B. (2010). Incarceration in fragile families. *The Future of Children*, *20*(2), 157–177. doi:10.1353/foc.2010.0006

Williams, M. (2020). *Racial trauma: Assessment and treatment techniques for trauma rooted in racism* [Training, PowerPoint slides]. Pesi.

Wofford, J., & Ohrt, J. (2018). An integrated approach to counseling children diagnosed with ADHD, ODD, and chronic stressors. *The Family Journal (Alexandria, Va.)*, *26*(1), 105–109. doi:10.1177/1066480718756594

Wolff, N., Shi, J., & Siegel, J. (2009). Patterns of victimization among male and female inmates: Evidence of an enduring legacy. *Violence and Victims*, *24*(4), 469–484.

World Health Organization. (n.d.). *Mental health and prisons*. https://www.who.int/mental_health/policy/mh_in_prison.pdf

Zabern, A., & Bouteyre, E. (2017). Leading protective factors for children living out of home: A literature review. *Child & Family Social Work*, *23*(2), 324–335. doi-org.proxy.libraries.uc.edu/10.111/cfs.12398

KEY TERMS AND DEFINITIONS

ACEs: An acronym that stands for Adverse Childhood Experiences. This rating system is used to determine that amount of experienced hardship and trauma for children and adolescents.

BIPOC: An acronym that stands for Black, Indigenous, and People of Color. This phrase is used to acknowledge multiple minority populations who have experienced injustices due to the color of their skin.

Incarceration: A legal removal from one's environment and confined into jail or prison.

Mental Health: The state of physiological, emotional, and social wellbeing of an individual.

Penal: Engaging in an act that is punishable by law.

Post-Incarceration Syndrome: A non-DSM disorder in which symptoms are akin to PTSD and develop as a result of spending a considerable amount of time incarcerated and in solitary confinement.

PTSD: A DSM diagnosis that stands for Post-Traumatic Stress Disorder. This disorder is often associated with those who encounter war and extreme violence.

Trauma: A psychological term used to describe an event that causes emotional harm and potentially physical distress.

Chapter 6
Supporting the Parent–Child Bond

R. Erin W. Berzins
Antioch University, Seattle, USA

ABSTRACT

This chapter examines the parent-child bond when a parent is incarcerated in state or federal prison. The purpose is to prepare helping professionals to support children who wish to maintain relationships with their parents during prison sentences. The nature of the parent-child relationship is discussed, and practical strategies are proposed for helping parents to stay a part of their children's lives. Topics include visitation, video visits, phone calls, letter writing, emails, and parental participation in education. Logistics of these activities are discussed, and child-friendly activities are suggested to help prepare children for interacting with their parent within the context of the correctional system. Contraindications for such contact are also noted. The chapter concludes with recommendations for professional advocacy.

INTRODUCTION

There are approximately 1.5 million minor children in the United States who have at least one parent incarcerated in a state or federal prison (Maruschak & Bronson, 2016). Some estimates, which include jail sentences, bring the number of children with a parent behind bars at any given time up to over two and a half million (Pew Charitable Trusts, 2010).

The personal challenges facing children of incarcerated parents can be extensive. Many children with incarcerated parents were in vulnerable situations prior to their parent's arrest, such as living in low socioeconomic conditions, living with a parent struggling with a substance abuse disorder, or living without both parents in the home. Some of these children went on to witness their parent's arrest, and many have felt traumatized by losing their parent to the prison system (Arditti, 2012; Turney & Goodsell, 2018). Higher rates of mental health conditions, such as depression, and physical health conditions, such as asthma, have also been observed in this population (Turney, 2014).

The impact of incarceration on the parent-child bond is also significant. The majority of children with an incarcerated parent live more than 100 miles from their parent's prison (Mumola, 2000), making it

DOI: 10.4018/978-1-7998-9209-0.ch006

difficult to maintain contact (Pleggenkuhle et al., 2018). The visitation process can be emotionally and logistically challenging even when the distance can be managed (Correa et al., 2021; Schubert et al., 2016), and custodial parents may have mixed feelings about facilitating the connection (Poehlmann et al., 2010; Saunders, 2016). Many children are left wondering what the relationship between themselves and their incarcerated parent will be.

Supporting healthy bonds while a parent is incarcerated can potentially benefit both parent and child. Incarcerated parents who are active in their children's lives tend to remain more focused on rehabilitation and their parenting role while incarcerated, and are less likely to reoffend when released (Carlson, 1998; Jbara, 2012). Meanwhile, children who wish to have a relationship with the incarcerated parent benefit from their guidance and love (Poehlmann et al., 2010). All adults in a child's life, including counselors, social workers, educators, and family members, can help to support this bond and the needs of children with incarcerated parents.

This chapter will discuss the benefits of supporting the parent-child bond, when appropriate, as well as provide practical strategies for keeping parents and children in contact during incarceration. Contraindications for this connection will also be discussed, such as abusive parent-child relationships. By the end of the chapter, readers will be familiar with research on parent-child relationships during incarceration, understand the benefits and limitations of supporting ongoing connection during incarceration, learn practical strategies for supporting a child who wishes to communicate with their incarcerated parent, and be aware of methods for accessing resources. Implications for allyship and advocacy will also be discussed.

HONORING CHILDREN OF THE INCARCERATED

Incarceration can be a life-changing event for an entire family. A marriage or partnership may be disrupted, daily interactions between parent and child will almost certainly end, and financial support from one parent will likely become negligible or nonexistent. One need not strain their imagination to envision the stress and worry that could be placed upon a child. In the early 2000s, a group of advocates, government staff, and members of the helping professions formed the San Francisco Children of Incarcerated Parents Partnership. This group released a bill of rights to advocate for children and families (listed in Table 1). These rights can serve as an overview of possible needs experienced by children with incarcerated parents.

The bill of rights is the result of extensive research and experience from its authors and speaks to the ways in which children *should* be respected. Unfortunately, the bill of rights is aspirational only in many cases. For example, access to physical contact, a voice in the process, and emotional support may be found lacking for many children. Readers are encouraged to consider the ways in which they can support these rights within their own work and community settings.

Table 1. Children of incarcerated parents: A bill of rights

1	I have the right to be kept safe and informed at the time of my parent's arrest.
2	I have the right to be heard when decisions are made about me.
3	I have the right to be considered when decisions are made about my parent.
4	I have the right to be well cared for in my parent's absence.
5	I have the right to speak with, see, and touch my parent.
6	I have the right to support as I face my parent's incarceration.
7	I have the right not to be judged, blamed, or labeled because my parent is incarcerated.
8	I have the right to a lifelong relationship with my parent.

Source: San Francisco Children of Incarcerated Parents Partnership (2005)

With a foundational assumption that the rights of these children matter, helping professionals should get to know each family and assess the support needs and desires of the children individually. It can be easy to lose sight of a child in the myriad of statistics available. A full examination of the effects of incarceration on children is beyond the scope of this chapter, but for example, as noted previously, increased mental health challenges have been found for children of incarcerated parents. It is notable, however, that results in the literature have been mixed (Davis & Shlafer, 2016), and correlation versus causation is difficult to firmly establish, given the number of confounding variables and the inability to randomize samples. Regardless of research statistics, it is important to recognize that each child, within each family, is a unique individual who will have their own response to the incarceration. Allyship is enhanced, and stigmatization reduced, when professionals avoid the temptation to view all children of incarcerated parents as the same (Phillips & Gates, 2011). This chapter contains information from various studies with aggregated data, and although generalizations are intended to highlight common themes, no child will perfectly match any written work. Additionally, it is important to remember that policies, resources, and programs also vary widely across the nation. Examples will be used to discuss important concepts, but readers are encouraged to research the application to their own state. Honoring the rights of children with incarcerated parents begins with an understanding of the policies and practices within one's own jurisdiction.

THE PARENT-CHILD RELATIONSHIP

When considering the parent-child bond during incarceration, it is important to contextualize the relationship in its own history. Children who lived with their parent prior to the start of their prison sentence may react differently than children who saw their parent only occasionally. The disruption of a historically warm and loving connection is likely more stressful than disruption to a distant or conflictual relationship. Unfortunately, if a child's relationship with their parent was strained prior to incarceration, it is prone to remaining so during the incarceration, particularly if the sentence is long (Saunders, 2016). Efforts to support, or build, a strong bond should begin with a realistic assessment of the current relationship, as well as the goals of the child for this connection.

Following arrest, children may have complex and mixed emotions about their parent. Some may work to cognitively separate the concept of their parent from the crime committed. A child might, for example, avoid talking about or thinking about their parent's crime, or they might discuss topics like the arrest in a detached manner. Other children may feel the desire to distance from their parent entirely (Luther, 2016). Even children who desire relationships with their incarcerated parents may experience feelings like anger, shame, or embarrassment about their situation or toward their parent. Children may also worry about their parent's well-being in what they imagine are scary surroundings (Saunders, 2016). Supportive adults can listen nonjudgmentally to all of the feelings children want to express and validate that these feelings are normal and acceptable. Helping professionals who facilitate visitation or communicate with parents may also wish to normalize for parents that their children are potentially processing conflicting emotions and prepare parents for moments of anger or avoidance.

A child's developmental stage will likely impact the child's experience of the incarceration, particularly as it pertains to understanding. Young children, engaging in developmentally appropriate egocentric thinking, may blame themselves for the incarceration, believing, for example, that if they had only been better behaved, their parent would still be home. Older children and teenagers may conceptualize that the parent's own decision-making is to blame, likely increasing feelings of anger.

Incarcerated parents likely also experience mixed emotions about the relationships with their children. Although contact with children can help a parent to feel loved, comforted, and excited for the future, many parents also feel guilty or ashamed, and they may experience stress about their parenting responsibilities and sadness about the distance between themselves and their children (Turanovic & Tasca, 2019). Contact with family, despite some hard emotions, seems to help many incarcerated individuals to remain more recovery-focused and, in many cases, reduces recidivism (Carlson, 1998; Jbara, 2012; La Vigne et al., 2005), even when relationships are maintained virtually (Duwe & McNeeley, 2021).

No matter the quality, a relationship through bars is inherently a different relationship than it was before. Contact may be reduced and elements of the relationship such as the frequency of calls and visits become beyond the immediate control of the incarcerated parent. Meanwhile, the irregular contact can be difficult for children, especially younger children, who may not understand why their parent is not more available to them (Saunders, 2016).

The stress of the incarceration may manifest for some children as mood disorders or behavioral problems (Turney, 2014). Crucially, strong parent-child relationships may mitigate some of the emotional consequences of the incarceration for the child, easing distress and negative outcomes. This makes it all the more important that children who are struggling have access to their parent if they choose to. It is noteworthy that research has suggested that in the context of higher adversity (such as experiencing poverty and systemic racism), the buffer of parental support may be less powerful (Davis & Shlafer, 2016). This does not mean that children with high adversity do not benefit from relationships with their parents; the opposite is in fact likely true. A child who is experiencing significant social and emotional challenges likely needs the love and validation of a parent all the more, even though the effects may not be strongly evident to observers. It can be assumed that any correlations between the parent-child bond and the child's mood and behavior are nuanced and deserving of careful consideration before decisions are made about ongoing interactions.

Helping professionals may need to assist children to advocate for themselves, or even speak up on the child's behalf, especially if other adults are skeptical of the benefits of the parent-child connection. If a child's stress about losing their parent, or mixed emotions toward their parent, are being expressed with behavioral acting out, adults may perceive that the relationship with the parent—and not the struggles to maintain it—are the cause of the child's behavior. Although severing contact with the child's parent may be done with the motivation of protection (Saunders, 2016; Turney & Wildeman, 2013), acting without thoroughly considering the child's needs and desires for relationship could be quite detrimental. Understandably, many children who desire a relationship with their incarcerated parent find it upsetting when adults do not understand or support this (Saunders, 2016). If a child's behavior or mood does not change positively with contact with the incarcerated parent, a helping professional could act as an advocate by checking in with the child regularly and inquiring about their experiences of being in contact with their parent.

Some research has suggested that children act out more before and after visits with incarcerated parents. This literature, however, may actually be capturing the problem of poor-quality visitation, including visiting spaces which are unwelcoming to children, short visit times, or the inability to have physical contact with parents (Schubert et al., 2016). Again, listening to children and carefully examining the situation in a holistic manner will help to contextualize challenges accurately and better support the needs of families.

It must be recognized that despite the high potential for distress, the parent-child bond can be full of joy and love during a prison sentence. Incarcerated parents can continue to participate in family decisions about school, discipline, and parenting practices through phone calls, letters, and visits. Visits can be fun and rich in connection for both parent and child (Toews et al., 2020). Quality visitation may also reduce the experience of parenting stress for the incarcerated parent and enhance child development (Beckmeyer & Arditti, 2014), as well as the attachment relationship between parent and child (La Vigne et al., 2005). Affirming parent-child interactions during the incarceration can communicate to children that they are still loved and cared for, as well as instill hope about the future, when the parent is released (Song et al., 2018).

Unfortunately, few families are able to maintain a regular schedule of visits while a parent is incarcerated (Pleggenkuhle et al., 2018). In the United States, courts have consistently affirmed a stance that inmate visits are a privilege, and not a right, and are therefore subject to suspension and termination at the discretion of prison facilities (Boudin et al., 2013). As a result, supporting the parent-child bond is best approached with numerous means of connection. Helping professionals can assist by advocating, connecting families with resources, and becoming educated about the logistics of navigating a relationship from behind bars. The quality of the relationship developed and maintained during an incarceration will likely affect the relationship after release (La Vigne et al., 2005), so it is clear that supporting a positive, loving bond while a parent is incarcerated can have a lasting effect for a family and the well-being of a child.

CONTRAINDICATIONS FOR CONTACT

Children with incarcerated parents have the same rights to parental relationships as other children. Concurrently, the best interests of the child must be preserved when considering whether or not the relationship is beneficial (Roberston, 2011). Unfortunately, some incarcerated parents are not positive participants in their children's lives. In other cases, environmental factors may prevent contact from being a positive experience.

In the United States, annual rates of child abuse and maltreatment are measured in the hundreds of thousands. In 2019, there were approximately 656,000 confirmed cases of maltreatment documented by the U.S. Department of Health and Human Services. These cases included medical neglect, physical neglect, psychological maltreatment, physical abuse, sexual abuse, and sexual trafficking. Younger children, including infants, are more likely to experience these events than are older children and teens. The majority of perpetrators (77.5%) were identified as the child's parent. Individual risk factors for families include poverty, substance use, and a multigenerational history of domestic violence (Administration on Children, Youth and Families, Children's Bureau, 2019).

Responses to, and developmental effects of, abuse vary widely across the population of mistreated children (Toth & Manly, 2019). For some children, contact with a prior abuser is completely contraindicated and, in some cases, has even been forbidden by the courts via a no-contact order. In such cases, it is clear that helping professionals and other supportive adults should not facilitate any contact. In other instances, families may be participating in formal reunification programs in an attempt to repair and reconnect. Therapeutic programs, supervised visits, parenting classes, and other interventions may be administered in an attempt to make possible a safe reunification of parent and child. These programs vary widely in quality, focus, modality, and outcomes (Maltais et al., 2019). Reunification is often a difficult process for families, and unfortunately many will reengage at some point with Child Protective Services, following another report of maltreatment (Terling, 1999). Whether a child has contact with their parent following mistreatment (formally reported or not) is a matter highly individual to the child and family. The child's physical and emotional safety should be considered first and foremost.

Even if the child was not subject to mistreatment by the incarcerated parent directly, emotional wellness may be a concern for children who witnessed their parents using substances, engaging in intimate partner violence, or otherwise behaving in a manner frightening to the child. In such cases, contact with an incarcerated parent may remind a child of past traumas (Arditti, 2012). In these instances, individual or family counseling could be a valuable resource to engage prior to assisting with parent-child contact.

Children with incarcerated parents have, on average, more traumatic experiences in their histories than children without incarcerated parents (Turney, 2018). The prison environment itself may be difficult for a child with trauma, due to stressors like noise, the unfamiliar environment, unfriendly staff, or the presence of many strangers. Exposure to a strange and scary place, as well as sitting in a room with other offenders, may be frightening for a child (Schubert et al., 2016), and especially for a child who associates these triggers with trauma memories. Children who can safely interact with their parent, but perhaps not the prison environment, may be better suited to visitation alternatives and may benefit from individual mental health counseling prior to more direct contact.

In conclusion, facilitating connection with parents and children during a prison sentence is an important consideration for the wellness of all involved. Careful attention must be paid to the risks and benefits, as well as to the long-term goals of the child and family.

VISITATION

Seeing a parent face-to-face is important for many children. Time spent together, physical touch, and sharing meals can help to maintain family bonds. Although visitation can be challenging, even an occasional visit may benefit both the parent and child; the amount of visitation has been found to be less important than the quality of the visits (Beckmeyer & Arditti, 2014).

An enjoyable, low-stress visit is more likely when family members are able to communicate effectively. Arguments or tension may cause distress for both the incarcerated parents and their family members. Helping professionals can support quality visitation by working with families on conflict resolution skills and clear communication (Turanovic & Tasca, 2019). Children may wish to write down notes ahead of visits to remember the topics that they wish to discuss with their parent during the visit, such as positive stories, important recent events, and accomplishments. Keeping a journal of topics that will be shared during a visit could also help some children to feel connected to their parent in between visits.

The design of visitation programs differs widely from facility to facility and state to state (Boudin et al., 2013; Poehlmann et al., 2010). The visitation room in the parent's prison may be cold and sterile or cheerful and colorful; the staff processing visitors may be friendly and welcoming to children or gruff and scary; the level of security of the prison may require that the exterior of the building be wrapped in razor wire, with tall lookout towers, or it might look more like a large school from the child's perspective. Some visiting areas may include outdoor space to play and feel quite comfortable (Toews et al., 2020). Understandably, these differences can result in a wide variety of experiences (Poehlmann et al., 2010).

The type of visit available to a family may also depend upon the prison's facilities or the parent's offense or security level. In some facilities, a parent and child can play on the floor together, while in others, it may be required to sit in chairs which are bolted to the floor. During a face-to-face visit in some prisons, children may be allowed one hug at the beginning and end of a visit only, while in others, children under a certain age may be allowed to sit in their parent's lap. Visits might also consist of the parent and child being separated by a barrier of plexiglass, which can be particularly challenging for young children who may not understand why they cannot reach their parent (Correa et al., 2021).

Visiting an incarcerated family member can be a taxing process, logistically, emotionally, and financially (Christian, 2005; Correa et al., 2021; Schubert et al., 2016). Adults and adolescents need state identification, transportation must be arranged, and at some facilities, parking fees must be paid. Overnight accommodations may need to be paid if the prison is too far from home for a day trip (Schubert et al., 2016), and other expenses like food, gasoline, or bus tickets may be financial burdens (Christian, 2005). Once on site, families must wait through long lines, as well as submit to person and property searches, before visits which may be so short that the time spent getting into the visiting room is longer than the visit itself (Correa et al., 2021). Guardians may need to provide birth certificates or other proof of guardianship in order to escort a minor into the facility (Shlafer et al., 2015). Facilities may also require a social security number for running a background check ahead of visits, deterring undocumented immigrants (Boudin et al., 2013).

Helping professionals can assist in facilitating visitation by aiding families to navigate some of these challenges. If a guardian is concerned that they do not have the correct documentation and is worried about possible exposure by calling the facility, a helping professional could reach out to the prison and ask about these policies on their behalf. In some states, requiring social security numbers or other proof of legal citizenship has been abolished in order to make visitation more accessible (Boudin et al., 2013), so clarification is important. Adults and teens may also need help acquiring identification from an appropriate agency.

Assistance with transportation to prisons varies state to state. A full listing of resources is beyond the scope of this chapter, but helping professionals are encouraged to research options in their area. Local nonprofits may be able to provide services such as free or low-cost transportation (e.g., Use What You've Got Ministry in Indiana), or overnight accommodations (e.g., Matthew House in Washington). Calling the prison itself may be a helpful first step for locating resources such as nonprofit contacts, bus vouchers, or other assistance. Staff who support family visitation within the prison may be called a title such as Community Partnership Coordinator (Washington State) or Rehabilitation Coordinator (New York State). The prison chaplain is also likely to be a good first contact. Many prisons' websites also contain links to community organizations that offer families support.

Most prisons have information on their webpages that describe the visitor application process, visiting hours, and policies that regulate visits. Helping professionals can make themselves familiar with these policies, which likely include dress code, types of acceptable identification, rules about physical contact, lists of which items may be brought in for babies and small children, and the required steps for scheduling a visit. Photos, videos, or descriptions of the visiting room may be available. It is worth investigating the visitation space to help the family prepare, as well as to possibly alleviate some worries for the guardian about the environment to which the child will be exposed. Some facilities offer orientation meetings for families, to provide information about visiting and other family-related topics, which a helping professional may be permitted to attend.

Providing children with honest, age-appropriate information about their parent's incarceration may support a more positive visitation experience and overall relationship (Dallaire et al., 2010; Poehlmann-Tynan et al., 2021). Young children may understand that their parent broke a rule and is required to be away from home for a while (similar, perhaps, to the familiar concept of a time-out), while older children and adolescents likely understand the concept of incarceration. Additionally, hands-on practice can help alleviate anxiety about the unknown before entering the facility. According to Bandura's (1976) social learning theory, children learn from watching others and trying on new behaviors with role models. This theory can be utilized to help children practice strategies for navigating the prison.

Roleplays and practice can be used to demystify and rehearse the visiting room environment. For example, to prepare for rules about physical contact, such as that they may be limited to a short hug or kiss at hello and goodbye, followed by taking a seat (Schubert et al., 2016), children can practice this routine with their custodial parent in a mock visiting room set-up. If a child will be expected to sit with their back against the chair for the duration of the visit, a helping professional could practice this with a child. This practice could also be turned into a game in which each player places a small object, such as a ping pong ball or eraser, between themselves and the chairback and competes to see who can go longer without dropping their object by leaning forward. The children's game Simon Says, in which children practice following directions, could be utilized to rehearse following the instructions of prison staff or a parent while in the facility. This game, or something similar, such as red-light/green-light (a game in which children move when "green light" is called and freeze when "red light" is called) could also be used to practice the important skill of not running in a prison, as this is typically not allowed. Children should be coached that if they are allowed to hug their parent, they should walk, and not run, to their parent in the visiting room.

The television show *Sesame Street* (Sesame Workshop, n.d.) has developed a series of videos and handouts for children of incarcerated parents. One of these resources is an animated video describing the visitation process. Showing young children this video, which is available on the Sesame Street website, may also help to demystify the process.

Children and teens can also be assisted with tasks like pre-selecting their clothing, to ensure compliance with dress code policies (Boudin et al., 2013). Children should be made aware that they will be asked to walk through a metal detector and that they could be subject to additional search. Refusal to be searched may result in being turned away (Boudin et al., 2013), so helping professionals can aid in making this process less scary for children by explaining what will likely happen, showing children pictures of metal detectors and wands, and doing roleplays. A doorway can substitute for a metal detector so that children can practice waiting in line, being waved through, and slowly walking through the detector.

It is important for children and families to be aware of the rules pertaining to visitation. Failure to follow rules while on prison property can result in a visit being ended or even family members being temporarily or permanently prohibited from entering the facility.

SPECIAL PROGRAMS

In addition to general visitation information, a website for a specific prison facility or the state's department of corrections may detail special programs available to families. Depending upon the facility, families may be eligible for opportunities like extended visits, overnight visits, or special celebrations for events like Father's Day or Mother's Day (Boudin et al., 2013). Facilities may also host family-friendly events for holidays and religious or cultural celebrations such as powwows. Volunteers often attend these events to provide extra activities in the visiting room such as family photographs, crafts and games, or toys for kids to take home (Melander, 2020).

Other programs provide support for the parent-child bond as well. Special Boy Scout or Girl Scout troops may be available in the child's area, which provide both social support and opportunities to engage in scouting activities with incarcerated parents, who host some of the troop meetings (Soltes, 2012; Washington State Department of Social and Health Services, 2009). Several programs, such as the Women's Storybook Project (Texas or Arkansas) and the Children's Literacy Foundation (New Hampshire and Vermont), allow inmates to record themselves reading a book to their child, which is then mailed to the child for reading along with the recording. Programs like Angel Tree (Prison Fellowship, n.d.) provide children with holiday gifts on behalf of their incarcerated parent to remind children that they are being thought of during the holidays.

Overnight visits (sometimes called "conjugal" or "trailer" visits) may be available to parents in certain facilities. Such visits allow families to interact in special home-like visiting areas. Families can share meals and spend a day together away from other inmates and staff. Incarcerated parents who are serving sentences in work release programs or other low-security facilities may also be eligible for furlough programs, during which the inmate can leave the prison and spend a partial day, or even several days, visiting family (Bülow & Dagan, 2020).

Awareness of special family-friendly programming may help a custodial guardian to be more comfortable with the visitation process. Participation may also give a child additional time with their parent and opportunities for bonding in more naturalistic interactions.

ALTERNATIVES TO VISITATION

Although being able to see and touch a parent are activities included in the bill of rights for children of incarcerated parents, this does not always happen. In addition to logistical challenges, decisions may be made on behalf of the child which prevent visits. Department of corrections policies may also prevent in-person contact. Understanding these barriers, as well as alternative ways to support the parent-child bond, is important for helping professionals.

Custodial guardians play a central role in whether or not visits occur. When a parent becomes incarcerated, the other parent, or a kinship caregiver such as a grandparent, often serves as the decision-maker, or gatekeeper, for contact with the incarcerated parent. This may be complicated by a strained relationship between the guardian and the incarcerated parent (Saunders, 2016). Incarceration often precedes separation or divorce (Turney & Wildeman, 2013), and a parent who is upset with their ex-partner may be less likely to facilitate visits (Poehlmann et al., 2010). Foster parents are also likely to be custodial guardians. Their feelings about the incarcerated individual or the prison setting itself may also inhibit visitation.

The incarcerated parent themselves could also prevent visits. Some incarcerated parents prefer that their children not visit, fearing, for example, that their child may be emotionally harmed by seeing them in prison or being unable to touch them because of visitation policies or glass barriers (Correa et al., 2021). Incarcerated parents may even prefer that their children believe that the parent is traveling or working out of town and may conceal the incarceration entirely (Pleggenkuhle et al., 2018). Other parents may ask their families not to visit because they do not want to ask anyone to incur the financial costs or manage the challenging logistics of coming to see them (Christian, 2005). Interestingly, despite parental concerns, children's perceptions of their parents may be less effected by the incarceration experience than by the quality of the relationship which existed pre-incarceration (Washington et al., 2018). Helping professionals may wish to gently explore the fears of parents in regard to facilitating visitation and help the child speak to their own desires about seeing their parent in a prison visiting room.

Prison policies require that potential visitors submit documentation for security background checks. Custodial guardians who are unable to pass a background check may be judged a possible threat to the safety of the facility and denied access, meaning that they cannot escort a minor child, who is unable to visit alone. Even with no criminal convictions, the guardian may not be eligible. In some states, individuals identified as a prior victim of the inmate may be unable to visit (Boudin et al., 2013). A guardian listed as a victim of past domestic violence, for example, is unlikely to be able to escort a child.

Even when all of the logistical and relational variables to enable visitation align well, prison policies may limit the number of visits an inmate can have in any given month (Boudin et al., 2013). Until more family-friendly visitation policies are enacted nationwide, alternatives to visitation will likely be necessary for many families if they wish to maintain regular contact.

Alternatives to visitation are discussed in the following sections. It may be important for a family to know that all phone calls, letters, and emails from family members are subject to monitoring by prison staff. Written materials in a language other than English may be delayed if the facility requires that they be reviewed by a translator prior to release to the inmate.

Phone Calls

Phone calls are the most common form of connection for children to incarcerated parents (Skora Horgan & Poehlmann-Tynan, 2020). A challenge with this modality is the expense to inmates and families. Various advocates have attempted to bring down costs, including by means of court actions. The Federal Communications Commission has capped rates on interstate calls, but intrastate rates are currently determined on a state-by-state basis (Fuchs, 2019). For-profit companies typically operate the phones in prisons, offering prepaid or collect calls. Costs can range from a couple of dollars to over 10 dollars for a 15-minute call (Zimmerman & Flaherty, 2007). To assist families, local nonprofit organizations may be available to provide phone cards. A facility may also be able to arrange a special call for family emergencies.

Children should be prepared for a time-limited phone call, as the line will likely cut off after a predetermined period. If a call is planned in advance, children should also be prepared for the possibility that the call is delayed or not possible. Inmates must often wait in unpredictable lines for the phone and may not be able to access a telephone before the allotted time is up. Unexpected events like cellblock lockdowns could also interfere with a parent's ability to make it to the phone when a child is expecting the call.

A number of prison policies apply to phone calls, which can vary state to state. For example, it may be forbidden for an inmate to call the residence of an identified victim, which would prohibit a parent from calling their child if the custodial parent was a victim of the inmate's domestic violence. The facility might also limit the number of phone numbers that an inmate can call or restrict the number of times per year that new numbers can be added to the list. A family with a new telephone number may need to wait for phone calls until the incarcerated parent has a chance to update their approved phone list.

Helping professionals can support children, especially young children, by practicing answering and speaking into the phone. It may be necessary, for example, to dial 1 to accept the call. Young children can also practice speaking clearly into the phone and not pushing extra buttons or hanging up without their guardian's permission.

Video Visits

Video visits can be a good alternative for young children who do not have the attention span for a phone call. Younger children also especially benefit from seeing body language and facial expressions. Seeing a parent's face on camera has been found to provide more of a sense of closeness than voice-only calls for children (Tarasuik et al., 2013), which makes this technology a valuable resource in enhancing and building the parent-child bond. Like phone calls, video visits can be costly to families (potentially around 30 cents per minute) because the technology is facilitated by for-profit companies (Charles et al., 2021; Skora Horgan & Poehlmann-Tynan, 2020).

Rules for video visits will likely be similar to in-person visitation. As such, nonapproved visitors, including family members not on the inmate's visitors list, will likely not be allowed to participate, and a visit could be ended if such an individual appears on screen or speaks off camera. Families must provide their own internet connection and webcam. Video visit software may be incompatible with tablets and phones, necessitating a laptop or desktop computer (Duwe & McNeeley, 2021). If a family intends to use a library service or other public space, they should be particularly attentive to the policies of the prison.

Children may benefit from roleplaying video visits just as they would in-person visits. Sitting still and speaking toward the microphone are important skills. A family might also want a young child to practice seeing a loved one on screen to facilitate the understanding that the parent will not be available for physical contact.

Letters

Mail can be a reliable way to maintain relationships from afar. Although the cost of postage stamps may be burdensome on both sides, a lot of information can be conveyed in each letter. As with visits, it is important to become familiar with department of corrections policies related to mail. Commonly, for example, it is forbidden for mail to be sent from inmate to inmate, and so a child with two incarcerated parents would not be allowed to include a note from their mom in a letter to their dad. The contents of an envelope may also be limited to correspondence from one individual, so siblings may need to send separate letters to ensure that their mail reaches their parent. Newspaper clippings, photographs, and other media are also likely regulated by special rules. Books and magazines can likely be sent only directly from a publisher or retailer. When a parent responds, families may want to be aware that a message such as "mailed from a correctional facility" is going to be stamped on the envelope.

Young children may wish to send artwork. In some facilities, artwork will be confiscated if it contains glitter, glue, or stickers. Supportive adults can help children create artwork which can be delivered to their parent without delay by reading the guidelines for mail carefully.

Emails

Some facilities may offer email services, though it is not the email to which many are accustomed. Family members can type messages into the website of the inmate email service, which is then delivered to a kiosk within the prison. The message will not arrive instantly. Short video clips may be allowed. As with other forms of communication, prison email is typically provided by a for-profit company and will incur charges. An email system which allows for video messages may be particularly well suited to young children, who can speak or sing to parents. Again, it is important to be familiar with the rules of such communicate and help children be prepared to follow them.

EDUCATION

Parent-child relationships include not just social time spent together but also the contributions that parents make to all elements of a child's life. School is one such factor which is central to most children's day-to-day lives. Including incarcerated parents in education facilitates a connection to a central part of the child's experience.

Children of incarcerated parents are more likely than their peers to struggle with academic achievement and in-school behavior (Shlafer et al., 2017). Both internalizing behaviors (things like reporting feeling sick frequently or socially withdrawing) and externalizing behaviors (acting out), may be more common (Dallaire et al., 2010). Some of these effects are directly mediated by parental involvement in the child's education. For example, children whose parents are actively involved in their educations tend to perform better academically (Hill et al., 2018) and have higher self-esteem related to academics (Wang & Sheikh-Khalil, 2014). Relatedly, teachers can also support higher achievement by challenging their own assumptions about children of incarcerated parents and demonstrating that they anticipate positive results from these students (Wildeman et al., 2017).

Educators and other helping professionals can support a family-based approach to education by understanding the logistics of life for families with an incarcerated parent. Incarcerated parents can join parent-teacher conferences by phone or video visit, where available (Melander, 2020; Turney, 2019), but this must be arranged ahead of time. Educational decisions such as moving a child to a different program, changing classrooms, or applying for an individualized education plan, can be made by both parents, but educators should be aware that the incarcerated parent may need more time to receive information in the mail, wait for access to the phone or a visit, and possibly need material translated prior to responding.

Educators and school staff can also support the parent-child bond by being understanding in regard to special needs. For example, children may need to miss school in order to visit their parent, especially if the prison is far from home (Saunders, 2016). Schools can also make time and space for children to talk about their feelings related to missing their parent (Shlafer & Poehlmann, 2010; Turney, 2019) and communicate understanding if a child acts out as a means of processing difficult emotions (Saunders, 2016). Such behaviors communicate to children that their families are accepted and respected by school staff.

Children with incarcerated parents may feel isolated in their classrooms. Activities at school such as sharing their parents' careers or making artwork for Mother's Day or Father's Day can inadvertently leave these children feeling left out (Dallaire et al., 2010). Teachers and other school staff can keep the diversity of families in mind when designing activities and discussing family structures in order to support a positive view of all parents.

ADVOCACY

The bill of rights for children with incarcerated parents should be more than a dream. Children are innocent victims in the mass incarceration occurring within the United States, and helping professionals can play an important role in improving outcomes for these families. It is apparent that the needs of families impacted by incarceration are varied, and readers are encouraged to consider their own resources and positions of privilege that may be leveraged on behalf of children.

One mechanism for supporting the parent-child bond is to support parenting skills. Outcomes data for parenting classes for incarcerated parents is mixed, but results suggest that the parent-child relationship can be enhanced by access to such resources (Armstrong et al., 2018), and that the risk for child behavioral problems may decline with select programs (Menting et al., 2014). Given that many parents experiencing incarceration may have lacked sufficient emotional support in their own lives, knowledge of parenting practices and child development, and time to consider their parenting preferences, having the opportunity to participate in parenting classes in prison could be a unique opportunity for growth. Social work and counseling researchers could also support this population by furthering studies of effective parenting classes and the generation of best practices (Tremblay & Sutherland, 2017).

The emotional and behavioral challenges of children with incarcerated parents could lead to a dismissive attitude about the nature of incarcerated parents' parenting skills and the impacts they have on their children. This would, however, discount the role that the system itself plays in creating positive or negative experiences for children in the visiting room (Poehlmann et al., 2010). Helping professionals can advocate for more family-friendly visitation, including approachable and well-trained staff, longer visits, and more accommodating visiting rooms, with art and furniture appropriate to children. In order to honor children's rights, visitation should not be conditioned upon the parent's behavior. It is reasonable and important to consider the needs of families when policies are made (Poehlmann et al., 2010; San Francisco Children of Incarcerated Parents Partnership, 2005).

Special programs to support the parent-child bond, such as holiday events and overnight visits, require special funding. In areas where the funding, or the motivation, to provide these programs does not exist, helping professionals can provide policy advocacy. Interested readers can also explore volunteer options within the visiting rooms of their local prisons by visiting the appropriate department of corrections website.

Supporting children of incarcerated parents and the bond with their parents is also facilitated, at a foundational level, when helping professionals examine and challenge any of their own personal biases (Dallaire et al., 2010; Phillips & Gates, 2011). Allies to these children will look beyond the circumstances of the incarceration and see the parent and child as they are: a unique, important and valuable family, deserving of the same choices, autonomy, and support as any other.

SUMMARY

This chapter has examined the parent-child bond when a parent is incarcerated in state or federal prison. When appropriate, it is proposed that parents and children have support to maintain a strong relationship throughout the prison sentence. This relationship can be enhanced in a variety of ways, including keeping the incarcerated parent active in the child's life through visitation, phone calls, written correspondence, and participation in the child's education. Helping professionals are encouraged to support the rights of children with incarcerated parents by becoming knowledgeable about the options available to families and by advocating for improved services for children.

The work of supporting a parent-child bond when a parent is incarcerated will be highly individual to the child and family. In general, consider these points for helping professionals:

- A child with an incarcerated parent likely has many feelings about the situation, their parent, and themselves. The child's self-concept, understanding of their family, and beliefs about the future are likely to be affected. Listen carefully and make space for all of the child's emotions. Validate and normalize having strong and disparate feelings.
- Research the prison in which the parent is currently incarcerated (be aware that this could change during the sentence). Read the policies related to visitation, video visits, mail, phone calls, emails, and special programs. Consider being available for the task of reaching out to prison staff to ask clarifying questions on behalf of a family.
- Help children prepare for contact with their incarcerated parents by utilizing the learning methods appropriate for the child's age, such as games, roleplays, and factual conversations.
- Advocate, as appropriate, for the incarcerated parent to be included in decision-making processes related to the child's education.
- Advocate for the overall welfare of children of incarcerated parents when it comes to policies, programs, and funding.

CRITICAL THINKING QUESTIONS

Readers are also encouraged to prepare themselves for this work by enhancing self-awareness and challenging preconceived notions. To enhance allyship, helping professionals can approach families impacted by incarceration with an open and accepting stance. Consider the following critical thinking questions:

- What beliefs do I hold about people who end up in prison? How might these beliefs shape the ways in which I interact with families?
- What beliefs do I hold about parenting and what it means to be a "good" parent? How might my biases and personal background influence my values in this area?
- How can I best prepare myself to be an unconditional advocate for a child's well-being, even if a family makes decisions different from those which I might have made?

CASE STUDY

Maya, age six, and her brother, Jordan, age fourteen, are brought to family counseling by their grandmother, Marie. Marie explains that she is currently legal guardian to Maya and Jordan while their mother, her daughter, is in prison. Maya was three years old when her mother was arrested for possession of a controlled substance. Marie tearfully explains that Jordan was present for the arrest and was terrified to see the police taking his mom away. Marie says that Jordan went through a period of crying spells, anger, and acting out at school in the year or so following his mother's incarceration. Marie says that Jordon was always very close to his mom and the adjustment to living with his grandparents and not seeing his mom every day was very difficult. Maya does not remember the days before her mom was in prison, but Maire explains that she enjoys going on their monthly visits. She is currently able to sit in her mom's lap during the visits, and likes telling her mom about her school, her dolls, and her drawings. Marie says that Jordan used to go on the visits, but he has been expressing more and more anger toward his mother and has recently refused to attend the visit days. He has also stopped taking his mom's phone calls and told his grandmother "Mom was selfish and ruined everything for us. I'm not giving her my time!" Marie was saddened to hear this and says she is not sure how much she should push Jordan to talk to his mom. Marie explains to the counselor that she is worried about both kids. She notes that when Maya turns seven in a couple of months, she will no longer be allowed, per the prison rules, to sit on her mom's lap during the visits. Marie says "I just have no idea how to tell her that. How do you say that to a six-year-old?" She also explains that the kids' mother is going to be getting out of prison in about a year and she worries that if Jordan does not work through some of his anger before then, the reunification will not go well. Marie would like the counselor to work with both kids, and hopefully, include their mom in sessions in the future.

If you were the counselor, how would you approach this family and address Marie's concerns?

REFERENCES

Administration on Children, Youth and Families, Children's Bureau. (2019). *Child maltreatment 2019.* U.S. Department of Health & Human Services, Administration for Children and Families. https://www.acf.hhs.gov/sites/default/files/documents/cb/cm2019.pdf

Arditti, J. A. (2012). Child trauma within the context of parental incarceration: A family process perspective. *Journal of Family Theory & Review*, *4*(3), 181–219. doi:10.1111/j.1756-2589.2012.00128.x

Armstrong, E., Eggins, E., Reid, N., Harnett, P., & Dawe, S. (2018). Parenting interventions for incarcerated parents to improve parenting knowledge and skills, parent well-being, and quality of the parent–child relationship: A systematic review and meta-analysis. *Journal of Experimental Criminology*, *14*(3), 279–317. doi:10.100711292-017-9290-6

Bandura, A. (1976). *Social learning theory*. Prentice-Hall.

Beckmeyer, J. J., & Arditti, J. A. (2014). Implications of in-person visits for incarcerated parents' family relationships and parenting experience. *Journal of Offender Rehabilitation*, *53*(2), 129–151. doi:10.1080/10509674.2013.868390

Boudin, C., Stutz, T., & Littman, A. (2013). Prison visitation policies: A fifty-state survey. *Yale Law & Policy Review*, *32*, 149–189.

Bülow, W., & Dagan, N. (2020). From rehabilitation to penal communication: The role of furlough and visitation within a retributivist framework. *Punishment & Society*, *23*(3), 376–393. doi:10.1177/1462474520953676

Carlson, J. R. (1998). Evaluating the effectiveness of a live-in nursery within a women's prison. *Journal of Offender Rehabilitation*, *27*(1-2), 73–85. doi:10.1300/J076v27n01_06

Charles, P., Kerr, M., Wirth, J., Jensen, S., Massoglia, M., & Poehlmann-Tynan, J. (2021). Lessons from the field: Developing and implementing an intervention for jailed parents and their children. *Family Relations*, *70*(1), 171–178. doi:10.1111/fare.12524

Christian, J. (2005). Riding the bus: Barriers to prison visitation and family management strategies. *Journal of Contemporary Criminal Justice*, *21*(1), 31–48. doi:10.1177/1043986204271618

Correa, N. P., Hayes, A. K., Bhalakia, A. M., Lopez, K. K., Cupit, T., Kwarteng-Amaning, V., Keefe, R. J., Greeley, C. S., & Van Horne, B. S. (2021). Parents' perspectives on the impact of their incarceration on children and families. *Family Relations*, *70*(1), 162–170. doi:10.1111/fare.12529

Dallaire, D. H., Ciccone, A., & Wilson, L. C. (2010). Teachers' experiences with and expectations of children with incarcerated parents. *Journal of Applied Developmental Psychology*, *31*(4), 281–290. doi:10.1016/j.appdev.2010.04.001

Davis, L., & Shlafer, R. J. (2016). Mental health of adolescents with currently and formerly incarcerated parents. *Journal of Adolescence*, *54*(1), 120–134. doi:10.1016/j.adolescence.2016.10.006 PMID:28011442

Duwe, G., & McNeeley, S. (2021). Just as good as the real thing? The effects of prison video visitation on recidivism. *Crime and Delinquency*, *67*(4), 475–497. doi:10.1177/0011128720943168

Fellowship, P. (n.d.). *Unwrapping the gift of connection.* https://www.prisonfellowship.org/about/angel-tree/angel-tree-christmas/

Fuchs, Z. (2019). Behind Bars: The urgency and simplicity of prison phone reform. *Harvard Law & Policy Review*, *14*, 205–229.

Hill, N. E., Witherspoon, D. P., & Bartz, D. (2018). Parental involvement in education during middle school: Perspectives of ethnically diverse parents, teachers, and students. *The Journal of Educational Research*, *111*(1), 12–27. doi:10.1080/00220671.2016.1190910

Jbara, A. E. (2012). The price they pay: Protecting the mother-child relationship through the use of prison nurseries and residential parenting programs. *Indiana Law Journal (Indianapolis, Ind.)*, *87*, 1825–1845.

La Vigne, N. G., Naser, R. L., Brooks, L. E., & Castro, J. L. (2005). Examining the effect of incarceration and in-prison family contact on prisoners' family relationships. *Journal of Contemporary Criminal Justice*, *21*(4), 314–335. doi:10.1177/1043986205281727

Luther, K. (2016). Stigma management among children of incarcerated parents. *Deviant Behavior*, *37*(11), 1264–1275. doi:10.1080/01639625.2016.1170551

Maltais, C., Cyr, C., Parent, G., & Pascuzzo, K. (2019). Identifying effective interventions for promoting parent engagement and family reunification for children in out-of-home care: A series of meta-analyses. *Child Abuse & Neglect*, *88*, 362–375. doi:10.1016/j.chiabu.2018.12.009 PMID:30579168

Maruschak, L. M., & Bronson, J. (2016). *Parents in prison and their minor children.* US Department of Justice, Bureau of Justice Statistics. https://www.bjs.gov/content/pub/pdf/pptmcspi16st.pdf

Melander, L. (2020). Keeping connected while living apart: An exploration of a prison contact maintenance program. *Journal of Offender Rehabilitation*, *59*(5), 267–284. doi:10.1080/10509674.2020.1745980

Menting, A. T., de Castro, B. O., Wijngaards-de Meij, L. D., & Matthys, W. (2014). A trial of parent training for mothers being released from incarceration and their children. *Journal of Clinical Child and Adolescent Psychology*, *43*(3), 381–396. doi:10.1080/15374416.2013.817310 PMID:23915290

Mumola, C. J. (2000). *Incarcerated parents and their children.* Bureau of Justice Statistics Special Report. https://www.bjs.gov/content/pub/pdf/iptc.pdf

Pew Charitable Trusts. (2010). *Collateral costs: Incarceration's effect on economic mobility.* https://www.pewtrusts.org/~/media/legacy/uploadedfiles/pcs_assets/2010/collateralcosts1pdf.pdf

Phillips, S. D., & Gates, T. (2011). A conceptual framework for understanding the stigmatization of children of incarcerated parents. *Journal of Child and Family Studies*, *20*(3), 286–294. doi:10.100710826-010-9391-6

Pleggenkuhle, B., Huebner, B. M., & Summers, M. (2018). Opting out: The role of identity, capital, and agency in prison visitation. *Justice Quarterly*, *35*(4), 726–749. doi:10.1080/07418825.2017.1339113

Poehlmann-Tynan, J., Cuthrell, H., Weymouth, L., Burnson, C., Frerks, L., Muentner, L., Holder, N., Milavetz, Z., Lauter, L., Hindt, L., Davis, L., Schubert, E., & Shlafer, R. (2021). Multisite randomized efficacy trial of educational materials for young children with incarcerated parents. *Development and Psychopathology*, *33*(1), 323–339. doi:10.1017/S0954579419001792 PMID:33616033

Roberston, O. (2011). *Collateral convicts: Children of incarcerated parents. Recommendations and good practice from the UN Committee on the Rights of the Child Day of General Discussion 2011.* Human Rights and Refugees Publications. https://www.quno.org/sites/default/files/resources/ENGLISH_Collateral%20Convicts_Recommendations%20and%20good%20practice.pdf

San Francisco Children of Incarcerated Parents Partnership. (2005). *Children of incarcerated parents: A bill of rights.* https://sfonline.barnard.edu/children/SFCIPP_Bill_of_Rights.pdf

Saunders, V. (2016). Children of prisoners–Children's decision making about contact. *Child & Family Social Work*, *22*(S2), 63–72. doi:10.1111/cfs.12281

Schubert, E. C., Duininck, M., & Shlafer, R. J. (2016). Visiting mom: A pilot evaluation of a prison-based visiting program serving incarcerated mothers and their minor children. *Journal of Offender Rehabilitation*, *55*(4), 213–234. doi:10.1080/10509674.2016.1159641 PMID:27867281

Shlafer, R. J., Loper, A. B., & Schillmoeller, L. (2015). Introduction and literature review: Is parent-child contact during parental incarceration beneficial? In J. Poehlmann-Tynan (Ed.), *Children's contact with incarcerated parents: Implications for policy and intervention* (pp. 1–21). Springer International. doi:10.1007/978-3-319-16625-4_1

Shlafer, R. J., & Poehlmann, J. (2010). Attachment and caregiving relationships in families affected by parental incarceration. *Attachment & Human Development*, *12*(4), 395–415. doi:10.1080/14616730903417052 PMID:20582847

Skora Horgan, E., & Poehlmann-Tynan, J. (2020). In-home video chat for young children and their incarcerated parents. *Journal of Children and Media*, *14*(3), 400–406. doi:10.1080/17482798.2020.1792082

Soltes, F. (2012). *Girl Scouts Beyond Bars: Providing a better path.* Office of Juvenile Justice and Delinquency Prevention. https://www.ojp.gov/pdffiles1/ojjdp/249001.pdf

Song, H., Woo, Y., Lee, H. D., & Cochran, J. K. (2018). The dynamics of intra-family relationships during incarceration and the implications for children of incarcerated parents. *International Journal of Offender Therapy and Comparative Criminology*, *62*(12), 3775–3796. doi:10.1177/0306624X18755481 PMID:29392971

Tarasuik, J. C. M., Kaufman, J., & Galligan, R. (2013). Seeing is believing but is hearing? Comparing audio and video communication for young children. *Frontiers in Psychology*, *4*(64). Advance online publication. doi:10.3389/fpsyg.2013.00064 PMID:23450846

Terling, T. (1999). The efficacy of family reunification practices: Reentry rates and correlates of reentry for abused and neglected children reunited with their families. *Child Abuse & Neglect*, *23*(12), 1359–1370. doi:10.1016/S0145-2134(99)00103-9 PMID:10626617

Toews, B., Wagenfeld, A., Stevens, J., & Shoemaker, C. (2020). Feeling at home in nature: A mixed method study of the impact of visitor activities and preferences in a prison visiting room garden. *Journal of Offender Rehabilitation*, *59*(4), 223–246. doi:10.1080/10509674.2020.1733165

Toth, S. L., & Manly, J. T. (2019). Developmental consequences of child abuse and neglect: Implications for intervention. *Child Development Perspectives*, *13*(1), 59–64. doi:10.1111/cdep.12317

Tremblay, M. D., & Sutherland, J. E. (2017). The effectiveness of parenting programs for incarcerated mothers: A systematic review. *Journal of Child and Family Studies*, *26*(12), 3247–3265. doi:10.100710826-017-0900-8

Turanovic, J. J., & Tasca, M. (2019). Inmates' experiences with prison visitation. *Justice Quarterly*, *36*(2), 287–322. doi:10.1080/07418825.2017.1385826

Turney, K. (2014). Stress proliferation across generations? Examining the relationship between parental incarceration and childhood health. *Journal of Health and Social Behavior*, *55*(3), 302–319. doi:10.1177/0022146514544173 PMID:25138199

Turney, K. (2018). Adverse childhood experiences among children of incarcerated parents. *Children and Youth Services Review*, *89*, 218–225. doi:10.1016/j.childyouth.2018.04.033

Turney, K. (2019). Understanding the needs of children with incarcerated parents: What educators should know. *American Educator*, *43*(2), 22–28.

Turney, K., & Goodsell, R. (2018). Parental incarceration and children's wellbeing. *The Future of Children*, *28*(1), 147–164. doi:10.1353/foc.2018.0007

Turney, K., & Wildeman, C. (2013). Redefining relationships: Explaining the countervailing consequences of paternal incarceration for parenting. *American Sociological Review*, *78*(6), 949–979. doi:10.1177/0003122413505589

Wang, M., & Sheikh-Khalil, S. (2014). Does parental involvement matter for student achievement and mental health in high school? *Child Development*, *85*(2), 610–625. doi:10.1111/cdev.12153 PMID:24033259

Washington, H. M., Juan, S. C., & Haskins, A. R. (2018). Incapacitated involvement: Incarceration and fatherhood in fragile families at age 9. *Journal of Family Issues*, *39*(13), 3463–3486. doi:10.1177/0192513X18783225

Washington State Department of Social and Health Services. (2009). *Beyond the walls: A guide to services for families affected by incarceration.* https://snohomishcountywa.gov/DocumentCenter/View/6011/Beyond-the-Walls?bidId=

Wildeman, C., Scardamalia, K., Walsh, E. G., O'Brien, R. L., & Brew, B. (2017). Paternal incarceration and teachers' expectations of students. *Socius: Sociological Research for a Dynamic World*, *3*, 1–14. doi:10.1177/2378023117726610

Workshop, S. (n.d.). *Coping with incarceration.* https://sesamestreetincommunities.org/topics/incarceration/

Zimmerman, P. R., & Flaherty, S. M. (2007). Location monopolies and prison phone rates. *The Quarterly Review of Economics and Finance*, *47*(2), 261–278. doi:10.1016/j.qref.2006.12.002

ADDITIONAL READING

Burgess, S., & Caselman, T. (2009). *Empowering children of incarcerated parents.* Youthlight.

Council on Crime and Justice. (2006). *Children of incarcerated parents.* A report for the Department of Justice. https://repositories.lib.utexas.edu/bitstream/handle/2152/15162/CCJ_CIP_FinalReport.pdf;sequence=2

Eddy, J. M., & Poehlmann-Tynan, J. (Eds.). (2019). *Handbook on children with incarcerated parents: Research, policy, and practice*. Springer Nature. doi:10.1007/978-3-030-16707-3

Gabel, K., & Johnston, D. (Eds.). (1995). *Children of incarcerated parents.* Lexington Books.

Hairston, C. F. (2007). *Focus on children with incarcerated parents: An overview of the research literature.* A report prepared for the Annie E. Casey Foundation. https://repositories.lib.utexas.edu/bitstream/handle/2152/15158/aecasey_children_incparents.pdf?sequence=2

Malone, P. A. (2016). Non-death loss in the lives of adolescents. In *Counseling adolescents through loss, grief, and trauma*. Routledge. doi:10.4324/9780203699638-3

Nesmith, A., & Ruhland, E. (2008). Children of incarcerated parents: Challenges and resiliency, in their own words. *Children and Youth Services Review*, *30*(10), 1119–1130. doi:10.1016/j.childyouth.2008.02.006

KEY TERMS AND DEFINITIONS

Advocacy: Proactive behaviors to support and enhance the rights, welfare, or needs of a person or community.

Child Abuse and Mistreatment: Actions of an adult toward a minor child which cause the child physical or psychological harm.

Helping Professionals: Individuals employed within fields designed to support the welfare of others, such as counselors, social workers, educators, and legal advocates.

Parent-Child Bond: The emotional and physical connection between a parent and child.

Social Learning Theory: A theory based on the work of Albert Bandura which states that new behaviors are developed by observing and imitating the behavior of others.

Stress: An emotional and physiological feeling of tension or anxiety, typically in reaction to increased demands being placed upon a person due to challenging or irregular circumstances.

Trauma: An event, or events, which were frightening to an individual and caused that individual to doubt their own safety or the safety of a loved one.

Chapter 7
Foster Care Youth With an Incarcerated Parent

Regina Gavin Williams
https://orcid.org/0000-0003-2424-0204
North Carolina Central University, USA

Jennifer Barrow
North Carolina Central University, USA

ABSTRACT

Children and adolescents are removed from their homes and placed within foster care due to various concerns. One entry point to foster care that presents various challenges to the mental, emotional, and behavioral stability and adult-sufficiency of youth are those with an incarcerated parent. Research indicated that 20-30% of foster care youth have an incarcerated parent. Yet, the children of incarcerated parents are often understudied when it comes addressing the issues and needs of foster care youth. This chapter will focus on the role out-of-home care plays on youth who are in foster care due to the incarceration of a parent. The barriers foster care youth with an incarcerated parent experience will be examined, and the intersection of parental criminal justice involvement and child welfare involvement will be explored. Protective factors, practice, and policy implications for human service professionals supporting youth in foster care who have an incarcerated parent will be shared.

INTRODUCTION

Children enter into the foster care systems in various ways. Foster care youth have been removed from their families by the court system or through voluntary foster care placement (i.e. a biological parent/guardian either unable or unwilling to take care of the child). Foster care is a temporary living situation in which youth can be placed temporarily with relatives (i.e., kinship foster care), in non-relative foster homes, in therapeutic or treatment care, or may live in a residential group home (Kirk, et l., 2013; Curtis, 1999). Longer-term placement options may include adoption or allowing the adolescent to age out of foster care at the age of 18 or 21 years-old. Some of the most common reasons that children are removed

DOI: 10.4018/978-1-7998-9209-0.ch007

from their homes and placed within foster care include neglect (61%), parental drug use (32%), the inability for caretaker to cope (14%), and physical abuse (13%) (U.S. Department of Health and Human Services, 2016). One entry point to foster care that presents various challenges to the mental, emotional, and behavioral stability and adult-sufficiency of youth are those with an incarcerated parent.

A risk factor for a child's involvement with a local child protective services (CPS) is parental involvement in the criminal justice system (Gifford et al., 2020). This may occur due to the parent violating criminal laws while also behaving in ways that could endanger their children, or violating laws related to parent abuse and neglect (Gifford et al., 2020). Child welfare involvement and parental incarceration may also occur due to other risk factors such as family instability and dysfunction, poverty, parental mental illness, increased neighborhood violence, maternal history of physical and sexual abuse, and parental substance abuse (Hoffman et al., 2010; Williams, 2017). For example, parents' substance use can lead to their criminal involvement while also insinuating that the home environment is unsafe for a child, thus leading to CPS involvement (Austin, 2016). It may also occur if the parent being involved in the criminal justice system causes a hindrance on familial resources which can then increase the risk for child maltreatment (Kirk & Wakefield, 2018). Moreover, it may occur when a parent's incarceration and absence from the home forces a child's placement into the foster care system (Gifford et al., 2020). According to U.S. data collected from 2002-2011, research found that higher adult incarceration rates were affiliated with higher caseloads for foster care (Edwards, 2016). In 2017, seven percent of youth were in foster care due to the incarceration of a parent (U.S. Department of Health and Human Services, Administration for Children and Families, Administration on Children, Youth and Families, & Children's Bureau, 2018). Other research indicated that 20-30% of foster care youth have an incarcerated parent (Seymore, 2001). Furthermore, parental incarceration is recognized as an adverse childhood experience (ACE) with a distinguishing factor from other ACE's being the combination of stigma, trauma, and shame associated with a child having an incarcerated parent (Hairston, 2007). Yet, the children of incarcerated parents are often understudied when it comes addressing the issues and needs of foster care youth (Haywood & DePanfilis, 2007).

Foster care youth tend to have a higher rate of juvenile justice system involvement as compared to non-foster care youth (Zlotnick et al., 2012). Research noted that foster care youth are more likely to engage in criminal behaviors as a result of a number of issues such as an unstable living environment, school issues and absences, and substance abuse and untreated mental health concerns (Bruskas, 2008; Neely-Barnes, 2011; Zlotnick et al., 2012). Furthermore, researchers noted that youth who "age out" of the foster care system at 18-years-old are more likely to be incarcerated as adults. In this regard, 25% of youth formerly in foster care will be incarcerated within the first two years upon leaving the foster care system (Zlotnick et al., 2012; Sloan, 2014). These concerns speak to the growing need for human service professionals and supportive adults to provide prevention services to youth while in foster care in an effort to reduce the number of foster care youth being dually involved in the juvenile justice system. It is, however, important to note that there is often a misperception that children who have an incarcerated parent are more likely to be predisposed to criminal activity or more likely to be incarcerated as compared to their peers, yet there is no existing research to confirm this notion (National Resource Center on Children & Families of the Incarcerated, 2014).

This chapter will focus on the role out-of-home care plays on youth who are in foster care due to the incarceration of a parent. The barriers foster care youth with an incarcerated parent experience will be examined, and the intersection of parental criminal justice involvement and child welfare involvement will be explored. Protective factors, such as a nurturing and strong caregiver experience, that buffer the effect of parental incarceration will be shared (Denby, 2012). Practice and policy implications for human service professionals (e.g. counselors, social workers, educators, advocates, and public figures) who support youth in foster care who have an incarcerated parent will be shared.

BARRIERS EXPERIENCED

Shaw et al., (2015) revealed a gap in literature on out-of-home care and the role parental incarceration has on the trajectory of children navigating the child welfare system, including placement. Foster care youth who have an incarcerated parent experience multiple barriers as it relates to family reunification, home stability, adult self-sufficiency, and education. The authors of this chapter highlight the various barriers herein.

Family Reunification

According to the Adoption and Safe Families Act (ASFA) of 1997 (P.L. 105-89), once a child or adolescent is placed in out-of-home care, the importance of achieving permanency for the youth via reunification with their families in a timely fashion is emphasized (U.S. Department of Health and Human Services [DHHS], 2000). In particular, the Adoption and Safe Families Act first had the goal of enhancing the permanency of foster care youth and limiting the time youth spent in foster care which simultaneously limited the time parents are able to reunify with their children (Williams, 2017). Research noted that of the approximately 251,359 children who exited foster care during the 2019 federal fiscal year, they spent a medium of 15.5 months in foster care (Child Welfare Information Gateway, 2019). In this regard, ASFA attempted to reduce the extended period that youth may spend in foster care without a connection to permanency. *Permanency* can be defined as "providing continuity of parenting, commitment to be a parent, and the legal and social status that comes from having a family of one's own" (Pasztor et al., 2015, p. 12). The term *family reunification* can be viewed on a continuum, ranging from family visitation to a child's physical return to their biological family (Maluccio et al., 1996). It is a process that is planned to safely reconnect youth who are in out-of-home care back with their families through the offering of various support and services to the children, families, foster caregivers or other service providers (Williams, 2017). Family reunification also attempts to support youth and their families with both achieving and maintaining their reconnection, whether it be the child fully reunifying with their families, visitations, phone calls, or any level of correspondence that might affirm the child's relationship with his or family (Pecora et al., 2010).

When a parent of a child is incarcerated, termination of parental rights (TPR) may be pursued faster than visitation and reunification, or visitation and reunification may not be pursued at all (Lee et al., 2005). Due to the ASFA, incarcerated parents tend to lose their parental rights at a disproportionate rate since it sets a concrete timeline for initiating the TPR, which is a child placement not exceeding 15 of the previous 22 months (National Resource Center on Children & Families of the Incarcerated, 2014). Yet, over the last few decades, the number of incarcerated parents has increased. Between 1991 and 2007, the number of parents who were incarcerated increased by 80 percent and in 2006, there were over 800,000 parents who were incarcerated (D'Andrade et al., 2012). One of the results of this growth was that foster care youth are more likely to have an incarcerated parent (D'Andrade et al., 2012). According to previous research, several factors impact parent-child reunification such as age, gender, race and ethnicity, child problems, family structure, and parental substance abuse, housing, and multiple problems. For instance, issues that might impact the likelihood to reunify include parental substance abuse, mental illness, and housing issues, difficulty find employment, difficulty obtaining public assistance, as well as children being placed in kinship care and prior removals from the home (Haywood & DePanfilis, 2007; (Phillips & Bloom, 1998). For instance, parents whose child has been removed from their care due to abuse or neglect are more than likely ordered by a juvenile court to complete a plan of services such as treatment for domestic violence, counseling, parenting classes, etc. (D'Andrade et al., 2012).

Agencies are required to assist parents with reunification such as offering services or making a community referral. This can assist the parent with resolving any of the issues that caused the child's removal from the home within twelve months, in order to be reunified. If the issues are not resolved in this timeframe, reunification services can end, and an agency may find a permanent home for the child (D'Andrade et al., 2012). In regard to reunification of a child with an incarcerated parent, the incarceration may not impact a parent's responsibility to both engage in these services, nor could it affect an agency's obligation to assist in the parent-child reunification process (D'Andrade et al., 2012). This, however, depends on the parent's incarceration sentence being no longer than the timeframe of the reunification process. Herein, it is conceivable that the incarceration of a parent can interfere with the reunification process that is administered by child welfare services. For example, there may be difficulty for incarcerated parents to gain access to available services, and these prison services may vary in quality and effectiveness (D'Andrade et al., 2012). As it relates to visitation, several factors are likely to be compromised due to parental incarceration such as a parent being incarcerated in a prison that is far away, as well as the challenges of transporting and accompanying the child to the prison by a caseworker or a foster caregiver. (D'Andrade et al., 2012). According to the National Resource Center on Children & Families of the Incarcerated (2014), 84 percent of parents in federal prisons and 62 percent of parents in state prisons are in prison over 100 miles away from where they lived; whereas 43 percent of parents in federal prisons are in prison over 500 miles away from where they used to live. Additionally, there are several prison visitation restrictions that are in place such as how often, how long, and what times individuals are able to visit (D'Andrade et al., 2012). This means that some children might never visit their incarcerated parent. According to research, 58 percent of mothers in prison reported having no visits from their children, whereas 59 percent of fathers reported having no visits from their children (National Resource Center on Children & Families of the Incarcerated, 2014). Correctional institutions also tend to restrict inmate communications, such as when a phone call could be made or received. Therefore, limited correspondence may hinder a caseworker from keeping an incarcerated parent informed on reunification matters (D'Andrade et al., 2012).

Research noted that when it comes to incarcerated mothers, 27 percent have had a child who had been placed in foster care at some time during the child's life (Moses, 2006). However, the mother's incarceration was not the reason the child was in foster care, with three-quarters of cases of foster care placement occurring prior to the mother experiencing her first incarceration (Moses, 2006). This finding helps to negate the myth that a mother's incarceration is a direct cause for a child's foster care placement. Furthermore, when it comes to the likelihood of reunification between an incarcerated mother and the child in comparison to all youth in foster care, other foster care youth are twice as likely to be reunited with their biological parents (40 percent) compared to youth in foster care with incarcerated mothers (20 percent; Moses, 2006). Impacting reunification are challenges with housing, economic challenges, placement setting, child's age and length of time in care (Howard & DePanfilis, 2007). Moreover, youth of incarcerated mothers are four times more likely to remain in foster care until they "age out" at 18-years old. These youth typically are not reunified with their parents but instead are either adopted, engage in independent living, decide to enter into some form of subsidized guardianship, or exit by some other form (Moses 2006). For instance, youth who have an incarcerated mother are more likely to be adopted compared to all foster care youth (Moses, 2006). These noted barriers speak to the ongoing concerns that must be addressed as it relates to the difficulty of family reunification for foster care youth with an incarcerated parent.

Kinship Foster Care Placement

Human services professionals will often seek placement (temporary to permanent) with family members or fictive kin (i.e., kinships foster caregivers and non-blood related familial connections) for youth entering foster care (Mackintosh, et al., 2006). The term *kinship care* was created by Child Welfare League of America (CWLA) and the National Foster Parent Association (NFPA) National Commission on Family Foster Care. Kinship care can be *formal* in that the child was taken into custody by protective services and then placed with a relative caregiver by the child welfare system (Pasztor & Petras, 2012). On the other hand, Kinship care can be *informal* in that the child is being taken care of by a relative caregiver without going through the formal process with the child welfare system (Pasztor & Petras, 2012).

Informal kinship foster care arrangements can present challenges addressing the child(ren)'s emotional and behavioral concerns (Phillips, Dettlaff, & Baldwin, 2010). For instance, frequent changes in schools, foster home placements, and a history of neglect and abuse all contribute to the need to address the behavioral and mental health needs of children in foster care. Lee, et al., (2015) reported that children in foster care are more likely to use multiple psychotropic medications than children not in the child welfare system. Further, children in foster care utilize mental health services at a rate five to eight times higher than other Medicaid eligible children (Lee, et al., 2015).

Kinship Foster care placements provide the child with a home setting and individuals the child may be familiar with. Children of incarcerated parents are typically placed with family caregivers via their removal by CPS or informal arrangement (Haywood & DePanfilis, 2007). Youth who are in kinship foster care placements are less likely to be reunified with their parents and tend to spend longer amounts of time within kinship foster care as compared to youth who are placed in non-relative care (Haywood & DePanfilis, 2007). However, placement with fictive kin/family caregivers may lead to conflicted loyalties with the child having to choose family friends over their blood relatives based on factors including, proximity to incarcerated parent(s), willingness to care for child, perceived stability of home environment, school, and other dependents in the family. Furthermore, placement with fictive kin/family caregivers may jeopardize the caregivers' ability to maintain social services benefits and result in discontinuation of care with a familial connection (Phillips, et al., 2010).

Educational, Adult Self-Sufficiency Needs

Shaw et al., (2015) have noted a paucity in research on the educational and career trajectory of foster children and those receiving child welfare benefits. Children in foster placement may enroll in multiple school settings resulting in academic losses, experience misidentification for special education programs, and inconsistent instruction across school districts and states. Furthermore, Kirk et al. (2013) noted that about 10% of former foster care youth were enrolled in college, and only 4% of these youth obtained a bachelor's degree. Foster care youth are also more likely to repeat a grade, be suspended or expelled or drop out of high school (Unrau, Font, & Rawls, 2012). In addition, little is known about foster care youth's readiness to engage in a postsecondary education, their developmental necessities during their transition to postsecondary education, and ways child welfare professionals can be of assistance (Williams et al., 2018; Unrau et al., 2012). In regard to adult self-sufficiency, only one third of foster care youth who have aged out of the foster care following their 18th birthday possessed a driver's license, own basic living necessities, or had money after leaving foster care (Pecora, Kessler, et al., 2006). These educational and adult self-sufficiency barriers experienced by foster care youth speak to the need for effective interventions and support that can be provided by human services professionals in order to improve their future outcomes.

HUMAN SERVICE INTERVENTIONS AND RECOMMENDATIONS

Human service professionals benefit from consultation and resource sharing. In order to address the barriers experienced by foster care youth with an incarcerated parent, human service professionals may benefit from information and solutions to address these barriers, while also providing protective factors such as practice implications, advocacy and theoretical approaches, and policy/practice chances. While these are not exhaustive recommendations, the authors' focus is to emphasize the psychosocial needs of foster care youth with an incarcerated parent and their foster families including data collection and tracking foster placements, preventions services and policy changes, Adverse Childhood Experiences (ACEs), engaging foster families, addressing educational needs and the use of evidenced-based therapeutic practices. Furthermore, the authors suggest future-oriented programming may generate positive outcomes and self-sufficiency for foster care youth with an incarcerated parent.

Data Collection and Tracking Foster Placements

Accurate data collection impacts effective intervention and requires accurate and timely data distribution (Phillips, Dettlaff, & Baldwin, 2010). While health professionals may know the number of children being placed in foster care, knowing the number of children in foster care due to the incarceration of a parent presents an opportunity to explore eventual family reunification needs. Furthermore, the needs of a child in foster care due to parental incarceration suggests their home may have been one without the trauma associated with abuse and neglect. The intervention needs of children placed because of neglect and abuse are different from the needs of a child in foster placement because the parent was removed from the home (James, 2004; Tonheim & Iversen, 2019). Providing foster families with support and follow-up contributes to fewer foster placements, improved behavioral outcomes, increased collaboration, and fewer placement mismatches that may contribute to placement disruptions (Crum, 2010; Geiger, et al., 2017; Konijn, et al., 2019; Tonheim & Iversen, 2019

Beginning with stronger local and state-level data collection will allow the needs of foster children of incarcerated parents to be tracked more efficiently. James (2004) noted the first 100 days of placement are critical in providing interventions. Too often familial placements are not tracked, not considered placement, and impact reunification after a parent's incarceration ends (Hayward & DePanfilis, 2007; James, 2004). Human service professionals can begin with tracking informal, kinship placements, and sibling placements. Tracking sibling sets will allow for family reunification efforts to be extended to siblings even when parental reunification is not possible. In order to build networks of data collection, local human services agencies should have a clearinghouse of shared data accessible statewide. The reliable input of demographic information, reasons for placement changes, and case notes with assessment and treatment interventions will allow for the continuation of care and services designed to address immediate needs, while also ensuring family reunification remains a primary treatment goal. Extending access to placement data across regions (e.g., southeast, mid-Atlantic, northeast) and at the federal level allows for interventions and reunification efforts to follow the child across placements.

Prevention Services and Policy Changes

It is important that the needs of foster families are addressed in order to meet the needs of foster care youth with an incarcerated parent. Utilizing prevention services coupled with behavioral interventions to generate positive outcomes will be essential to address the needs of these foster care youth and their caretaker(s). This may include policy changes that raise the age from 18 to 21 for youth to receive services by re-entering foster care or remaining in foster care when reunification is not possible due to the parent's incarceration term, or the ability for the parent to provide for the youth post-release. As it relates to diverse populations of foster care youth, implementing policies that may aid in changing the increasing number of African American children in foster care due to the incarceration of a parent is also needed (Williams, 2017). Herein, recognizing the unique needs of foster children who have an incarcerated parent, particularly those from diverse backgrounds, is a community initiative that requires involvement of multiple stakeholders, from human service professionals to state-level government officials, as well as from professionals who are champions for facilitating the needs of youth from diverse populations. These individuals must advocate for policy and funding structure changes designed to improve familial, health, and economic outcomes for families. For instance, human service professionals working with legislators may play an active role in sharing ideas, sponsoring partnerships, seeking grant funding, and developing relationships among stakeholders to provide programming designed to meet the needs of families and children (Williams-Mbengue, n.d.).

Adverse Childhood Experiences (ACEs) and Engaging Foster Families

Adverse Childhood Experiences (ACEs) are more common among foster care youth. Resulting from separation from parents, household substance use, violence, and abuse/neglect, children placed in foster care have experienced on average 2.5 ACEs. Furthermore, children in foster care are more likely to experience more ACEs and have a higher risk of ACEs than their non-foster placement counterparts (Turney & Wildeman, 2017). This data demonstrates the unique vulnerabilities of children in foster care and highlights the need for foster placement family counseling to address the mental health needs of foster care youth with an incarcerated parent who may have had exposure to multiple ACEs.

Foster families must be provided with on-going parental training to meet the specific needs of children, particularly those caring for children with a family history of trauma. The delivery of parenting education allows for foster families to access resources necessary to meet the needs of foster care youth with an incarcerated parent. Denby (2012) found that a strong, nurturing caregiver experience serves as a protective factor to buffer the effects of parental incarceration. Furthermore, the authors suggest providing for the needs of foster families will in turn aid them in better facilitating the needs of their foster children, as well as create a home environment that is stable and consistent.

Addressing mental health and behavioral needs is necessary to achieve permanence and combat any potential negative mental health outcomes of foster care youth. Engaging and educating foster families on the identification, assessment and treatment of mental health concerns builds upon change for the child and their host environment. Foster families can provide information that may be key to identifying the child's strengths and existing needs. Moreover, siblings may be able to offer insight into a foster child's current behaviors and any history from the family of origin. Overall, it is conceivable that foster families will benefit from connecting the needs of the child to treatment interventions, including foster parent education provided by a trained human services professional.

Addressing Educational Needs

Human services professionals may address the educational needs of students in foster care by connecting with their previous and current schools to ensure accurate educational records, such as 504 or Individual Education Plans (IEPs), are provided to the school. Receiving education records from previous schools will provide the school counselor or human services professional information needed for grade placement and implementation of federally mandated accommodations. Furthermore, school counselors or school social workers must be made aware of the home environment and familial status of the foster care youth in an effort to best advocate for their social/emotional, career, and academic developmental needs within the educational environment. This may be particularly important for students in foster care who may experience negative emotions at school related to their separation and loss of connection due to parental incarceration. For instance, using the American School Counselor Association (ASCA; 2019) model as a framework, school counselors can engage in direct and indirect student services such as individual or small-group counseling and referrals, consultation, collaboration with community stakeholders in an effort to provide the best support services for these foster care youth who have an incarcerated parent.

To further meet the needs of foster care youth with an incarcerated parent there needs to be a future planning focus. High school-aged students in foster care should be connected with vocational and career counseling resources to assess values, education plans, and career goals. The distribution of information for scholarships and state-level funding specific to foster care youth should be made readily available to human services professionals and further, to the foster care youth. Foster care youth must be made aware of state-level funding provided through programs like education training vouchers (ETV), Foster Care to Success (i.e. REACH funding), and federal grants made available through the completion of the Free Application for Federal Student Aid (FAFSA) (Foster Care to Success, n.d.). Pokempner (2019) noted the availability of Title IV-E funds to address the programming and policy changes necessary to serve older foster care youth. Increasing without the connection to another family through adoption, legal guardianship, or successful reunification, these youth are at a greater risk for poor adult outcomes (i.e., high school dropout/pushout, incarceration, employability/post-graduate training). Thus, funding for post-secondary education is necessary to meet the needs (e.g., financial, housing, educational costs) of children in foster care to obtain employment following their post-secondary training and foster care placement.

Use of Evidenced-Based Practices

In order to improve outcomes for youth in foster care, their mental health needs should be addressed through a number of evidence-based practices, including Trauma-Focused Cognitive Behavioral Therapy

(TF-CBT), Multi-Systemic Therapy (MST) for child abuse and neglect, Parent Child Interaction Therapy (PCIT), and Acceptance Commitment Therapy (ACT).

Trauma-Focused Cognitive Behavioral Therapy (TF-CBT)

Many youth experience multiple and chronic traumas which may be heightened for foster care youth with an incarcerated parent, such as experiencing maltreatment, domestic violence, neglect, or being separated from their biological family for extended periods of time. The cumulative effect of trauma may result in maladaptive coping, mental health diagnosis, the need to address posttraumatic stress disorder (PTSD), and associated behaviors (van der Kolk, 2007). Utilizing TF-CBT is one of many evidence-based practices that can be used by health services professionals to address the counseling needs of foster children with an incarcerated parent as well as their caregivers (Cohen, et al., 2012)

TF-CBT is designed to address a child's behaviors as a result of traumatic experiences, including abuse, neglect, and witness to violent acts. TF-CBT aims to improve a child's behavior and foster parents' skills and communication methods. Designed for children ages 3-18 years, TF-CBT incorporates techniques from cognitive therapy, behavioral therapy, and family system therapy. Cohen and Mannarino (2019) suggest TF-CBT be used to address the trauma related to separation. Addressing the fear children may have of further separation may be addressed with the foster family through the development of a safety plan. This may include the human services professional providing practical information related to how to access assistance, addressing questions about sibling placements, parent's safety, school changes, identifying trusted adults, addressing child's fear of separation, and fear of future interactions with law enforcement and child protective services. Human services professionals should provide factual information to the child to build a trusting relationship and address the psychosocial impact as a result of trauma. Moreover, addressing the parenting needs of foster families to manage behavioral problems may also use a TF-CBT approach. Cohen, et al. (2012) suggest an extended period of time be spent on addressing coping skills and safety, while recognizing there may be times of trial and error used to find the coping skills that lead to relaxation, sense of safety and addressing the neurological impact of trauma.

While the focus of TF-CBT is on the child, a trauma-focused professional will recognize the importance of using the foster family in treatment. Particular focus may be on the child and caregiver's relationship. Providing the foster family with the tools to identify problematic behaviors (e.g., self-injury), utilizing coping skills, recognizing source of behavior is trauma, and having factual information about previous trauma and social history (Cohen & Mannarino, 2019). Engaging the child in setting routines and leading activities may prove to create a sense of power and trust in the foster home (NCTSN, 2018). This will require foster parent commitment to the process that may include repeated intervention, practice, role play and through trial and error fine tuning unsuccessful coping strategies (Cohen, et al., 2012).

Multi-Systemic Therapy (MST)

MST is focused on meeting the needs of children with serious physical abuse or neglect in their history where services are provided within the home rather than in a human services professional's office (Schowenwald, 2008; Henggeler & Schaeffer, 2010). MST is an integration of theories and intervention models. The application of MST through family therapy may address the multiple risk factors impacting foster care youth who have an incarcerated parent. Social learning theory is incorporated in treatment, which is focused on addressing how parents interact and communicate with children who may have behavior problems. Utilizing family therapy for the delivery of behavioral interventions, MST has proven effective at improving familial relations, decreasing maladaptive behaviors, and improving interactions with other systems, including school and social services systems. This therapeutic approach is designed for families with children ages 6-17 years. MST assumes that individuals exist within a social ecology of multiple systems each influencing one another. Therefore, for proper assessment and introduction of interventions, health service professionals need to consider the reciprocal nature by which each system affects the children they serve through direct and indirect approaches (Henggeler & Schaeffer, 2010; Henggeler, Sheidow et al., 2009).

MST relies on caregivers as the conduit for interventions. This will require human service professionals to empower them with the resources, skills, and training needed to be effective with their foster children, and in turn, strengthen the family support system. Building upon the success of the family, a human services professional may begin to implement additional interventions across school and community contexts with the ultimate goal of building systems of support for the foster youth that promote positive mental well-being, academic outcomes, and post-placement employability.

MST's assessment process also recognizes the caregiver may need treatment for mental health needs. Caregivers may suggest the foster child be the focus of treatment, however, MST's effectiveness may be hindered by the caregiver's unmet mental health issues. Recognizing the caregiver's mental health needs are connected to the welfare of the child, human service professionals may have to convince the caregiver to seek treatment if needed. Therefore, dual treatment for caregiver and child allow for the MST approach to determine if the foster youth's behavioral problems are connected to trauma, co-existing condition (e.g., ADHD, anxiety, depression) and then employ evidence-based approaches recognizing the behaviors are connected to the system and not the individual.

Parent Child Interaction Therapy (PCIT)

PCIT is designed specifically for younger children to address defiance, aggression, and other behavioral problems. The goal of PCIT is to improve the child's social skills and improve the caretaker-child relationship. PCIT may take advantage of the foster family's influence in addressing acting out and misbehavior through short-term treatment, role play, modeling, coaching, and teaching the foster parents play therapy skills. This intervention is also useful at child-parent reunification and provides the parent coaching to address the parent-child relationship through improved communication and recognizing the importance of modeling desired behaviors (Woodfield & Cartwright, 2020).

PCIT is a combination of play therapy, behavioral play therapy and Filial Therapy. There are seven steps involved with PCIT: (a) pre-treatment assessment of child and foster family functioning and feedback, (b) teaching behavioral play therapy skills, (c) coaching behavioral play therapy, (d) teaching discipline techniques and approaches, (e) coaching discipline skills, (f) post-treatment assessment of child and foster family functioning and feedback, and (g) boosters, as needed to reinforce new skills learned. While there are limits to PCITs, it has demonstrated repeated success for addressing acting-out behaviors that may be connected to trauma history, conduct disorder, disruptive mood dysregulation, disorder,attention deficit hyperactivity disorder, and oppositional defiant disorder) (Eyberg & Funderbunk, 2011; Levac, et al., 2008; McNeil, et al., 2005).

Acceptance Commitment Therapy (ACT)

ACT addresses behavior change by connecting context and optimal outcomes to existing overt and covert behaviors that may be triggered by negative thought patterns. ACT grew out of cognitive-behavioral approaches and provides greater flexibility in understanding and changing behaviors (Hayes, et al., 2006; Hayes & Strosahl, 2004; Luoma & Vilardaga, 2013). Children with incarcerated parents experiencing foster placement may engage in new coping strategies to address feelings of loss, grief, confusion, and insecurity. They may engage in emotional outbursts (overt) or self-injurious behaviors (covert) designed to express frustration over their new reality. In this instance, the use of ACT can provide a focus on producing meaningful behavioral change through systematic interventions consistent with achieving positive client life outcomes (Hayes & Strosahl, 2004).

ACT uses behavioral interventions, such as skills acquisition, psychosocial education, shaping, goal setting, and contingency management to change the relationship between cognition and emotion (covert self) and overt behaviors that show up in school, work, and at home. ACT treatment seeks to broaden the behavioral repertoire that children-clients can pull from to govern their covert self. Using an ACT perspective suggests that context determines the function of a behavior rather than seeing that behavior as a property of the event itself. This suggests that employing ACT aids in manipulating the environment or context in which targeted behaviors occur. The goal is to alter the degree to which cognition and emotions impact the behaviors they evoke (Hayes & Strosahl, 2004).

ACT is characterized by its goal to promote psychological flexibility, which involves effectively adapting one's environment to behave in ways that best align with personally recognized values (Hayes & Strosahl, 2004). It is important for foster caregivers to understand the use of ACT does not thrive in rigid, rule-governed environments. Allowing the foster care youth an opportunity to share their understanding of and development of house rules and familial expectation may be beneficial in promoting ACTs goal for acceptance, cognitive defusion, contact with the present model, committed action, and values. This way of living is contrasted with rigid, rule-governed behavior dominated by avoidance, which is seen in ACT as the natural, but problematic consequence of language and cognition (Hayes & Strosahl, 2004). This quality is referred to as psychological inflexibility and is posited as a fundamental aspect of psychopathology (Coyne, et al., 2011; Hayes et al., 2012). Connecting interventions to psychological flexibility can increase one's use of behavioral contingencies aligned with goals and can increase alignment between the covert and overt self through behaviors designed to address environmental changes.

Human service professionals facilitating the needs of foster care youth who have an incarcerated parent, along with supporting their foster families, can provide meaningful outcomes for the foster care youth. In doing so, these professionals can aid in helping these youth achieve potential successful reunification, adult self-sufficiency, and improved educational and mental health outcomes. While it is conceivable that the recommendations presented in the chapter may help to facilitate the needs of *all* youth in foster care regardless of their parental care status; recognizing the unique concerns needs of foster care youth with an incarcerated parent may better encourage human service professionals to increase their advocacy efforts and support for this particular sub-population of foster care youth. In an effort to provide further resources to human service professionals, suggested websites and web-based resources are presented herein to address the needs of foster care youth with an incarcerated parent. These resources may be used to implement interventions or provide information to human services professionals engaged in work with foster care youth who have an incarcerated parent.

REFERENCES

American School Counselor Association. (2019). *ASCA national model: A framework for school counseling programs*. Author.

Austin, A. (2016). Is prior parental criminal justice involvement associated with child maltreatment? A systematic review. *Children and Youth Services Review*, *68*, 146–153. doi:10.1016/j.childyouth.2016.07.008

Bruskas, D. (2008). Children in foster care: A vulnerable population at risk. *Journal of Child and Adolescent Psychiatric Nursing*, *21*(2), 70–77. doi:10.1111/j.1744-6171.2008.00134.x PMID:18429837

Child Welfare Information Gateway. (2019). *Foster care statistics 2019*. Washington, DC: U.S. Department of Health and Human Services, Children's Bureau. Retrieved from https://www.childwelfare.gov/pubPDFs/foster.pdf

Cohen, J. A., & Mannarino, A. P. (2019). Trauma-Focused cognitive behavioral therapy for childhood traumatic separation. *Child Abuse & Neglect*, *92*, 179–195. doi:10.1016/j.chiabu.2019.03.006 PMID:30999167

Cohen, J. A., Mannarino, A. P., Kliethermes, M., & Murray, L. A. (2012). Trauma-focused CBT for youth with complex trauma. *Child Abuse & Neglect*, *36*(6), 528–541. doi:10.1016/j.chiabu.2012.03.007 PMID:22749612

Coyne, L. W., McHugh, L., & Martinez, E. R. (2011). Acceptance and commitment therapy (ACT): Advances and applications with children, adolescents, and families. *Child and Adolescent Psychiatric Clinics of North America*, *20*(2), 379–399. doi:10.1016/j.chc.2011.01.010 PMID:21440862

Crum, W. (2010). Foster parent parenting characteristics that lead to increased placement stability or disruption. *Children and Youth Services Review*, *32*(2), 185–190. doi:10.1016/j.childyouth.2009.08.022

Curtis, P. (1999). The chronic nature of the foster care crisis. In P. Curtis, G. Dale Jr, & J. Kendall (Eds.), *The foster care crisis: Translating research into policy and practice* (pp. 1–13). University of Nebraska Press.

D'Andrade, A., & Valdez, M. (2012). Reunifying from behind bars: A quantitative study of the relationship between parental incarceration, service use, and foster care reunification. *Social Work in Public Health*, *27*(6), 616–636. doi:10.1080/19371918.2012.713294 PMID:22963161

Denby, R. (2012). Parental incarceration and kinship care: Caregiver experiences, child well-being, and permanency intentions. *Social Work in Public Health*, *27*(1/2), 104–128. doi:10.1080/19371918.2012.639639 PMID:22239381

Edwards, F. (2016). Saving children, controlling families: Punishment, redistribution, and child protection. *American Sociological Review*, *81*(3), 575–595. doi:10.1177/0003122416638652

Eyberg, S. M., & Funderburk, B. (2011). *Parent-child interaction therapy protocol. PCIT International, INC*. PCIT International.

Geiger, J. M., Piel, M. H., & Julien-Chinn, F. (2017). Improving relationships in child welfare practice: Perspectives of foster care providers. *Child & Adolescent Social Work Journal*, *34*(1), 23–33. doi:10.100710560-016-0471-3

Gifford, E. J., Evans, K. E., Eldred Kozecke, L., & Sloan, F. A. (2020). Mothers and fathers in the criminal justice system and children's child protective services involvement. *Child Abuse & Neglect, 101*. https://doi-org.ezproxy.nccu.edu/10.1016/j.chiabu.2019.104306

Hairston, C. F. (2007). *Focus on the children with incarcerated parents: A overview of the research literature.* Annie E. Casey Foundation. Retrieved from https://assets.aecf.org/m/resourcedoc/aecf-FocusonChildrenwith_ncarceratedParentsOverviewofLiterature-2007.pdf

Hayes, S. C., Luoma, J. B., Bond, F. W., Masuda, A., & Lillis, J. (2006). Acceptance and Commitment Therapy: Model, processes and outcomes. *Behaviour Research and Therapy*, *44*(1), 1–25. doi:10.1016/j.brat.2005.06.006 PMID:16300724

Hayes, S. C., & Strosahl, K. D. (2004). *A Practical Guide to Acceptance and Commitment Therapy*. Springer Science & Business Media. doi:10.1007/978-0-387-23369-7

Hayward, R. A., & DePanfilis, D. (2007). Foster children with an incarcerated parent: Predictors of reunification. *Children and Youth Services Review*, *29*(10), 1320–1334. doi:10.1016/j.childyouth.2007.05.005

Henggeler, S. W., & Schaeffer, C. (2010). Treating serious antisocial behavior using multisystemic therapy. In J. R. Weisz & A. E. Kazdin (Eds.), *Evidence-based psychotherapies for children and adolescents* (2nd ed., pp. 259–276). Guilford Press.

Henggeler, S. W., Schoenwald, S. K., Borduin, C. M., Rowland, M. D., & Cunningham, P. B. (2009). *Multisystemic therapy for antisocial behavior in children and adolescents* (2nd ed.). Guilford Press.

Henggeler, S. W., Sheidow, A. J., & Lee, T. (2009). Multisystemic therapy (MST). In J. H. Bray & M. Stanton (Eds.), The Wiley-Blackwell handbook of family psychology. Wiley-Blackwell.

Hoffmann, H. C., Byrd, A. L., & Kightlinger, A. M. (2010). Prison programs and services for incarcerated parents and their underage children: Results from a national survey of correctional facilities. *The Prison Journal*, *90*(4), 397–416. doi:10.1177/0032885510382087

James, S. (2004). Why Do Foster Care Placements Disrupt? An Investigation of Reasons for Placement Change in Foster Care. *The Social Service Review*, *78*(4), 601–627. doi:10.1086/424546

Kirk, C. M., Lewis, R. K., Nilsen, C., & Colvin, D. Q. (2013). Foster care and college: The educational aspirations and expectations of youth in the foster care system. *Youth & Society*, *45*(3), 307–323. doi:10.1177/0044118X11417734

Kirk, D. S., & Wakefield, S. (2018). Collateral consequences of punishment: A critical review and path forward. *Annual Review of Criminology*, *1*(1), 171–194. doi:10.1146/annurev-criminol-032317-092045

Konijn, C., Admiraal, S., Baart, J., van Rooij, F., Stams, G., Colonnesi, C., Lindauer, R., & Assink, M. (2019). Foster care placement instability: A meta-analytic review. *Children and Youth Services Review*, *96*, 483–499. doi:10.1016/j.childyouth.2018.12.002

Lee, A. F., Genty, P. M., & Laver, M. (2005). *The impact of the adoption and safe families act on children of incarcerated parents*. Child Welfare League of America.

Lee, T., Fouras, G., & Brown, R.American Academy of Child and Adolescent Psychiatry (AACAP) Committee of Quality Issues (CQI). (2015). Practice parameter for the assessment and management of youth involved with the child welfare system. *Journal of the American Academy of Child and Adolescent Psychiatry*, *54*(6), 502–517. doi:10.1016/j.jaac.2015.03.005 PMID:26004666

Levac, A. M., McCay, E., Merka, P., & Reddon-D'Arcy, M. L. (2008). Exploring parent participation in a parent training program for children's aggression: Understanding and illuminating mechanisms of change. *Journal of Child and Adolescent Psychiatric Nursing*, *21*(2), 78–88. doi:10.1111/j.1744-6171.2008.00135.x PMID:18429838

Luoma, J. B., & Vilardaga, J. P. (2013). Improving therapist psychological flexibility while training acceptance and commitment therapy: A pilot study. *Cognitive Behaviour Therapy*, *42*(1), 1–8. doi:10.1080/16506073.2012.701662 PMID:23505991

Mackintosh, V. H., Myers, B. J., & Kennon, S. S. (2006). Children of incarcerated mothers and their caregivers: Factors affecting the quality of their relationship. *Journal of Child and Family Studies*, *15*(5), 581–596. doi:10.100710826-006-9030-4

Maluccio, A. N., Abramczyk, L. W., & Thomlison, B. (1996). Family reunification of children in out-of-home care: Research perspectives. *Children and Youth Services Review*, *18*(4/5), 287–305. doi:10.1016/0190-7409(96)00007-2

McNeil, C. B., Herschell, A. D., Gurwitch, R. H., & Clemens-Mowrer, L. (2005). Training foster parents in parent-child interaction therapy. *Education & Treatment of Children*, *28*(2), 182–196.

Moses, M. C. (2006). Correlating Incarcerated mothers, foster care and mother-child reunification. *Corrections Today*, *68*(6), 98–100.

National Child Traumatic Stress Network. (2018). *Giving voice to immigrant children: Understanding traumatic separation.* https://www.nctsn.org/resources/giving-immigrant-children-voice-understanding-traumatic-separation

National Resource Center on Children & Families of the Incarcerated. (2014). *Children and families of the incarcerated fact sheet*. Retrieved from https://nrccfi.camden.rutgers.edu/fil es/nrccfi-fact-sheet-2014.pdf

Neely-Barnes, S., & Whitted, K. (2011). Examining the social, emotional, and behavioral needs of youth involved in the child welfare and juvenile justice system. *Journal of Health & Human Services*, 206-239.

Pasztor, E. M., & Petras, D. D. (2012). Selecting foster parents: What to expect and ask. In K. Phagan-Hansel (Ed.), *The foster parenting toolbox: A practical, hands-on approach to parenting children in foster care* (pp. 4–8). EMK Press.

Pasztor, E. M., Petras, D. D., Stogel, S., Heilman, C., Chavez, R., & Boylan, B. (2015). *Essential requirements for permanency*. Fostering Families Today.

Pecora, P., Whittaker, J., Maluccio, A., Barth, R., DePanfilis, D., & Plotnik, R. (2010). *The child welfare challenge – Policy, practice, and research.* Transaction Publishers.

Phillips, S., & Bloom, B. (1998). In whose best interest? The impact of changing public policy on relatives caring for children with incarcerated parents. *Child Welfare*, *76*(5), 531–541. PMID:9744072

Phillips, S. D., Dettlaff, A. J., & Baldwin, M. J. (2010). An exploratory study of the range of implications of families' criminal justice system involvement in child welfare cases. *Children and Youth Services Review*, *32*(4), 544–550. doi:10.1016/j.childyouth.2009.11.008

Pokempner, J. (2019). Leveraging the FFPSA for older youth: Prevention Provisions. *Children's Rights Litigation*, *21*(2), 13–18.

Schoenwald, S. K. (2008). Towards evidence-based transport of evidence-based treatments: MST as an example. *Journal of Child & Adolescent Substance Abuse*, *17*(3), 69–91. doi:10.1080/15470650802071671

Schoenwald, S. K., Halliday-Boykins, C. A., & Henggeler, S. W. (2003). Client-level predictors of adherence to MST in community service settings. *Family Process*, *42*(3), 345–359. doi:10.1111/j.1545-5300.2003.00345.x PMID:14606199

Seymour, C. (2001). Children with parents in prison: Child welfare policy, program, and practice issues. In C. Seymour & C. F. Hairston (Eds.), *Children with parents in prison: Child welfare policy, program & practice issues*. Transaction Press.

Shaw, T. V., Bright, C. L., & Sharpe, T. L. (2015). Child welfare outcomes for youth in care as a result of parental death or parental incarceration. *Child Abuse & Neglect*, *42*, 112–120. doi:10.1016/j.chiabu.2015.01.002 PMID:25641050

Sloan, M. (2014). *Differentiating Factors between Foster Youth and Non-Foster Youth Involved in the Juvenile-Justice System* (Order No. 3622814). Available from ProQuest Central; ProQuest Dissertations & Theses Global. (1548983942). http://nclive.org.ezproxy.nccu.edu/cgi-bin/nclsm?url=http://search.proquest.com.ezproxy.nccu.edu/dissertations-theses/differentiating-factors-between-foster-youth-non/docview/1548983942/se-2?accountid=12713

Tonheim, M., & Iversen, A. C. (2019). "We felt completely left to ourselves." Foster parents' views on placement disruption. *Child & Family Social Work*, *24*(1), 90–97. http://dx.doi.org.ezproxy.nccu.edu/10.1111/cfs.12585. doi:10.1111/cfs.12585

Turney, K., & Wildeman, C. (2017). Adverse childhood experiences anoint children placed in and adopted from foster care: Evidence from a nationally representative survey. *Child Abuse & Neglect*, *64*, 117–129. doi:10.1016/j.chiabu.2016.12.009 PMID:28086178

Unrau, Y. A., Font, S. A., & Rawls, G. (2012). Readiness for college engagement among students who have aged out of foster care. *Children and Youth Services Review*, *34*(1), 76–83. doi:10.1016/j.childyouth.2011.09.002

U.S. Department of Health and Human Services. (2017). Administration for Children and Families, Administration on Children, & Youth and Families Children's Bureau (2018). *Child Maltreatment*, 1–261.

U.S. Department of Health and Human Services, Administration for Children and Families, Administration on Children, Youth and Families, & Children's Bureau (2018). *The AFCARS Report: Preliminary FY 2017 estimates as of September 24, 2018 - Number 251–6*. Author.

U.S. Department of Health and Human Services. (2018, November 8). *Trends in Foster Care & Adoption: FY 2010- 2019*. The Administration for Children and Families. https://www.acf.hhs.gov/cb/report/trends-foster-care-adoption-2019

van der Kolk, B. A. (2007). The Developmental Impact of Childhood Trauma. In L. J. Kirmayer, R. Lemelson, & M. Barad (Eds.), *Understanding trauma: Integrating biological, clinical, and cultural perspectives* (pp. 224–241). Cambridge University Press. doi:10.1017/CBO9780511500008.016

Williams, B. (2017). *The Impact on Reunification for Families with Incarcerated Parents: A Policy Analysis of the Adoption and Safe Families Act of 1997*. Available from ProQuest Central. (1964285542). http://nclive.org.ezproxy.nccu.edu/cgi-bin/nclsm?url=http://search.proquest.com.ezproxy.nccu.edu/dissertations-theses/impact-on-reunification-families-with/docview/1964285542/se-2?accountid=12713

Williams, R. G., Baker, S. B., & Williams-DeVane, C. R. (2018). Effects of customized Counseling Interventions on Career and College Readiness Self-Efficacy of Three Female Foster Care Youth. *The Professional Counselor*, *8*(2), 159–174. doi:10.15241/rgw.8.2.159

Williams-Mbengue, N. (n.d.) *The social and emotional well-being of children in foster care*. National Conference of State Legislatures. Retrieved from: https://www.ncsl.org/Portals/1/Documents/cyf/Social_Emotional_WellBeing_Newsletter.pdf

Woodfield, M. J., & Cartwright, C. (2020). Parent-Child Interaction Therapy from the Parents' Perspective. *Journal of Child and Family Studies*, *29*(3), 632–647. http://dx.doi.org.ezproxy.nccu.edu/10.1007/s10826-019-01611-5. doi:10.100710826-019-01611-5

Zlotnick, C., Tammy, T. W., & Soman, L. A. (2012). Life course outcomes on mental 104 and physical health: The impact of foster care on adulthood. *American Journal of Public Health*, *102*(3), 534–541. doi:10.2105/AJPH.2011.300285 PMID:22390519

Section 3

Developing Strategies to Support those Impacted by Incarceration and Reduce Recidivism

Chapter 8
Counseling Strategies to Disrupt the School–Prison Nexus

Joy Gray
Pennsylvania State University, USA

ABSTRACT

The school-prison nexus is comprised of all systems and services that reduce access to education and increase involvement with the justice system, particularly for clients of color. All professionals who come into contact with these services are in an ideal position to disrupt this system and address social inequities; however, they may overtly or covertly also be contributing to the nexus through inequitable practices. Consequently, this chapter will firstly explore how the school-prison nexus contributes to incarceration, including an exploration of how the systems in which counselors and other helping professionals are integral to this nexus through racist practices. The chapter then moves on to suggest ways in which helping professionals can work to disrupt this nexus in their work. These strategies to disrupt the school-prison nexus focus on how examining professional bias and applying a systems-based approach to practice can assist in achieving the social change necessary to end the criminalization of youth of color and address the impacts of incarceration before it happens.

INTRODUCTION

It is well documented that school disciplinary policies disproportionately impact children of color and that these practices retraumatize youth and contribute to the criminalization of children (Department of Education and Office for Civil Rights, 2017; Dutil, 2020; Muñiz, 2021; Nellis, 2016; Novak, 2019). They continue to experience explicit discrimination through the placing of Black students with disabilities into less inclusive environments in educational settings than their White counterparts (White et al., 2019). This segregation is seen within special education classrooms, within the school as a whole, and within the communities that these school are located, reducing access to education and resources and increasing isolation, seclusion, and stigmatization (White et al., 2019). The criminalization of youth of

DOI: 10.4018/978-1-7998-9209-0.ch008

color is also demonstrated when they are subjected to juvenile facilities and adult justice systems whilst they are still juveniles; experiences not reported by their White counterparts (Blankenship et al., 2018). Additionally, racism and bias in educational and mental health systems has historically interpreted race-based traumatic stress and resistance against racism as an individual problem of behavior conduct (Atkins-Loria et al., 2015). Atkins-Loria and colleagues (2015) noted one example of this pathologizing interpretation of race-based trauma includes disproportionate conduct disorder diagnoses, which leads to the modern colonization and criminalization of youth of color.

Recognition of the school-prison nexus has resulted in the recommendation of practices to disrupt inequities in the school system. Restorative justice practices are one practice recommended for use within schools to mitigate racial disparity in school disciplinary practices as a move away from punitive punishment and towards understanding and healing (Schiff, 2018), as well as implementation of non-pathologizing approach to diagnosing race-based traumatic stress (Carter, 1990; Carter et al., 2019). Researchers also suggest a model of optimal development and nurturing for all professionals that are involved with youth (Basile et al., 2019; Graham et al., 2017) as well as understanding of personal bias (Mcneal, 2014; Ratts et al., 2016) and identifying and elevating community strengths (Vera & Speight, 2003). Such approaches are consistent with the multicultural and social justice counseling competencies described by Ratts and colleagues (2016).

This chapter will firstly provide a comprehensive overview of how racist systems interconnect and result in criminalization and incarceration for youth of color. Topics covered include racism in school settings and the pathologizing of racial trauma and will focus on the role of helping professionals in the school-prison nexus and the harm that is being done when services are provided in a culturally unaware and insensitive manner. The chapter will then move to explore strategies that counselors can utilize to disrupt the harmful outcomes of the school-prison nexus previously described. These strategies include confronting and challenging personal biases, anti-racist counselor education, broaching, culturally aware diagnostic processes, restorative practices, and community social justice advocacy. Counselors must integrate these strategies into a systemic anti-racist, strength-based approach to their work to actively work against harmful structures that make up the school-prison nexus.

Defining the School-Prison Nexus

There is a significant literature base analyzing and describing the school-to-prison pipeline, as well as mass incarceration and the prison-industrial complex. This "pipeline" is described as comprising of school policies and social norms that introduce children to the justice system (Barnes, & Motz, 2018; Heitzeg, 2009; Meiners, 2011; Owens, 2017; Rocque, & Snellings, 2018). Rather than tracking students into further or specialized education, the school-to-prison pipeline tracks students out of school and into carceral facilities (Heitzeg, 2009). The tracking of children out of school can be through explicit means, such as expulsion and suspension, or through implicit processes that disengage students with the school system at large. Examples of such processes include interpreting and labelling normative behaviors as conduct problems and punishing those perceived problems and not engaging, acknowledging, or allowing students to express themselves in ways that are differing from majority culture.

Though this pipeline identifies some aspects of criminalization of children, the idea of a singular structure is misleading. For this reason, the school-to-prison pipeline terminology has been criticized as a simplistic metaphor that is in danger of missing more complex thinking needed to address all of the systems involved with the criminalization, punishment, and incarceration of youth (Mcgrew, 2016).

For example, a focus simply on zero-tolerance policies may miss implicit processes that encourage disengagement such as feelings of disconnectedness. Due to all of the processes that encourage disengagement in education and increase interactions with the justice system within schools education also needs to be considered as part of the prison-industrial complex (Meiners, 2011). It is important to note that the school-to-prison pipeline terminology is discussed throughout literature inconsistently; at times referring only to school-specific procedures in isolation (Owens, 2017), and at others acknowledging and including all of the systems that contextually inform the pipeline structures (Barnes & Motz, 2018; Heitzeg, 2009). The school-prison nexus, as coined by Meiners (2011), intentionally refers to systems and services that criminalize youth of color and place barriers to their success by decreasing access to education and increasing interactions with disciplinary processes and the justice system (Dutil, 2020; McCarter, 2017; Mcneal, 2014; Meiners, 2011). Given that these systems and services disproportionately target youth of color, a discussion of the connection between school and prison must include a discussion of racism and discrimination. This definition of a nexus includes and expands on the impact of school policies and describes the criminalization of youth as interconnected systems and services, including contextual and social factors. Additionally, the American Psychological Association has released guidelines on inclusive language which describe that the term pipeline is a microaggression regarding the historical and contemporary traumas experienced by Indigenous communities (American Psychological Association, 2021). This chapter will therefore be using the school-prison nexus as terminology to describe this phenomenon.

Brief History of the School-Prison Nexus

The recent funding and expansion of private prisons and the prison-industrial complex continues a long history of denying education to youth of color as well as youth of low social-economic status and with disabilities, which the school-prison nexus works to maintain. The racist systems and individuals that made explicit racial segregation and discrimination following the use of chattel slavery continue to ensure that access to resources, including education, is grossly inequitable (Meiners, 2011). Meiners (2011) describes how in the United States oppressed groups have historically been treated as necessary for exploited labor but excluded from full democratic rights. Utilizing residential schools to assist the cultural destruction of First Nations and apartheid segregation, education was one way in which groups of people were systematically oppressed, disadvantaged, and traumatized. This funneled oppressed groups into non-living wage labor and removed access to any further resources, education, or higher-wage positions. Though de jure segregation removes these outcomes in principle, the impact and continued implementation of de facto segregation continues to bolster the school-prison nexus for students of color.

Additionally, professionals in supposed 'helping' fields including physical and mental health staff have been historically instrumental in the oppression of certain groups. The unethical and extremely harmful experimentation in Tuskegee on African American men with syphilis demonstrates one way in which medical professionals have actively withheld treatments and caused generational pain and suffering in low-income, Black communities (Howell, 2017). This type of oppression continues today, with significant inequities in access to care and treatments and disproportionate rates of chronic health conditions and maternal mortality experienced by Black women (Chinn et al., 2021). The limiting of equitable, culturally responsive, and effective care is one way in which individuals are denied full democratic rights and denied resources within society. This systematic medical oppression perpetuates concerns of poverty, chronic and acute physical and mental illness, and lack of resources, feeding into the school-prison nexus indirectly. For example, limiting career opportunities based on eligibility for medical insurance coverage or keeping families and individuals in crisis to ensure basic needs are met. Furthermore, deliberate harm towards communities results in an adaptive survival strategy of distrust of future helping professionals. It is therefore clear that helping professionals have an imperative to work actively against complicity with the nexus and provide care that works to address inequities as a matter of civil rights.

COUNSELING AND THE SCHOOL-PRISON NEXUS

As described, the school-prison nexus includes any and all services and systems that criminalize youth, decrease their access to education, and increase their interactions with the justice system. Given the clinical and educational settings in which counselors work, it follows that they will be in ideal positions to make immediate and direct change within the nexus itself. This section will focus on the settings and roles of counselors and other helping professionals, and how the school-prison nexus operates within those contexts.

The Role of Discipline and School Policy

Even professionals who do not work within school settings will work with clients who are either currently in education or who have had previous experience with educational settings. It is therefore important to understand the impact of school culture, context, and policy on the lives of clients. This is of particular importance to school counselors, whose role as a leader and advocate within the school system tasks them with combatting oppression, systemic racism, and White supremacy (Mason et al., 2021). One causal process that has been suggested as contributing to the school-prison nexus is that race impacts the probability of receiving school-based punishment, which in turn impacts the probability of being arrested later in life (Barnes & Motz, 2018). More specifically, racism and racial bias directed towards youth of color by adult professionals and the systems within which they work increases the probability that youth of color will receive punishment and be targeted by law enforcement, and that the consequences of those interactions will be more severe than for their White counterparts.

School-Based Disciplinary Policies

One of the most readily apparent aspects of the school-prison nexus is how zero-tolerance policies aggressively penalize unwanted behaviors and apply a grossly disproportionate punitive response. These zero-tolerance policies apply harsh and mandatory consequences to students when a rule is violated without considerations for context, such as seriousness of the violation, intent of student, implicit bias, mitigating circumstances, developmental and normative behaviors within context, and others (Heitzeg, 2009; Skiba, 2000). These policies essentially eliminate the possibility for rehabilitation, second chances, and understanding for some students, particularly students of color. The emergence of zero-tolerance policies in schools was in response to a context of fear surrounding the use of drugs, anti-Black racism, and school shootings (Heitzeg, 2009). What on the surface appeared to target the presence of illicit substances and weapons in school buildings expanded to include a wide array of behavioral concerns and was then disproportionately then applied to youth of color. Heitzig (2009) notes that in principle these policies to reduce the use of firearms in school shootings ought to have been applied within suburban, majority White schools where school shootings had largely occurred, however the effects of the policies were mostly applied and enforced within urban schools with majority non-White students. Zero tolerance policies criminalize a large number of minor incidents of misbehavior whilst only targeting a very small number of the major incidents which they were designed to eliminate (Skiba, 2000). Barnes and Motz (2018) show how addressing the racial inequality in school-based punishment and disciplinary practices could alone reduce racial disparity in adult arrest rates by up to 16%.

The implementation of school resources officers (SROs) has similar implications. SROs are law enforcement officers who are employed and work within the school settings with a purported goal of maintaining safety for students and staff in the school. Though there is evidence that students may report a greater feeling of safety with the presence of SROs, they also report fears of becoming involved in justice systems, of being arrested and witnessing peers being arrested, and overall reduced school connectedness (Theriot, 2016). This integration of law enforcement within schools begins to blur the line between education and carceral settings; for example, a majority of SROs have reported that they would make an arrest in order to calm students down when they are perceived to be disrupting class (Wolf, 2014). Having a system within classrooms that uses arrest over alternative de-escalation techniques results both in the criminalization of normative behaviors, as well as increasing contact with the justice system with more arrests being made of children under the age of fifteen (Owens, 2017). Professionals in the school system must be skilled in emotional and behavioral de-escalation techniques, rather than rely on the removal or arrest of students experiencing emotional distress.

Other policies and practices put in place within school settings increase the overall policing of students with minimal impacts on safety and disproportionately impacting the lives of minoritized students. Often there is little evidence to support these practices as actually reducing harm or increasing safety in the school setting. These include the inclusion of metal detectors in school, locker searches, surveillance cameras, and uniforms (Muñiz, 2021; Skiba, 2000).

Removal From the School System

When punishment is applied in a school setting, and particularly in response to zero-tolerance policies, it often takes the form of expulsions and exclusions. These actions not only explicitly remove the child from the educational facility, but also increase the likelihood of future absences from school whether mandatory or not, decrease additional social, emotional, and behavioral outcomes (Heitzeg, 2009). Temporary removal from the school building or permanent removal from the school system is a very clear example of how interaction with the educational system can be reduced. When looking at the indirect effects the issue is compounded. With limited opportunities to connect with peers and staff in school settings youth may look for connectedness and belonging in other settings, reducing their social networks and supports within school and increasing their sense of isolation upon any future return to that educational setting. The opportunities to develop socially and emotionally are reduced, as well as the absence of formal educational, extra-curricular activities, and the structure of an organized school day. Without a school diploma, future work opportunities and earning potential is also significantly limited. Studies have shown that school districts looking to increase their testing scores can use exclusionary practices to remove students of color from their schools and benefit from increased scores, rather than providing those students with the education and services they need to succeed and thrive. Often there may be insufficient resources, programs, or services available to dedicated school staff who feel they have no other options to assist students (Heitzeg, 2009).

The Pathologizing of Racism and Racial Trauma

The diagnostic process and counseling profession itself is maintained by a White, Eurocentric perspective from a majority population of professionals (US Census Bureau, 2017) that gatekeeps access to resources and the legitimacy of suffering; diagnoses being the key to receiving services through many agencies and organizations. An alternative dimensional and non-pathologizing diagnostic system that focuses on symptoms and experiences has been suggested by many researchers and clinicians (Brunoni & Brunoni, 2017; Carter, 2007; Marecek & Gavey, 2013). Until a revised system is implemented across the mental health field clinicians are asked to assess all clients using criteria that cannot be adequately applied to every population (Carter, 2007) and may not be equipped with the skills to do so with a culturally sensitive approach (Carter, 1990; Mcneal, 2014). The absence of assessment and treatment with regards to racial trauma in the field in spite of the evidence of its need has been described expansively by researchers and clinicians, indicting one way in which racial bias within the mental health field presents and sustains discrimination in service for clients of color (Ann Payne & Welch, 2015; Carter, 2007; Dutil, 2020; Jernigan & Daniel, 2011). There is substantial literature on the psychological and physical impact of experiencing racism, with a major contribution by Carter (2007). Carter (2007) describes how the emotional and physiological responses to experiencing racism are identical symptomatically to other forms of chromic stress and trauma, and yet race-based traumatic stress is rarely assessed for as part of clinical assessments and screenings. The pathologizing of racial trauma through misdiagnosis and subsequent bias in treatment actively dismisses the psychological and physiological impact of oppression and results in counselors contributing to this criminalization by concluding that the externalizing symptoms of distress are the primary target of treatment, and not the systems that necessitated them (Atkins-Loria et al., 2015; Carter, 2007; Meiners, 2011).

It is hypothesized that a diagnosis of conduct disorder in response to external symptoms of distress may be given to White youth as a pre-requisite to receive mental health services, whereas in Black youth an absence of a diagnosis indicates instead a more direct attribution of symptoms to criminality rather than psychological distress (Pottick et al., 2007). Once in residential treatment, it has been found that a diagnosis of conduct disorder, whilst disproportionately applied to boys of color, does not even accurately reflect symptoms of externalizing behavior and that normative and nondisruptive behaviors were labelled as a conduct problem for boys of color (Cameron & Guterman, 2007). Receiving a diagnosis of conduct disorder is associated with several other negative outcomes, including educational and involvement with the justice system. When reviewing a nationally representative sample of adults, it was found that children with a trauma history who had received a diagnosis of conduct disorder were significantly more likely to drop out of high school before graduating than those who had not received such a diagnosis. The overall impact of trauma on the rate of high school drop-out was 1.65 times that of an individual without the experience of childhood trauma, however this increases to 2.38 times when the child received a diagnosis of conduct disorder (Porche et al., 2011). The need for culturally sensitive diagnosing of conduct disorder has previously been described (Mizock & Harkins, 2011) in response to the overrepresentation of youth of color in the population of youth who receive a conduct disorder diagnosis. The focus on externalizing behaviors rather than the experience of the youth as survivors of oppression misdirects fault to the individual level, allowing discriminatory systems to go unchallenged.

Other patterns of over- and misrepresentation in psychiatric diagnosing are indicated in literature. For example, along with conduct disorder, African American men are more likely to receive a diagnosis of schizophrenia and less likely to receive an affective disorder such as major depressive disorder (MDD) or generalized anxiety disorder (GAD) (Atkins-Loria et al., 2015; Schwartz et al., 2019). Clients who present with identical symptoms as rated by clinicians receive differential diagnoses based on race; with White clients receiving an affective disorder diagnosis and African American clients receiving a diagnosis of schizophrenia for the same presenting clinician rated symptoms (Schwartz et al., 2019). Misapplication and mistreatment of psychiatric disorders is far from the only way in which physical and mental health diagnoses disproportionately impact minoritized clients, however any clinical professionals must be aware of how bias in psychiatric diagnosing and treatment can contribute to the dehumanizing and criminalization of clients. Providing diagnosis and assessment from a culturally sensitive and empowering approach is one of great ethical importance (Ibrahim et al., 2011).

The Role of Helping Professionals in Sustaining the School-Prison Nexus

An aspect of the school-prison nexus that helping professionals must be willing to explore and engage with is the role that their field has in sustaining and advancing the criminalization of youth of color (Gonzalez & Cokley, 2021; Mason et al., 2021; Pinkney, 2021). Unexamined bias results in helping professionals engaging in the very systems that they desire to dismantle in providing equitable care and services. This will manifest in various ways dependent on the roles, responsibilities, and settings of each professional.

Bryan (2017) describes how White teachers are integral in sustaining the school-prison nexus, particularly given their positionality within educational settings. Firstly, by implementing disproportionate disciplinary actions, which are often described as the main component of the school-prison nexus. And furthermore, by modeling the dehumanization of students of color, White professionals in the classroom teach White students how to uphold racist biases and behaviors. (Bryan, 2017). There is also clear direction in the literature for other professionals on how to revise and develop practice in order to not to be complicit in school-prison nexus practices. Examples include utilizing the holistic and community focused approach of social work to include collaboration with school systems, include conversations regarding race and racism, and facilitating education to strengthen school climates (McCarter, 2017) and critically examining race in the context of medicine (Ibrahim et al., 2011; Matthew et al., 2021). The need for professionals to examine their own education and bias is application across all fields in order to provide truly culturally competent and effective care.

Implicit Bias

One reason that youth of color are disproportionately targeted by punishment and disciplinary processes can be explained by a number of processes informed by racial implicit bias. When a bias is unexamined, helping professionals apply their services and treatments following their own prejudices without the awareness of the harm they are perpetuating. This leads to differential labelling of behavior, as seen in the previous discussion of how identical symptoms may receive differential diagnoses. Similarly, when a youth is being criminalized by professionals operating from a lens of White supremacy, behavior is labeled as dysfunctional, aggressive, and disrespectful rather than age-normative, a strength, coping skill, or act of resistance (Basile, 2020; Basile et al., 2019). Additionally, harsher punishments are given for the same or less severe rule violations (Muñiz, 2021; Owens, 2017).

Recognizing the impact of personal bias reveals how wide-spread its impact can be on clients and broader society. Each of the previous sections of this chapter can be analyzed to find how implicit bias comes to affect clients, especially when applied through systems and policies that criminalize and oppress. For example, a counselor who is not attending to personal bias may perceive "acting out" behavior from a White client as symptomatic of posttraumatic stress syndrome and normative given previously reported experiences of violence. The same counselor with unaddressed racist bias may interpret identical behavior from a Black client as disordered conduct with a history of oppositional and dysfunctional relationships, labelling the symptoms, causes, and ultimately the client differently and following with different treatment plans accordingly. The impacts of such abstract hypotheticals are very real for clients who receive such biased services. The White client in such a scenario may receive specialized trauma-focused therapy alongside an understanding of how their history and experiences have impacted them. Their counterpart is instead interpreted through a lens that identifies the root of client's concerns lies solely with their own conduct and an absence of treatment that recognizes the personal history of the client and their cultural context; this disproportionate hyper focus on conduct is one of the channels through which criminalization occurs. Note how labeling behavior differently becomes codified in official practices through the use of a mental health diagnosis. Addressing personal bias has become a recent mandate in all fields across the helping professions, with an understanding that unaddressed bias will cause a provider to act in ways which are harmful to the client. Willingly not addressing this way in which a provider is actively causing harm breaks the ethical imperative of non-malfeasance in practice.

Case Study

Systemic and Cultural Assessment

A teacher has referred a student to the counselor due to disruptive behavior in the classroom. The teacher reports that the student, a Black boy in fourth grade, insists on keeping the hood of his sweatshirt up which is a violation of the school dress code. When confronted the student walked out of the classroom. When asked about the incident by the counselor, the student looks towards his feet and shrugs. The counselor notes that a previous mental health professional has provided the student with a diagnosis of Unspecified Disruptive, Impulse-Control, and Conduct Disorder. The treatment plan included behavioral interventions designed to address unwanted behaviors in the school setting.

If you were the counselor in this situation, what external and systemic factors may be impacting the student? How have deficit-focused approaches shaped the world of this student? What more do you need to know to fully understand the student's experience from a strengths-based and trauma-informed lens?

COUNSELING STRATEGIES FOR DISRUPTING THE NEXUS

The Multicultural and Social Justice Counseling Competencies (MSJCC) provides a framework for understanding how professionals can effectively serve marginalized clients (Ratts et al., 2016). The understanding of how privilege and marginalization work with regards to the school-prison nexus is essential in disrupting its work, and counselors can apply their work at all levels of work, including counselor self-awareness, understanding client worldview, the professional counseling relationship, and in advocacy. This section will explore multiple counseling strategies from a variety of perspectives to assist in disrupting the school-prison nexus.

An absence of culturally appropriate treatment, chronic trauma, poverty, and racism, contribute to the school-prison nexus (Novak, 2019; Oswald & Coutinho, 1996; Porche et al., 2011), whereas culturally appropriate treatments include approaches that center the impact of race and racism, are community focused and strengths-based, and emphasize critical self-examination (Joseph et al., 2020; Meiners, 2011; Miller et al., 2018; Vera & Speight, 2003). Helping professionals may not be equipped with the skills to assess clients with a culturally sensitive approach, and so understanding how to build these skills is essential. (Carter, 1990; Danzer et al., 2021; Hemmings & Evans, 2018; Mcneal, 2014). These skills may take a variety of forms, from personal introspection, to revising clinical and educational practices, to collaboration and advocacy within the community.

Understanding and Addressing Personal Bias

There has been a shift across fields to emphasize the importance of addressing personal bias within helping professions. This awareness is not a single-event learning, but an ongoing process of being authentic and congruent with oneself and following with intentional accountability and practice which actively seeks to be inclusive and non-oppressive. The idea of a congruent and authentic counselor is not new, as seen in person-centered counseling made famous by Rogers (1966). Counselors are simply being asked to ensure that this self-reflection and authenticity is extended to biases towards and against race. (Matthew et al., 2021). In doing so, counselors are able to both grow in their skills and meet the needs of diverse clients and clients with oppressed identities (Pinkney, 2021). Counselors who are unable to be authentic and avoid racial topics in their personal growth will not only be lacking in clinical skills but also do harm to clients by allowing their biases to influence their interactions, assumptions, and treatments. Additionally, it is an ethical imperative to provide culturally competent care to all clients (Ratts et al., 2016); being willfully ignorant of racialized contexts and societal factors that impact clients of color is both unethical and tacitly contributes to and upholds racism wand White supremacy within the mental health field. In addition to bias, understanding how personal privilege is influential in the professional's life and embracing any associated discomfort is essential as an effective and culturally competent helper (Moss & Singh 2015).

It is important to note that there may be resistance to this work, with the suggestion that anti-bias trainings and awareness may have the unintended consequences of being more divisive than inclusive. Understanding Helm's (1997) White racial identity model and adapting pedagogy accordingly will help to navigate resistance, as well as reviewing professional Codes of Ethics, which mandate this personal work (Ibrahim et al., 2011).

Anti-Racist Pedagogy and Training

In order to ensure that professionals are providing equitable services and not contributing to the school-prison nexus addressing personal biases are essential. Education throughout training and continued development can be intentionally planned to ensure this imperative is met (Bryan, 2017). The need for integrative and focused courses during counselor training goes beyond a cursory overview of multiculturalism and ethics. Indeed, the idea of introductory multicultural courses can be criticized as including the same pathologizing and deficit-focused approaches that contribute to the school-prison nexus. Additionally, they often allow the majority White counselors-in-education to intellectualize multicultural work and racism, both systemic and specific to counseling, without critically engaging with their own concepts of race, Whiteness, and at the expense of the learning of students of color (Gonzalez & Cokley, 2021). Effective counselors will be trained in understanding how systemic racism impacts clients in clinical and classroom settings. A call to action for counselor preparation programs to include core courses that educate counselors-in-training on anti-racism and anti-racist practice demonstrates that this has hitherto been neglected in counselor training programs (Gonzalez & Cokley, 2021; Hargons et al., 2017).

Gonzalez and Cokley (2021) propose a model for such a core anti-racist counseling course, providing counselor educators with a framework for implementing such a course, as well as the tools to infuse other courses with anti-racist pedagogy. They clearly describe the theory behind the course construction as well as concrete examples of assignments and course structure. Using a critical race theory (CRT) framework to discuss an approach to pedagogy and course goals, examples of course assignments they suggest include a racial-conscious digital autobiography, an activism project and interview, as well as dedicating space for group processing. Another model of how counselors can be prepared to work with an anti-racist lens has been proposed specifically to meet the needs of school counselors and their clients. Mason et al. (2021) revise and expand the tenets of the transforming school counseling initiative (TSCI) to outline how to create anti-racist school counselor preparation. They describe how leadership, advocacy, teaming and collaboration, counseling and coordination, and assessment and use of data can be used to more effectively work to dismantle racism systems that sustain the school-prison nexus within school settings themselves.

Broaching Within Individual Counseling

When providing individual counseling, there are skills that counselors can use to address systemic racism and its effects on the client in the room. Alongside the essential listening skills, counselors incorporate broaching into their work so that their multicultural awareness and knowledge is brought into practical application. Broaching refers to intentionally and actively addressing within counseling sessions how culture and power are present in the life and society of the client (King & Borders, 2019). The inclusion of broaching as a necessary part of school counseling work is needed to ensure culturally appropriate and strength-based services are provided for all students (Mason et al., 2021). Counselors must be willing, not just to understand the impact of racism and criminalization on clients, but to be able to appropriately integrate this aspect of socialization and experience into sessions with clients (Pinkney, 2021).

The Counselors for Social Justice (CSJ) (Ibrahim et al., 2011) make explicit in their Code of Ethics how counselors approach advocacy on an individual level. It includes being transparent with clients regarding the counselors' approach to social justice work, as well as their commitments and limits to advocacy. Broaching may also include the understanding and appropriate self-disclosure of power and privilege within the counseling relationship. King and Borders (2019) explore how racial identity factors, such as identification with one's race, may impact counselor broaching behaviors and the therapeutic relationship. Additionally, that the counselor's cultural responsiveness is enhanced when they are able to actively incorporate cultural dynamics within sessions; specifically, those of identity and power. Therefore, counselors ought to not only have an understanding of culture, power, and oppression, but be willing and able to use this directly in counseling sessions and be able to explore these topics openly.

Culturally Aware Diagnostic Approaches

Counselors and other mental health professionals are in positions of power regarding their roles as gatekeepers to services and care and the clinical decisions they are certified and licensed to make. In this regard, counselors occupy a privileged position with inherent power over a client (Ratts et al., 2016). As described in this chapter, the diagnostic choices that mental health professional make are impacted by more than merely the presenting clinical symptoms. One way in which a lack of understanding of how personal bias informs the school-prison nexus is seen through deficit-focused diagnosis and treatment. Experiences and opportunities of youth of color have been shaped by the institutional racism perpetuated by educational and mental health professionals, and bias within helping professionals contributes to deficit-focused interventions (Atkins-Loria et al., 2015; Carter, 1990; Mcneal, 2014; Nolan, 2011). Being aware of differential diagnoses and taking take to provide accurate, meaningful, diagnoses with minimal stigmatization and understanding of the impact of potential diagnoses on clients is essential. It is therefore and ethical imperative to reassess diagnosing and treatment practices to incorporate cultural awareness and counselor bias (Ibrahim et al., 2011).

Arriving at diagnostic decisions and appropriate treatments is often done so through various psychological testing. This may be done via structured or semi-structured interviews and with formal assessments, however these assessments may themselves be problematic and unchallenged acceptance of their validity can be very harmful to clients. Mental health professionals must critically review any psychological assessments they intend to use with clients, taking into account any bias in items and results, and how the assessment may be further harming clients through racist and pathologizing evaluation (Byrd et al., 2021; Ibrahim et al., 2011).

The limited assessment and treatment with regards to racial trauma and discrimination in the field has also been described expansively by researchers (Carter, 2007; Danzer et al., 2021; Dutil, 2020; Hemmings & Evans, 2018; Jernigan & Daniel, 2011; Payne & Welch, 2015). This gap in mental health assessment and treatment is resulting in significant harm to clients, and contributes to the dehumanization and criminalization of youth of color. Counselors must take into account the impact of racial trauma during the assessment process; not doing so may result in symptoms of trauma or affective disorders instead being attributed to antisocial or criminal behaviors (Pottick et al., 2007).

Utilizing strengths-based approaches to clinical work is also essential in providing effective and equitable treatment for all clients. This approach replaces the historically deficit-based approaches that, in part, inform the punitive and judgmental responses to unwanted or misunderstood behaviors. A strengths-based approach understands individuals as navigating the world and their situation as best as they can with the resources available to them. Additionally, the theoretical underpinnings of a positive approach to psychotherapy include understanding how social and cultural factors impede a person's capacity for growth, positive emotions and strengths are real and valid, and that these strengths can be used in an effective clinical relationship (Rashid, 2015). This approach can be applied with a critical assessment of personal bias and culture to ensure that clients are being viewed through a positive, empowering lens rather than the disempowering and dehumanizing lens that feeds the school-prison nexus. Meanwhile, all mental health professionals make moves to work together to introduce new systems of providing care that are more equitable for all, including access to care that is not dependent on diagnostic codes and access to medical insurance or financial resources.

Restorative Justice Practices

Integrating knowledge and practice of specific restorative justice techniques has been suggested as one way to make changes in the school-prison nexus. Restorative justice is a theory and approach to justice that emphasizes healing, respect, accountability, and empathy for all parties involved. Its practice includes involving all parties in the resolution when a harm, rule-violation, or offense has occurred (Tyner, 2020).

Counselors and other helping professionals working with groups can particularly be intentional about how to use restorative justice to resolve conflict within groups, which can be integrated seamlessly with a general person-centered approach to working with clients.

Integrating restorative justice principles and practices into school and community settings can assist in disrupting the school-prison nexus in a variety of ways. Tyner (2020) describes restorative justice as more than a set of practices; rather, it is an approach to life that embraces healing and community engagement and attributes its origins to indigenous societies. Schools and settings that incorporate this approach replace a punitive approach to harm with one that address harms, needs, encourages dialogue and responsibility and is respectful of all involved. Helping professionals can facilitate this by becoming trained to hold restorative justice circles and by ensuring the principles of restorative justice are infused throughout wider school and community policies. Circles can also be held for other purposes whilst centering community respect and dialogue. By using circles and the principle of respect for all whilst centering the harm that was done, restorative justice can be used as both a preventative and a reactive intervention. In a preventative manner, it builds communication skills, sense of community and belonging, self-esteem, improves behaviors and sets expectations, improved academic skills, and is culturally inclusive (Tyner, 2020). As an intervention following harm, it promotes prosocial behavior, encourages self-advocacy and self-efficacy in problem-solving, and builds relationships. All of these positive outcomes demonstrate how using restorative justice principles can resist the criminalization of students and actively works to increase their inclusion and sense of community within educational settings.

Community and Systems Social Justice Advocacy

Ratts et al. (2016) note the importance of balancing individual interventions with work in the community to bring about broader social change, and thereby providing a more equitable environment for clients to have their needs met and to thrive. Indeed, the MSJCC are rooted in human rights and a history of civil rights advocacy (Singh et al., 2020). The need for helping professionals to extend their work to include social justice advocacy in their private work and in wider systems has been recognized and delineated in recent literature for professionals across the helping fields. For example, Matthew et al. (2021) describe how pediatricians can engage families in anti-racist discourse and also attend to the deleterious impact of racism on children of color within clinical work. Within counseling psychology, the recognition of the importance of healing in activism is highlighted alongside the need for leaders in the field to be courageous in their involvement with the Black Lives Matter movement (Hargons et al., 2017). Counselors who work within school settings are tasked with championing advocacy within their schools and promoting safe, positive environments free from systemic barriers for all students (Mason et al., 2021; Moss & Singh 2015). Interventions, and especially school-based interventions, that work to build the strengths of low-income and culturally diverse students must be integrated throughout the educational and social experiences of youth. Howard and Solberg (2006) offer a specific curriculum, the Achieving Success Identity Pathways, to demonstrate how this would be incorporated within a school setting.

CSJ provide a Code of Ethics to clarify and expand how the American Counseling Association (ACA) Code of Ethics can be applied to a specifically social justice orientation (Ibrahim et al., 2011). With the goals of eradicating all forms of oppressions and centering the dignity of all persons, the CSJ Code of Ethics guides helping professionals on how to apply their advocacy skills. Examples of how to ensure advocacy work is effective and ethical, include developing alliances with groups working for change, providing and interpreting data that demonstrates the urgency for policy and practice change, and ensuring supervisees are aware of the impact of bias and privilege. They note that counselors are able to advocate for clients in pushing for wider social change, and in more targeted specific ways when the client's permission has been obtained.

Interdisciplinary work is essential when conducting social justice work to collaborate with scholars, practitioners, and activists who are knowledgeable and active in the variety of fields that are impacted by systemic inequities (Hargons et al., 2017; Ibrahim et al., 2011). It is therefore prudent to build community relationships and partnerships with professionals both within the counseling field and in other fields that clients will interact with. This may include staff and professionals working within justice or law enforcement, medical fields, social work, children and family services, community resources, case management, schools carceral settings, and others. Being able to provide clients with a nexus of support and to advocate on their behalf where necessary and appropriate helps aid positive, systemic change.

Nexus of Interventions

Much in the same way that it is important to understand the multitude of ways in which minoritized clients are criminalized, it is also important to understand how the multitude of ways in which we respond is inherently connected. Committing to engage in only one, isolated act of advocacy or intervention falls short of addressing the nexus as a whole. Indeed, the MSJCC includes counseling and advocacy interventions as one of the developmental domains for counselors (Ratts et al., 2016), and the CSJ Code of Ethics explicitly outlines that addressing systems are an ethical imperative for counselors (Ibrahim et al., 2011).

Case Study

Preparing Future Counselors

A new community mental health center has opened in a low-income neighborhood with a high percentage of families who are racially minoritized. One of the new counselors at the center recently graduated from a counseling program at a wealthy Predominantly White Institution (PWI). The counselor reports that they are excited to use their counseling theory in individual sessions but is not as interested in community advocacy work. The counselor is seeking supervision as many of their new clients are not returning after the initial session.

If you were the supervisor of this counselor, how would you approach supervising the counselor in their new role? What would you suggest for the counselor to be able to work most effectively with their new clients? How would you guide the counselor in providing ethical, culturally competent services?

FUTURE RESEARCH DIRECTIONS

The refocusing or expansion of the work of counselors and other helping professionals to include social justice advocacy, activism, and anti-racism is not new, but has recently found greater acceptance at the forefront of literature and discourse following high profile murders of Black citizens by police officers. Several researchers and clinicians have described what anti-racist, inclusive, and social justice work would look like both in counselor education and practice. The goal of future counselors and counselor educators is to ensure that these conceptual models are put into practice to provide equitable services for all clients and, through the changes made in systems in which counselors work, challenge and disrupt the school-prison nexus. Additionally, Meiners (2011) offers specific concerns for professionals in educational capacities with regards to addressing the school-prison nexus and the abolition of carceral systems, including questioning the ethical implications of focusing on youth, negotiating wider social structures that support punishment, stigma, and incarceration, and incorporating a comprehensive intersectional approach to social justice work. Future research may analyze the effectiveness and implementation of the models and interventions described in this chapter to ensure the most effective use of resources in meeting client needs.

SUMMARY AND CONCLUSION

This chapter described the impact of oppressive systems that increase incarceration for minoritized clients throughout the lifespan. School settings and mental health services have historically punished and pathologized students of color, resulting in harmful, traumatizing, and criminalizing outcomes. Using introspection to critically assess personal biases, culturally sensitive diagnostic and treatment procedures, restorative justice, and social justice advocacy, strategies were then suggested to guide professionals in fostering systemic change to disrupt how the school-prison nexus functions in their work. Overall, counselors are demanded to assess how systemic factors are impacting clients and work to foster change in these systems for lasting, positive change in the lives of our clients.

Counselors and other helping professionals must critique themselves and their contexts through the lens of the school-prison nexus, which results in oppression and incarceration for many marginalized clients and their communities. The immediate action and perseverance of all helping professionals is needed to disrupt the school-prison nexus and empower all clients to thrive. Though there are many dedicated educator and clinician activists, widespread implement of these new practices has been slow in the face of many systemic barriers. By using our work to interrupt the systems and services that criminalize youth, helping professionals can help reduce the number of people who are incarcerated and dismantle oppressive systems towards the abolition of the prison-industrial complex.

REFERENCES

American Psychological Association. (2021). Inclusive language guidelines. *Equity, Diversity, and Inclusion.* https://www.apa.org/about/apa/equitydiversity-inclusion/language-guidelines.pdf

Atkins-Loria, S., Macdonald, H., & Mitterling, C. (2015). Young African American Men and the Diagnosis of Conduct Disorder: The Neo-colonization of Suffering. *Clinical Social Work Journal*, *43*(4), 431–441. doi:10.100710615-015-0531-8

Barnes, J. C., & Motz, R. T. (2018). Reducing racial inequalities in adulthood arrest by reducing inequalities in school discipline: Evidence from the school-to-prison pipeline. *Developmental Psychology*, *54*(12), 2328–2340. doi:10.1037/dev0000613 PMID:30265031

Basile, V. (2020). Standin' tall: Criminalization and acts of resistance among elementary school boys of color. *Race, Ethnicity and Education*, *23*(1), 94–112. doi:10.1080/13613324.2018.1497964

Basile, V., York, A., & Black, R. (2019). Who Is the One Being Disrespectful? Understanding and Deconstructing the Criminalization of Elementary School Boys of Color. *Urban Education, 00*(0), 1–29. doi:10.1177/0042085919842627

Blankenship, K. M., del Rio Gonzalez, A. M., Keene, D. E., Groves, A. K., & Rosenberg, A. P. (2018). Mass incarceration, race inequality, and health: Expanding concepts and assessing impacts on well-being. *Social Science & Medicine, 215*, 45–52. doi:10.1016/j.socscimed.2018.08.042 PMID:30205278

Brunoni, A. R., & Brunoni, A. R. (2017). Beyond the DSM: Trends in psychiatry diagnoses. *Archives of Clinical Psychiatry, 44*(6), 154–158. doi:10.1590/0101-60830000000142

Bryan, N. (2017). White teachers' role in sustaining the school-to-prison pipeline: Recommendations for teacher education. *The Urban Review, 49*(2), 326–345. doi:10.100711256-017-0403-3

Byrd, D. A., Rivera Mindt, M. M., Clark, U. S., Clarke, Y., Thames, A. D., Gammada, E. Z., & Manly, J. J. (2021). Creating an antiracist psychology by addressing professional complicity in psychological assessment. *Psychological Assessment, 33*(3), 279–285. doi:10.1037/pas0000993 PMID:33779204

Carter, R. T. (1990). The Relationship Between Racism and Racial ldentity Among White Americans: An Exploratory Investigation. *Journal of Counseling and Development, 69*(1), 46–50. doi:10.1002/j.1556-6676.1990.tb01455.x

Carter, R. T. (2007). Racism and Psychological and Emotional Injury: Recognizing and Assessing Race-Based Traumatic Stress. *The Counseling Psychologist, 35*(1), 13–105. doi:10.1177/0011000006292033

Carter, R. T., Kirkinis, K., & Johnson, V. E. (2019). Relationships Between Trauma Symptoms and Race-Based Traumatic Stress. *Traumatology, 26*(1), 11–18. doi:10.1037/trm0000217

Chinn, J. J., Martin, I. K., & Redmond, N. (2021). Health equity among Black women in the United States. *Journal of Women's Health, 30*(2), 212–219. doi:10.1089/jwh.2020.8868 PMID:33237831

Danzer, G., Rieger, S., Schubmehl, S., & Cort, D. (2021). White Psychologists and African Americans' Historical Trauma: Implications for Practice. *Journal of Aggression, Maltreatment & Trauma, 25*(4), 351–370. doi:10.1080/10926771.2016.1153550

Department of Education and Office for Civil Rights. (n.d.). The use of restraint and seclusion on children with disabilities in K-12 schools. *Civil Rights Data Collection.* https://www2.ed.gov/about/offices/list/ocr/docs/restraint-and-seclusion.pdf

Dutil, S. (2020). Dismantling the School-to-Prison Pipeline: A Trauma-Informed, Critical Race Perspective on School Discipline. *Children & Schools, 42*(3), 171–178. doi:10.1093/cs/cdaa016

Gonzalez, I. A., & Cokley, R. K. (2021). The Case for a Core Anti-racist Course for Counselors in Training. *Teaching and Supervision in Counseling, 3*(2), 26–37. doi:10.7290/tsc030204

Grace, J. E., & Nelson, S. L. (2019). "Tryin' to Survive": Black Male Students' Understandings of the Role of Race and Racism in the School-to-Prison Pipeline. *Leadership and Policy in Schools, 18*(4), 664–680. doi:10.1080/15700763.2018.1513154

Graham, P. W., Yaros, A., Lowe, A., & McDaniel, M. S. (2017). Nurturing Environments for Boys and Men of Color with Trauma Exposure. *Clinical Child and Family Psychology Review*, *20*(2), 105–116. doi:10.100710567-017-0241-6 PMID:28547524

Hargons, C., Mosley, D., Falconer, J., Faloughi, R., Singh, A., Stevens-Watkins, D., & Cokley, K. (2017). Black lives matter: A call to action for counseling psychology leaders. *The Counseling Psychologist*, *45*(6), 873–901. doi:10.1177/0011000017733048 PMID:29217847

Heitzeg, N. A. (2009). Education or Incarceration: Zero Tolerance Policies and the School to Prison Pipeline. *Forum on Public Policy Online, 2009*(2), 1-21.

Helms, J. E. (1997). Toward a model of White racial identity development. In P. G. Altbach, K. Arnold, & I. C. King (Eds.), *College student development and academic life: Psychological, intellectual, social and moral issues* (pp. 207–224). Routledge.

Hemmings, C., & Evans, A. M. (2018). Identifying and Treating Race-Based Trauma in Counseling. *Journal of Multicultural Counseling and Development*, *46*(1), 20–39. doi:10.1002/jmcd.12090

Howard, K. A., & Solberg, V. S. H. (2006). School-based social justice: The achieving success identity pathways program. *Professional School Counseling*, *21*(1), 278–287. doi:10.5330/prsc.9.4.4587465231061304

Howell, J. (2017). Race and US medical experimentation: The case of Tuskegee. *Cadernos de Saude Publica*, *33*(1, suppl 1). Advance online publication. doi:10.1590/0102-311x00168016 PMID:28492710

Ibrahim, F. A., Dinsmore, J. A., Estrada, D., & D'Andrea, M.Counselors for Social Justice (CSJ) Ethi. (2011). The Counselors for Social Justice (CSJ) code of ethics. *Journal for Social Action in Counseling and Psychology*, *3*(2), 1–21. doi:10.33043/JSACP.3.2.1-21

Jernigan, M. M., & Daniel, J. H. (2011). Racial trauma in the lives of Black children and adolescents: Challenges and clinical implications. *Journal of Child & Adolescent Trauma*, *4*(2), 123–141. doi:10.1080/19361521.2011.574678

Joseph, A. A., Wilcox, S. M., Hnilica, R. J., & Hansen, M. C. (2020). Keeping Race at the Center of School Discipline Practices and Trauma-Informed Care: An Interprofessional Framework. *Children & Schools*, *42*(3), 161–170. doi:10.1093/cs/cdaa013

King, K. M., & Borders, L. D. (2019). An experimental investigation of White counselors broaching race and racism. *Journal of Counseling and Development*, *97*(4), 341–351. doi:10.1002/jcad.12283

Mason, E., Robertson, A., Gay, J., Clarke, N., & Holcomb-McCoy, C. (2021). Antiracist School Counselor Preparation: Expanding on the Five Tenets of the Transforming School Counseling Initiative. *Teaching and Supervision in Counseling, 3*(2), 2, 4-14.

Matthew, A. J., Clark, M. A., & McDavid, L. M. (2021). Combating racism: The role of the pediatrician. *Pediatric Research*, *90*(4), 1–3. doi:10.103841390-020-01345-x PMID:33469175

McCarter, S. (2017). The school-to-prison pipeline: A primer for social workers. *Social Work (United States)*, *62*(1), 53–61. doi:10.1093www078 PMID:28395045

Mcgrew, K. (2016). The dangers of pipeline thinking: How the school-to-prison pipeline metaphor squeezes out complexity. *Educational Theory*, *7*(3), 1–17. doi:10.1111/edth.12173

Mcneal, L. R. (2014). Managing Our Blind Spot: The Role of Bias in the School-to-Prison Pipeline. *Arizona State Law Journal*, *48*, 285–311. https://b.3cdn.net/advancement/d05cb2181a4545db07_r2im6caqe.pdf

Meiners, E. R. (2011). Ending the School-to-Prison Pipeline/Building Abolition Futures. *The Urban Review*, *43*(4), 547–565. doi:10.100711256-011-0187-9

Miller, M. J., Keum, B. T. H., Thai, C. J., Lu, Y., Truong, N. N., Huh, G. A., Li, X., Yeung, J. G., & Ahn, L. H. R. (2018). Practice recommendations for addressing racism: A content analysis of the counseling psychology literature. *Journal of Counseling Psychology*, *65*(6), 669–680. doi:10.1037/cou0000306 PMID:30091623

Mizock, L., & Harkins, D. (2011). Diagnostic bias and conduct disorder: Improving culturally sensitive diagnosis. *Child and Youth Services*, *32*(3), 243–253. doi:10.1080/0145935X.2011.605315

Moss, L. J., & Singh, A. A. (2015). White School Counselors Becoming Racial Justice Allies to Students of Color: A Call to the Field of School Counseling. *Journal of School Counseling*, *13*(5), 1–36.

Muñiz, J. O. (2021). Exclusionary Discipline Policies, School-Police Partnerships, Surveillance Technologies and Disproportionality: A Review of the School to Prison Pipeline Literature. *The Urban Review*, *53*(5), 1–26. doi:10.100711256-021-00595-1

Nellis, A. (n.d.). The Color of Justice: Racial and Ethnic Disparity in State Prisons. *The Sentencing Project.* http://www.sentencingproject.org/publications/color-of-justice-racial-and-ethnic-disparity-in-state-prisons

Nolan, K. M. (2011). Oppositional behavior in urban schooling: Toward a theory of resistance for new times. *International Journal of Qualitative Studies in Education: QSE*, *24*(5), 559–572. doi:10.1080/09518398.2011.600263

Novak, A. (2019). The School-To-Prison Pipeline: An Examination of the Association Between Suspension and Justice System Involvement. *Criminal Justice and Behavior*, *46*(8), 1165–1180. doi:10.1177/0093854819846917

Oswald, D. P., & Coutinho, M. J. (1996). Leaving School: The Impact of State Economic and Demographic Factors for Students with Serious Emotional Disturbance. *Journal of Emotional and Behavioral Disorders*, *4*(2), 114–125. doi:10.1177/106342669600400206

Owens, E. G. (2017). Testing the school-to-prison pipeline. *Journal of Policy Analysis and Management*, *36*(1), 11–37. doi:10.1002/pam.21954

Payne, A. A., & Welch, K. (2015). Restorative Justice in Schools: The Influence of Race on Restorative Discipline. *Youth & Society*, *47*(4), 539–564. doi:10.1177/0044118X12473125

Pinkney, K. E. (2021). Anti-Racist Practice: I Am Accountable. Are You? *Journal of Mental Health Counseling*, *43*(3), 277–280. doi:10.17744/mehc.43.3.10

Porche, M. V., Fortuna, L. R., Lin, J., & Alegria, M. (2011). Childhood Trauma and Psychiatric Disorders as Correlates of School Dropout in a National Sample of Young Adults. *Child Development*, *82*(3), 982–998. doi:10.1111/j.1467-8624.2010.01534.x PMID:21410919

Rashid, T. (2015). Positive psychotherapy: A strength-based approach. *The Journal of Positive Psychology*, *10*(1), 25–40. doi:10.1080/17439760.2014.920411

Ratts, M. J., Singh, A. A., Nassar-Mcmillan, S., Butler, S. K., & McCullough, J. R. (2016). Multicultural and Social Justice Counseling Competencies: Guidelines for the Counseling Profession. *Journal of Multicultural Counseling and Development*, *44*(1), 28–48. doi:10.1002/jmcd.12035

Rocque, M., & Snellings, Q. (2018). The new disciplinology: Research, theory, and remaining puzzles on the school-to-prison pipeline. *Journal of Criminal Justice*, *59*, 3–11. doi:10.1016/j.jcrimjus.2017.05.002

Rogers, C. R. (1966). *Client-centered therapy*. American Psychological Association.

Schiff, M. (2018). Can restorative justice disrupt the 'school-to-prison pipeline?'. *Contemporary Justice Review*, *21*(2), 121–139. doi:10.1080/10282580.2018.1455509

Schwartz, E. K., Docherty, N. M., Najolia, G. M., & Cohen, A. S. (2019). Exploring the racial diagnostic bias of schizophrenia using behavioral and clinical-based measures. *Journal of Abnormal Psychology*, *128*(3), 263–271. doi:10.1037/abn0000409 PMID:30762376

Singh, A. A., Nassar, S. C., Arredondo, P., & Toporek, R. (2020). The past guides the future: Implementing the multicultural and social justice counseling competencies. *Journal of Counseling and Development*, *98*(3), 238–252. doi:10.1002/jcad.12319

Skiba, R. J. (2000). Zero Tolerance, Zero Evidence: An Analysis of School Disciplinary Practice. Policy Research Report. Indiana University, Bloomington. Education Policy Center.

Theriot, M. T. (2016). The impact of school resource officer interaction on students' feelings about school and school police. *Crime and Delinquency*, *62*(4), 446–469. doi:10.1177/0011128713503526

Tyner, A. R. (2020). The Tangled Web of Mass Incarceration: Addressing the School-To-Prison Pipeline Through a Restorative Justice Approach. *University of St. Thomas Law Journal*, *17*(1), 59.

US Census Bureau. (n.d.). *Data USA: Counselors*. DataUSA. https://datausa.io/profile/soc/counselors#demographics

Vera, E. M., & Speight, S. L. (2003). Multicultural Competence, Social Justice, and Counseling Psychology: Expanding Our Roles. *The Counseling Psychologist*, *31*(3), 253–272. doi:10.1177/0011000003031003001

White, J. M., Li, S., Ashby, C. E., Ferri, B., Wang, Q., Bern, P., & Cosier, M. (2019). Same as it ever was: The nexus of race, ability, and place in one urban school district. *Educational Studies*, *55*(4), 453–472. doi:10.1080/00131946.2019.1630130

Wolf, K. C. (2014). Arrest decision making by school resource officers. *Youth Violence and Juvenile Justice*, *12*(2), 137–151. doi:10.1177/1541204013491294

ADDITIONAL READING

Carter, R. T. (2007). Racism and Psychological and Emotional Injury: Recognizing and Assessing Race-Based Traumatic Stress. *The Counseling Psychologist*, *35*(1), 13–105. doi:10.1177/0011000006292033

Carter, R. T., & Pieterse, A. L. (2020). *Measuring the effects of racism*. Columbia University Press.

Ibrahim, F. A., Dinsmore, J. A., Estrada, D., & D'Andrea, M.Counselors for Social Justice (CSJ) Ethi. (2011). The Counselors for Social Justice (CSJ) code of ethics. *Journal for Social Action in Counseling and Psychology*, *3*(2), 1–21. doi:10.33043/JSACP.3.2.1-21

Kim, C., Losen, D., & Hewitt, D. (2010). *The School-to-Prison Pipeline: Structuring Legal Reform*. NYU Press.

Meiners, E. R. (2010). *Right to be hostile: Schools, prisons, and the making of public enemies*. Routledge. doi:10.4324/9780203936450

Nellis, A. (n.d.). The Color of Justice: Racial and Ethnic Disparity in State Prisons. *The Sentencing Project*. http://www.sentencingproject.org/publications/color-of-justice-racial-and-ethnic-disparity-in-state-prisons

Ratts, M. J., Singh, A. A., Nassar-Mcmillan, S., Butler, S. K., & McCullough, J. R. (2016). Multicultural and Social Justice Counseling Competencies: Guidelines for the Counseling Profession. *Journal of Multicultural Counseling and Development*, *44*(1), 28–48. doi:10.1002/jmcd.12035

KEY TERMS AND DEFINITIONS

Anti-Racism: The practice of opposing systemic racism and racial oppression.

Criminalization: The treatment of normative and non-criminal behaviors and persons as if they were criminal acts and requiring of punishment or rehabilitation.

Implicit Bias: The ideas and opinions we hold, formed through our socialization processes, that judge identities or qualities of persons without conscious recognition of doing so.

Pathologizing: The treatment of normative behaviors as if they were psychologically abnormal.

Race-Based Traumatic Stress/Race-Based Trauma: The chronic presence of racial stressors which result in psychological and physical injury and symptoms. In this chapter the terms are considered interchangeably.

Restorative Justice: An approach to justice when harm to someone has been done that focuses on understanding, accountability, and healing. Practically, often includes meetings with the person harmed and the person who did the harm along with a mediator.

School-Prison Nexus: The systems and services that place barriers to success by decreasing access to education and increasing interactions with disciplinary processes and the justice system. The school-prison nexus is referred in some literature as the school-to-prison pipeline.

Social Justice: Equitable distribution and access to resources, privileges, rights, and opportunities for all persons.

Trauma-Informed: The understanding and integration into one's work of the prevalence, impact, and healing from all types of trauma on an individual.

Zero-Tolerance: A policy that mandates harsh punishment for certain behaviors or rule infractions without consideration of context.

Chapter 9
School Supports for Students Impacted by Incarceration

Erin M. Sappio
https://orcid.org/0000-0003-1130-1987
Stockton University, USA

Jessica Howland
Rutgers University, USA

ABSTRACT

This chapter describes the academic, behavioral, and mental health impact incarceration has on youth. It describes ways school counselors, school psychologists, and teachers can offer support for students during and post incarceration, as well as ways school personnel can support students with incarcerated parents. Implications for schools to intervene on behalf of the student impacted by incarceration and areas for future research are offered. Understanding educationally based supports available to children who are incarcerated or who have incarcerated parents can enhance outcomes for those youth. Counselors working with these youth in mental health settings can share knowledge of school-based supports with the families of affected youth. Counselors can also consult with school personnel to ensure affected youth are receiving appropriate services.

INTRODUCTION

The global well-being of youth is impacted when a student or their parent is incarcerated. Since students spend a significant amount of their young lives in school, school personnel are in a unique position to observe, monitor, and intervene on behalf of the impacted student. The objectives of this chapter are as follows:

1. Understand the impact that incarceration has on a student's academic performance, physical health, and mental health.

DOI: 10.4018/978-1-7998-9209-0.ch009

2. Understand the impact that parental incarceration can have on a student's health and academic performance.
3. Identify the roles school counselors, school psychologists, and teachers play when a student is incarcerated.
4. Identify the roles school counselors, school psychologists, and teachers play when a student's parent is incarcerated.
5. Offer implications for schools to intervene on behalf of a student impacted by incarceration.
6. Identify areas for future research to help support students in school who are impacted by incarceration.

BACKGROUND

In 2017, approximately 43,580 children were held overnight in a juvenile justice system residential placement (Children's Defense Fund, 2021). In 2019, 653 children were incarcerated in adult prisons (Children's Defense Fund, 2021). Ninety-three thousand school-age youth are arrested and incarcerated on any given day (National Juvenile Justice Network, 2009). Regardless of whether in juvenile or adult detention centers, the number of incarcerated children of color is significantly disproportionate to the number of White children. An estimated 2.7 million children had a parent who was incarcerated in 2020 (National Institute of Corrections, 2021). In total, almost three million American children are impacted by incarceration yearly. Children and adolescents who are incarcerated experience challenges to their physical, cognitive, and mental health development, as well as decreased future economic and social opportunities (Sawyer, 2019). Children with incarcerated parents (IP) are more likely to have school problems and less school engagement than their unaffected peers (Murphey & Cooper, 2015). Children with IP also have less parental monitoring of relationships and risky behaviors and greater levels of emotional difficulties (Murphey & Cooper, 2015). These hardships reveal the need for intense support services.

Educational systems can provide much needed assistance to both children who are in the juvenile justice system and youth with IP. The Committee on the Rights of the Child (2019) asserts that the child justice system should provide adequate education for the release and reintegration of the child into society; furthermore, children in juvenile justice systems have a right to an education that is appropriate for their needs and abilities; however, students in juvenile justice facilities receive fewer educational hours per week than students in public schools (Office for Civil Rights, 2016). Furthermore, two thirds of incarcerated youth do not return to school to obtain a high school diploma or GED (Roy-Stevens, 2004).

In contrast to the educational outcomes for incarcerated students, typically developing children in the United States spend approximately 1,000 hours per year in school (Organisation for Economic Co-operation and Development, 2021.) Given this significant amount of concentrated time with responsible adults who can monitor progress and intervene when necessary, the local school system can be a tremendous asset for students with IP.

School Support Personnel

This chapter focuses on three school support roles who work within the public education system: school counselors, school psychologists, and teachers. School counselors are professionals who have completed a graduate level education in the field of counseling. They must meet rigorous state certification and licensure requirements, and uphold the ethical and professional standards of the American School Counseling Association (ASCA). ASCA (2021) asserts school counselors help students improve academic achievement, increase their emotional well being, and counsel students on their future career endeavors. This chapter will highlight the important role that school counselors can play in assisting youth impacted by incarceration. As of 2021, in the United States, 24 states and the District of Columbia mandate that school counselors be employed in grades K–12; six states mandate that school counselors serve in public schools for grades 9–12 but not in elementary schools; and 20 states do not mandate school counselors in public schools. Table 1 presents the states which have mandates for school counselors to be employed in public schools.

Table 1. School Counselor Mandates by State

Yes Mandate for K–8 Yes Mandate for 9–12	No Mandate for K–8 Yes Mandate for 9–12	No Mandate for K–8 No Mandate for 9–12
Alabama Arkansas District of Columbia Georgia Idaho Iowa Maine Maryland Missouri Montana Nebraska New Hampshire New Jersey New Mexico North Dakota Oklahoma Oregon Rhode Island South Carolina Tennessee Vermont Virginia West Virginia Wisconsin Wyoming	Indiana Louisiana Mississippi Nevada Utah Washington	Alaska Arizona California Colorado Connecticut Delaware Florida Hawaii Illinois Kansas Kentucky Massachusetts Michigan Minnesota New York North Carolina Ohio Pennsylvania South Dakota Texas

School psychologists are graduate level professionals who work in public schools to support student learning through assessment, intervention monitoring, and school-based counseling. In addition, they support learning by offering teacher consultation on academic and behavioral strategies. The National Association of School Psychologists (2021a) indicates 48 states require a school district to employ at least one person who has a degree or certification in school psychology (Kansas and Tennessee are the two states that do not specify education in "school psychology"). School psychologists work with children in juvenile justice systems in a variety of ways: They conduct psychoeducational evaluations to assess a student's cognitive abilities, academic achievement, and social emotional functioning before students go into the juvenile system, when they are in the system, or when they are reintegrated into their home schools. They also provide recommendations for interventions to improve student success. School psychologists work with students with IP by providing psychoeducational evaluations, school-based counseling, teacher consultation, and writing and monitoring special education plans (referred to as Individual Education Programs or IEPs). This chapter will explain the ways in which school psychologists (and others who hold the school psychology training, though differently named) can assist youth impacted by incarceration.

Teachers provide direct instruction to our country's youth, as such, the teacher's approach can impact a student's readiness, willingness, and ability to learn. Each state has different requirements to obtain a teacher certification but the basic requirement is a bachelor's degree in education. Traditional public schools require instruction to be delivered by teachers certified for their grade level and content area. Teachers working with children who are incarcerated or teachers working in public education with students with IP can assist in the student's academic progress and social emotional development in impactful ways.

SCHOOL SUPPORTS WHEN THE STUDENT IS INCARCERATED

Students who are incarcerated are entitled to a public education that is delivered through the justice system. Attitudes and dispositions toward the students receiving education delivered through this system impact the student's educational progress. If a successful reintegration of students into the public school system postincarceration is expected, then students should be given a quality education delivered in a confidence-building manner.

Vélez Young-Alfaro (2017) conducted an ethnography which indicated that students in a youth prison school setting felt as though the majority of the direct (verbal) and indirect (nonverbal) interactions they had with adults treated them as if they were threats. This consistent messaging impacted identity development so that the youth began to see themselves as threats. Vélez Young-Alfaro points out the structural factors in youth prison schools give indirect messaging of dangerousness. For example, high levels of restriction with locked doors and the potential for physical restraint, the need for specific permission to use the bathroom or use specific school supplies, or even getting up from their desks, constantly reinforce the message that the youth are potentially dangerous.

As recommended in the 2009 National Juvenile Justice Network's policy platform, "All facilities must provide each youth with an appropriate education. Facilities must identify youth who have learning disabilities or other special needs and provide those youth with an individualized education program and accommodations to meet their needs. Facilities must provide other activities and programs that support a youth's healthy development into adulthood" (p.1). Research supports the need for this recommendation (e.g., Foley, 2001); however, the strategies required to accomplish this recommendation are not effectively implemented by juvenile justice agencies (Brazzell et al., 2009).

It is not uncommon for students who are incarcerated to be behind in earning the credits required by their state department of education for a high school diploma (Hagner et al., 2008). Hagner et al. found that participants felt they were too far behind in required credits once discharged back to their home schools. Further, discharge did not align with the school calendar, and did not coordinate with the beginning or end of a semester (Hagner et al., 2008). As a condition for parole, study participants noted that they were released with work to complete from unaligned syllabi, expected to attend school regularly, and to be academically successful (Hagner et al., 2008). It is not surprising that Foley (2001) found that 43% of youth offenders leave the criminal justice system without a high school diploma, and never return to school. Many juvenile correctional systems fail to provide appropriate educational programming to students in spite of the Elementary and Secondary Education Act (ESEA) 2015 amendment to Title I,

Part D, "Prevention and Intervention Programs for Children and Youth Who are Neglected," meant to support youth transitioning to and from the juvenile justice system by requiring educational planning, supports, and efficient reenrollment in appropriate educational placements (Office of Elementary and Secondary Education, 2015).

While it is difficult to accurately measure how many incarcerated youth are identified as having a disability, studies have found the rate to range between 40% and 70% (Bullis et al., 2002; Wolford, 2000). This inconsistent information can be attributed to undiagnosed or misdiagnosed disabilities. Many students who are deemed unlikely to succeed in a comprehensive high school setting are referred for special services and out of district placement (Foley, 2001). Bullis et al. (2002) reported that juveniles with disabilities were 2.8 times more likely to be reincarcerated.

Students who arrive as eligible for special education and related services continue to have that statutory right while incarcerated; additionally, these students are eligible to receive transition planning and vocational training (Hagner et al., 2008). Unruh and Bullis (2005) found a lack of transition services available to incarcerated juveniles created employment-related barriers. Incarcerated juveniles are generally not afforded the opportunity to utilize transition services in the form of job sampling, resulting in job experiences being limited. While transition coordinators may assist juveniles in securing a position, the adjudicated juvenile learns their job skills in real time, subjecting them to real-life consequences as well, such as being laid off or fired (Unruh & Bullis, 2005). As a result, juvenile offenders receive vocational training in high-stakes situations. Non-adjudicated juveniles, particularly those with disabilities, are afforded more opportunities to practice job skills in a structured, supported, low-risk environment. The National Juvenile Justice Network policy platform (2009) advocated in their recommendations,

When appropriate, youth should be allowed to temporarily leave facilities for supervised community service activities, jobs, job training, and home visits in order to maintain prosocial connections to the community. In addition, community, volunteer, and faith-based groups should be permitted access to facilities in order to provide youth with classes, workshops, and other services and activities. (p. 2)

This practice has safety, security, and fiscal ramifications that are not addressed in the recommendation.

As with the research regarding female offenders with disabilities, transition information on incarcerated female juveniles is sparse and typically not examined with a separation in the data according to male versus female offenders (Unruh & Bullis, 2005). The research shows that both males and females involved in the juvenile justice system display problems at home and at school prior to being placed in the system, and to adjust poorly back to school and the community, resulting in an unlikeliness to adapt successfully into adult life (Unruh & Bullis, 2005).

Hagner et al. (2008) asked their study participants to describe what supports they felt would provide the best possible outcomes postincarceration. Thirty-three participants, age 14–17 years old, had been in the criminal justice system for at least two weeks (Hagner et al., 2008). Ninety percent of the participants in the study stated that the ability of their community school to engage the student upon transitioning from the criminal justice system would determine if their outcome was successful or not (Hagner et al., 2008).

The National Juvenile Justice Network recommended in 2009,

All youth must receive a thorough initial evaluation of their mental, emotional, and physical health needs upon entry into any facility and must be provided with appropriate treatment and services during their

time in confinement. Prior to their return to the community, adequate preparation for their subsequent educational, emotional, physical, and mental health care needs must be made. (p. 1)

As the research continues to show, this recommendation is either not adhered to with fidelity, or there are barriers to fulfilling this recommendation.

Allen and Lloyd-Hazlett (2021) explored perspectives on postincarceration success through narrative inquiry with six participants. All six participants pointed to education as being the most important component of success after incarceration. A quality education gave these participants confidence to go forward and make changes in their lives after incarceration. Similarly, Metcalf (2002) asserts that "optimum educational placement, counseling, mentoring, employment assistance, and tutoring are examples of the extra encouragement that can make the difference between graduation and chronic incarceration." Therefore, proper educational supports for incarcerated youth are critical.

The Role of the School Counselor When a Student Is Incarcerated

School counselors provide direct and indirect services which benefit students. Direct services include individual and group school-based counseling, career counseling, and academic support. Indirect services include consultation with teachers, consultation with parents, and coordination with community support providers. When a student is incarcerated, the facilitation of educational continuity is an indirect service provided. Stone and Zibulsky (2015) assert that the lack of educational continuity is a major obstacle for student success in the juvenile justice system. Students' educational backgrounds should be shared with educators in the system when students enter the facilities. Likewise, educational records should be shared with the public school district when the students reintegrate into public schools postincarceration. Therefore, it is necessary for school personnel to be involved in coordinating the educational services of students as they enter the juvenile justice system and when they exit by sharing educational records. Since school counselors are highly familiar with maintaining educational records, this is a crucial role they should play in assisting these students.

School counselors can also provide educational continuity when reintegrating students into schools postincarceration by coordinating communication with external counselors. Students, postincarceration, benefit from ongoing counseling and mentoring services (e.g., Allen, & Lloyd-Hazlett, 2021; Lopez-Humphreys & Teater, 2019). Communication between the school counselor and the external counselor would provide the students with more success in school academically, behaviorally, and in terms of social-emotional wellbeing (Appling et al., 2020).

Research is lacking in the area of the direct services school counselors can offer incarcerated students. However, much can be surmised about the school counselor's role when one considers the services that are offered in the public schools. The American School Counselor Association (2021) explains that school counselors create school counseling programs which aim to improve the student's academic and social emotional success while at school while also helping students achieve career goals. The school counselor working in a juvenile justice system can help the student approach each of these goals. School counselors can offer individual and group counseling to students who are incarcerated to improve student attitudes toward education and career. School counselors can also assist in transitioning students to vocational placements when appropriate—either coordinating vocational training while incarcerated or transitioning a student to a vocational school postincarceration.

As noted above, two thirds of incarcerated youth do not complete a high school diploma or GED (Roy-Stevens, 2004). School counselors could decrease this number by supporting the youths' mindset on the importance of education. Belief in one's control over career goals is a powerful motivator and predictor of success (Shane et al., 2012). By helping incarcerated youth identify and work toward career goals, youth may be more likely to return to school after incarceration to complete their diplomas or GEDs.

Likewise, when students reintegrate into schools after incarceration, it is important for the school counselor to work closely with the students to focus specifically on their academic, social-emotional, and career goal improvement. These students may be more reluctant to attend school regularly and engage with school support personnel (Hawkins et al., 2011). Therefore, the school counselor needs to reach out to this at-risk population to help them feel included in the school body and to feel as though positive postsecondary school opportunities are possible. This outreach can be done through individual, school-based counseling as well as group counseling, if an appropriate group exists in the school. Increasing social capital through connections with school personnel may enhance the outcomes for the reintegrated youth (Hawkins et al., 2011).

The Role of the School Psychologist When a Student Is Incarcerated

The Council of State Governments Justice Center (2015) identified that one in three incarcerated youth were identified as being in need of special education; more than 50% of incarcerated youth have reading and math skills significantly below grade level; 60% of incarcerated youth have repeated a grade. These statistics signal the need for academic interventions that would be appropriately evaluated and recommended by school psychologists. The National Association of School Psychologists (NASP) endorses the role of school psychologists working in juvenile justice systems (NASP, 2021b). Crespi and Lovelace (2010) address the training needs of school psychologists in nontraditional settings, such as juvenile justice facilities.

Regardless of whether students are receiving their education in juvenile justice systems or public schools, the Individuals with Disabilities Education Act (2004) specifies that youth under the age of 18 with disabilities are entitled to a free appropriate public education (FAPE). This federal law further specifies that local educational agencies (LEAs) have a responsibility to identify and service all students with disabilities within their district, including those students who are incarcerated in juvenile and adult justice systems. When students are incarcerated, the school psychologist can provide evaluations, educational monitoring through the IEP, and educational consultation to teachers, and can assist in transition planning. Geib et al. (2011) suggest that disability screening can be carried out during the intake process into the juvenile justice system. Furthermore, they advocate for youth to be tracked or supervised throughout their educational experience in the juvenile justice system so that their educational progress can be documented in an IEP, which can then be transitioned into the public school system postincarceration.

Stone and Zibulsky (2015) make the case for involvement of a school psychologist to improve academic and social emotional outcomes for incarcerated youth. They call for school psychologists to create comprehensive, school-based health and mental health programming which functions through a tiered model such as Multitiered Systems of Support (MTSS). The MTSS model typically provides services in three tiers: Tier 1 consists of preventative programming and resilience-building services offered to all students in the student body; Tier 2 consists of interventions targeting at-risk populations within a school; Tier 3 consists of specifically-tailored intervention services for individual students who have been identified as needing such. Tier 3 services would be most relevant to incarcerated students. An example of a Tier 3 service would be having the school psychologist create a reintegration plan which would include social emotional welfare planning as well as parent coordination.

The Role of the Teacher When a Student Is Incarcerated

Teachers have a demanding job in that they have to attend to the various needs of each student while educating them as a group. Teachers of incarcerated students have the same demands as teachers in public schools with the additional complications of managing behaviors and attempting to implement inspiring and confidence-building activities in a highly restrictive setting. The professional needs of teachers working in the juvenile justice system and working with students who have been released from incarceration must be addressed.

Regardless of the state in which a student is incarcerated, all students are entitled to equal access to opportunities that promote educational excellence (U.S. Department of Education, 2021). Research continually shows that educational programs in correctional facilities span a spectrum of provision, from below the minimum, to meeting the individual educational needs of students (e.g., Foley, 2001.) The available special education programs vary even more. As a result, the role of the teacher in correctional facilities also varies greatly.

States vary as widely regarding their requirements for teaching in a correctional facility as they do on their philosophies of education and programming. The Federal Bureau of Prisons requires teachers to show eligibility to teach in one of three ways: They need to a) have a minimum of a bachelor's degree, coursework in four pertinent areas of student functioning and development, student teaching experience, and 24 semester hours of coursework in teaching principles; b) demonstrate that they have a bachelor's degree and one year of teaching experience that included lesson plan preparation and student evaluation, or c) have a valid teaching certificate or license; the other requirements, such as student teaching or specific coursework, are not required with this option. Special education teachers are required to have 24 semester hours of special education coursework. They are not required to have any experience working with special education students (Federal Bureau of Prisons, 2021), nor are they required to have experience working with incarcerated youth.

While students entering the justice system have typically already experienced academic failure, difficulties with attendance, behavioral impediments to success, and a lack of home supports to meet their needs, only one option to become a teacher with the Federal Bureau of Prisons requires any coursework in general psychology and child development, and no experience or training in handling students with traumatic experiences, behavioral difficulties or classroom management is noted (Federal Bureau of Prisons, 2021).

Once teachers are hired for a teaching position in a correctional facility, the teaching models, daily schedule, and access to students and resources are typically dictated to them by the facility. The National Juvenile Justice Network (2016) reports that incarcerated youth face numerous barriers to reaching their educational goals. They state that students are provided "a substandard education" (p. 1) with curricula that are not aligned to the state standards, delays in the transfer of educational records to and from the correctional facility, and policies that can prevent reenrollment in schools once their term of incarceration has been fulfilled. In addition to the lack of cohesion in educational programs, even when a facility does utilize the local curriculum, incarcerated youth generally lack access to the technology that is used by schools to teach the curriculum (Leone & Wruble, 2015). Other supplies and resources are also limited, whether due to differences in funding or for other reasons such as safety in the setting. Leone and

Wruble found that it was not uncommon for classes to be cancelled due to a staffing shortage. Classes can be cancelled for individual students based upon movement restrictions, or cancelled entirely due to facility lockdowns (Brazzell et al., 2009). Therefore, it is unlikely that they are receiving the reported number of hours of education on a daily basis.

Research shows the majority of instruction seems to take place as direct, whole-group instruction for both students with and without disabilities (Foley, 2001). This can be due to many reasons, including those above as well as a lack of updated materials, large class sizes, lack of substitute teachers, and lack of staff development (Leone & Wruble, 2015). Funding for educational programs in the corrections system does not keep up with increases in enrollment, and these programs are typically the first to receive fiscal cuts (Brazzell et al., 2009). As a result, students are not afforded the materials, access to technology, or even the space required to effectively run a classroom. The role of the teacher, then, is quite limited by a number of factors outside of their control.

Foley (2001) found that special education services vary across the United States. Research to determine the extent to which IDEA mandates are followed within correctional facilities is extremely limited (Foley, 2001). It was found that educators in correctional facilities will typically find a mixture of general and special education students in their classes, placing the responsibility to modify instruction and accommodate all student needs within the class upon the classroom teacher, whether qualified or not to do so.

SOCIAL EMOTIONAL LEARNING IN SCHOOLS TO REDUCE STUDENT INCARCERATION

From a MTSS model, school-wide prevention level services are referred to as Tier 1 services. These are services which all school personnel are involved with implementing: school counselors, school psychologists, teachers, school administrators, etc. Tier 2 consists of services targeted toward a small group of students who have been identified as being at risk. Of relevance to incarcerated students, school delinquency is a risk factor for incarceration (Denning & Homel, 2008); therefore, students who demonstrate delinquent behavior may be included in Tier 2 services.

School-wide social emotional learning programs can be considered Tier 1 or Tier 2 services. The Collaborative for Academic and Social Emotional Learning (CASEL, 2019) defines social emotional learning (SEL) as “the process through which children and adults understand and manage emotions, set and achieve positive goals, feel and show empathy for others, establish and maintain positive relationships, and make responsible decisions.” Table 2 presents the five competencies that should be included in SEL programs according to CASEL.

Table 2. CASEL's 5 SEL competencies (2013 CASEL Guide, p. 9)

Self-awareness: The ability to accurately recognize one's emotions and thoughts and their influence on behavior. This includes accurately assessing one's strengths and limitations and possessing a well-grounded sense of confidence and optimism.
Self-management: The ability to regulate one's emotions, thoughts, and behaviors effectively in different situations. This includes managing stress, controlling impulses, motivating oneself, and setting and working toward achieving personal and academic goals.
Social awareness: The ability to take the perspective of and empathize with others from diverse backgrounds and cultures, to understand social and ethical norms for behavior, and to recognize family, school, and community resources and supports.
Relationship skills: The ability to establish and maintain healthy and rewarding relationships with diverse individuals and groups. This includes communicating clearly, listening actively, cooperating, resisting inappropriate social pressure, negotiating conflict constructively, and seeking and offering help when needed.
Responsible decision making: The ability to make constructive and respectful choices about personal behavior and social interactions based on consideration of ethical standards, safety concerns, social norms, the realistic evaluation of consequences of various actions, and the well-being of self and others.

At this time, all 50 states require SEL goals to be included in the curriculum at some point between preschool and 12th grade (CASEL, 2019). Research on the benefits of SEL programming in schools suggests that social emotional learning opportunities in schools reduce delinquent behavior in the early school-aged years (e.g., Choudhury & Moses, 2016; Frey et al., 2005). Since early-age delinquent behavior is a risk factor for later incarceration, SEL programs in schools may offer the potential to reduce incarceration for youth. SEL programming needs to start as early as preschool. Early intervention in preschool can increase the IQ of preschool children, increase their academic readiness, and improve student behaviors (i.e., Barnett & Hustedt, 2005). Ensuring that students enter school with the behavioral and academic readiness skills to learn and stay on grade level sets children up for academic success. Without this early intervention, students from urban and low-income areas are often below grade level from the beginning, which can lead to behavioral problems (e.g., Schweinhart, 2013).

Additionally, Durlak et al. (2011) found that SEL programs in school can significantly enhance attitudes, behaviors, and academic performance. Bridgeland et al. (2006) conducted a national survey of individuals who had dropped out of high school. They described that participants indicated they would have stayed in school until graduation if there had been more of a focus on social emotional skills during school. This research signals a need for school personnel to continue developing and implementing effective SEL programs in school to improve the academic achievement and behavioral and social emotional well-being of children.

SCHOOL SUPPORTS WHEN A PARENT IS INCARCERATED

Adverse Childhood Experiences (ACEs) are experiences of youth between 0 and 17 years old that can be potentially traumatic. ACEs can cause long-term physical health and mental health problems (e.g., Chang et al., 2019). The incarceration of a school-age child's parent is an ACE.

Lee et al. (2014) demonstrated that there is a correlation between the stress experienced by youth who had a parent with a history of incarceration and poor health, highlighting the needs for emotional and physical health support. Sullivan (2020) points out the many struggles experienced by children of IP including residential instability, food insecurity, and lack of adult support for educational, medical, developmental, and emotional needs.

Turney and Goodsell (2018) describe the impairments students suffer when their parents are incarcerated across four domains of well-being: (1) behavior, (2) education, (3) health, and (4) hardship and deprivation. Children with IP will be impacted to varying degrees, with the most common risk factors being race and social class (Turney & Goodsell, 2018). Black and Hispanic children experience parental incarceration most frequently; children of parents without high school diplomas are also at an increased risk. In the category of Black children whose parents are without high school diplomas, 62.1% of those surveyed in the Fragile Families and Child Wellbeing Study experienced parental incarceration (Turney & Goodsell, 2018).

Behavioral Impact

Possibly the most commonly discussed domain of impact when a student has one or more parents incarcerated is related to behavior (Turney & Goodsell, 2018). Turney (2017) reports higher rates of social exclusion for children with IP. Turney and Goodsell (2018) describe how paternal incarceration tends to result in children displaying aggressive or destructive behaviors, while maternal incarceration leads to increases in depressive symptoms.

Longitudinal studies support that parental incarceration is associated with increased behavioral problems and reduced prosocial behaviors (Bradshaw et al., 2021). Youth with IP were significantly more likely to experience depression, anxiety, conduct/behavioral problems, attention deficit hyperactivity disorder, and substance use disorders (Bomysoad & Francis, 2021). In a school setting, these behavioral problems can manifest in the classroom, impacting the child's time on academic tasks and disruptions to the classroom learning in general. Behavioral problems in school can also cause social difficulties between the student and peers.

Educational Impact

Examining the educational impact of parental incarceration, Turney and Goodsell (2018) found correlations between paternal incarceration and children being held back in a grade, lower reading and math comprehension scores, a higher rate of school absences, and being placed in special education. The influence of maternal incarceration has been studied less, and the effects on younger children are harder to discern since the entire family unit seems to be more heavily disrupted in this situation (Turney & Goodsell, 2018).

These educational deficits may be attributed to the lack of parental support on schoolwork, as the parent who is incarcerated is not physically present to support learning and the custodial parent may have limited time to give to support the child's educational success. These educational deficits may also be attributed to the child's inability to concentrate on schoolwork because they are struggling with their own mental health, such as depression, anxiety, or ADHD (Bomysoad & Francis, 2021.)

Physical Health Impact

Parental incarceration and the effect on a child's physical health has been widely researched. Because of both the financial impact as well as the availability of care when a parent is incarcerated, these children are more likely to have their healthcare neglected (Turney & Goodsell, 2018). Studies find children exposed to parental incarceration have a higher risk of asthma and obesity, and longitudinal studies have found those children become adults with an increased likelihood for being diagnosed with high cholesterol, migraines, and overall poor health (Turney & Goodsell, 2018). Turney (2017) also reported a higher rate of infant mortality. Unmet healthcare needs in children with IP are similar across race/ethnicity (Turney, 2017). Parks et al. (2020) found that youth with IP use tobacco products more than youth whose parents have never been incarcerated.

Hiolski et al. (2019) compared physical health indicators of children with IP (in grades 8–11) to those of physical health indicators of children without IP (in grades 8–11). Six physical health indicators were measured as dependent variables in this study: overall health, physical activity, fruit and vegetable consumption, fast food consumption, sugar-sweetened beverage consumption, and hours of nightly sleep. For all six indicators, students with IP had health indicators which fared more poorly compared to those students without IP.

Hardship and Deprivation Impact

Children with IP are more greatly impacted by financial hardships, even after accounting for their socioeconomic status prior to the parent being removed from the home (Turney & Goodsell, 2018). As a result, these children are more likely to experience life events such as eviction, homelessness, and food insecurity. Additionally, the economic and lifestyle hardships due to parental incarceration disproportionately impact the Black population (Wildeman, 2014).

Intergenerational incarceration refers to the incidents of increased involvement in the justice system that children with IP experience. Supports offered through the educational system may disrupt this intergenerational process and mediate the negative outcomes associated with parental incarceration.

The Role of the School Counselor When a Student's Parent Is Incarcerated

As previously stated, school counselors provide direct and indirect services that benefit students. With regard to students with IP, direct supports such as school-based counseling and academic monitoring are important services school counselors can offer.

School-based counseling can take the form of individual counseling sessions, group counseling sessions, or SEL programming. School counselors do not engage students in long-term psychotherapy. Rather, counseling sessions are intended to be brief and targeted on specific needs such as teaching coping skills, improving mood regulation, and enhancing self-confidence. Often, counseling sessions address goal setting and positive decision making. School counselors may approach counseling with a variety of therapeutic modalities, such as cognitive-behavioral, solution-focused, or person-centered. When working with a student with IP, the student may be working on several social emotional goals based on the behavioral, physical, mental, or academic impact they are experiencing. School counselors can decide whether those students would benefit from one-on-one counseling or group counseling in school. The school counselor can also decide whether the student should see the counselor on a weekly, biweekly, or monthly basis.

School counselors can provide academic monitoring for students with IP. One route for academic monitoring is through referral to the Intervention and Referral Services Teams (also known as Pupil Assistance Committee). This type of team, typically facilitated by the school counselor, consists of the school nurse and teachers. This team will review a student's academic progress and needs and will make recommendations for accommodations for assistance, allowing specialized attention to be given to students in need. In the case of a student with IP, accommodations could include academic intervention to reduce homework assignments, provide positive behavioral supports in the classroom, and/or include health monitoring by the school nurse.

Career counseling and career goal attainment are services that school counselors assist students with. Oftentimes, schools facilitate parent night events to bring parents into the school to discuss postsecondary options for the students. When parents are unable to attend due to incarceration, or when the custodial parent is unable to attend due to caregiving responsibilities, the child with IP is left vulnerable to being overlooked. School counselors can take time to assess students' career goals. If the student is interested in a vocational career, the school counselor can assist the student in applying to vocational school programs. If the student is interested in college, the school counselor can assist the student in applying to schools and have application fees waived. Additionally, the school counselor can assist the student in obtaining loans to pay for college.

Indirect services offered by school counselors include consultation with teachers, coordinating career goal attainment, and coordinating wraparound services, such as community-based mental health and welfare services that could assist the youth and their families. School counselors can consult with teachers to approach working with students from a perspective of trauma-sensitive care. Many times, school personnel do not know when students have a parent who is incarcerated since there are no mandates for reporting such circumstances. Therefore, it is helpful when teachers approach all students delicately, with respect for their life situations. A school approaching trauma-sensitive care includes professional development for teachers to identify signs and symptoms of trauma, learn to respond to students carefully when they are showing these signs and symptoms, and build positive connections among staff and students (Trauma-Informed Care Implementation Resource Center, 2021). School counselors can offer this type of professional development/training to teaching staff in the school as an indirect service to enhance the learning experience of students.

Increasing relationships between school personnel and students by forming a mentorship can be helpful for affected students (Sullivan, 2020; Rossen, 2011). School counselors can assist affected youth and their families to obtain community-based mental health services. The school counselors often know community-based mental health counselors who have expertise in different areas and with different populations, so they are in a unique position to make an appropriate referral.

School counselors can assist families in securing the necessary welfare supports that may alleviate some of the hardships they are experiencing. Within the school, students of low-income families can receive free or reduced lunch and breakfast. Furthermore, those free or reduced cost meals can be received throughout the entire summer, even when school is not in session. When these forms are sent home with a student but not returned, the school counselor can follow up with the family to ensure that forms are signed to initiate the meal service.

Financial assistance for utility bills can be obtained through the Low Income Home Energy Assistance Program (LIHEAP). School counselors can share this information, as well as information about other federal welfare support programs such as the Supplemental Nutrition Assistance Program (SNAP) and Temporary Assistance for Needy Families (TANF) with families to ensure they have the necessary supports for safe, daily living. Additionally, school counselors can assist families in securing free or reduced cost internet service in their home so that students can continue to access their homework assignments and study materials online. Helping families to understand the need for and obtaining these free or reduced cost services can reinforce the importance of education for the students.

The Role of the School Psychologist When a Student's Parent Is Incarcerated

If a student with IP is referred to the intervention and referral service or pupil assistance team, a school psychologist should be invited to participate in the meeting as an ad hoc member. The school psychologist can advise whether a more thorough child study team evaluation should take place to allow for more in-depth evaluation of the student. Such evaluation could assess the student's cognitive, academic, and social emotional functioning to identify whether school-based counseling services or an IEP is needed. In some cases, ACEs can cause such an intense level of stress for a child that the child demonstrates behaviors which could meet special education eligibility. In such a case, an IEP would be written and educational progress monitoring would ensue.

When a student with IP is already receiving special education services through an IEP, an IEP review meeting might be appropriate to review the student's progress and to ensure that all needs are continuing to be met. School-based counseling may be a related service added to an IEP when an eligible student has an ACE. School-based counseling is typically included when the student's social emotional factors are impacting their ability to access their education. In such cases, school-based counseling as an IEP-driven related service may address goals based around the need for improved organization, executive functioning, and task completion.

School psychologists working with students with IP should give added attention to relationship-building and academic monitoring of affected students. Additional outreach would likely be needed to ensure communication with the student's guardian. Oftentimes, general school paperwork (e.g., program announcements, extracurricular announcements, school lists, Parent-Teacher Association messages) is mailed or emailed to families. Child study team paperwork, such as invitations to evaluation planning meetings, when a child is being reviewed for a disability, or IEP meetings, to monitor student progress, is also often sent home through mail or email. These forms of communication may be missed by families who are working through increased stressors, such as incarceration. To build trust and relationships for students with IP, school psychologists could reach out to create relationships with the student's caregiver (Rossen, 2011). To improve this outreach, school psychologists should take a more active and direct role in communicating with parents through phone calls or, in some cases, through house visits. Personalized and individualized attention in this way can strengthen trust and a working relationship to benefit the student.

Finally, like the school counselor, the school psychologist can assist in teacher consultation using a trauma-sensitive approach. Ormiston et al. (2020) described that due to the comprehensive training of school psychologists in counseling strategies, teacher consultation, and child assessments, school psychologists are uniquely qualified to build MTSS using trauma-informed practices. The goal of this approach is to support students by helping teachers implement empathetic and preventative practices in the classroom.

The Role of the Teacher When a Student's Parent Is Incarcerated

It is important that teachers maintain high expectations for students despite their family dynamics (Rossen, 2011). Teachers strive to help students feel seen as individuals who are still progressing towards their own potential. Students are not defined by their family dynamic even though they are impacted by it. Being trained in a trauma-sensitive approach would give the teacher necessary preparation and tools to work most effectively with students from a variety of family dynamics (Trauma-Informed Care Implementation Resource Center, 2021).

Teachers might make curricular decisions being mindful of family dynamics. For example, teachers might take a creative approach to the acknowledgement of Mother's Day or Father's Day, as these holidays may pose an increased emotional challenge for the student with IP. To describe differentiated instruction in the classroom to be more inclusive of family styles is beyond the scope of this chapter. We will leave the discussion by offering resources at the end of this chapter that might be helpful for teachers. Knowledge of these resources is important for counselors working with youth with IP to offer strategies or consultation when needed.

IMPLICATIONS

There is an implication for educational advocacy for juveniles who are currently incarcerated. Youth receiving their education within the juvenile justice system must have access to quality education which is appropriate to meet their educational needs. School counselors, school psychologists, and all mental health professionals who work with youth can advocate for these services. In a justice system which aims to remediate youth to reintegrate into society, education is paramount. Mental health professionals who recognize this need can effectively advocate for these developmentally appropriate services.

Advocacy efforts would also be appropriate to increase SEL programming in schools. Currently, all 50 states require SEL goals to be included in preschool, but far fewer require SEL goals to be included through grade 12 (CASEL, 2019). SEL services may be an effective tool used within an MTSS model to benefit students impacted by incarceration.

Since students entering the justice system typically have already experienced a number of behavioral, academic, and mental health concerns, coursework in child psychology or training in trauma-sensitive care is indicated. Likewise, teachers working with students with IP will be better equipped to enhance students' learning and forge stronger connections when trained in trauma-sensitive approaches.

The law and the perspectives of professionals indicate that schools have the ability to offer supports that can help students impacted by incarceration. School counselors, school psychologists, and teachers need to think expansively about their roles in the schools to ensure they are meeting the needs of all youth, whether in traditional or nontraditional settings. Active outreach is needed to work with students impacted by incarceration.

FUTURE RESEARCH DIRECTIONS

Although there are supports to be obtained through schools, more research into the educational opportunities offered to incarcerated youth is needed. Research is needed into the ways that youth in justice systems are receiving education. Research can investigate the adherence to teacher certification standards and the amount of time on task that incarcerated students actually receive.

Due to the prevalence of youth with disabilities who are incarcerated, critical questions regarding the delivery of special education services remain. Specifically, research is needed into the extent to which IDEA regulations are being followed. Are students receiving special education evaluations? Are IEPs being written and implemented accordingly? Is educational monitoring taking place?

To improve the high school graduation rate postincarceration, more research is needed to find out where the educational discontinuity between incarceration and postincarceration is happening. More research into the extent to which vocational assessments and vocational placement postincarceration are being conducted is needed. Research into the efficacy of SEL programming during and postincarceration is also needed to identify whether there are evidence-based programs which can benefit this population to improve their graduation rate.

CONCLUSION

Yearly, almost 3 million children in America are impacted by incarceration, either by being incarcerated themselves or having a parent who is incarcerated. Incarcerated youth require services while incarcerated and postincarceration to support their social emotional growth and their educational attainment. School counselors, school psychologists, and teachers can support incarcerated youth by enhancing educational continuity, increasing the coordination of services between the public school and the juvenile justice system, increasing positive behavioral supports, increasing academic monitoring, improving vocational assessment and training, and offering SEL programming focused on career counseling goals. When students return to the public school system postincarceration, school personnel can refer them to student support committees such as the intervention and referral services team or the child study team, offer school-based counseling to actively engage the student in the school community, provide academic monitoring through graduation, and coordinate services with community mental health providers.

Likewise, school counselors, school psychologists, and teachers need to support students with IP by implementing academic monitoring of students on multiple tiers in order to identify students at risk. When a student with IP is identified, outreach should be made to the custodial parent to ensure the coordination of services with community mental health providers and welfare services in order to mitigate the hardships the student faces. Ongoing academic monitoring, school-based counseling, SEL programming, and assistance with postsecondary planning should be given individualized attention.

With the amount of time youth spend in educational services and the quality of the training and education of school personnel, students impacted by incarceration can benefit from enhanced support provided by the public school system.

REFERENCES

Allen, S., & Lloyd-Hazlett, J. (2021). Success stories of males convicted of a violent offense. *International Journal for the Advancement of Counseling*, *43*(2), 147–163. doi:10.100710447-021-09421-5

American School Counselor Association (ASCA). (2021). *The role of the school counselor.* Retrieved June 24, 2021 from https://www.schoolcounselor.org/

Appling, B. M., Tuttle, M., & May, V. S. (2020). The experiences of school counselors who collaborate with clinical mental health counselors. *Professional School Counseling*, *23*(1), 1–10. 10.1177%2F2156759X19882660

Barnett, W. S., & Hustedt, J. T. (2005). Head Start's lasting benefits. *Infants and Young Children, 18*(1), 16–24. doi:10.1097/00001163-200501000-00003

Bomysoad, R. N., & Francis, L. A. (2021). Associations between parental incarceration and youth mental health conditions: The mitigating effects of adolescent resilience and positive coping strategies. *Current Psychology (New Brunswick, N.J.)*. Advance online publication. doi:10.100712144-021-01351-0

Bradshaw, D., Creaven, A.-M., & Muldoon, O. T. (2021). Parental incarceration affects children's emotional and behavioral outcomes: A longitudinal cohort study of children aged 9 to 13 years. *International Journal ofBehavioral Development, 45*(4), 310–316. Advance online publication. doi:10.1177/0165025421995918

Brazzell, D., Crayton, A., Mukamal, D. A., Solomon, A. L., & Lindahl, N. (2009). *From the classroom to the community: Exploring the role of education during incarceration and reentry.* The Urban Institute, John Jay College. Retrieved July 25, 2021 from https://www.urban.org/sites/default/files/publication/30671/411963-From-the-Classroom-to-the-Community.PDF

Bridgeland, J., Dilulio, J. Jr, & Morison, K. (2006). *The silent epidemic: Perspectives of high school dropouts*. Civic Enterprises.

Bullis, M., Yovanoff, P., Mueller, G., & Havel, E. (2002). Life on the "outs": Examination of the facility-to-community transition of incarcerated youth. *Exceptional Children, 69*(1), 7–22. doi:10.1177/001440290206900101

Chang, X., Jiang, X., Mkandarwire, T., & Shen, M. (2019). Associations between adverse childhood experiences and health outcomes in adults aged 18–59 years. *PLoS One, 14*(2), e0211850. Advance online publication. doi:10.1371/journal.pone.0211850 PMID:30730980

Children's Defense Fund. (2021). *The state of America's children® 2020: Youth justice*. Retrieved June 22, 2021 from https://www.childrensdefense.org/policy/resources/soac-2020-youth-justice/

Choudhury, S., & Moses, J. M. (2016). Mindful interventions: Youth, poverty, and the developing brain. *Theory & Psychology, 26*(5), 591–606. doi:10.1177/0959354316669025

Collaborative for Academic and Social Emotional Learning (CASEL). (2013). *CASEL Guide: Effective social and emotional learning programs: Preschool and elementary school edition*. CASEL.

Collaborative for Academic and Social Emotional Learning (CASEL). (2019). *SEL is...* Retrieved July 8, 2021 from https://casel.org/what-is-sel/

Committee on the Rights of the Child. (2019, September 18). General comment No. 24 (2019) on children's rights in the child justice system. United Nations.

Council of State Governments Justice Center & the Council of Juvenile Correctional Administrators. (2015, November). *Locked out: Improving educational and vocational outcomes for incarcerated youth.* Retrieved July 31, 2021 from https://csgjusticecenter.org/publications/locked-out-improving-educational-and-vocational-outcomes-for-incarcerated-youth/

Crespi, T. D., & Lovelace, J. R. (2010). Adolescent incarceration and children's psychiatric hospitalization: Training school psychologists for nontraditional settings. In E. García-Vásquez, T. D. Crespi, & C. A. Riccio (Eds.), Handbook of education, training, and supervision of school psychologists in school and community, Vol 1: Foundations of professional practice (pp. 279–294). Routledge/Taylor & Francis Group.

Denning, R., & Homel, R. (2008). Predicting recidivism in juvenile offenders on community-based orders: The impact of risk factors and service delivery. *Probation and Parole: Current Issues*, *46*(3–4), 189–215. doi:10.1080/10509670802143508

Durlak, J. A., Weissberg, R. P., Dymnicki, A. B., Taylor, R. D., & Schellinger, K. B. (2011). The impact of enhancing students' social and emotional learning: A meta-analysis of school-based universal interventions. *Child Development*, *82*(1), 405–432. doi:10.1111/j.1467-8624.2010.01564.x PMID:21291449

Federal Bureau of Prisons. (2021). *Teacher: Job series number: 1710*. Retrieved July 24, 2021 from https://www.bop.gov/jobs/positions/index.jsp?p=Teacher#:~:text=Basic%20Requirements&text=You%20have%20a%20Bachelor's%20degree,and%2For%20philosophy%20of%20education

Foley, R. (2001). Academic characteristics of incarcerated youth and correctional educational programs: A literature review. *Journal of Emotional and Behavioral Disorders*, *9*(4), 248–259. doi:10.1177/106342660100900405

Frey, K. S., Nolen, S. B., Van Schoiack Edstrom, L., & Hirschstein, M. K. (2005). Effects of a school-based social-emotional competence program: Linking children's goals, attributions, and behavior. *Journal of Applied Developmental Psychology*, *26*(2), 171–200. doi:10.1016/j.appdev.2004.12.002

Geib, C. F., Chapman, J. F., D'Amaddio, A. H., & Grigorenko, E. L. (2011). The education of juveniles in detention: Policy considerations and infrastructure development. *Learning and Individual Differences*, *21*(1), 3–11. doi:10.1016/j.lindif.2010.05.002

Hagner, D., Malloy, J. M., Mazzone, M. W., & Cormier, G. M. (2008). Youth with disabilities in the Criminal Justice System. *Journal of Emotional and Behavioral Disorders*, *16*(4), 240–247. doi:10.1177/1063426608316019

Hawkins, R. L., Vashchenko, M., & Davis, C. (2011). Making a place for youth: Social capital, resilience, and communities. In F. T. Sherman & F. H. Jacobs (Eds.), *Juvenile Justice: Advancing Research, Policy, and Practice* (pp. 245–266). John Wiley & Sons, Inc. doi:10.1002/9781118093375.ch12

Hiolski, K., Eisenberg, M. E., & Shlafer, R. J. (2019). Youth self-reported health and their experience of parental incarceration. *Families, Systems & Health*, *37*(1), 38–45. doi:10.1037/fsh0000394 PMID:30920262

Individuals with Disabilities Education Act, 20 U.S.C. § 1400 (2004).

Lee, H., Wildeman, C., Wang, E. A., Matusko, N., & Jackson, J. S. (2014). A heavy burden: The cardiovascular health consequences of having a family member incarcerated. *American Journal of Public Health*, *104*(3), 421–427. doi:10.2105/AJPH.2013.301504 PMID:24432879

Leone, P. E., & Wruble, P. C. (2015). Education services in juvenile corrections: 40 years of litigation and reform. *Education & Treatment of Children*, *38*(4), 587–604. doi:10.1353/etc.2015.0026

Lopez-Humphreys, M., & Teater, B. (2019). "It's what's on the inside that counts": A pilot study of the subjective changes among returned citizens participating in a peer-mentor support initiative. *Journal of Social Service Research, 46*(6), 741–755. doi:10.1080/01488376.2019.1656699

Metcalf, R. (2002). Role of the school psychologist in juvenile forensics. In N. G. Ribner (Ed.), *The California School of Professional Psychology handbook of juvenile forensic psychology* (pp. 432–453). Jossey-Bass/Wiley.

Murphey, D., & Cooper, P. M. (2015). *Parents behind bars: What happens to their children?* Child Trends. Retrieved June 22, 2021 from https://www.childtrends.org/wp-content/uploads/2015/10/2015-42ParentsBehindBars.pdf

National Association of School Psychologists (NASP). (2021a). *School psychology credentialing resources*. Retrieved July 5, 2021 from https://www.nasponline.org/standards-and-certification/school-psychology-credentialing-resources

National Association of School Psychologists (NASP). (2021b). *Who are school psychologists*. Retrieved July 6, 2021 from https://www.nasponline.org/about-school-psychology/who-are-school-psychologists

National Institute of Corrections. (2021). *Children of incarcerated parents*. National Institute of Corrections. The United States Department of Justice. Retrieved June 22, 2021 from https://nicic.gov/children-of-incarcerated-parents#:~:text=Recent%20estimates%20show%20that%202.7,or%20jail%20at%20some%20point

National Juvenile Justice Network. (2009). *National Juvenile Justice Network policy platform: Conditions of confinement*. Retrieved July 11, 2021 from http://www.njjn.org/uploads/policy-platforms/Conditions-of-Confinement-Policy-Platform-5-18-12-fin.pdf?phpMyAdmin=14730ab3483c51c94ca868bccffa06ef

National Juvenile Justice Network. (2016). *Improving educational outcomes for youth in the juvenile justice system*. Retrieved July 24, 2021 from https://www.njjn.org/our-work/improving-education-for-youth-in-juvenile-justice-snapshot?phpMyAdmin=14730ab3483c51c94ca868bccffa06ef

Office for Civil Rights. (2016). *2013–2014 Civil rights data collection: A first look* [New Release for 2016]. U.S. Department of Education.

Office of Elementary and Secondary Education, U.S. Department of Education. (2015). *Title I, Part D, Neglected, Delinquent or At-Risk Program*. Retrieved August 3, 2021 from https://oese.ed.gov/offices/office-of-formula-grants/school-support-and-accountability/prevention-intervention-programs-children-youths-neglected-delinquent-risk/

Organisation for Economic Co-operation and Development. (2021). *Teaching hours*. Retrieved June 22, 2021 from https://data.oecd.org/teachers/teaching-hours.htm

Ormiston, H. E., Nygaard, M. A., & Heck, O. C. (2020). The role of school psychologists in the implementation of trauma-informed multi-tiered systems of support in schools. *Journal of Applied School Psychology*. Advance online publication. doi:10.1080/15377903.2020.1848955

Parks, M. J., Davis, L., Wilhelm, A. K., McMorris, B. J., Borowsky, I. W., & Shlafer, R. J. (2020). Parental incarceration and youth tobacco product use: Implications for prevention and the e-cigarette epidemic. *Addictive Behaviors*, *107*, 106428. Advance online publication. doi:10.1016/j.addbeh.2020.106428 PMID:32311626

Rossen, E. (2011, November). Supporting students with incarcerated parents. *Principal Leadership.* Retrieved July 23, 2021 from https://www.nasponline.org/Documents/Resources%20and%20Publications/Handouts/Families%20and%20Educators/Incarcerated_Parents_Nov2011.pdf

Roy-Stevens, C. (2004, October). *Overcoming barriers to school reentry* [Fact sheet]. Office of Juvenile Justice and Delinquency Prevention, U.S. Department of Justice. https://www.ojp.gov/pdffiles1/ojjdp/fs200403.pdf

Sawyer, W. (2019, December 19). *Youth confinement: The whole pie 2019.* Prison Policy Initiative. Retrieved August 4, 2021 from https://www.prisonpolicy.org/reports/youth2019.html

Schweinhart, L. J. (2013). Long-term follow-up of a preschool experiment. *Journal of Experimental Criminology*, *9*(4), 389–409. doi:10.100711292-013-9190-3

Shane, J., Heckhausen, J., Lessard, J., Chen, C., & Greenberger, E. (2012). Career-related goal pursuit among post-high school youth: Relations between personal control beliefs and control strivings. *Motivation and Emotion*, *36*(2), 159–169. doi:10.100711031-011-9245-6

Stone, S., & Zibulsky, J. (2015). Maltreatment, academic difficulty, and systems-involved youth: Current evidence and opportunities. *Psychology in the Schools*, *52*(1), 22–39. doi:10.1002/pits.21812

Sullivan, M. (2020). Research and best practices to support students with incarcerated parents. In E. Rossen (Ed.), *Supporting and educating traumatized students: A guide for school-based professionals* (2nd ed., pp. 165–179). Oxford University Press. doi:0.1093/med-psych/9780190052737.003.0009

Trauma-Informed Care Implementation Resource Center. (2021). *What is trauma-informed care?* Retrieved July 22, 2021 from https://www.traumainformedcare.chcs.org/what-is-trauma-informed-care/

Turney, K. (2017). Unmet health care needs among children exposed to parental incarceration. *Maternal and Child Health Journal*, *21*(5), 1194–1202. doi:10.100710995-016-2219-2 PMID:28108834

Turney, K., & Goodsell, R. (2018). Parental incarceration and children's wellbeing. *The Future of Children*, *28*(1), 147–164. doi:10.1353/foc.2018.0007

Unruh, D., & Bullis, M. (2005). Female and male juvenile offenders with disabilities: Differences in the barriers to their transition to the community. *Behavioral Disorders*, *30*(2), 105–117. doi:10.1177/019874290503000207

U.S. Department of Education. (2021). *The federal role in education.* Retrieved July 24, 2021 from https://www2.ed.gov/about/overview/fed/role.html

Vélez Young-Alfaro, M. (2017). Students as threats: Schooling inside a youth prison. *Anthropology & Education Quarterly*, *48*(3), 301–317. doi:10.1111/aeq.12201

Wildeman, C. (2014). Parental incarceration, child homelessness, and the invisible consequences of mass imprisonment. *The Annals of the American Academy of Political and Social Science*, *651*(1), 74–96. doi:10.1177/0002716213502921

Wolford, B. I. (2000). Youth education in the juvenile justice system. *Corrections Today*, *62*, 128–130.

KEY TERMS AND DEFINITIONS

American School Counselor Association (ASCA): ASCA is an organization, with over 40,000 members, which advocates for the best practices of school counselors. This organization advocates for research-based practices which support school counselors in their work with children.

Americans With Disabilities Act (ADA): ADA is a civil rights law, enacted in 1990, to prohibit discrimination against individuals with disabilities within agencies receiving federal financial assistance.

Free Appropriate Public Education (FAPE): The Individuals with Disabilities Education Act requires public schools to offer students a free appropriate public education, also known as FAPE. Student programming for special education students is measured against the standard of FAPE, particularly when ensuring that students have appropriate special education services offered to them through their Individualized Education Plan (IEP).

Individualized Education Program (IEP): The IEP is a legal document under the Individuals with Disabilities Education Act which specifies the special education services that a student will receive through the public school district. The IEP is written by the child study team, consisting of a representative from the school district, the case manager, a parent, a regular education teacher, and a special education teacher. Goals and objectives are based upon identified needs through evaluations conducted by the child study team.

Individuals With Disabilities Education Act (IDEA): IDEA is a federal law which ensures the rights of children with disabilities to receive a free, appropriate public education between the ages of 3 and 21. IDEA specifies the regulations regarding evaluations, parental involvement, and services to be given.

Intervention and Referral Services Team: An intervention and referral services team is a general education, student progress monitoring team. Typically, the team consists of a school counselor, a school nurse, and at least one teacher. The team can create short-term interventions for students to assist them when they are having a hard time. When those services are not enough, students can be referred for a higher level of services, such as a 504 plan or child study team evaluation.

Multitiered Systems of Support (MTSS): An MTSS framework is an approach used by schools to give students supports at different levels. Student data is collected at each stage of intervention to monitor progress. Stages range from preventative practices such as social emotional learning programming which are given to all students in the school, to individualized practices which are given to targeted students.

National Association of School Psychologists (NASP): NASP is an organization with over 25,000 members which advocates for best practices for school psychologists. This organization advocates for practices to advance student learning, behavior, and mental health. Roughly 30 pages of sample writing from the book.

Pupil Assistance Team: A pupil assistance team is another name for an intervention and referral services team.

Related Services: Related services are services given to a student through an IEP to help them make developmentally appropriate progress in school. Some examples include school-based counseling, speech therapy, occupational therapy, physical therapy, nursing services, and positive behavioral supports.

Social Emotional Learning (SEL): SEL refers to a process through which students learn skills to manage their emotions and enhance their self-confidence. SEL programming refers to school-based activities and classroom management styles which deliver SEL goals to students.

Chapter 10
Preventing Students' Incarceration and Supporting Students With Incarcerated Family Members

Pao-Yin Huang
University of Florida, USA

ABSTRACT

This chapter aims to discover incarceration issues in school settings and corresponding interventions from school counseling and promote a systemic change. This chapter will mainly focus on two incarceration issues that students might experience: students with incarcerated household members and students with behavioral issues in school that might potentially lead to detention and incarceration in the school-to-prison pipeline context. In order to stop the school-to-prison pipeline, school counselors and mental health professionals in school serve a critical role to intervene and support students at an early stage while they encounter incarceration issues. The content in this chapter includes (1) understanding students' experiences around incarceration issues through trauma, grief, and loss lenses in the school-to-prison pipeline context; (2) supporting students through existing school counseling systems and resources; and (3) advocacy.

INTRODUCTION

The goal of this chapter is to outline two incarceration issues that students can encounter in the school-to-prison pipeline context: (1) household members' incarceration; (2) and students with behavioral issues in school which might potentially lead to suspension, expulsion, detention, and later incarceration. This chapter aims to provide an understanding of students' experience of facing these two incarceration issues from a trauma, grief and loss perspective (Alvarez, 2020; Malone, 2016; Morgan-Mullane, 2018; Skinner-Osei & Levenson, 2018) and provide interventions for school counselors and mental health professionals in school settings. This chapter is organized as follows: (1) introduce the background of the

DOI: 10.4018/978-1-7998-9209-0.ch010

school-to-prison pipeline, understand students' experiences related to the two incarceration issues that this chapter aim to highlight through trauma, and grief and loss lens; (2) provide interventions through implementing ASCA National Model (2016) and trauma-informed school; (3) propose advocacy for school counselors and mental health professionals in schools to effectively support students and create a systemic change to rewrite the school-to-prison pipeline.

BACKGROUND

The USA has the highest rate of incarcerated people and the highest impression rate in the world (World Prison Brief, 2020). 29% of Black residents, 24% of Hispanic residents, and 12% of White residents are incarcerated (U.S. Department of Justice, 2020). Black and Native American people experience a higher rate of incarceration compared to other racial groups according to the result of the report, Prisoner in 2019 (U.S. Department of Justice, 2020). Black youth has always composed the highest portion of juvenile arrest rate, followed by other racial minority groups, American Indian, White, and Asian (Office of Juvenile Justice and Delinquency Prevention [OJJDP], 2019). Asian, Pacific Islander, and Native American populations were not presented in these reports on incarceration rate, reflecting the marginalized status and larger societal invisibility perpetuated within US society regarding these communities

A similar situation reflects in the juvenile justice system as well. 2,083 people between 10 to 17 years old were arrested in 2019 (OJJDP, 2019). Native American youths have a 1.5 times higher possibility; and Black youths have a 2.4 times higher possibility of being arrested compared to their White peers (OJJDP, 2019). Students of color are more likely to be incarcerated, which composed nearly 70% of the population of juveniles in correctional facilities consistently across fifteen years (OJJDP, 2019). On top of the criticism of racial inequity in the US justice system, there is also the concern of over usage of incarcerating people, not because of the increasing violence but because of policies that criminalized mental health issues, low SES, immigrants, and disability (Perez, Leifman, & Estrada, 2003; Abrego, et. al, 2017; Marwick, Fontaine, & Boyd, 2017; Nanda, 2019). These social locations are often associated with racial minority groups which put them into a more marginalized state in society and reflect in the phenomenon of the school-to-prison pipeline.

Take the arrest rate of Black students, for example, 31.6% of Black students were arrested in school from 2017 to 2018 (U.S. Department of Education Office of Civil Rights, 2021). The School system is argued to contribute to the injustice of the US justice system. The school-to-prison pipeline refers to the effect of school disturbance laws, zero-tolerance policies, and practices, and school policing that leads to expelling students from schools and putting them into prison (Evans & Didlick-Davis, 2012; Meiners, 2011). School policies at any level are usually associated with disciplinary protocols that mostly are punitive and disproportionately impact students with minoritized identities, such as race/ethnicity, disability, low SES, and LGBTQIA+ (Skiba, Arrendondo, & Williams, 2017). These factors put schools into the position of regulating students through suspension, detention, and expulsion which makes students' behavioral issues seem "criminal" (Welton & Harris, 2022). It is important for school counselors and mental health professionals in schools to be aware of the context while intervening in students' "behavioral issues".

UNDERSTAND STUDENTS' EXPERIENCES RELATED TO INCARCERATION ISSUES

Intersectionality

Intersectionality was proposed by Kimberlé Crenshaw (1989) and later broadly used in understanding people's lived experiences. Intersectionality indicates people's lived experiences were shaped by their diverse social identities, such as race/ethnicity, sexuality, gender identity, disability, age, socioeconomic status, and religion/faith (United Nation Development Programme, 2017). The overlapping of two or more marginalized identities can create more oppression in an individual's life. For example, the study showed that racial differences appeared in boys who were involved in the juvenile justice system compared to girls (Goodkind et al., 2013). Therefore, before diving into identifying students who struggle with incarceration issues and providing intervention, school counselors and mental health professionals who work in school settings need to work on monitoring and challenging their own biases about different identities, cultures, values, and worldviews. Through these efforts, they can further decriminalize students' behavior to prevent the school-to-prison pipeline and close the opportunity gap with students.

Grief and Loss Lens

Students experience the incarceration of a household member as a form of loss because the family member is absent in the student's life. Those family members can no longer provide emotional, parental, and financial support for months to years (Arditti, Smock, & Parkman, 2005). Students might also face the loss of attachment with the family member, and the cutoff of mother-child attachment associates a higher possibility for the kid to be incarcerated in the future (Dallarie, 2007). The left parent or household members might be less responsive and unavailable to kids since they have to take responsibility for the incarcerated member (Malone, 2016). The effect of household members' incarceration might result in the relocation of students, like moving to other relatives' households or being put in foster care (Graham & Harris, 2013), which contributes to other forms of loss, including loss of friendship and familiar environment.

Trauma Lens

"Trauma results from an event, series of events, or set of circumstances that is experienced by an individual as physically or emotionally harmful or threatening and that has lasting adverse effects on the individual's functioning and physical, social, emotional, or spiritual well-being" (SAMHSA, 2012, p. 2). Trauma can happen to anyone from individuals, families, groups, communities, and spread across generations. The complexity of trauma can impact people's behavioral health refers to a state of mental/emotional being and/or choices and actions that affect wellness (SAMHSA, 2014. p. xvi). Students who experienced household member incarceration can be traumatized, as the entire process of witnessing their family members involved in the arrest, trial, and subsequent incarceration impacts them (Malone, 2016). The traumatic change might reflect on students' physical, social, emotional, and cognitive responses (Malone, 2007). Considering the demographic of justice-involved youth, the majority are students of color. Therefore, intergenerational trauma and racialized trauma need to be taken into consideration. Intergenerational trauma indicates traumas that people inherit from their upbringing even though they do not experience it by themselves, and the trauma is passed down from generation to generation (Prager, 2016). Racialized trauma refers to trauma experiences related to race including but not limited to racially motivated attacks and assault, ongoing racially discriminatory incidents (Saleem, Anderson, & Williams, 2020).

A common way to construct trauma response is the fight-flight-freeze model (Bracha, et al., 2004). Fight responses can present as physical and/or verbal behaviors, such as kicking, punching, or threatening; flight responses present as people try to avoid, run away, or escape the current source of trigger; freeze responses are unable to respond to the source of trigger, physically freeze, and follow other people's direction without thinking twice (Katz & Barnetz, 2014; Kaysen, et al., 2005). Students who presented more fight responses are more likely to be kids who experienced physical abuse at home (Katz & Barnetz, 2014). That is, if students present behavioral issues in school, this might be a trauma response coming from their traumatic experiences. A trauma lens is a possible way to comprehend both students with incarcerated family members and students with behavioral issues more precisely.

Identifying Significant Signs

Identifying students with incarcerated household members is the very first step. Students of incarcerated household members face multiple emotional and social difficulties, such as witnessing family members' criminal activities, seeing them be arrested and involved in court, experiencing the change of family financial status, housing stability, change of caregiving format or caregiver, stressful visits with the incarcerated family member, and shame and stigma towards the incarcerated family member (Murray, Farrington, & Sekol, 2012). Incarceration of a family member is very likely toimpact a variety of mental health concerns for these students, such as but not limited to: anxiety, depression, intrusive thoughts, suicidal ideation, suicidal attempt; and behavioral issues like aggressive behaviors, delinquency, crime, self-injury behaviors, and school-related issues (Davis & Shlafer, 2017; Johnson & Easterling, 2015; Kjellstrand, Reinke, and Eddy, 2018; Murray, Loeber, & Pardini, 2012). It might be difficult to recognize signs of students experiencing incarcerated household members since it is very similar to the signs of experiencing stress.

There are some ways to identify significant signs of students with behavioral issues, including school personnel's observation and Office Discipline Referrals (ODR). Spaulding and colleagues (2010) also present the occurrence of different types of ODRs throughout K-12 schools. At the elementary level, the top three ODRs were fighting, defiance, and disruption. In middle school, the most common ODRs were defiance, disruption, and fighting. The most frequent ODRs appeared in high school were defiance, tardy, and truancy. ODRs might lead to suspension and eventually expulsion. More frequent suspension and expulsion are associated with more and quicker recidivism (Novak & Fagan, 2022). It is possible that students who are suspended experience more challenges in establishing their social and academic skills, labeling, and more adverse school experiences without receiving appropriate support which can possibly progress to more suspensions. Girvan and colleagues (2017) reported subjective ODRs, which require school personnel to make a judgment of students' behaviors, showed the most variances in racial discipline compared to objective ODRs. Across all school levels, the most common location of students' behavioral issues occurs in the classroom (Spaulding et al., 2010) which emphasizes the intense involvement of teachers, paraprofessionals, and all the school personnel who engage in classroom settings in identifying students' behavioral issues in the first place. Justice-involved-youths are more likely to be those who are exposed to child abuse, household dysfunction, and four or more adverse childhood experiences (ACEs) (Clements-Nolle & Waddington, 2019). According to the Centers for

Disease Control and Prevention (2019), ACEs are defined as "potentially traumatic events that occur in childhood...include violence, abuse, and growing up in a family with mental health or substance use problems." Experiencing family member's incarceration is one of the ACEs (CDC, 2019). People who are exposed to more ACEs are more likely to be negatively impacted on their mental and physical health, like depression, substance use, and heart disease (CDC, 2019). The School-to-prison pipeline is a combination of various systemic issues that trickle down to schools that make schools not a safer place for students, especially students of color.

INTERVENTION

Identifying Protective Factors

For school counselors and mental health professionals in school to work with students with incarcerated family members and students with behavioral issues, they can firstly begin with identifying the protective factors, resources, and strengths that students have. Protective factors can be students' external and internal sources, such as resilience. External resilience includes strong family communication, positive peer role model, school connectedness, and nonparental role model (Clements-Nolle & Waddington, 2019). Having a trusting adult in life is a key protective factor (Malone, 2016; Washington, 2015; Wasserman et al., 2003). The trusting adult can be the students' guardian, a community member, a teacher, a school counselor, or any adult that can establish a stable and sustainable relationship with these students. Additionally, school connectedness can buffer the psychological distress related to ACEs exposure (Clements-Nolle & Waddington, 2019). Internal resilience includes but is not limited to personal competence, positive mindset to challenges and changes, meaning-making, and assertiveness (Clements-Nolle & Waddington, 2019; Connor & Davidson, 2003).

School counselors and mental health professionals in school are highly encouraged to assess protective and risk factors with students more thoroughly through exploring with students, communicating with students' families, guardians, or caregiving, collaborating with a community partner who has been working with these students (e.g. social workers, mental health counselors), and learning from school personnel who has more contacts with these students. Other than observing students' behavioral change, school counselors can implement universal screening to monitor students' mental health. Including questions that assess grief, loss, and trauma in the universal screening questionnaire can obtain more data on recognizing students' needs.

Support

There are many ways that school counselors and mental health professionals in school can support students with incarcerated family members and students with behavioral issues. School counselors and mental health professionals in schools can provide direct support through periodic quick check-ins, individual counseling, group counseling, and classroom guidance. They can also support students through collaborations including connecting students with resources embedded in the school and community, and partnering with teachers to create plans to intervene in students' behavioral, emotional, and mental health issues. Bryan and Henry (2012) proposed the idea of school-family-community partnerships that these three parties work together to support students. There are seven stages in the partnership model: (a) preparing to partner, (b) assessing needs and strengths, (c) coming together, (d) creating shared vision and plans, (e) taking action, (f) evaluating and celebrating progress, and (g) maintaining momentum (Bryan & Henry, 2012). Implementing this model requires a lot of preparation beforehand. Communication is the key for school counselors, families, and the community to establish a collaborative relationship in order to neat the safety net for students. The partnership is a democratic collaboration which indicates three parties share the ownership and responsibility for decision making. The average school counselor to student ratio is 1:455 in the school year of 20220 to 2021 (ASCA, 2022). Consider the limited funding and resources that school counselors can utilize and the huge numbers of students they need to work with, it is necessary to integrate resources from family and community to better support students.

Educate

School counselors have the ethical responsibility to receive ongoing education with knowledge and skills related to working with diverse populations, local law, resources in the community, common delinquency issues that students present in the building (ASCA, 2019; Brown, 2020). School counselors can provide psychoeducation sessions for students of incarcerated household members about the process of experiencing grief and loss and let them have these vocabularies in mind (Malone, 2016). School counselors and mental health professionals in school can educate students to advocate for their needs and always game plan with students to return to class. School counselors can include some education sessions around incarceration issues in the comprehensive school counseling programs in response to the need of students. That way, all students are exposed to the conversation around incarceration issues, helping them to destigmatize students with incarcerated family members and students with behavioral issues. However, school counselors need maintain awareness that they do not share any identifiable information about the particular students who experience incarceration issues (Warren, Coker, & Collins, 2019).

In the study of Bryan and colleagues (2012), race was a predictor of English teacher behavioral referrals to school counselors and gender was a predictor for both English and math teacher referrals of students' behavioral issues. Black students and Black and multiracial girls have a higher possibility to be referred to school counselors due to disruptive behaviors which reflects that disciplinary referrals in school settings were not race and gender neutral (Bryan, 2012; Gregory et al., 2010; Skiba et al., 2011). Therefore, besides educating students, adults in schools need to continually receive education to actively be a part of transforming the school-to-prison pipeline. Educating adults in schools is paramount to breaking the school-to-prison pipeline. From a counseling professional standpoint, school counselors can recommend adults in schools resources about the school-to-prison pipeline, trauma, ACEs, grief, and loss, trauma-informed care while working with students with incarcerated household members or students with behavioral issues.

Advocate

Advocacy is a critical component of promoting social justice and systemic change and it is one of the professional competencies that counselors need to be equipped with. (ASCA, 2019; Ratts et al., 2016; Toporek, & Daniels, 2018). School counselors and mental health professionals in schools need to be prepared to advocate on behalf of students for appropriate accommodation, support, and resources through in-service training (Warren, Coker, & Collins, 2019). Sometimes school counselors might have to take a step further to advocate for including more resources to support the function of the system that students are in. For instance, some incarcerated fathers shared that it has been difficult to be a father when they are physically distant from their children and they encountered difficulties in parenting after returning to their family (Arditti, Smock, & Parkman, 2005). School counselors advocate on behalf of students' well-being to provide workshops and flyers about parenting skills for their caregivers and collaborate with organizations in the community to address other needs of students.

To serve the purpose of stopping the school-to-prison pipeline, school counselors and mental health professionals in school can practice advocacy through engaging in difficult conversations with adults in schools to call out people's implicit biases, support people to unlearn their biases, manifest changes in schools, and enhance community building. The Association for Specialist in Group Work (Gruth et al., 2019) proposed 10 strategies for people to facilitate difficult conversations in group settings: (1) acknowledge that culture and power are always present; (2) develop multicultural and social justice competencies; (3) create brave, affirming, and humanizing spaces; (4) process group experiences with purpose; (5) cultivate cultural humanity; (6) engage in intentional unity building; (7) practice mindful and reflexive group facilitation; (8) lean in and keep going; (9) consider possibilities of action; (10) assess the impact. These ten strategies can serve as a guide for school counselors and mental health professionals in schools to actively promote social justice on a daily basis in their work. Promoting policy change is another advocacy that school counselors and mental health professionals in school can pursue. It is necessary to investigate how policies at various levels contribute to the school-to-prison pipeline and challenges for students with incarcerated family members and students with behavioral issues. Changing the school-to-prison pipeline is not work that can be done only by intervening in one individual's behavior, instead requires the work from allparties that are involved in the system that students are in.

BUILD UPON EXISTING FOUNDATIONS

ASCA Model

According to the ASCA National Model (2016), all school counselors are encouraged to practice data-driven school counseling. It is perhaps difficult to identify what exactly happened to students at first, but data from various aspects will show students' tendency for counselors to know where to begin the work. Rich data can help school counselors and mental health professionals in school identify students' behavioral patterns. Some common programs and assessment instruments that schools adopt to track students' behaviors, academic performance, and mental health status are PBIS, universal screening, ClassDojo, and ASCA national model app. Further, we can utilize a loss, grief, and trauma lens to recognize the reactions of students who have incarcerated household members. Besides observing students' behavioral change, schools can also implement universal screening to monitor students' mental health. Including questions that assess grief, loss, and trauma in the universal screening questionnaire can obtain more data on recognizing students' needs.

The accountability of intervention and school counseling programs comes from thick data as well. Collecting data is an ongoing process for school counselors to understand students' needs, and it serves as the foundation for school counselors to design a comprehensive school counseling plan and prevention service (ASCA, 2016; Beslser et al., 2016). ASCA national model (2016) also highlights a collective effort of the system that school counselors should collaborate with teachers, administrators, families, and stakeholders to support students.

However, multicultural issues, social justice issues, gender issues, and racial inequity issues need to be taken into consideration throughout the process of collecting data. When a student, especially a student of color, is reported with behavioral issues, school counselors are encouraged to be mindful of the context around this report. Research also emphasized the importance of implementing culturally responsive school counseling programs and interventions (Bryan et al., 2012).

Trauma-Informed School

Trauma-informed school came from a trauma-informed approach. The trauma-informed approach contains three key elements: "(1) realizing the prevalence of trauma; (2) recognizing how trauma affects all individuals involved with the program, organization, or system, including its workforce; and (3) responding by putting this knowledge into practice" (SAMHSA, 2012, p 4). The trauma-informed approach provides school counselors and school personnel a lens of understanding the effect of trauma and responding to it accordingly. It starts from using trauma-informed language to approach students, school counselors, and school personnel as they are encouraged to ask "what happened to you" instead of "what is wrong with you" to students with delinquent issues. Building a trauma-informed school requires all school personnel's collective effort to cultivate a culture that includes immersive collaborations and constant advocacy for training and resources. Trauma-informed school is an approach that intentionally fosters the organizational culture of prioritizing everyone's wellness and staff's self-care that requires stakeholders from a higher level to encourage adults in schools to do so (SAMHSA, 2014). It is crucial to implement a culturally responsive/sustaining (Paris, 2012) trauma-informed practice to include students' unique needs.

CASE STUDY

Kelab is an 8th grader, a third-generation Asian immigrant who comes from a low SES household and lives in a community with a higher crime rate with substance use issues. He used to perform well academically throughout 6th and 7th grade. He had no problem with turning in homework assignments on time and kept himself on track. However, in the recent two months, his teachers reported that Kelab missed assignments and could not focus on class. He also has more conflicts with his peers and talks back to teachers while receiving task instructions in class. Kelab has been sent to the disciplinary office twice this semester. His homeroom teacher also noticed that he became more isolated, as evidenced in not sitting with his friends during lunchtime and playing alone during recess.

The entire school had a universal screening earlier in the semester. Kelab showed a medium level of anxiety and depression on the result of the screening. The school counselor scheduled an appointment with Kelab right after seeing the result. Kelab only shared that the rising scores on his anxiety and depression were associated with the academic stress along with 8th grade. He was concerned a lot about the upcoming high school stage and would like to keep his grades up for college applications. The school counselor contacted Kelab's parents and found out his mom was incarcerated in the middle of summer vacation and he witnessed the process of his mom being arrested. Kelab had to move to his grandparents' place due to the loss of financial support from his mother. Kelab's school counselor and teachers work together with Kelab to provide additional support in class and invite a student to be Kelab's peer mentor. Kelab, Kelab's teachers, and school counselor agreed that if Kelab found himself feeling overwhelmed or activated in a class, he can request to go to the counseling office to get some quiet time and process with the school counselor. The school counselor connected Kelab's guardian with resources from the school and community to gain financial support and afterschool programs. Kelab attends a local grief and loss support group with the school counselor's recommendation and meets with the school counselor weekly for a 10 minutes check-in session to keep him on track.

QUESTIONS

1. What are the pieces in this scenario that can contribute to the school-to-prison pipeline?
2. What resources embedded in school can be utilized to support students who struggle with incarceration issues?
3. What support can be included through the partnership with community and family to support students who struggle with incarceration issues?
4. What are the ethical and legal issues that school counselors and school personnel need to be aware of while working with students who struggle with incarceration issues? How to address and respond to these issues?
5. What are the areas that school counselors can advocate for students with behavioral issues?

CONCLUSION

An effective school counselor, especially when working with students of color, is considered to have knowledge about the student and be present in the picture, trust and have faith in students, and show warmth and positivity (Washington, 2015). As we aim to build an equitable school system for all students, school counselors and mental health professionals in schools are highly encouraged to support students with a holistic understanding of students, including their diverse identities, intersectionality, trauma, familial relationships, mental health status, their community, and how all the factors intertwined then contribute to their behaviors. School counselors and mental health professionals in school need to look closely into lived experiences of students with incarcerated family members and students with behavioral issues with a critical mind and social justice eyes. Placing one kid in the juvenile justice system consumes more money than putting them in school (Morones, 2014). The School-to-prison pipeline is a systemic issue that requires a collective effort to make the system function for all students. It takes a village to raise a child. It takes society as a whole to heal from systemic issues around incarceration and we can start from school to change the narrative to school-to-success.

"It takes a village."

REFERENCES

Abrego, L., Coleman, M., Martínez, D. E., Menjívar, C., & Slack, J. (2017). Making immigrants into criminals: Legal processes of criminalization in the post-IIRIRA era. *Journal on Migration and Human Security*, *5*(3), 694–715. doi:10.1177/233150241700500308

Alvarez, A. (2020). Seeing race in the research on youth trauma and education: A critical review. *Review of Educational Research*, *90*(5), 583–626. doi:10.3102/0034654320938131

American School Counselor Association. (2016). *The ASCA National Model Implementation Guide: Foundation, Management, and Accountability*. Author.

American School Counselor Association. (2019). *ASCA school counselor professional standards & competencies.* Author.

American School Counselor Association. (2022). *Student-to-School-Counselor Ratio 2020–2021.* American School Counselor Association. https://www.schoolcounselor.org/getmedia/238f136e-ec52-4bf2-94b6-f24c39447022/Ratios-20-21-Alpha.pdf

Arditti, J. A., Smock, S. A., & Parkman, T. S. (2005). "It's been hard to be a father": A qualitative exploration of incarcerated fatherhood. *Fathering*, *3*(3), 267–288. doi:10.3149/fth.0303.267

Belser, C. T., Shillingford, M., & Joe, J. R. (2016). The ASCA model and a multi-tiered system of supports: A framework to support students of color with problem behavior. *The Professional Counselor*, *6*(3), 251–262. doi:10.15241/cb.6.3.251

Bracha, S. H., Ralston, T. C., Matsukawa, J. M., Williams, A. E., & Bracha, A. S. (2004). Does "Fight or Flight" need updating? *Psychosomatics (Washington, D.C.)*, *45*(5), 448–449. doi:10.1176/appi.psy.45.5.448 PMID:15345792

Brown, E. C. (2020). School counselor conceptualizations of the needs of children of incarcerated parents. *Children and Youth Services Review, 112*, 104936. doi:10.1016/j.childyouth.2020.104936

Bryan, J., Day-Vines, N. L., Griffin, D., & Moore-Thomas, C. (2012). The disproportionality dilemma: Patterns of teacher referrals to school counselors for disruptive behavior. *Journal of Counseling and Development*, *90*(2), 177–190. doi:10.1111/j.1556-6676.2012.00023.x

Bryan, J., & Henry, L. (2012). A Model for Building School-Family-Community Partnerships: Principles and Process. *Journal of Counseling and Development*, *90*(4), 408–420. doi:10.1002/j.1556-6676.2012.00052.x

Centers for Disease Control and Prevention. (2019, November 5). *Adverse childhood experiences (ACES).* Centers for Disease Control and Prevention. https://www.cdc.gov/vitalsigns/aces/index.html

Connor, K. M., & Davidson, J. R. (2003). Development of a new resilience scale: The Connor-Davidson resilience scale (CD-RISC). *Depression and Anxiety*, *18*(2), 76–82. doi:10.1002/da.10113 PMID:12964174

Crenshaw, K. (1989). Demarginalizing the intersection of race and sex: A black feminist critique of antidiscrimination doctrine, feminist theory and antiracist politics. *U. Chi. Legal F., 139.*

Dallaire, D. H. (2007). Incarcerated mothers and fathers: A comparison of risks for children and families. *Family Relations*, *56*(5), 440–453. doi:10.1111/j.1741-3729.2007.00472.x

Davis, L., & Shlafer, R. J. (2017). Mental health of adolescents with currently and formerly incarcerated parents. *Journal of Adolescence*, *54*(1), 120–134. doi:10.1016/j.adolescence.2016.10.006 PMID:28011442

Evans, M. P., & Didlick-Davis, C. (2012). Organizing to end the school-to-prison pipeline: An analysis of grassroots organizing campaigns and policy solutions. *e-Journal of Education Policy*. Retrieved from http://nau.edu/COE/ eJournal/Fall-2012/

Girvan, E. J., Gion, C., McIntosh, K., & Smolkowski, K. (2017). The relative contribution of subjective office referrals to racial disproportionality in school discipline. *School Psychology Quarterly*, *32*(3), 392–404. doi:10.1037pq0000178 PMID:27736122

Goodkind, S., Shook, J. J., Kim, K. H., Pohlig, R. T., & Herring, D. J. (2013). From child welfare to juvenile justice: Race, gender, and system experiences. *Youth Violence and Juvenile Justice*, *11*(3), 249–272. doi:10.1177/1541204012463409

Graham, J. A., & Harris, Y. R. (2013). Children of color and parental incarceration: Implications for research, theory, and practice. *Journal of Multicultural Counseling and Development*, *41*(2), 66–81. doi:10.1002/j.2161-1912.2013.00028.x

Gregory, A., Skiba, R. J., & Noguera, P. A. (2010). The achievement gap and the discipline gap: Two sides of the same coin? *Educational Researcher*, *39*(1), 59–68. doi:10.3102/0013189X09357621

Guth, L. J., Pollard, B. L., Nitza, A., Puig, A., Chan, C. D., Singh, A. A., & Bailey, H. (2019). Ten strategies to intentionally use group work to transform hate, facilitate courageous conversations, and enhance community building. *Journal for Specialists in Group Work*, *44*(1), 3–24. doi:10.1080/01933922.2018.1561778

Johnson, E. I., & Easterling, B. A. (2015). Coping with confinement: Adolescents' experiences with parental incarceration. *Journal of Adolescent Research*, *30*(2), 244–267. doi:10.1177/0743558414558593

Katz, C., & Barnetz, Z. (2014). The behavior patterns of abused children as described in their testimonies. *Child Abuse & Neglect*, *38*(6), 1033–1040. doi:10.1016/j.chiabu.2013.08.006 PMID:24035397

Kaysen, D., Morris, M. K., Rizvi, S. L., & Resick, P. A. (2005). Peritraumatic Responses and Their Relationship to Perceptions of Threat in Female Crime Victims. *Violence Against Women*, *11*(12), 1515–1535. doi:10.1177/1077801205280931 PMID:16247114

Kjellstrand, J. M., Reinke, W. M., & Eddy, J. M. (2018). Children of incarcerated parents: Development of externalizing behaviors across adolescence. *Children and Youth Services Review*, *94*, 628–635. doi:10.1016/j.childyouth.2018.09.003

Malone, P. A. (2007). The impact of peer death on adolescent girls: A task-oriented group intervention. *Journal of Social Work in End-of-Life & Palliative Care*, *3*(3), 23–37. doi:10.1300/J457v03n03_04 PMID:18077294

Malone, P. A. (2016). *Counseling adolescents through loss, grief, and trauma*. Routledge. doi:10.4324/9780203699638

Marwick, A., Fontaine, C., & Boyd, D. (2017). "Nobody sees it, nobody gets mad": Social media, privacy, and personal responsibility among low-SES youth. *Social Media+ Society, 3*(2). doi:10.1177/2056305117710455

Meiners, E. R. (2011). Ending the School-to-Prison Pipeline/Building Abolition Futures. *The Urban Review, 43*(4), 547–565. doi:10.100711256-011-0187-9

Morgan-Mullane, A. (2018). Trauma Focused Cognitive Behavioral Therapy with Children of Incarcerated Parents. *Clinical Social Work Journal, 46*(3), 200–209. doi:10.100710615-017-0642-5 PMID:30100639

Morones, A. (2014). Juvenile-Justice System Not Meeting Educational Needs, Report Says; "Systemic" problems outlined in report.(Brief article). *Education Week, 33*(29), 6–6.

Murray, J., Farrington, D. P., & Sekol, I. (2012). Children's antisocial behavior, mental health, drug use, and educational performance after parental incarceration: A systematic review and meta-analysis. *Psychological Bulletin, 138*(2), 175-210. doi:10.1037/a0026407

Murray, J., Loeber, R., & Pardini, D. (2012). Parental involvement in the criminal justice system and the development of youth theft, marijuana use, depression, and poor academic performance. *Criminology, 50*(1), 255–302. doi:10.1111/j.1745-9125.2011.00257.x

Nanda, J. (2019). The construction and criminalization of disability in school incarceration. *Colum. J. Race & L., 9*, 265.

Novak, A., & Fagan, A. (2022). Expanding research on the school-to-prison pipeline: Examining the relationships between suspension, expulsion, and recidivism among justice-involved youth. *Crime and Delinquency, 68*(1), 3–27. doi:10.1177/0011128721999334

Office of Juvenile Justice and Delinquency Prevention. (2019). *Juvenile Arrests. Demographic characteristics of Juvenile arrests, 2019.* https://www.ojjdp.gov/ojstatbb/crime/qa05104.asp?qaDate=2019

Paris, D. (2012). Culturally Sustaining Pedagogy: A Needed Change in Stance, Terminology, and Practice. *Educational Researcher, 41*(3), 93–97. doi:10.3102/0013189X12441244

Perez, A., Leifman, S., & Estrada, A. (2003). Reversing the criminalization of mental illness. *Crime and Delinquency, 49*(1), 62–78. doi:10.1177/0011128702239236

Prager, J. (2016). Disrupting the Intergenerational Transmission of Trauma: Recovering Humanity, Repairing Generations. In Breaking Intergenerational Cycles of Repetition (1st ed.). Verlag Barbara Budrich. doi:10.2307/j.ctvdf03jc.7

Ratts, M., Singh, A. A., Nassar-McMillan, S., Butler, S. K., & McCullough, J. R. (2016). Multicultural and Social Justice Counseling Competencies: Guidelines for the Counseling Profession. *Journal of Multicultural Counseling and Development, 44*(1), 28–48. doi:10.1002/jmcd.12035

Saleem, F. T., Anderson, R. E., & Williams, M. (2020). Addressing the "myth" of racial trauma: Developmental and ecological considerations for youth of color. *Clinical Child and Family Psychology Review, 23*(1), 1–14. doi:10.100710567-019-00304-1 PMID:31641920

SAMHSA ReleasesBehavioral Health. (2013). SAMHSA Releases *Behavioral Health, United States, 2012. Psychiatric Services (Washington, D.C.), 64*(12), 1281–1281. doi:10.1176/appi.ps.6412News1 PMID:24292740

Skiba, R. J., Arrendondo, M. I., & Williams, N. T. (2017). In and of itself a risk factor: Exclusionary discipline and the school-to-prison pipeline. In K. J. Fasching- Varner, L. L. Martin, R. W. Mitchell, K. P. Bennett-Haron & A. Daneshzadeh (Eds.), Understanding dismantling, and disrupting the prison-to-school pipeline (pp. 111–130). Rowman & Littlefield.

Skiba, R. J., Horner, R. H., Chung, C., Rausch, M. K., May, S., & Tobin, T. (2011). Race is not neutral: A national investigation of African American and Latino disproportionality in school discipline. *School Psychology Review, 40*(1), 85–107. doi:10.1080/02796015.2011.12087730

Skinner-Osei, P., & Levenson, J. S. (2018). Trauma-informed services for children with incarcerated parents. *Journal of Family Social Work, 21*(4-5), 421–437. doi:10.1080/10522158.2018.1499064

Spaulding, S. A., Irvin, L. K., Horner, R. H., May, S. L., Emeldi, M., Tobin, T. J., & Sugai, G. (2010). Schoolwide social-behavioral climate, student problem behavior, and related administrative decisions: Empirical patterns from 1,510 schools nationwide. *Journal of Positive Behavior Interventions, 12*(2), 69–85. doi:10.1177/1098300708329011

Substance Abuse and Mental Health Services Administration. (2014). *SAMHSA's concept of trauma and guidance for a trauma-informed approach.* Author.

Toporek, R., & Daniels, J. (2018). *American Counseling Association advocacy competencies. In Youthful offenders in the federal system.* United States Sentencing Commission.

United Nations development programme. (2017). Article. *New Zealand Journal of Medical Laboratory Science, 71*(1), 23.

US Department of Education. (2021). *2017–18 Civil Rights Data Collection: School Climate and Safety.* Author.

Warren, J. G., Coker, G. L., & Collins, M. L. (2019). Children of Incarcerated Parents: Considerations for Professional School Counselors. *The Professional Counselor (Greensboro, N.C.), 9*(3), 185–199. doi:10.15241/jmw.9.3.185

Washington, A. R. (2015). "It's like he'll be there for you": Middle School African American Males' Stories of Effective Professional School Counselors. *Journal of African American Males in Education, 6*(2), 1–16.

Wasserman, G. A. (2003). *Risk and protective factors of child delinquency.* U.S. Dept. of Justice, Office of Justice Programs, Office of Juvenile Justice and Delinquency Prevention. doi:10.1037/e501772006-001

Welton, A. D., & Harris, T. O. (2022). Youth of Color Social Movements for Racial Justice: The Politics of Interrogating the School-to-Prison Pipeline. *Educational Policy (Los Altos, Calif.), 36*(1), 57–99. doi:10.1177/08959048211059728

World Prison Brief, Institute for Crime & Justice Policy Research. (2020). *Highest to lowest - prison population total.* Highest to Lowest - Prison Population Total | World Prison Brief. https://www.prison-studies.org/highest-to-lowest/prison-population-total?field_region_taxonomy_tid=All

Chapter 11
Mitigating Juvenile Incarceration in Nigeria Through the Lens of Counseling

Abel Ebiega Enokela
https://orcid.org/0000-0003-4488-8614
Ambrose Alli University, Nigeria

ABSTRACT

This chapter critically examines juvenile incarceration in Nigeria with emphasis on pupils and students of basic and post basic education schools that are not up to the age of 18. Juvenile incarceration has a lot of implications for children and young persons like trauma reaction and behavioral and emotional challenges. Cases of prison congestion with children and young persons staying with adults and hardened criminals in hazardous and dehumanizing conditions imposed on them by 'endless' incarceration continue to thrive in our society, particularly in Nigeria. This chapter, in proffering solutions to juvenile incarceration considered the roles of school counselors as pivotal to mitigating behaviors that could be precursors to incarceration. Sutherland's differential association theory and Bandura's social learning theory provided the theoretical direction for this effort.

INTRODUCTION

Juvenile incarceration is a disturbing social eyesore as many children and adolescents within the age bracket of juvenility could be exposed to tortuous and dehumanizing conditions if efforts are not directed towards reducing its prevalence. Oxford Reference (n.d.) defines incarceration as "the process of being institutionalized, by a carceral organization such as the prison service, in a prison, mental hospital, juvenile detention center, or other carceral institution which isolates inmates from the wider society." From the definition offered by Oxford Reference, juvenile incarceration in this chapter is conceptualized as the detention or the imprisonment of persons considered to be within the age bracket of juvenility. The Children and Young Persons Act (CYPA) of Nigeria as cited by James (2013), defines a child as "a person under the age of fourteen years," and a young person as "a person who has attained the age of

DOI: 10.4018/978-1-7998-9209-0.ch011

fourteen years." Furthermore, James (2013) quoting the Beijing Rules of the United Nations Standard Minimum Rules for the Administration of Juvenile Justice notes that a juvenile is "a child or young person who, under the respective legal systems, may be dealt with for an offence in a manner which is different from an adult." Okagbue (n.d) postulates that the word "juvenile" was not defined in Nigeria's legislative system, and that Children and Young Persons Law (CYPL) simply considers a child to be a person under the age of 14, and a young person, as a person up to 14, but less than 18. Hence, aligning this term to the Nigerian context, a juvenile is a person who has not attained the age of 18. Thus, throughout this a juvenile is perceived as person below age of 18.

A number of researches have concentrated so much on juvenile delinquency in terms of its prevalence, causes and impacts on schools and other social contexts, but perhaps with little efforts towards providing scholarship voices aimed at mitigating juvenile incarceration from a counseling perspective. Juvenile incarceration requires coordinated emphasis from experts, especially those in the helping profession or behavior science because of the lifelong implications it has on children and young persons, family members and significant others. Johns (2021) postulates that mass incarceration is a societal burden because it could affect both the person incarcerated and family members with negative implications on classroom development, as a result of trauma reaction, and behavioral and emotional maladjustments. Some negative effects of incarceration include: the possibility of the children of incarcerated parents becoming incarcerated; children not being able to complete school; increased health and psychological challenges of children from families of incarcerated parents; Poverty, unemployment, lower wages, and unstable housing; and rise in marital and relationships challenges which could lead to dysfunctional families (Michelle, 2012). Ajah and Ugwuoke (2018) lament that the Nigerian prisons are congested with juveniles who are not usually separated from adult and hardened criminals, contrary to the provisions of the law. These under aged individuals usually face hazards and dehumanizing conditions as a result of incarceration, including poor feeding and clothing, exposure to disease, and the risk of physical and sexual abuse. In addition to these dehumanizing conditions, Atilola (2012) reports that several studies have revealed a high prevalence of mental and behavioral disorders like anxiety, depression and disruptive behavioral disorders among incarcerated adolescents in Ibadan, the capital city of Oyo State. Considering the condition of children or young persons incarcerated in prison, there is an urgent need to put structures in place to mitigate juvenile crimes or delinquencies that could lead to incarceration. The root of behaviors that could be termed juvenile delinquency could be traceable to faulty psychological and developmental processes.

In addressing juvenile incarceration, counseling has a role to play because of its therapeutic potentials that could help in modifying behavior and refocusing individuals to maintain adaptive life. Counselling is a professional relationship that could help diverse individuals, families, and groups to access mental health, fitness, education, and career goals (Kaplan, Arvydas, & Gladding, 2014). Egbochukwu (2008) opines that counselling is a process by which a troubled individual could be assisted to feel free and behave in a more personally satisfying manner through interaction with a counsellor who could stimulate him or her to develop appropriate adaptation in his/her environmental contexts. Skill You Need (2021) perceives counseling as "the act of helping the client to see things more clearly, possibly from a different view-point. This can enable the client to focus on feelings, experiences or behavior, with a goal of facilitating positive change." Thus, counseling services in schools could help learners to access their psychosocial endowments to foster proper character formation which could in turn mitigate juvenile crime and incarceration. Counseling services could help to detect early propensities of some pupils or students to delinquent behavior that could lead to incarceration. Some behavioral challenges manifested by pupils and students in schools that are considered by many as just "childish" adolescent behavior (Crews, 2016), could serve as precursors to juvenile crimes that could lead to incarceration. Thus, counseling as a therapeutic relationship between therapists and clients could help to ameliorate juvenile behavioral maladjustments before they get out of hands. Abnormal behavior is the rooted of juvenile delinquency. This is line with the postulate of Tappan (1972; cited in Abubakar,2018) which states that "the nature of juvenile delinquency sprang up from different abnormal behaviour such as stealing or shoplifting, drunkenness, burglary, robbery, rape, homicide, idleness, truancy, prostitution, disobedience, running away from home, kleptomanism and sexual promiscuity." If abnormal or antisocial behavior is allowed to thrive, it may become a big behavioral problem to the person expressing it, school, peer, family members and the community at large. This makes it crucial for counselors, especially school counselors to explore all avenues to ensure juvenile delinquency is minimized among pupils and students in schools.

Looking at what have been said so far, this chapter, intends to provide a voice aimed at producing an antidote to juvenile incarceration with emphasis on children and young persons under the age of 18. The scope of this chapter is limited to juvenile pupils and students who are in basic and post basic schools within the Nigerian educational system. Persons under this category are chosen as the focus of this chapter because the Federal Government of Nigeria through its National Policy on Education (NPE) makes provision for guidance and counseling services in schools in Nigeria (FRN, 2013). Thus, this population could have access to counseling services that could enhance adaptive behavior which could ward off delinquencies. It is the firm belief of this contribution that delinquency-incarceration nexus could be controlled through appropriate counseling approaches. Though, this review effort is focused on Nigeria's contexts, it has a universal application and could be helpful to all counselors, social workers, psychologists, researchers and related stakeholders worldwide.

METHODOLOGY

This chapter adopts a theoretical approach to address mitigation of juvenile incarceration in Nigeria with focus on pupils and students of basic and post basic schools. The chapter also relies on secondary data drawn from literature available on the internet. The contribution aligns with differential association theory of Edwin H. Sutherland and social learning theory of Albert Bandura as the major theoretical foundations. The narrative review model is also adopted in this chapter, in keeping with the understanding of Charles Sturt University Library (2021) which defines narrative review as "a comprehensive, critical and objective analysis of the current knowledge on a topic." The scope of this chapter is delimited to mitigation of incarceration of juveniles in basic and post basic schools as obtainable in the Nigerian educational system as contained in its National Policy on education (FRN, 2013). Juveniles who are not in basic or post schools are outside the focus of this contribution. Counselors in this chapter are to a large extent, perceived as school counselors who work with pupils and students in various basic and post basic schools in Nigeria. Though, the Nigerian juvenile pupils and students are adopted as the target population of this review, it is merely to serve a scoping purpose to enhance effective coverage of the chapter, and does not diminish its universal applicability.

THEORETICAL FRAMEWORKS

This review is hinged on two theories, one from the field of criminology, the differential association theory of Edwin H. Sutherland and another from the field of Psychology, the social learning theory of Albert Bandura.

Differential Association Theory

Edwin H. Sutherland (1947) postulates that people learn delinquent behavior through association with people who violate social norms, meaning that individuals' associations with members of delinquent groups could provide the platform for them to learn and adopt delinquent habits prevalent in those groups. By associating with such persons, individuals could behave contrary to acceptable social norms. Sutherland (Sutherland & Cressey, 1970, pp. 75–77; cited in Trappen 2018)), presents 9 postulates to explain the thrust of differential association theory as: 1. Criminal behavior is learned; 2. Criminal behavior is a process of communication, learned in interaction with other persons; 3. The principal part of the learning of criminal behavior occurs within intimate personal groups; 4. When criminal behavior is learned, the learning includes (a) techniques of committing the crime; and (b) the specific direction of motives, drives, rationalizations, and attitudes; 5. The specific direction of the motives and drives is learned from definitions of the legal codes as favorable or unfavorable; 6. A person becomes delinquent because of an excess of definitions favorable to violation of law over definitions unfavorable to violation of law – this is the principle of differential association; 7. Differential association may vary in frequency, duration, priority, and intensity; 8. The process of learning criminal behavior by association with criminal and anti-criminal patterns involves all of the mechanisms that are involved in any other type of learning; and 9. While criminal behavior is an expression of general needs and values, it is not explained by those general needs and values since noncriminal behavior is an expression of the same needs and values. Each of these postulates provides a counseling concern which should be carefully considered by counselors who are to mitigate delinquent behavior to prevent juvenile incarceration, especially among pupils and students.

Social Learning Theory

Bandura's (1977) social learning theory opines that people learn from one another, through observation, imitation, and modeling. Behavior of aggression, bravery and fear could be learnt through models (Bandura, 2006). The thrust of this theory is that children could learn and imitate behaviors they observe in other people around them. Thus, in line with the social learning theory, it could be stated that human behavior could be regulated based on exposure to adaptive learning experiences since individuals could observe, assimilate and imitate behaviors of others. Hence, juvenile delinquencies could be curtailed if pupils or students are exposed to good models, that could be observed and imitated.

These theories have much in common in terms of the influence of their psychosocial contents as possible influencers of human behavior. Through the lens of these theories, school counselors could mitigate juvenile incarceration by influencing the psychosocial environments of pupils and students under their counseling services. Adeboye (2015, cited in Ajah et al, 2018) sees juvenile delinquency as the resistant antisocial, illegal or criminal behavior of children or adolescents that could not be controlled or corrected by their parents, thereby endangering the lives of people in a community and by implication, attracting law enforcement agency. Abubakar (2018) also posits that juvenile delinquency is the behavior of children which could, under the law, subject them to juvenile court. Considering the implications of juvenile delinquency, counselors should through appropriate counseling strategies influence juveniles by influencing character formation actors or structures to enhance adaptive behavior to mitigate antisocial behaviors that could be precursors to juvenile crimes.

JUVENILE INCARCERATION IN NIGERIA

Juvenile incarceration or imprisonment cases in Nigeria are well documented in literature as proof of its prevalence. Incarceration of children and young persons have very serious societal implications which can affect various social contexts (Johns, 2021; Stanko, & Crews, 2016).

Ejekwonyilo (2019) a reporter with The Cable, reports a horrible situation about juvenile incarceration across Nigeria. The report stresses that there were juvenile inmates in Minna Remand Home which was overcrowded with emaciated juveniles with torn clothes, who were facing challenges of food. The reporter also says that the situation in Minna, Suleja, Markurdi and Port Harcourt presented similar conditions of juveniles who were languishing in prisons or in borstal institutions across the country without education; and in most cases, were incarcerated in adult prisons, contrary to one's expectation. In buttressing the plight of these young prisoners, the reporter presents quoted voices of some of them, among whom was Suleiman Adamu, a 12-year-old boy and pupil of Alfitrah Primary School, Tunga, Minna, who lamented saying: "I was brought here by my father whom I was living with together with my step-mother. My step-mother accused me of stealing her wrapper. Immediately I got here, I was put in chains so that I do not runaway; you can see I'm still in chains and I don't know who will rescue me from this problem."

Collaborating the report of Ejekwonyilo (2019) is the report of Atilola (2014) which posits that a large proportion of Nigeria's arrestees were minor offenders to whom available facilities were not up to the standard to sustain appropriate mental health. This means that these juveniles who found themselves in incarceration facilities were likely experienced psychopathological challenges. The Centre for Socio-Legal Studies (2009) points out that the three borstal homes in Nigeria situated in Kaduna, Ilorin and Abeokuta whose mandate are to reform young offenders, and to separate them from adults' criminals in prison custody were not effective because of lack of proper policy, legal and institutional framework that could prevent juvenile delinquency or aid in correctional processes of juvenile offenders. The center further lamented that the number of borstal homes in Nigeria were inadequate and unable to cope with the rising cases and the proliferation of juvenile offences. The report of the Centre for Socio-Legal studies (2009), portends danger for juvenile offenders in Nigeria as they are unlikely to receive the necessary reformations, they need from the borstal homes which are inadequate in number and quality.

A CASE STUDY OF JUVENILE INCARCERATION IN IBADAN REMAND HOME, IBADAN, OYO STATE, NIGERIA

The Method of the Case Study

This case study is based on a study carried out by Bella, Atilola, and Omigbodun (2010) on 59 children (60%) males and 40% females) who were incarcerated at Ibadan remand home, a juvenile correctional center built in 1955 by the state government. The mean age of the participants was 11.68 years (SD:4.8). The study sought to explore and identify the psychosocial needs and psychopathology among incarcerated children in the correctional center. The researcher adopted a Sociodemographic Questionnaire to collect data on child's age, gender, school and class, religion, family type, occupation and marital status of the parents, present abode, and the reason for admission into the home. The researchers sought approval for the study from the Oyo state Ministry of women affairs, community development and social welfare and were granted the permission to embark on the project. Furthermore, the participants' consent was also obtained from children above 13 years. Parental consent was waived in line with world best practice since the parents of the children would have been difficult to reach. Monthly visitation to the remand home was maintained to interview all the children remanded in the home from the first visit, and the new inmates face to face over a year. Trained clinicians carried the interviews which lasted approximately 30-40 minutes. Furthermore, descriptive statistics such as means and standard deviations, were used to explain continuous variables; percentages were used to explain categorical variables. The chi-squared test at 0.05 alpha level was used to compare two proportions and to examine the relationship between two qualitative variables.

Description of the Remand Home

The remand home was located on about four acres of land with one dormitory that was partitioned for male and female inmates. There was a central administrative area attached to a building under renovation to be used as a classroom. Two other bungalows served as residential apartments for the staff members. The members of staff consisted of three wardens, two part time nurses, one caterer, and two-night guards. The nurses worked between 8 – 4 pm from Monday to Friday only. The remand home had no provision for emergency services. In addition, the home lacked first-aid box.

Results of the Study

The study confirms that 51(90%) of the incarcerated children had need of care. The study further reveals that 2(3%) of the incarcerated children in the home committed juvenile offences of stealing and 4 (7%) had challenges beyond parental control. 54 children (96%) showed evidence of psychosocial disruption as a result of separation from parents, family and abandonment. Only 5(8%) of these incarcerated children were attending school while in the remand home during the period of the research.

In addition, 55 (97%) of the children showed evidence of Psychopathology. The study reported anxious preoccupation and depressive symptomatology as the most common among the participants. It was also observed that depressive symptoms (21.9% vs 17.9%), suicidal ideation (28% vs 21.4%) and attempts (12.5% vs 7.1%) were prevalent among the participants. Prevalence level was higher among male participants than female participants, but not statistically significant. The study concluded that most of the children in the Ibadan Remand Home had significant challenges with behavioral adaption, support, social and educational systems.

The case study above reveals the impact of juvenile incarceration. The impact as could be observed from the study ranges from psychosocial needs to psychopathology. The condition of the incarcerated children in this case study makes mitigation of incarceration very important.

MITIGATING JUVENILE INCARCERATION THROUGH COUNSELING INTERVENTIONS

Juvenile incarceration comes as result of juvenile delinquency or crime. The child or young person exhibiting antisocial behavior may end up being incarcerated. Hence, pupils and students in schools, especially those in Nigeria who are the main focus of this study need the support of school counselors to overcome antisocial behaviors that could create problems for them, their family members or the society as a whole. In trying to mitigate juvenile crimes or incarceration, this chapter rests on the planks of the differential association theory of Sutherland and the social learning theory of Badura. The differential theory has 9 postulates which are summarized as follows: criminal behavior is learned; learned in interaction with other persons, within intimate personal groups; learning includes (a) techniques of committing the crime; and (b) the specific direction of motives, drives, rationalizations, and attitudes; from definitions of the legal codes as favorable or unfavorable; a person becomes delinquent because of an excess of definitions favorable to violation (principle of differential association);differential association may vary in frequency, duration, priority, and intensity; process of learning criminal behavior by association involves all of the mechanisms that are involved in any other type of learning; and criminal behavior is an expression of general needs and values, but not explained by those general needs and values since noncriminal behavior is an expression of the same needs and values. (Sutherland, et al, 1978).

Since the process of learning criminal behavior involves all the mechanisms involved in any other type of learning, counseling strategy should aim at mitigating the learning processes of criminal acts. Each of these 9 postulates provides a platform to aid counseling processes to help pupils and students to overcome criminality. The social learning theory of Bandura provides directions in terms of learning through observation, imitation, and modeling (Bandura, 1977). Counseling processes should consider aiding pupils and students to learn adaptive behavior through observation, imitation and modeling. Thus, counseling processes should aim at how to positively influence pupils and students' psychosocial contexts or environments to create room for adaptive character formation. Carey, Fan, He, and Jin, (2020) observe five dimensions of the roles of school-based counselors as: counselling services; prevention programs; advocacy and systematic improvement; administrator role; and educational and career planning. Each of these roles provides the Nigerian school counselors the opportunity to engage in helping pupils or students to cope with the pressures that could lure them to embracing delinquent acts

School counselors could mitigate delinquency of school children under them by assessing the psychosocial environments that may be upholding delinquencies or crimes that could lead to incarceration. Bronfenbrenner's (1974), ecological system theory shows five psychological environments that could shape individuals' behavior. These systems are microsystem, referring to settings individuals relate closely with (e.g. Parents, teachers and peer group); mesosystem, the linkages or interactions of individuals' microsystems (e.g. relationship between teacher and parents, peers and parents influences); exosystem, referring to microsystems of individuals who are not embedded directly in a person's psychosocial environment, but have influence on his or her behavior(e.g. associates of parents, friends of peers); macrosystem, referring to settings that are external, but have influence on individuals (e.g. cultural values, religious beliefs, and written and unwritten laws in the society); and chronosystem, changes in psychosocial environments over time (Bronfenbrenner, 1978; 1986; Ettekal & Mahoney, 2017). In keeping with Sutherland's 9 postulates in his differential association theory, school counselors have to beam their torchlights on these ecological environments that are possible platforms for juveniles to learn criminal behavior through observation, imitation and modeling. School counselors, keeping in mind their roles as preventative and counseling actors (Carey et al, 2020, Aluede, 2020), should put in place counseling approaches that could neutralize maladaptive behavior that could thrive in pupils and students' psychosocial environments.

There are cases of Nigerian juvenile delinquencies that have been captured in empirical studies that are of interest to this chapter because they provide practical examples of delinquent behaviors that could lead to incarceration if they continue to thrive among pupils and students. Adeleke, (2019) reports gap in family communication, regulation and control mechanism deficiency, institutional and social lapses, excessive drugs abuse, persistent economic hardship and social disorganization, long communal hatred, and negative social variables as the reasons for delinquency statuses of children in areas experiencing communal crisis conflict in southwestern Nigeria. Similarly, Osagie-Obazee and Eduwen (2016) finds family factors, such as parent-child rearing style, family type and socio-economic status, assault from mass media, cultural and ethnic beliefs as causes of delinquent adolescents in secondary schools in Edo South Senatorial District of Edo State. Again, Sanni, Udoh, Okediji, Modo, and Eze, (2010) observes lack of family stability, family cohesiveness, and family adaptability as strong factors impacting on juvenile delinquency among secondary school students in Uyo metropolis in Akwa Ibom state. Furthermore, Adegoke (2015) notes broken home, poverty and peer influence as main sustainers of juvenile delinquency among learners from ten schools across Ikorodu Local Government Area of Lagos State. In addition, Ukwueze, (2015) notices negative study behaviors, truancy, cultism, alcoholism, assaults, and lateness to school, as major forms of adolescents' inappropriate behaviors in a population of 5,433 SS 2 students, with 600 students as sample in public senior secondary schools in Eti-Osa and Lagos Mainland Local Government Areas of Lagos State.

Looking at the cases presented in this chapter, it could be observed that social contexts like peer group, family, mass media and the society could serve as sustainers of delinquent behavior. Thus, school counselors must help pupils and students to navigate through these social contexts without their being influenced negatively to embrace delinquent acts. Consequently, counseling approach has to touch pupils or students themselves and the influencing psychosocial environments around them. School counselors have the responsibility of applying preventative and curative counseling tools on juveniles to keep them psychologically healthy to be able to overcome delinquent behavior. Preventative measures should aim at manipulating social contexts that could serve as sources of learning criminal acts to pupils or students. The family setting is pivotal to the child's learning and other developmental processes. School counselors' roles extend to collaborating with parents, families and communities to help pupils or students' developmental processes. The family unit features prominently as a source of delinquent behavior among Nigerian children and young persons (Adeleke, 2019; Osagie-Obazee et al, 2016; Sanni, et al, 2010; Adegoke, 2015) based on empirical findings from Nigeria. The family unit could prevent delinquent behavior if the psychosocial environment supports good personality development of the children or young persons. Counselors through their liaison roles with families should help parents to see the need of making their homes conducive for proper character formation for juveniles.

Children could acquire various experiences in family settings as they are exposed to a number of influences and expectations (Ceka & Murati, 2016; Roostin, 2018) which could help them to acquire family values that could in turn help them to be resistant to deviant behavior from peers and other social contexts. Nigerian counselors could reach out to families by organizing fora where issues about child's training would be discussed. Schools' Open Days could also be used by counselors to enlighten parents on the need of making the family unit psychosocially healthy for children and young persons. Another social context that counselors need to stimulate to enhance adaptive behavior are peer groups. Adegoke (2015) finds peer influence as a source of juvenile delinquency. Students' cultism is on the increase as a result of peer influence. Corroborating this is assertion, Ukwueze (2015) notices cultism as a major cause of juvenile delinquency. Thus, the Peer influence and delinquency nexus among adolescence should be given a special attention in order to mitigate antisocial behaviors.

School counselors could facilitate preventative counseling by providing an atmosphere for students to learn through appropriate models. This can be done by inviting eminent persons in the community who are good role models to give talks to learners in schools. Career weeks, career conferences, field trips, seminars and workshops could be organized by school counselors where professionals who are role models could share life and professional experiences with children and young persons. Such programs could make children and young persons to appreciate hard work and dignity of labor, instead of embracing criminality as a way of climbing the ladder of success. As part of preventative counseling aimed at mitigating juvenile delinquency and incarceration, school counselors need to stimulate communal social contexts. This is necessary because Adeleke, (2019) observes institutional, social lapses, and long communal hatred; and Osagie-Obazee and colleague (2016) finds assault from mass media, cultural and ethnic beliefs as causes of juvenile delinquency in their separate studies. Similarly, according to Federman (1998); cited in Agarwal and Dhanasekaran (2012), a national television violence study, finds an alarming number of violent contents in television programs viewed by children and adolescents in America. The study claimed that these violent contents in television programs contributed to antisocial behavior like aggression, desensitization to violence and fear of being victimized. These reports show that community social contexts are contributory to juvenile delinquency. School counselors should work with other key players in the community, like community chiefs to help in checking activities that could lead to negative character formations.

School counselors could also influence school administrators who could influence relevant government agents to ensure that programs shown on television or transmitted through other means of the mass media are controlled. Preventative counseling is a proactive and forward-looking counseling intervention strategy. It is very important for school counselors to know that children and young persons need to be properly guided for them to fit into society adaptively. They need to teach juveniles the necessity of being law abiding. Drawing on Hirschi's (1969), social control theory, individuals from birth are bad apples which need laws, rules and regulations in order to maintain a sane society. Hirschi's social control theory explains that individuals are not born with a conscience but that it is developed over time as result of their interactions within social contexts like family, churches and schools (Crawford, 2014). The theory emphasizes four bonds that could mitigate criminality- attachment, commitment, involvement and belief. Michael, Wiatrowski, Griswold, and Roberts (1981) explain these bonds as follows: attachment; relates to the affective ties individuals has towards significant others like the family unit which teaches children and young ones adaptive behavior; commitment, which relates to investment in conventional behavior that could bring fulfilment to individuals, but could be ruined through delinquent behavior; involvement, which relates to participating in societally acceptable activities that could enhance socially valued success and status objectives; and belief, which is individual's alignment with the overall social-value system in a social context. School counselors should endeavor to teach children and young persons the need to embrace these four bonds in order to live a good and fulfilling life. Juvenile delinquency will be reduced drastically if juvenile pupils and students appreciate the value system of the society they live in and have respect for the law of the land. Therefore, it is safe to theorize that juvenile delinquency and incarceration could be mitigated if counselors are mindful of the fact that criminal acts could be learnt from others, could be unlearnt through observation, imitation and modeling; and if children and young persons could be helped to establish attachment, commitment, involvement, and belief ties towards socially acceptable values.

Having looked at the preventative counseling approach to mitigating juvenile delinquency and incarceration, it is in important to look at the curative counseling dimension. Learners who manifest delinquent acts need curative counseling to be helped to change their maladaptive thoughts about criminal acts in order to accept adaptive thoughts through a process of cognitive restructuring, which could be achieved through the presentation of models they could observe and imitate during counseling processes. These models could be pictures or videos of successful people with exemplary lifestyles. This in line with the postulate of Bandura (1977; 2006) which reveal the potentials of models in shaping behavior. Individuals could pay attention to people (models), encode their behavior, and imitate or copy the observed behavior (McLeod, 2016). Thus, school counselors need to help students with delinquent behaviors to unlearn them through appropriate behavior modification strategies. Behavior psychologists like Skinner (1938; 1948) believes that behavior could be modified through operant (environmental) conditioning with appropriate reinforcements; while Pavlov, another behaviorist, emphasizes classical conditioning (stimulus substitution) for effecting changes in behavior (Pavlov,1902; McLeod, 2014).

In addition, Pupils and students under curative counseling could go through bibliotherapy processes to have exposure to adaptive models that could help in modifying their antisocial behaviors. The purpose of bibliotherapy is to provide suitable books, or audio / visual materials to juveniles to enhance their understanding of the danger of juvenile crimes and the incarceration that may follow as an aftermath. Association of Hospital and Institution Libraries (1971) defined bibliotherapy as "the use of selected reading materials as therapeutic adjuvants in medicine and psychiatry; also, guidance in the solution of personal problems through directed reading." Adomeh and Enokela (2020) find that bibliotherapy was effective in fostering students' emotional stability among 482 students drawn from junior secondary schools within the six area councils of the FCT, Abuja, Nigeria. Thus, bibliotherapy could provide appropriate models for learners to imitate to enhance adaptation that could strengthen them against juvenile crimes; and by implication mitigate incarceration.

Another strategy that could help learners to maintain adaptive behavior is peer counseling. White Swan Foundation (2016) defines Peer counseling as "a helping process that involves one-on-one interaction or interaction between members of a group, who have several things in common. In an academic setting, it usually refers to students helping their fellow students. It is a way of relating, responding and helping people, aimed at exploring thoughts, feelings, issues and concerns, with the hope of reaching a clear understanding and make informed decisions." Considering the definition offered by White Swan Foundation (2016), peer counseling processes could involve pupils or students for the purpose of helping them to modify maladaptive behaviors of some through the adaptive models of others. In this situation, the school counselors could raise a group for peer counseling where students that are of good behavior can serve as models for others who manifest antisocial behavior. School counselors must monitor the peer counseling group carefully, so that those with negative behavior patterns do not affect others negatively. Bururia, Marangu, and Nyaga, (2014) in a study establishes that peer counseling was important in mentoring other students as it addressed issues related to youth peer group, giving it the opportunity to model good behavior in Secondary Schools in Maara Sub County, Kenya. The finding of this study is a pointer to the effectiveness of peer counseling which could be incorporated into counseling processes to mitigate delinquency and incarceration of children and young persons in Nigeria.

SUMMARY AND CONCLUSION

This review critically evaluates the potentials of mitigating juvenile crimes and incarceration of children and young persons, with focus on the situation of the Nigerian pupils and students. The review relies on secondary sources of data gleaned from reliable sources from the internet. The differential association theory of Sutherland and the social learning theory of Bandura provide the theoretical direction for this effort. Sutherland contends that criminal behaviors could be learnt just like any other behavior (Sutherland, 1947; Sutherland, Cressey, & Luckenbill, 1992). Similarly, Bandura postulates that behavior could be learnt through observation, imitation and modeling (Bandura, 1947; 1973, McLeod, 2016). Both theories lay emphasis on the impacts of social contexts as influencers of human behavior. Therefore, to mitigate juvenile delinquency and incarceration, school counselors who have the noble roles of counselling services; prevention programs; advocacy and systematic improvement; administrator role; and educational and career planning (Carey, et al, 2020; Aluede, et al 2020) should feature significantly on the counseling scene to help in mitigating juvenile incarceration. School counselors based on this review, need to understand the psychosocial environments that could influence juvenile behavior so as to plan towards stimulating those environments to enhance adaptive behavior. These psychological settings- microsystem, mesosystem, exosystem, macrosystem and chronosystem (Bronfenbrenner, 1974; 1986; Ettekal et al, 2017) are systems that could determine the psychological healthiness of pupils and students to mitigate antisocial behaviors. School counselors are also advised to help pupils and students to positively see dignity in being law abiding, in line with Hirschi's (1969) social control theory which emphasizes four bonds of attachment, commitment, involvement and belief as antidote to delinquencies.

Furthermore, in keeping with Osagie and colleagues (2016), the federal, state and local governments in Nigeria should carry out a thorough campaign against programs that promote maladaptive behavior on mass media; and counselors are to encourage parents for them to see need of raising children and young persons with proper regards for social values. In addition, community counselling will enhance comprehensive interventions and promote a supportive and a psychologically healthy environment for all (Lazarus, Baptiste, & Seedat, 2009).

Mitigating juvenile incarceration involves quite a number of factors, but the role of the school counselors is central to helping pupils and students to combat delinquent behavior that could lay the foundation for incarceration.

In summary, Juvenile incarceration could pose a great deal of problem for a nation. Thus, all stakeholders involved in the training of children or young persons should show interest in fighting against social vices that can promote antisocial behavior. The Nigerian government at all levels need to invest more in school counselling services so that children can be properly guided in their formative ages before it becomes difficult to mold them.

REFERENCES

Abubakar, L. A. (2018). *The nature and causes of juvenile delinquency in Nigeria.* https://abubakarlawanku-ra.wordpress.com/2018/07/16/the-nature-and-causes-of-juvenile-delinquencyinnigeria/#:~:text=The%20 Nigerian%20constitution%20of%201979,pressure%20or%20certain%20emotional%20stimulation

Adegoke, N. (2015). Factors responsible for juvenile delinquency in nigeria: a case study of selected primary schools in Ikorodu, Lagos State, Nigeria. *Research on Humanities and Social Science, 5*(5), 78-84.

Adeleke, F. (2019). Child delinquency in communal conflict areas in southwestern Nigeria. *Journal of Community Psychology, 47*(4), 790–804. Advance online publication. doi:10.1002/jcop.22153 PMID:30644105

Adomeh, I. O. C., & Enokela, E. A. (2020). Perception of the effectiveness of bibliotherapy in fostering emotional adjustment among junior secondary school students in FCT, Abuja. *International Research Journal of Humanities, Language and Literature, 7*(1), 10–20.

Agarwal, V., & Dhanasekaran, S. (2012). Harmful Effects of Media on Children and Adolescents. *Journal Indian Association for Child and Adolescent Mental Health, 8*(2), 38–45.

Ajah, O. B., & Ugwuoke, O. C. (2018). Juvenile justice administration and child prisoners in Nigeria. *International Journal of Criminal Justice Sciences, 13*(2), 438–446. 110.5281/zenodo.2658065

Aluede, O., & Adubale, A. A. (2020). School-based Counsellors' Role as Perceived by Nigerian Counsellors. *Journal of School-Based Counseling Policy and Evaluation, 2*(1), 56–62. doi:10.25774/ppbt-6k45

Association of Hospital and Institution Libraries. (1971). *Bibliotherapy: Methods and Materials.* American Library Association.

Atilola, O. (2012). Prevalence and correlates of psychiatric disorders among residents of a juvenile remand home in Nigeria: Implications for mental health service planning. Nigerian Journal of Medicine. *Journal of the National Association of Resident Doctors of Nigeria, 21*, 416–426. PMID:23304950

Atilola, O. (2014). Different points of a continuum? Cross sectional comparison of the current and pre-contact psychosocial problems among the different categories of adolescents in institutional care in Nigeria. *BMC Public Health, 12*(1), 554. doi:10.1186/1471-2458-12-554 PMID:22835146

Bandura, A. (1977). Self-efficacy: Toward a unifying theory of behavioral change. *Psychological Review, 84*(2), 191–215. doi:10.1037/0033-295X.84.2.191 PMID:847061

Bandura, A. (2006). Toward a psychology of human agency. *Perspectives on Psychological Science, 1*(2), 164–180. doi:10.1111/j.1745-6916.2006.00011.x PMID:26151469

Bella, T.T., Atilola1, O. & Omigbodun, O.O. (2010). Children within the juvenile justice system in Nigeria: Psychopathology and psychosocial needs. *Annals of Ibadan Postgraduate Medicine, 8*(1), 34–39.

Bronfenbrenner, U. (1974). Developmental research, public policy, and the ecology of childhood. *Child Development, 45*(1), 1–5. doi:10.2307/1127743

Bronfenbrenner, U. (1978). The social role of the child in ecological perspective. *Zeitschrift für Soziologie*, *7*(1), 4–20. doi:10.1515/zfsoz-1978-0101

Bronfenbrenner, U. (1986). Ecology of the family as a context for human development: Research perspectives. *Developmental Psychology*, *22*(6), 723–742. doi:10.1037/0012-1649.22.6.723

Bururia, D. N., Marangu, P. G., & Nyaga, J. N. (2014). Contribution of Peer Counseling to Student Behavior Change in Secondary Schools in Maara Sub County. *Kenya Journal of Educational Policy and Entrepreneurial Research*, *1*(2), 86–93.

Ceka, A., & Murati, R. (2016). The Role of Parents in the Education of Children. *Journal of Education and Practice*, *7*(5), 61–64.

Charles Sturt University Library. (2021). *Literature review: Traditional or narrative literature reviews.* https://libguides.csu.edu.au/review/Traditional

Crawford, M. (2014). *Social Control Theory*. https://www.researchgate.net/publication/275154441_Social_Control_Theory doi:10.13140/RG.2.1.2360.7847

Crews, G. A. (2016). *School killers speak: A comprehensive examination of perpetrators, events, and characteristics of K-12 school violence in America*. The Veritas Group.

Egbochukwu, E. O. (2008). *Guidance and counselling: A comprehensive text*. Uniben Press.

Ejekwonyilo, A. (2019). *Inside the world of Nigeria child prisoners*. https://www.thecable.ng/inside-the-world-of-nigerias-child-prisoners

Ettekal, A. V., & Mahoney, J. L. (2017). Ecological systems theory. In K. Peppler (Ed.), *The Sage encyclopedia of out-of-school learning* (pp. 239–241). Sage.

Federal Republic of Nigeria (FRN). (2013). National policy on education. Lagos: Nigerian Educational Research Council (NERDC) Press.

Federman, J. (Ed.). (1998). *National Television Violence Study* (Vol. 3). Sage.

Hirschi, T. (1969). *Causes of Delinquency*. University of California Press.

James, G. (2013). Assessment of the Administration and Practice of Juvenile Justice System in Abuja, Nigeria. *Mediterranean Journal of Social Sciences*, *4*(1), 331–338.

Johns, J., & Barnes, N. (2021). The Locked Cage: Understanding the Impact of Incarceration on Children and Families within the School. In M. A. Rausch & L. L. Gallo (Eds.), *Strengthening School Counselor Advocacy and Practice for Important Populations and Difficult Topics* (pp. 162–174). IGI Global. doi:10.4018/978-1-7998-7319-8.ch009

Kaplan, D. M., Tarvydas, V. M., & Gladding, S. T. (2014). A vision for the future of counseling: the new consensus definition of counseling. *Journal of Counselling and Development*. https://onlinelibrary.wiley.com/doi/full/10.1002/j.1556-6676.2014.00164.x

Lazarus, S., Baptiste, D., & Seedat, M. (2009). Community Counselling: Values and Practices. *Journal of Psychology in Africa*, *19*(3), 449–454. doi:10.1080/14330237.2009.10820314

McLeod, S. A. (2014). *Classical conditioning*. www.simplypsychology.org/classical-conditioning.html

McLeod, S. A. (2016). *Bandura - social learning theory*. www.simplypsychology.org/bandura.html

Michelle, A. (2012). *The New Jim Crow: Mass Incarceration in the Age of Colorblindness*. The New Press.

Okagbue, I. (n.d.). *Children in Conflict with the Law: The Nigerian Experience*. https://www.unicef-irc.org/portfolios/documents/487_nigeria.htm

Osagie-Obazee, G., & Eduwen, F. (2016). The influence of family factors on delinquent adolescents in secondary schools in Edo South Senatorial District of Edo State. AFRREV IJAH. *An International Journal of Arts and Humanities*, *5*(3), 231–243. doi:10.4314/ijah.v5i3.19

Oxford Reference. (n.d.). *Incarceration*. https://www.oxfordreference.com/view/10.1093/oi/authority.20110803095959949

Pavlov, I. P. (1902). *The work of the digestive glands*. Griffin.

Roostin, E. (2018). Family influence on the development of children. *Journal of Elementary Education*, *1*(1), 1–12. doi:10.22460/pej.v1i1.654

Sanni, K. B., Udoh, N. A., Okediji, A. A., Modo, F. N., & Ezeh, L. N. (2010). Family Types and Juvenile Delinquency Issues among Secondary School Students in Akwa Ibom State, Nigeria: Counseling Implications. *Journal of Social Science*, *23*(1), 21–28.

Schreck, C., & Hirschi, T. (2009). *Social control theory*. https://www.researchgate.net/publication/337873997_Social_Control_Theory

Skill You Need. (2021). *What is counselling?* https://www.skillsyouneed.com/learn/counselling.html

Skinner, B. F. (1938). *The Behaviour of organisms: An experimental analysis*. Appleton-Century.

Skinner, B. F. (1948). Superstition' in the pigeon. *Journal of Experimental Psychology*, *38*(2), 168–172. doi:10.1037/h0055873 PMID:18913665

Stanko, S. C., & Crews, G. A. (2016). The Impact of Mass Incarceration and Social Issues of Institutionalization on School Violence in Youths. In A. C. Gordon (Ed.), *Critical Examinations of School Violence and Disturbance in K-12 Education* (pp. 29–37). IGI Global. doi:10.4018/978-1-4666-9935-9.ch003

Sutherland, E. H. (1947). *Principles of criminology* (4th ed.). Lippincott.

Sutherland, E. H., Cressey, D. R., & Luckenbill, D. F. (1992). Principles of criminology (11th ed.). Lanham, MD: Alta Mira Press.

Trappen, S. (2018). *Theories of Delinquency*. https://sandratrappen.com/2018/12/30/theories-of-delinquency/

Ukwueze, A. C. (2015). Adolescents' inappropriate behaviours affecting academic performance in senior secondary schools: Need for counselling interventions. *Sokoto International Journal of Counselling Psychology*, *3*(2), 138–154.

White Swan Foundation. (2016). *Peer counseling in an academic setting*. https://www.whiteswanfoundation.org/education/peer-counselling-in-academic-setting

Wiatrowski, M. D., Griswold, D. B., & Roberts, M. K. (1981). Social control theory and delinquency. *American Sociological Review*, *46*(5), 525–341. doi:10.2307/2094936

KEY TERMS AND DEFINITIONS

Basic School: In line with National Policy on Education, basic school covers preprimary, primary and junior secondary schools in the Nigerian education system. Learners spend 1 year in preprimary school, 6 years in primary school and 3 years in junior secondary school. The basic education takes 10 years put together.

Counseling: Counseling is a professional relationship that could help individual to achieve mental health, fitness, education, and career goals. It is also a process of helping an individual to behave in a more personally satisfying way to foster appropriate adaptation in his/her environmental contexts. In this chapter, counseling was particularly perceived as a therapeutic relationship between the counselor and learners to assist the latter to develop adaptive skills or competences to be able to resist juvenile delinquency or crimes.

Incarceration: Incarceration is a process of someone being placed in prison, remand home or juvenile detention center, where he or she would be cut off from the wider society. Juvenile incarceration in this chapter is perceived as the detention or the imprisonment of persons considered to be under the age of 18.

Juvenile: Juvenile refers to child and young person under the age 18, more specifically, a child under the age of 14 and a young person up 14 but less than 18.

Juvenile Delinquency: Juvenile delinquency refers to offences or crimes of persons under the age of 18. It is an antisocial behavior which include stealing or shoplifting, fighting, burglary, rape, homicide, and so on. Juvenile delinquency could lead to incarceration of those who express it.

Post Basic School: The post basic schools include secondary schools, technical schools and their equivalents. Learners spend 3 years in post basic schools. Those who are more than 18 years, still in any of the post basic schools are no longer juvenile and are not the target population of this chapter.

Pupils: Pupils are learners in preprimary and primary levels of the basic school.

School Counselors: School counselors are counselors who work with pupils or students. They provide counseling services to pupils or students to help to them to achieve mental health, adaptive behavior, education, and career goals. This chapter aligned with 5 key roles of school-based counselors as: counselling services; prevention programs; advocacy and systematic improvement; administrator role; and educational and career planning.

Students: Students are learners in junior secondary school level of basic school and post basic schools, comprising senior secondary school, technical school, and their equivalents.

Chapter 12
Trauma-Engaged and Culturally Responsive Schools:
Changing the School-to-Prison Pipeline

Liliana Burciaga
Lewis University, USA

ABSTRACT

An abundance of research on the prevalence of traumatic experiences in childhood and their impact on the brain, behavior, and learning led to discourse on how schools can provide trauma-informed services to prevent further re-traumatization and provide support. Over the last two decades, research has highlighted the integration of trauma-responsive practices in schools in place of traditional school discipline. Traditional school discipline policies disproportionately impact students of color and help support the school-to-prison pipeline. This chapter addresses the issue of schools creating trauma-engaged learning environments. However, there is less direction in the literature about why or how creating trauma-engaged schools should happen from a culturally affirming lens and social justice perspective since it is minoritized students that are more likely to feed the school-to-prison pipeline. Therefore, this chapter aims to provide an overview on creating trauma-engaged and culturally responsive schools to dismantle the school-to-prison pipeline.

INTRODUCTION

The school-to-prison pipeline is widely understood as the trajectory from the educational system to the United States criminal justice system (McCarter, 2016). This pipeline was created by a system that presents as disciplining youth in schools by imposing suspensions, expulsions, and juvenile justice referrals that lead to higher risks of them being pushed out of the education system and into the criminal justice system; thus, criminalizing youth. Students from minoritized groups are disproportionately affected by this funneling system, especially students of color, LGBTQ+ youth, and those with disabilities (Aleguire, 2016; Annamma et al., 2016; Gregory et.al, 2010; Whitford et al., 2019). Moreover, students who have experienced trauma in their lives are at risk for being entrapped in the school-to-prison pipeline when

DOI: 10.4018/978-1-7998-9209-0.ch012

schools are not equipped to respond to these students (Aleguire, 2016). This chapter will begin with understanding the prevalence of trauma and how schools' poor response to trauma can lead to youth interacting with the criminal justice system.

Bringing trauma into the discussion of dismantling the school-to-prison pipeline is critical for addressing this cycle that our society is confronted with. Creating trauma-engaged and culturally responsive schools is a social justice imperative. Without understanding the effects that trauma and chronic stress can have on students, youth who have experienced trauma are seen as exhibiting problematic behaviors instead of children who are adapting and trying to survive as best as they can (Aleguire et al., 2016). It is well documented in research literature that when youth have experienced trauma they are more vulnerable to experiencing negative consequences in schools, especially when school professionals are not trained in identifying and responding to signs of trauma (Aleguire et al., 2016). This chapter will discuss the issues with traditional discipline in schools and how they contribute to the perpetuation of the school-to-prison pipeline.

Trauma is at the core of many of the problem behaviors that are seen in schools that lead to school discipline (Aleguire, 2016; National Council of State Education Associations, 2019). In order to know how to transform school cultures, school professionals must understand trauma and its effects so that they can change school culture and respond to trauma rather than problem behaviors. Several successful frameworks for creating trauma sensitive school cultures, implementing trauma-informed care or practice, and establishing an overall trauma-responsive, engaged school system are available (Alaska Department of Education and Early Development, 2019; Cole et al., 2005; Substance Abuse and Mental Health Services Administration, 2014; Wolpow et al., 2009). This chapter will provide an overview of trauma-informed care and frameworks for creating trauma-responsive schools. Since there are racial disparities in who is impacted by the school-to-prison pipeline, this chapter will also discuss the role of race in understanding trauma responsiveness in schools and how this can be addressed through increasing cultural competence and culturally responsive teaching in schools.

BACKGROUND

Framing the Issue of Trauma

Trauma can take many forms, but generally refers to the emotional response when experiencing a distressing and possibly life-changing event or circumstance (SAMHSA, 2014). It is a widespread and costly public health problem (SAMHSA, 2014). The lifetime prevalence of a person experiencing at least one traumatic event in their lifetime, is more than people might assume. Traumatic events are a lot more common than some people think.

Decades of research have provided insight on the prevalence of trauma and its consequences. The Center for Disease Control-Keiser Permanente study, on adverse childhood experiences [ACEs], is one of the largest studies that provides knowledge on the prevalence of adverse childhood experiences and their consequences (Center for Disease Control and Prevention [CDC], 2021). These are traumatic experiences that occur in childhood that can have an impact throughout one's life. ACEs can include: experiences of abuse, neglect, and household challenges such as witnessing a parent behave violently towards another; having a household member with substance abuse or mental health issues; parental separation or divorce; experiencing economic hardship; or living in a household with a family member who has been incarcerated, as well as community-level stressors like witnessing community violence; living in unsafe neighborhoods; experiencing racism; living in foster care; and being bullied (CDC, 2021; Child Trends, 2019; Wade et al., 2016).

There are higher levels of ACEs in the general population than previously imagined. The original Keiser Permanente ACEs study took place between 1995-1997 and included data from over 17,000 individuals that answered questions regarding their childhood experiences, health status, and behaviors, with over 50% reporting that they experienced at least one adverse childhood experience [ACE] (CDC, 2021). ACEs have been studied extensively since the original study was conducted.

Data from the 2018 National Survey of Children's Health [NSCH] showed that between 2017-2018, one in three children under the age of 18 have experienced at least one ACE and 14% experienced two or more ACEs (Health Resources and Services Administration). An analysis of the trends in the NSCH data showed that there are racial and ethnic disparities in who experiences ACEs, with 61% of Black children and 51% of Latino or Hispanic children experiencing at least one ACE compared to 40% of white non-Latino or Hispanic children and 23% Asian non-Latino or Hispanic children (Child Trends, 2016). Children who live in poverty or near-poverty are also twice as likely than peers who are more affluent to have three or more adverse experiences in childhood (Child Trends, 2016). In short, studies have uncovered that children who have experienced ACEs are more likely to exhibit negative behaviors in school and to also develop other risky behaviors that impact their health, well-being, and opportunities throughout their life-course (Morton, 2018; Frieze, 2015; Reuben et al., 2016; Chartier et al., 2010; Chapman et al., 2004). There is a substantial correlation between child adversity and negative life outcomes. The more ACEs a child has experienced, the higher the risk of them experiencing negative life outcomes compared to those who have only experienced one (Reuben et al., 2016; Chartier et al., 2010; Chapman et al. 2004). A considerable concern is that youth of color report greater prevalence of trauma than White youth and this is likely to be due to racial trauma (Saleem et al., 2020).

Considering how widespread ACEs are, schools are more likely to encounter children who may experience emotional turmoil due to trauma. Educators may be well-trained in many areas and may have engaging lesson plans, but they frequently lack training in the understanding of trauma and how to respond to it (Cummings et al., 2017). They also are not likely to understand the neurobiology that drives some student behavior or may not know how to acknowledge the role of trauma in those behaviors (Craig, 2016; Cummings et al., 2017; Dutro, 2017). Teachers are also likely to lack diversity training to work with the students they serve so students of color can feel that they are targets of discrimination, trauma, and stress that is associated with racial trauma (Hardy, 2013; Sawyer et al., 2012). Teachers' lack of trauma and diversity training often leads them to interpret student behaviors as defiant, misconduct, and dysregulated and may respond with punitive behavior management programs that have been put into place to respond to such behaviors. The emotional and behavioral outburst and the punishments that usually follow in a traditional school setting impact both the mental health and safety of educators, staff, and students. When informed about trauma, the issues that may arise in a classroom can be understood from a different perspective that can lead to taking a positive approach to discipline. When these issues are not examined and understood as being likely connected to trauma, they contribute to the school- to-prison pipeline.

Racial Trauma in Schools

For students of color, the experience of racial trauma in schools is grave. Racial trauma is defined as "trauma that results from the actual and perceived experiences of students of color due to the immutable characteristic of race." (Aleguirre et al., 2016). Williams et al. adds that this includes:

...race-related experiences that are collectively characterized as racism, including acts of prejudice, discrimination, or violence against a subordinate racial group based on attitudes of superiority held by the dominant group...[and] can be caused by overt or covert actions carried out by individuals or society (e.g., aversive racism, modern/ symbolic racism, racial microaggressions, etc.). (2018, p. 181)

Racial trauma is the byproduct of racism when it impairs individuals in psychological and physical ways. Research on racial trauma has highlighted that anticipating prejudice and experiencing racial stress leads to psychological and physical distress, including cardiovascular reactivity, anxiety, hypertension, and sleep disturbances (Krieger, 1990; Sawyer et al., 2012; Williams & Mohammed, 2009). Specifically, Black youth experience traumatic symptoms as a result of racism, such as hypervigilance about anticipated racism, decreased self-esteem, depression, poor academic self-concept and academic performance, and decreased school engagement (Chavous et al., 2008; Jernigan & Daniel, 2011; Wang & Huguley, 2012; Wong, Eccles, & Sameroff, 2003). Youth of color undergo these debilitating experiences in various parts of society, including schools.

In his research, Kenneth Hardy (2013) indicates that few educators understand the deeply destructive impact of racial trauma. In a 2020 study by the National Center for Education Statistics, in the 2017-2018 school year, 79 percent of public school teachers were White, and only 7 percent were Black and 9 percent were Latino (Taie & Westat, 2020). Among private school teachers, 85 percent were White, 3 percent were Black, and 7 percent were Latino (Taie & Westat, 2020). This means that the vast majority of teachers have not personally experienced the effects of racism since most educators are White. These teachers are less likely to understand the role that racial trauma can play in school.

When there are cross-racial interactions people can experience feelings of threat and discomfort, also known as racial anxiety. Students of color may have anxiety about unavoidably experiencing racism and this can result in them becoming distant, avoiding eye contact, less friendly and engaging in the classroom (Johnson & Godsil, 2014). White teachers can also have anxiety about being perceived as racist towards students of color (Johnson & Godsil, 2014). When these aspects of racial anxiety are present in the classroom, student-teacher interactions can be perceived as negative and this can spiral into students becoming hostile towards teachers that they perceive as hostile (Johnson & Godsil, 2014). These interactions between aspects of racial anxiety can contribute to racial trauma. Racial anxiety can also be impacted by one's stereotypes of other racial groups and implicit biases. For example, teachers and school officials are likely to perceive Black children as being older, more aggressive and guiltworthy, despite exhibiting the same developmentally-appropriate behaviors as their White counterparts (Intercultural Development Research Association, 2021). This highlights the need for schools to address trauma and diversity training at all levels.

A Student's Brain on Trauma

The research on trauma and the ACEs data helps us understand how learning, behavior, and the brain are affected by trauma and why schools need to evaluate their approaches in the classroom and the overall school culture. The brain is overwhelmed and becomes disorganized so it shuts down and goes into survival mode, which then impacts students' ability to regulate themselves in the classroom and learn. When trauma is experienced, the brain and nervous system can become disorganized, resulting in a variety of responses such as flight, fight, freeze, fawn. This disorganization impacts each student differently, but the overall result is shutting down the area of the brain that is responsible for self-regulation, learning, and problem solving. Clearly, this directly impacts a student's ability to learn and participate constructively in a classroom. Trauma research states that:

Trauma can impact learning in ways that can be seen and hidden in the classroom. Given that the educational system is based on the ability to regulate behavior and the ability to take in and recall previous information and learning, students with trauma histories are at a marked disadvantage for academic achievement, through no fault of their own. (Morton, 2018, p. 75)

There is a connection between trauma, academic performance, social functioning, and behavioral problems (Blaustein & Kinniburgh, 2019; Craig, 2016; Cole et al., 2005; Morton, 2018; Morton & Berardi, 2017; National Scientific Council on the Developing Child [NSCDC], 2010; The National Child Traumatic Stress Network, 2018). Students need access to the executive functioning skills of the cerebral cortex in order to learn and succeed in schools. To recognize this connection, there needs to be an understanding that trauma impacts our ability to use executive functioning.

Executive functioning skills can include our ability to think critically, plan, organize, manage time, control and monitor our behavior, focus, adaptability, and impulse control. Executive functioning is referred to as "The captain of the cognitive ship" (Blaustein & Kinniburgh, 2018, p. 259). Essentially, it includes skills that impact both academic and social competence, including reading comprehension, writing, language arts, memorizing and problem-solving (Blaustein & Kinniburgh, 2018; Craig, 2016). Trauma leaves the brain in a heightened state of awareness, making it difficult to access executive functioning and instead rely on the body's automatic system for stress response- also known as the fight, flight, freeze, fawn response. During this heightened state, the body is triggered by real or perceived danger, so students are left with the inability to access higher reasoning and language expression, which leaves them unable to express their feelings or ask for assistance (Cole et al., 2005; Morton & Berardi, 2017; The National Child Traumatic Stress Network, 2018). Experiencing child adversity can lead to permanent changes to the brain architecture (Franke, 2014; NSCDC, 2005/2014, 2010; Nemeroff, 2016). Toxic stress, when the fight, flight, or freeze response is activated too often or for long periods of time, impacts development of the brain and its structure, including impairing executive functioning (Franke, 2014; NSCDC, 2005/2014, 2010; Nemeroff, 2016).

How does this translate to the day to day in a classroom setting? A student that has had traumatic experiences may be triggered and can interpret something that is not threatening, such as not understanding the directions for an assignment or not being able to do a specific task, and feel intense emotion associated with the traumatic event/s. The student is not able to control this response because their brain is overloaded by the stress reaction. This means that they may respond in ways that are disproportionate to the situation. Children who have been traumatized can experience times of their brain not being available for learning, like when they have flashbacks, intrusive thoughts, or dissociation and can appear to be daydreaming or withdrawn. They can have difficulties managing their emotions when they are stressed.

Their stress reactions can impact their relationships not only with peers but also with adults, especially authority figures, since trauma may lead to having difficulty trusting others. Even for the most motivated student, trauma can have long-term interference in their ability to succeed academically, socially, and emotionally. Students' trauma responses are often misunderstood for being misbehavior and this often leads to punitive consequences.

Traditional School Discipline Fails

Zero tolerance policies were developed in the 1990's by the federal government as a prevention response to drug use and gun violence in schools (Thompson, 2018). Zero tolerance school discipline policies and practices mandate punishment for misconduct through suspensions and expulsions, and sometimes this leads to interactions with the justice system. The way that this has been interpreted is broad and can vary from school to school, but one popular interpretation was to create strict zero tolerance policies (Thompson, 2018). There is no official definition of the term zero tolerance, but in general it refers to harsh predetermined mandatory consequences that are applied to a violation of school rules without consideration for the gravity of the behavior, extenuating circumstances, or situational context (American Psychological Association, 2008).

There is substantial data that corporal punishment is ineffective and detrimental to children (American Academy of Child and Adolescent Psychiatry, 2012; American Academy of Pediatrics, 1998; Gershoff, 2008, 2013; Durrant & Ensom, 2012). Alfie Kohn (2005, 1993) makes the argument that what is known about the harm of physical punishment can also be attributed to other forms of punishment stating that any kind of punishment is ineffective because it makes people angry, teaches power, eventually loses its effectiveness, erodes, relationships with kids, distracts kids from the important issues, and makes kids more self-centered.

The use of suspensions and expulsions creates all these issues that Kohn emphasizes but rarely are these things consistent with what educators and school staff hope to accomplish with discipline. In fact, to date there is no substantial data that supports that suspensions are effective strategies that improve student behavior and academic performance, yet schools continue to use them as a form of discipline (International Child and Youth Care Network, 2009).

Data has consistently shown that there are vulnerable populations that are affected at greater rates by suspensions and expulsions. For instance, according to the National Association for the Education of Young Children (NAEYC), a 2014 report stated that 8,700 three and four-year-old children were expelled from their state-funded preschool or prekindergarten classrooms each year, with Black boys being twice as likely to be expelled as their white peers (2017). The 2020 United States [U.S.] Department of Education Office for Civil Rights report revealed that in the 2017-2018 school year, Black students, who accounted for 15.1% of total student enrollment, were expelled at twice and a half their share of total student enrollment—38.8% of expulsions with educational services and 33.3% of expulsions without educational services. Latino and Alaskan Native/American Indian students have also been shown to be disproportionately affected by expulsions and suspensions compared to white students, but not at the same rate as Black students (Alguire, 2016; U.S. Department of Education's Office for Civil Rights, 2020; Whitford et al., 2019). This is consistent with research that states that Black youth are more likely to be disciplined than youth of other races (Aleguirre, 2016; Ryberg et al., 2021). Suspensions in grades K-12 showed that Black girls received in-school suspensions (11.2%) and out-of-school suspensions (13.3%) at rates almost two times their overall enrollment (7.4%) and Black boys received both in-school suspensions (20.1%) and out-of-school suspensions (24.9%) suspensions at rates more than three times their total student enrollment (7.7%); this is the largest disparity across all race/ethnicity and sex groups (U.S. Department of Education's Office for Civil Rights, 2020). The data consistently supports the disproportionate impact of

On average, students with disabilities were more than twice as likely to be suspended compared to students without disabilities in the 2017-2018 school year (Ryberg et al., 2021). Black, male students with intellectual, emotional, or physical disabilities have a 33.8% chance of being suspended in a given school year, compared with only a 16.2% chance for their white male peers (Aleguire, 2016). Latino male students with disabilities are suspended at a rate of about 23.2%, and Black female students with disabilities are suspended more often than white male students with disabilities (Aleguire, 2016). In the 2017-2018 school year, there was a 5.2% increase in rates of suspensions for students with disabilities in K-12 schools and a 1.1% increase in secondary schools (Ryberg et al., 2021). Students of color with disabilities are the most vulnerable group for harsh discipline in schools.

LGBTQ+ students also face disproportionately high levels of school discipline due to hostile school climates. In a 2019 School Climate Survey by the Gay, Lesbian & Straight Education Network, over 3% of students who were surveyed that identified as LGBTQ+ reported being disciplined for simply identifying as LGBTQ+ (Kosciw et al., 2020). LGBTQ+ students are twice as likely (46.8%) to be disciplined (e.g. detention or suspension) when they report being victimized or bullied at school (Kosciw et al., 2020).

According to research, harsh disciplinary methods push students to drop out, and eventually contributes to the school-to-prison pipeline since high school dropouts are more likely to be arrested and end up in jail or prison (Aleguire, 2016). A great deal of the research on suspension and expulsion shows that they do little to change behavior and they tend to push kids out of school altogether. A study from the Everyone Graduates Center at John Hopkins University (Balfanz et al., 2014) found that being suspended once in ninth grade was related to increased risk of dropping out. In this study suspension increased the probability of leaving school before graduation from 16% to 32%, with each additional suspension raising the chances of dropping out by 10% (Balfanz et al., 2014). Similar outcomes have been found in other studies looking at student suspensions and expulsions (APA, 2008; Skiba et al., 2014; Noltemeyer et al., 2015). With studies making it clear that suspension and expulsion fails, it is critical to rethink the purpose of our education systems and act to implement alternatives to traditional discipline approaches in school. Zero tolerance policies have received much criticism for this reason as well as its connection to criminalizing youth.

Trouble at School Means Incarceration

The growing concerns about crime in schools led to the creation of federal policies that mandated suspensions for bringing weapons to schools (Thompson, 2018). Since many schools have outsourced police to discipline, whether it is through the use of police resource officers or by referring students to law enforcement as a way of punishment, it becomes much easier for youth to build a juvenile record. Punishments can then become harsher after the first offense. What used to be small violations (e.g. talking back, disrupting class, horseplay, disobedience) that school officials would deal with have easily become criminal behavior. Most suspensions are handed down for minor rule breaking, such as nonviolent issues, as opposed to major infractions (e.g. harassment or bullying, possession of a dangerous weapon, defacing school property, gang related activity). A systematic review found that chronic absences and classroom disruption were the most common reasons for suspension (Skiba et al., 2014). When schools rely on police to discipline students, they essentially push youth into the justice system.

The way that zero tolerance policies are used today causes more harm than good since there is no support that they actually create safer environments. In fact, several studies have noted that zero tolerance policies are misused and abused (APA, 2008; Gregory and Evans, 2020; Heitzeg, 2009; Losen et al. 2015). What's more, there is overwhelming evidence that these punishments are harsher on some students than others. These policies are associated with racial disproportionality. Punitive discipline policies disproportionately affect students of color and students with disabilities, making it more difficult for them to learn and be successful in their learning environment. Black and Brown youth, students in special education, LGBTQ+, and low-income students are consistently overrepresented in the number of students who are disciplined due to no tolerance policies (Annamma et al., 2016; Gregory et al., 2010; Whitford et al., 2019). One of the most comprehensive analyses of school suspensions and expulsions tracked 1 million students in Texas and highlighted the racial disproportionality (Fabelo et al. 2011). Studies have found overwhelming evidence that Black students receive more of these consequences than their white counterparts (Gopalan & Nelson 2019; Owens & McLanahan, 2019). A study highlighted that differential treatment and support in school is an important but understudied mechanism in the early criminalization of Black students (Owens & McLanahan, 2020).

According to the U.S. Department of Education Office for Civil Rights (2014), Black students are three times more likely to be suspended or expelled than white students. The national and longitudinal data collected suggests that decreased use of corporal punishment in schools predicts lower rates of suspension overall but higher suspension rates can be predicted in school districts that serve larger proportions of students of color (U.S. Department of Education Office for Civil Rights, 2014). While the most current data shows that the disproportion has closed somewhat, this is happening at a lower rate for Black students (U.S. Department of Education Office for Civil Rights, 2021).

These differences in how students are disciplined can be explained by structural racism and educator bias. These findings are consistent with Michelle Alexander's (2010) influential book, *The New Jim Crow: Mass Incarceration in the Age of Colorblindness*, where it is highlighted that communities of color, especially Black communities, are targeted by mass incarceration. Parallels are drawn between the post–Civil Rights Era system of mass incarceration and the Jim Crow segregation system that reigned from 1877 to 1965. In both cases, Blacks are controlled and constrained from being able to fully be protected as citizens and be equal to Whites (Alexander, 2010; Horsdord, 2018). Jim Crow laws legalized segregation and kept millions of children from getting an education because of the color of their skin. Even after these laws were deemed unconstitutional, the discrimination and systemic racism continues embedded in society and shapes how Black people can operate in society today (Alexander, 2010; Horsdord, 2018; IDRA, 2021). At the same time, overt and implicit biases were passed down in other communities, and the inequities that were rooted in racism have persisted in various systems like healthcare, housing, and education (IDRA, 2021). Specifically, in the education system this has been evident in the disproportionate discipline, criminalization, and harsh treatment of Black youth that pushes them out of the classroom and into the pipeline (IDRA, 2021). Marrus (2015) posits that to keep the education of Black youth from becoming the new Jim Crow three steps must be taken. These are: 1. address implicit racial bias that leads to disproportionate numbers of Black youth in foster care, school discipline, and juvenile justice systems, 2. the number of children in these systems must be reduced, and 3. quality, nurturing education must be provided for those who are in these systems (Marrus, 2015). When the power in these systems is not confronted, institutional racism persists by allowing unconscious issues related to race to keep perpetuating the narratives that eventually lead to feeding the pipeline. Students of color are at higher risk of racial trauma that is inherent in systemic racism and racial bias from school officials.

Racial bias is less likely to be explicit in the present day than years ago but it is more likely to take form through implicit bias (Johnson & Godsil, 2014). The disparities in school discipline are impacted by the implicit bias of teachers, administrators, and other school staff. The Equal Justice Society lists implicit bias as being a key instigating factor for youth of color, LGBTQ+, and youth with disabilities being treated more harshly than their white counterparts in schools (Aleguire, 2016). Implicit biases are unconscious thought patterns and attitudes that are rooted in learned stereotypes. Johnson & Godsil (2014) notes that stereotypes are often learned from the messages that one comes across in popular media, that people tend to favor their own groups and are likely to dehumanize other groups. The "Implicit Association Test" (IAT) has shown that a significant number of people have anti-black bias (Johnson & Godsil, 2014). A Texas A&M study found that 97.3% of suspensions, expulsions, and other disciplinary measures are discretionarily-imposed based on a school policy or an administrator's decision (Carmichael, 2011). This becomes a biased imposition of punishment since school officials' assessments of the situation can include their own racialized stereotypes. The lack of self-awareness of these biases suggests that the adults interacting with youth in the school system may feel justified in how they react to a disciplinary situation and not be aware of how their implicit biases impact the interaction or decision making. That means that if an authority figure has implicit biases about certain groups of youth then they are more likely to view them as more threatening or more guilty and will respond with harsher discipline methods compared to how they respond to white students in similar situations. For example, if a teacher has an implicit bias that Black boys tend to be troublemakers then they are more likely to assume that a Black student initiated a fight and advocate for an out of school suspension while recommending an in school suspension for a student in a similar situation. The negative impact that Whiteness can have on teachers' understanding of children of color and urban schools is detrimental, especially since White teachers often enter the profession viewing students of color and their communities as dangerous and at fault for the educational challenges they face (Picower, 2009).

Responding to Trauma in Schools

The effect of stress and trauma can be mitigated with the right supports to promote healing and prevent re-traumatization. Adverse childhood experiences can be prevented through educating caregivers, communities, and policymakers so that adults can provide more stable and supportive environments where children can thrive (CDC, 2021). Schools can help students learn self-regulation skills and through a whole-school approach, they can support positive brain development, mitigating the effects of ACEs. The ACEs data has motivated communities to respond to trauma because it is known that at least half of adults have experienced adversity in childhood (Cole et al., 2013; Prewitt, 2014).

Trauma-informed care is an approach to the delivery of mental health services that assumes that an individual is more likely to have a history of trauma. Trauma-informed care includes having an understanding and awareness of the impact of trauma; using an environmental and cultural lens to recognize the context that plays a role in how someone experiences trauma; being purposeful about avoiding retraumatizing individuals who have a history of trauma; and the role of the client's participation in the services they receive (Substance Abuse and Mental Health Services Administration [SAMHSA], 2014). The focus of trauma-informed care is on providing safe, supportive, and inclusive environments so that exposure of trauma is minimized and where if exposure does happen there are practices in place to buffer against its impact. This includes culturally responsive interventions and the promotion of resilience.

The Four R's have been used as the key assumptions to help programs or systems provide trauma-informed care (SAMHSA, 2014). These are: Realize, Recognize, Respond, and Resist (SAMHSA, 2014). In the context of schools, the Four R's provide key assumptions for how to begin to think about transforming schools:

1. Realize: Understand the widespread impact of trauma, how it impacts learning, and that there are ways to mitigate its impact.
2. Recognize: Identify the signs and symptoms of trauma in students, families, and educational staff.
3. Respond: Integrate the knowledge about trauma into the school culture by addressing policies, procedures, and practices.
4. Resist: School-wide trauma-sensitivity allows for the prevention of further retraumatization and blaming.

A collaboration between the CDC and SAMHSA (2020) also provides six principles as a guide to a trauma-informed approach. These include: safety, trustworthiness and transparency, peer support, collaboration and mutuality, empowerment and choice, and cultural, historical and gender issues.

Becoming trauma-informed is a social justice action because it addresses the impact of stress and trauma on minoritized communities and individuals in a society where privilege and marginalization exist. In schools, it also means addressing what contributes to the pipeline. Schools around the nation are recognizing the connection between trauma and the pipeline and several are making efforts to transform their systems and are seeing success. In a recent study, for example, a school using trauma and culturally responsive tools to target dropout recovery saw a consistently high graduation rate with each graduate having a plan for post-secondary success (Basford et al., 2020). These are the tools needed to break the pipeline, but they must be used with race at the center of all discourse.

Responding to racial trauma includes identifying the means that can address the structural racism and educator bias that contribute to interrupt and eventually break the school-to-prison pipeline. Grinage (2019) emphasizes the importance of using strength-based, healing centered approaches to work towards racial justice in education. Current research suggests ways to address structural racism in schools and educator bias:

- Remove police from school buildings and end exclusionary discipline practices (e.g. suspension and expulsion).
- Create a safe climate that affirms discussion about race, racial identity, and racism.
- Provide safe spaces and coping options for students (e.g. cultural student associations, ethnic studies).
- Integrate cultural competent curriculums and increase training for staff on culturally sustaining pedagogy and practices.
- Train staff, students, and families on restorative practices and monitor the implementation of these practices closely.
- Engage in safe and supported opportunities for growth for all-district wide to include administrators, staff, teachers, students, and caregivers.
- Develop a district plan to address racial bullying. (Anderson, 2019; Gringe, 2019; IDRA, 2021).

CREATING TRAUMA-ENGAGED SCHOOLS

With new, irrefutable understanding about the impact that childhood trauma has on the brain, learning, and behavior, schools have been empowered to provide students the support and tools that they need to break the cycle of trauma and dismantle the pipeline. To address the effects of trauma and racially disproportionate school suspensions and expulsions, a majority of school counselors and social workers have implemented trauma-informed care and multi-tiered socio-emotional learning programming (Joseph et al., 2020; Walkley & Cox, 2013). An analysis of these services in schools found that these supports alone do not lead to consistent changes in student's behavioral problems and social skills, even when disciplinary data demonstrated a decrease in suspensions each year (Báez et al., 2019). When factoring in the effects of trauma, major differences were in the pre and post interventions (Báez et al., 2019). This data suggests that students who have experienced more trauma are likely to need greater support in schools. A recent study found that, "Positive experiences and supportive relationships provide the buffering that allows children to withstand, or recover, from adverse experiences." (Sege et al., 2017). Children need to feel safe and connected to adults and peers everywhere in a school community. One teacher, counselor, social worker, psychologist, or school administrator cannot do it alone. It is about the embodiment of a school culture where interactions and services are coordinated to help students feel safe and supported throughout the school day. This requires the teamwork of everyone in the school system to apply trauma-informed principles to schools.

In the literature, there are often various terms used to refer to trauma-informed care, such as trauma-focused, and trauma-specific (Zakszeski, et al., 2017). These are terms that are more often related to mental health treatment and some professionals may use them synonymously. There has been some criticism about trauma-informed care not providing clear and practical application. This has led to research on the practice elements of trauma-informed care, for example screening, assessment, and referral to treatment (Berliner & Kolko, 2016). There can be confusion regarding what trauma-informed care means in the context of schools since several frameworks use different terms, such as trauma-informed, trauma-sensitive, trauma-responsive, and trauma-engaged.

The Institute for Child and Family Well-being (ICFW) differentiates between trauma-informed, trauma-focused, and trauma-sensitive practices. In Issue Brief: Translating Trauma-Informed Principles into Trauma-Responsive Practices (2018), the ICFW states that trauma-informed care principles can be applied to practices by professionals with moderate level of training while trauma-focused or trauma-specific practices are interventions only implemented by highly trained professionals that specialize in trauma; the former facilitates the latter. When considering counseling implementation in schools, trauma-focused or trauma-specific treatments are programs like Trauma Focused Cognitive Behavioral Therapy (TF-CBT) and Cognitive Behavioral Intervention for Trauma in Schools (CBITS) that are evidenced-based treatments that can be used with populations with trauma history that are experiencing emotional and behavioral difficulties. On the other hand, school interventions that have been commonly used and can have trauma-informed principles applied are multitiered and reach the whole student population rather than a targeted population; Multi-tier Systems of Support (MTSS) and Positive Behavior Intervention Supports (PBIS) are well-known examples. Trauma-sensitive practices are usually associated with school-based initiatives that train teachers and school staff and administrators to use a trauma lens for developing a school culture and implementing policies and procedures (ICFW, 2018). The main difference between trauma-informed and trauma-sensitive frameworks is in the context of setting where the staff trained are not trained to implement trauma-informed care because it is beyond the scope of most staff (ICFW, 2018).

To better illustrate the differences between trauma-informed, trauma-focused, and trauma-sensitive practices, consider the following example: A trauma assessment tool is a trauma-informed care instrument. While a school mental health professional or school nurse may be trained to utilize the trauma assessment tool, a teacher would not be trained to administer the trauma assessment. If the teacher has been trained to recognize the signs of trauma through a trauma-sensitive framework, they can refer a student to be assessed while also providing a safe and inclusive environment in the classroom. Some teachers may have more specialized training and may provide non-clinical forms of trauma-focused programming, which helps to offer support to students experiencing symptoms of trauma. A school mental health professional may implement school wide programming using trauma-informed care principles and may refer a student whose trauma assessment indicates that signs of trauma are interfering with their daily functioning to a community counselor who can provide trauma-focused treatment. They may also implement trauma-focused interventions with students who need them while also connecting them to a trauma specialist in the community. Other school personnel, teachers, and administrators may use a trauma-sensitive approach to the school day and to develop policies and procedures for the school, which provide the foundation that facilitates the use of trauma-informed and trauma-focused approaches with students.

The ICFW emphasizes that it is crucial for us to "move from trauma awareness to trauma responsiveness by translating TIC [trauma-informed care] principles into practices that mitigate the effects of trauma or prevent it altogether" (ICFW, 2018, p. 2). They differentiate between trauma-sensitive and trauma responsiveness by defining trauma responsiveness as being the movement towards preventative measures and practices that will help reduce the impact of ACEs throughout the lifespan. Experts on trauma-informed care provide two definitions to differentiate between trauma-sensitive and trauma-responsive frameworks:

Trauma-sensitive: The organization values a trauma-informed lens and identifies trauma and resilience in policies. Trauma training is institutionalized for all staff. Staff feel supported and understood in the workplace.

Trauma-responsive: Staff applies knowledge of trauma and resilience in work. Staff utilizes language that supports safety, choice, collaboration, trustworthiness, and empowerment. (Trauma Matters Delaware, 2021, para. 4)

In their Transforming Schools guide the Alaska Department of Education and Early Development describes trauma-engaged schools as going a step further from being trauma-sensitive and trauma-informed because the approaches to learning, discipline, support services, policies, and procedures are trauma-reducing (2018). The University of Chicago Trauma-Responsive Educational Practices Project frames trauma-responsiveness in schools as having the goals of moving away from educator emotional reactivity towards being developmentally responsive to the needs of students dealing with trauma (Keels, 2020). Trauma-engagement is tantamount to trauma-responsiveness since there is a shared approach of how understanding trauma and resilience is used to support and mitigate trauma impact or prevent traumatization. The terms trauma-responsive and trauma-engaged schools are less common in the literature, but it is important to consider that the trauma-informed care in schools research is still relatively new and has largely focused on trying to define what it means in a school context and the effectiveness of trauma-informed and trauma-focused approaches. Moving towards trauma-engagement, allows schools to revolutionize their systems so that students are less likely to be funneled through the pipeline and instead be provided with tools to help them be resilient and empowered. To illustrate how a trauma-engaged perspective is different from traditional discipline in schools, Figure 1 compares both approaches:

Figure 1. Comparison of traditional and trauma-engaged school perspectives
Source: (Milakovic, 2020; Alaska Department of Education and Early Development, 2018; Wolpow et al., 2009, 2016)

Traditional School Perspective	Trauma-Engaged School Perspective
Students choose their behavior and need punitive consequences	Knowledge of the prevalence of trauma: Student behaviors can be a result of an automatic stress response
Punitive discipline is implemented through zero tolerance policies	Restorative practices and positive, respectful discipline are used to strengthen the student's abilities
Student behavior is characterized negatively by labeling, and understood as a result of deficits	Student behavior is characterized constructively and reframed to focus on strengths and changing the environment
Authoritarian and hierarchical decision-making	Collaborative- offer flexibility, empower student to make choices, positive relationships
Coping strategies are undervalued.	Behavior is a way of communicating and has a purpose Prosocial behavior and self-regulations skills needs to be taught
Academic focused	Holistic view of the student
School counseling professionals offer the support to students who have experienced trauma	Teamwork: All school personnel share the responsibility of offering a trauma sensitive environment
Supports a system where students must demonstrate a need to get the supports	Supports are offered school-wide regardless of perceived need Trauma-specific interventions are accessible
Staff-centered culture	Student-centered culture
Uses jargon with students, parents, and noneducators. Personnel are the experts	Uses language that all can understand Families, community partners, and all school personnel are collaborators
Lack of cultural responsiveness and integration of families' culture into the school environment Adults working with students may or may not be culturally competent	Culture of families is valued and celebrated and integrated into the school environment Adults are always working on their cultural competency
Compassion fatigue, secondary trauma, and personal trauma of adults working with students can impact how they respond to them	The role of wellness is recognized and supported so that adults that work with students also care for themselves so that they are better able to respond to students
Policies and procedures maintain implicit, structural, and institutional bias	Implicit, structural and institutional bias are recognized so that their impact can be diminished through training and restructuring of policies and procedures

Successful Frameworks and Approaches

The American School Counseling Association [ASCA] (2016) states that school counselors can be key players in encouraging a trauma sensitive culture at their schools because they can identify students affected by trauma and provide the support and resources needed. Understanding successful frameworks and approaches to creating trauma-responsiveness in schools allows them to promote these practices and to carry out their role at all levels of education outlined by the ASCA (2016). Two frameworks have led the way of transforming schools through district-wide approaches. These are the Flexible Framework in Massachusetts (Cole et al., 2005, 2013) and Washington's Compassionate Schools (Wolpow et al., 2009, 2016). Schools began implementing their approaches to using trauma-informed principles in 2005, with the approaches from Massachusetts and Washington states providing some key takeaways: 1. Successful change requires the participation of all schools in a district 2. The entire school community must support the changes. 3. More than one school district is needed to have a long-term impact in a state. 4. There is no one size fits all approach. The approach needs to be tailored to the culture of the school community (Cole et al., 2005, 2013; Wolpow et al., 2009, 2016) .

A brief summary of The Flexible Framework and Compassionate Schools provides some foundational work for the Transforming Schools: A Framework for Trauma-Engaged Practice in Alaska, a trauma and culturally responsive approach to schools (Alaska Department of Education and Early Development, 2018).

The Flexible Framework

The Flexible Framework provides a guide for creating trauma-sensitive schools. Trauma-sensitive schools aim to offer a school culture where all students feel safe and supported and where there is a whole-school commitment to addressing the impact of trauma on learning. Each trauma-sensitive school can look different since no two schools are exactly alike and all have various strengths and needs. The framework was created by the Trauma and Learning Policy Initiative (TLPI), a partnership between Massachusetts Advocates for Children and Harvard Law School. TLPI (Cole et al., 2005, 2013) provides two publications that outline the Flexible Framework and explore how this tool can be used by schools to create their own action plans. The Flexible Framework provides six operational functions trauma-sensitive school initiatives (Cole et al., 2005, 2013):

- Leadership sets the foundation and culture that promotes trauma sensitivity.
- Professional Development is necessary for all school personnel to understand the prevalence and impact of trauma, foster positive relationships, and develop new skills as alternatives to punitive discipline.
- Access to Resources for students and staff through collaborative community partnerships.
- Academic and Nonacademic Strategies help to build competence in students and help foster their physical, psychological, and academic well-being.
- Policies and Protocols should be reviewed so that they are consistent with trauma-sensitivity.
- Collaboration with Families engages them in students' education and creates sensitivity to their diverse needs.

Compassionate Schools

The state of Washington Compassionate Schools Initiative is a trauma-responsive approach with the aim to reduce ACEs, specifically children's exposure to violence (Wolpow et al., 2009, 2016). It provides a platform for educators to gain trauma-responsive strategies so that they have tools and resources. This process guide is meant to help school communities develop their own unique compassionate personality and was developed through empirically validated data (Wolpow et al., 2009, 2016). There are ten principles that are provided as a guide as well as a three-domain curriculum that provides a framework for the content and strategies that are suggested be taught. The ten principles of Compassionate Schools are:

- Focus on culture and climate in the school and community.
- Train and support all staff regarding trauma and learning.
- Encourage and sustain open and regular communication for all.
- Develop a strengths-based approach in working with students and peers.
- Ensure discipline policies are both compassionate and effective (Restorative Practices).
- Weave compassionate strategies into school improvement planning.
- Provide tiered support for all students based on what they need.
- Create flexible accommodations for diverse learners.
- Provide access, voice, and ownership for staff, students, and community.
- Use data to identify vulnerable students and determine outcomes and strategies for continuous quality improvement. (Wolpow et al., 2009, 2016).

The three-domain curriculum focuses on: 1) Safety and Connection 2) Improving Self-Regulation and 3) Competencies of Personal Agency, Social Skills, and Academic Skills (Wolpow et al., 2009, 2016). The curriculum starts with teaching psychoeducation to provide so students feel safe and assured so they can learn to attune to themselves and the cues of others. Students then learn to control their feelings and behaviors in states of arousal. The final domain helps students build or rebuild those developmental competencies that were disrupted by trauma.

Transforming Schools

Transforming Schools: A Framework for Trauma-Engaged Practice in Alaska is a guide that has been developed to integrate trauma-engaged practice and policies to improve student outcomes. This is done through a holistic lens with the foundational understanding of the impact that trauma has on learning and success. The emphasis is on relationship building across various avenues, with students, parents, school staff, and community partners. This framework is described as having the foundation of trauma-sensitive schools but also adds that it is trauma-responsive by using "approaches to learning and discipline [that] are trauma-shielding or trauma-reducing. They are reflective and collaborative, they promote a culture of learning, and they make meaning out of the past. They are also prevention-oriented and have relational leadership." (Alaska Department of Education and Early Development, 2018, p. 7). To transform schools, a mindset shift is needed for all stakeholders: students, administrators, school staff, and community members (Alaska Department of Education and Early Development, 2018). Figure 2 demonstrates the eleven areas that must all function together for true trauma-engaged transformation.

Figure 2. Transforming schools framework
Source: (Alaska Department of Education and Early Development, 2018)

This framework also identifies seven steps that are viewed as being essential for thoughtful preparation and eventual success (Alaska Department of Education and Early Development, 2018). First, the school should develop a clear motivation and vision for transforming the school. Next, it is important to determine the school community's readiness for change, the capacity to move practices forward, and if the infrastructure and supports exist so that districts know where to get started. Third, buy-in and commitment from all is needed because this determines the success of transforming. Fourth, a school culture that is respectful and safe needs to be promoted and standards set for how this will be done. Next, a common understanding or language so everyone understands the terms referred to. Sixth, realize that there will be challenges and mishaps and view these as opportunities for learning. Lastly, the guide is a resource and encourages schools to take any of the areas in any order to work on and adapt as necessary since each school system is different.

Race at The Center of Trauma-Engaged Schools

The pipeline is a public health crisis and racial equity issue for youth of color. These cultural shifts in school systems should be both trauma-responsive and race centered, addressing the discipline disproportion that contributes to the school-to prison pipeline and making it a commitment to social justice. Considering that youth of color are more likely to experience adverse childhood experiences and the prominence of race and racial bias impacting discipline decisions, it is imperative to incorporate tenets of Critical Race Theory into creating trauma-engaged schools (Dutil, 2020; Joseph et al., 2020). Trauma-informed care by nature is aligned with Critical Race Theory's main principles of empowerment, history, gender, and culture (Crosby, 2016). This makes a race centered approach easily aligned with trauma-engaged initiatives, like restorative. Three of the key tenets of Critical Race Theory that can be applied are: 1) color blindness or neutrality 2) interest convergence, and 3) the use of narrative (Dutil, 2020). This includes recognizing racial bias and discrimination in disciplinary methods so that racially conscious changes are made to existing policy, discipline, and training of teachers to support students (Gregory and Fergus, 2017). It is also asking critical questions about who certain policies serve so that a change is made to benefit students not those in positions of power. It also includes allowing for the student narrative or perspective to be heard so that narratives are not one sided.

Restorative Initiatives

Restorative practices are an integral part of trauma-responsive or trauma-engaged school environments since this approach aims to repair and prevent the lasting impact from trauma. They allow for engagement of the student voice, affirm students' strengths, recognize the inequities they experience, and co-develop solutions (Joseph et al., 2020). Restorative justice practices are effective, sustainable, and equitable alternative discipline methods. They strengthen relationships, increase skills in solving interpersonal conflict, and reduce staff members' punitive reaction towards students (Anfara et al., 2013). Restorative justice practices can prevent some of the harm done by suspensions and expulsions. There is substantial evidence that restorative initiatives can reduce suspensions and they also show promise for reducing racial disparities in punitive discipline (Griffith & Tyner, 2019). Additionally, studies indicate that restorative practices improve relationships and increase educator respect towards racially diverse students (Lustick, 2017). Many studies indicate that restorative initiatives have promise for improving school climate and interactions among students (McCluskey et al., 2008). Examples of restorative initiatives are: peacemaking circles, community conferencing, peer juries, peer mediation, and mentorship. Socioemotional learning and mindfulness tools taught in schools also go hand in hand with restorative justice practices because they teach tools for regulation, improve communication, and problem solving in positive ways. These skills are vital for student success in their academic and personal lives.

Cultural Competence in Education

For trauma-engaged schools to work, change needs to occur in how students of color are treated in academic settings. Trauma-engagement cannot exist without cultural value and respect. The National Education Association Diversity Toolkit: Cultural Competence for Educators states that:

Cultural competence is the ability to successfully teach students who come from a culture or cultures other than our own. It entails developing certain personal and interpersonal awareness and sensitivities, understanding certain bodies of cultural knowledge, and mastering a set of skills that, taken together, underlie effective cross-cultural teaching and culturally responsive teaching. (2021).

School personnel need to be culturally competent to have the foundation for cultural responsiveness. Effective implementation of culturally responsive practices in schools means a change in how school professionals perceive and respond to students of color. This requires training and exploration of cultural competence that include identifying their biases and how they impact their decision-making, learning how to implement culturally responsive practices in the classroom, active reflection and challenging of how one interprets experiences, and building skills for addressing challenging behaviors (The National Education Association, 2021). Educator preparation programs and professional development workshops across the U.S. are not adequately preparing educators to bring culturally responsive teaching to classrooms (Muñiz, 2019). A 2018 study of New York teachers found that less than one in three teachers received ongoing professional development addressing issues of race and ethnicity in the classroom (Bryan-Gooden & Hester).

Research on cultural responsiveness in education states that these practices work well together with other reform efforts in education, for example initiatives that improve school climate and implement social-emotional learning (Osher and Berg, 2018). It is consistent with the goals of trauma-engaged schools. A recent review of all U.S. states' culturally responsive competencies identified eight competencies that promote culturally responsive teaching:

- Reflect on one's cultural lens.
- Recognize and redress bias in the system.
- Draw on students' culture to share curriculum and instruction.
- Bring real-world issues into the classroom.
- Model high expectations for all students.
- Model and promote respect for student differences.
- Collaborating with families and the local community.
- Communicate in linguistically and culturally responsive ways. (Muñiz, 2019).

The Role of Counselors in Transforming Schools

In agreement with the ASCA's (2016) position that school counselors are key players in promoting trauma sensitive school climates, Howell et al. (2019) asserts that school counselors need a voice at the table when it comes to leading school-wide decisions surrounding moving schools towards trauma responsiveness. If the mental health expertise role of school counselors is accepted to lead trauma responsiveness in schools, then education can see transformative change (Howell et al., 2019). School Counselors have a substantial role in transforming the culture in schools. Counselors are presently underutilized in leadership for school systemic change but their understanding of mental health problems, advocacy, and role in consultation makes them ideal leaders for the trauma-responsive movement (Howell et al., 2019; Pincus et al., 2020). Counselors can improve the school system by promoting trauma-sensitive environments and providing trauma-informed care to students that need the support. Their competency in trauma is necessary. Counselors respond to trauma in schools by using trauma-informed practice and trauma-focused interventions for the students that need the support. They implement trauma-informed care by recognizing and understanding the effects of trauma, avoid retraumatization, and they infuse awareness and knowledge to others. This can contribute to the school culture and influence school policies. Counselors can collaborate within their school and district to create policies that: 1) support trauma and cultural responsiveness 2) ensure staffing for trauma screening, and 3) provide trauma-focused services (Martinez et al., 2020).

The ASCA (2016) also acknowledges the role of school counselors as consultants, educators of school staff, and collaborators in the movement towards school trauma responsiveness. This is also consistent with trauma-informed practices supported by SAMHSA (2014). School counselors work with community partners and stakeholders to promote recovery and resilience. They are part of promoting a welcoming and safe school environment to prevent re-traumatization. Their relationship building with students, their families, and school staff helps build the rapport needed so that their knowledge is welcomed. Since trauma-engaged schools and cultural responsiveness requires collaboration, counselors may also serve as consultants and provide training or professional development for parents and teachers. Counselors need to develop multidisciplinary partnerships with educators. School mental health professionals may sometimes play a role in helping educators and other school personnel develop trauma and culturally responsive competency. School counselors can also be trained to use restorative justice practices to help build community and as a positive way of problem-solving or approaching conflict. Working towards trauma responsiveness in schools builds safe connections for students, which improves their resilience.

Developments in the field of interpersonal neurobiology has brought an understanding of resilience as a teachable tool (Siegel, 2012). Resilience to adversity can be promoted through resilience resources and prompt interventions that alleviate the negative effects of ACEs by building individual coping skills (Iniquez & Stankowski, 2016). Supportive relationships can mitigate the negative effect of childhood trauma by helping to build resilience (Arincorayan et al., 2017). Siegel's research provides extensive support for the development of resilience through relationships. The brain can foster resilience when youth are provided with opportunities to practice skills that allow the left and right parts of the brain to come together and integrate (Siegel, 2012). Siegel refers to integration as a linkage of different parts of the brain; when a system is integrated it moves to a harmonious flow that leads to the emergence and reception of new things (Siegel, 2012). Integration is honoring differences and promoting linkages, it is how secure attachment is created, and well-being can be created through integration in the brain, which is a fundamental basis for self-regulation (Siegel, 2012). Mindfulness practice and activities allows the brain to practice learning to be fully present with feelings (Siegel, 2012). When integration is practiced, people learn to be in touch with themselves; this leads to insight, which leads to empathy to understand another person's experience, and eventually integration that leads to healthier relationships (Siegel, 2012).

Creating a trauma-responsive culture is an example of how healthy connections and opportunities for integration can foster resilience in youth to reduce the effects of trauma.

Resilience research has consistently shown that the single most important factor for building resilience against trauma is having consistent presence of one or more caring adults (Arincorayan et al., 2017; Iniquez & Stankowski, 2016; Siegel 2012). When those that have experienced trauma are consistently met with empathy and tools then systems allow for them to thrive, adapt to their stressors, and learn to cope with the impact of trauma. Prevent Child Abuse America (2016) outlines strategies that can be adapted to help to build resilience in schools and align with the tenets of transforming schools to break the school-to-prison pipeline:

Strategy 1: Change the discussion from "what's wrong with you?" to "what happened to you?" When the ACEs research and neuroscience informs understanding, responses are led with empathy. Caring relationships are valuable in trauma-responsive systems.

Strategy 2: Recognize how systemic racism contributes to toxic stress. The role of systemic racism and racial bias in how schools respond to students who have been traumatized need to be acknowledged so that at all steps of transforming schools a racial equity approach is taken.

Strategy 3: Recognize toxic stress as the largest public health issue of our generation. Child adversity has a long term impact throughout the lifespan and is costly. Reducing the effects of ACEs benefits all of society.

Strategy 4: Build critical collaborations. Being able to work together and collaborate to transform school systems allows for a greater chance of improving long-term outcomes for children. Collaborate within the school, with families, and community partners so that everyone works toward one common goal.

Strategy 5: Promote safe, stable, nurturing relationships & environments. Having stability and nurturing relationships in trauma sensitive environments provides safety for building resilience and healing.

Strategy 6: Prevent intergenerational transmission of toxic stress. Healthy adults are able to be present and engaged. To create good outcomes for children the adults also need support from community partners so that families that deal with trauma receive support.

Strategy 7: Promote hope. The effects of trauma do not have to be permanent. When there is prevention and response, the effects can be prevented or mitigated. Work together to establish trauma-engaged schools.

Case Vignette

Marcus is a 12 year old Black male in the seventh grade with inconsistent academic performance. As of last week he is living with his aunt and her family of four along with his two siblings. His mother was recently arrested for violating parole and his father has not been in his life since he was murdered when Marcus was three years old. On this particular day, Marcus is visibly angry. He storms into class late and is pacing and cursing before he tips over a chair.

From the perspective of a school without the knowledge and tools to implement trauma-responsive practices, Macus' teacher is likely to call the office so that he can be disciplined for being disrespectful in the classroom. The school resource officer is likely to be called to the classroom since Marcus is angry and aggressive. This is likely to escalate from there.

Marcus' school, however, has worked to transform their school system to one that is trauma-engaged and culturally responsive. Marcus' teacher has been trained in understanding trauma and the school has a Peace Room for when students need a safe space to calm down and practice the socioemotional skills that they learn throughout the week. The teacher recognizes that Marcus has experienced adversity throughout his childhood and that due to this he has a hard time trusting others so she and other staff have worked to build a relationship with him [as with all students] daily by greeting him, allowing him to help out with tasks, and encouraging him to use his art skills as a way to cope with emotions. Since she has good rapport with Marcus, she feels comfortable acknowledging that he is struggling at the moment and offers some time in the Peace Room. She calls the school counselor for assistance.

The school counselor models emotional regulation for Marcus and leads him on a short exercise that Marcus is familiar with because they have practiced it in school. In the Peace Room Marcus is able to draw some comics to help him cope. Once he is calm, he shares that he heard some rumors that another student made fun of his mom being in prison. Marcus states that he feels disrespected and that he needs to confront this student to keep his respect. His counselor is able to set up a mediation session with the student and another trained staff so that they can resolve the conflict. Marcus is able to learn that there was a misunderstanding regarding what was said by the other student and the other student has a better understanding about how Marcus feels when they talk about his home life. They are also able to better understand one another on a cultural level since Marcus can share how respect plays a role in how he feels. Since Marcus is struggling with the recent difficulties in his home life and is adjusting to the changes, the school counselor reaches out to his aunt and connects the family to a counselor in the community for family support. The school counselor will also follow up with Marcus at school so that he can participate in a school group and continue building on his coping skills.

Reflection Questions

1. How are connection and relationship the foundation of how this situation was handled?
2. In what way is resilience fostered in this situation?
3. How is racial bias less likely to occur in the way that this situation was handled?
4. How could this situation have gone if Marcus' school was not working towards trauma-engagement and cultural responsiveness?

FUTURE RESEARCH DIRECTIONS

This chapter provides considerations to creating trauma-engaged schools with the integration of cultural responsiveness, where race and social justice are integrated. This provides a foundation for how the work that counselors do can contribute to dismantling of the pipeline. This can be a tool when thinking about the strategies that clinicians use in school settings and can also empower them to see themselves as catalysts for change.

It is clear that to truly create change, school approaches to implementing trauma-informed care need to focus on the healing and prevention of hardship to students that are most affected by traditional school systems. To do this, schools must recognize that the efforts towards trauma-informed care needs to include responsiveness to mitigate the negative effects of trauma and of systemic factors and biases at all levels. While trauma-informed care is not new, more research is needed for evaluating the effectiveness of trauma-engaged schools that are also culturally responsive and the impact that they have on changing the pipeline.

CONCLUSION AND SUMMARY

Existing research has found that there is a gap in research on cultural adaptations of school-based social, emotional, behavioral interventions for students of color (Brown et al., 2018). Trauma-engagement and cultural responsiveness in schools challenges traditional views on schools and serve as social justice actions. As advocates for social justice, counselors are tasked with providing support for all students in schools by providing trauma-responsive interventions and promoting cultural responsiveness to meet the needs of minoritized students.

This chapter aimed to discuss the connection between the school-to-prison pipeline, systemic racism and racial bias, and trauma. Students from minoritized groups, such as students of color, LGBTQ+, and students with disabilities are more likely to be impacted by harsh disciplinary actions in schools as a result of bias from school staff. Understanding the prevalence of trauma and how it impacts student behavior in the schools provides a foundation for conceptualizing how the effects of trauma can be misinterpreted and punished. By engaging in the approaches to prevent trauma and to address trauma effects, schools can reduce trauma and better address the root of the problem to disrupt the school-to-prison pipeline. Trauma is the impelling cause of many of the issues at schools that interrupt learning yet too often the response is one that does not lead to providing the supports needed to build student resilience. To do so, adults that work with students need a foundation of understanding trauma and its effects.

School counselors serve a pivotal role in consultation, training, collaboration, and providing direct services that foster the changes in schools that create a trauma-engaged system. School counselors are in a unique position to lead and promote the transformation of schools into systems that prevent trauma and remove systemic barriers that lead to the criminalization of traumatized students. School counselors must understand the foundations of trauma-responsive schools and successful frameworks so that they understand their role in promoting and sustaining these practices. By addressing the issues with traditional discipline that lead to grave consequences for certain students, ensuring cultural competence, and integrating culturally responsive teaching schools can stop the vitality of the school-to prison-pipeline.

REFERENCES

Alaska Department of Education and Early Development. (2019). *Transforming schools: A framework for trauma-engaged practice in Alaska*. https://education.alaska.gov/

Aleguire, Z., Basallaje, A., Bridges, C., Dudley, K. K., Elgart, A., Paterson, E., Singh, J., Stack, A., Williams, B., & Yakar, I. (2016). *Breaking the chains: The school-to-prison pipeline, implicit bias, and racial trauma*. https://equaljusticesociety.org/breakingthechains/

Alexander, M. (2010). *The new Jim Crow: Mass incarceration in the age of colorblindness*. The New Press.

American Academy of Child and Adolescent Psychiatry. (2012). *Corporal punishment*. https://www.aacap.org/AACAP/Policy_Statements/2012/Policy_Statement_on_Corporal_Punishment.aspx

American Academy of Pediatrics. (1998). Guidance for effective discipline. *Pediatrics*, *101*(4), 723–728. doi:10.1542/peds.101.4.723 PMID:9521967

American Psychological Association. (2008). Are zero tolerance policies effective in the schools?: An evidentiary review and recommendations. *The American Psychologist*, *63*(9), 852–862. doi:10.1037/0003-066X.63.9.852 PMID:19086747

American School Counselor Association. (2016). *The school counselor and trauma-informed practice*. https://www.schoolcounselor.org/Standards-Positions/Position-Statements/ASCA-Position-Statements

Anderson, R. E., Saleem, F. T., & Huguley, J. P. (2019). Choosing to see the racial stress that afflicts our black students. *Phi Delta Kappan, 101*(3), 20–25. doi:10.1177/0031721719885911

Anfara, V. A. Jr, Evans, K. R., & Lester, J. N. (2013). Restorative justice in education: What we know so far. *Middle School Journal, 44*(5), 57–63. doi:10.1080/00940771.2013.11461873

Annamma, S. A., Anyon, Y., Joseph, N. M., Farrar, J., Greer, E., Downing, B., & Simmons, J. (2016). Black girls and school discipline: The complexities of being overrepresented and understudied. *Urban Education, 54*(2), 211–242. doi:10.1177/0042085916646610

Arincorayan, C. D., Applewhite, L., Garrido, M., Cashio, V., & Bryant, M. (2017). Resilience-enhancing relationships: what we can learn from those with a history of adverse childhood experiences. *U.S. Army Medical Department Journal, 2*(17), 25-32.

Báez, J. C., Renshaw, K. J., Bachman, L. E., Kim, D., Smith, V. D., & Stafford, R. E. (2019). Understanding the necessity of trauma-informed care in community schools: A mixed-methods program evaluation. *Children & Schools, 41*(2), 101–110. doi:10.1093/cs/cdz007

Balfanz, R., Byrnes, V., & Fox, J. (2014). Sent home and put off-track: The antecedents, disproportionalities, and consequences of being suspended in the ninth grade. *The Journal of Applied Research on Children, 5*(2).

Basford, L., Lewis, J., & Trout, M. (2020). It can be done: How one charter school combats the school-to-prison pipeline. *The Urban Review, 53*(3), 540–562. doi:10.100711256-020-00583-x

Berliner, L., & Kolko, D. J. (2016). Trauma informed care. *Child Maltreatment, 21*(2), 168–172. doi:10.1177/1077559516643785 PMID:27152025

Blaustein, M., & Kinniburgh, K. M. (2019). *Treating traumatic stress in children and adolescents: How to foster resilience through attachment, self-regulation, and competency*. The Guilford Press.

Brown, C., Maggin, D. M., & Buren, M. (2018). Systematic review of cultural adaptations of school-based social, emotional, and behavioral interventions for students of color. *Education & Treatment of Children, 41*(4), 431–456. doi:10.1353/etc.2018.0024

Bryan-Gooden, J., & Hester, M. (2018). *Is NYC preparing teachers to be culturally responsive? Data snapshot*. https://steinhardt.nyu.edu/metrocenter/ejroc

Carmichael, D. (2011). *Breaking schools' rules*. https://ppri.tamu.edu/portfolio-items/page/2/

Centers for Disease Control and Prevention. (2021). *About the CDC-Kaiser ace study*. https://www.cdc.gov/violenceprevention/aces/about.html

Centers for Disease Control and Prevention and Substance Abuse and Mental Health Services Administration. (2020). *Infographic: 6 guiding principles to a trauma-informed approach*. https://www.cdc.gov/cpr/infographics/6_principles_trauma_info.htm

Chapman, D. P., Whitfield, C. L., Felitti, V. J., Dube, S. R., Edwards, V. J., & Anda, R. F. (2004). Adverse childhood experiences and the risk of depressive disorders in adulthood. *Journal of Affective Disorders, 82*(2), 217–225. doi:10.1016/j.jad.2003.12.013 PMID:15488250

Chartier, M. J., Walker, J. R., & Naimark, B. (2010). Separate and cumulative effects of adverse childhood experiences in predicting adult health and Health Care Utilization. *Child Abuse & Neglect, 34*(6), 454–464. doi:10.1016/j.chiabu.2009.09.020 PMID:20409586

Chavous, T. M., Rivas-Drake, D., Smalls, C., Griffin, T., & Cogburn, C. (2008). Gender matters, too: The influences of school racial discrimination and racial identity on academic engagement outcomes among African American adolescents. *Developmental Psychology, 44*(3), 637–654. doi:10.1037/0012-1649.44.3.637 PMID:18473633

Child Trends. (2019). *Trends in adverse childhood experiences.* https://www.childtrends.org

Cole, S., Eisner, A., Gregory, M., & Ristuccia, J. (2013). *Helping traumatized children learn: Creating and advocating for trauma-sensitive schools* (Vol. 2). Massachusetts Advocates for Children.

Cole, S. F., O'Brien, J. G., Gadd, M. G., Ristuccia, J., Wallace, D. L., & Gregory, M. (2005). *Helping traumatized children learn: Supportive school environments for children traumatized by family violence.* Massachusetts Advocates for Children.

Craig, S. E. (2016). *Trauma-sensitive schools: Learning communities transforming children's lives, K-5.* Teachers College Press.

Crosby, S. D. (2016). Trauma-informed approaches to juvenile justice: A critical race perspective. *Juvenile & Family Court Journal, 67*(1), 5–18. doi:10.1111/jfcj.12052

Cummings, K. P., Addante, S., Swindell, J., & Meadan, H. (2017). Creating supportive environments for children who have had exposure to traumatic events. *Journal of Child and Family Studies, 26*(10), 2728–2741. doi:10.100710826-017-0774-9

Durrant, J., & Ensom, R. (2012). Physical punishment of children: Lessons from 20 years of research. *Canadian Medical Association Journal, 184*(12), 1373–1377. doi:10.1503/cmaj.101314 PMID:22311946

Dutil, S. (2020). Dismantling the school-to-prison pipeline: A trauma-informed, critical race perspective on school discipline. *Children & Schools, 42*(3), 171–178. doi:10.1093/cs/cdaa016

Dutro, E. (2017). Let's start with heartbreak: The perilous potential of trauma in literacy. *Language Arts, 95*(5), 326–337.

Fabelo, T., Thompson, M. D., Plotkin, M., Carmichael, D., Marchbanks, M. P., III, & Booth, E. A. (2011). *Breaking schools' rules: A statewide study of how school discipline relates to students' success and juvenile justice involvement.* https://csgjusticecenter.org/publications/breaking-schools-rules/

Franke, H. (2014). Toxic stress: Effects, prevention and treatment. *Children (Basel, Switzerland), 1*(3), 390–402. doi:10.3390/children1030390 PMID:27417486

Frieze, S. (2015). How Trauma Affects Student Learning and Behaviour. *BU Journal of Graduate Studies in Education, 7*(2), 27–34.

Gershoff, E. T. (2008). *Report on Physical Punishment in the United States: What Research Tells Us About Its Effects on Children.* https://phoenixchildrens.org/

Gershoff, E. T. (2013). Spanking and Child Development: We know enough now to stop hitting our children. *Child Development Perspectives*, *7*(3), 133–137. doi:10.1111/cdep.12038 PMID:24039629

Gopalan, M., & Nelson, A. A. (2019). Understanding the racial discipline gap in schools. *AERA Open*, *5*(2), 1–26. doi:10.1177/2332858419844613 PMID:34012995

Gregory, A., & Evans, K. (2020). *The starts and stumbles of restorative justice in education: Where do we go from here?* https://nepc.colorado.edu/publication/restorative-justice

Gregory, A., & Fergus, E. (2017). Social and emotional learning and equity in school discipline. *The Future of Children*, *27*(1), 117–136. doi:10.1353/foc.2017.0006

Gregory, A., Skiba, R. J., & Noguera, P. A. (2010). The achievement gap and the discipline gap. *Educational Researcher*, *39*(1), 59–68. doi:10.3102/0013189X09357621

Griffith, D., & Tyner, A. (2019). *Discipline reform through the eyes of teachers*. https://fordhaminstitute.org/national/research/discipline-reform-through-the-eyes-of-teachers

Grinage, J. (2019). Endless mourning: Racial melancholia, black grief, and the transformative possibilities for racial justice in Education. *Harvard Educational Review*, *89*(2), 227–250. doi:10.17763/1943-5045-89.2.227

Hardy, K. V. (2013). Healing the Hidden Wounds of Racial Trauma. *Reclaiming Children and Youth*, *22*(1), 24–28.

Health Resources and Services Administration. (2020, March 4). *New HRSA data show one in three US children have suffered an adverse childhood experience*. https://www.hrsa.gov/about/news/press-releases/

Heitzeg, N. A. (2009). Education or incarceration: Zero tolerance policies and the school to prison pipeline. *Forum on Public Policy*, 1–21.

Horsford, S. D. (2018). School integration in the new Jim Crow: Opportunity or oxymoron? *Educational Policy*, *33*(1), 257–275. doi:10.1177/0895904818810526

Howell, P. B., Thomas, S., Sweeney, D., & Vanderhaar, J. (2019). Moving beyond schedules, testing and other duties as deemed necessary by the principal: The school counselor's role in Trauma Informed Practices. *Middle School Journal*, *50*(4), 26–34. doi:10.1080/00940771.2019.1650548

Iniguez, K. C., & Stankowski, R. V. (2016). Adverse childhood experiences and health in adulthood in a rural population-based sample. *Clinical Medicine & Research*, *14*(3-4), 126–137. doi:10.3121/cmr.2016.1306 PMID:27503793

Institute for Child and Family Well-Being. (2018). *Issue brief: Translating trauma-informed principles into trauma-responsive practices*. https://uwm.edu/icfw/issuebriefs/

Intercultural Development Research Association. (2021). *Understanding and addressing racial trauma and supporting black students in schools – policy brief*. https://www.idra.org/education_policy

International Child and Youth Care Network. (2009). *Rethinking the effectiveness of suspensions*. Discipline. https://cyc-net.org/cyc-online/cyconline-dec2009-sautner.html

Jernigan, M. M., & Daniel, J. H. (2011). Racial trauma in the lives of black children and adolescents: Challenges and clinical implications. *Journal of Child & Adolescent Trauma*, *4*(2), 123–141. doi:10.1080/19361521.2011.574678

Johnson, A. M., & Godsil, R. D. (2014). *Transforming Perception: Black Men and Boys*. https://perception.org/publications/transforming-perception

Joseph, A. A., Wilcox, S. M., Hnilica, R. J., & Hansen, M. C. (2020). Keeping race at the center of school discipline practices and trauma-informed care: An interprofessional framework. *Children & Schools*, *42*(3), 161–170. doi:10.1093/cs/cdaa013

Keels, M. (2020). Building racial equity through trauma-responsive discipline. *ASCD: Trauma-Sensitive Schools*, *78*(2), 40–45.

Kohn, A. (1993). *Punished by rewards the trouble with gold stars, incentive plans, A's, praise, and other bribes*. Houghton Mifflin.

Kohn, A. (2005). *Unconditional parenting: Moving from rewards and punishments to love and reason*. Atria Books.

Kosciw, J. G., Clark, C. M., Truong, N. L., & Zongrone, A. D. (2020). *The 2019 national school climate survey: The experiences of lesbian, gay, bisexual, transgender, and queer youth in our nation's schools*. https://www.glsen.org/

Krieger, N. (1990). Racial and gender discrimination: Risk factors for high blood pressure? *Social Science & Medicine*, *30*(12), 1273–1281. doi:10.1016/0277-9536(90)90307-E PMID:2367873

Losen, D. J., Hodson, C. L., Keith, M. A., II, Morrison, K., & Belway, S. (2015). *Are we closing the school discipline gap?* https://escholarship.org/uc/item/2t36g571

Lustick, H. (2017). "Restorative justice" or restoring order? restorative school discipline practices in urban public schools. *Urban Education*, *56*(8), 1269–1296. doi:10.1177/0042085917741725

Martinez, R. R. Jr, Gavin Williams, R., & Green, J. (2019). The role of school counselors delivering a trauma-informed care approach to supporting youth in Foster Care. *Professional School Counseling*, *23*(1), 2156759X2094774. doi:10.1177/2156759X20947747

Martinez, R. R. Jr, Gavin Williams, R., & Green, J. (2019). The role of school counselors delivering a trauma-informed care approach to supporting youth in Foster Care. *Professional School Counseling*, *23*(1), 2156759X2094774. doi:10.1177/2156759X20947747

McCarter, S. (2016). The school-to-prison pipeline: A primer for social workers. *Social Work*, *62*(1), 53–61. doi:10.1093www078 PMID:28395045

McCluskey, G., Lloyd, G., Stead, J., Kane, J., Riddell, S., & Weedon, E. (2008). 'I was dead restorative today': From restorative justice to restorative approaches in school. *Cambridge Journal of Education*, *38*(2), 199–216. doi:10.1080/03057640802063262

Milakovic, D. (2020). *Supporting through an equitable trauma-informed lens* [PowerPoint slides]. Pennsylvania Department of Education. https://www.pattan.net/

Morton, B. M. (2018). The grip of trauma: How trauma disrupts the academic aspirations of Foster Youth. *Child Abuse & Neglect*, *75*, 73–81. doi:10.1016/j.chiabu.2017.04.021 PMID:28478934

Morton, B. M., & Berardi, A. A. (2017). Trauma-informed school programing: Applications for mental health professionals and educator partnerships. *Journal of Child & Adolescent Trauma*, *11*(4), 487–493. doi:10.100740653-017-0160-1 PMID:32318170

Muñiz, J. (2019). *Culturally responsive teaching: A 50-state survey of teaching standards*. https://www.newamerica.org/education-policy/reports/culturally-responsive-teaching/

National Association for the Education of Young Children. (2017). *Standing together against suspension & expulsion in early childhood*. https://www.naeyc.org/

National Child Traumatic Stress Network. (2018). *Effects*. The National Child Traumatic Stress Network. https://www.nctsn.org/what-is-child-trauma/trauma-types/complex-trauma/effects

National Council of State Education Associations. (2019). *Addressing the epidemic of trauma in schools*. https://www.nea.org/professional-excellence/student-engagement/trauma-informed-schools

National Education Association. (2021). *Diversity toolkit: Cultural competence for educators*. https://www.nea.org/professional-excellence/just-equitable-schools

National Scientific Council on the Developing Child. (2005). *Excessive Stress Disrupts the Architecture of the Developing Brain: Working Paper No. 3*. https://developingchild.harvard.edu/resources/

National Scientific Council on the Developing Child. (2010). *Persistent Fear and Anxiety Can Affect Young Children's Learning and Development*. https://developingchild.harvard.edu/resources/

Nemeroff, C. B. (2016). Paradise lost: The Neurobiological and clinical consequences of child abuse and neglect. *Neuron*, *89*(5), 892–909. doi:10.1016/j.neuron.2016.01.019 PMID:26938439

Noltemeyer, A. L., Ward, R. M., & Mcloughlin, C. (2015). Relationship between school suspension and student outcomes: A meta-analysis. *School Psychology Review*, *44*(2), 224–240. doi:10.17105pr-14-0008.1

Osher, D., & Berg, J. (2019). *School climate and social and emotional learning the integration of two approaches. Issue Brief.* http:// prevention.psu.edu/uploads/files/rwjf443059.pdf

Owens, J., & McLanahan, S. S. (2020). Unpacking the drivers of racial disparities in school suspension and expulsion. *Social Forces*, *98*(4), 1548–1577. doi:10.1093foz095 PMID:34017149

Picower, B. (2009). The unexamined whiteness of teaching: How white teachers maintain and enact dominant racial ideologies. *Race, Ethnicity and Education*, *12*(2), 197–215. doi:10.1080/13613320902995475

Pincus, R., Hannor-Walker, T. S., Wright, L., & Justice, J. (2020). Covid-19's effect on students: How school counselors rise to the rescue. *NASSP Bulletin*, *104*(4), 241–256. doi:10.1177/0192636520975866

Prewitt, E. (2014, May 13). *State, federal lawmakers take action on trauma-informed policies, programs*. https://acestoohigh.com/2014/04/30/state-federal-lawmakers-take-action/

Reuben, A., Moffitt, T. E., Caspi, A., Belsky, D. W., Harrington, H., Schroeder, F., Hogan, S., Ramrakha, S., Poulton, R., & Danese, A. (2016). Lest we forget: Comparing retrospective and prospective assessments of adverse childhood experiences in the prediction of Adult Health. *Journal of Child Psychology and Psychiatry, and Allied Disciplines*, *57*(10), 1103–1112. doi:10.1111/jcpp.12621 PMID:27647050

Ryberg, R., Her, S., Temkin, D., & Harper, K. (2021). *Despite reductions since 2011-12, black students and students with disabilities remain more likely to experience suspension.* https://www.childtrends.org/publications/black-students-disabilities-out-of-school-suspensions

Saleem, F. T., Anderson, R. E., & Williams, M. (2020). Addressing the "myth" of racial trauma: Developmental and ecological considerations for youth of color. *Clinical Child and Family Psychology Review*, *23*(1), 1–14. doi:10.100710567-019-00304-1 PMID:31641920

Sawyer, P. J., Major, B., Casad, B. J., Townsend, S. S. M., & Mendes, W. B. (2012). Discrimination and the stress response: Psychological and physiological consequences of anticipating prejudice in interethnic interactions. *American Journal of Public Health*, *102*(5), 1020–1026. doi:10.2105/AJPH.2011.300620 PMID:22420818

Sege, R. D., & Harper Browne, C. (2017). Responding to ACES with hope: Health outcomes from positive experiences. *Academic Pediatrics*, *17*(7), S79–S85. doi:10.1016/j.acap.2017.03.007 PMID:28865664

Siegel, D. J. (2012). *Pocket guide to interpersonal neurobiology: An integrative handbook of the mind.* W.W. Norton & Co.

Skiba, R. J., Arredondo, M. I., & Williams, N. T. (2014). More than a metaphor: The contribution of exclusionary discipline to a school-to-prison pipeline. *Equity & Excellence in Education*, *47*(4), 546–564. doi:10.1080/10665684.2014.958965

Stop Child Abuse America. (2016). *The Facilitator's Guide to Resilience.* https://www.onecaringadult.co/wp-content/uploads/2016/08/KPJR-Facilitators-Guide.pdf

Substance Abuse and Mental Health Services Administration. (2014). *SAMHSA's concept of trauma and guidance for a trauma-informed approach.* https://ncsacw.samhsa.gov/

Taie, S., & Westat, R. G. (2020). *Characteristics of public and private elementary and secondary school teachers in the United States: results from the 2017–18 national teacher and principal survey.* https://nces.ed.gov/pubs2020/2020142.pdf

Thompson, K. (2018). *Zero-tolerance policies and the school to prison pipeline.* https://www.sharedjustice.org/most-recent/2017/12/21/zero-tolerance-policies-and-the-school-to-prison-pipeline

Trauma Matters Delaware. (2021). *Organizational Transition to Trauma Responsiveness.* https://traumamattersdelaware.org/what-is-trauma-informed-care/

United States Department of Education Office for Civil Rights. (2014). *Civil rights data collection data snapshot: School discipline. Issue Brief No. 1.* https://ocrdata.ed.gov/

United States Department of Education Office for Civil Rights. (2021). *Civil Rights Data Collection.* https://www2.ed.gov/about/offices/list/ocr/data.html

Walkley, M., & Cox, T. L. (2013). Building trauma-informed schools and Communities. *Children & Schools*, *35*(2), 123–126. doi:10.1093/cs/cdt007

Wang, M.-T., & Huguley, J. P. (2012). Parental racial socialization as a moderator of the effects of racial discrimination on educational success among African American adolescents. *Child Development*, *83*(5), 1716–1731. doi:10.1111/j.1467-8624.2012.01808.x PMID:22717004

Whitford, D. K., Gage, N. A., Katsiyannis, A., Counts, J., Rapa, L. J., & McWhorter, A. (2019). The exclusionary discipline of American Indian and Alaska native (AI/an) students with and without disabilities: A civil rights data collection (CRDC) national analysis. *Journal of Child and Family Studies*, *28*(12), 3327–3337. doi:10.100710826-019-01511-8

Williams, D. R., & Mohammed, S. A. (2008). Discrimination and racial disparities in health: Evidence and needed research. *Journal of Behavioral Medicine*, *32*(1), 20–47. doi:10.100710865-008-9185-0 PMID:19030981

Williams, T. M., Printz, D., Ching, T., & Wetterneck, T. C. (2018). Assessing PTSD in ethnic and racial minorities: Trauma and racial trauma. *Directions in Psychiatry*, *38*(3), 179–196.

Wolpow, R., Johnson, M. M., Hertel, R., & Kincaid, S. (2009). *The heart of learning and teaching: Compassion, resiliency, and academic success*. Office of Superintendent of Public Instruction (OSPI) Compassionate Schools.

Wolpow, R., Johnson, M. M., Hertel, R., & Kincaid, S. (2016). *The heart of learning and teaching: Compassion, resiliency, and academic success*. Office of Superintendent of Public Instruction (OSPI) Compassionate Schools.

Wong, C. A., Eccles, J. S., & Sameroff, A. (2003). The influence of ethnic discrimination and ethnic identification on African American adolescents' School and Socioemotional Adjustment. *Journal of Personality*, *71*(6), 1197–1232. doi:10.1111/1467-6494.7106012 PMID:14633063

Zakszeski, B. N., Ventresco, N. E., & Jaffe, A. R. (2017). Promoting resilience through trauma-focused practices: A critical review of school-based implementation. *School Mental Health*, *9*(4), 310–321. doi:10.100712310-017-9228-1

ADDITIONAL READING

Morton, B. M., & Berardi, A. (2016). *Trauma-informed school initiative*. National Child Traumatic Stress Network: https://www.nctsn.org/

Siegel, D. J. (2010). *Mindsight: The new science of personal transformation*. Bantam Books.

Siegel, D. J., & Bryson, T. P. (2012). *The whole-brain child: 12 revolutionary strategies to nurture your child's developing mind*. Delacorte Press.

Substance Abuse and Mental Health Services Administration. (2014). Trauma-informed care in behavioral health services. Treatment Improvement Protocol (TIP) Series 57. HHS Publication No. (SMA) pp. 13-4801. Rockville, MD: Author.

Substance Abuse and Mental Health Services Administration. (2017). *Adverse childhood events*. Author.

van der Kolk, B. (2014). *The body keeps the score: Brain, mind, and body in the healing of trauma*. Penguin.

KEY TERMS AND DEFINITIONS

Adverse Childhood Experiences: Traumatic experiences that occur in childhood that can have an impact throughout one's life.

Executive Functioning Skills: Our ability to plan, organize, manage time, control, and monitor our behavior, focus, and control ourselves.

Fight, Flight, Freeze, Fawn Response: The body's automated system for stress response.

Implicit Bias: Unconscious thought patterns and attitudes that are rooted in learned stereotypes.

School-to-Prison Pipeline: The trajectory from the educational system to the United States criminal justice system.

Toxic Stress: When the fight, flight, freeze, fawn response is activated too often or for long periods of time it impacts development of the brain and its structure, including impairing executive functioning.

Trauma: The emotional and physical experience had when a distressing and possibly life-changing event is experienced.

Zero Tolerance Policies: Policies and practices that mandate punishment for misconduct through suspensions and expulsions.

Section 4
The Re-Entry Process

Chapter 13
Parental Incarceration and Family Reunification

My'Kayla Bowser
University of Arkansas, USA

Erin Kern Popejoy
University of Arkansas, USA

ABSTRACT

Incarceration-induced separation is challenging for families. However, the family reunification process can be just as challenging. This chapter is divided into two primary sections exploring parallel processes both during incarceration and after reentry into society through the lens of the family stress-proximal processes model. The authors present commonly faced hardships such as financial insecurity, housing insecurity, and difficulty finding work after release. Additionally, discussion of challenges to parent-child and partner relationships is provided, both during and after incarceration. A case example is provided throughout the chapter to illustrate the concepts presented, and suggestions for mental health providers are offered.

INTRODUCTION

Incarceration has many challenging and negative impacts on communities, individuals, and families. Separation within families, especially, is difficult. However, less often discussed is the reunification period, in which many families struggle to reorganize family system roles and reestablish personal relationships, trust, and attachment. This chapter reviews theories of family systems and stress, along with common family issues faced both during and after incarceration, along with suggestions for therapeutic practice.

DOI: 10.4018/978-1-7998-9209-0.ch013

FAMILY SYSTEMS THEORY

Murray Bowen (1966, 1978) introduced one of the first comprehensive theories of family systems functioning. Bowen's systems theory continues to be a foundational theory in the conceptualization of families and the practice of family therapy in the U.S. Bowen suggested that families develop patterns of functioning that help to diffuse feelings of stress or anxiety, which often develop from feeling either too close or too distant from others in the system. The degree of anxiety in any particular family system is determined by external stressors and sensitivity to transgenerational themes within relationships, such as roles, expectations, and ways of relating to one another. This systems approach led to the eventual development of the family stress model, which examines the impact of external stressors on children by way of caregiver interpersonal conflict.

Family Stress Model

Rueben Hill (1958) developed the foundational framework for studying family stress called the ABC-X Model. Hill posited that family stress is distinguished by three factors: (A) the provoking event or stressor, (B) the family's resources at the time of event, and (C) the meaning attached to the event – individually by family members and collectively as a unit. The ABC-X family stress model was first established to indicate the relational process of stress on individuals moving through a family system. Hill's model demonstrates that the initiating stressor originates with a parent or caregiver, spreads to interpersonal conflict with a partner, and in turn results in negative impact on the child(ren) by way of parental stress and conflict. Based on Hill's previous work, Boss's (2002) adaptation, the contextual family stress model, posits that families and the individuals within them are more likely to demonstrate resilience to adversity when they have access to both external and internal resources for coping, as family stress is influenced by both external and internal contexts. External contexts are often environmental issues that are out of the family's control, and internal contexts include family dynamics (boundaries, rules, roles) and the experience of loss (Boss, 2002).

Family Stress-Proximal Process Model for Incarceration

Joyce Arditti (2016) developed a family stress-proximal process model for better understanding the impact of incarceration on families and children. Arditti added to the original family stress model by specifying the initial stressor as parental incarceration, and, much like Boss's contextual model, included the consideration of person-environment interactions that may contribute to emotional distress and alter family and individual functioning. The term *proximal processes* was coined by Urie Bronfenbrenner for use in his bioecological model, and refers to the enduring interactions between object or caregiver and child (Bronfenbrenner & Morris, 1998). Critical proximal processes when considering incarceration involve the nature of loss and who is considered to be included with or excluded from the family. Ambiguous losses, where levels of uncertainty are high, are thought to be harder to resolve and more difficult to find effective resources to cope with, often causing more negative effects for the family.

Arditti's family stress-proximal processes model connects both developmental and sociological lenses by situating psychological and family processes within a broader context of social inequality. As seen in Figure 1, the model demonstrates the influence of contextual factors on incarceration and the family system, viewing parental incarceration as both a result of and contributor to disadvantage. Additionally, bidirectional lines are seen between psychological distress and relational processes, reflecting the dynamic nature of family systems.

Figure 1. A family stress-proximal process model of incarceration demonstrates the impacts on both non-incarcerated caregivers and children
(Adapted from Arditti, 2016).

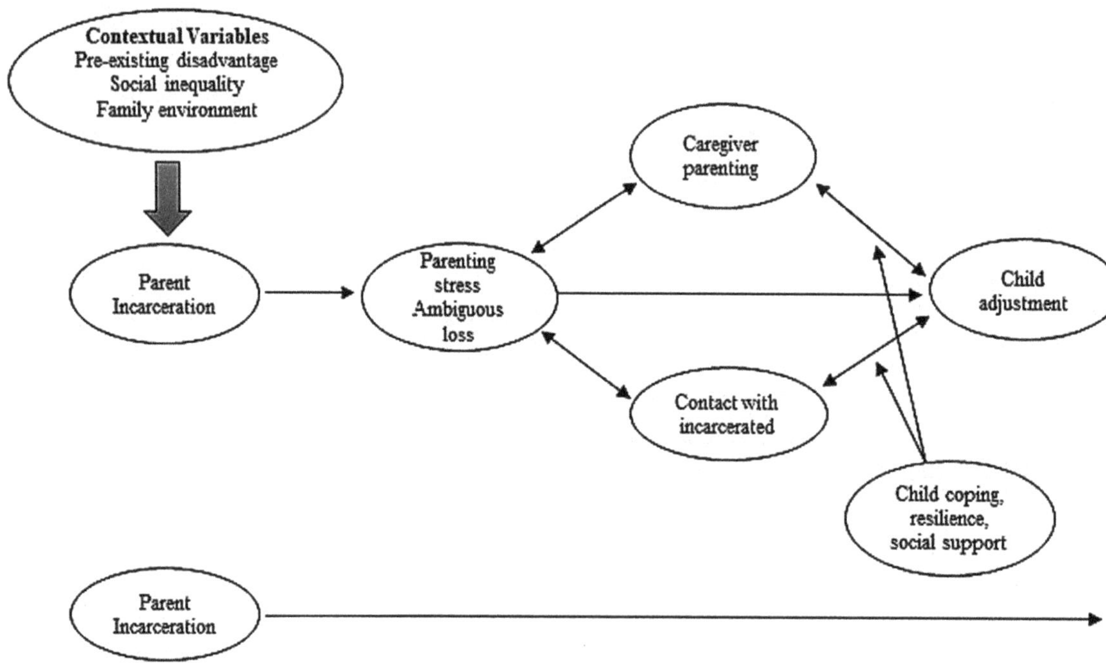

SOCIAL INEQUALITY

In her book, *The New Jim Crow*, Michelle Alexander stated, "As a criminal, you have scarcely more rights, and arguably less respect, than a black man living in Alabama at the height of Jim Crow. We have not ended racial caste in America; we have merely redesigned it" (p. 2, 2010). Similarly, Ming Liu, Pickett and Ivey (2007), concurred that "America's blind spot is social class" (p.194). Within the social ecology of the United States, there are clear and blatant inequities. Privilege, in certain forms, provides the ability to evade or soften the impacts and ripple effects that incarceration has on individuals, families, and communities. This chapter will provide a focus on those who are at higher risk for incarceration and who often feel the impacts more harshly.

Racial Profiling

Black and brown individuals experience higher rates of encounters with law enforcement than their White counterparts, demonstrating that racial profiling continues to be an active practice in the United States. In fact, Black and Latinx individuals are three times more likely to be searched during a traffic stop, and Black individuals are twice as likely to be arrested and almost four time as likely to experience use of force during interactions with law enforcement (National Association for the Advancement of Colored People [NAACP], 2018). The impact of this profiling is widespread, including higher rates of incarceration and longer sentencing than White counterparts.

The New Jim Crow

Black and Brown individuals are faced with the implicit racial prejudices of judges, and other systemic and structural inequities, even before they enter the criminal-justice system (Simon, 2016). Over 50% of Black males are arrested before they are 24 years old, which is a substantial obstruction to finding work, going to school and contributing fully to their communities. Additionally, separation from families as a result of incarceration negatively impacts social and familial roles, such as being a father, husband, brother, and engaged community member. Re-learning these skills after incarceration can seem insurmountable, especially for those who had a long-term sentence (Durrah, 2013). For example, finding stable employment is a crucial step to protect an individual from re-offending. However, having a criminal record can reduce the likelihood of being hired – or even being offered an interview – by half. This can make supporting a family, or even contributing to family finances, impossible.

Socioeconomic Status

Family wellbeing is heavily influenced by parental figures' social standing or socioeconomic status. Comprised of education, income, and occupation, a parent's socioeconomic status significantly affects how the family unit views and interacts in the world and how the world views the family system and the individuals that establish it. It also determines the accessibility of food, shelter, and general stability that impacts overall health. Thus, socioeconomic status ultimately determines the success or failure of the parents, children, and family unit's lives. For families with a history of engagement with the criminal legal system, it is common to experience higher economic and social strain due to systems of domination (i.e., racism, classism, sexism, etc.). Such social placement has a profound impact on the welfare of families, romantic partners, and children. Therefore, when considering the implications of parental incarceration on family wellbeing, it is critical to assess how imprisonment results from and contributes to social inequality.

Mass incarceration and poverty are intimately linked, so it is difficult not to interact with the penal system for marginalized families who experience a higher percentage of social inequality by birthright. Parental incarceration reinforces accumulated family adversity by exacerbating preexisting disadvantages (Arditti & Johnson, 2020). Most prisoners have a history characterized by adversity and disadvantage (i.e., family victimization, low education, neighborhood inequity, substance misuse and addiction, mental health difficulties, etc.). These risks integrated with the compounding issues of adversity and loss from maintaining the family unit can cause significant stress. Such stress can manifest in various ways, especially for children, where it can reinforce life narratives that become present in their adult lives.

KYLEE, SAM, AND ANTHONY: A CASE EXAMPLE

Kylee is making dinner. Her 11 year old son, Sam, is in the living room watching television. This is their typical weeknight routine – Sam takes the bus home from school and does his homework before

Kylee gets home from work each day. Kylee makes dinner, they talk about their day, and watch their shows until it is time for Sam to go to bed. Once Sam is asleep, Kylee makes both of their lunches for the next day, looks over household bills and prioritizes which need immediate attention, and gets ready for bed herself. Her last task of the day is to write a quick e-mail to her husband, Anthony, who has been incarcerated in a state prison for 4 years.

Prior to his incarceration, Kylee and Anthony lived in a small, middle class suburb of a large city. She worked at an insurance company, and he was employed by the city doing construction and electrical work. They lived paycheck to paycheck, with a small savings account for emergencies, and described their lifestyle as "comfortable." Anthony was hurt in a construction accident and was prescribed Percocet and Oxycodone for his pain. He began selling some of his prescribed medication to others who worked with him, in order to bring in extra income while he was unable to perform some job responsibilities for a while after the accident. One of his co-workers reported him to the police, resulting in Anthony's arrest. He received a sentence of 10 years for distribution of a Schedule II substance.

Kylee's family will be discussed from various perspectives throughout this chapter, to highlight the different concepts put forth.

DURING INCARCERATION

The period of incarceration is often one of stress and survival, as the incarcerated individual is suddenly absent, and the family system must adjust to cover their roles and obligations. There are issues within family role assignments, financial hardship, and connection between parents and children as well as with romantic partners.

Family Functioning and Role Assignments

Systems theory states that the system is greater than the sum of its parts. When applied to families, which act as living organisms, each has its unique unit that experiences varying systemic and interpersonal change levels. Those diverse experiences mean that each family has its own set of structures and boundaries that it must maintain to ensure growth and survival. Family units are dependent on the relationships and memories shared, and as a result, all successes and failures are experienced together. The goal of family systems is to maintain homogeneity; however, that stability is not always possible when parental incarceration is involved. Incarceration becomes a stressor to the family system that becomes a disruptive force in family life, even for only short periods. During imprisonment, the family structure shifts to accommodate the missing family member. As a result, the management of tasks and patterns of authority, communication, and general interactions become misaligned (Nichols & Schwartz, 2008, pg. 185). When this occurs, families are unable to regulate, and thus, the roles assumed within the system must be reassessed and repurposed to fit the current structure of the unit.

Accumulated Family Adversity

After Anthony's arrest, Kylee and Sam stayed in their home for 2 years. Kylee fell behind on the mortgage, which she could not afford on her single income. The house was foreclosed on and Kylee and Sam moved to a more affordable apartment in a different part of the city, leaving behind Sam's neighborhood friends and his school. Kylee struggled to adjust to her role of single mother while also grieving the loss of Anthony in their day to day life. Anthony had brought in the primary income, had covered their health insurance, and had been the primary disciplinarian for Sam. With him gone, Kylee was forced to take on these roles herself. Now, 4 years later, Kylee has adapted to the changes as best she can. She and Sam qualify for Medicaid health insurance, they have settled into their new home, and she has enough income to cover basic needs. Sam and Kylee visit Anthony together once a month, and Kylee visits on her own every other week. She often feels guilty that she is not able to visit more frequently, but the prison is a 3 hour drive from their home and she cannot afford the gas money. They stay in more regular contact through phone calls, e-mail, and the postal service.

Anthony, Kylee, and Sam are clear examples of how parental incarceration uproots families and jeopardizes their established way of living. Kylee and Sam had to set a new standard of living while learning to operate against a complex penal system. Such navigation is standard for families such as theirs. The relationship between parental incarceration and outcomes related to family stability becomes more prominent during imprisonment. Structural disadvantages that result from transgenerational trauma are usually present pre-incarceration and become relevant to the family system's overall functioning during incarceration. Transgenerational disadvantages (i.e., economic limitations, socioeconomic status, and social attitudes regarding access and opportunity) are reinforced during this destabilization period. As a result, the family must reckon with living in a dual reality of longing and surviving.

Financial Hardship

Within U.S. society, money is the catalyst for economic and social prosperity. It is pivotal to establishing a quality standard of living, providing access to higher quality education and career opportunities, and allowing greater flexibility to live freely. For families impacted by the criminal legal system, the lack of money becomes the heaviest burden to carry. It is difficult for families to maintain a quality of life like the standard established pre-incarceration after a partner and parental figure has been imprisoned. Therefore, parental incarceration introduces the family structure to material hardship and economic burdens that transition them to a lower socioeconomic status than previously held. The comfort that the unit once established ceases as the family must now adapt and struggle to accommodate a typically stricter lifestyle. Consequently, the responsibility to maintain the family system during parental incarceration falls to the nonincarcerated partner for the duration of the sentencing. For family units with one sole parental provider who becomes incarcerated, the child-rearing and family preservation then falls to a respective guardian (i.e., foster care, fictive kin, etc.) willing to provide labor to maintain the family structure.

Loss of Income

The lack of financial support necessary to support the incarcerated individual during confinement (i.e., legal fees and fines, expenses associated with prison visits, phone calls, etc.) along with managing family duties causes strain and stress that further burdens under-resourced families. Hence, parental incarceration transfers hyper-marginalization from the individual to the family system to the individuals within the unit, especially the children, and reinforces social instability tenfold.

Parental incarceration is a distinct and risky form of family instability because of the visible and invisible ways imprisonment contributes to social stratification. The family rupture can also result in guardianship changes, mainly when maternal incarceration occurs (Tasca et al., 2011). Such system changes can place undue stress on a family, resulting in significant changes in roles within the system, such as moving from co-parenting to living as a single parent. Older children may consequently become parentified themselves and expected to care for any younger children or help provide financial support for the household. Upon reunification, both partners and children may find it challenging to relinquish their newly established roles. As a result, the incarcerated parent more often struggles to find a sense of purpose within the family system.

Housing Insecurity

The most significant change area for the family unit during parental incarceration is the lack of secure housing. Of the basic needs vital to sustaining life, physiological conditions are at the base, including food, water, clothing, and most importantly, shelter. Parental incarceration is the antithesis of those basic needs as it is associated with a high rate of residential instability and homelessness for children of jailed and imprisoned parents (Wakefield & Wildeman, 2014). Families of incarcerated persons are more likely to live in high-poverty areas due to the penal system. As previously stated, many of the families impacted by incarceration already occupy lower socioeconomic and marginalized statuses and experience greater levels of housing insecurity. When reinforced by imprisonment, the struggle to maintain safe, decent housing intensifies.

When a partner and parental figure is incarcerated, the family experiences "downward mobility" or the movement to a lower social class. The family unit is forced to live in more socioeconomically disadvantaged communities due to budget constraints and evictions. An incarcerated parental figure means one less wage earner in the home, maintaining their livelihood and financing their children's lives. Families with single source incomes have fewer options for where to reside and, as a result, may move often. Thus, the neighborhoods they move to have almost predominantly higher percentages of single mother residents that sustain a livelihood without the support of public assistance and live below the poverty line (Wakefield & Wildeman, 2014). For children, constant relocation to neighborhoods with a lower standard of life means fewer quality schools and more access to trauma and adversity. The nonincarcerated parent means greater chances of holding multiple jobs and unemployment. For family entities, it means higher rates of crime and violence that shape the family's identity and can lead to antisocial behaviors with each other and the incarcerated parent.

RELATIONSHIPS AND ATTACHMENT: STAYING CONNECTED

In his book, *A Secure Base,* John Bowlby (1988) outlined a developmental theory of personality termed attachment theory that describes the emotional connection formed between people. The basic tenets of the theory posit that human beings are wired for social, physical, and emotional connection and, therefore, form attachments that serve as a representation of how connection is performed historically and in future settings (Johnson, 2019). Such bonds are established in early childhood as a means for survival and aid in creating emotionally secure bases for relationships.

For children experiencing parental incarceration, the bond between parent and child becomes severed as they lose the proximity, comfort, and protection of an influential life figure. Through an attachment lens, the parental figure becomes inaccessible and less responsive, so the child adopts secondary models of connection (i.e., secondary insecure models) that take the form of vigilant, hyperactivated, avoidant, or dismissive (Johnson, 2019). As a result, parents and children experience varying symptoms of psychological distress that negatively impact the quality of the relationship and ability to connect.

Current literature suggests prolonged separation resulting from incarceration poses a significant risk to the well-being of the family unit. Nonparental care heightens youths' exposure to adverse childhood experiences, behavioral and emotional difficulties, and parentification. In Joyce Arditti's article (2016), she uses the family stress-proximal process (FSPP) model to examine the stressors children experience because of parental incarceration. Psychological distress relating to parents and children, unresolved loss, and familial alterations are a critical part of the person-environment process that encompasses FSPP. Parental engagement is a necessary function of parenting, but it becomes hindered during parental incarceration, where parents, partners, and children physically and emotionally experience distance. Such a separation can drastically impact the attachment bonds established pre-incarceration needed to form relationships.

Arditti describes the experience of living with an incarcerated parent and partner as ambiguous loss or the "mismatch between physical and psychological presence" (p. 70). The attachment between incarcerated parents and their families is physically severed and results in an insecure attachment that manifests itself as grief, anxiety, and insecurity. For example, nonincarcerated parents and children experience this most commonly through the physical absence of the incarcerated parent while maintaining psychological connection through phone or video calls. Feelings of anger, withdrawal, and hostility are common during this stage as the family unit experiences missing their missing person. Incarceration is highly stigmatized, so the added loss and lack of social support cause the family to become more isolated and lonelier.

Similarly, the increase in parenting stress caused by the need to maintain childcare becomes heightened and more persistent. The economic strain caused by parental incarceration results in nonincarcerated parents employing harsher, more authoritarian, and negative parenting behavior (Arditti, 2016). Such a response is expected as the nonincarcerated parent caregivers become physically, emotionally, and financially drained from acting as the sole provider for the children. However, the shift in parenting by the nonincarcerated parent directly correlates to observed and reported adverse child behavior problems that reinforce the ambiguous loss and antisocial behaviors.

Parent-Child

Sam struggles to feel connected to his father. He used to look forward to visiting and to receiving phone calls several times a week, but now feels awkward and uncomfortable. He shares that he does not feel like he knows Anthony and does not have many clear memories of him being present. As he gets older, Sam is beginning to focus more on spending time with friends and beginning extracurricular activities. He does not often speak of his father to his friends, and dodges the subject when others ask. Kylee can see the sadness in Sam, which usually manifests as anger, embarrassment, and resentment. The two argue more often than they used to, as Sam pushes against the rules that Kylee attempts to set and enforce. Sam also argues with Anthony when he tries to support Kylee as the disciplinarian. Although he would not admit it to many people, Sam is scared that his father will not return to the family. He finds that, despite missing Anthony's presence, it feels safer to keep a distance between them.

As showcased above, the relationship between parent and child is necessary and can become strained as a result of parental incarceration. The attachment to parental figures is among the first that children make and is critical to forming emotional, physical, and social bonds that will sustain a person throughout their life. Yet when that relationship becomes nonexistent or strained due to imprisonment and its inevitable distance, it can rupture the foundation of the parental attachments and be replaced by other more prominent and immediate attachments. For Sam, it is easier to distance himself from his father to protect himself from feelings of abandonment, much like many other children experiencing parental incarceration today.

In their book, *Children of the Prison Boom*, Wakefield, and Wildeman (2014) explicitly state how parental incarceration negatively harms children and their relationship with their parents. Using the Fragile Families and Child Wellbeing Study, a longitudinal study of parents, Wakefield and Wildeman compared family units' adaptability and resiliency when facing parental incarceration and those who were not. Based on parental demographics, household characteristics, and paternal characteristics, the authors determined the significance of parental incarceration's impact on children. The results found that children of incarcerated parents have on average, more harmful experiences that lead to mental and developmental issues.

Children of incarcerated parents must adapt faster and become more resilient than children of nonincarcerated parents and thus, have higher exposure to adverse childhood experiences (ACE). Youth with higher ACE scores are more likely to have poor attention, excessive anxiety, and externalizing behaviors like rule-breaking and temper outbursts due to the instability of parental incarceration. Children raised in instability are more likely to maintain a lower socioeconomic status as adults, and parents with low education are more likely to have difficulty raising their children. When compounded with parental imprisonment, a highly stigmatizing experience, the emotional suffering imparted on parents and children leave the family unit experiencing extended uncertainty and grief. The attachment between parent-child then becomes strained as the child's loss manifests in emotions and behaviors ranging from anger, withdrawal, and profound sadness (Arditti, 2016). It is not easy to promote healthy, functioning relationships when a child's mental, emotional, and verbal development is significantly impaired.

Partners

Like the parent-child relationship, the couple must intentionally foster the romantic relationship during imprisonment to ensure connection is maintained. Relationships require investment and accessibility, two of the most limiting factors due to the penal system. During incarceration, the relationship quality between partners often deteriorates based on myriad variables, many of which are beyond the couple's control.

Based on Kristin Turney's (2015) article, the overall relationship quality of romantic partners deteriorates due to lack of shared time, the economic costs of maintaining contact, and the emotional toll experienced by both partners. The financial burden alone (i.e., managing food, clothing and book requests, family visits, legal cases, appeals, etc.) associated with the imprisonment of partners and families results in the compromising of necessary bonding time to nurture the relationship. Similarly, when children are a factor in the romantic relationship, the overall relationship quality decreases further as shared parental responsibility becomes the sole responsibility of one person, which increases the risk of stress-related health conditions. The necessity to manage paid work and caregiving of self and children on top of partner connection leaves the relationship between the couple strained or nonexistent (Wakefield and Wildeman, 2014).

The strain on the relationship resulting from incarceration may encourage the nonincarcerated partner to pursue new partners to close the missing gap that the incarcerated person is no longer filling.

Many mothers who sought new romantic partnerships during the incarceration period found that they received the support, emotional stability, and physical care absent in their relationship before incarceration (Turney, 2015). Mothers who did not pursue new romantic partners reported an overall decrease in relationship quality with less supportiveness and emotional support and more physical abuse. Turney (2015) found for the incarcerated fathers that incarceration did not appear to affect their perception of relationship quality. Thus, the ability to sustain a romantic partnership is perceived to be more difficult by the non-incarcerated individual.

POST INCARCERATION

Just as families must adjust when an individual is incarcerated, they must readjust when that same individual is released. Often, the expectation is that each person will happily and easily fall back into their original roles upon reunification—however, it is rarely this simple. The family members who stepped into new roles may be reluctant to give them up for a variety of reasons. They may feel they do a better job in the role, they may enjoy the responsibility, or they may fear that the individual will become re-incarcerated requiring another system adjustment. Holding on to the responsibility of a role may feel safer than returning it to the formerly incarcerated individual. Additionally, families may still face financial hardship in new ways, with difficulty finding work and facing housing insecurity for some different reasons than when one partner was incarcerated. Relationships must be addressed as well, both romantic partnerships and parent-child relationships that have been strained by extended absence and other stressors.

Financial Hardship

Just as when a partner is incarcerated, financial hardship is a common theme within families of formerly incarcerated individuals. However, the situation changes as it is not necessarily due to having a single income household or to sending supplies or goods to someone who is incarcerated. Often, financial hardship comes from difficulty finding appropriate work for the incarcerated individual. Additionally, housing insecurity is still a concern for many released individuals, as they may not be able to join their partner and/or children in their home, depending on where they live. This means possibly having to pay a second rent at another location to have a place to live. These collateral consequences of incarceration are just a few faced by individuals who are reintegrating back into society and their families (Turanovic, Rodriguez, & Pratt, 2012).

Finding Work

Securing stable employment is critical to preventing recidivism. However, a criminal record can reduce the likelihood of even being interviewed by as much as 50%. Many employers will not hire anyone with a felony on their record, greatly reducing the prospects for obtaining a livable income in a legal manner. This can make supporting a family, or even contributing to family finances, impossible (Turanovic, Rodriguez, & Pratt, 2012).

There has been movement in recent years around the equitable and inclusive selection of employees, such as the Ban the Box movement, which prohibits employers from asking candidates about their criminal history on initial job applications, and the consideration of "Green factors." Green factors were created around the enforcement of Title VII of the Civil Rights Act of 1964, and consider the nature and gravity of the offense, the time passed since the offense and any time served, and the nature of the job being sought after. The term comes from the case of *Green v. Missouri Pacific Railroad*, in which the court determined that a complete bar on employment based on any criminal activity was unlawful under Title VII (U.S. Equal Employment Opportunity Coalition, 2012).

In addition to barriers to finding employment, formerly incarcerated individuals face obstacles from their conditioning during imprisonment. While incarcerated there is a heavy emphasis on routine and schedule, having days planned and tasks completed in a timely manner, and adaptation to the subjugating nature of prison where there is little room for individual decision making or autonomy. This environment has been noted as "antithetical" to successful reintegration, and certainly opposes many workforce settings that desire flexibility, autonomy, and quick decision making (Anazodo, Ricciardelli, & Chan, 2019). As such, many formerly incarcerated individuals find that they are restricted in the types of employment they can find, and the length of time they are able to hold a position.

Housing Insecurity

As demonstrated through Kylee's story, it is not uncommon for the nonincarcerated partner to be forced to relocate to different housing due to financial issues resulting from loss of dual income. However, housing issues can continue to pervade post-release as well. Similar to employment, there are many barriers to individuals with felony records around renting property, even sometimes obtaining a home loan. For formerly incarcerated individuals who are married or in a relationship, this means that much of the weight falls on the nonincarcerated partner to carry. For example, when purchasing a home, it may be easier to secure a loan only in the nonincarcerated partner's name—which means using only their income, thereby reducing the maximum amount able to be borrowed. Additionally, if the nonincarcerated partner is living in a rental property when the incarcerated individual is released, and they plan on living together, the formerly incarcerated partner will need to be listed on the lease. This can be problematic if the landlords are not willing to rent to individuals who have certain criminal backgrounds and may force the family to relocate.

RELATIONSHIPS AND ATTACHMENT: RECONNECTION

During incarceration, the focus is on maintaining attachment with loved ones. Once released, that focus shifts to reconnection. There is an expectation, to some extent, that distance is inevitable—particularly with extended time apart. When an individual is released they may try to finds ways to bridge that distance with partners and children. However, it is rarely a simple process.

Parent-Child

One of the core tenets of attachment theory (Bowlby, 1973) is that "variation of security and thus the [internal working model] are a direct function of lived experiences, especially experiences in the earliest portion of the life span (i.e., first 3-5 years of life)" (Belsky, 2002). Given the large numbers of young children of incarcerated parents, it would be negligent to overlook the impact of separation due to incarceration on parental attachment. If children do not feel secure in their attachment, they are more likely to develop negative self- and other perceptions, creating obstacles for any close relationships. Additionally, because emotional regulation is closely linked with the behaviors and patterns within close relationships, it may be that some of these children begin to have problems with appropriate regulation of their emotions (Belsky, 2002). While these challenges to attachment may not be permanent, they certainly add additional stress to the family that is already facing adversity. Finding a way to foster secure attachment throughout incarceration is not always possible, as secure attachment may not have been presented to begin with, but it is integral to successfully maintaining any pre-existing attachment bonds.

Reconnection can be challenging for newly released parent and their child. The parent has likely missed a significant amount of time with the child, and various developmental milestones. Even if the child has been visiting and conversing with the parent on a regular basis, they may feel disconnected or distant from the parent now that they are back in the home or in their daily life. Often there is an awkwardness that accompanies reintegrating the parent back into the household. Additionally, children may protect themselves out of fear of the parent leaving again. This can look like anger or disrespect toward the parent, or an unwillingness to incorporate the parent into their daily life and routine. Parents may have to earn the trust of the child back with consistent behavior, regardless of how the child may be acting out. This can be challenging as the formerly incarcerated parent is also adjusting to their release and may not be capable of consistency and stability immediately. Sometimes parents may be so consumed with fear of re-incarceration that they withdraw further from the family, causing them to miss milestone celebrations that facilitate connection (Goffman, 2009).

Partners

Strong and stable relationships appear to be protective factors which reduce the risk of reoffending. However, incarceration places undue stress on marriages and other romantic relationships; twenty-two percent of marriages result in divorce or separation after incarceration. Even if relationships can survive the adversity of incarceration, they may emerge significantly changed. While many incarcerated individuals are in nonmarital romantic relationships, relatively few are legally married. For the purpose of this section, the term "divorce" is used but can apply to any separation or breakup between two partners.

Divorce is considered to be yet another collateral consequence of incarceration, along with financial hardship, difficulty finding employment, and a variety of health issues. While this outcome may be intuitive to anyone who understands the challenges of incarceration, it also rests on strong empirical evidence. Both Lopoo and Western (2005) and Apel et al. (2010) found that the probability of marital dissolution among incarcerated men is three times higher than in groups of nonincarcerated men. However, the understanding around why this happens is still unclear. Some research posits that when a partner is incarcerated, the nonincarcerated partner begins to lean on the community around them – sometimes to an extent that causes the support system to burn out, leaving them with nowhere to turn and eventually choosing to leave the relationship to find a new partner.

Massoglia, Remster, and King (2011) thought it boiled down to two possibilities found throughout the literature – either the stigma of incarceration was too great to bear by the nonincarcerated partner, or the separation due to incarceration was too much of a strain on the relationship. What they found was that the stigma around incarceration is actually weakened by the shared history and degree of intimacy between partners, causing it to hold less salience within these relationships. Rather than stigma, their research findings point to extended separation as a direct contributor to marital dissolution. Separation can cause many strains not only to the relationship, but also to the partner left behind to manage a household on their own. Maintaining a romantic relationship during incarceration is economically, emotionally, and logistically complicated. This can cause the non-incarcerated partner to look elsewhere for both financial and emotional support, possibly leading to the development of a new relationship. Further, the challenges associated with partner incarceration do not remit after release—in fact, in some cases they may be magnified while the family system transitions back to pre-incarceration roles (Turney, 2015). A survey of heterosexual couples with an incarcerated male partner found that men rated relationship happiness much higher than their partner during the incarceration, but both partners rated satisfaction low after release (Comfort, 2018). Female partners sometimes valued the independence gained during the time apart and felt that their autonomy may be threatened by their partner's return. Overall, female partner's expectation of the male partner's reintegration into the family and household were drastically different from the male's expectations, which can deliver substantial blows to the relationship satisfaction upon reintegration

Coparenting

In addition to the romantic relationship, many partners have children that they coparent. In heterosexual relationships, female partners have more often expressed expectations that male partners would take on various household responsibilities, such as childcare, after being released, but instead they are faced with new challenges (Comfort, 2018). Male partners are typically inclined to prioritize securing employment over any other endeavors following release, but the record of incarceration often makes this difficult, as discussed earlier in this chapter. While chances of employment can be increased by maintaining family ties while incarcerated, as has been demonstrated, this is not easily accomplished (McKay, Comfort, Grove, Bir, & Lindquist, 2018). Conviction history can also be a barrier to cohabitation, which can negatively impact the provision of child support or adequately contributing to family finances.

Anthony served a total of 8 years in state prison and was released with additional years of parole. Upon his release he moved into temporary transitional housing. Kylee was not able to find a rental within her price range that would allow a felon to be listed on the lease and she did not want to move Sam into a new school district when he was close to finishing high school, as he had just begun his junior year. Anthony was not able to be employed by the city any longer but was able to find a job in construction relatively easily. He was transparent with his new employer about his past, and they agreed to take him on with certain stipulations regarding drug testing—which he was required to do for his parole as well. Once he had acquired several months of steady income, he and Kylee were able to obtain a home loan and purchase a home in Sam's current school district. Both Anthony and Kylee attribute the ability to stay in regular contact and visit on a regular basis to their marital success. This is not to say that they are without stressors or conflict in their relationship, but they were able to maintain a commitment to one another that is not always present when one partner is facing long-term incarceration. Kylee used her employee assistant program benefits to connect all three of them with marriage and family counseling to help with release and reunification, and she has kept them active in their local church, which provides a sense of community and support.

IMPLICATIONS FOR MENTAL HEALTH PROVIDERS

Mental health providers—counselors, social workers, psychologists, marriage and family therapists, etc.—are at the front lines for caring for individuals and families who have moved through incarceration. Unfortunately, due to stigma, and some of the issues mentioned in this chapter such as financial hardship, it may be challenging to find services that they trust and can afford. On top of stigma due to the incarceration itself, many incarcerated individuals and their families are from minoritized groups that have mistrust for the medical and mental health field, and who value keeping personal information within the immediate family (Avent Harris & Wong, 2018). This can make it difficult to reach certain populations. However, there are certain perspectives and tools that can be used for outreach and to provide a positive experience for those who seek help.

A Systems Perspective

While various types of mental health clinicians are found throughout the prison system, marriage and family therapists are not often employed in incarcerated settings. Criminal activity is often viewed as an individual undertaking, and the impact of conviction and incarceration on the family is not frequently discussed (Datchi et al., 2016). The result is a slew of individually focused services and a dearth of family or systems approaches, despite the evidence of need for systemic treatment in incarcerated settings (Datchi & Sexton, 2013; Tadros et al., 2019; Tadros & Finney, 2018; Tadros & Ogden, 2020).

Inclusion of family therapists can help to strengthen family system relationships, reducing family dysfunction, and facilitate better reintegration into society. Family therapy can increase involvement and support from the non-incarcerated family members and can support the family to strengthen resilience during times of adversity. It can also facilitate healthy communication, mutual respect, and strengthen interpersonal relationships between partners, parents, and children (Datchi & Sexton, 2013; May et al., 2014)

The family stress-proximal processes model (Arditti, 2016) introduced at the beginning of this chapter is a useful perspective to work from, as it provides the various pieces for understanding the components and processes at play within families experiencing incarceration. This model helps to outline the individuals involved as well as the external processes acting upon them, which can help a clinician to know where to start when treating a family who is experiencing incarceration or reunification.

Culturally Informed Care

As discussed earlier in the chapter, a great deal of the U.S. incarcerated population are from already minoritized groups, particularly disadvantaged socioeconomic status and minoritized racial and ethnic populations. Therefore, any clinician providing services to incarcerated individuals or their families must take cultural competency into consideration. Tadros and Owens (2019) make the following recommendations for working with incarcerated individuals while using a culturally informed lens:

1. Counseling with incarcerated individuals must come from a holistic perspective. Counselors must be comfortable with addressing the realities of being a racially minoritized individual in the United States and the mental, physical, and spiritual effects of microaggressions. Understanding techniques such as broaching race and ethnicity will be important and useful.

2. Therapists must have an understanding that many racially minoritized individuals often come from families that operate as a collective unit. Understanding cultural nuances is key to becoming culturally competent as a counselor. Incarcerated individuals, then, may carry deep shame around the impact they have had on their family and, possibly, the family's standing in society. They may also be estranged from family who felt it better to cut them off than face any embarrassment brought on by their incarceration.
3. Navigating any disconnect between family and support systems with those who are incarcerated is imperative. Exploring topics of reintegration in both the family system and the community are necessary. Additionally, discussion of auxiliary support systems is critical. If the family does not want to accept the incarcerated individual back into their folds, they must be able to seek support and belonging elsewhere.
4. Therapists must have a clear understanding of reentry into society. Understanding the intersectionality of issues that someone faces as they are released, and the various stressors that accompany reentry into society, is imperative to helping individuals and their families navigate the multifaceted aspects of reintegration.
5. Exploring values and messaging about diversity topics within the family system is necessary. Growing up, what messages did individuals receive from their family or other important figures in their lives about race, gender, socioeconomic status, and their place in the world? Many incarcerated individuals carry values imparted from parents and other authority figures that hold salience to their self-worth and self-awareness. Additionally, exploring and combatting cultural values and messages around what it means to be incarcerated could be helpful for these clients.
6. Explore conditions of self-worth for clients. Those clients who have higher external levels of self-worth are likely to be higher risk for emotional concerns. High levels of external self-worth would include having a lot of money, a need for admiration from large groups of people, and a strong focus on acquiring and showing off material possessions. External self-worth can be difficult to control, and often takes time to achieve, therefore making it an unstable measure of self-worth. High internal levels of self-worth could include spirituality, kindness, and other character traits that are stable and intrinsically motivated (Burger, 2015).
7. Spirituality/religion is often a protective factor to stress for marginalized individuals. Therapists should consider exploration of these topics during the counseling process. The effects of incarceration on a client's spiritual being are warranted. This does not mean imposing a particular type of religion or spiritual practice on a client, but inquiring to their beliefs and values around spirituality and utilizing any existing views to underpin support and belonging.
8. Clinicians are encouraged to join social justice branches of their professional organizations, such as the Association for Multicultural Counseling and Development (a branch of the American Counseling Association). Joining these organizations will allow the clinician to embrace ongoing growth and development through continuing education, conferences, and access to timely research and news.
9. Engaging therapists or therapists in training in the privilege walk exercise, originating from the work of Peggy McIntosh (1989), can help build awareness and understanding of white privilege and systemic oppression in the United States. This can be used a teambuilding or training exercise in almost any setting.

10. Clinicians must accept that becoming culturally competent is an ongoing, dynamic, and active process. Multicultural competence is not passive; it requires continuous engagement. Additionally, no one will ever fully reach competence to the point of being able to say, "I am done."
11. Counselors must have a strong understanding around how systemic inequality contributes to the racial and ethnic inequities in the criminal justice system and for-profit corrections. Michelle Alexander's book *The New Jim Crow* (2010) outlines many of the issues within the current legal system and the criminalization of minoritized groups.

Understanding Attachments

An understanding of Bowlby's (1973) attachment theory and Ainsworth et al.'s (1978) types of secure and insecure attachment is important for all clinicians but is of particular salience in this context. With extended separation between family members, it is imperative to be knowledgeable in these theories of attachment, as they may help to conceptualize family challenges. Additionally, working from theoretical lenses or utilizing techniques that are directly related to attachment and connection may be especially helpful for clinicians. Use of Sue Johnson's (2019) emotionally focused therapy (EFT) for couples, or the varying offshoots utilized for parent-child dyads, or individuals, can be helpful when attending to attachment wounds within the incarcerated individual or their family members. Similarly, practitioners of relational cultural theory (RCT; Jordan, 2010; Miller, 1988) address the need for authenticity and connection in relation to the messaging received from other individuals as well as the culture at large. RCT theorists posit that shame around personal identities causes them to disconnect and isolate, facilitating chronic depression. Use of these attachment and connection focused modalities may help begin to address many of the connection hardships that so many incarcerated families face. Similarly, conceptualizing such families through the family stress-proximal processes model (Arditti, 2016), or similar models that consider external and internal stressors alongside the context of incarceration and social inequities, may help to develop a stronger understanding of these families.

CONCLUSION

Family reunification after incarceration is challenging, at best. There is a plethora of obstacles that families must face both during and after incarceration, both internal and external to the family and the self, creating chronic stressors and adversity for these individuals. For clinicians working with these families, an understanding of a systems perspective, attachment, and continual striving for cultural competence are all integral to effective therapeutic intervention.

REFERENCES

Ainsworth, M. D. S., Blehar, M. C., Waters, E., & Wall, S. (1978). *Patterns of attachment: A psychological study of the strange situation*. Erlbaum.

Alexander, M. (2010). *The new Jim Crow: Mass incarceration in the age of colorblindness*. The New Press.

Anazodo, K. S., Ricciardelli, R., & Chan, C. (2019). Employment after incarceration: Managing a socially stigmatized identity. *Equality, Diversity and Inclusion*, *38*(5), 564–582. doi:10.1108/EDI-09-2018-0175

Apel, R., Blokland, A. A. J., Nieuwbeerta, P., & van Schellen, M. (2010). The impact of imprisonment on marriage and divorce: A risk set matching approach. *Journal of Quantitative Criminology*, *26*(2), 269–300. doi:10.100710940-009-9087-5

Arditti, J. (2016). A family stress-proximal process model for understanding the effects of parental incarceration on children and their families. *Couple & Family Psychology*, *5*(2), 65–88. doi:10.1037/cfp0000058

Avent Harris, J. R., & Wong, C. D. (2018). African American college students, the Black church, and counseling. *Journal of College Counseling*, *21*(1), 15–28. doi:10.1002/jocc.12084

Belsky, J. (2002). Developmental origins of attachment styles. *Attachment & Human Development*, *4*(2), 166–170. doi:10.1080/14616730210157510 PMID:12467508

Boss, P. (2002). *Family stress management: A contextual approach* (2nd ed.). Sage., doi:10.4135/9781452233895

Bowlby, J. (1973). *Separation, anxiety and anger* (Vol. 2). The Hogarth Press and the Institute of Psycho-Analysis.

Bowlby, J. (1988). *A secure base*. Basic Books.

Bronfenbrenner, U., & Morris, P. A. (1998). The ecology of developmental processes. In Handbook of child psychology: Vol. 1. Theoretical models of human development (5th ed., pp. 993–1028). New York: Wiley.

Burger, J. M. (2015). *Personality*. Brooks/Cole Publishing, Co.

Datchi, C. C., Barretti, L. M., & Thompson, C. M. (2016). Family services in adult detention centers: Systemic principles for prisoner reentry. *Couple & Family Psychology*, *5*(2), 89–104. doi:10.1037/cfp0000057

Datchi, C. C., & Sexton, T. L. (2013). Can family therapy have an effect on adult criminal conduct? Initial evaluation of functional family therapy. *Couple & Family Psychology*, *2*(4), 278–293. doi:10.1037/a0034166

Durrah, D. A. J. (2013). *Understanding African American male inmates' decisions to seek mental health treatment while incarcerated (No. 3604412)*. ProQuest Dissertations & Theses.

Goffman, A. (2009). On the run: Wanted men in a Philadelphia ghetto. *American Sociological Review*, *74*(3), 339–357. doi:10.1177/000312240907400301

Johnson, S. M. (2019). *Attachment Theory in Practice*. Guilford Press.

Jordan, J. (2010). *Relational-cultural therapy*. American Psychological Association.

Lopoo, L. M., & Western, B. (2005). Incarceration and the formation and stability of marital unions. *Journal of Marriage and Family*, *67*(3), 721–734. doi:10.1111/j.1741-3737.2005.00165.x

Massoglia, M., Remster, B., & King, M. (2011). Stigma or separation?: Understanding the incarceration-divorce relationship. *Social Forces*, *90*(1), 133–155. doi:10.1093f/90.1.133

May, J., Osmond, K., & Billick, S. (2014). Juvenile delinquency treatment and prevention: A literature review. *The Psychiatric Quarterly*, *85*(3), 295–301. doi:10.100711126-014-9296-4 PMID:24610601

McIntosh, P. (1989). White privilege: Unpacking the invisible knapsack. *Peace and Freedom*, (July/August), 10–12.

Miller, J. B. (1988). *Connections, disconnections, and violations.* Work in Progress No. 33. Wellesley, MA: Stone Center Working Paper Series.

Nichols, M. N., & Schwartz, R. C. (2008). *Family therapy: Concepts and methods* (8th ed.). Pearson.

Simon, C. (2016). *There is a stunning gap between the number of white and black inmates in America's prisons.* Business Insider. Retrieved from http://www.businessinsider.com/study-finds-huge-racial-disparity-in-americas-prisons-2016-6/#incarceration-ratio-for-blacks-versus-whites-by-state-1

Tadros, E., & Finney, N. (2018). Structural family therapy with incarcerated families. *The Family Journal (Alexandria, Va.)*, *26*(2), 253–261. doi:10.1177/1066480718777409

Tadros, E., Fye, J. M., McCrone, C. L., & Finney, N. (2019). Incorporating multicultural couple and family therapy into incarcerated settings. *International Journal of Offender Therapy and Comparative Criminology*, *63*(4), 641–658. doi:10.1177/0306624X18823442 PMID:30628499

Tadros, E., & Ogden, T. E. (2020). Conceptualizing incarcerated coparenting through a structural family theory lens. *Marriage & Family Review*, *56*(6), 535–552. doi:10.1080/01494929.2020.1728007

Tadros, E., & Owens, D. (2019). Clinical implications for culturally informed counseling with incarcerated individuals. *The American Journal of Family Therapy*, *49*(4), 344–355. doi:10.1080/01926187.2020.1813659

Turanovic, J. J., Rodriguez, N., & Pratt, T. C. (2012). The collateral consequences of incarceration revisited: A qualitative analysis of the effects on caregivers of children of incarcerated parents. *Criminology*, *50*(4), 913–960. doi:10.1111/j.1745-9125.2012.00283.x

Turney, K. (2015). Hopelessly devoted? Relationship quality during and after incarceration. *Journal of Marriage and Family*, *77*(2), 480–495. doi:10.1111/jomf.12174

U.S. Equal Employment Opportunity Coalition. (2012). *Enforcement guidance on the consideration of arrest and conviction records in employment decisions under Title VII of the Civil Rights Act.* Retrieved April 5, 2022 from https://www.eeoc.gov/laws/guidance/enforcement-guidance-consideration-arrest-and-conviction-records-employment-decisions#VB6

Wakefield, S., & Wildeman, C. (2014). *Children of the prison boom: Mass incarceration and the future of American inequality.* Oxford University Press.

Chapter 14
Returning Home:
The Re-Entry Process

Debra M. Perez
Liberty University, USA

Tricia M. Mikolon
University of the Cumberlands, USA

Sarah Littlebear
University of the Cumberlands, USA

ABSTRACT

Reentering the community is a difficult process for those released from incarceration and is a topic that is addressed with the individual by staff prior to their release. This often focuses on determining where they want to live, follow up care, as well as where they will work. However, the process of integrating back into the family is not necessarily always addressed with the individual, let alone their family. In the absence of the incarcerated individual, the family has needed to reconfigure itself to adjust to the empty space created by the imprisonment of the individual. The family has taken on different roles and responsibilities, filling in for the missing person, while managing their own adjustment and reactions to the incarceration. This is rarely supported by additional external support for the family members and is not included in the re-entry planning for the released individual. This chapter will focus on the needs of the family as they navigate the re-entry of the released individual back into the family dynamic.

INTRODUCTION

Re-entry is a process of returning to the community from incarceration which thousands of people face each year (Mancini et al., 2016; Morenoff & Harding, 2014). These individuals are mothers or fathers, sons or daughters, sisters or brothers, and members of families and communities. Research has been conducted focusing on this process from both the correctional staff point of view to enhance their role in assisting in this process (Austin, 2021; Barack & Stebbins, 2017; Galletta et al., 2021; Matthews,

DOI: 10.4018/978-1-7998-9209-0.ch014

2021; Steen, 2021) as well as from the experience of the individual (Cook & Haynes, 2021; Gomes & Rocker, 2021; Matthews, 2021; Nuño, 2021). Little research has focused on the process of integration back into the family (Hood & Gaston, 2021; Mancini et al., 2016; Rankins, 2022). The family needed to adjust to the loss of the individual due to their incarceration from the daily life of the household. The remaining family members have assumed different roles and responsibilities allowing for the absorption of obligations that the incarcerated individual once held.

Along with this change was each member's need to process their own reactions and emotions to this loss, as well as the incarceration itself. Upon return of the incarcerated individual, this family dynamic will change yet again, this time shifting to incorporate the individual back into the family. This adjustment may bring with it feelings of resentment for the time the person was missing from the family, fear of their re-incarceration, frustration about the conditions of release the individual has brought onto the family, confusion over the perception of the incarceration, and excitement of the homecoming (Hood & Gaston, 2021). This mix of conflicting emotions may increase the pressure of this adaption and influence the duration of this transition.

This chapter will provide an overview of the re-entry process and a discussion of the impact this has on the family of the returning individual. Considerations of the released individual's re-entry on the family will be explored, including how the perceptions of incarceration and assumed responsibilities play a role. Changes within the family dynamic will be explored with attention to family systems and appropriate interventions to assist the members of the home.

OVERVIEW OF RE-ENTRY PROCESS

As release from incarceration approaches, the staff of the institution will begin to prepare the individual for re-entry into the community. This process often focuses on the need to secure housing, employment, and follow-up care. Some individuals may be released under the supervision of probation or parole, which brings with it additional expectations and responsibilities, failure of which results in various consequences up to and including re-incarceration.

Re-entry begins at the start of incarceration with the individual being received into the jail or prison according to their sentence. At this time, an evaluation is completed to determine treatment and programming needs to assist in their adjustment but also to help ensure that their return to the community will be a productive one, a release of a stronger and healthier individual equipped with positive coping skills and healthy support systems.

Exploration of their employment needs and skill development occurs, with the focus of gaining employment upon release. Evaluation of their physical, mental, and emotional states are completed with attention to what will be needed upon release to enable them to maintain stability within the community. Treatment is provided to reduce recidivism related to criminal thinking as well as increase positive coping skills to manage daily stressors. The hope is to return a healthier version of the individual to the community.

Family support has been found to increase successful re-entry when provided and increase recidivism when absent (Liu & Visher, 2021). However, the return of an individual from confinement may also increase the stress of the family system already stretched to extremes to compensate for their absence (Hood & Gaston, 2021). An exploration into the impact of re-entry on the family is necessary to assist in transforming this process from one of increased stress and strain to one of support and adjustment for all involved.

IMPACT OF RE-ENTRY ON THE FAMILY

How a family adapts to the re-entry of the returning individual depends tremendously on both the experience of the family with that person prior to their incarceration as well as their perception of the incarceration. Was the individual a responsible family member prior to their incarceration or someone who brought chaos and drama to the family? Was incarceration viewed as a logical consequence of the person's behaviors and choices or as something that happened to the person, placing the individual as well as the family in a victim role of the authorities? Is the return a wonderful event that the family has been waiting for, one to be celebrated, or has this moment been dreaded since the returning individual first left, rooted in feelings of resentment and fear? Complicating this dynamic more are the emotions that may be coexisting within family members which differ from person to person depending on their relationship with the returning individual and the role that person had in their life prior to incarceration. Such conflicts may result in increased stress within individual and between family members.

Role of the Returning Member Within the Family

The family's experience of the return of the individual depends heavily on the role of the individual prior to their incarceration as well as their involvement with the family and each member during confinement. What the relationship with the individual was like prior to their imprisonment often influences their relationships while confined. The amount and quality of communication during their incarceration with each family member determines the foundation upon which the relationship is built prior to their return and greatly influences how each person will view the relationship upon their return. A significant factor is the family members' ability to express their emotions throughout this process, as open and healthy discussion from the onset of incarceration paves the way for this to continue in person upon the reintegration.

Prior to returning home, discussions that explore the current family members' roles within the home and the expectations of the returning member upon re-entry to the home are necessary. Waiting to explore these topics once the individual has already physically returned to the home may increase inhibition of frank discussions which need to occur. These conversations are often had with staff and the incarcerated individual prior to their release, but rarely include the family. To what extent these dialogues occur with the family is dependent on the incarcerated individual. Rarely does the family incorporate external support during the transition of re-entry into the home as this is often viewed as a personal experience and not one requiring outside assistance or involvement. The family may also encounter limited resources to assist them during this time (Rankins, 2022).

Impact of Conditions of Release on the Family

In many cases, the release of an individual from incarceration comes under the supervision of probation or parole for some period. Such releases involve mandates in place to attempt to ensure a positive transition back into the community with supervision by the probation/parole agent. Mandates may include the need for consistent employment, restrictions from having a cell phone or alcohol/controlled substances and firearms in the home, and consistent treatment involvement for criminality, substance use, and/or mental health concerns.

These restrictions, by the very nature of the individual returning to the home, extend then to the family as well. While the restrictions are intended to support the family and assist the returning individual in being a productive member of society, the household priorities may differ from those of supervision. Finding employment may be a condition of parole but hindered by incarceration, placing the burden of finding opportunities on the family prior to release (Mornoff & Harding, 2014; Silver et al., 2021). Home plans are often investigated prior to release, placing the family into the evaluative process to determine if the home is a healthy environment. Such mandates as removal of firearms, alcohol, or other concerning elements for the incarcerated individual will be necessary prior to approval.

Upon re-entry into the home, securing employment may take time but the increase in resources within the family will occur immediately. Youth may be required to attend educational programming to increase their academic standing in additional to daily school programs (Strnadová et al., 2022). The availability of resources in the community to comply with these mandates is also an important consideration as extensive travel may be required to comply with treatment, education, employment, or supervision requirements (Desai et al., 2021). Prior debt incurred by the individual may also become due upon their release (Harper et al., 2021). Singularly any one of these puts an additional strain on family finances and structure, combined they may become a significant burden for the family as well as the community at large (Franco-Paredes et al., 2021).

Needing to function within the restrictions of supervision may also frustrate some family members, making them feel as if they too are on probation or parole, and further paying the consequences of the choices of someone outside of themselves. Role confusion, based on the returning individual's perceptions prior to their confinement and expectations upon return, may clash with those of the family members who have assumed their responsibilities during the absence. Confusion and resentments may occur throughout this process, leading to frustration on behalf of all involved.

Changes of Responsibilities for Family Members

As discussed, the conditions of release the individual re-entering the community must follow impact that person who is attempting to stabilize and learn a new identity as well as the family members who provide emotional, physical, and financial support. Upon re-entry, an individual must establish an address for visits from supervision, and they oftentimes reside with family members. Generally, the safety and support family may provide helps the individual re-entering feel more comfortable with the transition. This is a time for reconnection with family members and renewal of life outside of being incarcerated.

Are families of individuals with a criminal history considered agents of change in the community, or do they view themselves as victims of the system? Regardless of how family members view themselves, they must spend some time figuring out how the individual who has returned to their lives has changed since release. The formerly incarcerated individual may not have sharpened employment skills, and families may bear the brunt of filling in these gaps, particularly in assisting with technology.

Financial responsibilities within the family are impacted as well. Changes in obligations may have occurred in the budgetary roles within the family. Contributions to the household income may shift from what they once were. Remaining family members may be put in the position to pursue higher paying or potentially laborious jobs. Furthermore, the impact of incarceration may limit the employment options available to the returning family member, further complicating the family's overall financial plan.

Family Perceptions of Incarceration

When considering the perceptions family members have regarding a loved one's incarceration, the relationship the family member has with the returning individual is important. There is already a stigma families may be cognizant of surrounding a loved one's incarceration. Incarcerated individuals are often left in the dark regarding court appearances due to security reasons, and this became more pronounced during the COVID-19 pandemic as courts struggled to keep up with cases. The lack of information the individual may have about their court appearances can flow to the family members themselves, thus creating uncertainty within the household (Correa et al., 2021). Children may become uneasy when they already have a lack of communication with a parent in jail or prison, and not having a timeline for court dates and possible release may be anxiety-provoking. Encouraging open communication and offering programs to assist families and children of those incarcerated may help families navigate the uncertainty of incarceration more effectively (Correa et al., 2021).

Children may look forward to their parent's transition back, and this can bring about a multitude of emotions. Although there is at least one caregiver in place while a parent is incarcerated, children are often excited yet anxious when a parent is coming home. Children may experience worry and attach themselves to the parent once they are home. In general, parental incarceration has been viewed to have negative consequences on children. However, the consequences do not have to be negative as the social context of the parental incarceration may lessen the impact on the children's perceptions (Johnson & Easterling, 2012). Incarceration's stigma may lend itself to the concept of ambiguous loss, where the children do not talk about their parent's confinement, and therefore, experience distress, while also balancing that with eagerness to have their parent home and spend more time with them (Johnson & Easterling, 2012).

Impact of These Changes on Family Members

According to Comfort (2016), the frequency of incarcerations and time placed on community supervision matters to loved ones. If a family member is frequently arrested and incarcerated for even low-level criminal activity, disruptions in jobs and roles within the family occur frequently impacting the entire system. Even with stipulations set by community supervision to seek and maintain employment upon re-entry, the time it takes to obtain employment may be lengthened with a criminal background and more so with certain offenses.

Many re-entering the community are hesitant to discuss their criminal background. Applicants approach employment in different ways, which includes attempting to prove themselves prior to disclosing their background or being honest with potential employers on the front end (Cherney & Fitzgerald, 2016). Employers may view the lack of initial disclosure as dishonest and use this to deny employment, while the honesty could be praised and regarded as a welcome change from the criminal mindset. When jobs are difficult to obtain and maintain, the family has the challenge of financial support. However, successful employment may bring with it long hours and absence from the home.

Romantic partners of the re-entering individual may experience various emotions. Marriages may dissolve in the aftermath, and if a relationship remains intact, partners may be impacted by the individual's decreased social status due to criminal history (Wildeman & Western, 2010). Fear of judgement from other family members and friends can be difficult to endure. The stigma of a partner's criminal record may be challenging, and couples may decide to receive counseling or other services to work through issues and determine relationship status.

One issue can be the potential for recidivism or rearrest. There is greater likelihood of returning to a correctional facility if previously incarcerated. Families may also need to support individuals struggling with mental health or addiction needs such as attending appointments or paying for services.

Overall, family perceptions may be conflicting regarding the re-entry of the individual. Excitement and tension resonate among families. Many are hopeful that their family member will not return to jail or prison, but they do not always know the proper resources to address the full spectrum of needs within the family. Community supervision, such as parole or probation, may feel intrusive, but it also can provide a safety net for families. Struggles establishing employment and keeping appointments may be difficult but results in a renewed sense of freedom for the household and increased independence for the reintegrating member once in place.

Changes Within the Family Dynamic

The structure of a family depends largely on who the members are and the complex interactions among members (Minuchin, 1974). Viewing the interactions of a family allows the therapist to see the influence each member has on another and vice versa. Focusing on the family, rather than on an individual, gives the social context that the client is part of as the family is a natural social group. As one family member interacts with another, the two members influence each other and additionally impact the remaining family members which in turn impacts the two original interacting members. By changing the behaviors of one member of the family, the entire family changes in response.

In an intact family, there is a parental subunit in charge of a sibling subunit (Minuchin, 1974). When the parental subunit is disrupted, a member of the sibling subunit may be expected to fill the empty parental role impacting the sibling subunit as well. When the missing family member is from the sibling subunit, the remaining siblings must adjust and carry on without the missing sibling.

Depending on which family member was incarcerated, the impact of their return may be quite different. When the returning member was a parent, the parental subsystem would adjust to include the reintegration of the missing parent. Parental roles and responsibilities will need to be renegotiated. Additionally, the child that stepped in to assume the missing parent's role will have to return to the sibling subunit, a shift in roles that may not be appreciated or respected, and depending on the length of incarceration, may not be realistic. If the returning member is from the sibling subunit, reintegration into the family requires less negotiation depending on which siblings remain in the home. Regardless of the returning member's relationship position, the family structure will be rigid in their absence as family members have moved on with their new role for several years so change will be slow and will take a great amount of intentionality and renegotiation.

Overview of Family Systems

The family is viewed as an emotional unit and conceptualized as a complete system (Bowen, 1978). By approaching the family from a systems approach, the members are seen as a whole rather than evaluated as parts. In this circular approach, relationships and interactions are explored as each member is interconnected to and impacts the others. Change occurs within the system rather than just within one individual, noting that the system will attempt to return to homeostasis, rejecting change. The therapist works to reinforce changes made in the system for lasting transformation.

Families must work together to provide for each person's needs (Bowen, 1978). This level of cooperation and cohesiveness also encourages emotional interdependence where one member's emotional state influences or impacts the emotional state of the remaining family members. Emotional reactivity can be both a positive or negative experience within the family system, depending on the emotion and subsequent impact. A change in one person will ripple out causing changes in the rest of the family. Because of the interdependence the family experiences, it is vital that family members are given the opportunity prior to release to resolve emotions related to the incarceration as well as prepare for changing roles within the family system.

Changes the Family Encounters During Re-Entry

From both a structural and systems approach, a change in the makeup of the family will affect all members. The family will need to be restructured and the roles renegotiated. The family will have to work out each member's new roles and responsibilities. Depending on the age of the member and the impact of incarceration, renegotiation may be met with resistance or outright refusal.

After release, it will need to be decided which family member takes the released individual to required appointments, such as probation/parole meetings, job interviews, and eventually work. The family will need to address any limitations that are imposed on them by the released individual returning home, such as the removal of firearms or alcohol. The family will also need to adjust to the released individual now being physically present and the impact their presence has on the family dynamic.

Needing to function within the restrictions of supervision may also frustrate some family members, making them feel as if they too are on probation or parole, and further paying the consequences of the choices of someone outside of themselves. Role confusion, based on the returning individual's perceptions of this prior to their confinement and expectations upon return may clash with those of the family members who have assumed their responsibilities during the absence. Confusion and resentments may occur throughout this process, leading to frustration on behalf of all involved.

The impact of stigma that the family has experienced throughout the period of incarceration, including during re-integration, is another change that will need to be addressed. Additionally, how they have coped with that in the past and how they will continue to deal with that moving forward will need to be explored. While the incarcerated individual has been serving the time mandated by their sentence, the family has been left to deal with the community response to the crime which can often be directed towards them. The shame they may feel about the crime committed or about the family member themselves will need to be addressed and also a plan made for how to cope with potential community reactions to release. Once returned to the family and society, the formerly incarcerated individual will need to face community reactions as well as those from their family regarding the crime they committed.

INTERVENTIONS FOR ASSISTING THE FAMILY THROUGH THE RE-ENTRY PROCESS

Interventions for the family needs to begin before the person is released from prison. Each member of the family will need individual therapy to address their feelings surrounding the incarceration, the crime that was committed, community response, and the loss of the individual in their lives. Additionally, each member will need to process the grief surrounding the loss they experienced when the person was incarcerated and what role that person will play in their lives upon return. Each family member will also need to deal with any shame they have experienced as a result of the returning individual's crime and the response from the community that they have had to navigate during the criminal proceedings, incarceration, or release. Ideally, individual therapy will occur shortly after the family member is incarcerated and will be revisited prior to release.

Upon release from incarceration, each member will need to be involved in family therapy. It will be important for the family to learn how to communicate with each other and to express feelings about what they have all experienced. Additionally, it will be important to address the changes that have to occur to reintegrate the missing family member, the roles that will adjust, the expectations, the responsibilities, and the overall impact to the family.

By focusing on the structure and functioning of the family itself, change occurs. By adjusting the organization of the family, members' positions are altered and every member of the family experiences change (Minuchin, 1974). By the counselor joining the family in recreating its structure and functioning, the counselor becomes a temporary additional family member during session, encouraging healthy changes and helping navigate conflict and struggles.

Family therapy would begin with a genogram, outlining the members of the family and demonstrating structurally where each member fits into the greater family system (Minuchin, 1974). In creating this analysis, the counselor can explore the roles members have had to take on with the absence of the incarcerated individual and provide a clear picture of the manner in which the family will need to be restructured to allow for re-entry. While exploring the structure of the family, interactions among members (boundaries) are addressed and rules and expectations developed to facilitate successful reunification. Typical daily routines can be explained but then adjusted to incorporate the returning family member, and an exploration of decision making within the family system completed to include the impact of the returning person. Additionally, family finances can be addressed as the burden on the family increases with the addition of the returning member, while also potentially decreasing with the returning member gaining employment and contributing to the overall financial picture.

As the amount of time in the home increases following re-entry, the family dynamics and conflicts will need to be addressed regularly. Rules, roles, and responsibilities will need to continue to adjust as the returning member integrates back into the family, gains employment, adheres to probation/parole requirements, and attends therapy appointments. To address family conflict, the counselor can utilize enactment to encourage the family to act out their disagreements, rather than to talk about it (Minuchin, 1974). This allows the counselor to make changes in the interactions among family members as they occur to create a healthier family interaction. Additionally, in addressing the various issues impacting the family, the counselor can strengthen each members' differentiation of self, creating a clear separation of emotional and intellectual functioning among family members, therefore creating an overall healthier system (Bowen, 1978).

IMPLICATIONS FOR COUNSELOR EDUCATORS, COUNSELORS, AND COMMUNITY AND SOCIAL JUSTICE ADVOCATES

Counselor educators are responsible for the development of knowledge, skill, and identity of those they teach. Understanding the barriers, issues, concerns, and stigma associated with release from confinement is necessary for counselors if they are to be a support to the individual, family, or both during this transition

(Salem et al., 2021). Understanding the unique needs of the released individual's criminogenic thinking, experiences within the incarcerated culture, their current plans for change, and the impact this has on their family and support system is significant and varies from those of the general population (Singer & Kopak, 2021). Focusing on developing a healthy support system while being able to be objective and holding the individual accountable for their consequences and change is important to any counselor, but especially so for those working with individuals returning to society (Kjellstrand et al., 2021).

The counselor educator must be aware of the unique cultural and personality factors of the criminogenic mind and the multifaceted re-entry needs they have. Sharing this knowledge with students will allow the future counselor to not only understand this unique population, but better plan for their treatment concerns throughout the incarceration and re-entry process. It is important that the family be included in this process (Baker et al., 2021; Hood & Gaston, 2021; Mancini et al., 2016; Rankins, 2022) and that the counselor learns to view the family as both a potential support for the individual but also a system that is made of up individuals who have their own thoughts, experiences, and roles within the re-entry process. This wholistic approach to counseling the re-entry population and their families ensures that each member is considered, and their needs met, thus enabling the process to be one of healthy growth and development for all involved.

Counselors who work with the families during re-integration will need to assist family members in renegotiating their roles and responsibilities within the family system. The role that the formerly incarcerated individual will play in the home will have to be made clear and the expectations laid out. Counselors in the community will need to work with the family prior to release and continue to provide family therapy for several months following re-entry. It is important that each family member be able to process the experience of incarceration and the loss they have felt from the missing family member while also adjusting to the member's return. Additionally, counselors within the prison can work with the incarcerated individual prior to release to understand the importance of the family's involvement in release preparation and planning and ongoing family therapy following release.

Community support and advocacy for families when re-integration occurs is vital. Popular Education (PE) is a theory and practice that utilizes a community-academic partnership wherein individuals share their life experiences to help others cope with stress thus increasing empowerment and improving well-being (Grieb, et al., 2014). PE may be facilitated in-person or virtually and may be led through efforts in academic institutions, churches, legal programs, or other similar organizations. It is a challenge to advocate for community change when it comes to re-integrating families. Within communities, change is occurring regarding perceptions of previously incarcerated individuals. Potential employers may be offered monetary incentives for hiring workers with a criminal record but may still view individuals re-entering as a liability.

Advocating for better mental health and addiction services for returning individuals within communities is critical, as well as counseling services for family members. Counseling benefits all family members and the community in which they reside. Communities and schools need to understand how to best support children of incarcerated parents in order to avoid behavioral or academic problems. Education is essential to raise awareness among community stakeholders to increase support programs.

SUMMARY

Incarceration impacts both the individual and their family. The individual is expected to work on themselves, improve their decision-making and coping skills, and return to the community as a healthy member of society. The family, left with a void the person once physically filled, must adjust to this by changing their roles and responsibilities to compensate for this loss. While re-entry is a main focus with the individual while incarcerated, it rarely involves family members in the process. How this transition transpires depends not only on the changes of the released person, but on the family's willingness to adjust roles and responsibilities again, their perception of the individual prior to and during confinement, and their experience of the incarceration overall. Additionally, the family's response to conditions of release placed on them simply by receiving the individual back into the home plays a role.

Changes within the family dynamic must be explored as each ripple throughout the family system. Interactions between and among members need to occur and may require outside assistance to allow for a healthy transition. Counselors, counselor educators, social justice advocates, and the community at large benefit from understanding the process of reentry for both the formerly incarcerated individual and their families. By strengthening the communication and understanding of this change, families will no longer find shame in asking for assistance during this realignment within the family dynamic and professionals in the field will be better prepared to assist them to ensure success for all involved. This results in healthier families, communities, and society.

REFERENCES

Austin, J. (2001). Prisoner reentry: Current trends, practices, and issues. *Crime and Delinquency*, *47*(3), 314–334. doi:10.1177/0011128701047003002

Baker, T., Mitchell, M. M., & Gordon, J. A. (2021). Prison visitation and concerns about reentry: Variations in frequency and quality of visits are associated with reentry concerns among people incarcerated in prison. *International Journal of Offender Therapy and Comparative Criminology*. Advance online publication. doi:10.1177/0306624X211013516 PMID:33940994

Barak, A., & Stebbins, A. (2017). Re-entry as performance: Reflections from Institution X. *Critical Social Policy*, *37*(2), 287–309. doi:10.1177/0261018316676732

Bowen, M. (1978). *Family Theory in Clinical Practice* (Vol. J). Aronson.

Comfort, M. (2016). "A twenty-hour-a-day job": The impact of frequent low-level criminal justice involvement on family life. *The Annals of the American Academy*, *665*(1), 63–79. doi:10.1177/0002716215625038 PMID:28935993

Cook, A., & Haynes, S. H. (2021). Imprisonment pains, reentry strains, and perceived likelihood of reoffending. *Criminal Justice Studies*, *34*(1), 16–32. doi:10.1080/1478601X.2020.1771332

Correa, N. P., Hayes, A. K., Bhalakia, A. M., Lopez, K. K., Cupit, T., Kwarteng-Amaning, V., Keefe, R. J., Greeley, C. S., & Van Horne, B. S. (2021). Parents' perspectives on the impact of their incarceration on children and families. *Family Relations*, *70*(1), 162–170. doi:10.1111/fare.12529

Desai, A., Durham, K., Burke, S. C., NeMoyer, A., & Heilbrun, K. (2021). Releasing individuals from incarceration during COVID-19: Pandemic-related challenges and recommendations for promoting successful reentry. *Psychology, Public Policy, and Law*, *27*(2), 242–255. doi:10.1037/law0000279

Franco-Paredes, C., Ghandnoosh, N., Latif, H., Krsak, M., Henao-Martinez, A. F., Robins, M., Vargas Barahona, L., & Poeschla, E. M. (2021). Decarceration and community re-entry in the COVID-19 era. *The Lancet. Infectious Diseases*, *21*(1), e11–e16. doi:10.1016/S1473-3099(20)30730-1 PMID:33007225

Galletta, E., Fagan, T. J., Shapiro, D., & Walker, L. E. (2021). Societal reentry of prison inmates with mental illness: Obstacles, programs, and best practices. *Journal of Correctional Health Care*, *27*(1), 58–65. doi:10.1089/jchc.19.04.0032 PMID:34232765

Gomes, S., & Rocker, D. (2021). Gender, incarceration and reentry: An analysis of the barriers to reentry of male and female adult prisoners in Portugal. In *Incarceration and Generation* (Vol. 1, pp. 255–299). Palgrave Macmillan. doi:10.1007/978-3-030-82265-1_8

Grieb, S. M. D., Crawford, A., Fields, J., Smith, H., Harris, R., & Matson, P. (2014). "The stress will kill you": Prisoner reentry as experienced by family members and the urgent need for support services. *Journal of Health Care for the Poor and Underserved*, *25*(3), 1183–1200. doi:10.1353/hpu.2014.0118 PMID:25130233

Harper, A., Ginapp, C., Bardelli, T., Grimshaw, A., Justen, M., Mohamedali, A., Thomas, I., & Puglisi, L. (2021). Debt, incarceration, and re-entry: A scoping review. *American Journal of Criminal Justice*, *46*(2), 250–278. doi:10.100712103-020-09559-9 PMID:32837173

Hood, B. J., & Gaston, S. (2021). How families respond to the collateral consequences of incarceration and prisoner reentry. *Family Relations*, fare.12616. Advance online publication. doi:10.1111/fare.12616

Johnson, E. I., & Easterling, B. (2012). Understanding unique effects of parental incarceration on children: Challenges, progress, and recommendations. *Journal of Marriage and Family*, *74*(2), 342–356. doi:10.1111/j.1741-3737.2012.00957.x

Kjellstrand, J., Matulis, J., Jackson, A., Smith, J., & Eddy, J. M. (2021). The Importance of Positive Social Support During Reentry From Prison: Examining the Role of Volunteer Mentoring. *International Journal of Offender Therapy and Comparative Criminology*.

Liu, L., & Visher, C. A. (2021). Decomposition of the role of family in reentry: Family support, tension, gender, and reentry outcomes. *Crime and Delinquency*, *67*(6-7), 970–996. doi:10.1177/0011128720987195

Mancini, C., Baker, T., Sainju, K. D., Golden, K., Bedard, L. E., & Gertz, M. (2016). Examining external support received in prison and concerns about reentry among incarcerated women. *Feminist Criminology*, *11*(2), 163–190. doi:10.1177/1557085115579483

Matthews, E. (2021). Peer focused pirsion re-entry programs: Which peer characteristics matter most? *Incarceration*, *2*(2), 1–19. doi:10.1177/26326663211019958

Minuchin, S. (1974). *Families and Family Therapy*. Harvard University Press. doi:10.4159/9780674041127

Morenoff, J. D., & Harding, D. J. (2014). Incarceration, prisoner reentry, and communities. *Annual Review of Sociology*, *40*(1), 411–429. doi:10.1146/annurev-soc-071811-145511 PMID:25400321

Nuño, L. F. (2021). Prisoner Re-Entry and Desistance. *Global Perspectives on People, Process, and Practice in Criminal Justice*, 99-109.

Rankins, L. (2022). *The Family Connection: Examining the Transitional Impact on Family Members of Returning Citizens Reentering Society*. Academic Press.

Salem, B. E., Kwon, J., Ekstrand, M. L., Hall, E., Turner, S. F., Faucette, M., & Slaughter, R. (2021). Transitioning into the community: Perceptions of barriers and facilitators experienced by formerly incarcerated, homeless women during reentry—A qualitative study. *Community Mental Health Journal*, *57*(4), 609–621. doi:10.100710597-020-00748-8 PMID:33387178

Silver, I. A., D'Amato, C., & Wooldredge, J. (2021). The cycle of reentry and reincarceration: Examining the influence on employment over a period of 18 years. *Journal of Criminal Justice*, *74*, 101812. doi:10.1016/j.jcrimjus.2021.101812

Singer, A. J., & Kopak, A. M. (2021). Jail reentry and gaps in substance use disorder treatment in rural communities. *Corrections: Policy, Practice and Research*, 1–23. doi:10.1080/23774657.2021.1967816

Steen, A. A. (2021). *From Bunks and Bars to Sidewalks and Skies: Support for Reentry from Incarceration*. Academic Press.

Strnadová, I., Clark, H. G., O'Neill, S. C., Cumming, T. M., Mathur, S. R., Wells, T. C., & Danker, J. (2022). Barriers to Community Re-entry for Incarcerated Youth: Stakeholders' Perspectives in Australia and the United States. In *Transition Programs for Children and Youth with Diverse Needs*. Emerald Publishing Limited. doi:10.1108/S1479-363620220000018017

Turanovic, J. J., Rodriguez, N., & Pratt, T. C. (2012). The collateral consequences of incarceration revisited: A qualitative analysis of the effects on caregivers of children of incarcerated parents. *Criminology*, *50*(4), 913–959. doi:10.1111/j.1745-9125.2012.00283.x

Wildeman, C., & Western, B. (2010). Incarceration in fragile families. *The Future of Children*, *2*(20), 157–177. doi:10.1353/foc.2010.0006 PMID:20964136

Chapter 15
Collateral Consequences:
Incarceration, Communities, and Reintegration

Eugenie Joan Looby
Mississippi State University, USA

Chiquita Long Holmes
Mississippi State University, USA

Tinmuk Li
Mississippi State University, USA

Lindsey Donald
Mississippi State University, USA

ABSTRACT

This chapter focuses on incarceration, communities, and the impact of community reentry programs on recidivism and reintegration. The authors provide demographic data on incarceration and recidivism and present information on community implications of incarceration. The authors also examine challenges facing previously incarcerated individuals as they return to their former communities and components of community reentry programs. The authors provide commentary on the efficacy of community reentry programs, advocacy initiatives, suggestions and recommendations, directions for future research, suggested readings, and a glossary of key terms and definitions.

INTRODUCTION

Most inmates in correctional institutions, when eventually released, attempt to reenter and reintegrate into communities or neighborhoods, some familiar, some adopted, and some new (Brine et al., 2021). This has resulted in increasing numbers of formerly incarcerated individuals who face innumerable obstacles, some greatly exacerbated by imprisonment, as they try to attain success post-release (Brine et

DOI: 10.4018/978-1-7998-9209-0.ch015

al., 2021; Ivery, 2020). Further, they are often confronted by an unforgiving public beset with negative attitudes about prison rehabilitation and a reluctance to grant "second chances." The social, economic, interpersonal, and psychological challenges that persist and impact this population and their surrounding networks are not clearly understood. These challenges can result in a plethora of difficulties that may result in severe collateral damage and lead to further reincarceration if not addressed. Counselors, social workers, community organizations, community reentry programs, corrections personnel, policymakers, politicians, and many other agents are positioned to articulate the concerns of this population. They can also provide needed resources and develop strategies to engender post-release benefits and reduce recidivism for previously incarcerated individuals.

This chapter focuses on community implications of incarceration and the impact of community reentry programs on recidivism and reintergration. The chapter begins with incarceration, release, and reentry data and the impact of high incarceration rates on communities. This is followed by information on challenges facing previously incarcerated individuals, components of community reentry programs, and research on their effectiveness. The chapter concludes with advocacy initiatives, suggestions, recommendations, future research directions, suggested readings, and a glossary of key terms and definitions.

BACKGROUND

There are nearly 2.3 million individuals, 25% of the world's prison population, incarcerated in the United States (U.S.) penal system, including federal, state, county, and military jails and psychiatric, reservation, and immigration detention centers (Sawyer & Wagner, 2020). State prison systems house the greatest number of inmates, with three states, Texas at 154,479, California at 122,417, and Florida at 96,009, holding the largest share (Sawyer & Wagner, 2020). Additionally, the federal prison system reports over 155,000 incarcerated individuals (Federal Bureau of Prisons, 2021).

Alper and colleagues (2018) examined rates of recidivism among individuals released from prison. The study reviewed the frequency of arrests for nine years following the initial prison release in 2005. They found that of the individuals released, 83% were rearrested, averaging five arrests per individual (Alper et al., 2018). Notably, rearrests do not constitute convictions of new crimes. It is challenging to ascertain a concise measure of recidivism based on new convictions, as most state correctional systems do not track this data (Sawyer & Wagner, 2020).

Many reasons are given as to why individuals reoffend, including limited legal employment opportunities, lack of available resources, challenges in funding and securing housing, denied public assistance, poverty, lack of education, and much more (Li, 2018; Western, 2018). The following section discusses community perspectives and experiences frequently faced by previously incarcerated individuals.

COMMUNITY PERSPECTIVES AND EXPERIENCES

This section discusses the reactions to previously incarcerated individuals reintegrating into communities. Discussed are stigma, support networks, neighborhoods and crime, family, employer attitudes, and police involvement.

Stigma

While reintegration forms an opportunity for previously incarcerated individuals to become functioning members of society (Quinn-Hogan, 2021), they face challenges reentering the community (Moore et al., 2013, 2016). While these challenges are numerous, a prominent issue is societal stigma (Moore et al., 2013). Referring to individuals as *ex-offenders* and *ex-prisoners* creates stigma by perceiving them as criminals (Obatusin & Ritter-Williams, 2019). The connotation associated with *ex-offender* lends the idea that a person is capable of deviance and recidivism.

Unfortunately, the stigmas associated with the previously incarcerated form barriers on the individual to receive necessary resources such as housing and education (Rade et al., 2016). These attitudes are typically associated with the offense type, rehabilitation participation, and mental illness (Rade et al., 2016). Specifically, community members report fears for safety (Barak & Stebbins, 2021) and disapprove of voting rights for previously incarcerated individuals (Rade et al., 2016). Previously incarcerated individuals who recidivate have often experienced stigmatization by their community members (Moore et al., 2013, 2016; Quinn-Hogan, 2021). Labels and discrimination impact one's social life causing previously incarcerated individuals to withdraw from others. This increases the probability of reconnection with other offenders (Moore et al., 2016), where criminal behavior is deemed acceptable and encouraged (Quinn-Hogan, 2021). Correlations were found between stigma and previously incarcerated individuals related to poor psychological and social functioning, depression, and low self-esteem (Moore et al., 2013).

Support Networks

The community also includes those in the previously incarcerated individual's support network upon reentry. The community members may be individuals within their original community or members of a new community. Quinn-Hogan (2021) noted that forming relationships in new communities generated decreases in recidivism rates. Additionally, creating new relationships resulted in improvement in psychosocial well-being. Nonetheless, the new communities may also lack the needed social and familial support to facilitate successful reintegration (Barak & Stebbins, 2021).

Neighborhoods and Crime

While numerous previously incarcerated individuals return to communities, a limited number of neighborhoods house them (Kirk, 2015). Typically, previously incarcerated individuals reside in a small region in metropolitan areas leaving these locations at risk for high crime rates (Chamberlain & Wallace, 2016).

Social bonds, institutional barriers, and parole policies often impact the decision-making process for residents living in these communities (Kirk, 2015). Heavily populated areas housing other previously incarcerated individuals may contribute to increases in criminal behavior (Chamberlain & Wallace, 2016). Kirk (2015) postulates a contagion effect by reinforcing criminal mindset and practices from the previously incarcerated to the neighborhood resident. Communities with high numbers of previously incarcerated individuals may reinforce increased criminal behavior. Neighborhoods with high crime rates experience continuous residential turnover, impacting the community members' ability to form sufficient social bonds (Chamberlain & Wallace, 2016).

Family

Once a family member faces incarceration, there are detrimental impacts on social bonds. More specifically, strained relationships result from an individual being incarcerated (Mowen & Visher, 2016). McKay et al. (2016) indicate that family relationships are pivotal when an individual is reintegrating into society. Upon being released into the community, previously incarcerated individuals rely on family and friends to survive; consequently, their reentry often places financial burdens on the family members (Chamberlain & Wallace, 2016). Individuals who have faced multiple convictions typically experience poorer relationships with their family members (Mowen & Visher, 2016). Results from a qualitative survey by Arditti & Parkman (2011) of perceptions of previously incarcerated males regarding reentry highlighted the importance of family support. Additionally, these results also showed that support from the family was conditional upon the individual's ability to be a contributing family member.

Employer Perspectives

As previously incarcerated individuals face negative perceptions from the community upon reentry (Obatusin & Ritter-Williams, 2019), they are denied employment opportunities and other constitutional rights such as voting (Rade et al., 2016). Upon being released into the community, previously incarcerated individuals seek out employment opportunities without success (Atkin & Armstrong, 2013). Successful reentry has been contingent on obtaining employment by allowing these individuals to earn wages and reconnect with lost relationships. Research indicates that unemployed individuals may often recidivate and go back to prison (Decker et al., 2015; Obatusin & Ritter-Williams, 2019). Obtaining employment post-release is challenging for previously incarcerated individuals due to lack of skill set, geographic location (Atkin & Armstrong, 2013), and education (Obatusin & Ritter-Williams, 2019), among other factors.

In addition to these personal barriers, previously incarcerated individuals have difficulty finding employment due to employer's negative perceptions (Bowman & Travis, 2012). Previously incarcerate individuals report beliefs of unsuccessful employment resulting from their identity and experiences with incarceration (Atkin & Armstrong, 2013). While laws protect individuals from workplace discrimination based on various aspects of identity, this lacks the protection of discriminating towards the label of an *offender*.

Earlier research delineates reluctance on behalf of employers to hire previously incarcerated individuals for reasons such as fear of harm, customer loss, and offender skill deficits (Giguere & Dundes, 2002). Other research illustrates other reasons for employer reluctance, including coworker and customer discomfort (Atkin & Armstrong, 2013; Obatusin & Ritter-Williams, 2019). One influence over employer perceptions of hiring previously incarcerated individuals is the criminal offense. As with people in the community (Rade et al., 2016), some employers have negative perceptions against specific crimes such as murder and sex offenses (Atkin & Armstrong, 2013). On the other hand, employers are less reluctant to hire individuals who have obtained a driving under the influence offense. In addition, geographic location plays a role due to the lack of employment in the areas where previously incarcerated individuals reside post-release.

Police Involvement

In recent years, research has been focused on high police involvement in areas that experience high crime rates (Kochel & Weisburd, 2017; Ratcliffe et al., 2015; Weisburd et al., 2011). These communities, known as *hot spots,* are typically located in urban areas and include heavy police involvement. Over 20 studies have demonstrated that heavy police involvement in *hot spot* areas decreases crime rates; nonetheless, there have been community concerns surrounding the increased police involvement (Kochel & Weisburd, 2017). Critics postulate that heavily policed areas may leave individuals in the community fearing they are the targets of the police involvement rather than being collaborators with the police in crime prevention (Ratcliffe et al., 2015). Individuals in these communities experience frustration and possible discrimination by the police, causing a reduction in trust (Kochel & Weisburd, 2017).

Additionally, living in a community labeled as a *hot spot* raises concerns for safety in its members by perceiving their environment as unsafe (Ratcliffe et al., 2015). The fear caused by over-police involvement eventually leads individuals to withdraw from their communities, increasing criminal behavior due to the perception of loss of social control (Weisburd et al., 2011). In addition to community obstacles, previously incarcerated individuals experience a plethora of circumstances that seem to discourage their successful reintegration. Some of these challenges are discussed below.

CHALLENGES FACING PREVIOUSLY INCARCERATED INDIVIDUALS

The consequences of incarceration place significant hardships on individuals returning to their communities. Incarceration disproportionately impacts racial minorities, amplifying the systematic challenges and discrimination faced by the previous incarcerated (The Sentencing Project, 2018; Western, 2018). This section discusses the physical and mental health challenges and the social, economic, and housing barriers faced by previously incarcerated individuals and offers strategies to support this population.

Physical Health

Research indicates that incarceration increases the risk for many health concerns, as previously incarcerated individuals report higher instances of chronic illness and infectious disease (Massoglia & Pridemore, 2015; Schnittker & John, 2007). Compared to the general population, incarcerated individuals are infected with hepatitis C up to 20 times the rate of other citizens (Varan et al., 2014). The risks of HIV and sexually transmitted diseases are also prevalent among incarcerated individuals. Moreover, higher instances of chronic physical illness, such as cancer, asthma, and hypertension, are found among the previously incarcerated (Massoglia & Pridemore, 2015; Wang et al., 2009).

Upon release, poor health outcomes are largely due to limited access to services and low help-seeking behaviors (Wildeman & Wang, 2017). Researchers argue that individuals incarcerated during young adulthood, when health attitudes are crystalized, sometimes lack the opportunity to explore and formalize positive health practices. Often, when released from prison, unhealthy habits persist, including smoking and poor diet and eating habits, leading to an increased risk of hypertension, diabetes, and cancer (Porter, 2014).

Further, the daily prison regimen, need for security, and lack of autonomy in the penal system do little to provide health education and patient navigation that promote disease management post-release

(Simon, 2013). Therefore, individuals returning to the community struggle to manage their illnesses and locate adequate and affordable healthcare to address their needs. Due to limited access to health services, communicable and chronic diseases often go untreated, leading to more severe illness and increased morbidity among the previously incarcerated (Massoglia & Pridemore, 2015).

Healthcare providers are essential to support previously incarcerated individuals. They address acute healthcare needs, provide necessary adjunctive medical support, including treatment navigation, disease management, and education, and link the previously incarcerated individuals to crucial resources such as Medicaid and reduced or free dental and pharmacy services (Wang et al., 2012). To support continuity of care, a peer support model that includes community healthcare managers who have also been incarcerated can be a helpful strategy in reducing the stigma and marginalization faced by previously incarcerated individuals. These peer health managers can normalize the post-release experience and provide guidance and support in navigating health system challenges (Tyler & Brockmann, 2017).

Mental Health

Mental health concerns, particularly those linked to trauma and stress, are more prevalent among previously incarcerated individuals (Massoglia, 2008). To illustrate, the Bureau of Justice Statistics (BJS) explains that more than 60% of individuals in county and city jails and 50% of individuals in statewide and federal prison systems report mental health concerns compared to 10% of the overall U.S. population (Bronson & Berzofsky, 2017). Further, the BJS revealed that severe and persistent mental illness, such as schizophrenia and severe depression, is approximately 2 to 4 times more prevalent among incarcerated individuals when compared to the general public (Bronson & Berzofsky, 2017; Tyler & Brockmann, 2017).

The structure and characteristics of correctional institutions are not conducive to emotional wellness, triggering mental illness for some. In other instances, the criminalization of substance-addicted individuals and those diagnosed with pre-existing mental illness translates into an increased number of individuals experiencing mental illness post-release (Steinberg et al., 2015). Though the need for mental health treatment among the previously incarcerated is great, barriers related to treatment access, including transportation and affordability, are significant roadblocks for this population (DeMartini et al., 2020). The inability to access treatment for mental health and substance use concerns is also linked to higher instances of recidivism. Referral, access, and continuation of mental health services are more likely to occur when the previously incarcerated individual is completing parole or probation and other post-release stipulations (Hamilton & Belenko, 2016).

The cumulative stress associated with community reentry can negatively impact the mental health of the previously incarcerated. Often probation and parole are contingent upon maintaining employment, suitable housing, and reliable transportation. Failure to comply with these requirements in a timely fashion can mean the revocation of probation or parole, with immediate return to prison. The obstacles of adjusting to living in the community and meeting the post-release demands can cause significant emotional distress for the previously incarcerated (Western, 2018). Further, Semenza & Link (2019) argue that repeated experiences of bias and marginalization around job seeking, housing, and access to services can diminish mental health over time.

The Mental Health Courts Program is a promising community-based strategy addressing the needs of the mentally ill while avoiding further criminalization and recidivism. A meta-analytic study conducted by Fox and colleagues (2021), examining 30 studies on mental health courts, found that mental health courts decreased incarceration rates by more than 70%. Additionally, state and city government jurisdictions report a reduction in criminal justice expenditures due to the implementation of mental health courts (Costopoulos & Wellman, 2017; Steinberg et al., 2015).

Social Impact of Incarceration

The social implication of prior incarceration is delineated by several factors that impact housing, help-seeking, physical and mental health, and family support. Supportive relationships positively affect community reentry and increase physical and emotional wellness (DeMartini et al., 2020; Wallace et al., 2016). Incarceration places a substantial burden on family integration and the maintenance of relationships, weakening the protective factors that positive socialization and healthy relationships provide against mental illness, homelessness, and financial hardships (Wallace et al., 2016; Western, 2018).

Even with a supportive family relationship, addressing the needs of the previously incarcerated individual can sometimes create strain for family members attempting to provide housing, transportation, financial, and emotional support for the previously incarcerated family member while managing their own needs. Additionally, many previously incarcerated individuals return to the family to find that many factors have changed, and significant family milestones have occurred while away. Navigating the changes and discovering where they fit in the family unit can be difficult and lead to emotional distress for the previously incarcerated individual and their family members (Mowen & Visher, 2016; Western, 2018).

In some instances, post-release rules and conditions stipulate where and with whom the previously incarcerated individuals can interact. As a result, reconnecting with friends and family members whom themselves have had previous criminal involvement, despite the family or friends' rehabilitation or their having no further criminal offenses, can place probation or parole in jeopardy. These policies may leave the previously incarcerated individual with a limited support group, fueling alienation and distress (Binnall, 2019). To encourage social reintegration into communities and families, previously incarcerated individuals may benefit from a broad array of social supports. For example, mentoring, apprenticeships, specialized support groups, and spiritual engagement all help to encourage prosocial behaviors (Price-Tucker et al., 2019).

Housing

Stable housing is an essential link in successful community reentry for the previously incarcerated individual, as it provides a foundation for successful post-release activities. Without stable housing, it is challenging to rebuild and maintain social relationships, gain employment, and access services (Keene et al., 2018). However, discriminatory housing practices make it difficult for the previously incarcerated to secure stable housing. Moreover, the rising cost of housing in the private market, coupled with the shortage of subsidized and low-income housing in communities, disproportionately impacts the previously incarcerated. Though Public Housing Authorities (PHAs) have the discretion to rent to previously incarcerated individuals, they are typically highly selective and exclusionary when considering these individuals as tenants (Curtis et al., 2013). Federal laws further restrict previously incarcerated individuals' access to low-income housing, including the Cranston-Gonzalez National Affordable Housing Act of 1990 (NAHA). This law imposes a 3-year moratorium on access to subsidized housing on former tenants convicted of crimes, including substance-related offenses. Housing policies that evaluate prospective tenants individually and avoid making negative assumptions about previously incarcerated individuals can help decrease housing discrimination and sigma (Curtis et al., 2013; Keene et al., 2018).

Employment

Securing stable employment supports previously incarcerated individuals' financial, housing, and food security and decreases recidivism. However, the stigma of having spent time incarcerated often makes it challenging to find employment that provides a living wage. Consequently, despite their skill set, individuals returning to the community may be relegated to low-wage jobs that offer limited financial security and little opportunity for advancement (Western, 2018).

Previously incarcerated individuals experience unemployment five times the rate of the general U.S. population (Semenza & Link, 2019; Western, 2018). The authors also explain that systemic barriers and stigma associated with incarceration and physical and mental health challenges adversely impact employment. Moreover, securing employment post-incarceration is significantly more difficult for previously incarcerated Black men when compared to their White counterparts (Couloute & Kopf, 2018; Garretson, 2016; Western, 2018). For example, a study conducted by Pager et al. (2009) found that the African American candidate was significantly less likely to be offered employment of applicants with similar qualifications and matching resumes. Certificates of employment and rehabilitation may decrease the challenge of securing a job and reduce collateral consequences that adversely impact previously incarcerated individuals (Garretson, 2016).

The next section discusses reentry programs. These are programs designed to help previously incarcerated individuals reintegrate into society by developing skills for success and reducing reoffending.

CREATING SUCCESSFUL REENTRY PROGRAMS

A salient element of effective crime prevention initiatives is evaluating the effectiveness of community integration practices and programs targeting reducing recidivism. Called reentry programs or community reentry programs, they cover a variety of interventions, skill sets, and services designed to help previously incarcerated individuals to reintegrate back into society successfully (Gill & Wilson, 2016; Festen et al., 2002; Griffiths et al., 2007; Morenoff & Harding, 2014). Components may include employment and vocational training, substance abuse and mental health treatment, housing, and developing effective interpersonal skills and peer support (Coates, 2015; Cortes & Rogers, 2010; Gill & Wilson, 2016; Li, 2018; Visher & Mallik-Kane, 2007).

These initiatives present a concerted effort by many stakeholders, including but not limited to the justice system, community agencies, and faith-based and other organizations targeting specific populations of previously incarcerated individuals. These initiatives target specific risk factors and challenges aligned with recidivism, such as the following: substance abuse, unemployment, lack of job skills, limited education, limited housing, mental health issues, limited or poor social networks, poor life skills, financial constraints, health and psychosocial problems, legal issues, and loss of civil rights (Coates, 2015; Cortes & Rogers, 2010; Denckla & Berman, 2001; Dougherty, 2012; Festen et al., 2002; Hammett et al.,1999; McVey, 2001; Nelson & Trone, 2000; Ortiz, 2000; Travis et al., 2001). Others may focus on specific groups, for example, chronic repeaters, drug addicts, women, youths, or children of incarcerated parents (Griffiths et al., 2007).

Elements of Community-Based Reentry Programs

Reentry programs can be classified into several categories: institutional programs, surveillance programs, support programs (community-based programs), and integrated programs. Each has its strengths, challenges, focus, and needs. Community-based reentry programs are designed to provide a continuum of care begun during incarceration, with the end goal being successful community integration of previously incarcerated individuals. The previously incarcerated individual and a case manager identify, analyze, document, and create a plan to achieve specific goals (Hunter et al., 2016). According to Ivery (2020), the individual utilizes the program's offerings to complete the stated goals, with the understanding that the individual's needs should be matched with specific program types. Each program has different components and criteria; not all programs offer every service. If the previously incarcerated individual's needs do not match the program type, referral to another program is made (Ivery, 2020). Articulated below are some of the more common components of community reentry programs.

Housing

As mentioned earlier, previously incarcerated individuals are challenged to find stable, suitable living accommodations because of restrictive policies, discriminatory practices, and financial insecurity (Cortes & Rogers, 2010; Curtis et al., 2013; Li, 2018). Further, the lack of stable housing may lead to homelessness, drug use, and further crime (Baldry et al., 2003; Fontaine, 2013; Li, 2018). Some returning incarcerated individuals reside with families, close friends, or significant others (Roman & Travis, 2004). If those options are not available, having access to a secure living facility such as community-based correctional housing, a variety of inexpensive housing options, and halfway houses, instead of homeless shelters or cheap and dilapidated hotels and motels in high crime areas, facilitates a more successful community transition and lessens the possibility of reoffending. Community reentry programs that include housing as part of their services address these needs and promote the dissolution of policies that promote housing discrimination against this population. Several researchers have found an indirect link between the lack of accommodations and recidivism, unemployment, education, and substance abuse (Harper & Chitty, 2004; Nilsson, 2003).

Education

Brazzell and colleagues (2009) reported that 65% of prisoners have some high school education compared with 82% of the general population, while Holzer et al. (2003) claim that 70% of released offenders have dropped out of high school, 50% classified as illiterate, and 19% have under eight years of education. Brazzell et al. (2009) and Harlow (2003) contend that the number of prisoners with a GED (General Education Diploma) has increased because they were obtained in prison; however, those having school diplomas have declined. Research has further indicated that inmates who successfully complete secondary GED programs or adult basic education in prison have significantly reduced recidivism rates and improved chances of employment after release (Steurer & Smith, 2003).

Because education is an essential element of workforce participation and reduced recidivism, many community-based reentry programs have inserted focused educational initiatives for previously incarcerated individuals. These programs vary in activity and intensity. For example, some programs offer GED preparation courses and post-secondary education, career and technical education, employment training, college enrollment assistance and referrals, special education, vocational training, financial incentives, and tutoring (Taliaferro & Pham, 2018). Research has found that inmates who take advantage of prison education programs are 43% less likely to engage in criminal activity; however, educational programs are sparse in prisons and even less common in the reentry communities. Because each dollar spent on prison education saves close to four dollars on re-incarceration costs (Brazell et al., 2009), all community reentry programs and entities that promote prison rehabilitation must provide these services.

Employment

Employment is a determining factor in affecting successful community reentry. For previously incarcerated individuals, barriers to securing gainful employment include lack of job contacts, no callbacks for interviews, inadequate or poor basic skills, limited qualifications, limited education, spotty work history, limited training, credentialing, licensure or certification to perform the job, and employer stigma towards hiring previously incarcerated individuals (Fletcher, 2002; Holzer et al., 2003; McGrew & Hanks, 2017). Many states deny jobs to previously incarcerated individuals; therefore, they are forced to occupy low-skill jobs that provide limited benefits and little upward and financial mobility (Brazell et al., 2009; Li, 2018). Additionally, previously incarcerated individuals who find jobs are hired at wages lower than before their incarceration (Visher et al., 2008).

Some community reentry programs have included vocational training and employment assistance as part of their offerings. However, these programs must offer opportunities to obtain high-quality jobs with upward trajectories, longevity, and decent wage-earning potential as these elements play a significant factor in determining successful reentry (Griffiths et al., 2007). Participation in legitimate workforce for over six months can reduce recidivism rates, help develop social capital in previously incarcerated individuals, and limit exposure to criminal behavior (Gill & Wilson, 2016; Ramakers et al., 2017). Additionally, employed previously incarcerated individuals are more likely than their unemployed counterparts to remain arrest-free. Participants in prison-based vocational training are more likely to find employment after release (Wilson et al., 2000). Ethridge and colleagues (2014) explain that vocational programs in prisons and communities are designed to help previously incarcerated individuals with specific skill sets transferable upon release into communities. However, many individuals may not take advantage of these programs while in prison, and many of these programs may not be available during incarceration. This does not limit their participation in these programs upon release; however, they may find themselves with skill deficits and unable to pursue immediate viable employment.

Vocational Training

Many programs require their participants to receive certifications and vocational training before being considered for employment. Studies have shown that when an employer sees credentials on a previously incarcerated individual's resume, it sets that person apart from other candidates applying for the same job (National Institute of Corrections, 2019). Community-based programs that provide training and placement services to previously incarcerated individuals may include educational employment training, holistic support, soft skills training, GED classes, one on one mentorship, entrepreneurial skills, writing business plans, filing taxes, meeting etiquette resumes, job readiness classes, vocational education, job training, placement, and monitoring (Klein & Mohan, 2016; Visher & Mallik-Kane, 2007). These programs have had varied outcomes and are not available in enough numbers to service previously incarcerated individuals needing gainful employment.

Griffiths and colleagues (2007) emphasized the following: individual needs of previously incarcerated individuals must be identified and matched with specific services; employment services must be provided continuously from the time of incarceration until release; and assessments must occur early and be used to determine employment delivery services. The success of employment readiness of previously incarcerated individuals is contingent on collaboration with critical stakeholders such as prisons and parole agencies, program staff, public and private job sectors, community reentry programs, and the previously incarcerated person who is not hampered by barriers that limit employability (Decker et al., 2015; Ethridge et al., 2014; Griffiths et al., 2007).

Substance Abuse and Mental Health

Substance use and addiction represent major challenges for previously incarcerated individuals, and many have had past drug abuse histories (Begun et al., 2016; Belenko, 2006; Li, 2018). For example, participants in a returning home study used drugs and drank alcohol to intoxication at least weekly prior to prison; about 83% of state inmates had a history of drug use; 70% reported drug use regularly; only 24% of inmates in state prison participate in drug treatment programs while incarcerated; nearly half of state prisons offer no treatment or minimal treatment; thus, substance abusers returning to their communities relapse quickly (Foley & Gao, 2002; Visher et al., 2010). Certain drugs are strongly linked to criminal behavior, especially to maintain the drug habit (Gottfredson et al., 2003; Uggen & Thompson, 2003). Few individuals receive drug treatment in prison, and still fewer are able to continue their treatment in the community (Hunter et al., 2016), limiting their ability to secure gainful employment and affordable housing and increasing their chances to reoffend (Belenko, 1998).

Substance abuse and mental health treatment programs are offered in some community reentry programs. Treatment interventions are provided via residential programs, outpatient treatment programs, detoxification services, therapeutic communities, aftercare, and drug court and may include social skills training, drug testing, individual and group counseling, case management and supervision, and counseling (Chanhatasilpa et al., 2000). Research indicates that successes made during prison treatment can be maintained if the previously incarcerated individual is provided with aftercare support upon release. Those who participate both in prison treatment and aftercare programming fare best in reducing recidivism outcomes and successful community reentry (Chanhatasilpa et al., 2000).

Families and Social Supports

As mentioned earlier, family members provide critical support for previously incarcerated individuals as they attempt to reintegrate into post-prison life. Some studies have found a positive relationship between solid family support and reduced reoffending (Baldry et al., 2003; McKay et al., 2016; Women's Prison Association, 1996). However, additional challenges such as ambivalence about the previously incarcerated individual's return, strained relationships, parent-child incarceration issues, dependency on others, and struggles with role identity and responsibilities may further distress everyone involved.

To address some of these barriers, community reentry programs must address creating successful family relationships, especially since attitudes about the previously incarcerated individual may differ pre and post-release. Services that address financial hardships, family support and cohesion, reentry resource support, financial management and stability, transitional living assistance, peer mentoring, counseling, employment support, maintaining contact with family and incarcerated members, parenting classes for incarcerated individuals, and parent support groups can be much-needed additions (McKay et al., 2016; Price-Tucker et al., 2019). Festen (2002) suggests that family therapy, anger management and conflict resolution classes, parenting skills training, family bridge-building, and child reunification are extremely beneficial family services.

Interpersonal Skills

According to Nelson & Trone (2000), previously incarcerated individuals need training in managing time, communicating effectively, problem-solving and addressing conflicts, prosocial activities, managing anger effectively, and making sound decisions. The authors reiterate the utility of applying cognitive-behavioral interventions, common in correctional environments, to help previously incarcerated individuals address these deficits. This training can be done close to release as well. Some community reentry programs include these components, as they are vital to successful community engagement, employment, and integration.

Mentoring

Because of limited or severely weakened social relationships, previously incarcerated individuals make significant gains by engaging in mentoring relationships as they prepare for community reentry. Community-based reentry programs may provide extensive mentoring for previously incarcerated individuals, utilizing mentors from all strata of life as positive role models of guidance and support (Hucklesby & Wincup, 2014). Mentors serve as peer supports during tough times, accountability guides, decision-making helpers, and advocates. For example, mentoring has increased job obtainment and security and decreased recidivism rates (Fletcher & Sherk, 2009; McDaniel, 2014). Results from a study by Kavanagh & Borrill (2013) indicated that mentors had a positive experience building their mentees' trust, while Buck's (2016) study found that mentees admired their mentors and desired to engage in social imitation of their mentors to improve themselves.

Case Management

Previously incarcerated individuals in community-based reentry programs have case managers to help them navigate the challenges inherent in the community reentry process. Case managers perform the following essential services: goal attainment and resource building between client needs and external services; conduct intakes to get client background information, readiness for the program, and best fit; and administer needs assessments to ascertain client-program matching and placement (Hunter et al., 2016). According to Hunter and colleagues (2016), they also engage in service planning focused on client goals and objectives, adjusting these plans when necessary and coordinating service delivery. Most importantly, they monitor client progress, evaluate the effectiveness of that progress, and serve as the client's first line of defense against challenges and risks of recidivism (Ivery, 2020).

COMMUNITY COLLABORATION AND PROGRAM INTEGRATION

Community reentry programs thrive because of community collaboration and commitment to helping previously incarcerated individuals flourish upon release from prison. Communities play a key role in successful integration. However, efforts must be collaborative, integrated, needs-based, and reflect a seamless structure of support and assistance from stakeholders. This section discusses developing successful community collaboration, elements of successful community reentry programs, and reviews existing research on these programs.

Community Collaboration

Griffiths and colleagues (2007) and Shaw (2006) offer recommendations for developing successful community collaboration initiatives. Among the most salient are the following: glean active and committed support; create multiple avenues of delivering information; employ multifaceted initiatives to addressing crime; employ best communication strategies; create parallel partnerships and reduce duplication of efforts; engage underserved and vulnerable populations in planning; design transparent decision making and accountability models; employ evidence-based evaluation and assessment; provide incentives for local ownership of initiatives; match programs to previously incarcerated individual's needs; and mobilize system-wide, integrative, consistent approaches and responses to behavior.

Elements of Successful Community Reentry Programs

Andrews & Bonta (2010) developed a list of interventions to guide successful reentry programs. They include the following: program and individual needs match; comprehensive needs assessment; accountability; varying and balanced surveillance; wrap-around comprehensive and integrative services; multiple agency support and partnerships; transparent roles and responsibilities; appropriate service and delivery timelines; comprehensive case and management systems; programs matched with community issues; community investment; evidence-based evaluation methods; program begins from incarceration confinement through stabilization and reintegration.

What Works

Gill & Wilson (2016) reported that special needs reentry programs (e.g., vocational training, drug treatment) may or may not reduce recidivism, while generalized services (e.g., halfway houses) did not. Similarly, Seiter & Kadela (2003) found variations in the impact of specific types and combinations of services in reentry programs. Services addressing employment and housing were less successful than those addressing substance abuse and education. James (2015) reviewed 22 studies on the effectiveness of reentry programs focused on substance abuse, adult basic education, GED training, and halfway houses. They concluded that methodological flaws and poor program evaluation, among a variety of other factors, impact the success or failure of a program. The research on recidivism suggests that it may be more beneficial for previously incarcerated individuals to access reentry services their first year after release; this is when they are most vulnerable to recidivate (James, 2015).

Additionally, several reasons are given for the mixed program's lack of success. They are as follows: theory or program failure; poor program; poor needs matching; the highest risk populations not targeted;

risk factors, learning styles, gender, race/ethnicity not considered; gaps between service provision and reentry; therapeutic philosophy; poor resources; limited collaboration between prison and community; and most importantly, a lack of fit (Andrews & Bonta, 2010; Lipsey, 2009; Seiter & Kadela, 2003).

A report issued by Muhlhausen (2018) focused on reentry programs and promising practices about adult recidivism. The conclusion was that lack of empirical rigor casts doubt on the effectiveness of community reentry programs, and the reason for their success or failure are complex. To reinforce whether or not community reentry programs reduce recidivism, Muhlhausen (2018) cited several major studies. First, Seven Second Chance Adult Demonstration Programs across different sites and involving 966 participants were evaluated. The Second Chance Act includes reentry programs funded by the U.S. Department of Justice and offers comprehensive services (e.g., case management, education, employment counseling, and housing) to previously incarcerated individuals. At the 18 and 30-month follow-up, the programs had little effect on arrests, convictions, and incarcerations.

Similarly, in examining six different employment programs involving over 8,000 participants, there was no significant diminishing of arrests or incarceration at the two-year and three-year follow-up. What gains that were made faded by the third year. Muhlhausen (2018) pointed out that employment and training are paramount in preventing reoffending; however, scant employment programs show success in reducing recidivism, and programs focused solely on jobs do not bode well for success. Successful reentry is a much more multifaceted undertaking.

ADVOCACY

The U.S. leads the world in the number of citizens incarcerated; however, until recently, the implications of mass incarceration on the individual, family, and community have not been fully understood. People of color are most impacted by incarceration, and the fallout is multidimensional (Wiseman et al., 2017). The resultant sequelae of mass incarceration experienced by families have left profound collateral damage in many life domains, particularly for underserved populations. For example, family well-being, family structure, overall family quality of life, loss of income, children with disengaged parents, multigenerational trauma, parentified children, and impoverished communities with lost social capital are some of some of the consequences engendered by the ongoing systemic failures of the U.S. criminal justice system (Savat, 2021).

Addressing mass incarceration is a social justice, human dignity, professional and personal imperative (Lee, 2018; Pettus-Davis & Epperson, 2015). Therefore, developing an array of strategies that focus on prevention, intervention, and rehabilitation is key. Additionally, supportive modalities to prevent recidivism and help underserved families and communities adversely impacted by mass incarceration are necessary (Pettus-Davis & Epperson, 2015). Advocacy on several levels is critical for addressing the systemic challenges of mass incarceration in the U.S. This section outlines professional and policy advocacy initiatives to address incarceration, rehabilitation, and community reintegration.

Professional Advocacy

- Advocate for prison reforms and minimum sentencing laws.
- Advocate for funding for initiatives that address the needs of previously incarcerated individuals and their families.

- Address local school district policies that favor police involvement over prevention and age-appropriate behavioral interventions to disrupt the school-to-prison pipeline.
- Encourage community engagement that addresses mass incarceration and over-policing on previously incarcerated individuals and their families.
- Provide and disseminate information to previously incarcerated individuals about food banks, legal aid, community and religious organizations, shelters, free healthcare, and social support.
- Advocate for strengths-based opportunities for volunteerism and community engagement that decreases stigma and allows for personal atonement.
- Engage and educate counseling professionals through scholarship, research, and creating courses for counselor trainees that delineate the mental health risks and challenges of incarceration.
- Develop multidisciplinary community teams to address the needs of children and families impacted by incarceration.
- Collaborate with community stakeholders to provide resource fairs inside jails and prisons that provide essential information related to mental and physical health, employment, mentoring, internet access, skills for daily living, and links to community support.

Policy Initiatives

- Require all law enforcement jurisdictions to maintain a full range of recidivism data.
- Increase federal and state funding that addresses substance dependence and mental illness.
- Encourage city governments to address discriminatory housing policies that disenfranchise previously incarcerated individuals.
- Evaluate policies that keep individuals in jail without being formally convicted.
- Establish community resource centers and apprenticeship programs that focus on job skills and trades to support employment.

SOLUTIONS AND RECOMMENDATIONS

Price-Tucker and colleagues (2019) provided solutions and recommendations integral to the success of community reentry programs. Areas included health, employment, housing, education, skill development, mentorship, social networks, and institutional intervention. Programs must address the following components:

Health

Employ integrative physical, mental, and substance abuse care; include support groups and a continuum of treatment and counseling services; partner with correctional facilities and state governments to obtain critical health data; provide comprehensive health and trauma coverage to females.

Employment

Emphasize training and job placement; focus on placement in a job with future growth potential; vocational education, GED training, and entrepreneurship are critical; ascertain job opportunities in reentry neighborhoods; create partnerships with prisons to re-direct incarcerated individuals to healthy neighborhoods.

Housing

Integrate services (e.g., employment services, health services, social skills); focus on groups vulnerable to housing insecurities (women, underserved racial and ethnic populations, and the elderly); housing for reentry women must consider safety, security, and affordability issues; provide a variety of available housing.

Education

Include employment training, college entry, referral service, GED assistance, and vocational training; match programs to different age demographics.

Interpersonal Skills

Offer programs that develop skills such as anger management, goal setting, parenting, and conflict resolution; target antisocial peer involvement; employ evidenced-based cognitive-behavioral practices to reduce specific behaviors.

Mentorship

Promote mentoring programs; engage in mentor-mentee matching of similar backgrounds; create same gender and needs matching; pair on racial, SES, and other demographics; determine priorities for each group.

Social Networks

Stress family support and connection; help previously incarcerated women before release to build strong family ties; provide wrap-around services to address gender-specific needs; provide financial incentives as needed.

Institutional Intervention

Develop collaborative partnerships between the prison and community reentry programs, health care facilities, employers, educational institutions, and faith-based organizations that complement each other's strengths and weaknesses to facilitate continuity of care and avoid recidivism; teach incarcerated individuals skills necessary for successful real-life transition.

DIRECTIONS FOR FUTURE RESEARCH

Below are some suggestions for future research on the community impact of incarceration and community reentry programs.

- Develop rigorous empirical research designs focused on recidivism.
- Explore research investigating the impact of "heavy" policing on public safety.
- Engage in research focused on the school to prison pipeline.
- Examine research focused on interrupting generational incarceration.

CASE STUDY

The Case of Janessa

Janessa is a 25-year-old biracial lesbian. She served five years in prison and has struggled to find employment and develop meaningful family connections. Her mother was incarcerated for forgery and mail fraud when Janessa was 14. During her mother's incarceration, Janessa's parents divorced. A year later, her father remarried. Janessa did not feel connected to her stepmother and stepsiblings, as she was an only child. Because of the strained relationship between Janessa, her father, and her stepmother, Janessa lived with her maternal grandmother. When Janessa's mother was released from prison, Janessa was 19. Once released from prison, Janessa's mother moved in with Janessa and her grandmother, who had several health challenges and limited income. Janessa's mother's prison record prevented her from engaging in substantive employment to support the family financially. As a result, Janessa, who had a lot of automotive knowledge and worked at a local upscale car dealership, began to engage in opportunities to support the family. Such opportunities began with "taking" parts from abandoned cars and selling them. Soon Janessa learned that parts such as catalytic converters from newer cars brought much higher prices. Gradually, she began to steal catalytic converters from cars at work, sometimes one over several weeks, until she was stealing three or four per week. The management noticed the missing parts, which Janessa admitted to taking. Janessa was fired from the dealership and charged with theft. Janessa pleaded guilty and was sentenced to five years in prison. While in prison, her father visited her often, and they have seemingly reconciled.

QUESTIONS FOR CONSIDERATION

1. Not all individuals faced with difficult circumstances commit crimes. In Janessa's case, what might have been some factors that contributed to the choices she made?
2. What are some early interventions or preventative measures that could have been employed in this situation?
3. What are the most important components required for Janessa's reentry into the community?
4. What struggles might Janessa experience during this process (e.g., psychological, social, economic, physical)?

5. How would you support Janessa in reintegrating with her family, including the mother, grandmother, father, stepmother, and stepsiblings?
6. Develop an advocacy initiative that addresses Janessa's needs. Choose any initiative that stands out for you.

CONCLUSION

Previously incarcerated individuals experience a plethora of social, economic, psychological, and environmental challenges that may impede their successful reintegration into communities. These challenges also inflict substantial collateral damage to their families. Professionals can serve as conduits of understanding and change by providing needed resources and advocating for revamping policies and entrenched systems that undermine previously incarcerated individuals' success and human dignity. In doing so, the previously incarcerated individual, the family, and society benefit. Successful community integration is contingent upon collaboration and participation by everyone. This is an ethical and legal imperative.

REFERENCES

Alper, M., Durose, M. R., & Markman, J. (2018). *2018 Update on prisoner recidivism: A 9-year follow-up period (2005-2014)* (NCJ 250975). Bureau of Justice Statistics. https://bjs.ojp.gov/content/pub/pdf/18upr9yfup0514.pdf

Andrews, D. A., & Bonta, J. (2010). *The psychology of criminal conduct* (5th ed.). LexisNexis.

Arditti, J. A., & Parkman, T. (2011). Young men's reentry after incarceration: A developmental paradox. *Family Relations Interdisciplinary Journal of Applied Family Science*, *60*(2), 205–220. doi:10.1111/j.1741-3729.2010.00643.x

Atkin, C. A., & Armstrong, G. S. (2013). Does the concentration of parolees in a community impact employer attitudes toward the hiring of ex-offenders? *Criminal Justice Policy Review*, *24*(1), 71–93. doi:10.1177/0887403411428005

Baldry, E., McDonnell, D., Maplestone, P., & Peeters, M. (2003). *Ex-prisoners and accommodation: What bearing do different forms of housing have on social reintegration?* (No.46). Australian Housing and Urban Research Institute. https://www.ahuri.edu.au/__data/assets/pdf_file/0005/2210/AHURI_Final_Report_No46_Ex_prisoners_and_accomodation.pdf

Barak, A., & Stebbins, A. (2021). Anticipated alienation and critical social work: Ex-offenders' perspectives on re-entry. *British Journal of Social Work*, *51*(1), 38–56. doi:10.1093/bjsw/bcaa069

Begun, A. L., Early, T. J., & Hodge, A. (2016). Mental health and substance abuse service engagement by men and women during community reentry following incarceration. *Administration and Policy in Mental Health*, *43*(2), 207–218. doi:10.100710488-015-0632-2 PMID:25663094

Belenko, S. (1998). Research on drug courts: A critical review. *National Drug Court Institute Review, 1*(1), 1-42. https://www.ndci.org/sites/default/files/ndci/CASA.Bekenko.1998.pdf

Belenko, S. (2006). Assessing released inmates for substance-abuse-related service needs. *Crime and Delinquency, 52*(1), 94–113. doi:10.1177/0011128705281755

Binnall, J. M. (2019). Divided we fall: Parole supervision conditions prohibiting "inter-offender" associations. *University of Pennsylvania Journal of Law and Social Change, 22*(1), 25-69. https://scholarship.law.upenn.edu/jlasc/vol22/iss1/3

Bowman, S. W., & Travis, R. Jr. (2012). Prisoner reentry and recidivism according to the formerly incarcerated and reentry service providers: A verbal behavior approach. *The Behavior Analyst Today, 13*(3-4), 9–19. doi:10.1037/h0100726

Brazzell, D., Crayton, A., Mukamal, D. A., Solomon, A. L., & Lindahl, N. (2009). *From the classroom to the community: Exploring the role of education during incarceration and reentry*. Urban Institute: Justice Policy Center. https://files.eric.ed.gov/fulltext/ED508246.pdf

Brine, K., Power, J., Smith, H. P., & Nolan, A. (2021). A qualitative study of success in postrelease federal inmates with mental health issues. *Journal of Correctional Health Care, 27*(1), 40–50. doi:10.1089/jchc.19.02.0009 PMID:34232766

Bronson, J., & Berzofsky, M. (2017). *Indicators of mental health problems reported by prisoners and jail inmates, 2011–12* [Special report] (NCJ 250612). Bureau of Justice Statistics. https://bjs.ojp.gov/content/pub/pdf/imhprpji1112.pdf

Buck, G. (2016). "I wanted to feel the way they did": Mimesis as a situational dynamic of peer mentoring by ex-offenders. *Deviant Behavior, 38*(9), 1027–1041. doi:10.1080/01639625.2016.1237829

Chamberlain, A. W., & Wallace, D. (2016). Mass reentry, neighborhood context and recidivism: Examining how the distribution of parolees within and across neighborhoods impacts recidivism. *Justice Quarterly, 33*(5), 912–941. doi:10.1080/07418825.2015.1012095

Chanhatasilpa, C., MacKenzie, D. L., & Hickman, L. J. (2000). The effectiveness of community-based programs for chemically dependent offenders: A review and assessment of research. *Journal of Substance Abuse Treatment, 19*(4), 383–393. doi:10.1016/S0740-5472(00)00131-8 PMID:11166503

Coates, T. N. (2015). *The Black family in the age of mass incarceration*. The Atlantic. https://www.theatlantic.com/magazine/archive/2015/10/the-black-family-in-the-age-of-mass-incarceration/403246/

Cortes, K., & Rogers, S. (2010). *Reentry housing options: The policymakers' guide*. The Council of State Governments. https://csgjusticecenter.org/wp-content/uploads/2020/02/Reentry_Housing_Options-1.pdf

Costopoulos, J. S., & Wellman, B. L. (2017). The effectiveness of one mental health court: Overcoming criminal history. *Psychological Injury and Law, 10*(3), 254–263. doi:10.100712207-017-9290-x

Couloute, L., & Kopf, D. (2018). *Out of prison & out of work: Unemployment among formerly incarcerated people*. Prison Policy Initiative. https://www.prisonpolicy.org/reports/outofwork.html

Curtis, M. A., Garlington, S., & Schottenfeld, L. S. (2013). Alcohol, drug, and criminal history restrictions in public housing. *Cityscape: A Journal of Policy Development and Research, 15*(3), 37-52. https://www.huduser.gov/periodicals/cityscpe/vol15num3/ch2.pdf

Decker, S. H., Ortiz, N., Spohn, C., & Hedberg, E. (2015). Criminal stigma, race, and ethnicity: The consequences of imprisonment for employment. *Journal of Criminal Justice, 43*(2), 108–121. doi:10.1016/j.jcrimjus.2015.02.002

DeMartini, L., Mizock, L., Drob, S., Nelson, A., & Fisher, W. (2020). The barriers and facilitators to serious mental illness: Recovery postincarceration. *Psychological Services*, 1–10. doi:10.1037er0000431 PMID:32551728

Denckla, D., & Berman, G. (2001). *Rethinking the revolving door: A look at mental illness in the courts.* Center for Court Innovation. https://www.courtinnovation.org/sites/default/files/rethinkingtherevolvingdoor.pdf

Dougherty, J. (2012). *Survey reveals barriers to successful ex-offender re-entry.* Judicial Process Commission. http://www.rocjpc.org/images/Survey-Reveals-Barriers-to-Successful-Ex-Offender-Re-Entry.pdf

Ethridge, G., Dunlap, P. N., Boston, Q., & Staten, B. H. (2014). Ex-offenders in rural settings seeking employment. *Journal of Applied Rehabilitation Counseling, 45*(4), 56–63. doi:10.1891/0047-2220.45.4.56

Federal Bureau of Prisons. (2021). *Statistics.* https://www.bop.gov/about/statistics/population_statistics.jsp

Festen, M., Waul, M., Solomon, A., & Travis, J. (2002, January 30-31). *From prison to home: The effect of incarceration and reentry on children, families, and communities* [Conference Report]. Office of the Assistant Secretary for Planning and Evaluation. https://www.urban.org/sites/default/files/publication/60716/410632-Background-Paper-The-Effect-of-Incarceration-and-Reentry-on-Children-Families-and-Communities.PDF

Fletcher, D. R. (2002). Ex-offenders, the labour market and the new public administration. *Public Administration, 79*(4), 871–891. doi:10.1111/1467-9299.00284

Fletcher, R. C., & Sherk, J. (2009). *Mentoring former prisoners: A guide for reentry programs.* Public/Private Ventures. https://eric.ed.gov/?id=ED507378

Foley, R. M., & Gao, J. (2002). Correctional education programs serving incarcerated juveniles: A status report. *Journal of Correctional Education, 53*(4), 131–138. https://www.ojp.gov/ncjrs/virtual-library/abstracts/correctional-education-programs-serving-incarcerated-juveniles

Fontaine, J. (2013). The role of supportive housing in successful reentry outcomes for disabled prisoners. *Cityscape: A Journal of Policy Development and Research, 15*(3), 53-75. https://www.huduser.gov/portal/periodicals/cityscpe/vol15num3/ch3.pdf

Fox, B., Miley, L. N., Kortright, K. E., & Wetsman, R. J. (2021). Assessing the effect of mental health courts on adult and juvenile recidivism: A meta-analysis. *American Journal of Criminal Justice, 46*(4), 644–664. doi:10.100712103-021-09629-6

Garretson, H. J. (2016). Legislating forgiveness: A study of post-conviction certificates as policy to address the employment consequences of a conviction. *The Boston University Public Interest Law Journal*, *25*(1), 1–42. https://papers.ssrn.com/sol3/papers.cfm?abstract_id=2733215

Giguere, R., & Dundes, L. (2002). Help wanted: A survey of employer concerns about hiring ex-convicts. *Criminal Justice Policy Review*, *13*(4), 396–408. doi:10.1177/088740302237806

Gill, C., & Wilson, D. B. (2016). Improving the success of reentry programs: Identifying the impact of service-need fit on recidivism. *Criminal Justice and Behavior*, *44*(3), 336–359. doi:10.1177/0093854816682048

Gottfredson, D. C., Najaka, S. S., & Kearley, B. (2003). Effectiveness of drug treatment courts: Evidence from a randomized trial. *Criminology & Public Policy*, *2*(2), 171–196. doi:10.1111/j.1745-9133.2003.tb00117.x

Griffiths, C. T., Dandurand, Y., & Murdoch, D. (2007). *The social reintegration of offenders and crime prevention*. National Crime Prevention Centre, Public Safety Canada. https://curtgriffiths.com/wp-content/uploads/pdfs/social-reintegration.pdf

Hamilton, L., & Belenko, S. (2016). Effects of pre-release services on access to behavioral health treatment after release from prison. *Justice Quarterly*, *33*(6), 1080–1102. doi:10.1080/07418825.2015.1073771

Hammett, T. M., Harmon, P., & Maruschak, L. M. (1999). *1996-1997 Update: HIV/AIDS, STDs, and TB in correctional facilities*. National Institute of Justice. doi:10.1037/e514772006-001

Harlow, C. W. (2003). *Education and correctional population* [Special report] (NCJ 195670). Bureau of Justice Statistics. https://bjs.ojp.gov/content/pub/pdf/ecp.pdf

Harper, G., & Chitty, C. (2004). The impact of corrections on re-offending: A review of 'what works': Home office research study 291. *PsycEXTRA Dataset*. doi:10.1037/e455022008-001

Holzer, H. J., Raphael, S., & Stoll, M. A. (2003). *Employment barriers facing ex-offenders*. Urban Institute. https://www.urban.org/sites/default/files/publication/59416/410855-Employment-Barriers-Facing-Ex-Offenders.PDF

Hucklesby, A., & Wincup, E. (2014). Assistance, support and monitoring? The paradoxes of mentoring adults in the criminal justice system. *Journal of Social Policy*, *43*(2), 373–390. doi:10.1017/S0047279413001013

Hunter, B. A., Lanza, A. S., Lawlor, M., Dyson, W., & Gordon, D. M. (2016). A strengths-based approach to prisoner reentry: The fresh start prisoner reentry program. *International Journal of Offender Therapy and Comparative Criminology*, *60*(11), 1298–1314. doi:10.1177/0306624X15576501 PMID:25805715

Ivery, E. A. (2020). *The influence of community-based reentry programs on reintegrating ex-offenders in Ohio* [Doctoral dissertation, Walden University]. Walden Dissertations and Doctoral Studies. https://scholarworks.waldenu.edu/cgi/viewcontent.cgi?article=11229&context=dissertations

James, N. (2015). *Offender reentry: Correctional statistics, reintegration into the community, and recidivism* (RL34287). Congressional Research Service. https://sgp.fas.org/crs/misc/RL34287.pdf

Kavanagh, L., & Borrill, J. (2013). Exploring the experiences of ex-offender mentors. *Probation Journal*, *60*(4), 400–414. doi:10.1177/0264550513502247

Keene, D. E., Smoyer, A. B., & Blankenship, K. M. (2018). Stigma, housing and identity after prison. *Sociological Review. Mongraph*, *66*(4), 799–815. doi:10.1177/0038026118777447 PMID:32855574

Kirk, D. S. (2015). A natural experiment of the consequences of concentrating former prisoners in the same neighborhoods. *Proceedings of the National Academy of Sciences of the United States of America*, *112*(22), 6943–6948. doi:10.1073/pnas.1501987112 PMID:25976097

Klein, J., & Mohan, L. (2016). *Prison to proprietor: Entrepreneurship as a re-entry strategy*. The Aspen Institute. https://www.aspeninstitute.org/wp-content/uploads/2016/09/AFN-PrisonToProprietor.pdf

Kochel, T. R., & Weisburd, D. (2017). Assessing community consequences of implementing hot spots policing in residential areas: Findings from a randomized field trial. *Journal of Experimental Criminology*, *13*(2), 143–170. doi:10.100711292-017-9283-5

Lee, C. C. (2018). Final thoughts: The counselor as agent of social justice: The process of becoming. In C. C. Lee (Ed.), *Counseling for social justice* (pp. 249–254). American Counseling Association Foundation.

Li, M. (2018). *From prisons to communities: Confronting re-entry challenges and social inequality*. American Psychological Association. https://www.apa.org/pi/ses/resources/indicator/2018/03/prisons-to-communities

Lipsey, M. W. (2009). The primary factors that characterize effective interventions with juvenile offenders: A meta-analytic overview. *Victims & Offenders*, *4*(2), 124–147. doi:10.1080/15564880802612573

Massoglia, M. (2008). Incarceration as exposure: The prison, infectious disease, and other stress-related illnesses. *Journal of Health and Social Behavior*, *49*(1), 56–71. doi:10.1177/002214650804900105 PMID:18418985

Massoglia, M., & Pridemore, W. A. (2015). Incarceration and health. *Annual Review of Sociology*, *41*(1), 291–310. doi:10.1146/annurev-soc-073014-112326 PMID:30197467

McDaniel, K. (2014). *Recidivism prevention through prosocial support: A systematic review of empirical research* [Thesis, University of Central Florida]. HIM 1990-2015. University of Central Florida. https://stars.library.ucf.edu/honorstheses1990-2015/1598

McGrew, A., & Hanks, A. (2017). *The case for paid apprenticeships behind bars*. Center for American Progress. https://www.americanprogress.org/issues/economy/reports/2017/04/27/431384/case-paid-apprenticeships-behind-bars/

McKay, T., Comfort, M., Lindquist, C., & Bir, A. (2016). If family matters: Supporting family relationships during incarceration and reentry. *Criminology & Public Policy*, *15*(2), 529–542. doi:10.1111/1745-9133.12209

McVey, C. C. (2001). Coordinating effective health and mental health continuity of care (NCJ 190462). *Corrections Today*, *63*(5), 58–62. https://www.ojp.gov/ncjrs/virtual-library/abstracts/coordinating-effective-health-and-mental-health-continuity-care

Moore, K., Stuewig, J., & Tangney, J. (2013). Jail inmates' perceived and anticipated stigma: Implications for post-release functioning. *Self and Identity*, *12*(5), 527–547. doi:10.1080/15298868.2012.702425 PMID:25045324

Moore, K. E., Stuewig, J. B., & Tangney, J. P. (2016). The effect of stigma on criminal offenders' functioning: A longitudinal mediational model. *Deviant Behavior*, *37*(2), 196–218. doi:10.1080/01639625.2014.1004035 PMID:26973364

Morenoff, J. D., & Harding, D. J. (2014). Incarceration, prisoner reentry, and communities. *Annual Review of Sociology*, *40*(1), 411–429. doi:10.1146/annurev-soc-071811-145511 PMID:25400321

Mowen, T. J., & Visher, C. A. (2016). Changing the ties that bind: How incarceration impacts family relationships. *Criminology & Public Policy*, *15*(2), 503–528. doi:10.1111/1745-9133.12207

Muhlhausen, D. (2018, June 12). *Research on returning offender programs and promising practices* [Paper presentation]. Secretaries Innovation Group, National Institute of Justice. https://nij.ojp.gov/speech/research-returning-offender-programs-and-promising-practices

National Institute of Corrections. (2019). *Provide certified technical skills training*. Correctional Industries. https://info.nicic.gov/cirs/node/37

Nelson, M., & Trone, J. (2000). *Why planning for release matters*. Vera Institute of Justice. https://biblioteca.cejamericas.org/bitstream/handle/2015/3728/IIB%2Bplanning_for_release.pdf?sequence=1&isAllowed=y

Nilsson, A. (2003). Living conditions, social exclusion and recidivism among prison inmates. *Journal of Scandinavian Studies in Criminology and Crime Prevention*, *4*(1), 57–83. doi:10.1080/14043850310005321

Obatusin, O., & Ritter-Williams, D. (2019). A phenomenological study of employer perspectives on hiring ex-offenders. *Cogent Social Sciences*, *5*(1), 1571730. doi:10.1080/23311886.2019.1571730

Ortiz, M. (2000). Managing special populations (NCJ 186711). *Corrections Today*, *62*(7), 64–68. https://www.ojp.gov/ncjrs/virtual-library/abstracts/managing-special-populations

Pager, D., Bonikowski, B., & Western, B. (2009). Discrimination in a low-wage labor market: A field experiment. *American Sociological Review*, *74*(5), 777–799. doi:10.1177/000312240907400505 PMID:20689685

Pettus-Davis, C., & Epperson, M. W. (2015). *From mass incarceration to smart decarceration* (CSD Working Papers No. 14-31). Center for Social Development. https://openscholarship.wustl.edu/cgi/viewcontent.cgi?article=1575&context=csd_research

Porter, L. C. (2014). Incarceration and post-release health behavior. *Journal of Health and Social Behavior*, *55*(2), 234–249. doi:10.1177/0022146514531438 PMID:24872468

Price-Tucker, A., Zhou, A., Charroux, A., Tenzin, C., Robertson, E., Abdalla, H., Gu, J., Barton, J., Keselj, M., Bernstein, O., Alexis, P., Odayappan, S., & Escalante, T. (2019). *Successful reentry: A community-level analysis*. The Harvard University Institute of Politics Criminal Justice Policy Group. https://iop.harvard.edu/sites/default/files/sources/program/IOP_Policy_Program_2019_Reentry_Policy.pdf

Quinn-Hogan, A. N. (2021). The stain of a criminal label: Post-release stigmatization and its effects on reintegration and recidivism among ex-offenders. *Sociology Publications,* 52. https://ir.lib.uwo.ca/sociologypub/52/

Rade, C. B., Desmarais, S. L., & Mitchell, R. E. (2016). A meta-analysis of public attitudes toward ex-offenders. *Criminal Justice and Behavior*, *43*(9), 1260–1280. doi:10.1177/0093854816655837

Ramakers, A., Nieuwbeerta, P., Van Wilsem, J., & Dirkzwager, A. (2017). Not just any job will do: A study on employment characteristics and recidivism risks after release. *International Journal of Offender Therapy and Comparative Criminology*, *61*(16), 1795–1818. doi:10.1177/0306624X16636141 PMID:26975405

Ratcliffe, J. H., Groff, E. R., Sorg, E. T., & Haberman, C. P. (2015). Citizens' reactions to hot spots policing: Impacts on perceptions of crime, disorder, safety and police. *Journal of Experimental Criminology*, *11*(3), 393–417. doi:10.100711292-015-9230-2

Roman, C. G., & Travis, J. (2004). *Taking stock: Housing, homelessness, and prisoner reentry*. Urban Institute. https://www.urban.org/sites/default/files/publication/58121/411096-Taking-Stock.PDF

Savat, S. (2021). *For 50 years, mass incarceration has hurt American families. Here's how to change it.* Phys.org. https://phys.org/news/2021-10-years-mass-incarceration-american-families.html

Sawyer, W., & Wagner, P. (2020) *Mass incarceration: The whole pie 2020*. Prison Policy Initiative. https://www.prisonpolicy.org/reports/pie2020.html

Schnittker, J., & John, A. (2007). Enduring stigma: The long-term effects of incarceration on health. *Journal of Health and Social Behavior*, *48*(2), 115–130. doi:10.1177/002214650704800202 PMID:17583269

Seiter, R. P., & Kadela, K. R. (2003). Prisoner reentry: What works, what does not, and what is promising. *Crime and Delinquency*, *49*(3), 360–388. doi:10.1177/0011128703049003002

Semenza, D. C., & Link, N. W. (2019). How does reentry get under the skin? Cumulative reintegration barriers and health in a sample of recently incarcerated men. *Social Science & Medicine*, *243*, 1–9. doi:10.1016/j.socscimed.2019.112618 PMID:31665655

Shaw, M. (2006). *Communities in action for crime prevention* [Background paper]. 6th Annual Colloquium on Crime Prevention, Canberra, Australia. https://www.unodc.org/pdf/criminal_justice/Handbook_on_Crime_Prevention_Guidelines_-_Making_them_work.pdf

Simon, J. (2013). From health to humanity: Re-reading Estelle v. Gamble after Brown v. Plata. *Federal Sentencing Reporter, 25*(4), 276-280.

Steinberg, D., Mills, D., & Romano, M. (2015). When did prisons become acceptable mental healthcare facilities? *Stanford Law School.* https://law.stanford.edu/wp-content/uploads/sites/default/files/publication/863745/doc/slspublic/Report_v12.pdf

Steurer, S. J., & Smith, L. G. (2003). *Education reduces crime: Three-state recidivism study. Executive summary.* Correctional Education Association. https://files.eric.ed.gov/fulltext/ED478452.pdf

Taliaferro, W., & Pham, D. (2018). *Incarceration to reentry: Education & training pathways in Ohio*. Center for Law and Social Policy, Inc. (CLASP). https://files.eric.ed.gov/fulltext/ED586093.pdf

The Sentencing Project. (2018). *Report to the United Nations on racial disparities in the US criminal justice system*. https://www.sentencingproject.org/publications/un-report-on-racial-disparities/

Travis, J., Solomon, A. L., & Waul, M. (2001). *From prison to home: The dimensions and consequences of prisoner reentry*. The Dimensions & Consequences of Prisoner Reentry.

Tyler, E. T., & Brockmann, B. (2017). Returning home: Incarceration, reentry, stigma and the perpetuation of racial and socioeconomic health inequity. *The Journal of Law, Medicine & Ethics*, *45*(4), 545–557. doi:10.1177/1073110517750595

Uggen, C., & Thompson, M. (2003). The socioeconomic determinants of ill-gotten gains: Within-person changes in drug use and illegal earnings. *American Journal of Sociology*, *109*(1), 146–185. doi:10.1086/378036

Varan, A. K., Mercer, D. W., Stein, M. S., & Spaulding, A. C. (2014). Hepatitis C seroprevalence among prison inmates since 2001: Still high but declining. *Public Health Reports*, *129*(2), 187–195. doi:10.1177/003335491412900213 PMID:24587554

Visher, C., Debus-Sherrill, S., & Yahner, J. (2008). *Employment after prison: A longitudinal study of releasees in three states*. Urban Institute. https://www.urban.org/research/publication/employment-after-prison-longitudinal-study-releasees-three-states

Visher, C., Yahner, J., & La Vigne, N. (2010). *Life after prison: Tracking the experiences of male prisoners returning to Chicago, Cleveland, and Houston*. Urban Institute. https://www.urban.org/sites/default/files/publication/28671/412100-Life-after-Prison-Tracking-the-Experiences-of-Male-Prisoners-Returning-to-Chicago-Cleveland-and-Houston.PDF

Visher, C. A., & Mallik-Kane, K. (2007). Reentry experiences of men with health problems. In R. B. Greifinger (Ed.), *Public Health Behind Bars* (pp. 434–460). Springer. doi:10.1007/978-0-387-71695-4_25

Wallace, D., Fahmy, C., Cotton, L., Jimmons, C., McKay, R., Stoffer, S., & Syed, S. (2016). Examining the role of familial support during prison and after release on post-incarceration mental health. *International Journal of Offender Therapy and Comparative Criminology*, *60*(1), 3–20. doi:10.1177/0306624X14548023 PMID:25156422

Wang, E. A., Hong, C. S., Shavit, S., Sanders, R., Kessell, E., & Kushel, M. B. (2012). Engaging individuals recently released from prison into primary care: A randomized trial. *American Journal of Public Health*, *102*(9), 22–29. doi:10.2105/AJPH.2012.300894 PMID:22813476

Wang, E. A., Pletcher, M., Lin, F., Vittinghoff, E., Kertesz, S. G., Kiefe, C. I., & Bibbins-Domingo, K. (2009). Incarceration, incident hypertension, and access to health care: Findings from the coronary artery risk development in young adults (CARDIA) study. *Archives of Internal Medicine*, *169*(7), 687–693. doi:10.1001/archinternmed.2009.26 PMID:19364998

Weisburd, D., Hinkle, J. C., Famega, C., & Ready, J. (2011). The possible "backfire" effects of hot spots policing: An experimental assessment of impacts on legitimacy, fear and collective efficacy. *Journal of Experimental Criminology*, *7*(4), 297–320. doi:10.100711292-011-9130-z

Western, B. (2018). *Homeward: Life in the year after prison*. Russell Sage Foundation. doi:10.7758/9781610448710

Wildeman, C., & Wang, E. A. (2017). Mass incarceration, public health, and widening inequality in the USA. *Lancet*, *389*(10077), 1464–1474. doi:10.1016/S0140-6736(17)30259-3 PMID:28402828

Wilson, D. B., Gallagher, C. A., & MacKenzie, D. L. (2000). A meta-analysis of corrections-based education, vocation, and work programs for adult offenders. *Journal of Research in Crime and Delinquency*, *37*(4), 347–368. doi:10.1177/0022427800037004001

Women's Prison Association. (1996). *When a mother is arrested: How the criminal justice and child welfare systems can work together more effectively: A needs assessment initiated by the Maryland department of human resources* (NCJ 174111). U.S. Department of Justice Office of Justice Programs. https://www.ojp.gov/ncjrs/virtual-library/abstracts/when-mother-arrested-how-criminal-justice-and-child-welfare-systems

ADDITIONAL READING

DeMartini, L., Mizock, L., Drob, S., Nelson, A., & Fisher, W. (2020). The barriers and facilitators to serious mental illness: Recovery postincarceration. *Psychological Services*. Advance online publication. doi:10.1037er0000431 PMID:32551728

Dyer, L., Hardeman, R., Vilda, D., Theall, K., & Wallace, M. (2019). Mass incarceration and public health: The association between Black jail incarceration and adverse birth outcomes among Black women in Louisiana. *BMC Pregnancy and Childbirth*, *19*(1), 525. Advance online publication. doi:10.118612884-019-2690-z PMID:31881857

Gill, C., & Wilson, D. B. (2016). Improving the success of reentry programs: Identifying the impact of service-need fit on recidivism. *Criminal Justice and Behavior*, *44*(3), 336–359. doi:10.1177/0093854816682048

Quinn-Hogan, A. N. (2021). The stain of a criminal label: Post-release stigmatization and its effects on reintegration and recidivism among ex-offenders. *Sociology Publications*, 52. https://ir.lib.uwo.ca/sociologypub/52/

Semenza, D. C., & Link, N. W. (2019). How does reentry get under the skin? Cumulative reintegration barriers and health in a sample of recently incarcerated men. *Social Science & Medicine*, *243*, 1–9. doi:10.1016/j.socscimed.2019.112618 PMID:31665655

Turney, K. (2014). The intergenerational consequences of mass incarceration: Implications for children's co-residence and contact with grandparents. *Social Forces*, *93*(1), 299–327. doi:10.1093fou062

Tyler, E. T., & Brockmann, B. (2017). Returning home: Incarceration, reentry, stigma and the perpetuation of racial and socioeconomic health inequity. *The Journal of Law, Medicine & Ethics*, *45*(4), 545–557. doi:10.1177/1073110517750595

Western, B. (2018). *Homeward: Life in the year after prison*. Russell Sage Foundation., doi:10.7758/9781610448710

KEY TERMS AND DEFINITIONS

Collateral Consequences: Residual negative impact of incarceration.

Community Collaboration: Individuals working together to achieve a specific goal.

Community Reentry Programs: Programs designed to help previously incarcerated people transition successfully into society.

Correctional Institutions: Facilities where incarcerated people are housed.

Ex-Offender: A pejorative term referring to an individual who has been released from a correctional institution.

Inmate: An individual housed in a correctional institution.

Mass Incarceration: The pervasive and systemic incarceration of underserved populations.

Over Policing: A disproportionate level of police presence that impacts the community negatively.

Recidivism: A relapse into criminal behavior.

Reintegrate: Adjustment and assimilation of previously incarcerated individuals to their former or another community upon prison release.

Stigma: Pejorative and biased beliefs.

Underserved Populations: Individuals representing a marginalized and disenfranchised group.

Compilation of References

Abram, K. M., & Teplin, L. A. (1991). Co-occurring disorders among mentally ill jail detainees: Implications for public policy. *The American Psychologist*, *46*(10), 1036–1045. doi:10.1037/0003-066X.46.10.1036 PMID:1746771

Abrego, L., Coleman, M., Martínez, D. E., Menjívar, C., & Slack, J. (2017). Making immigrants into criminals: Legal processes of criminalization in the post-IIRIRA era. *Journal on Migration and Human Security*, *5*(3), 694–715. doi:10.1177/233150241700500308

Abubakar, L. A. (2018). *The nature and causes of juvenile delinquency in Nigeria.* https://abubakarlawankura.wordpress.com/2018/07/16/the-nature-and-causes-of-juvenile-delinquencyinnigeria/#:~:text=The%20Nigerian%20constitution%20of%201979,pressure%20or%20certain%20emotional%20stimulation

Adam, A., & McNeely, J. (2020). *Substance use screening and risk assessment in adults.* Johns Hopkins University.

Adams, S., Houston-Kolnik, J., & Reichert, J. (2017). *Trauma-informed and evidence-based practices and programs to address trauma in correctional settings.* https://icjia.illinois.gov/researchhub/articles/trauma-informed-and-evidence-based-practices-and-programs-to-address-trauma-in-correctional-settings

Adegoke, N. (2015). Factors responsible for juvenile delinquency in nigeria: a case study of selected primary schools in Ikorodu, Lagos State, Nigeria. *Research on Humanities and Social Science, 5*(5), 78-84.

Adeleke, F. (2019). Child delinquency in communal conflict areas in southwestern Nigeria. *Journal of Community Psychology*, *47*(4), 790–804. Advance online publication. doi:10.1002/jcop.22153 PMID:30644105

Administration on Children, Youth and Families, Children's Bureau. (2019). *Child maltreatment 2019.* U.S. Department of Health & Human Services, Administration for Children and Families. https://www.acf.hhs.gov/sites/default/files/documents/cb/cm2019.pdf

Adomeh, I. O. C., & Enokela, E. A. (2020). Perception of the effectiveness of bibliotherapy in fostering emotional adjustment among junior secondary school students in FCT, Abuja. *International Research Journal of Humanities, Language and Literature*, *7*(1), 10–20.

Agarwal, V., & Dhanasekaran, S. (2012). Harmful Effects of Media on Children and Adolescents. *Journal Indian Association for Child and Adolescent Mental Health*, *8*(2), 38–45.

Agnew, R. (1992). Foundation for a general strain theory of crime and delinquency. *Criminology*, *30*(1), 47–87. doi:10.1111/j.1745-9125.1992.tb01093.x

Agyepong, T. E. (2018). *The criminalization of Black children: Race, gender, and delinquency in Chicago's juvenile justice system, 1899-1945.* University of North Carolina Press. doi:10.5149/northcarolina/9781469636443.001.0001

Ainsworth, M. D. S., Blehar, M. C., Waters, E., & Wall, S. (1978). *Patterns of attachment: A psychological study of the strange situation*. Erlbaum.

Ajah, O. B., & Ugwuoke, O. C. (2018). Juvenile justice administration and child prisoners in Nigeria. *International Journal of Criminal Justice Sciences, 13*(2), 438–446. 110.5281/zenodo.2658065

Akesson, B., Smyth, J., Mandell, D., Doan, T., Donina, K., & Hoven, C. (2012). Parental involvement with the criminal justice system and the effects on their children: A collaborative model for researching vulnerable families. *Social Work in Public Health, 27*(1-2), 148–164. doi:10.1080/19371918.2012.629898 PMID:22239383

Alaska Department of Education and Early Development. (2019). *Transforming schools: A framework for trauma-engaged practice in Alaska*. https://education.alaska.gov/

Aleguire, Z., Basallaje, A., Bridges, C., Dudley, K. K., Elgart, A., Paterson, E., Singh, J., Stack, A., Williams, B., & Yakar, I. (2016). *Breaking the chains: The school-to-prison pipeline, implicit bias, and racial trauma*. https://equaljusticesociety.org/breakingthechains/

Alexander, L., & Alexander, M. (2021). Fear. In N. Hannah-Jones, C. Roper, I. Silverman, & J. Silverstein (Eds.), A New Origin Story: The 1619 Project (pp.97–122). One World.

Alexander, M. (2010). *The New Jim Crow: Mass Incarceration in the Age of Colorblindness*. New Press.

Alexander, M. (2010). *The new Jim Crow: Mass incarceration in the age of colorblindness*. The New Press.

Alisic, E., Jongman, M., van Wesel, F., & Kleber, R. (2011). Building child trauma theory from longitudinal studies: A meta-analysis. *Clinical Psychology Review, 31*(5), 736–747. doi:10.1016/j.cpr.2011.03.001 PMID:21501581

Allen, S., & Lloyd-Hazlett, J. (2021). Success stories of males convicted of a violent offense. *International Journal for the Advancement of Counseling, 43*(2), 147–163. doi:10.100710447-021-09421-5

Alper, M., Durose, M. R., & Markman, J. (2018). *2018 Update on prisoner recidivism: A 9-year follow-up period (2005-2014)* (NCJ 250975). Bureau of Justice Statistics. https://bjs.ojp.gov/content/pub/pdf/18upr9yfup0514.pdf

Aluede, O., & Adubale, A. A. (2020). School-based Counsellors' Role as Perceived by Nigerian Counsellors. *Journal of School-Based Counseling Policy and Evaluation, 2*(1), 56–62. doi:10.25774/ppbt-6k45

Alvarez, A. (2020). Seeing race in the research on youth trauma and education: A critical review. *Review of Educational Research, 90*(5), 583–626. doi:10.3102/0034654320938131

American Academy of Child and Adolescent Psychiatry. (2012). *Corporal punishment*. https://www.aacap.org/AACAP/Policy_Statements/2012/Policy_Statement_on_Corporal_Punishment.aspx

American Academy of Pediatrics. (1998). Guidance for effective discipline. *Pediatrics, 101*(4), 723–728. doi:10.1542/peds.101.4.723 PMID:9521967

American Psychiatric Association. (2013). *Diagnostic and statistical manual of mental disorders* (5th ed.). Author.

American Psychological Association. (2008). Are zero tolerance policies effective in the schools?: An evidentiary review and recommendations. *The American Psychologist, 63*(9), 852–862. doi:10.1037/0003-066X.63.9.852 PMID:19086747

American Psychological Association. (2021). Inclusive language guidelines. *Equity, Diversity, and Inclusion*. https://www.apa.org/about/apa/equitydiversity-inclusion/language-guidelines.pdf

American Psychological Association. (2022). *Socioeconomic status*. https://www.apa.org/topics/socioeconomic-status

American Psychological Association. (2022). *Trauma*. https://www.apa.org/topics/trauma#:~:text=Trauma%20is%20an%20emotional%20response,symptoms%20like%20headaches%20or%20nausea

American School Counselor Association (ASCA). (2021). *The role of the school counselor.* Retrieved June 24, 2021 from https://www.schoolcounselor.org/

American School Counselor Association. (2016). *The ASCA National Model Implementation Guide: Foundation, Management, and Accountability*. Author.

American School Counselor Association. (2016). *The school counselor and trauma-informed practice*. https://www.schoolcounselor.org/Standards-Positions/Position-Statements/ASCA-Position-Statements

American School Counselor Association. (2019). *ASCA national model: A framework for school counseling programs*. Author.

American School Counselor Association. (2019). *ASCA school counselor professional standards & competencies*. Author.

American School Counselor Association. (2022). *Student-to-School-Counselor Ratio 2020–2021*. American School Counselor Association. https://www.schoolcounselor.org/getmedia/238f136e-ec52-4bf2-94b6-f24c39447022/Ratios-20-21-Alpha.pdf

Aminawung, J., Chamberlain, A., Fox, A., Nyamu, S., Shavit, S., & Wang, E. (2019). Illicit substance use after release from prison among formerly incarcerated primary care patients: A cross-sectional study. *Addiction Science & Clinical Practice*. https://ascpjournal.biomedcentral.com/articles/10.1186/s13722-019-0136-6

Anazodo, K. S., Ricciardelli, R., & Chan, C. (2019). Employment after incarceration: Managing a socially stigmatized identity. *Equality, Diversity and Inclusion*, *38*(5), 564–582. doi:10.1108/EDI-09-2018-0175

Anda, R. F., Felitti, V. J., Bremner, J. D., Walker, J. D., Whitfield, C. H., Perry, B. D., Dube, S. R., & Giles, W. H. (2006). The enduring effects of abuse and related adverse experiences in childhood. *European Archives of Psychiatry and Clinical Neuroscience*, *256*(3), 174–186. doi:10.100700406-005-0624-4 PMID:16311898

Anderson, R. E., Saleem, F. T., & Huguley, J. P. (2019). Choosing to see the racial stress that afflicts our Black students. *Phi Delta Kappan: The Professional Journal for Educators*. https://kappanonline.org/racial-stress-black-students-anderson-saleem-huguley/

Anderson, C. (2016). *White Rage: The Unspoken Truth of Our Racial Divide*. Bloomsbury.

Anderson, J. D., Pitner, R. O., & Wooten, N. R. (2019). A gender-specific model of trauma and victimization in incarcerated women. *Journal of Human Behavior in the Social Environment*. Advance online publication. doi:10.1080/10911359.2019.1673272

Anderson, R. E., Saleem, F. T., & Huguley, J. P. (2019). Choosing to see the racial stress that afflicts our black students. *Phi Delta Kappan*, *101*(3), 20–25. doi:10.1177/0031721719885911

Andrews, D. A., & Bonta, J. (2010). *The psychology of criminal conduct* (5th ed.). LexisNexis.

Anfara, V. A. Jr, Evans, K. R., & Lester, J. N. (2013). Restorative justice in education: What we know so far. *Middle School Journal*, *44*(5), 57–63. doi:10.1080/00940771.2013.11461873

Annamma, S. A., Anyon, Y., Joseph, N. M., Farrar, J., Greer, E., Downing, B., & Simmons, J. (2016). Black girls and school discipline: The complexities of being overrepresented and understudied. *Urban Education*, *54*(2), 211–242. doi:10.1177/0042085916646610

Annie E. Casey Foundation. (2020). *Children in poverty by race and ethnicity in the United States*. https://datacenter.kidscount.org/data/tables/44-children-in-poverty-by-race-and-ethnicity

Apel, R., Blokland, A. A. J., Nieuwbeerta, P., & van Schellen, M. (2010). The impact of imprisonment on marriage and divorce: A risk set matching approach. *Journal of Quantitative Criminology*, *26*(2), 269–300. doi:10.100710940-009-9087-5

Appling, B. M., Tuttle, M., & May, V. S. (2020). The experiences of school counselors who collaborate with clinical mental health counselors. *Professional School Counseling*, *23*(1), 1–10. 10.1177%2F2156759X19882660

Arditti, J. (2012). Child trauma within the context of parental incarceration: A family process perspective. *Journal of Family Theory & Review*, *4*(3), 181–219. doi:10.1111/j.1756-2589.2012.00128.x

Arditti, J. (2016). A family stress-proximal process model for understanding the effects of parental incarceration on children and their families. *Couple & Family Psychology*, *5*(2), 65–88. doi:10.1037/cfp0000058

Arditti, J. A. (2005). Families and incarceration: An ecological approach. *Families in Society*, *86*(2), 251–260. doi:10.1606/1044-3894.2460

Arditti, J. A. (2012b). *Parental Incarceration and the Family: Psychological and Social Effects of Imprisonment on Children, Parents, and Caregivers*. New York University Press.

Arditti, J. A., & Parkman, T. (2011). Young men's reentry after incarceration: A developmental paradox. *Family Relations Interdisciplinary Journal of Applied Family Science*, *60*(2), 205–220. doi:10.1111/j.1741-3729.2010.00643.x

Arditti, J. A., Smock, S. A., & Parkman, T. S. (2005). "It's been hard to be a father": A qualitative exploration of incarcerated fatherhood. *Fathering*, *3*(3), 267–288. doi:10.3149/fth.0303.267

Arincorayan, C. D., Applewhite, L., Garrido, M., Cashio, V., & Bryant, M. (2017). Resilience-enhancing relationships: what we can learn from those with a history of adverse childhood experiences. *U.S. Army Medical Department Journal*, *2*(17), 25-32.

Armstrong, E., Eggins, E., Reid, N., Harnett, P., & Dawe, S. (2018). Parenting interventions for incarcerated parents to improve parenting knowledge and skills, parent well-being, and quality of the parent–child relationship: A systematic review and meta-analysis. *Journal of Experimental Criminology*, *14*(3), 279–317. doi:10.100711292-017-9290-6

Arya, N., & Augarten, I. (2008). Critical condition: African American youth in the justice system. *Race Ethnicity*, 1–49.

Association of Hospital and Institution Libraries. (1971). *Bibliotherapy: Methods and Materials*. American Library Association.

Atilola, O. (2012). Prevalence and correlates of psychiatric disorders among residents of a juvenile remand home in Nigeria: Implications for mental health service planning. Nigerian Journal of Medicine. *Journal of the National Association of Resident Doctors of Nigeria*, *21*, 416–426. PMID:23304950

Atilola, O. (2014). Different points of a continuum? Cross sectional comparison of the current and pre-contact psychosocial problems among the different categories of adolescents in institutional care in Nigeria. *BMC Public Health*, *12*(1), 554. doi:10.1186/1471-2458-12-554 PMID:22835146

Atkin, C. A., & Armstrong, G. S. (2013). Does the concentration of parolees in a community impact employer attitudes toward the hiring of ex-offenders? *Criminal Justice Policy Review*, *24*(1), 71–93. doi:10.1177/0887403411428005

Atkins, C. (2014). *Co-occurring disorders: Integrated assessment and treatment of substance use and mental disorders*. PESI Publishing and Media.

Atkins-Loria, S., Macdonald, H., & Mitterling, C. (2015). Young African American Men and the Diagnosis of Conduct Disorder: The Neo-colonization of Suffering. *Clinical Social Work Journal*, *43*(4), 431–441. doi:10.100710615-015-0531-8

Austin, A. (2016). Is prior parental criminal justice involvement associated with child maltreatment? A systematic review. *Children and Youth Services Review*, *68*, 146–153. doi:10.1016/j.childyouth.2016.07.008

Austin, J. (2001). Prisoner reentry: Current trends, practices, and issues. *Crime and Delinquency*, *47*(3), 314–334. doi:10.1177/0011128701047003002

Avent Harris, J. R., & Wong, C. D. (2018). African American college students, the Black church, and counseling. *Journal of College Counseling*, *21*(1), 15–28. doi:10.1002/jocc.12084

Báez, J. C., Renshaw, K. J., Bachman, L. M., Kim, D., Smith, V. D., & Stafford, R. E. (2019). Understanding the necessity of trauma-informed care in community schools: A mixed-methods program evaluation. *Children & Schools*, *41*(2), 101–110. Advance online publication. doi:10.1093/cs/cdz007

Baglivio, M. T., & Wolff, K. T. (2021). Positive childhood experiences (PCE): Cumulative resiliency in the face of adverse childhood experiences. *Youth Violence and Juvenile Justice*, *19*(2), 139–162. doi:10.1177/1541204020972487

Baker, T., Mitchell, M. M., & Gordon, J. A. (2021). Prison visitation and concerns about reentry: Variations in frequency and quality of visits are associated with reentry concerns among people incarcerated in prison. *International Journal of Offender Therapy and Comparative Criminology*. Advance online publication. doi:10.1177/0306624X211013516 PMID:33940994

Baldry, E., McDonnell, D., Maplestone, P., & Peeters, M. (2003). *Ex-prisoners and accommodation: What bearing do different forms of housing have on social reintegration?* (No.46). Australian Housing and Urban Research Institute. https://www.ahuri.edu.au/__data/assets/pdf_file/0005/2210/AHURI_Final_Report_No46_Ex_prisoners_and_accomodation.pdf

Balfanz, R., Byrnes, V., & Fox, J. (2014). Sent home and put off-track: The antecedents, disproportionalities, and consequences of being suspended in the ninth grade. *The Journal of Applied Research on Children*, *5*(2).

Balingit, M. (2018). Racial disparities in school discipline are growing, federal data show. *The Washington Post*. https://www.washingtonpost.com/local/education/racial-disparities-in-school-discipline-are-growing-federal-data-shows/2018/04/24/67b5d2b8-47e4-11e8-827e-190efaf1f1ee_story.html?noredirect=on&utm_term=.303a447ba026

Bandura, A. (1976). *Social learning theory*. Prentice-Hall.

Bandura, A. (1977). Self-efficacy: Toward a unifying theory of behavioral change. *Psychological Review*, *84*(2), 191–215. doi:10.1037/0033-295X.84.2.191 PMID:847061

Bandura, A. (2006). Toward a psychology of human agency. *Perspectives on Psychological Science*, *1*(2), 164–180. doi:10.1111/j.1745-6916.2006.00011.x PMID:26151469

Barak, A., & Stebbins, A. (2017). Re-entry as performance: Reflections from Institution X. *Critical Social Policy*, *37*(2), 287–309. doi:10.1177/0261018316676732

Barak, A., & Stebbins, A. (2021). Anticipated alienation and critical social work: Ex-offenders' perspectives on re-entry. *British Journal of Social Work*, *51*(1), 38–56. doi:10.1093/bjsw/bcaa069

Barnes, J. C., & Motz, R. T. (2018). Reducing racial inequalities in adulthood arrest by reducing inequalities in school discipline: Evidence from the school-to-prison pipeline. *Developmental Psychology*, *54*(12), 2328–2340. doi:10.1037/dev0000613 PMID:30265031

Barnett, W. S., & Hustedt, J. T. (2005). Head Start's lasting benefits. *Infants and Young Children*, *18*(1), 16–24. doi:10.1097/00001163-200501000-00003

Basford, L., Lewis, J., & Trout, M. (2020). It can be done: How one charter school combats the school-to-prison pipeline. *The Urban Review*, *53*(3), 540–562. doi:10.100711256-020-00583-x

Basile, V. (2020). Standin' tall: Criminalization and acts of resistance among elementary school boys of color. *Race, Ethnicity and Education*, *23*(1), 94–112. doi:10.1080/13613324.2018.1497964

Basile, V., York, A., & Black, R. (2019). Who Is the One Being Disrespectful? Understanding and Deconstructing the Criminalization of Elementary School Boys of Color. *Urban Education*, *00*(0), 1–29. doi:10.1177/0042085919842627

Bath, E., Brown, L., Conrad, S., Folk, J., Kemp, K., Marshall, B., Ramos, L., Rosen, B., & Tolou-Shams, M. (2021). The prospective impact of adverse childhood experiences on justice-involved youth's psychiatric symptoms and substance abuse. *Journal of Consulting and Clinical Psychology*, *89*(6), 483–498. doi:10.1037/ccp0000655 PMID:34264697

Beatty, L., & Snell, T. (2021). *U.S. department of justice profile of prison inmates 2016.* https://bjs.ojp.gov/content/pub/pdf/ppi16.pdf

Beaty, B., Binswanger, I., Calcaterra, S., Min, S., & Mueller, S. (2014). The association between social stressors and drug use/hazardous drinking among former prison inmates. *Journal of Substance Abuse Treatment*, *47*(1), 41–49. doi:10.1016/j.jsat.2014.02.002 PMID:24642070

Beck, A. J. (2021). Race and ethnicity of violent crime offenders and arrestees, 2018. U.S. Department of Justice. Office of Justice Programs. Bureau of Justice Statistics.

Beckmeyer, J. J., & Arditti, J. A. (2014). Implications of in-person visits for incarcerated parents' family relationships and parenting experience. *Journal of Offender Rehabilitation*, *53*(2), 129–151. doi:10.1080/10509674.2013.868390

Begun, A. L., Early, T. J., & Hodge, A. (2016). Mental health and substance abuse service engagement by men and women during community reentry following incarceration. *Administration and Policy in Mental Health*, *43*(2), 207–218. doi:10.100710488-015-0632-2 PMID:25663094

Belenko, S. (1998). Research on drug courts: A critical review. *National Drug Court Institute Review*, *1*(1), 1-42. https://www.ndci.org/sites/default/files/ndci/CASA.Bekenko.1998.pdf

Belenko, S. (2006). Assessing released inmates for substance-abuse-related service needs. *Crime and Delinquency*, *52*(1), 94–113. doi:10.1177/0011128705281755

Belenko, S., Hiller, M., & Hamilton, L. (2013). Treating substance use disorders in the criminal justice system. *Current Psychiatry Reports*, *15*(11), 414. doi:10.100711920-013-0414-z PMID:24132733

Bella, T.T., Atilola1, O. & Omigbodun, O.O. (2010). Children within the juvenile justice system in Nigeria: Psychopathology and psychosocial needs. *Annals of Ibadan Postgraduate Medicine*, *8*(1), 34–39.

Belser, C. T., Shillingford, M., & Joe, J. R. (2016). The ASCA model and a multi-tiered system of supports: A framework to support students of color with problem behavior. *The Professional Counselor*, *6*(3), 251–262. doi:10.15241/cb.6.3.251

Belsky, J. (2002). Developmental origins of attachment styles. *Attachment & Human Development*, *4*(2), 166–170. doi:10.1080/14616730210157510 PMID:12467508

Bender, K. (2018). *Education opportunities in prison are key to reducing crime.* https://www.americanprogress.org/article/education-opportunities-prison-key-reducing-crime/

Bengtson, V. L., & Roberts, R. E. I. (1991). Intergenerational solidarity in aging families: Anexample of formal theory construction. *Journal of Marriage and Family*, *53*(4), 856–870. doi:10.2307/352993

Bennett, E., Lewis, M., & Hunsaker, E. (2012). Counseling kids with incarcerated caregivers. In *Proceedings of the ACA Conference (vol. 1)*. VISTAS.

Berg, J., Roberts, M., Bock, B., Martin, R., Stein, L., Parker, D., McGovern, A., Shuford, S., & Clarke, J. (2016). Changes in depression and stress after release from a tobacco-free prison in the united states. *International Journal of Environmental Research and Public Health*, *13*(1). PMID:26771622

Berliner, L., & Kolko, D. J. (2016). Trauma informed care. *Child Maltreatment*, *21*(2), 168–172. doi:10.1177/1077559516643785 PMID:27152025

Bethell, C., Jones, J., Gombojav, N., Linkenbach, J., & Sege, R. (2019). Positive childhood experiences and adult mental and relational health in a statewide sample: Associations across adverse childhood experiences levels. *JAMA Pediatrics*, *173*(11), e193007. Advance online publication. doi:10.1001/jamapediatrics.2019.3007 PMID:31498386

Biederman, J., Faraone, S. V., Monuteaux, M. C., & Feighner, J. A. (2000). Patterns of alcohol and drug use in adolescents can be predicted by parental substance use disorders. *American Academy of Pediatrics*, *106*(4), 792–797. doi:10.1542/peds.106.4.792 PMID:11015524

Billingsley, A., & Giovannoni, J. M. (1972). *Children of the storm: Black children and American child welfare*. Harcourt Brace Jovanovich.

Binnall, J. M. (2019). Divided we fall: Parole supervision conditions prohibiting "inter-offender" associations. *University of Pennsylvania Journal of Law and Social Change*, *22*(1), 25-69. https://scholarship.law.upenn.edu/jlasc/vol22/iss1/3

Binswanger, I. A., Stern, M. F., Deyo, R. A., Heagerty, P. J., Cheadle, A., Elmore, J. G., & Koepsell, T. D. (2007). Release from prison—A high risk of death for former inmates. *The New England Journal of Medicine*, *356*(2), 157–165. doi:10.1056/NEJMsa064115 PMID:17215533

Black, C. (2010). Understanding the pain of abandonment. *Psychology Today*. https://www.psychologytoday.com/us/blog/the-many-faces-addiction/201006/understanding-the-pain-abandonment

Black, D. W. (2015). The natural history of antisocial personality disorder. *Canadian Journal of Psychiatry*, *60*(7), 309–314. doi:10.1177/070674371506000703 PMID:26175389

Blankenship, K. M., del Rio Gonzalez, A. M., Keene, D. E., Groves, A. K., & Rosenberg, A. P. (2018). Mass incarceration, race inequality, and health: Expanding concepts and assessing impacts on well-being. *Social Science & Medicine*, *215*, 45–52. doi:10.1016/j.socscimed.2018.08.042 PMID:30205278

Blaustein, M., & Kinniburgh, K. M. (2019). *Treating traumatic stress in children and adolescents: How to foster resilience through attachment, self-regulation, and competency*. The Guilford Prcss.

Blumer, H. (1969). *Symbolic interactionism: Perspectives and method*. Prentice-Hall.

Bomysoad, R. N., & Francis, L. A. (2021). Associations between parental incarceration and youth mental health conditions: The mitigating effects of adolescent resilience and positive coping strategies. *Current Psychology (New Brunswick, N.J.)*. Advance online publication. doi:10.100712144-021-01351-0

Boppre, B., & Boyer, C. (2021). "The traps started during my childhood": The role of substance abuse in women's responses to adverse childhood experiences (ACEs). *Journal of Aggression, Maltreatment & Trauma*, *30*(4), 429–449. doi:10.1080/10926771.2019.1651808

Boss, P. (2002). *Family stress management: A contextual approach* (2nd ed.). Sage., doi:10.4135/9781452233895

Boudin, C., Stutz, T., & Littman, A. (2013). Prison visitation policies: A fifty-state survey. *Yale Law & Policy Review*, *32*, 149–189.

Bowen, M. (1978). *Family Theory in Clinical Practice* (Vol. J). Aronson.

Bowlby, J. (1973). *Separation, anxiety and anger* (Vol. 2). The Hogarth Press and the Institute of Psycho-Analysis.

Bowlby, J. (1988). *A secure base*. Basic Books.

Bowles, M. A., DeHart, D., & Webb, J. R. (2012). Family influences on female offenders's substance use: The role of adverse childhood events among incarcerated women. *Journal of Family Violence*, *27*(7), 681–686. doi:10.100710896-012-9450-4

Bowman, S. W., & Travis, R. Jr. (2012). Prisoner reentry and recidivism according to the formerly incarcerated and re-entry service providers: A verbal behavior approach. *The Behavior Analyst Today*, *13*(3-4), 9–19. doi:10.1037/h0100726

Bracha, S. H., Ralston, T. C., Matsukawa, J. M., Williams, A. E., & Bracha, A. S. (2004). Does "Fight or Flight" need updating? *Psychosomatics (Washington, D.C.)*, *45*(5), 448–449. doi:10.1176/appi.psy.45.5.448 PMID:15345792

Bradshaw, D., Creaven, A.-M., & Muldoon, O. T. (2021). Parental incarceration affects children's emotional and behavioral outcomes: A longitudinal cohort study of children aged 9 to 13 years. *International Journal of Behavioral Development*, *45*(4), 310–316. Advance online publication. doi:10.1177/0165025421995918

Branje, S., Keijsers, L., Loeber, R., Meeus, W., Pardini, D., & Rekker, R. (2015). Moving in and out of poverty: The within-individual association between socioeconomic status and juvenile delinquency. *PLoS One*, *10*(11). https://www.ncbi.nlm.nih.gov/pmc/articles/PMC4648521/#:~:text=Socioeconomic%20status%20(SES)%20is%20one,treated%20as%20a%20static%20characteristic PMID:26575271

Brazzell, D., Crayton, A., Mukamal, D. A., Solomon, A. L., & Lindahl, N. (2009). *From the classroom to the community: Exploring the role of education during incarceration and reentry.* The Urban Institute, John Jay College. Retrieved July 25, 2021 from https://www.urban.org/sites/default/files/publication/30671/411963-From-the-Classroom-to-the-Community.PDF

Brazzell, D., Crayton, A., Mukamal, D. A., Solomon, A. L., & Lindahl, N. (2009). *From the classroom to the community: Exploring the role of education during incarceration and reentry*. Urban Institute: Justice Policy Center. https://files.eric.ed.gov/fulltext/ED508246.pdf

Bridgeland, J., Dilulio, J. Jr, & Morison, K. (2006). *The silent epidemic: Perspectives of high school dropouts*. Civic Enterprises.

Brine, K., Power, J., Smith, H. P., & Nolan, A. (2021). A qualitative study of success in postrelease federal inmates with mental health issues. *Journal of Correctional Health Care*, *27*(1), 40–50. doi:10.1089/jchc.19.02.0009 PMID:34232766

Brinkley-Rubinstein, L., Craven, K. L., & McCormack, M. M. (2014). Shifting perceptions of race and incarceration as adolescents age: Addressing disproportionate minority contact by understanding how social environment informs racial attitudes. *Child & Adolescent Social Work Journal*, *31*(1), 25–38. doi:10.100710560-013-0306-4

Brinkley-Rubinstein, L., Zaller, N., Martino, S., Cloud, D. H., McCauley, E., Heise, A., & Seal, D. (2018). Criminal justice continuum for opioid users at risk of overdose. *Addictive Behaviors*, *86*, 104–110. doi:10.1016/j.addbeh.2018.02.024 PMID:29544869

Bronfenbrener, U. (1989). Ecological systems theory. *Annals of Child Development*, *6*, 187–249.

Bronfenbrenner, U., & Morris, P. A. (1998). The ecology of developmental processes. In Handbook of child psychology: Vol. 1. Theoretical models of human development (5th ed., pp. 993–1028). New York: Wiley.

Bronfenbrenner, U. (1974). Developmental research, public policy, and the ecology of childhood. *Child Development, 45*(1), 1–5. doi:10.2307/1127743

Bronfenbrenner, U. (1978). The social role of the child in ecological perspective. *Zeitschrift für Soziologie, 7*(1), 4–20. doi:10.1515/zfsoz-1978-0101

Bronfenbrenner, U. (1986). Ecology of the family as a context for human development: Research perspectives. *Developmental Psychology, 22*(6), 723–742. doi:10.1037/0012-1649.22.6.723

Bronson, J., & Berzofsky, M. (2017). *Indicators of mental health problems reported by prisoners and jail inmates, 2011–12* [Special report] (NCJ 250612). Bureau of Justice Statistics. https://bjs.ojp.gov/content/pub/pdf/imhprpji1112.pdf

Brooks, M., Gaynes, E., Krupat, T., & Lemaster-Schipani, D. (2013). Stronger together: Volume I, experiences of children of incarcerated parents. The Osborne Association.

Brown, E. (2018). *Imprisoned parents, challenged children.* ASCA SC. https://www.ascaschoolcounselordigital.org/ascaschoolcounselor/january_february_2018/MobilePagedArticle.action?articleId=1329904#articleId1329904

Brown, E. C. (2020). School counselor conceptualizations of the needs of children of incarcerated parents. *Children and Youth Services Review, 112*, 104936. doi:10.1016/j.childyouth.2020.104936

Brown, C., Maggin, D. M., & Buren, M. (2018). Systematic review of cultural adaptations of school-based social, emotional, and behavioral interventions for students of color. *Education & Treatment of Children, 41*(4), 431–456. doi:10.1353/etc.2018.0024

Brown, S. L., Wanamaker, K. A., Greiner, L., Scott, T., & Skilling, T. A. (2021). Complex trauma and criminogenic needs in a youth justice sample: A gender-informed latent profile analysis. *Criminal Justice and Behavior, 48*(2), 175–194. doi:10.1177/0093854820964513

Brown, S., Fite, P. J., DiPierro, M., & Bortolato, M. (2017). Links between stressful life events and proactive and reactive functions of aggression. *Journal of Aggression, Maltreatment & Trauma, 6*(6), 691–699. doi:10.1080/10926771.2017.1322658 PMID:31223229

Brunoni, A. R., & Brunoni, A. R. (2017). Beyond the DSM: Trends in psychiatry diagnoses. *Archives of Clinical Psychiatry, 44*(6), 154–158. doi:10.1590/0101-60830000000142

Bruskas, D. (2008). Children in foster care: A vulnerable population at risk. *Journal of Child and Adolescent Psychiatric Nursing, 21*(2), 70–77. doi:10.1111/j.1744-6171.2008.00134.x PMID:18429837

Bryan-Gooden, J., & Hester, M. (2018). *Is NYC preparing teachers to be culturally responsive? Data snapshot.* https://steinhardt.nyu.edu/metrocenter/ejroc

Bryan, J., Day-Vines, N. L., Griffin, D., & Moore-Thomas, C. (2012). The disproportionality dilemma: Patterns of teacher referrals to school counselors for disruptive behavior. *Journal of Counseling and Development, 90*(2), 177–190. doi:10.1111/j.1556-6676.2012.00023.x

Bryan, J., & Henry, L. (2012). A Model for Building School-Family-Community Partnerships: Principles and Process. *Journal of Counseling and Development, 90*(4), 408–420. doi:10.1002/j.1556-6676.2012.00052.x

Bryan, N. (2017). White teachers' role in sustaining the school-to-prison pipeline: Recommendations for teacher education. *The Urban Review, 49*(2), 326–345. doi:10.100711256-017-0403-3

Buck, G. (2016). "I wanted to feel the way they did": Mimesis as a situational dynamic of peer mentoring by ex-offenders. *Deviant Behavior*, *38*(9), 1027–1041. doi:10.1080/01639625.2016.1237829

Bullis, M., Yovanoff, P., Mueller, G., & Havel, E. (2002). Life on the "outs": Examination of the facility-to-community transition of incarcerated youth. *Exceptional Children*, *69*(1), 7–22. doi:10.1177/001440290206900101

Bülow, W., & Dagan, N. (2020). From rehabilitation to penal communication: The role of furlough and visitation within a retributivist framework. *Punishment & Society*, *23*(3), 376–393. doi:10.1177/1462474520953676

Buntin, M., & Ayanian, J. (2017). Social risk factors and equity in medicare payment. *The New England Journal of Medicine*, *376*(6), 507–510. doi:10.1056/NEJMp1700081 PMID:28177864

Bureau of Justice Assistance. (2022). *Managing substance withdrawal in jails: A legal brief.* https://bja.ojp.gov/doc/managing-substance-withdrawal-in-jails.pdf

Burger, J. M. (2015). *Personality*. Brooks/Cole Publishing, Co.

Bururia, D. N., Marangu, P. G., & Nyaga, J. N. (2014). Contribution of Peer Counseling to Student Behavior Change in Secondary Schools in Maara Sub County. *Kenya Journal of Educational Policy and Entrepreneurial Research*, *1*(2), 86–93.

Butler, P. (2013). Poor people lose: Gideon and the critique of rights. *The Yale Law Journal*, *122*(8), 2176–2204.

Byrd, D. A., Rivera Mindt, M. M., Clark, U. S., Clarke, Y., Thames, A. D., Gammada, E. Z., & Manly, J. J. (2021). Creating an antiracist psychology by addressing professional complicity in psychological assessment. *Psychological Assessment*, *33*(3), 279–285. doi:10.1037/pas0000993 PMID:33779204

Carli, L. L. (2020). Women, gender equality and COVID-19. *Gender in Management*, *35*(7/8), 647–655. doi:10.1108/GM-07-2020-023

Carlson, E., Smith, S., & Dalenberg, C. (2013). Can sudden, severe emotional loss be a traumatic stressor? *Journal of Trauma & Dissociation*, *14*(5), 519–528. doi:10.1080/15299732.2013.773475 PMID:24060034

Carlson, J. R. (1998). Evaluating the effectiveness of a live-in nursery within a women's prison. *Journal of Offender Rehabilitation*, *27*(1-2), 73–85. doi:10.1300/J076v27n01_06

Carmichael, D. (2011). *Breaking schools' rules*. https://ppri.tamu.edu/portfolio-items/page/2/

Carroll, K. M., Rounsaville, B. J., Nich, C., Gordon, L. T., Wirtz, P. W., & Gawin, F. (1994). One-Year Follow-up of Psychotherapy and Pharmacotherapy for Cocaine Dependence. *Archives of General Psychiatry*, *51*(12), 989–997. doi:10.1001/archpsyc.1994.03950120061010 PMID:7979888

Carson, A. (2021). *U.S. department of justice prisoners in 2020-statistical tables*. https://bjs.ojp.gov/content/pub/pdf/p20st.pdf

Carson, A., Sandler, D., Bhaskar, R., Fernandez, L., & Porter, S. (2021). *Employment of persons released from federal prison in 2010*. https://bjs.ojp.gov/content/pub/pdf/eprfp10.pdf

Carson, E. A. (2021, December). *Prisoners in 2020 – Statistical Tables* (NCJ 302776). US Department of Justice, Office of Justice Programs, Bureau of Justice Statistics. https://bjs.ojp.gov/library/publications/prisoners-2020-statistical-tables

Carson, E. A., & Anderson, E. (2016). *Prisoners in 2015*. United States Department of Justice, Bureau of Justice Statistics. https://www.bjs.gov/content/pub/pdf/p15.pd

Carson, E. A. (2020). *Prisoners in 2019*. U.S. Department of Justice. Office of Justice Programs. Bureau of Justice Statistics.

Carter, R. T. (1990). The Relationship Between Racism and Racial ldentity Among White Americans: An Exploratory Investigation. *Journal of Counseling and Development*, *69*(1), 46–50. doi:10.1002/j.1556-6676.1990.tb01455.x

Carter, R. T. (2007). Racism and Psychological and Emotional Injury: Recognizing and Assessing Race-Based Traumatic Stress. *The Counseling Psychologist*, *35*(1), 13–105. doi:10.1177/0011000006292033

Carter, R. T., Kirkinis, K., & Johnson, V. E. (2019). Relationships Between Trauma Symptoms and Race-Based Traumatic Stress. *Traumatology*, *26*(1), 11–18. doi:10.1037/trm0000217

Ceka, A., & Murati, R. (2016). The Role of Parents in the Education of Children. *Journal of Education and Practice*, *7*(5), 61–64.

Center for Disease Control. (2021, April 6). *About the CDC-Kaiser ACE Study*. https://www.cdc.gov/violenceprevention/aces/about.html

Center for Health Care Strategies. (2021). *What is trauma?* https://www.traumainformedcare.chcs.org/what-is-trauma/

Center for Substance Abuse Treatment. (2012). *Managing chronic pain in adults with or in recovery from substance use disorders*. Substance Abuse and Mental Health Services Administration. https://www.ncbi.nlm.nih.gov/books/NBK92053/table/ch2.t5/

Centers for Disease Control and Prevention and Substance Abuse and Mental Health Services Administration. (2020). *Infographic: 6 guiding principles to a trauma-informed approach*. https://www.cdc.gov/cpr/infographics/6_principles_trauma_info.htm

Centers for Disease Control and Prevention. (2019, November 5). *Adverse childhood experiences (ACES)*. Centers for Disease Control and Prevention. https://www.cdc.gov/vitalsigns/aces/index.html

Centers for Disease Control and Prevention. (2021). *About the CDC-Kaiser ace study*. https://www.cdc.gov/violenceprevention/aces/about.html

Centers for Disease Control and Prevention. (2021, March 3). *Drug overdose deaths: Drug overdose deaths remain high*. https://www.cdc.gov/drugoverdose/deaths/index.html

Cerda, M., Fink, K., Gaidus, A., Greunwald, P., Keyes, K., Martins, S., Pear, P., Ponicki, W., & Rivera-Aguirre, A. (2019). Urban-rural variation in the socioeconomic determinants of opioid overdose. *Drug and Alcohol Dependence*, *195*, 66–73. doi:10.1016/j.drugalcdep.2018.11.024 PMID:30592998

Chamberlain, A. W., & Wallace, D. (2016). Mass reentry, neighborhood context and recidivism: Examining how the distribution of parolees within and across neighborhoods impacts recidivism. *Justice Quarterly*, *33*(5), 912–941. doi:10.1080/07418825.2015.1012095

Chandler, R. K., Fletcher, B. W., & Volkow, N. D. (2009). Treating drug abuse and addiction in the criminal justice system: Improving public health and safety. *Journal of the American Medical Association*, *301*(2), 183–190. doi:10.1001/jama.2008.976 PMID:19141766

Chandler, R. K., Peters, R. H., Field, G., & Juliano-Bult, D. (2004). Challenges in Implementing evidence-based treatment practices for co-occurring disorders in the criminal justice system. *Behavioral Sciences & the Law*, *22*(4), 431–448. doi:10.1002/bsl.598 PMID:15282833

Chang, X., Jiang, X., Mkandarwire, T., & Shen, M. (2019). Associations between adverse childhood experiences and health outcomes in adults aged 18–59 years. *PLoS One*, *14*(2), e0211850. Advance online publication. doi:10.1371/journal.pone.0211850 PMID:30730980

Chanhatasilpa, C., MacKenzie, D. L., & Hickman, L. J. (2000). The effectiveness of community-based programs for chemically dependent offenders: A review and assessment of research. *Journal of Substance Abuse Treatment*, *19*(4), 383–393. doi:10.1016/S0740-5472(00)00131-8 PMID:11166503

Chapman, D. P., Whitfield, C. L., Felitti, V. J., Dube, S. R., Edwards, V. J., & Anda, R. F. (2004). Adverse childhood experiences and the risk of depressive disorders in adulthood. *Journal of Affective Disorders*, *82*(2), 217–225. doi:10.1016/j.jad.2003.12.013 PMID:15488250

Charles Sturt University Library. (2021). *Literature review: Traditional or narrative literature reviews.* https://libguides.csu.edu.au/review/Traditional

Charles, P., Kerr, M., Wirth, J., Jensen, S., Massoglia, M., & Poehlmann-Tynan, J. (2021). Lessons from the field: Developing and implementing an intervention for jailed parents and their children. *Family Relations*, *70*(1), 171–178. doi:10.1111/fare.12524

Chartier, M. J., Walker, J. R., & Naimark, B. (2010). Separate and cumulative effects of adverse childhood experiences in predicting adult health and Health Care Utilization. *Child Abuse & Neglect*, *34*(6), 454–464. doi:10.1016/j.chiabu.2009.09.020 PMID:20409586

Chavous, T. M., Rivas-Drake, D., Smalls, C., Griffin, T., & Cogburn, C. (2008). Gender matters, too: The influences of school racial discrimination and racial identity on academic engagement outcomes among African American adolescents. *Developmental Psychology*, *44*(3), 637–654. doi:10.1037/0012-1649.44.3.637 PMID:18473633

Chiappini, S., & Schifano, F. (2022). What about "pharming?" issues regarding the misuse of prescription and over the counter drugs. *Brain Sciences*, *10*(10), 736. doi:10.3390/brainsci10100736 PMID:33066476

Child Trends. (2019). *Trends in adverse childhood experiences*. https://www.childtrends.org

Child Welfare Information Gateway. (2019). *Foster care statistics 2019.* Washington, DC: U.S. Department of Health and Human Services, Children's Bureau. Retrieved from https://www.childwelfare.gov/pubPDFs/foster.pdf

Child Welfare Information Gateway. (2021). *Child welfare practice to address racial disproportionality and disparity.* U.S. Department of Health and Human Services, Administration for Children and Families, Children's Bureau. https://www.childwelfare.gov/pubs/issue-briefs/racial-disproportionality/

Children's Bureau. (2020). *The AFCARS report: Preliminary FY 2019 estimates as of June 23, 2020 – No. 27.* U.S. Department of Health and Human Services, Administration for Children and Families. https://www.acf.hhs.gov/cb/resource/afcars-report-27

Children's Defense Fund. (2021). *The state of America's children® 2020: Youth justice*. Retrieved June 22, 2021 from https://www.childrensdefense.org/policy/resources/soac-2020-youth-justice/

Chinn, J. J., Martin, I. K., & Redmond, N. (2021). Health equity among Black women in the United States. *Journal of Women's Health*, *30*(2), 212–219. doi:10.1089/jwh.2020.8868 PMID:33237831

Cho, R. (2010). Maternal incarceration and children's adolescent outcomes: Timing and Dosage. *The Social Service Review*, *84*(2), 257–282. doi:10.1086/653456

Choudhury, S., & Moses, J. M. (2016). Mindful interventions: Youth, poverty, and the developing brain. *Theory & Psychology*, *26*(5), 591–606. doi:10.1177/0959354316669025

Christian, J. (2005). Riding the bus: Barriers to prison visitation and family management strategies. *Journal of Contemporary Criminal Justice*, *21*(1), 31–48. doi:10.1177/1043986204271618

Cicchetti, D. (2010). Resilience under conditions of extreme stress: a multilevel perspective. *World Psychiatry, 9*(3), 145. doi:10.1186/1471-2458-13-3

Clark, D. B., Cornelius, J. R., Kirisci, L., & Tarter, R. E. (2005). Childhood risk categories for adolescent substance involvement: A general liability typology. *Drug and Alcohol Dependence, 77*(1), 13–21. doi:10.1016/j.drugalcdep.2004.06.008 PMID:15607837

Clemens, V., Berthold, O., Witt, A., Sachser, C., Brähler, E., Plener, P. L., Strauß, B., & Fegert, J. M. (2019). Child maltreatment is mediating long-term consequences of household dysfunction in a population representative sample. *European Psychiatry, 58*, 10–18. doi:10.1016/j.eurpsy.2019.01.018 PMID:30743239

Clements-Nolle, K., & Waddington, R. (2019). Adverse childhood experiences and psychological distress in juvenile offenders: The protective influence of resilience and youth assets. *The Journal of Adolescent Health, 64*(1), 49–55. doi:10.1016/j.jadohealth.2018.09.025 PMID:30579436

Coates, T. N. (2015). *The Black family in the age of mass incarceration*. The Atlantic. https://www.theatlantic.com/magazine/archive/2015/10/the-black-family-in-the-age-of-mass-incarceration/403246/

Cohen, J. A., & Mannarino, A. P. (2019). Trauma-Focused cognitive behavioral therapy for childhood traumatic separation. *Child Abuse & Neglect, 92*, 179–195. doi:10.1016/j.chiabu.2019.03.006 PMID:30999167

Cohen, J. A., Mannarino, A. P., Kliethermes, M., & Murray, L. A. (2012). Trauma-focused CBT for youth with complex trauma. *Child Abuse & Neglect, 36*(6), 528–541. doi:10.1016/j.chiabu.2012.03.007 PMID:22749612

Cole, S. F., O'Brien, J. G., Gadd, M. G., Ristuccia, J., Wallace, D. L., & Gregory, M. (2005). *Helping traumatized children learn: Supportive school environments for children traumatized by family violence*. Massachusetts Advocates for Children.

Cole, S., Eisner, A., Gregory, M., & Ristuccia, J. (2013). *Helping traumatized children learn: Creating and advocating for trauma-sensitive schools* (Vol. 2). Massachusetts Advocates for Children.

Collaborative for Academic and Social Emotional Learning (CASEL). (2013). *CASEL Guide: Effective social and emotional learning programs: Preschool and elementary school edition*. CASEL.

Collaborative for Academic and Social Emotional Learning (CASEL). (2019). *SEL is...* Retrieved July 8, 2021 from https://casel.org/what-is-sel/

Collins, P. H. (1990). Black feminist thought in the matrix of domination. In Black feminist thought: Knowledge, Consciousness, and the Politics of Empowerment (pp. 221 – 238). Unwin Hyman.

Colman, I., Eljdupovic, G., Martin, M., & Mckenzie, K. (2016). Risk of violence by inmates with childhood trauma and mental health needs. *Law and Human Behavior, 39*(6), 614–623. PMID:26214301

Comfort, M. (2016). "A twenty-hour-a-day job": The impact of frequent low-level criminal justice involvement on family life. *The Annals of the American Academy, 665*(1), 63–79. doi:10.1177/0002716215625038 PMID:28935993

Comfort, M., McKay, T., Landwehr, J., Kennedy, E., Lindquist, C., & Bir, A. (2016). The cost of incarceration for families of prisoners. *International Review of the Red Cross, 98*(903), 783–798. doi:10.1017/S1816383117000704

Committee on the Rights of the Child. (2019, September 18). General comment No. 24 (2019) on children's rights in the child justice system. United Nations.

Compassion Prison Project. (2022). *How common are adverse childhood experiences*. https://compassionprisonproject.org/childhood-trauma-statistics/

Conaway, D., & Strickler, M. (2018, January 8). *What is the difference between state and federal prisons?* https://www.conawayandstrickler.com/blog/what_is_the_difference_between_state_and_federal_prisons/

Connor, K. M., & Davidson, J. R. (2003). Development of a new resilience scale: The Connor-Davidson resilience scale (CD-RISC). *Depression and Anxiety, 18*(2), 76–82. doi:10.1002/da.10113 PMID:12964174

Conyne, C., & Cook, E. (Eds.). (2004). *Ecological counseling: An innovative approach to conceptualizing person-environment interaction.* American Counseling Association.

Cook, A., & Haynes, S. H. (2021). Imprisonment pains, reentry strains, and perceived likelihood of reoffending. *Criminal Justice Studies, 34*(1), 16–32. doi:10.1080/1478601X.2020.1771332

Corbett, A. D., Henderson, G., McKnight, A. T., & Paterson, S. J. (2006). 75 years of opioid research: The exciting but vain quest for the Holy Grail. *British Journal of Pharmacology, 147*(S1), 153–162. doi:10.1038j.bjp.0706435 PMID:16402099

Correa, N. P., Hayes, A. K., Bhalakia, A. M., Lopez, K. K., Cupit, T., Kwarteng-Amaning, V., Keefe, R. J., Greeley, C. S., & Van Horne, B. S. (2021). Parents' perspectives on the impact of their incarceration on children and families. *Family Relations, 70*(1), 162–170. doi:10.1111/fare.12529

Cortes, K., & Rogers, S. (2010). *Reentry housing options: The policymakers' guide.* The Council of State Governments. https://csgjusticecenter.org/wp-content/uploads/2020/02/Reentry_Housing_Options-1.pdf

Costa Duriguetto, G., & Araujo, R. (2020). Psychopathology and criminality. *International Journal of Psychiatry Research, 3*(3), 1–7. doi:10.33425/2641-4317.1063

Costopoulos, J. S., & Wellman, B. L. (2017). The effectiveness of one mental health court: Overcoming criminal history. *Psychological Injury and Law, 10*(3), 254–263. doi:10.100712207-017-9290-x

Couloute, L. (2018). *Getting back on course: Educational exclusion and attainment among formerly incarcerated people.* https://www.prisonpolicy.org/reports/education.html#:~:text=GEDs%20in%20prison&text=We%20found%20that%20of%20the,attained%20a%20GED%20while%20incarcerated

Couloute, L., & Kopf, D. (2018) *Out of prison & out of work: Unemployment among formerly incarcerated people.* https://www.prisonpolicy.org/reports/outofwork.html

Couloute, L., & Kopf, D. (2018). *Out of prison & out of work: Unemployment among formerly incarcerated people.* Prison Policy Initiative. https://www.prisonpolicy.org/reports/outofwork.html

Council of State Governments Justice Center & the Council of Juvenile Correctional Administrators. (2015, November). *Locked out: Improving educational and vocational outcomes for incarcerated youth.* Retrieved July 31, 2021 from https://csgjusticecenter.org/publications/locked-out-improving-educational-and-vocational-outcomes-for-incarcerated-youth/

Cox, R. M., Skirius, M. S., Lenz, A. S., James, R. K., & Packard, C. (2017). The effects of repeated exposure to the ARRAY program with offenders with mental illness. *Journal of Addictions & Offender Counseling, 38*(2), 98-114. doi:10.1002/jaoc.12033

Coyne, L. W., McHugh, L., & Martinez, E. R. (2011). Acceptance and commitment therapy (ACT): Advances and applications with children, adolescents, and families. *Child and Adolescent Psychiatric Clinics of North America, 20*(2), 379–399. doi:10.1016/j.chc.2011.01.010 PMID:21440862

Craig, J. M., Intravia, J., Wolff, K. T., & Baglivio, M. T. (2019). What can help? Examining levels of substance (non)use as a protective factor in the effect of ACEs on crime. *Youth Violence and Juvenile Justice, 17*(1), 42–61. doi:10.1177/1541204017728998

Craig, J. M., Piquero, A. R., Farrington, D. P., & Ttofi, M. M. (2017). A little early risk goes a long bad way: Adverse childhood experiences and life-course offending in the Cambridge study. *Journal of Criminal Justice*, *53*, 34–45. doi:10.1016/j.jcrimjus.2017.09.005

Craig, S. E. (2016). *Trauma-sensitive schools: Learning communities transforming children's lives, K-5*. Teachers College Press.

Crawford, M. (2014). *Social Control Theory*. https://www.researchgate.net/publication/275154441_Social_Control_Theory doi:10.13140/RG.2.1.2360.7847

Crenshaw, K. (1989). Demarginalizing the intersection of race and sex: A black feminist critique of antidiscrimination doctrine, feminist theory and antiracist politics. *U. Chi. Legal F., 139.*

Crespi, T. D., & Lovelace, J. R. (2010). Adolescent incarceration and children's psychiatric hospitalization: Training school psychologists for nontraditional settings. In E. García-Vásquez, T. D. Crespi, & C. A. Riccio (Eds.), Handbook of education, training, and supervision of school psychologists in school and community, Vol 1: Foundations of professional practice (pp. 279–294). Routledge/Taylor & Francis Group.

Crews, G. A. (2016). *School killers speak: A comprehensive examination of perpetrators, events, and characteristics of K-12 school violence in America*. The Veritas Group.

Crosby, S. D. (2016). Trauma-informed approaches to juvenile justice: A critical race perspective. *Juvenile & Family Court Journal*, *67*(1), 5–18. doi:10.1111/jfcj.12052

Crouch, E., Smith, H. P., & Andersen, T. S. (2022). An examination of caregiver incarceration, positive childhood experiences, and school success. *Children and Youth Services Review*, *133*, 106345. doi:10.1016/j.childyouth.2021.106345

Crum, W. (2010). Foster parent parenting characteristics that lead to increased placement stability or disruption. *Children and Youth Services Review*, *32*(2), 185–190. doi:10.1016/j.childyouth.2009.08.022

Cummings, K. P., Addante, S., Swindell, J., & Meadan, H. (2017). Creating supportive environments for children who have had exposure to traumatic events. *Journal of Child and Family Studies*, *26*(10), 2728–2741. doi:10.100710826-017-0774-9

Currie, J., & Tekin, E. (2006). *Does Child Abuse Cause Crime?* National Bureau of Economic Research. doi:10.3386/w12171

Curtis, M. A., Garlington, S., & Schottenfeld, L. S. (2013). Alcohol, drug, and criminal history restrictions in public housing. *Cityscape: A Journal of Policy Development and Research, 15*(3), 37-52. https://www.huduser.gov/periodicals/cityscpe/vol15num3/ch2.pdf

Curtis, P. (1999). The chronic nature of the foster care crisis. In P. Curtis, G. Dale Jr, & J. Kendall (Eds.), *The foster care crisis: Translating research into policy and practice* (pp. 1–13). University of Nebraska Press.

D'Andrade, A., & Valdez, M. (2012). Reunifying from behind bars: A quantitative study of the relationship between parental incarceration, service use, and foster care reunification. *Social Work in Public Health*, *27*(6), 616–636. doi:10.1080/19371918.2012.713294 PMID:22963161

Dallaire, D. H. (2007). Incarcerated mothers and fathers: A comparison of risks for children and families. *Family Relations*, *56*(5), 440–453. doi:10.1111/j.1741-3729.2007.00472.x

Dallaire, D. H., Ciccone, A., & Wilson, L. C. (2010). Teachers' experiences with and expectations of children with incarcerated parents. *Journal of Applied Developmental Psychology*, *31*(4), 281–290. doi:10.1016/j.appdev.2010.04.001

Damron, N. (2010). *Poverty fact sheet: Life beyond bars: Children with an incarcerated parent.* Institute for Research on Poverty. https://www.irp.wisc.edu/publications/factsheets/pdfs/Factsheet7-Incarceration.pdf

Danzer, G., Rieger, S., Schubmehl, S., & Cort, D. (2021). White Psychologists and African Americans' Historical Trauma: Implications for Practice. *Journal of Aggression, Maltreatment & Trauma*, *25*(4), 351–370. doi:10.1080/10926771.2016.1153550

Datchi, C. C., Barretti, L. M., & Thompson, C. M. (2016). Family services in adult detention centers: Systemic principles for prisoner reentry. *Couple & Family Psychology*, *5*(2), 89–104. doi:10.1037/cfp0000057

Datchi, C. C., & Sexton, T. L. (2013). Can family therapy have an effect on adult criminal conduct? Initial evaluation of functional family therapy. *Couple & Family Psychology*, *2*(4), 278–293. doi:10.1037/a0034166

Davis, A. J. (2017). The prosecution of black men. In A. Davis (Ed.), Policing the black man: Arrest, prosecution, and imprisonment (pp. 178-208). First Vintage.

Davis, L., & Shlafer, R. J. (2017). Mental health of adolescents with currently and formerly incarcerated parents. *Journal of Adolescence*, *54*(1), 120–134. doi:10.1016/j.adolescence.2016.10.006 PMID:28011442

Davis, L., & Shlafer, R. J. (2017). Substance use among youth with currently and formerly incarcerated parents. *Smith College Studies in Social Work*, *87*(1), 43–58. doi:10.1080/00377317.2017.1246797 PMID:29170570

Day, P. J., & Schiele, J. (2013). *A New History of Social Welfare* (7th ed.). Pearson.

Decker, K., Manis, A., & Paylo, M. (2015). Infusing social justice advocacy into counselor education: Strategies and recommendations. *The Journal of Counselor Preparation and Supervisor*, *8*(3). Advance online publication. doi:10.7729/83.1092

Decker, S. H., Ortiz, N., Spohn, C., & Hedberg, E. (2015). Criminal stigma, race, and ethnicity: The consequences of imprisonment for employment. *Journal of Criminal Justice*, *43*(2), 108–121. doi:10.1016/j.jcrimjus.2015.02.002

Delaney, R., Subramanian, R., Shames, A., & Turner, N. (2018). *American History, Race, and Prison.* Vera Institute of Justice.

DeMartini, L., Mizock, L., Drob, S., Nelson, A., & Fisher, W. (2020). The barriers and facilitators to serious mental illness: Recovery postincarceration. *Psychological Services*, 1–10. doi:10.1037er0000431 PMID:32551728

Denby, R. (2012). Parental incarceration and kinship care: Caregiver experiences, child well-being, and permanency intentions. *Social Work in Public Health*, *27*(1/2), 104–128. doi:10.1080/19371918.2012.639639 PMID:22239381

Denckla, D., & Berman, G. (2001). *Rethinking the revolving door: A look at mental illness in the courts.* Center for Court Innovation. https://www.courtinnovation.org/sites/default/files/rethinkingtherevolvingdoor.pdf

Denning, R., & Homel, R. (2008). Predicting recidivism in juvenile offenders on community-based orders: The impact of risk factors and service delivery. *Probation and Parole: Current Issues*, *46*(3–4), 189–215. doi:10.1080/10509670802143508

Department of Education and Office for Civil Rights. (n.d.). The use of restraint and seclusion on children with disabilities in K-12 schools. *Civil Rights Data Collection.* https://www2.ed.gov/about/offices/list/ocr/docs/restraint-and-seclusion.pdf

Desai, A., Durham, K., Burke, S. C., NeMoyer, A., & Heilbrun, K. (2021). Releasing individuals from incarceration during COVID-19: Pandemic-related challenges and recommendations for promoting successful reentry. *Psychology, Public Policy, and Law*, *27*(2), 242–255. doi:10.1037/law0000279

DeVuono-Powell, S., Schweilder, C., Walters, A., & Zohrabi, A. (2015). *Who pays? The true cost of incarceration on families.* http://whopaysreport.org/executive-summary/pdf-executive-summary/

Dewan, S. (2018). Family separation: It's a problem for U.S. citizens, too. *The New York Times.* https://www.nytimes.com/2018/06/22/us/family-separation-americans-prison-jail.html

Dillard, N. (2020). Designing research to dismantle oppression. Utilizing critical narrative analysis and critical participatory action research in research on mothering and work and beyond. *Journal of International Women's Studies*, *21*(7), 1–9.

Dillon, S. (2009). Study finds high rate of imprisonment among dropouts. *The New York Times.* https://www.nytimes.com/2009/10/09/education/09dropout.html

Dougherty, J. (2012). *Survey reveals barriers to successful ex-offender re-entry.* Judicial Process Commission. http://www.rocjpc.org/images/Survey-Reveals-Barriers-to-Successful-Ex-Offender-Re-Entry.pdf

Drug Policy Alliance. (2021). *A brief history of the drug war.* https://drugpolicy.org/issues/brief-history-drug-war

Dube, S. R., Anda, R. F., Felitti, V. J., Croft, J. B., Edwards, V. J., & Giles, W. H. (2001). Growing up with parental alcohol abuse: Exposure to childhood abuse, neglect, and household dysfunction. *Child Abuse & Neglect*, *25*(12), 1627–1640. doi:10.1016/S0145-2134(01)00293-9 PMID:11814159

Dube, S. R., Anda, R. F., Felitti, V. J., Edwards, V. J., & Croft, J. B. (2002). Adverse childhood experiences and personal alcohol abuse as an adult. *Addictive Behaviors*, *27*(5), 713–725. doi:10.1016/S0306-4603(01)00204-0 PMID:12201379

Dube, S. R., Felitti, V. J., Dong, M., Chapman, D. P., Giles, W. H., & Anda, R. F. (2003). Childhood abuse, neglect, and household dysfunction and the risk of illicit drug use: The adverse childhood experiences study. *Pediatrics*, *111*(3), 564–572. doi:10.1542/peds.111.3.564 PMID:12612237

Durlak, J. A., Weissberg, R. P., Dymnicki, A. B., Taylor, R. D., & Schellinger, K. B. (2011). The impact of enhancing students' social and emotional learning: A meta-analysis of school-based universal interventions. *Child Development*, *82*(1), 405–432. doi:10.1111/j.1467-8624.2010.01564.x PMID:21291449

Durrah, D. A. J. (2013). *Understanding African American male inmates' decisions to seek mental health treatment while incarcerated (No. 3604412).* ProQuest Dissertations & Theses.

Durrant, J., & Ensom, R. (2012). Physical punishment of children: Lessons from 20 years of research. *Canadian Medical Association Journal*, *184*(12), 1373–1377. doi:10.1503/cmaj.101314 PMID:22311946

Dutil, S. (2020). Dismantling the School-to-Prison Pipeline: A Trauma-Informed, Critical Race Perspective on School Discipline. *Children & Schools*, *42*(3), 171–178. doi:10.1093/cs/cdaa016

Dutra, L., Stathopoulou, G., Basden, S. L., Leyro, T. M., Powers, M. B., & Otto, M. W. (2008). A Meta-Analytic Review of Psychosocial Interventions for Substance Use Disorders. *The American Journal of Psychiatry*, *165*(2), 179–187. doi:10.1176/appi.ajp.2007.06111851 PMID:18198270

Dutro, E. (2017). Let's start with heartbreak: The perilous potential of trauma in literacy. *Language Arts*, *95*(5), 326–337.

Duwe, G., & McNeeley, S. (2021). Just as good as the real thing? The effects of prison video visitation on recidivism. *Crime and Delinquency*, *67*(4), 475–497. doi:10.1177/0011128720943168

Dyer, W. J., Day, R. D., & Wiley, A. R. (2018). Jailed fathers and family complexity. *Social Work Research*, *42*(3), 210–222. doi:10.1093wrvy015

Eason, J., Zucker, D., & Wildeman, C. (2017). Mass imprisonment across the rural-urban interface. *The Annals of the American Academy of Political and Social Science*, *671*(1), 202–216. doi:10.1177/0002716217705357

Eaves, E., Camplain, R., Lininger, M., & Trotter, I. I. R. (2020). Adverse childhood experiences in relation to drug and alcohol use in 30 days prior to incarceration in a county jail. *International Journal of Prisoner Health*. Advance online publication. doi:10.1108/IJPH-06-2020-0038 PMID:34745314

Edwards, F. (2016). Saving children, controlling families: Punishment, redistribution, and child protection. *American Sociological Review*, *81*(3), 575–595. doi:10.1177/0003122416638652

Egbochukwu, E. O. (2008). *Guidance and counselling: A comprehensive text*. Uniben Press.

Ejekwonyilo, A. (2019). *Inside the world of Nigeria child prisoners*. https://www.thecable.ng/inside-the-world-of-nigerias-child-prisoners

Elder, G. H. (1995). The life course paradigm: Social change and individual development. In P. Moen, G. H. Elder, & K. Luscher (Eds.), *Examining lives in context: Perspectives on the ecology of human development* (pp. 101–139). doi:10.1037/10176-003

Eldridge, T., & Thompson, C. (2018). *Treatment denied: The mental health crisis in federal prisons*. https://www.themarshallproject.org/2018/11/21/treatment-denied-the-mental-health-crisis-in-federal-prisons

Equal Justice Initiative. (2020). *Reconstruction in America: Racial violence after the civil war, 1865 – 1876*. Author.

Equal Justice Initiative. (2021). https://eji.org/criminal-justice-reform/

Erford, B., Bardhoshi, G., Ross, M., Gunther, C., & Duncan, K. (2015). Meta-analysis of counseling outcomes for youth with conduct disorder. *Journal of Counseling and Development*, *95*(1), 35–44. doi:10.1002/jcad.12115

Erwin, B. A., Newman, E., McMackin, R. A., Morrissey, C., & Kaloupek, D. G. (2000). PTSD, malevolent environment, and criminality among criminally involved male adolescents. *Criminal Justice and Behavior*, *27*(2), 196–215. doi:10.1177/0093854800027002004

Ethridge, G., Dunlap, P. N., Boston, Q., & Staten, B. H. (2014). Ex-offenders in rural settings seeking employment. *Journal of Applied Rehabilitation Counseling*, *45*(4), 56–63. doi:10.1891/0047-2220.45.4.56

Ettekal, A. V., & Mahoney, J. L. (2017). Ecological systems theory. In K. Peppler (Ed.), *The Sage encyclopedia of out-of-school learning* (pp. 239–241). Sage.

Evans, M. P., & Didlick-Davis, C. (2012). Organizing to end the school-to-prison pipeline: An analysis of grassroots organizing campaigns and policy solutions. *e-Journal of Education Policy*. Retrieved from http://nau.edu/COE/ eJournal/ Fall-2012/

Ewert, S., Sykes, B., & Pettit, B. (2013). The degree of disadvantage: Incarceration and inequality in education. *The Annals of the American Academy of Political and Social Science*, *651*(1), 24–43. doi:10.1177/0002716213503100

Eyberg, S. M., & Funderburk, B. (2011). *Parent-child interaction therapy protocol. PCIT International, INC*. PCIT International.

Fabelo, T., Thompson, M. D., Plotkin, M., Carmichael, D., Marchbanks, M. P., III, & Booth, E. A. (2011). *Breaking schools' rules: A statewide study of how school discipline relates to students' success and juvenile justice involvement*. https://csgjusticecenter.org/publications/breaking-schools-rules/

Fagan, A. A., & Novak, A. (2018). Adverse childhood experiences and adolescent delinquency in a high-risk sample: A comparison of white and black youth. *Youth Violence and Juvenile Justice*, *16*(4), 395–417. doi:10.1177/1541204017735568

Federal Bureau of Prisons. (2021). *Federal bureau of prisons program fact sheet*. Author.

Federal Bureau of Prisons. (2021). *Inmate race* [chart]. https://www.bop.gov/about/statistics/statistics_inmate_race.jsp

Federal Bureau of Prisons. (2021). *Statistics*. https://www.bop.gov/about/statistics/population_statistics.jsp

Federal Bureau of Prisons. (2021). *Teacher: Job series number: 1710*. Retrieved July 24, 2021 from https://www.bop.gov/jobs/positions/index.jsp?p=Teacher#:~:text=Basic%20Requirements&text=You%20have%20a%20Bachelor's%20degree,and%2For%20philosophy%20of%20education

Federal Bureau of Prisons. (2022). *Substance abuse treatment*. https://www.bop.gov/inmates/custody_and_care/substance_abuse_treatment.jsp

Federal Republic of Nigeria (FRN). (2013). National policy on education. Lagos: Nigerian Educational Research Council (NERDC) Press.

Federal Student Aid. (2021). *Federal student adult for adults in correctional and juvenile justice facilities*. https://studentaid.gov/sites/default/files/aid-info-for-incarcerated-individuals.pdf

Federman, J. (Ed.). (1998). *National Television Violence Study* (Vol. 3). Sage.

Felitti, V. J., Anda, R. F., Nordenberg, D., Williamson, D. F., Spitz, A. M., Edwards, V., & Marks, J. S. (1998). Relationship of childhood abuse and household dysfunction to many of the leading causes of death in adults: The adverse childhood experiences (ACE) study. *American Journal of Preventive Medicine*, *14*(4), 245–258. doi:10.1016/S0749-3797(98)00017-8 PMID:9635069

Fellner, J., Parker, A., & Rau Barriga, S. (2015). *Callous and cruel: Use of force against inmates with mental disabilities in U.S. jails and prisons*. https://www.hrw.org/report/2015/05/12/callous-and-cruel/use-force-against-inmates-mental-disabilities-us-jails-and#page

Fellowship, P. (n.d.). *Unwrapping the gift of connection*. https://www.prisonfellowship.org/about/angel-tree/angel-tree-christmas/

Festen, M., Waul, M., Solomon, A., & Travis, J. (2002, January 30-31). *From prison to home: The effect of incarceration and reentry on children, families, and communities* [Conference Report]. Office of the Assistant Secretary for Planning and Evaluation. https://www.urban.org/sites/default/files/publication/60716/410632-Background-Paper-The-Effect-of-Incarceration-and-Reentry-on-Children-Families-and-Communities.PDF

Finkelhor, D. (2020). Trends in adverse childhood experiences (ACEs) in the United States. *Child Abuse & Neglect*, *108*, 104641. Advance online publication. doi:10.1016/j.chiabu.2020.104641 PMID:32739600

Fleming, C. M., & Nurius, P. S. (2020). Incarceration and adversity histories: Modeling life course pathways affecting behavioral health. *The American Journal of Orthopsychiatry*, *90*(3), 312–323. doi:10.1037/ort0000436 PMID:31829646

Fletcher, R. C., & Sherk, J. (2009). *Mentoring former prisoners: A guide for reentry programs*. Public/Private Ventures. https://eric.ed.gov/?id=ED507378

Fletcher, D. R. (2002). Ex-offenders, the labour market and the new public administration. *Public Administration*, *79*(4), 871–891. doi:10.1111/1467-9299.00284

Foley, R. (2001). Academic characteristics of incarcerated youth and correctional educational programs: A literature review. *Journal of Emotional and Behavioral Disorders*, *9*(4), 248–259. doi:10.1177/106342660100900405

Foley, R. M., & Gao, J. (2002). Correctional education programs serving incarcerated juveniles: A status report. *Journal of Correctional Education*, *53*(4), 131–138. https://www.ojp.gov/ncjrs/virtual-library/abstracts/correctional-education-programs-serving-incarcerated-juveniles

Fontaine, J. (2013). The role of supportive housing in successful reentry outcomes for disabled prisoners. *Cityscape: A Journal of Policy Development and Research, 15*(3), 53-75. https://www.huduser.gov/portal/periodicals/cityscpe/vol15num3/ch3.pdf

Ford, K., Barton, E., Newbury, A., Hughes, K., Bezeczky, Z., Roderick, J., & Bellis, M. (2019). Understanding the prevalence of adverse childhood experiences (ACEs) in a male offender population in Wales: The prisoner ACE survey. *Public Health Wales*. https://research.bangor.ac.uk/portal/files/23356885/PHW_Prisoner_ACE_Survey_Report_E.pdf

Ford, M. (5, April 2019). The everyday brutality of American's prison. *The New Republic*. https://newrepublic.com/article/153473/everyday-brutality-americas-prisons

Ford, K., Bellis, M., Hughes, K., Barton, E., & Newbury, A. (2020). Adverse childhood experiences: A retrospective study to understand their associations with lifetime mental health diagnosis, self-harm or suicide attempt, and current low mental wellbeing in a male welsh prison population. *Health & Justice*, *8*(1), 13. doi:10.118640352-020-00115-5 PMID:32533348

Forste, R., & Fox, K. (2012). Household labor, gender roles, and family satisfaction: A cross-national comparison. *Journal of Comparative Family Studies*, *43*(5), 613–631. doi:10.3138/jcfs.43.5.613

Foster, H., & Hagan, J. (2009). The mass incarceration of parents in America: Issues of race/ethnicity, collateral damage to children, and prisoner reentry. *The Annals of the American Academy of Political and Social Science*, *623*(1), 179–194. doi:10.1177/0002716208331123

Foster, H., & Hagan, J. (2013). Maternal and paternal imprisonment in the stress process. *Social Science Research*, *42*(3), 650–669. doi:10.1016/j.ssresearch.2013.01.008 PMID:23521986

Fox, B., Miley, L. N., Kortright, K. E., & Wetsman, R. J. (2021). Assessing the effect of mental health courts on adult and juvenile recidivism: A meta-analysis. *American Journal of Criminal Justice*, *46*(4), 644–664. doi:10.100712103-021-09629-6

Franco-Paredes, C., Ghandnoosh, N., Latif, H., Krsak, M., Henao-Martinez, A. F., Robins, M., Vargas Barahona, L., & Poeschla, E. M. (2021). Decarceration and community re-entry in the COVID-19 era. *The Lancet. Infectious Diseases*, *21*(1), e11–e16. doi:10.1016/S1473-3099(20)30730-1 PMID:33007225

Franke, H. (2014). Toxic stress: Effects, prevention and treatment. *Children (Basel, Switzerland)*, *1*(3), 390–402. doi:10.3390/children1030390 PMID:27417486

Freudenberg, N., Daniels, J., Crum, M., Perkins, T., & Richie, B. (2005). Coming home from jail: The social and health consequences of community reentry for women, male adolescents, and their families and communities. *American Journal of Public Health*, *95*(10), 11725–11736. doi:10.2105/AJPH.2004.056325 PMID:16186451

Frey, K. S., Nolen, S. B., Van Schoiack Edstrom, L., & Hirschstein, M. K. (2005). Effects of a school-based social-emotional competence program: Linking children's goals, attributions, and behavior. *Journal of Applied Developmental Psychology*, *26*(2), 171–200. doi:10.1016/j.appdev.2004.12.002

Frieze, S. (2015). How Trauma Affects Student Learning and Behaviour. *BU Journal of Graduate Studies in Education*, *7*(2), 27–34.

Fuchs, Z. (2019). Behind Bars: The urgency and simplicity of prison phone reform. *Harvard Law & Policy Review*, *14*, 205–229.

Galletta, E., Fagan, T. J., Shapiro, D., & Walker, L. E. (2021). Societal reentry of prison inmates with mental illness: Obstacles, programs, and best practices. *Journal of Correctional Health Care*, *27*(1), 58–65. doi:10.1089/jchc.19.04.0032 PMID:34232765

Garland, D. (2001). Introduction. In D. Garland (Ed.), Mass imprisonment: Social causes and consequences (pp. 1-3). Sage.

Garland, D. (1990). *Punishment and modern society: A study in social theory*. Oxford University Press. doi:10.7208/chicago/9780226922508.001.0001

Garland, D. (2001). The meaning of mass imprisonment. In D. Garland (Ed.), *Mass imprisonment: Social cause and consequences* (pp. 1–2). Sage. doi:10.4135/9781446221228.n1

Garretson, H. J. (2016). Legislating forgiveness: A study of post-conviction certificates as policy to address the employment consequences of a conviction. *The Boston University Public Interest Law Journal*, *25*(1), 1–42. https://papers.ssrn.com/sol3/papers.cfm?abstract_id=2733215

Geib, C. F., Chapman, J. F., D'Amaddio, A. H., & Grigorenko, E. L. (2011). The education of juveniles in detention: Policy considerations and infrastructure development. *Learning and Individual Differences*, *21*(1), 3–11. doi:10.1016/j.lindif.2010.05.002

Geiger, J. M., Piel, M. H., & Julien-Chinn, F. (2017). Improving relationships in child welfare practice: Perspectives of foster care providers. *Child & Adolescent Social Work Journal*, *34*(1), 23–33. doi:10.100710560-016-0471-3

Gershoff, E. T. (2008). *Report on Physical Punishment in the United States: What Research Tells Us About Its Effects on Children*. https://phoenixchildrens.org/

Gershoff, E. T. (2013). Spanking and Child Development: We know enough now to stop hitting our children. *Child Development Perspectives*, *7*(3), 133–137. doi:10.1111/cdep.12038 PMID:24039629

Giano, Z., O'Neil, A., & Hubach, R. (2021). The effects of individual and dual ACE domains on binge drinking: Comparisons by gender. *Substance Use & Misuse*, *56*(11), 1–9. doi:10.1080/10826084.2021.1949604 PMID:34279181

Gicquelais, R. E., Mezuk, B., Foxman, B., Thomas, L., & Bohnert, A. S. B. (2019). Justice involvement patterns, overdose experiences, and naloxone knowledge among men and women in criminal justice diversion addiction treatment. *Harm Reduction Journal*, *16*(1), 1–11. doi:10.118612954-019-0317-3 PMID:31311572

Gifford, E. J., Evans, K. E., Eldred Kozecke, L., & Sloan, F. A. (2020). Mothers and fathers in the criminal justice system and children's child protective services involvement. *Child Abuse & Neglect, 101*. https://doi-org.ezproxy.nccu.edu/10.1016/j.chiabu.2019.104306

Giguere, R., & Dundes, L. (2002). Help wanted: A survey of employer concerns about hiring ex-convicts. *Criminal Justice Policy Review*, *13*(4), 396–408. doi:10.1177/088740302237806

Giliberti, M. (2015). *It's outrageous: Jails and prisons are no place to treat mental illness; just ask Paton Blough*. https://stepuptogether.org/updates/its-outrageous-jails-and-prisons-are-no-

Gill, C., & Wilson, D. B. (2016). Improving the success of reentry programs: Identifying the impact of service-need fit on recidivism. *Criminal Justice and Behavior*, *44*(3), 336–359. doi:10.1177/0093854816682048

Girvan, E. J., Gion, C., McIntosh, K., & Smolkowski, K. (2017). The relative contribution of subjective office referrals to racial disproportionality in school discipline. *School Psychology Quarterly*, *32*(3), 392–404. doi:10.1037pq0000178 PMID:27736122

Gjelsvik, A., Dumont, D. M., Nunn, A., & Rosen, D. L. (2014). Adverse childhood events: Incarceration of household members and health-related quality of life in adulthood. *Journal of Health Care for the Poor and Underserved*, *25*(3), 1169–1182. doi:10.1353/hpu.2014.0112 PMID:25130232

Gladding, S. T. (2011). Courtland Lee: A global advocate for counseling. *Journal of Counseling and Development*, *89*, 493–499.

Glaze, L. E., & Maruschak, L. L. M. (2008). *Parents in prison and their minor children.* U.S. Department of Justice. https://www.ncjrs.gov/App/abstractdb/AbstractDBDetails.aspx?id=244893

Glaze, L., & Maruschak, L. (2010). *Bureau of justice statistics special report: Parents in prison and their minor children.* U.S. Department of Justice. https://bjs.ojp.gov/content/pub/pdf/pptmc.pdf

Goddard, T., & Pooley, J. (2019). The impact of childhood abuse on adult male prisoners: A systematic review. *Journal of Police and Criminal Psychology*, *34*(2), 215–230. doi:10.100711896-018-9260-6

Goffman, A. (2009). On the run: Wanted men in a Philadelphia ghetto. *American Sociological Review*, *74*(3), 339–357. doi:10.1177/000312240907400301

Golden, L. (2009). Counseling children: Working with families. *Counseling and Human Development*, *41*(6), 1–10.

Gomes, S., & Rocker, D. (2021). Gender, incarceration and reentry: An analysis of the barriers to reentry of male and female adult prisoners in Portugal. In *Incarceration and Generation* (Vol. 1, pp. 255–299). Palgrave Macmillan. doi:10.1007/978-3-030-82265-1_8

Gonzalez, I. A., & Cokley, R. K. (2021). The Case for a Core Anti-racist Course for Counselors in Training. *Teaching and Supervision in Counseling*, *3*(2), 26–37. doi:10.7290/tsc030204

Goodkind, S., Shook, J. J., Kim, K. H., Pohlig, R. T., & Herring, D. J. (2013). From child welfare to juvenile justice: Race, gender, and system experiences. *Youth Violence and Juvenile Justice*, *11*(3), 249–272. doi:10.1177/1541204012463409

Gopalan, M., & Nelson, A. A. (2019). Understanding the racial discipline gap in schools. *AERA Open*, *5*(2), 1–26. doi:10.1177/2332858419844613 PMID:34012995

Gotsch, K. (2018, April 24). Families of mass incarceration. *The Sentencing Project.* https://www.sentencingproject.org/publications/6148/

Gottfredson, D. C., Najaka, S. S., & Kearley, B. (2003). Effectiveness of drug treatment courts: Evidence from a randomized trial. *Criminology & Public Policy*, *2*(2), 171–196. doi:10.1111/j.1745-9133.2003.tb00117.x

Grabenstein, H. (2018). *Inside Mississippi's notorious Parchman prison.* PBS NewsHour.

Grace, J. E., & Nelson, S. L. (2019). "Tryin' to Survive": Black Male Students' Understandings of the Role of Race and Racism in the School-to-Prison Pipeline. *Leadership and Policy in Schools*, *18*(4), 664–680. doi:10.1080/15700763.2018.1513154

Graf, G. H. J., Chihuri, S., Blow, M., & Li, G. (2021). Adverse childhood experiences and justice system contact: A systematic review. *Pediatrics*, *147*(1), e2020021030. doi:10.1542/peds.2020-021030 PMID:33328338

Graham, J. A., & Harris, Y. R. (2013). Children of color and parental incarceration: Implications for research, theory, and practice. *Journal of Multicultural Counseling and Development*, *41*(2), 66–81. doi:10.1002/j.2161-1912.2013.00028.x

Graham, P. W., Yaros, A., Lowe, A., & McDaniel, M. S. (2017). Nurturing Environments for Boys and Men of Color with Trauma Exposure. *Clinical Child and Family Psychology Review*, *20*(2), 105–116. doi:10.100710567-017-0241-6 PMID:28547524

Gramlich, J. (2021, August 16). *America's incarceration rate falls to lowest level since 1995.* PEW Research Center. https://www.pewresearch.org/fact-tank/2021/08/16/americas-incarceration-rate-lowest-since-1995/

Greene, J. (2002). *Getting Tough on Crime: The History and Political Context of Sentencing Reform Developments Leading to the Passage of the 1994 Crime Act.* https://www.justicestrategies.org/sites/default/files/Judy/GettingToughOnCrime.pdf

Greenfield, L. A., & Snell, T. L. (1999). *Women offenders* (NCJ 175688). US Department of Justice, Office of Justice Programs, Bureau of Justice Statistics. https://bjs.ojp.gov/content/pub/pdf/wo.pdf

Gregory, A., & Evans, K. (2020). *The starts and stumbles of restorative justice in education: Where do we go from here?* https://nepc.colorado.edu/publication/restorative-justice

Gregory, A., & Fergus, E. (2017). Social and emotional learning and equity in school discipline. *The Future of Children, 27*(1), 117–136. doi:10.1353/foc.2017.0006

Gregory, A., Skiba, R. J., & Noguera, P. A. (2010). The achievement gap and the discipline gap: Two sides of the same coin? *Educational Researcher, 39*(1), 59–68. doi:10.3102/0013189X09357621

Grieb, S. M. D., Crawford, A., Fields, J., Smith, H., Harris, R., & Matson, P. (2014). "The stress will kill you": Prisoner reentry as experienced by family members and the urgent need for support services. *Journal of Health Care for the Poor and Underserved, 25*(3), 1183–1200. doi:10.1353/hpu.2014.0118 PMID:25130233

Griffith, D., & Tyner, A. (2019). *Discipline reform through the eyes of teachers.* https://fordhaminstitute.org/national/research/discipline-reform-through-the-eyes-of-teachers

Griffiths, C. T., Dandurand, Y., & Murdoch, D. (2007). *The social reintegration of offenders and crime prevention.* National Crime Prevention Centre, Public Safety Canada. https://curtgriffiths.com/wp-content/uploads/pdfs/social-reintegration.pdf

Grinage, J. (2019). Endless mourning: Racial melancholia, black grief, and the transformative possibilities for racial justice in Education. *Harvard Educational Review, 89*(2), 227–250. doi:10.17763/1943-5045-89.2.227

Grinspoon, P. (2021). *Poverty, homelessness, and stigma make addiction more deadly.* https://www.health.harvard.edu/blog/poverty-homelessness-and-social-stigma-make-addiction-more-deadly-202109282602

Grummitt, L., Kelly, E., Barrett, E., Keyes, K., & Newton, N. (2021). Targets for intervention to prevent substance use in young people exposed to childhood adversity: A systematic review. *PLoS One, 16*(6), e0252815. Advance online publication. doi:10.1371/journal.pone.0252815 PMID:34097711

Guarino, H., Mateu-Gelabert, P., Quinn, K., Sirikantraporn, S., Ruggles, K. V., Syckes, C., Goodbody, E., Jessell, L., & Friedman, S. R. (2021). Adverse childhood experiences predict early initiation of opioid use behaviors. *Frontiers in Sociology, 6*, 620395. Advance online publication. doi:10.3389/fsoc.2021.620395 PMID:34055961

Gupta, H., Pettigrew, S., Lam, T., & Tait, R. J. (2016). A systematic review of the impact of exposure to internet-based alcohol-related content on young people's alcohol use behaviours. *Alcohol (Fayetteville, N.Y.), 51*(6), 763–771. PMID:27522028

Guth, L. J., Pollard, B. L., Nitza, A., Puig, A., Chan, C. D., Singh, A. A., & Bailey, H. (2019). Ten strategies to intentionally use group work to transform hate, facilitate courageous conversations, and enhance community building. *Journal for Specialists in Group Work, 44*(1), 3–24. doi:10.1080/01933922.2018.1561778

Hadden, S. E. (2001). *Slave patrols: Law and violence in Virginia and the Carolinas.* Harvard University Press.

Hagan, B. O., Wang, E. A., Aminawung, J. A., Albizu-Garcia, C. E., Zaller, N., Nyamu, S., Shavit, S., Deluca, J., Fox, A. D., & Transitions Clinic Network. (2018). History of solitary confinement is associated with post-traumatic stress disorder symptoms among individuals recently released from prison. *Journal of Urban Health, 95*(2), 141-148. doi:10.1007/s11524-017-0138-1

Hagner, D., Malloy, J. M., Mazzone, M. W., & Cormier, G. M. (2008). Youth with disabilities in the Criminal Justice System. *Journal of Emotional and Behavioral Disorders*, *16*(4), 240–247. doi:10.1177/1063426608316019

Hairston, C. F. (2007). *Focus on the children with incarcerated parents: A overview of the research literature.* Annie E. Casey Foundation. Retrieved from https://assets.aecf.org/m/resourcedoc/aecf-FocusonChildrenwith_ncarceratedParentsOverviewofLiterature-2007.pdf

Hairston, C. (2018). Family relationships during incarceration and when fathers return home. *Journal of Offender Rehabilitation*, *57*(2), 67–68.

Hambrick, E. P., Brawner, T. W., & Perry, B. D. (2019). Timing of early-life stress and the development of brain-related capacities. *Frontiers in Behavioral Neuroscience, 13*, 183. Advance online publication. doi:10.3389/fnbeh.2019.00183 PMID:31447660

Hamilton, L., & Belenko, S. (2016). Effects of pre-release services on access to behavioral health treatment after release from prison. *Justice Quarterly*, *33*(6), 1080–1102. doi:10.1080/07418825.2015.1073771

Hammett, T. M., Harmon, P., & Maruschak, L. M. (1999). *1996-1997 Update: HIV/AIDS, STDs, and TB in correctional facilities*. National Institute of Justice. doi:10.1037/e514772006-001

Haney, C. (2001). *The psychological impact of incarceration: Implications for post-prison adjustment.* https://aspe.hhs.gov/basic-report/psychological-impact-incarceration-implications-post-prison-adjustment

Haney, C. (2003). Mental health issues in long-term solitary and "Supermax" confinement. *Crime and Delinquency, 49*(1), 124–156. https://doi.org/10.1177/0011128702239239

Hardy, K. V. (2013). Healing the Hidden Wounds of Racial Trauma. *Reclaiming Children and Youth*, *22*(1), 24–28.

Harer, M. D., & Langan, N. P. (2001). Gender differences in predictors of prison violence: Assessing the predictive validity of a risk classification system. *Crime and Delinquency*, *47*(4), 513–536. doi:10.1177/0011128701047004002

Hargons, C., Mosley, D., Falconer, J., Faloughi, R., Singh, A., Stevens-Watkins, D., & Cokley, K. (2017). Black lives matter: A call to action for counseling psychology leaders. *The Counseling Psychologist*, *45*(6), 873–901. doi:10.1177/0011000017733048 PMID:29217847

Harlow, C. W. (2003). *Education and correctional population* [Special report] (NCJ 195670). Bureau of Justice Statistics. https://bjs.ojp.gov/content/pub/pdf/ecp.pdf

Harper, G., & Chitty, C. (2004). The impact of corrections on re-offending: A review of 'what works': Home office research study 291. *PsycEXTRA Dataset*. doi:10.1037/e455022008-001

Harper, A., Ginapp, C., Bardelli, T., Grimshaw, A., Justen, M., Mohamedali, A., Thomas, I., & Puglisi, L. (2021). Debt, incarceration, and re-entry: A scoping review. *American Journal of Criminal Justice*, *46*(2), 250–278. doi:10.100712103-020-09559-9 PMID:32837173

Hawkins, R. L., Vashchenko, M., & Davis, C. (2011). Making a place for youth: Social capital, resilience, and communities. In F. T. Sherman & F. H. Jacobs (Eds.), *Juvenile Justice: Advancing Research, Policy, and Practice* (pp. 245–266). John Wiley & Sons, Inc. doi:10.1002/9781118093375.ch12

Hayes, S. C., Luoma, J. B., Bond, F. W., Masuda, A., & Lillis, J. (2006). Acceptance and Commitment Therapy: Model, processes and outcomes. *Behaviour Research and Therapy*, *44*(1), 1–25. doi:10.1016/j.brat.2005.06.006 PMID:16300724

Hayes, S. C., & Strosahl, K. D. (2004). *A Practical Guide to Acceptance and Commitment Therapy*. Springer Science & Business Media. doi:10.1007/978-0-387-23369-7

Hayward, R. A., & DePanfilis, D. (2007). Foster children with an incarcerated parent: Predictors of reunification. *Children and Youth Services Review*, *29*(10), 1320–1334. doi:10.1016/j.childyouth.2007.05.005

Health Resources and Services Administration. (2020, March 4). *New HRSA data show one in three US children have suffered an adverse childhood experience*. https://www.hrsa.gov/about/news/press-releases/

Heitzeg, N. A. (2009). Education or Incarceration: Zero Tolerance Policies and the School to Prison Pipeline. *Forum on Public Policy Online, 2009*(2), 1-21.

Heitzeg, N. A. (2009). Education or incarceration: Zero tolerance policies and the school to prison pipeline. *Forum on Public Policy*, 1–21.

Helms, J. E. (1997). Toward a model of White racial identity development. In P. G. Altbach, K. Arnold, & I. C. King (Eds.), *College student development and academic life: Psychological, intellectual, social and moral issues* (pp. 207–224). Routledge.

Hemmings, C., & Evans, A. M. (2018). Identifying and Treating Race-Based Trauma in Counseling. *Journal of Multicultural Counseling and Development*, *46*(1), 20–39. doi:10.1002/jmcd.12090

Henggeler, S. W., Sheidow, A. J., & Lee, T. (2009). Multisystemic therapy (MST). In J. H. Bray & M. Stanton (Eds.), The Wiley-Blackwell handbook of family psychology. Wiley-Blackwell.

Henggeler, S. W., & Schaeffer, C. (2010). Treating serious antisocial behavior using multisystemic therapy. In J. R. Weisz & A. E. Kazdin (Eds.), *Evidence-based psychotherapies for children and adolescents* (2nd ed., pp. 259–276). Guilford Press.

Henggeler, S. W., Schoenwald, S. K., Borduin, C. M., Rowland, M. D., & Cunningham, P. B. (2009). *Multisystemic therapy for antisocial behavior in children and adolescents* (2nd ed.). Guilford Press.

Henry, B. F. (2020). Typologies of adversity in childhood & adulthood as determinants of mental health & substance use disorders of adults incarcerated in US prisons. *Child Abuse & Neglect*, *99*, 104251. Advance online publication. doi:10.1016/j.chiabu.2019.104251 PMID:31726246

Herrera, M. (2017). *A child's mental health and antisocial behavior: A close look at effects of parent incarceration based on timing*. https://pqdtopen.proquest.com/doc/1970070524.html?FMT=AI

Higgins, S. T., Wong, C. J., Badger, G. J., Ogden, D. E., & Dantona, R. L. (2000). Contingent reinforcement increases cocaine abstinence during outpatient treatment and one year of follow-up. *Journal of Consulting and Clinical Psychology*, *68*(1), 64–72. doi:10.1037/0022-006X.68.1.64 PMID:10710841

Hill, A.J. & Jones, D.B. (2021). The effect of school closings on teacher labor market outcomes and teacher effectiveness. *Education Finance and Policy*, 1 – 25. . doi:10.1162/edfp_a_00317

Hill, N. E., Witherspoon, D. P., & Bartz, D. (2018). Parental involvement in education during middle school: Perspectives of ethnically diverse parents, teachers, and students. *The Journal of Educational Research*, *111*(1), 12–27. doi:10.1080/00220671.2016.1190910

Hinton, E., & Cook, D. (2021). The mass criminalization of Black Americans: A Historical overview. *Annual Review of Criminology*, *4*(1), 261–286. doi:10.1146/annurev-criminol-060520-033306

Hiolski, K., Eisenberg, M. E., & Shlafer, R. J. (2019). Youth self-reported health and their experience of parental incarceration. *Families, Systems & Health*, *37*(1), 38–45. doi:10.1037/fsh0000394 PMID:30920262

Hirschi, T. (1969). *Causes of Delinquency*. University of California Press.

Hoeve, M., Colins, O., Mulder, E., Loeber, R., Stams, G., & Vermeiren, R. (2015). Trauma and mental health problems in adolescent males. *Criminal Justice and Behavior*, *42*(7), 685–702.

Hoffmann, H. C., Byrd, A. L., & Kightlinger, A. M. (2010). Prison programs and services for incarcerated parents and their underage children: Results from a national survey of correctional facilities. *The Prison Journal*, *90*(4), 397–416. doi:10.1177/0032885510382087

Hogan, P. T., & Siu, S. (1998). Minority children and the child welfare system: An historical perspective. *Social Work*, *33*(6), 493–498. doi:10.1093w/33.6.493

Holzer, H. J., Raphael, S., & Stoll, M. A. (2003). *Employment barriers facing ex-offenders*. Urban Institute. https://www.urban.org/sites/default/files/publication/59416/410855-Employment-Barriers-Facing-Ex-Offenders.PDF

Honore-Collins, C. P. (2005). The impact of African American incarceration on African American children in the child welfare system. *Race, Gender, & Class*, *12*(3/4), 107–118.

Hood, B. J., & Gaston, S. (2021). How families respond to the collateral consequences of incarceration and prisoner reentry. *Family Relations*, fare.12616. Advance online publication. doi:10.1111/fare.12616

Horsford, S. (2019). School Integration in the New Jim Crow: Opportunity or Oxymoron? *Educational Policy*, *33*(1), 257–275. doi:10.1177/0895904818810526

Howard, K. A., & Solberg, V. S. H. (2006). School-based social justice: The achieving success identity pathways program. *Professional School Counseling*, *21*(1), 278–287. doi:10.5330/prsc.9.4.4587465231061304

Howard, R., & Karatzias, T. (2016). From childhood trauma to self-harm: An investigation of theoretical pathways among female prisoners. *Clinical Psychology & Psychotherapy*. Advance online publication. doi:10.1002/cpp.2058 PMID:27878907

Howell, J. (2017). Race and US medical experimentation: The case of Tuskegee. *Cadernos de Saude Publica*, *33*(1, suppl 1). Advance online publication. doi:10.1590/0102-311x00168016 PMID:28492710

Howell, P. B., Thomas, S., Sweeney, D., & Vanderhaar, J. (2019). Moving beyond schedules, testing and other duties as deemed necessary by the principal: The school counselor's role in Trauma Informed Practices. *Middle School Journal*, *50*(4), 26–34. doi:10.1080/00940771.2019.1650548

Hser, Y., & Schulte, M. (2014). Substance use and associated health conditions throughout the lifespan. *Public Health Reviews*, *39*(2). https://www.ncbi.nlm.nih.gov/pmc/articles/PMC5373082/

Hucklesby, A., & Wincup, E. (2014). Assistance, support and monitoring? The paradoxes of mentoring adults in the criminal justice system. *Journal of Social Policy*, *43*(2), 373–390. doi:10.1017/S0047279413001013

Hunter, B. A., Lanza, A. S., Lawlor, M., Dyson, W., & Gordon, D. M. (2016). A strengths-based approach to prisoner reentry: The fresh start prisoner reentry program. *International Journal of Offender Therapy and Comparative Criminology*, *60*(11), 1298–1314. doi:10.1177/0306624X15576501 PMID:25805715

Ibrahim, F. A., Dinsmore, J. A., Estrada, D., & D'Andrea, M.Counselors for Social Justice (CSJ) Ethi. (2011). The Counselors for Social Justice (CSJ) code of ethics. *Journal for Social Action in Counseling and Psychology*, *3*(2), 1–21. doi:10.33043/JSACP.3.2.1-21

Individuals with Disabilities Education Act, 20 U.S.C. § 1400 (2004).

Iniguez, K. C., & Stankowski, R. V. (2016). Adverse childhood experiences and health in adulthood in a rural population-based sample. *Clinical Medicine & Research*, *14*(3-4), 126–137. doi:10.3121/cmr.2016.1306 PMID:27503793

Inman, S. (2020). *Racial disparities in criminal justice: How lawyers can help.* American Bar Association. https://www.americanbar.org/groups/young_lawyers/publications/after-the-bar/public- service/racial-disparities-criminal-justice-how-lawyers-can-help/

Institute for Child and Family Well-Being. (2018). *Issue brief: Translating trauma-informed principles into trauma-responsive practices.* https://uwm.edu/icfw/issuebriefs/

Intercultural Development Research Association. (2021). *Understanding and addressing racial trauma and supporting black students in schools – policy brief.* https://www.idra.org/education_policy

Intercultural Developmental Research Association. (2021). *Understanding and Addressing Racial Trauma and Supporting Black Students in Schools.* www.idra.org/wp-content/uploads/2021/02/Understanding-and-Addressing-Racial-Trauma-and Supporting-Black-Students-in-Schools-IDRA.pdf

International Child and Youth Care Network. (2009). *Rethinking the effectiveness of suspensions.* Discipline. https://cyc-net.org/cyc-online/cyconline-dec2009-sautner.html

Ivery, E. A. (2020). *The influence of community-based reentry programs on reintegrating ex-offenders in Ohio* [Doctoral dissertation, Walden University]. Walden Dissertations and Doctoral Studies. https://scholarworks.waldenu.edu/cgi/viewcontent.cgi?article=11229&context=dissertations

Jackson, K. M., Janssen, T., & Gabrielli, J. (2018). Media/marketing influences on adolescent and young adult substance abuse. *Current Addiction Reports*, *5*(2), 146–157. doi:10.100740429-018-0199-6 PMID:30393590

Jaggi, L., Mezuk, B., Watkins, D., & Jackson, J. (2016). The relationship between trauma, arrest, and incarceration history among black Americans: Findings from the national survey of American life. *Society and Mental Health*, *6*(3), 187–206.

Jaggi, L., Mezuk, B., Watkins, D., & Jackson, J. (2016). The relationship between trauma, arrest, and incarceration history among black americans: Findings from the national survey of American life. *Society and Mental Health*, *6*(3), 187–206. doi:10.1177/2156869316641730 PMID:27795871

James, N. (2015). *Offender reentry: Correctional statistics, reintegration into the community, and recidivism* (RL34287). Congressional Research Service. https://sgp.fas.org/crs/misc/RL34287.pdf

James, G. (2013). Assessment of the Administration and Practice of Juvenile Justice System in Abuja, Nigeria. *Mediterranean Journal of Social Sciences*, *4*(1), 331–338.

James, S. (2004). Why Do Foster Care Placements Disrupt? An Investigation of Reasons for Placement Change in Foster Care. *The Social Service Review*, *78*(4), 601–627. doi:10.1086/424546

Jbara, A. E. (2012). The price they pay: Protecting the mother-child relationship through the use of prison nurseries and residential parenting programs. *Indiana Law Journal (Indianapolis, Ind.)*, *87*, 1825–1845.

Jernigan, D. H., Padon, A., Ross, C., & Borzekowski, D. (2017). Self-reported youth and adult exposure to alcohol marketing in traditional and digital media: Results of a pilot survey. *Alcoholism, Clinical and Experimental Research*, *41*(3), 618–625. doi:10.1111/acer.13331 PMID:28219114

Jernigan, D., Noel, J., Landon, J., Thornton, N., & Lobstein, T. (2017). Alcohol marketing and youth alcohol consumption: A systematic review of longitudinal studies published since 2008. *Addiction (Abingdon, England)*, *112*(1), 7–20. doi:10.1111/add.13591 PMID:27565582

Jernigan, M. M., & Daniel, J. H. (2011). Racial trauma in the lives of Black children and adolescents: Challenges and clinical implications. *Journal of Child & Adolescent Trauma*, *4*(2), 123–141. doi:10.1080/19361521.2011.574678

Jewkes, Y., & Laws, B. (2021). Liminality revisited: Mapping the emotional adaptations of women in carceral spaces. *Punishment & Society*, *23*(3), 394–412. doi:10.1177/1462474520959623

Johns, J., & Barnes, N. (2021). The Locked Cage: Understanding the Impact of Incarceration on Children and Families within the School. In M. A. Rausch & L. L. Gallo (Eds.), *Strengthening School Counselor Advocacy and Practice for Important Populations and Difficult Topics* (pp. 162–174). IGI Global. doi:10.4018/978-1-7998-7319-8.ch009

Johnson, A. M., & Godsil, R. D. (2014). *Transforming Perception: Black Men and Boys*. https://perception.org/publications/transforming-perception

Johnson, E. I., & Easterling, B. (2012). Understanding unique effects of parental incarceration on children: Challenges, progress, and recommendations. *Journal of Marriage and Family*, *74*(2), 342–356. doi:10.1111/j.1741-3737.2012.00957.x

Johnson, E. I., & Easterling, B. A. (2015). Coping with confinement: Adolescents' experiences with parental incarceration. *Journal of Adolescent Research*, *30*(2), 244–267. doi:10.1177/0743558414558593

Johnson, S. M. (2019). *Attachment Theory in Practice*. Guilford Press.

Jones, C. M., Clayton, H. B., Deputy, N. P., Roehler, D. R., Ko, J. Y., Esser, M. B., ... Hertz, M. F. (2020). Prescription opioid misuse and use of alcohol and other substances among high school students—Youth Risk Behavior Survey, United States, 2019. *MMWR Supplements*, *69*(1), 38. doi:10.15585/mmwr.su6901a5

Jordan, J. (2010). *Relational-cultural therapy*. American Psychological Association.

Joseph, A. A., Wilcox, S. M., Hnilica, R. J., & Hansen, M. C. (2020). Keeping Race at the Center of School Discipline Practices and Trauma-Informed Care: An Interprofessional Framework. *Children & Schools*, *42*(3), 161–170. doi:10.1093/cs/cdaa013

Justice Strategies. (2017, June 14). *How can schools, teachers, and counselors help children impacted by incarceration?* [Blog post]. https://www.justicestrategies.org/coip/blog/2017/06/how-can-schools-teachers-and-counselors-help-children-impacted-incarceration

Juvenile Law Center. (2018). *What is the foster care-to-prison pipeline?* https://jlc.org/news/what-foster-care-prison-pipeline

Kaeble, D. (2018). *Time served in state prison 2016*. https://bjs.ojp.gov/content/pub/pdf/tssp16.pdf

Kaeble, D., & Cowhig, M. (2018). *Correctional populations in the United States, 2016*. U.S. Department of Justice. https://www.bjs.gov/content/pub/pdf/cpus16.pdf

Kaeble, D., Maruschak, L. M., & Bonczar, T. P. (2015). *Probation and parole in the United States, 2014*. U.S. Department of Justice. Office of Justice Programs. Bureau of Justice Statistics.

Kaplan, D. M., Tarvydas, V. M., & Gladding, S. T. (2014). A vision for the future of counseling: the new consensus definition of counseling. *Journal of Counselling and Development*. https://onlinelibrary.wiley.com/doi/full/10.1002/j.1556-6676.2014.00164.x

Karberg, J. C., & James, D. J. (2005). *Substance dependence, abuse, and treatment of jail inmates, 2002*. Bureau of Justice Statistics.

Katz, C., & Barnetz, Z. (2014). The behavior patterns of abused children as described in their testimonies. *Child Abuse & Neglect*, *38*(6), 1033–1040. doi:10.1016/j.chiabu.2013.08.006 PMID:24035397

Kavanagh, L., & Borrill, J. (2013). Exploring the experiences of ex-offender mentors. *Probation Journal*, *60*(4), 400–414. doi:10.1177/0264550513502247

Kaysen, D., Morris, M. K., Rizvi, S. L., & Resick, P. A. (2005). Peritraumatic Responses and Their Relationship to Perceptions of Threat in Female Crime Victims. *Violence Against Women*, *11*(12), 1515–1535. doi:10.1177/1077801205280931 PMID:16247114

Keels, M. (2020). Building racial equity through trauma-responsive discipline. *ASCD: Trauma-Sensitive Schools*, *78*(2), 40–45.

Keene, D., Smoyer, A., & Blankenship, K. (2018). Stigma, housing and identity after prison. *The Sociological Review*, *66*(4), 799–815. doi:10.1177/0038026118777447

Kelly, S., Jeremie-Brink, G., Chambers, A., & Smith-Bynum, M. (2020). The Black Lives Matter movement: A call to action for couple and family therapists. *Family Process*, *59*(4), 1374–1388.

Kerr, E. (2021). *See high school graduation rates by state*. https://www.usnews.com/education/best-high-schools/articles/see-high-school-graduation-rates-by-state#:~:text=The%20high%20school%20graduation%20rate,News%20Best%20High%20Schools%20rankings

Kia-Keating, M., Dowdy, E., Morgan, M. L., & Noam, G. G. (2011). Protecting and promoting: An integrative conceptual model for healthy development of adolescents. *The Journal of Adolescent Health*, *48*(3), 220–228. doi:10.1016/j.jadohealth.2010.08.006

Kim, H., Wildeman, C., Jonson-Reid, M., & Drake, B. (2017). Lifetime prevalence of investigating child maltreatment among US children. *American Journal of Public Health*, *107*(2), 274–280. doi:10.2105/AJPH.2016.303545 PMID:27997240

Kim, S., & Peterson, C. (2020). The health effects of gendered and devalued work: Health outcomes of incarcerated women engaging in sex work and care/service work. *Health & Justice*, *8*(1), 23. doi:10.118640352-020-00124-4 PMID:33206239

King, K. M., & Borders, L. D. (2019). An experimental investigation of White counselors broaching race and racism. *Journal of Counseling and Development*, *97*(4), 341–351. doi:10.1002/jcad.12283

Kirk, C. M., Lewis, R. K., Nilsen, C., & Colvin, D. Q. (2013). Foster care and college: The educational aspirations and expectations of youth in the foster care system. *Youth & Society*, *45*(3), 307–323. doi:10.1177/0044118X11417734

Kirk, D. S. (2015). A natural experiment of the consequences of concentrating former prisoners in the same neighborhoods. *Proceedings of the National Academy of Sciences of the United States of America*, *112*(22), 6943–6948. doi:10.1073/pnas.1501987112 PMID:25976097

Kirk, D. S., & Wakefield, S. (2018). Collateral consequences of punishment: A critical review and path forward. *Annual Review of Criminology*, *1*(1), 171–194. doi:10.1146/annurev-criminol-032317-092045

Kizielewicz, C. (2018). Black men have higher rates of recidivism despite lower risk factors. *Eurek Alert!* https://www.eurekalert.org/pub_releases/2018-10/cajr-bmh101818.php

Kjellstrand, J., Matulis, J., Jackson, A., Smith, J., & Eddy, J. M. (2021). The Importance of Positive Social Support During Reentry From Prison: Examining the Role of Volunteer Mentoring. *International Journal of Offender Therapy and Comparative Criminology.*

Kjellstrand, J. M., Reinke, W. M., & Eddy, J. M. (2018). Children of incarcerated parents: Development of externalizing behaviors across adolescence. *Children and Youth Services Review*, *94*, 628–635. doi:10.1016/j.childyouth.2018.09.003

Klein, J., & Mohan, L. (2016). *Prison to proprietor: Entrepreneurship as a re-entry strategy.* The Aspen Institute. https://www.aspeninstitute.org/wp-content/uploads/2016/09/AFN-PrisonToProprietor.pdf

Knight, K., & Farabee, D. (2004). *Treating addicted offenders: A continuum of effective practices.* Civic Research Institute.

Knott, T., & Donovan, K. (2010). Disproportionate representation of African-American children in foster care: Secondary analysis of the National Child Abuse and Neglect Data System, 2005. *Children and Youth Services Review*, *32*(5), 679–684. doi.org/10.1016/j.childyouth.2010.01.003

Kochel, T. R., & Weisburd, D. (2017). Assessing community consequences of implementing hot spots policing in residential areas: Findings from a randomized field trial. *Journal of Experimental Criminology*, *13*(2), 143–170. doi:10.100711292-017-9283-5

Koegler, E., Preble, K., Cimino, A., Stevens, J., & Diehl, S. (2019). Examining recidivism in a prostitution diversion program. *International Journal of Offender Therapy and Comparative Criminology.* Advance online publication. doi:10.1177/0306624X19866115 PMID:31364427

Kohli, R., Johnson, R. N., & Perez, L. H. (2006). Naming racism: A conceptual look at internalized racism in US schools. *Chicano/Latino. Law Review*, 183–206.

Kohn, A. (1993). *Punished by rewards the trouble with gold stars, incentive plans, A's, praise, and other bribes.* Houghton Mifflin.

Kohn, A. (2005). *Unconditional parenting: Moving from rewards and punishments to love and reason.* Atria Books.

Kois, L., Hill, K., Gonzales, L., Hunter, S., & Chauhan, P. (2019). Correctional officer mental health training: Analysis of 52 u.s. jurisdictions. *Criminal Justice Policy Review*, *31*(4), 555–572. doi:10.1177/0887403419849624

Konijn, C., Admiraal, S., Baart, J., van Rooij, F., Stams, G., Colonnesi, C., Lindauer, R., & Assink, M. (2019). Foster care placement instability: A meta-analytic review. *Children and Youth Services Review*, *96*, 483–499. doi:10.1016/j.childyouth.2018.12.002

Kopt, D. (2018). New data clearly illustrate the poverty-to-prison pipeline. *Quartz.* https://qz.com/1233966/new-data-clearly-illustrate-the-poverty-to-prison-pipeline/

Korgaonkar, M., Antees, C., Williams, L., Gatt, J., Bryant, R., Cohen, R., Paul, R., O'Hara, R., & Grieve, S. (2013). Early exposure to traumatic stressors impairs emotional brain circuitry. *PLOS ONE*, *8*(9), 1-8. doi:.org/ doi:10.1371/journal.pone.0075524

Kosciw, J. G., Clark, C. M., Truong, N. L., & Zongrone, A. D. (2020). *The 2019 national school climate survey: The experiences of lesbian, gay, bisexual, transgender, and queer youth in our nation's schools.* https://www.glsen.org/

Krase, K. S. (2013). Differences in racially disproportionate reporting of child maltreatment across report sources. *Journal of Public Child Welfare*, *7*(4), 351–369. doi:10.1080/15548732.2013.798763

Krieger, N. (1990). Racial and gender discrimination: Risk factors for high blood pressure? *Social Science & Medicine, 30*(12), 1273–1281. doi:10.1016/0277-9536(90)90307-E PMID:2367873

La Vigne, N. G., Naser, R. L., Brooks, L. E., & Castro, J. L. (2005). Examining the effect of incarceration and in-prison family contact on prisoners' family relationships. *Journal of Contemporary Criminal Justice, 21*(4), 314–335. doi:10.1177/1043986205281727

Lamb, H. R., & Bachrach, L. L. (2001). Some perspectives on deinstitutionalization. *Psychiatric Services, 52*(8), 1039–1045. doi:10.1176/appi.ps.52.8.1039

Langan, N. P., & Pelissier, B. M. (2001). Gender differences among prisoners in drug treatment. *Journal of Substance Abuse, 13*(3), 291–301. doi:10.10160899-3289(01)00083-9

Lazarus, S., Baptiste, D., & Seedat, M. (2009). Community Counselling: Values and Practices. *Journal of Psychology in Africa, 19*(3), 449–454. doi:10.1080/14330237.2009.10820314

Lee, A. F., Genty, P. M., & Laver, M. (2005). *The impact of the adoption and safe families act on children of incarcerated parents.* Child Welfare League of America.

Lee, C. C. (2018). Final thoughts: The counselor as agent of social justice: The process of becoming. In C. C. Lee (Ed.), *Counseling for social justice* (pp. 249–254). American Counseling Association Foundation.

Lee, H., Wildeman, C., Wang, E. A., Matusko, N., & Jackson, J. S. (2014). A heavy burden: The cardiovascular health consequences of having a family member incarcerated. *American Journal of Public Health, 104*(3), 421–427. doi:10.2105/AJPH.2013.301504 PMID:24432879

Lee, T., Cornell, D., Gregory, A., & Fan, X. (2011). High suspension schools and dropout rates for black and white students. *Education & Treatment of Children, 34*(2), 167–192. doi:10.1353/etc.2011.0014

Lee, T., Fouras, G., & Brown, R.American Academy of Child and Adolescent Psychiatry (AACAP) Committee of Quality Issues (CQI). (2015). Practice parameter for the assessment and management of youth involved with the child welfare system. *Journal of the American Academy of Child and Adolescent Psychiatry, 54*(6), 502–517. doi:10.1016/j.jaac.2015.03.005 PMID:26004666

Leonardi-Bee, J., Nderi, M., & Britton, J. (2016). Smoking in movies and smoking initiation in adolescents: Systematic review and meta-analysis. *Addiction (Abingdon, England), 111*(10), 1750–1763. doi:10.1111/add.13418 PMID:27043456

Leone, P. E., & Wruble, P. C. (2015). Education services in juvenile corrections: 40 years of litigation and reform. *Education & Treatment of Children, 38*(4), 587–604. doi:10.1353/etc.2015.0026

Levac, A. M., McCay, E., Merka, P., & Reddon-D'Arcy, M. L. (2008). Exploring parent participation in a parent training program for children's aggression: Understanding and illuminating mechanisms of change. *Journal of Child and Adolescent Psychiatric Nursing, 21*(2), 78–88. doi:10.1111/j.1744-6171.2008.00135.x PMID:18429838

Levitt, S. (2004). Understanding why crime fell in the 1990s: Four factors that explain the decline and six that do not. *The Journal of Economic Perspectives, 18*(1), 163–190.

Lhamon, C. E., & Samuels, J. (2014). *Dear colleague letter from the U.S. Department of Justice and the U.S. Department of Education.* https://www2.ed.gov/about/offices/list/ocr/letters/colleague-201401-title-vi.pdf

Li, M. (2018). *From prisons to communities: Confronting re-entry challenges and social inequality.* American Psychological Association. https://www.apa.org/pi/ses/resources/indicator/2018/03/prisons-to-communities

Liam, M., & Kunst, M. (2013). Is there a recognizable post-incarceration syndrome among released "lifers"? *International Journal of Law and Psychiatry*, *36*(3-4), 333–337.

Lipari, R., & VanHorn, S. (2017). *Trends in substance use disorders among adults aged 18 or older*. https://www.samhsa.gov/data/sites/default/files/report_2790/ShortReport-2790.html

Lipsey, M. W. (2009). The primary factors that characterize effective interventions with juvenile offenders: A meta-analytic overview. *Victims & Offenders*, *4*(2), 124–147. doi:10.1080/15564880802612573

Liu, J., Abdin, E., Vaingankar, J. A., Lim, M. S. M., Verma, S., Tang, C., . . . Subramaniam, M. (2021). Positive mental health framework of transdiagnostic protective factors in elucidating the association between adverse childhood experiences and severe mental disorders. *Australian & New Zealand Journal of Psychiatry*. https://doi.org/00048674211053568

Liu, L., & Visher, C. A. (2021). Decomposition of the role of family in reentry: Family support, tension, gender, and reentry outcomes. *Crime and Delinquency*, *67*(6-7), 970–996. doi:10.1177/0011128720987195

Looney, A., & Turner, N. (2018). *The Brookings Institution work and opportunity before and after incarceration.* https://www.brookings.edu/wp-content/uploads/2018/03/es_20180314_looneyincarceration_final.pdf

Lopez-Humphreys, M., & Teater, B. (2019). "It's what's on the inside that counts": A pilot study of the subjective changes among returned citizens participating in a peer-mentor support initiative. *Journal of Social Service Research*, *46*(6), 741–755. doi:10.1080/01488376.2019.1656699

Lopoo, L. M., & Western, B. (2005). Incarceration and the formation and stability of marital unions. *Journal of Marriage and Family*, *67*(3), 721–734. doi:10.1111/j.1741-3737.2005.00165.x

Losen, D. J., & Martinez, T. E. (2013). Out of school & off track: The overuse of suspensions in American middle and high schools. The Center for Civil Rights Remedies at the Civil Rights Project (UCLA).

Losen, D. J., Hodson, C. L., Keith, M. A., II, Morrison, K., & Belway, S. (2015). *Are we closing the school discipline gap?* https://escholarship.org/uc/item/2t36g571

Low, K. (16, February 2018). Understanding punishment and oppositional behavior. *Verywellmind.* https://www.verywellmind.com/punishment-and-oppositional-behavior-20730

Luoma, J. B., & Vilardaga, J. P. (2013). Improving therapist psychological flexibility while training acceptance and commitment therapy: A pilot study. *Cognitive Behaviour Therapy*, *42*(1), 1–8. doi:10.1080/16506073.2012.701662 PMID:23505991

Lustick, H. (2017). "Restorative justice" or restoring order? restorative school discipline practices in urban public schools. *Urban Education*, *56*(8), 1269–1296. doi:10.1177/0042085917741725

Luthar, S., Cicchetti, D., & Becker, B. (2000). The construct of resilience: A critical evaluation and guidelines for future work. *Child Development*, *71*, 543–562.

Luther, K. (2016). Stigma management among children of incarcerated parents. *Deviant Behavior*, *37*(11), 1264–1275. doi:10.1080/01639625.2016.1170551

Lu, Y. E., Landsverk, J., Ellis-Macleod, E., Newton, R., Ganger, W., & Johnson, I. (2004). Race, ethnicity, and case outcomes in child protective services. *Children and Youth Services Review*, *26*(5), 447–461. doi:10.1016/j.childyouth.2004.02.002

Mackintosh, V. H., Myers, B. J., & Kennon, S. S. (2006). Children of incarcerated mothers and their caregivers: Factors affecting the quality of their relationship. *Journal of Child and Family Studies*, *15*(5), 581–596. doi:10.100710826-006-9030-4

Magill, M., & Ray, L. A. (2009). Cognitive-behavioral treatment with adult alcohol and illicit drug users: A meta-analysis of randomized controlled trials. *Journal of Studies on Alcohol and Drugs*, *70*(4), 516–527. doi:10.15288/jsad.2009.70.516 PMID:19515291

Maguire-Jack, K., Font, S. A., & Dillard, R. (2020). Child protective services decision-making: The role of children's race and county factors. *The American Journal of Orthopsychiatry*, *90*(1), 48–62. doi:10.1037/ort0000388 PMID:31081655

Malone, P. A. (2007). The impact of peer death on adolescent girls: A task-oriented group intervention. *Journal of Social Work in End-of-Life & Palliative Care*, *3*(3), 23–37. doi:10.1300/J457v03n03_04 PMID:18077294

Malone, P. A. (2016). *Counseling adolescents through loss, grief, and trauma*. Routledge. doi:10.4324/9780203699638

Maltais, C., Cyr, C., Parent, G., & Pascuzzo, K. (2019). Identifying effective interventions for promoting parent engagement and family reunification for children in out-of-home care: A series of meta-analyses. *Child Abuse & Neglect*, *88*, 362–375. doi:10.1016/j.chiabu.2018.12.009 PMID:30579168

Maluccio, A. N., Abramczyk, L. W., & Thomlison, B. (1996). Family reunification of children in out-of-home care: Research perspectives. *Children and Youth Services Review*, *18*(4/5), 287–305. doi:10.1016/0190-7409(96)00007-2

Mancini, C., Baker, T., Sainju, K. D., Golden, K., Bedard, L. E., & Gertz, M. (2016). Examining external support received in prison and concerns about reentry among incarcerated women. *Feminist Criminology*, *11*(2), 163–190. doi:10.1177/1557085115579483

Martinez, R. R. Jr, Gavin Williams, R., & Green, J. (2019). The role of school counselors delivering a trauma-informed care approach to supporting youth in Foster Care. *Professional School Counseling*, *23*(1), 2156759X2094774. doi:10.1177/2156759X20947747

Maruschak, L. M., & Bronson, J. (2016). *Parents in prison and their minor children*. US Department of Justice, Bureau of Justice Statistics. https://www.bjs.gov/content/pub/pdf/pptmcspi16st.pdf

Maruschak, L., & Buehler, E. (2021). *Census of state and federal adult correctional facilities*. https://bjs.ojp.gov/content/pub/pdf/csfacf19st.pdf

Maruschak, L., Bronson, J., & Alper, M. (2021) *Parents in prison and their minor children: Survey of Prison Inmates 2016*. https://bjs.ojp.gov/library/publications/parents-prison-and-their-minor-children-survey-prison-inmates-2016#:~:text=An%20estimated%20684%2C500%20state%20and,of%20federal%20prisoners%20(58%25)

Maruschak, L. M., Bronson, J., & Alper, M. (2021). *Survey of prison inmates, 2016: Parents in prison and their minor children. U.S. Department of Justice. Office of Justice Programs*. Bureau of Justice Statistics.

Marwick, A., Fontaine, C., & Boyd, D. (2017). "Nobody sees it, nobody gets mad": Social media, privacy, and personal responsibility among low-SES youth. *Social Media+ Society*, *3*(2). doi:10.1177/2056305117710455

Mason, E., Robertson, A., Gay, J., Clarke, N., & Holcomb-McCoy, C. (2021). Antiracist School Counselor Preparation: Expanding on the Five Tenets of the Transforming School Counseling Initiative. *Teaching and Supervision in Counseling*, *3*(2), 2, 4-14.

Massoglia, M. (2008). Incarceration as exposure: The prison, infectious disease, and other stress-related illnesses. *Journal of Health and Social Behavior*, *49*(1), 56–71. doi:10.1177/002214650804900105 PMID:18418985

Massoglia, M. (2008). Incarceration, health, and racial disparities in health. *Law & Society Review*, *42*(2), 275–306. doi:10.1111/j.1540-5893.2008.00342.x

Massoglia, M., Pare, P., Schnittker, J., & Gagnon, A. (2014). The relationship between incarceration and premature adult mortality: Gender specific evidence. *Social Science Research*, *46*, 142–154. doi:10.1016/j.ssresearch.2014.03.002

Massoglia, M., & Pridemore, W. A. (2015). Incarceration and health. *Annual Review of Sociology*, *41*(1), 291–310. doi:10.1146/annurev-soc-073014-112326 PMID:30197467

Massoglia, M., Remster, B., & King, M. (2011). Stigma or separation?: Understanding the incarceration-divorce relationship. *Social Forces*, *90*(1), 133–155. doi:10.1093f/90.1.133

Masten, A. S. (2001). Ordinary magic: Resilience processes in development. *The American Psychologist*, *56*(3), 227.

Masten, A. S. (2014). Global perspectives on resilience in children and youth. *Child Development*, *85*(1), 6–20.

Masten, A. S., & Barnes, A. J. (2018). Resilience in children: Developmental perspectives. *Children*, *5*(7), 98.

Matthew, A. J., Clark, M. A., & McDavid, L. M. (2021). Combating racism: The role of the pediatrician. *Pediatric Research*, *90*(4), 1–3. doi:10.103841390-020-01345-x PMID:33469175

Matthews, E. (2021). Peer focused pirsion re-entry programs: Which peer characteristics matter most? *Incarceration*, *2*(2), 1–19. doi:10.1177/26326663211019958

May, J., Osmond, K., & Billick, S. (2014). Juvenile delinquency treatment and prevention: A literature review. *The Psychiatric Quarterly*, *85*(3), 295–301. doi:10.100711126-014-9296-4 PMID:24610601

Mayo Clinic. (2017). *Drug addiction substance use disorder*. https://www.mayoclinic.org/diseases-conditions/drug-addiction/symptoms-causes/syc-20365112

McCarter, S. (2017). The school-to-prison pipeline: A primer for social workers. *Social Work (United States)*, *62*(1), 53–61. doi:10.1093www078 PMID:28395045

McClellan, C., Lambdin, B. H., Ali, M. M., Mutter, R., Davis, C. S., Wheeler, E., Pemberton, M., & Kral, A. H. (2018). Opioid-overdose laws association with opioid use and overdose mortality. *Journal of Addictive Behaviors*, *86*, 90–95. doi:10.1016/j.addbeh.2018.03.014 PMID:29610001

McCluskey, G., Lloyd, G., Stead, J., Kane, J., Riddell, S., & Weedon, E. (2008). 'I was dead restorative today': From restorative justice to restorative approaches in school. *Cambridge Journal of Education*, *38*(2), 199–216. doi:10.1080/03057640802063262

McDaniel, K. (2014). *Recidivism prevention through prosocial support: A systematic review of empirical research* [Thesis, University of Central Florida]. HIM 1990-2015. University of Central Florida. https://stars.library.ucf.edu/honorstheses1990-2015/1598

McGrew, A., & Hanks, A. (2017). *The case for paid apprenticeships behind bars*. Center for American Progress. https://www.americanprogress.org/issues/economy/reports/2017/04/27/431384/case-paid-apprenticeships-behind-bars/

Mcgrew, K. (2016). The dangers of pipeline thinking: How the school-to-prison pipeline metaphor squeezes out complexity. *Educational Theory*, *7*(3), 1–17. doi:10.1111/edth.12173

McHugh, R. K., Hearon, B. A., & Otto, M. W. (2010). Cognitive behavioral therapy for substance use disorders. *The Psychiatric Clinics of North America*, *33*(3), 511–525. doi:10.1016/j.psc.2010.04.012 PMID:20599130

McIntosh, P. (1989). White privilege: Unpacking the invisible knapsack. *Peace and Freedom*, (July/August), 10–12.

McKay, T., Comfort, M., Grove, L., Bir, A., & Lindquist, C. (2018). Whose punishment, whose crime? Understanding parenting and partnership in a time of mass incarceration. *Journal of Offender Rehabilitation*, *57*(2), 69–82. doi:10.1080/10509674.2017.1294640

McKay, T., Comfort, M., Lindquist, C., & Bir, A. (2016). If family matters: Supporting family relationships during incarceration and reentry. *Criminology & Public Policy*, *15*(2), 529–542. doi:10.1111/1745-9133.12209

McKay, T., Landwehr, J., Lindquist, C., Feinberg, R., Comfort, M., Cohen, J., & Bir, A. (2018). Intimate partner violence in couples navigating incarceration and reentry. *Journal of Offender Rehabilitation*, *57*(5), 273–293.

McLeod, S. A. (2014). *Classical conditioning*. www.simplypsychology.org/classical-conditioning.html

McLeod, S. A. (2016). *Bandura - social learning theory*. www.simplypsychology.org/bandura.html

Mcneal, L. R. (2014). Managing Our Blind Spot: The Role of Bias in the School-to-Prison Pipeline. *Arizona State Law Journal*, *48*, 285–311. https://b.3cdn.net/advancement/d05cb2181a4545db07_r2im6caqe.pdf

McNeil, C. B., Herschell, A. D., Gurwitch, R. H., & Clemens-Mowrer, L. (2005). Training foster parents in parent-child interaction therapy. *Education & Treatment of Children*, *28*(2), 182–196.

McNeil, C., Capage, L., & Bennett, G. (2002). Cultural issues in the treatment of young African American children diagnosed with disruptive behavior disorders. *Journal of Pediatric Psychology*, *27*(4), 339–350. doi.org/10.1093/jpepsy/27.4.339

McVay, D. (2022). *Drug policy facts arrests and the criminal legal system*. https://www.drugpolicyfacts.org/chapter/crime_arrests

McVey, C. C. (2001). Coordinating effective health and mental health continuity of care (NCJ 190462). *Corrections Today*, *63*(5), 58–62. https://www.ojp.gov/ncjrs/virtual-library/abstracts/coordinating-effective-health-and-mental-health-continuity-care

Meier, P. S. (2011). Alcohol marketing research: The need for a new agenda. *Addiction (Abingdon, England)*, *106*(3), 466–471. doi:10.1111/j.1360-0443.2010.03160.x PMID:21299664

Meiners, E. R. (2011). Ending the School-to-Prison Pipeline/Building Abolition Futures. *The Urban Review*, *43*(4), 547–565. doi:10.100711256-011-0187-9

Melander, L. (2020). Keeping connected while living apart: An exploration of a prison contact maintenance program. *Journal of Offender Rehabilitation*, *59*(5), 267–284. doi:10.1080/10509674.2020.1745980

Mennis, J., Stahler, G., & Mason, M. (2016). Risky substance use environments and addiction: A new frontier for environmental justice. *International Journal of Environmental Research and Public Health*, *13*(6), 607. Advance online publication. doi:10.3390/ijerph13060607 PMID:27322303

Menting, A. T., de Castro, B. O., Wijngaards-de Meij, L. D., & Matthys, W. (2014). A trial of parent training for mothers being released from incarceration and their children. *Journal of Clinical Child and Adolescent Psychology*, *43*(3), 381–396. doi:10.1080/15374416.2013.817310 PMID:23915290

Metcalf, R. (2002). Role of the school psychologist in juvenile forensics. In N. G. Ribner (Ed.), *The California School of Professional Psychology handbook of juvenile forensic psychology* (pp. 432–453). Jossey-Bass/Wiley.

Meyer, S. (2016). *Women in prison: Histories of trauma and abuse highlight the need for specialized care*. https://theconversation.com/women-in-prison-histories-of-trauma-and-abuse-highlight-the-need-for-specialised-care-68668

Middleton, S. (2020). *Repressive legislation: Slave codes, northern Black laws, and southern Black codes*. Oxford Research Encyclopedias. American History., doi:10.1093/acrefore/9780199329175.013.634

Milakovic, D. (2020). *Supporting through an equitable trauma-informed lens* [PowerPoint slides]. Pennsylvania Department of Education. https://www.pattan.net/

Miley, K. K., O'Melia, M. W., & DuBois, B. L. (2022). *Generalist social work practice: An empowering approach* (9th ed.). Pearson.

Miller, J. B. (1988). *Connections, disconnections, and violations.* Work in Progress No. 33. Wellesley, MA: Stone Center Working Paper Series.

Miller, M. J., Keum, B. T. H., Thai, C. J., Lu, Y., Truong, N. N., Huh, G. A., Li, X., Yeung, J. G., & Ahn, L. H. R. (2018). Practice recommendations for addressing racism: A content analysis of the counseling psychology literature. *Journal of Counseling Psychology, 65*(6), 669–680. doi:10.1037/cou0000306 PMID:30091623

Miller, N., & Najavits, L. (2012). Creating trauma-informed correctional care. *European Journal of Psychotraumatology, 3*(1), 17246. doi:10.3402/ejpt.v3i0.17246 PMID:22893828

Minton, D., & Zeng, Z. (2021). *U.S. department of justice jail inmates in 2020- Statistical tables.* https://bjs.ojp.gov/content/pub/pdf/ji20st.pdf

Minton, T. D., Zeng, Z., & Maruschak, L. M. (2021). *Impact of COVID-19 on the local jail population, January-June 2020.* US Department of Justice, Office of Justice Programs, Bureau of Justice Statistics. https://copafs.org/wp-content/uploads/2021/09/icljpjj20.pdf

Minuchin, S. (1974). *Families and Family Therapy.* Harvard University Press. doi:10.4159/9780674041127

Mitchell, O., & Caudy, M. S. (2013). Examining racial disparities in drug arrests. *Justice Quarterly, 32*(2), 288–313. https://perma.cc/T3XU-JZVF. doi:10.1080/07418825.2012.761721

Mizock, L., & Harkins, D. (2011). Diagnostic bias and conduct disorder: Improving culturally sensitive diagnosis. *Child and Youth Services, 32*(3), 243–253. doi:10.1080/0145935X.2011.605315

Monahan, K. C., VanDerhei, S., Bechtold, J., & Cauffman, E. (2014). From the school yard to the squad car: School discipline, truancy, & arrest. *Youth & Adolescence, 43*(7), 1110–1122. doi:10.100710964-014-0103-1 PMID:24526497

Moore, K., Stuewig, J., & Tangney, J. (2014). The effects of stigma on criminal offenders' functioning: A longitudinal mediational model. *Defiant Behavior, 37*(2), 196-218. doi:10.1080/01639625.2014.1004035

Moore, K., Stuewig, J., & Tangney, J. (2013). Jail inmates' perceived and anticipated stigma: Implications for post-release functioning. *Self and Identity, 12*(5), 527–547. doi:10.1080/15298868.2012.702425 PMID:25045324

Morenoff, J., & Harding, D. (2014). Incarceration, prisoner reentry, and communities. *Annual Review of Sociology, 40*, 411–429. doi:10.1146/annurev-soc-071811-145511

Morgan-Mullane, A. (2018). Trauma Focused Cognitive Behavioral Therapy with Children of Incarcerated Parents. *Clinical Social Work Journal, 46*(3), 200–209. doi:10.100710615-017-0642-5 PMID:30100639

Morones, A. (2014). Juvenile-Justice System Not Meeting Educational Needs, Report Says; "Systemic" problems outlined in report.(Brief article). *Education Week, 33*(29), 6–6.

Morris, M. (2016). *Pushout: The criminalization of Black girls in schools.* The New Press.

Morton, B. M. (2018). The grip of trauma: How trauma disrupts the academic aspirations of Foster Youth. *Child Abuse & Neglect, 75*, 73–81. doi:10.1016/j.chiabu.2017.04.021 PMID:28478934

Morton, B. M., & Berardi, A. A. (2017). Trauma-informed school programing: Applications for mental health professionals and educator partnerships. *Journal of Child & Adolescent Trauma, 11*(4), 487–493. doi:10.100740653-017-0160-1 PMID:32318170

Moses, M. C. (2006). Correlating Incarcerated mothers, foster care and mother-child reunification. *Corrections Today, 68*(6), 98–100.

Moss, L. J., & Singh, A. A. (2015). White School Counselors Becoming Racial Justice Allies to Students of Color: A Call to the Field of School Counseling. *Journal of School Counseling, 13*(5), 1–36.

Mowen, T. J., & Visher, C. A. (2016). Changing the ties that bind: How incarceration impacts family relationships. *Criminology & Public Policy, 15*(2), 503–528. doi:10.1111/1745-9133.12207

Muhlhausen, D. (2018, June 12). *Research on returning offender programs and promising practices* [Paper presentation]. Secretaries Innovation Group, National Institute of Justice. https://nij.ojp.gov/speech/research-returning-offender-programs-and-promising-practices

Muller, C. (2012). Northward migration and the rise of racial disparity in American incarceration, 1880 – 1950. *American Journal of Sociology, 118*(2), 281–326. doi:10.1086/666384

Mumola, C. J. (2000). *Incarcerated parents and their children.* Bureau of Justice Statistics Special Report. https://www.bjs.gov/content/pub/pdf/iptc.pdf

Mumola, C. J. (2000). Incarcerated parents and their children. US Department of Justice. Office of Justice Programs. Bureau of Justice Statistics.

Mumola, C. J., & Karberg, J. C. (2006). *Drug use and dependence, state and federal prisoners, 2004.* Bureau of Justice Statistics. doi:10.1037/e560272006-001

Muñiz, J. (2019). *Culturally responsive teaching: A 50-state survey of teaching standards.* https://www.newamerica.org/education-policy/reports/culturally-responsive-teaching/

Muñiz, J. O. (2021). Exclusionary Discipline Policies, School-Police Partnerships, Surveillance Technologies and Disproportionality: A Review of the School to Prison Pipeline Literature. *The Urban Review, 53*(5), 1–26. doi:10.100711256-021-00595-1

Murphey, D., & Cooper, P. M. (2015). *Parents behind bars.* Child Trends. http://www.childtrends.org/wp-content/uploads/2015/10/2015-42ParentsBehindBars.pdf

Murphey, D., & Cooper, P. M. (2015). *Parents behind bars: What happens to their children?* Child Trends. Retrieved June 22, 2021 from https://www.childtrends.org/wp-content/uploads/2015/10/2015-42ParentsBehindBars.pdf

Murphy-Erby, Y., Christy-McMullin, K., Stauss, K., & Schriver, J. (2010). Multi-systems life course: A new practice perspective and its application in advanced practice with racial and ethnic populations. *Journal of Human Behavior in the Social Environment, 20*(5), 672–687. doi:10.1080/10911351003751868

Murray, J., Farrington, D. P., & Sekol, I. (2012). Children's antisocial behavior, mental health, drug use, and educational performance after parental incarceration: A systematic review and meta-analysis. *Psychological Bulletin, 138*(2), 175-210. doi:10.1037/a0026407

Murray, J., Loeber, R., & Pardini, D. (2012). Parental involvement in the criminal justice system and the development of youth theft, marijuana use, depression, and poor academic performance. *Criminology, 50*(1), 255–302. doi:10.1111/j.1745-9125.2011.00257.x

NAACP. (n.d.). *Criminal justice fact sheet.* https://www.naacp.org/criminal-justice-fact-sheet/

Nance, P. (2016). Over-Disciplining students, racial bias, and the school-to-prison-pipeline. *University of Richmond Law Review. University of Richmond*, *50*, 1063–1074.

Nanda, J. (2019). The construction and criminalization of disability in school incarceration. *Colum. J. Race & L.*, *9*, 265.

National Alliance on Mental Illness. (2022). *Mental health treatment while incarcerated.* https://www.nami.org/Advocacy/Policy-Priorities/Improving-Health/Mental-Health-Treatment-While-Incarcerated

National Association for the Education of Young Children. (2017). *Standing together against suspension & expulsion in early childhood.* https://www.naeyc.org/

National Association of School Psychologists (NASP). (2021a). *School psychology credentialing resources.* Retrieved July 5, 2021 from https://www.nasponline.org/standards-and-certification/school-psychology-credentialing-resources

National Association of School Psychologists (NASP). (2021b). *Who are school psychologists.* Retrieved July 6, 2021 from https://www.nasponline.org/about-school-psychology/who-are-school-psychologists

National Child Traumatic Stress Network. (2018). *Effects.* The National Child Traumatic Stress Network. https://www.nctsn.org/what-is-child-trauma/trauma-types/complex-trauma/effects

National Child Traumatic Stress Network. (2018). *Giving voice to immigrant children: Understanding traumatic separation.* https://www.nctsn.org/resources/giving-immigrant-children-voice-understanding-traumatic-separation

National Council of State Education Associations. (2019). *Addressing the epidemic of trauma in schools.* https://www.nea.org/professional-excellence/student-engagement/trauma-informed-schools

National Education Association. (2021). *Diversity toolkit: Cultural competence for educators.* https://www.nea.org/professional-excellence/just-equitable-schools

National Institute of Corrections. (2019). *Provide certified technical skills training.* Correctional Industries. https://info.nicic.gov/cirs/node/37

National Institute of Corrections. (2021). *Children of incarcerated parents.* National Institute of Corrections. The United States Department of Justice. Retrieved June 22, 2021 from https://nicic.gov/children-of-incarcerated-parents#:~:text=Recent%20estimates%20show%20that%202.7,or%20jail%20at%20some%20point

National Institute of Justice. (2022). *Recidivism.* https://nij.ojp.gov/topics/corrections/recidivism

National Institute on Drug Abuse. (2020). *Criminal justice drugfacts.* https://www.drugabuse.gov/publications/drugfacts/criminal-justice

National Institutes on Drug Abuse. (2020). *Common comorbidities with substance use disorders research report.* https://www.ncbi.nlm.nih.gov/books/NBK571451/

National Juvenile Justice Network. (2009). *National Juvenile Justice Network policy platform: Conditions of confinement.* Retrieved July 11, 2021 from http://www.njjn.org/uploads/policy-platforms/Conditions-of-Confinement-Policy-Platform-5-18-12-fin.pdf?phpMyAdmin=14730ab3483c51c94ca868bccffa06ef

National Juvenile Justice Network. (2016). *Improving educational outcomes for youth in the juvenile justice system.* Retrieved July 24, 2021 from https://www.njjn.org/our-work/improving-education-for-youth-in-juvenile-justice-snapshot?phpMyAdmin=14730ab3483c51c94ca868bccffa06ef

National Resource Center on Children & Families of the Incarcerated. (2014). *Children and families of the incarcerated fact sheet*. Retrieved from https://nrccfi.camden.rutgers.edu/fil es/nrccfi-fact-sheet-2014.pdf

National Resource Center on Children & Families of the Incarcerated. (2014). *Children and families of the incarcerated fact sheet.* Rutgers University.

National Scientific Council on the Developing Child. (2005). *Excessive Stress Disrupts the Architecture of the Developing Brain: Working Paper No. 3.* https://developingchild.harvard.edu/resources/

National Scientific Council on the Developing Child. (2010). *Persistent Fear and Anxiety Can Affect Young Children's Learning and Development.* https://developingchild.harvard.edu/resources/

Neely-Barnes, S., & Whitted, K. (2011). Examining the social, emotional, and behavioral needs of youth involved in the child welfare and juvenile justice system. *Journal of Health & Human Services*, 206-239.

Nellis, A. (n.d.). The Color of Justice: Racial and Ethnic Disparity in State Prisons. *The Sentencing Project.* http://www.sentencingproject.org/publications/color-of-justice-racial-and-ethnic-disparity-in-state-prisons

Nelson, M., & Trone, J. (2000). *Why planning for release matters.* Vera Institute of Justice. https://biblioteca.cejamericas.org/bitstream/handle/2015/3728/IIB%2Bplanning_for_release.pdf?sequence=1&isAllowed=y

Nemeroff, C. B. (2016). Paradise lost: The Neurobiological and clinical consequences of child abuse and neglect. *Neuron*, *89*(5), 892–909. doi:10.1016/j.neuron.2016.01.019 PMID:26938439

Nichols, M. N., & Schwartz, R. C. (2008). *Family therapy: Concepts and methods* (8th ed.). Pearson.

Nilsson, A. (2003). Living conditions, social exclusion and recidivism among prison inmates. *Journal of Scandinavian Studies in Criminology and Crime Prevention*, *4*(1), 57–83. doi:10.1080/14043850310005321

Nolan, K. M. (2011). Oppositional behavior in urban schooling: Toward a theory of resistance for new times. *International Journal of Qualitative Studies in Education: QSE*, *24*(5), 559–572. doi:10.1080/09518398.2011.600263

Noltemeyer, A. L., Ward, R. M., & Mcloughlin, C. (2015). Relationship between school suspension and student outcomes: A meta-analysis. *School Psychology Review*, *44*(2), 224–240. doi:10.17105pr-14-0008.1

Novak, A. (2019). The School-To-Prison Pipeline: An Examination of the Association Between Suspension and Justice System Involvement. *Criminal Justice and Behavior*, *46*(8), 1165–1180. doi:10.1177/0093854819846917

Novak, A., & Fagan, A. (2022). Expanding research on the school-to-prison pipeline: Examining the relationships between suspension, expulsion, and recidivism among justice-involved youth. *Crime and Delinquency*, *68*(1), 3–27. doi:10.1177/0011128721999334

Nuño, L. F. (2021). Prisoner Re-Entry and Desistance. *Global Perspectives on People, Process, and Practice in Criminal Justice*, 99-109.

Nusslock, R., & Miller, G. E. (2016). Early-life adversity and physical and emotional health across the lifespan: A neuroimmune network hypothesis. *Biological Psychiatry*, *80*(1), 23–32. doi:10.1016/j.biopsych.2015.05.017

O'Donnell, D. (2013). *BJA policy brief.* https://bja.ojp.gov/sites/g/files/xyckuh186/files/Publications/WomensPathwaysToJail.pdf

Obatusin, O., & Ritter-Williams, D. (2019). A phenomenological study of employer perspectives on hiring ex-offenders. *Cogent Social Sciences*, *5*(1), 1571730. doi:10.1080/23311886.2019.1571730

Odafe, M., Salami, T., & Walker, R. (2017). Race-related stress and hopelessness in the community-based African American adults: Moderating role of social support. *Cultural Diversity & Ethnic Minority Psychology*, *23*(4), 561–569. doi.org/10.1037/cdp0000167

Office for Civil Rights. (2016). *2013–2014 Civil rights data collection: A first look* [New Release for 2016]. U.S. Department of Education.

Office of Elementary and Secondary Education, U.S. Department of Education. (2015). *Title I, Part D, Neglected, Delinquent or At-Risk Program.* Retrieved August 3, 2021 from https://oese.ed.gov/offices/office-of-formula-grants/school-support-and-accountability/prevention-intervention-programs-children-youths-neglected-delinquent-risk/

Office of Juvenile Justice and Delinquency Prevention. (2019). *Juvenile Arrests. Demographic characteristics of Juvenile arrests, 2019.* https://www.ojjdp.gov/ojstatbb/crime/qa05104.asp?qaDate=2019

Okagbue, I. (n.d.). *Children in Conflict with the Law: The Nigerian Experience.* https://www.unicef-irc.org/portfolios/documents/487_nigeria.htm

Oliver, M. B. (2003). African American men as "criminal and dangerous": Implications of media portrayals of crime on the "criminalization" of African American men. *Journal of African American Studies*, *7*(2), 3–18.

Opsal, T., & Foley, A. (2013). Making it on the outside: Understanding barriers to women's post-incarceration reintegration. *Sociology Compass*, *7*(4), 265–277. doi:10.1111oc4.12026

Organisation for Economic Co-operation and Development. (2021). *Teaching hours.* Retrieved June 22, 2021 from https://data.oecd.org/teachers/teaching-hours.htm

Ormiston, H. E., Nygaard, M. A., & Heck, O. C. (2020). The role of school psychologists in the implementation of trauma-informed multi-tiered systems of support in schools. *Journal of Applied School Psychology.* Advance online publication. doi:10.1080/15377903.2020.1848955

Ortiz, M. (2000). Managing special populations (NCJ 186711). *Corrections Today*, *62*(7), 64–68. https://www.ojp.gov/ncjrs/virtual-library/abstracts/managing-special-populations

Osagie-Obazee, G., & Eduwen, F. (2016). The influence of family factors on delinquent adolescents in secondary schools in Edo South Senatorial District of Edo State. AFRREV IJAH. *An International Journal of Arts and Humanities*, *5*(3), 231–243. doi:10.4314/ijah.v5i3.19

Osher, D., & Berg, J. (2019). *School climate and social and emotional learning the integration of two approaches. Issue Brief.* http:// prevention.psu.edu/uploads/files/rwjf443059.pdf

Oswald, D. P., & Coutinho, M. J. (1996). Leaving School: The Impact of State Economic and Demographic Factors for Students with Serious Emotional Disturbance. *Journal of Emotional and Behavioral Disorders*, *4*(2), 114–125. doi:10.1177/106342669600400206

Owens, E. G. (2017). Testing the school-to-prison pipeline. *Journal of Policy Analysis and Management*, *36*(1), 11–37. doi:10.1002/pam.21954

Owens, J., & McLanahan, S. S. (2020). Unpacking the drivers of racial disparities in school suspension and expulsion. *Social Forces*, *98*(4), 1548–1577. doi:10.1093foz095 PMID:34017149

Oxford Reference. (n.d.). *Incarceration.* https://www.oxfordreference.com/view/10.1093/oi/authority.20110803095959949

Pager, D., Bonikowski, B., & Western, B. (2009). Discrimination in a low-wage labor market: A field experiment. *American Sociological Review*, *74*(5), 777–799. doi:10.1177/000312240907400505 PMID:20689685

Paris, D. (2012). Culturally Sustaining Pedagogy: A Needed Change in Stance, Terminology, and Practice. *Educational Researcher*, *41*(3), 93–97. doi:10.3102/0013189X12441244

Parks, M. J., Davis, L., Wilhelm, A. K., McMorris, B. J., Borowsky, I. W., & Shlafer, R. J. (2020). Parental incarceration and youth tobacco product use: Implications for prevention and the e-cigarette epidemic. *Addictive Behaviors*, *107*, 106428. Advance online publication. doi:10.1016/j.addbeh.2020.106428 PMID:32311626

Pasztor, E. M., & Petras, D. D. (2012). Selecting foster parents: What to expect and ask. In K. Phagan-Hansel (Ed.), *The foster parenting toolbox: A practical, hands-on approach to parenting children in foster care* (pp. 4–8). EMK Press.

Pasztor, E. M., Petras, D. D., Stogel, S., Heilman, C., Chavez, R., & Boylan, B. (2015). *Essential requirements for permanency*. Fostering Families Today.

Pathan, H., & Williams, J. (2012). Basic opioid pharmacology: An update. *British Journal of Pain*, *6*(1), 11–16. doi:10.1177/2049463712438493 PMID:26516461

Pavlov, I. P. (1902). *The work of the digestive glands*. Griffin.

Payne, A. A., & Welch, K. (2015). Restorative Justice in Schools: The Influence of Race on Restorative Discipline. *Youth & Society*, *47*(4), 539–564. doi:10.1177/0044118X12473125

Pearl, B. (2018, June 27). *Ending drug war numbers*. https://www.americanprogress.org/issues/criminaljustice/reports/2018/06/27/452819/ending-war-drugs-numbers/

Pecora, P., Whittaker, J., Maluccio, A., Barth, R., DePanfilis, D., & Plotnik, R. (2010). *The child welfare challenge – Policy, practice, and research*. Transaction Publishers.

Peniston, D. (2014). *Incarceration and Father-Absence: An Exploration of Fatherhood after Prison*. https://search.proquest.com/openview/d412d35c2e69a374307aafc59825e88f/1.pdf?pq-origsite=gscholar&cbl=18750&diss=y

Perez, A., Leifman, S., & Estrada, A. (2003). Reversing the criminalization of mental illness. *Crime and Delinquency*, *49*(1), 62–78. doi:10.1177/0011128702239236

Perry, S. (2016). *Coming Home: Challenges Related to Reentry and Recidivism for Previously Incarcerated New Mother.* Retrieved from https://scholarworks.wm.edu/cgi/viewcontent.cgi?article=1960&context=honorstheses

Petersilia, J. (2011, October). Beyond the prison bubble. *National Institute of Justice Journal*, *268*. https://nij.ojp.gov/topics/articles/beyond-prison-bubble

Petitclerc, A., & Brooks-Gunn, J. (2022). Home visiting and early childhood education for reducing justice system involvement. *Prevention Science*, 1–14. doi:10.100711121-022-01363-7 PMID:35267178

Petry, N. M., & Martin, B. (2002). Low-cost contingency management for treating cocaine- and opioid-abusing methadone patients. *Journal of Consulting and Clinical Psychology*, *70*(2), 398–405. doi:10.1037/0022-006X.70.2.398 PMID:11952198

Petry, N. M., Martin, B., Cooney, J. L., & Kranzler, H. R. (2000). Give them prizes, and they will come: Contingency management for treatment of alcohol dependence. *Journal of Consulting and Clinical Psychology*, *68*(2), 250–257. doi:10.1037/0022-006X.68.2.250 PMID:10780125

Pettit, B. (2012). *Invisible men: Mass incarceration and the myth of black progress*. Russell Sage Foundation.

Pettit, B., & Western, B. (2004). Mass imprisonment and the life course: Race and class inequality in U.S. incarceration. *American Sociological Review*, *69*(2), 151–169. doi:10.1177/000312240406900201

Pettus-Davis, C., & Epperson, M. W. (2015). *From mass incarceration to smart decarceration* (CSD Working Papers No. 14-31). Center for Social Development. https://openscholarship.wustl.edu/cgi/viewcontent.cgi?article=1575&context=csd_research

Pew Charitable Trusts. (2010). *Collateral costs: Incarceration's effect on economic mobility.* https://www.pewtrusts.org/~/media/legacy/uploadedfiles/pcs_assets/2010/collateralcosts1pdf.pdf

Phillips, S. D., Dettlaff, A. J., & Baldwin, M. J. (2010). An exploratory study of the range of implications of families' criminal justice system involvement in child welfare cases. *Children and Youth Services Review*, *32*(4), 544–550. doi:10.1016/j.childyouth.2009.11.008

Phillips, S. D., & Gates, T. (2011). A conceptual framework for understanding the stigmatization of children of incarcerated parents. *Journal of Child and Family Studies*, *20*(3), 286–294. doi:10.100710826-010-9391-6

Phillips, S., & Bloom, B. (1998). In whose best interest? The impact of changing public policy on relatives caring for children with incarcerated parents. *Child Welfare*, *76*(5), 531–541. PMID:9744072

Phillips, S., Burns, B., Wagner, R., Kramer, T., & Robbins, J. (2002). Parental incarceration among adolescents receiving mental health services. *Journal of Child and Family Studies*, *11*(4), 385–399. doi-org.proxy.libraries.uc.edu/10.1023/A:1020975106679

Phillips, S., & O'Brien, P. (2012). Learning from the ground up: Responding to children affected by parental incarceration. *Social Work in Public Health*, *27*, 29–44. doi:10.1080/19371918.2012.629914

Picower, B. (2009). The Unexamined Whiteness of teaching: How White teachers maintain and enact dominant racial ideologies. *Race, Ethnicity and Education*, *12*(2), 197–215. doi:10.1080/13613320902995475

Pincus, R., Hannor-Walker, T. S., Wright, L., & Justice, J. (2020). Covid-19's effect on students: How school counselors rise to the rescue. *NASSP Bulletin*, *104*(4), 241–256. doi:10.1177/0192636520975866

Pinkney, K. E. (2021). Anti-Racist Practice: I Am Accountable. Are You? *Journal of Mental Health Counseling*, *43*(3), 277–280. doi:10.17744/mehc.43.3.10

Piper, A., & Berle, D. (2019). The association between trauma experienced during incarceration and PTSD outcomes: A systematic review and meta-analysis. *Journal of Forensic Psychiatry & Psychology*, *30*(5), 854–875.

Pleggenkuhle, B., Huebner, B. M., & Summers, M. (2018). Opting out: The role of identity, capital, and agency in prison visitation. *Justice Quarterly*, *35*(4), 726–749. doi:10.1080/07418825.2017.1339113

Poehlmann-Tynan, J., Cuthrell, H., Weymouth, L., Burnson, C., Frerks, L., Muentner, L., Holder, N., Milavetz, Z., Lauter, L., Hindt, L., Davis, L., Schubert, E., & Shlafer, R. (2021). Multisite randomized efficacy trial of educational materials for young children with incarcerated parents. *Development and Psychopathology*, *33*(1), 323–339. doi:10.1017/S0954579419001792 PMID:33616033

Pokempner, J. (2019). Leveraging the FFPSA for older youth: Prevention Provisions. *Children's Rights Litigation*, *21*(2), 13–18.

Porche, M. V., Fortuna, L. R., Lin, J., & Alegria, M. (2011). Childhood Trauma and Psychiatric Disorders as Correlates of School Dropout in a National Sample of Young Adults. *Child Development*, *82*(3), 982–998. doi:10.1111/j.1467-8624.2010.01534.x PMID:21410919

Porter, L. C. (2014). Incarceration and post-release health behavior. *Journal of Health and Social Behavior*, *55*(2), 234–249. doi:10.1177/0022146514531438 PMID:24872468

Powledge, T. M. (1999). Addiction and the brain: The dopamine pathway is helping researchers find their way through the addiction maze. *Bioscience*, *49*(7), 513–519. doi:10.2307/1313471

Prager, J. (2016). Disrupting the Intergenerational Transmission of Trauma: Recovering Humanity, Repairing Generations. In Breaking Intergenerational Cycles of Repetition (1st ed.). Verlag Barbara Budrich. doi:10.2307/j.ctvdf03jc.7

Prewitt, E. (2014, May 13). *State, federal lawmakers take action on trauma-informed policies, programs*. https://acestoohigh.com/2014/04/30/state-federal-lawmakers-take-action/

Price-Tucker, A., Zhou, A., Charroux, A., Tenzin, C., Robertson, E., Abdalla, H., Gu, J., Barton, J., Keselj, M., Bernstein, O., Alexis, P., Odayappan, S., & Escalante, T. (2019). *Successful reentry: A community-level analysis*. The Harvard University Institute of Politics Criminal Justice Policy Group. https://iop.harvard.edu/sites/default/files/sources/program/IOP_Policy_Program_2019_Reentry_Policy.pdf

Prins, S. J. (2011). Does transinstitutionalization explain the overrepresentation of people with serious mental illnesses in the criminal justice system? *Community Mental Health Journal*, *47*, 716–722. https://doi.org/10.1007/s10597-011-9420-y

Pullen, E., & Oser, C. (2014). Barriers to substance abuse treatment in rural and urban communities: Counselor perspectives. *Substance Use & Misuse*, *49*(7), 891–901. doi:10.3109/10826084.2014.891615 PMID:24611820

Quinn-Hogan, A. N. (2021). The stain of a criminal label: Post-release stigmatization and its effects on reintegration and recidivism among ex-offenders. *Sociology Publications,* 52. https://ir.lib.uwo.ca/sociologypub/52/

Rade, C. B., Desmarais, S. L., & Mitchell, R. E. (2016). A meta-analysis of public attitudes toward ex-offenders. *Criminal Justice and Behavior*, *43*(9), 1260–1280. doi:10.1177/0093854816655837

Ramakers, A., Nieuwbeerta, P., Van Wilsem, J., & Dirkzwager, A. (2017). Not just any job will do: A study on employment characteristics and recidivism risks after release. *International Journal of Offender Therapy and Comparative Criminology*, *61*(16), 1795–1818. doi:10.1177/0306624X16636141 PMID:26975405

Rankins, L. (2022). *The Family Connection: Examining the Transitional Impact on Family Members of Returning Citizens Reentering Society*. Academic Press.

Raphael, S. (2011). Incarceration and prisoner reentry in the United States. *The Annals of the American Academy of Political and Social Science*, *635*(1), 192–215. doi:10.1177/0002716210393321

Rashid, T. (2015). Positive psychotherapy: A strength-based approach. *The Journal of Positive Psychology*, *10*(1), 25–40. doi:10.1080/17439760.2014.920411

Ratcliffe, J. H., Groff, E. R., Sorg, E. T., & Haberman, C. P. (2015). Citizens' reactions to hot spots policing: Impacts on perceptions of crime, disorder, safety and police. *Journal of Experimental Criminology*, *11*(3), 393–417. doi:10.100711292-015-9230-2

Ratts, M. J., Singh, A. A., Nassar-Mcmillan, S., Butler, S. K., & McCullough, J. R. (2016). Multicultural and Social Justice Counseling Competencies: Guidelines for the Counseling Profession. *Journal of Multicultural Counseling and Development*, *44*(1), 28–48. doi:10.1002/jmcd.12035

Rawson, R. A., Huber, A., McCann, M., Shoptaw, S., Farabee, D., Reiber, C., & Ling, W. (2002). Comparison of contingency management and cognitive-behavioral approaches during methadone maintenance treatment for cocaine dependence. *Archives of General Psychiatry*, *59*(9), 817–824. doi:10.1001/archpsyc.59.9.817 PMID:12215081

Reisig, M., Bales, W., Hay, C., & Wang, X. (2007). The effect of racial inequality on black male recidivism. *Justice Quarterly*, *24*(3), 408–434.

Renaud, J. (2018). *Who's really bringing contraband into jails? Our 2018 survey confirms it's staff not visitors.* https://www.prisonpolicy.org/blog/2018/12/06/jail-contraband/

Reuben, A., Moffitt, T. E., Caspi, A., Belsky, D. W., Harrington, H., Schroeder, F., Hogan, S., Ramrakha, S., Poulton, R., & Danese, A. (2016). Lest we forget: Comparing retrospective and prospective assessments of adverse childhood experiences in the prediction of Adult Health. *Journal of Child Psychology and Psychiatry, and Allied Disciplines*, *57*(10), 1103–1112. doi:10.1111/jcpp.12621 PMID:27647050

Richetelli, D. M., Hartstone, E. C., & Murphy, K. L. (2009). *A second reassessment of disproportionate minority contact in Connecticut's juvenile justice system.* The Office of Juvenile Justice Programs. U.S. Department of Justice to the state of Connecticut.

Roberston, O. (2011). *Collateral convicts: Children of incarcerated parents. Recommendations and good practice from the UN Committee on the Rights of the Child Day of General Discussion 2011.* Human Rights and Refugees Publications. https://www.quno.org/sites/default/files/resources/ENGLISH_Collateral%20Convicts_Recommendations%20and%20good%20practice.pdf

Roberts, D. (2012). Prison, foster care, and the systemic punishment of Black mothers. *UCLA Law Review. University of California, Los Angeles. School of Law*, *59*, 1474–1500.

Rocque, M., & Snellings, Q. (2018). The new disciplinology: Research, theory, and remaining puzzles on the school-to-prison pipeline. *Journal of Criminal Justice*, *59*, 3–11. doi:10.1016/j.jcrimjus.2017.05.002

Rogers, C. R. (1966). *Client-centered therapy.* American Psychological Association.

Roman, C. G., & Travis, J. (2004). *Taking stock: Housing, homelessness, and prisoner reentry.* Urban Institute. https://www.urban.org/sites/default/files/publication/58121/411096-Taking-Stock.PDF

Roostin, E. (2018). Family influence on the development of children. *Journal of Elementary Education*, *1*(1), 1–12. doi:10.22460/pej.v1i1.654

Rosenblum, A., Marsch, L. A., Joseph, H., & Portenoy, R. K. (2008). Opioids and the treatment of chronic pain: Controversies, current status, and future directions. *Experimental and Clinical Psychopharmacology*, *16*(5), 405–416. doi:10.1037/a0013628 PMID:18837637

Rosenthal, A. (2018). *Common application bans the box.* https://ccresourcecenter.org/2018/08/09/common-application-bans-the-box/

Rossen, E. (2011, November). Supporting students with incarcerated parents. *Principal Leadership.* Retrieved July 23, 2021 from https://www.nasponline.org/Documents/Resources%20and%20Publications/Handouts/Families%20and%20Educators/Incarcerated_Parents_Nov2011.pdf

Roy-Stevens, C. (2004, October). *Overcoming barriers to school reentry* [Fact sheet]. Office of Juvenile Justice and Delinquency Prevention, U.S. Department of Justice. https://www.ojp.gov/pdffiles1/ojjdp/fs200403.pdf

Ryberg, R., Her, S., Temkin, D., & Harper, K. (2021). *Despite reductions since 2011-12, black students and students with disabilities remain more likely to experience suspension.* https://www.childtrends.org/publications/black-students-disabilities-out-of-school-suspensions

Sack, D. (2014, August 14). We can't afford to ignore drug addiction in prison. *The Washington Post.* https://www.washingtonpost.com/news/to-your-health/wp/2014/08/14/we-cant-afford-to-ignore-drug-addiction-in-prison/?noredirect=on

Saleem, F. T., Anderson, R. T., & Williams, M. (2019). Addressing the "Myth" of racial trauma: Developmental and ecological considerations for youth of color. *Clinical Child and Family Psychology Review*, *23*(1), 1–14. doi:10.100710567-019-00304-1 PMID:31641920

Salem, B. E., Kwon, J., Ekstrand, M. L., Hall, E., Turner, S. F., Faucette, M., & Slaughter, R. (2021). Transitioning into the community: Perceptions of barriers and facilitators experienced by formerly incarcerated, homeless women during reentry—A qualitative study. *Community Mental Health Journal*, *57*(4), 609–621. doi:10.100710597-020-00748-8 PMID:33387178

SAMHSA ReleasesBehavioral Health. (2013). SAMHSA Releases *Behavioral Health, United States, 2012. Psychiatric Services (Washington, D.C.)*, *64*(12), 1281–1281. doi:10.1176/appi.ps.6412News1 PMID:24292740

San Francisco Children of Incarcerated Parents Partnership. (2005). *Children of incarcerated parents: A bill of rights.* https://sfonline.barnard.edu/children/SFCIPP_Bill_of_Rights.pdf

Sanni, K. B., Udoh, N. A., Okediji, A. A., Modo, F. N., & Ezeh, L. N. (2010). Family Types and Juvenile Delinquency Issues among Secondary School Students in Akwa Ibom State, Nigeria: Counseling Implications. *Journal of Social Science*, *23*(1), 21–28.

Santos, M. (2021). *RDAP introduction.* https://prisonprofessors.com/rdap-introduction/

Saunders, V. (2016). Children of prisoners–Children's decision making about contact. *Child & Family Social Work*, *22*(S2), 63–72. doi:10.1111/cfs.12281

Savat, S. (2021). *For 50 years, mass incarceration has hurt American families. Here's how to change it.* Phys.org. https://phys.org/news/2021-10-years-mass-incarceration-american-families.html

Sawyer, W. (2019, December 19). *Youth confinement: The whole pie 2019.* Prison Policy Initiative. Retrieved August 4, 2021 from https://www.prisonpolicy.org/reports/youth2019.html

Sawyer, W., & Wagner, P. (2020) *Mass incarceration: The whole pie 2020.* Prison Policy Initiative. https://www.prisonpolicy.org/reports/pie2020.html

Sawyer, W., & Wagner, P. (2020). *Mass incarceration: The whole pie 2020.* Prison Policy Initiative. https://www.prisonpolicy.org/reports/pie2020.html

Sawyer, W., & Wagner, P. (2022). *Mass incarceration: The whole pie 2022.* https://www.prisonpolicy.org/reports/pie2022.html

Sawyer, P. J., Major, B., Casad, B. J., Townsend, S. S. M., & Mendes, W. B. (2012). Discrimination and the stress response: Psychological and physiological consequences of anticipating prejudice in interethnic interactions. *American Journal of Public Health*, *102*(5), 1020–1026. doi:10.2105/AJPH.2011.300620 PMID:22420818

Schappell, A., Docherty, M., & Boxer, P. (2016). Violence and victimization during incarceration: Relations to psychosocial adjustment during reentry to the community. *Violence and Victims*, *31*(2), 361-378. http://dx.doi.org.uc.idm.oclc.org/10.1891/0886-6708.VV-D-13-00188

Schiele, J. H. (2000). *Human services and the Afrocentric paradigm.* Haworth Press.

Schiff, M. (2018). Can restorative justice disrupt the 'school-to-prison pipeline?'. *Contemporary Justice Review*, *21*(2), 121–139. doi:10.1080/10282580.2018.1455509

Schilling, E. A., Aseltine, R. H. Jr, & Gore, S. (2007). Adverse childhood experiences and mental health in young adults: A longitudinal survey. *BMC Public Health*, *7*(1), 1–10. doi:10.1186/1471-2458-7-30 PMID:17343754

Schnittker, J., & John, A. (2007). Enduring stigma: The long-term effects of incarceration on health. *Journal of Health and Social Behavior*, *48*(2), 115–130. doi:10.1177/002214650704800202 PMID:17583269

Schoenwald, S. K. (2008). Towards evidence-based transport of evidence-based treatments: MST as an example. *Journal of Child & Adolescent Substance Abuse*, *17*(3), 69–91. doi:10.1080/15470650802071671

Schoenwald, S. K., Halliday-Boykins, C. A., & Henggeler, S. W. (2003). Client-level predictors of adherence to MST in community service settings. *Family Process*, *42*(3), 345–359. doi:10.1111/j.1545-5300.2003.00345.x PMID:14606199

Schreck, C., & Hirschi, T. (2009). *Social control theory*. https://www.researchgate.net/publication/337873997_Social_Control_Theory

Schubert, E. C., Duininck, M., & Shlafer, R. J. (2016). Visiting mom: A pilot evaluation of a prison-based visiting program serving incarcerated mothers and their minor children. *Journal of Offender Rehabilitation*, *55*(4), 213–234. doi:10.1080/10509674.2016.1159641 PMID:27867281

Schwartz, E. K., Docherty, N. M., Najolia, G. M., & Cohen, A. S. (2019). Exploring the racial diagnostic bias of schizophrenia using behavioral and clinical-based measures. *Journal of Abnormal Psychology*, *128*(3), 263–271. doi:10.1037/abn0000409 PMID:30762376

Schweinhart, L. J. (2013). Long-term follow-up of a preschool experiment. *Journal of Experimental Criminology*, *9*(4), 389–409. doi:10.100711292-013-9190-3

Sege, R. D., & Harper Browne, C. (2017). Responding to ACES with hope: Health outcomes from positive experiences. *Academic Pediatrics*, *17*(7), S79–S85. doi:10.1016/j.acap.2017.03.007 PMID:28865664

Seiter, R. P., & Kadela, K. R. (2003). Prisoner reentry: What works, what does not, and what is promising. *Crime and Delinquency*, *49*(3), 360–388. doi:10.1177/0011128703049003002

Semenza, D. C., & Link, N. W. (2019). How does reentry get under the skin? Cumulative reintegration barriers and health in a sample of recently incarcerated men. *Social Science & Medicine*, *243*, 1–9. doi:10.1016/j.socscimed.2019.112618 PMID:31665655

Sexton, T. (2016). Incarceration as a family affair: Thinking beyond the individual. *Couples and Family Psychology: Research and Practice*, *5*(2), 61–64.

Seymour, C. (2001). Children with parents in prison: Child welfare policy, program, and practice issues. In C. Seymour & C. F. Hairston (Eds.), *Children with parents in prison: Child welfare policy, program & practice issues*. Transaction Press.

Seymour, C., & Hairston, C. F. (Eds.). (1998). *Children with parents in prison: Child welfare policy, program, and practice issues*. Transaction.

Shane, J., Heckhausen, J., Lessard, J., Chen, C., & Greenberger, E. (2012). Career-related goal pursuit among post-high school youth: Relations between personal control beliefs and control strivings. *Motivation and Emotion*, *36*(2), 159–169. doi:10.100711031-011-9245-6

Shaw, M. (2006). *Communities in action for crime prevention* [Background paper]. 6th Annual Colloquium on Crime Prevention, Canberra, Australia. https://www.unodc.org/pdf/criminal_justice/Handbook_on_Crime_Prevention_Guidelines_-_Making_them_work.pdf

Shaw, T., Bright, C., & Sharpe, T. (2015). Child welfare outcomes for youth in care as a result of parental death or incarceration. *Child Abuse and Neglect*, *42*, 112-120. doi:org/ doi:10.1016/j.chiabu.2015.01.002

Shlafer, R. J., Loper, A. B., & Schillmoeller, L. (2015). Introduction and literature review: Is parent-child contact during parental incarceration beneficial? In J. Poehlmann-Tynan (Ed.), *Children's contact with incarcerated parents: Implications for policy and intervention* (pp. 1–21). Springer International. doi:10.1007/978-3-319-16625-4_1

Shlafer, R. J., & Poehlmann, J. (2010). Attachment and caregiving relationships in families affected by parental incarceration. *Attachment & Human Development*, *12*(4), 395–415. doi:10.1080/14616730903417052 PMID:20582847

Shonkoff, J. P., Garner, A. P., Siegel, B. S., Dobbins, M. I., Earls, M. F., Garner, A. S., McGuinn, L., Pascoe, J., & Wood, D. L. (2012). The lifelong effects of early childhood adversity and toxic stress. *Pediatrics*, *129*(1), e232–e246. doi:10.1542/peds.2011-2663 PMID:22201156

Shrider, E., Kollar, M., Chen, F., & Semega, J. (2021). *Income and poverty in the united states*. https://www.census.gov/content/dam/Census/library/publications/2021/demo/p60-273.pdf

Shulman, E. P., Steinberg, L. D., & Piquero, A. R. (2013). The age-crime curve in adolescence and early adulthood is not due to age differences in economic status. *Journal of Youth and Adolescence*, *42*(6), 848–860. doi:10.100710964-013-9950-4 PMID:23595417

Sickmund, M., & Puzzanchera, C. (Eds.). (2014). *Juvenile offenders and victims: 2014 national report*. National Center for Juvenile Justice.

Siegel, D. J. (2012). *Pocket guide to interpersonal neurobiology: An integrative handbook of the mind*. W.W. Norton & Co.

Silver, I. A., D'Amato, C., & Wooldredge, J. (2021). The cycle of reentry and reincarceration: Examining the influence on employment over a period of 18 years. *Journal of Criminal Justice*, *74*, 101812. doi:10.1016/j.jcrimjus.2021.101812

Simon, C. (2016). *There is a stunning gap between the number of white and black inmates in America's prisons*. Business Insider. Retrieved from http://www.businessinsider.com/study-finds-huge-racial-disparity-in-americas-prisons-2016-6/#incarceration-ratio-for-blacks-versus-whites-by-state-1

Simon, J. (2013). From health to humanity: Re-reading Estelle v. Gamble after Brown v. Plata. *Federal Sentencing Reporter*, *25*(4), 276-280.

Sindelar, J., Elbel, B., & Petry, N. M. (2007). What do we get for our money? Cost effectiveness of adding contingency management. *Addiction (Abingdon, England)*, *102*(2), 309–316. doi:10.1111/j.1360-0443.2006.01689.x PMID:17222286

Singer, A. J., & Kopak, A. M. (2021). Jail reentry and gaps in substance use disorder treatment in rural communities. *Corrections: Policy, Practice and Research*, 1–23. doi:10.1080/23774657.2021.1967816

Singh, A. A., Nassar, S. C., Arredondo, P., & Toporek, R. (2020). The past guides the future: Implementing the multicultural and social justice counseling competencies. *Journal of Counseling and Development*, *98*(3), 238–252. doi:10.1002/jcad.12319

Skiba, R. J. (2000). Zero Tolerance, Zero Evidence: An Analysis of School Disciplinary Practice. Policy Research Report. Indiana University, Bloomington. Education Policy Center.

Skiba, R. J., Arrendondo, M. I., & Williams, N. T. (2017). In and of itself a risk factor: Exclusionary discipline and the school-to-prison pipeline. In K. J. Fasching- Varner, L. L. Martin, R. W. Mitchell, K. P. Bennett-Haron & A. Daneshzadeh (Eds.), Understanding dismantling, and disrupting the prison-to-school pipeline (pp. 111–130). Rowman & Littlefield.

Skiba, R. J., Arredondo, M. I., & Williams, N. T. (2014). More than a metaphor: The contribution of exclusionary discipline to a school-to-prison pipeline. *Equity & Excellence in Education*, *47*(4), 546–564. doi:10.1080/10665684.2014.958965

Skiba, R. J., Horner, R. H., Chung, C., Rausch, M. K., May, S., & Tobin, T. (2011). Race is not neutral: A national investigation of African American and Latino disproportionality in school discipline. *School Psychology Review*, *40*(1), 85–107. doi:10.1080/02796015.2011.12087730

Skill You Need. (2021). *What is counselling?* https://www.skillsyouneed.com/learn/counselling.html

Skinner, B. F. (1938). *The Behaviour of organisms: An experimental analysis*. Appleton-Century.

Skinner, B. F. (1948). Superstition' in the pigeon. *Journal of Experimental Psychology*, *38*(2), 168–172. doi:10.1037/h0055873 PMID:18913665

Skinner-Osei, P., & Levenson, J. S. (2018). Trauma-informed services for children with incarcerated parents. *Journal of Family Social Work*, *21*(4-5), 421–437. doi:10.1080/10522158.2018.1499064

Skora Horgan, E., & Poehlmann-Tynan, J. (2020). In-home video chat for young children and their incarcerated parents. *Journal of Children and Media*, *14*(3), 400–406. doi:10.1080/17482798.2020.1792082

Sloan, M. (2014). *Differentiating Factors between Foster Youth and Non-Foster Youth Involved in the Juvenile-Justice System* (Order No. 3622814). Available from ProQuest Central; ProQuest Dissertations & Theses Global. (1548983942). http://nclive.org.ezproxy.nccu.edu/cgi-bin/nclsm?url=http://search.proquest.com.ezproxy.nccu.edu/dissertations-theses/differentiating-factors-between-foster-youth-non/docview/1548983942/se-2?accountid=12713

Slocum, L. A., Medel, J., Doherty, E. E., & Simpson, S. S. (2022). Unpacking the Criminogenic Aspects of Stress Over the Life Course: The Joint Effects of Proximal Strain and Childhood Abuse on Violence and Substance Use in a High-Risk Sample of Women. *Journal of Research in Crime and Delinquency*. Advance online publication. doi:10.1177/00224278211068188

Smiley, C. J., & Fakunle, D. (2016). From "brute" to "thug:" The demonization and criminalization of unarmed Black male victims in America. *Journal of Human Behavior in the Social Environment*, *26*(3-4), 350–366.

Smith, L. A., & Foxcroft, D. R. (2009). The effect of alcohol advertising, marketing and portrayal on drinking behaviour in young people: Systematic review of prospective cohort studies. *BMC Public Health*, *9*(1), 1–11. doi:10.1186/1471-2458-9-51 PMID:19200352

Snell, T. L. (1995). *Correctional populations in the United States,1993*. Department of Justice. https://www.bjs.gov/content/pub/pdf/cpop93bk.pdf

Soler, M., & Gary, L. M. (2009). *Disproportionate minority contact: Addressing disproportionate minority contact in juvenile justice*. Office of Juvenile Justice and Delinquency Prevention.

Soltes, F. (2012). *Girl Scouts Beyond Bars: Providing a better path*. Office of Juvenile Justice and Delinquency Prevention. https://www.ojp.gov/pdffiles1/ojjdp/249001.pdf

Song, H., Woo, Y., Lee, H. D., & Cochran, J. K. (2018). The dynamics of intra-family relationships during incarceration and the implications for children of incarcerated parents. *International Journal of Offender Therapy and Comparative Criminology*, *62*(12), 3775–3796. doi:10.1177/0306624X18755481 PMID:29392971

Spaulding, S. A., Irvin, L. K., Horner, R. H., May, S. L., Emeldi, M., Tobin, T. J., & Sugai, G. (2010). Schoolwide social-behavioral climate, student problem behavior, and related administrative decisions: Empirical patterns from 1,510 schools nationwide. *Journal of Positive Behavior Interventions*, *12*(2), 69–85. doi:10.1177/1098300708329011

Speight, S. L. (2007). Internalized racism: One more piece of the puzzle. *The Counseling Psychologist*, *35*(1), 126–134. doi:10.1177/0011000006295119

Sripada, C. (2022). Impaired control in addiction involves cognitive distortions and unreliable self-control not compulsive desires and overwhelmed self-control. *Behavioural Brain Research*, *418*, 113639. doi:10.1016/j.bbr.2021.113639 PMID:34710509

Staats, C. (2014). *Implicit racial bias and school discipline disparities: Exploring the connection.* Kirwan Institute for the Study of Race and Ethnicity. Special Report. 1-20.

Stainbrook, K., Hanna, J., & Salomon, A. (2017). *The rsat study: The characteristics and components of funded treatment and aftercare services.* https://www.ojp.gov/pdffiles1/nij/grants/250715.pdf

Stanko, S. C., & Crews, G. A. (2016). The Impact of Mass Incarceration and Social Issues of Institutionalization on School Violence in Youths. In A. C. Gordon (Ed.), *Critical Examinations of School Violence and Disturbance in K-12 Education* (pp. 29–37). IGI Global. doi:10.4018/978-1-4666-9935-9.ch003

Staton, M., Dickson, M., Tillson, M., & Winston, E. (2019). *Criminal Justice Kentucky Treatment Outcome Study.* https://corrections.ky.gov/Divisions/ask/Documents/CJKTOS%20FInal%20Report%202019.pdf

Stauffer, B. (2016, October 12). *Interview: Why the U.S. should de-criminalize drug use.* https://www.hrw.org/news/2016/10/12/interview-why-us-should-decriminalize-drug-use

Stautz, K., Brown, K. G., King, S. E., Shemilt, I., & Marteau, T. M. (2016). Immediate effects of alcohol marketing communications and media portrayals on consumption and cognition: A systematic review and meta-analysis of experimental studies. *BMC Public Health*, *16*(1), 1–18. doi:10.118612889-016-3116-8 PMID:27278656

Steen, A. A. (2021). *From Bunks and Bars to Sidewalks and Skies: Support for Reentry from Incarceration.* Academic Press.

Steinberg, D., Mills, D., & Romano, M. (2015). When did prisons become acceptable mental healthcare facilities? *Stanford Law School.* https://law.stanford.edu/wp-content/uploads/sites/default/files/publication/863745/doc/slspublic/Report_v12.pdf

Steiner, M. (2022). *What is parole? How does parole work?* https://www.nolo.com/legal-encyclopedia/how-does-parole-work.html#:~:text=Parole%20Conditions&text=maintain%20employment%20and%20a%20residence,or%20alcohol%20recovery%20meetings%2C%20and

Stemen, D. (2017, July). *The prison paradox: More incarceration will not make us safer.* https://www.vera.org/publications/for-the-record-prison-paradox-incarceration-not-safer

Steurer, S. J., & Smith, L. G. (2003). *Education reduces crime: Three-state recidivism study. Executive summary.* Correctional Education Association. https://files.eric.ed.gov/fulltext/ED478452.pdf

Stitzer, M., & Petry, N. (2006). Contingency management for treatment of substance abuse. *Annual Review of Clinical Psychology*, *2*(1), 411–434. doi:10.1146/annurev.clinpsy.2.022305.095219 PMID:17716077

Stone, S., & Zibulsky, J. (2015). Maltreatment, academic difficulty, and systems-involved youth: Current evidence and opportunities. *Psychology in the Schools*, *52*(1), 22–39. doi:10.1002/pits.21812

Stop Child Abuse America. (2016). *The Facilitator's Guide to Resilience.* https://www.onecaringadult.co/wp-content/uploads/2016/08/KPJR-Facilitators-Guide.pdf

Strnadová, I., Clark, H. G., O'Neill, S. C., Cumming, T. M., Mathur, S. R., Wells, T. C., & Danker, J. (2022). Barriers to Community Re-entry for Incarcerated Youth: Stakeholders' Perspectives in Australia and the United States. In *Transition Programs for Children and Youth with Diverse Needs.* Emerald Publishing Limited. doi:10.1108/S1479-363620220000018017

Substance Abuse and Mental Health Services Administration. (2014). *SAMHSA's concept of trauma and guidance for a trauma-informed approach.* https://ncsacw.samhsa.gov/

Substance Abuse and Mental Health Services Administration. (2014). *SAMHSA's concept of trauma and guidance for a trauma-informed approach.* Substance Abuse and Mental Health Services Administration.

Substance Abuse and Mental Health Services Administration. (2017). *Implementation guide.* https://store.samhsa.gov/sites/default/files/d7/priv/sma16-4998.pdf

Substance Abuse and Mental Health Services Administration. (2018). *2018 national survey of drug use and health (NSDUH) releases.* https://www.samhsa.gov/data/release/2018-national-survey-drug-use-and-health-nsduh-releases

Sue, D. W., Capodilupo, C. M., Torino, G. C., Bucceri, J. M., Holder, A. M. B., Nadal, K. L., & Esquilin, M. (2007). Racial microaggressions in everyday life: Implications for clinical practice. *The American Psychologist, 64*(4), 271–286. doi:10.1037/0003-066X.62.4.271 PMID:17516773

Sullivan, M. (2020). Research and best practices to support students with incarcerated parents. In E. Rossen (Ed.), *Supporting and educating traumatized students: A guide for school-based professionals* (2nd ed., pp. 165–179). Oxford University Press. doi:0.1093/med-psych/9780190052737.003.0009

Sutherland, E. H., Cressey, D. R., & Luckenbill, D. F. (1992). Principles of criminology (11th ed.). Lanham, MD: Alta Mira Press.

Sutherland, E. H. (1947). *Principles of criminology* (4th ed.). Lippincott.

Sutton, J. R. (2013). Symbol and substance: Effects of California's three strikes law on felony sentencing. *Law & Society Review, 47*(1), 37–72.

Swopes, R. M., Simonet, D. V., Jaffe, A. E., Tett, R. P., & Davis, J. L. (2013). Adverse childhood experiences, posttraumatic stress disorder symptoms, and emotional intelligence in partner aggression. *Violence and Victims, 28*(3), 513–530. doi:10.1891/0886-6708.VV-D-12-00026 PMID:23862313

Sykes, B. L., & Pettit, B. (2014). Mass incarceration, family complexity, and the reproduction of childhood disadvantage. *The Annals of the American Academy of Political and Social Science, 654*(1), 127–149. doi:10.1177/0002716214526345

Tadros, E., & Finney, N. (2018). Structural family therapy with incarcerated families. *The Family Journal (Alexandria, Va.), 26*(2), 253–261. doi:10.1177/1066480718777409

Tadros, E., Fye, J. M., McCrone, C. L., & Finney, N. (2019). Incorporating multicultural couple and family therapy into incarcerated settings. *International Journal of Offender Therapy and Comparative Criminology, 63*(4), 641–658. doi:10.1177/0306624X18823442 PMID:30628499

Tadros, E., & Ogden, T. E. (2020). Conceptualizing incarcerated coparenting through a structural family theory lens. *Marriage & Family Review, 56*(6), 535–552. doi:10.1080/01494929.2020.1728007

Tadros, E., & Owens, D. (2019). Clinical implications for culturally informed counseling with incarcerated individuals. *The American Journal of Family Therapy, 49*(4), 344–355. doi:10.1080/01926187.2020.1813659

Taie, S., & Westat, R. G. (2020). *Characteristics of public and private elementary and secondary school teachers in the United States: results from the 2017–18 national teacher and principal survey.* https://nces.ed.gov/pubs2020/2020142.pdf

Taliaferro, W., & Pham, D. (2018). *Incarceration to reentry: Education & training pathways in Ohio.* Center for Law and Social Policy, Inc. (CLASP). https://files.eric.ed.gov/fulltext/ED586093.pdf

Talik, E., & Skowronski, B. (2017). The sense of quality of life and religious strategies of coping with stress in prison inmates. *Journal of Religion and Health*, *57*(3), 915–937. doi:10.100710943-017-0455-4

Tang, S., Jones, C. M., Wisdom, A., Lin, H. C., Bacon, S., & Houry, D. (2021). Adverse childhood experiences and stimulant use disorders among adults in the United States. *Psychiatry Research*, *299*, 113870. doi:10.1016/j.psychres.2021.113870 PMID:33780857

Tarasuik, J. C. M., Kaufman, J., & Galligan, R. (2013). Seeing is believing but is hearing? Comparing audio and video communication for young children. *Frontiers in Psychology*, *4*(64). Advance online publication. doi:10.3389/fpsyg.2013.00064 PMID:23450846

Terling, T. (1999). The efficacy of family reunification practices: Reentry rates and correlates of reentry for abused and neglected children reunited with their families. *Child Abuse & Neglect*, *23*(12), 1359–1370. doi:10.1016/S0145-2134(99)00103-9 PMID:10626617

The Hamilton Project. (2015). *Rates of drug use and sales, by race; rates of drug related criminal justice measures, by race*. https://www.hamiltonproject.org/charts/rates_of_drug_use_and_sales_by_race_rates_of_drug_related_criminal_justice

The National Center on Addiction and Substance Abuse. (2009). *From CASA's 2009 shoveling up II: The impact of substance abuse on federal, state and local budgets report*. https://www.ojp.gov/ncjrs/virtual-library/abstracts/shoveling-ii-impact-substance-abuse-federal-state-and-local-budgets

The Oxford Treatment Center. (2020). *The kindling effect: Alcohol withdrawal issues*. https://oxfordtreatment.com/substance-abuse/alcohol/kindling-effect/

The Pew Charitable Trusts. (2012). *Time served: The high cost, low return of longer prison terms*. The Pew Charitable Trusts. https://www.pewtrusts.org/~/media/assets/2012/06/06/time_served_report.pdf

The Pew Charitable Trusts. (2015). *Federal drug sentencing laws bring high cost, low return*. https://www.pewtrusts.org/-/media/assets/2015/08/federal_drug_sentencing_laws_bring_high_cost_low_return.pdf

The Pew Charitable Trusts. (2018, March 8). *More imprisonment does not reduce state drug problems*. https://www.pewtrusts.org/en/research-and-analysis/issue briefs/2018/03/more-imprisonment-does-not-reduce-state-drug-problems

The Scottish Government. (2018, May). *Understanding Childhood Adversity, Resilience, and Crime*. APS Group Scotland. https://www.gov.scot

The Sentencing Project. (2012). *Parents in prison*. https://www.sentencingproject.org/wp-content/uploads/2016/01/Parents-in-Prison.pdf

The Sentencing Project. (2018). *Report to the United Nations on racial disparities in the US criminal justice system*. https://www.sentencingproject.org/publications/un-report-on-racial-disparities/

The Sentencing Project. (2020, November). *Fact sheet: Incarcerated women and girls*. https://www.sentencingproject.org/wp-content/uploads/2016/02/Incarcerated-Women-and-Girls.pdf

The Sentencing Project. (n.d.). *Criminal justice facts*. https://www.sentencingproject.org/criminal-justice-facts/

Theerathitiwong, S. (2017). *The encyclopedia of corrections*. John Wiley & Sons.

Theriot, M. T. (2016). The impact of school resource officer interaction on students' feelings about school and school police. *Crime and Delinquency*, *62*(4), 446–469. doi:10.1177/0011128713503526

Thompson, K. (2018). *Zero-tolerance policies and the school to prison pipeline*. https://www.sharedjustice.org/most-recent/2017/12/21/zero-tolerance-policies-and-the-school-to-prison-pipeline

Thompson, R., & Haskins, R. (2014). Early stress gets under the skin: Promising initiatives to help children facing chronic adversity. *The Future of Children*, *24*(1), 1–8.

Tkach, M. J. (2018). A psychosocial linguistic exploration of the use of alcoholic as a social label of self-identity in AA and 12-step programs. *Alcoholism Treatment Quarterly*, *36*(1), 101–114. doi:10.1080/07347324.2017.1355221

Toews, B., Wagenfeld, A., Stevens, J., & Shoemaker, C. (2020). Feeling at home in nature: A mixed method study of the impact of visitor activities and preferences in a prison visiting room garden. *Journal of Offender Rehabilitation*, *59*(4), 223–246. doi:10.1080/10509674.2020.1733165

Tonheim, M., & Iversen, A. C. (2019). "We felt completely left to ourselves." Foster parents' views on placement disruption. *Child & Family Social Work*, *24*(1), 90–97. http://dx.doi.org.ezproxy.nccu.edu/10.1111/cfs.12585. doi:10.1111/cfs.12585

Toporek, R., & Daniels, J. (2018). *American Counseling Association advocacy competencies. In Youthful offenders in the federal system*. United States Sentencing Commission.

Torrey, F. E., Kennard, A. D., Eslinger, D., Lamb, R., & Pavle, J. (2010). *More mentally ill persons are in jails and prisons than hospitals: A survey of the states*. https://knox.oh.networkofcare.org/library/final_jails_v_hospitals_study.pdf

Toth, S. L., & Manly, J. T. (2019). Developmental consequences of child abuse and neglect: Implications for intervention. *Child Development Perspectives*, *13*(1), 59–64. doi:10.1111/cdep.12317

Trappen, S. (2018). *Theories of Delinquency*. https://sandratrappen.com/2018/12/30/theories-of-delinquency/

Trauma Matters Delaware. (2021). *Organizational Transition to Trauma Responsiveness*. https://traumamattersdelaware.org/what-is-trauma-informed-care/

Trauma-Informed Care Implementation Resource Center. (2021). *What is trauma-informed care?* Retrieved July 22, 2021 from https://www.traumainformedcare.chcs.org/what-is-trauma-informed-care/

Travis, J., & Western, B. (2017). Poverty, violence, and black incarceration. In A. Davis (Ed.), Policing the black man: Arrest, prosecution, and imprisonment (pp. 294-321). First Vintage.

Travis, J., Solomon, A. L., & Waul, M. (2001). *From prison to home: The dimensions and consequences of prisoner reentry*. The Dimensions & Consequences of Prisoner Reentry.

Travis, J., Western, B., & Redburn, S. (2014). *The growth in incarceration in the United States: Exploring causes and consequences*. The National Academics Press.

Tremblay, M. D., & Sutherland, J. E. (2017). The effectiveness of parenting programs for incarcerated mothers: A systematic review. *Journal of Child and Family Studies*, *26*(12), 3247–3265. doi:10.100710826-017-0900-8

Turanovic, J. J., Rodriguez, N., & Pratt, T. C. (2012). The collateral consequences of incarceration revisited: A qualitative analysis of the effects on caregivers of children of incarcerated parents. *Criminology*, *50*(4), 913–960. doi:10.1111/j.1745-9125.2012.00283.x

Turanovic, J. J., & Tasca, M. (2019). Inmates' experiences with prison visitation. *Justice Quarterly*, *36*(2), 287–322. do i:10.1080/07418825.2017.1385826

Turney, K. (2014). Stress proliferation across generations? Examining the relationship between parental incarceration and childhood health. *Journal of Health and Social Behavior*, *55*(3), 302–319. doi:10.1177/0022146514544173 PMID:25138199

Turney, K. (2015). Hopelessly devoted? Relationship quality during and after incarceration. *Journal of Marriage and Family*, *77*(2), 480–495. doi:10.1111/jomf.12174

Turney, K. (2017). Unmet health care needs among children exposed to parental incarceration. *Maternal and Child Health Journal, 21*(5), 1194–1202. doi:10.100710995-016-2219-2 PMID:28108834

Turney, K. (2018). Adverse childhood experiences among children of incarcerated parents. *Children and Youth Services Review, 89*, 218–225. doi:10.1016/j.childyouth.2018.04.033

Turney, K. (2019). Understanding the needs of children with incarcerated parents: What educators should know. *American Educator, 43*(2), 22–28.

Turney, K., & Goodsell, R. (2018). Parental incarceration and children's wellbeing. *The Future of Children, 28*(1), 147–164.

Turney, K., & Haskins, A. R. (2014). Falling behind? Children's early grade retention after paternal incarceration. *Sociology of Education, 87*(4), 241–258. doi:10.1177/0038040714547086

Turney, K., & Wildeman, C. (2013). Redefining relationships: Explaining the countervailing consequences of paternal incarceration for parenting. *American Sociological Review, 78*(6), 949–979. doi:10.1177/0003122413505589

Turney, K., & Wildeman, C. (2015). Detrimental for some? Heterogeneous effects of maternal incarceration on child wellbeing. *Criminology & Public Policy, 14*(1), 125–156. doi-org.proxy.libraries.uc.edu/10.1111/1745-9133.12109

Turney, K., & Wildeman, C. (2017). Adverse childhood experiences anoint children placed in and adopted from foster care: Evidence from a nationally representative survey. *Child Abuse & Neglect, 64*, 117–129. doi:10.1016/j.chiabu.2016.12.009 PMID:28086178

Tye, C., & Mullen, P. (2006). Mental disorder in female prisoners. *The Australian and New Zealand Journal of Psychiatry, 40*(3), 266–271. doi:10.1080/j.1440-1614.2006.01784.x PMID:16476155

Tyler, E. T., & Brockmann, B. (2017). Returning home: Incarceration, reentry, stigma and the perpetuation of racial and socioeconomic health inequity. *The Journal of Law, Medicine & Ethics, 45*(4), 545–557. doi:10.1177/1073110517750595

Tyner, A. R. (2020). The Tangled Web of Mass Incarceration: Addressing the School-To-Prison Pipeline Through a Restorative Justice Approach. *University of St. Thomas Law Journal, 17*(1), 59.

U.S. Department of Education. (2021). *The federal role in education.* Retrieved July 24, 2021 from https://www2.ed.gov/about/overview/fed/role.html

U.S. Department of Health and Human Services, Administration for Children and Families, Administration on Children, Youth and Families, & Children's Bureau (2018). *The AFCARS Report: Preliminary FY 2017 estimates as of September 24, 2018 - Number 251–6.* Author.

U.S. Department of Health and Human Services. (2017). Administration for Children and Families, Administration on Children, & Youth and Families Children's Bureau (2018). *Child Maltreatment*, 1–261.

U.S. Department of Health and Human Services. (2018, November 8). *Trends in Foster Care & Adoption: FY 2010-2019.* The Administration for Children and Families. https://www.acf.hhs.gov/cb/report/trends-foster-care-adoption-2019

U.S. Department of Justice. (2016). *RSAT for state prisoners program.* https://bja.ojp.gov/sites/g/files/xyckuh186/files/media/document/BJA-2016-9023.pdf

U.S. Department of Justice. (2021). *Drug courts.* https://www.ojp.gov/pdffiles1/nij/238527.pdf

U.S. Equal Employment Opportunity Coalition. (2012). *Enforcement guidance on the consideration of arrest and conviction records in employment decisions under Title VII of the Civil Rights Act.* Retrieved April 5, 2022 from https://www.eeoc.gov/laws/guidance/enforcement-guidance-consideration-arrest-and-conviction-records-employment-decisions#VB6

U.S. Government Accountability Office. (2007). *African American children in foster care: Additional HHS assistance needed to help states reduce the proportion in care* (GAO-07-816). https://www.gao.gov/products/GAO-07-816

Uggen, C., & Thompson, M. (2003). The socioeconomic determinants of ill-gotten gains: Within-person changes in drug use and illegal earnings. *American Journal of Sociology, 109*(1), 146–185. doi:10.1086/378036

Ukwueze, A. C. (2015). Adolescents' inappropriate behaviours affecting academic performance in senior secondary schools: Need for counselling interventions. *Sokoto International Journal of Counselling Psychology, 3*(2), 138–154.

United Nations development programme. (2017). Article. *New Zealand Journal of Medical Laboratory Science, 71*(1), 23.

United States Census Bureau. (2019). *Quick facts: United States* [Census Data]. https://www.census.gov/quickfacts/fact/table/US/IPE120219

United States Census Bureau. (2019). *QuickFacts United States.* https://www.census.gov/quickfacts/fact/table/US/PST045219

United States Department of Education Office for Civil Rights. (2014). *Civil rights data collection data snapshot: School discipline. Issue Brief No. 1.* https://ocrdata.ed.gov/

United States Department of Education Office for Civil Rights. (2021). *Civil Rights Data Collection.* https://www2.ed.gov/about/offices/list/ocr/data.html

United States Department of Education. (2012). *Civil rights data collection.* United States Department of Education.

United States Department of Justice Archives. (2017). *Report and recommendations concerning the use of restrictive housing.* https://www.justice.gov/archives/dag/report-and-recommendations-concerning-use-restrictive-housing

United States Sentencing Commission. (2017). *Recidivism among federal drug trafficking offenders.* https://www.ussc.gov/research/research-reports/recidivism-among-federal-drug-trafficking-offenders

Unrau, Y. A., Font, S. A., & Rawls, G. (2012). Readiness for college engagement among students who have aged out of foster care. *Children and Youth Services Review, 34*(1), 76–83. doi:10.1016/j.childyouth.2011.09.002

Unruh, D., & Bullis, M. (2005). Female and male juvenile offenders with disabilities: Differences in the barriers to their transition to the community. *Behavioral Disorders, 30*(2), 105–117. doi:10.1177/019874290503000207

US Census Bureau. (n.d.). *Data USA: Counselors.* DataUSA. https://datausa.io/profile/soc/counselors#demographics

US Department of Education. (2021). *2017–18 Civil Rights Data Collection: School Climate and Safety.* Author.

van der Kolk, B. A. (2007). The Developmental Impact of Childhood Trauma. In L. J. Kirmayer, R. Lemelson, & M. Barad (Eds.), *Understanding trauma: Integrating biological, clinical, and cultural perspectives* (pp. 224–241). Cambridge University Press. doi:10.1017/CBO9780511500008.016

Varan, A. K., Mercer, D. W., Stein, M. S., & Spaulding, A. C. (2014). Hepatitis C seroprevalence among prison inmates since 2001: Still high but declining. *Public Health Reports, 129*(2), 187–195. doi:10.1177/003335491412900213 PMID:24587554

Vélez Young-Alfaro, M. (2017). Students as threats: Schooling inside a youth prison. *Anthropology & Education Quarterly, 48*(3), 301–317. doi:10.1111/aeq.12201

Vera, E. M., & Speight, S. L. (2003). Multicultural Competence, Social Justice, and Counseling Psychology: Expanding Our Roles. *The Counseling Psychologist, 31*(3), 253–272. doi:10.1177/0011000003031003001

ViceNews. (2015). *Institutionalized: Mental health behind bars* [Video]. YouTube. www.youtube.com/watch?v=-fQ50a-m92Y

Visher, C., Debus-Sherrill, S., & Yahner, J. (2008). *Employment after prison: A longitudinal study of releasees in three states*. Urban Institute. https://www.urban.org/research/publication/employment-after-prison-longitudinal-study-releasees-three-states

Visher, C., Yahner, J., & La Vigne, N. (2010). *Life after prison: Tracking the experiences of male prisoners returning to Chicago, Cleveland, and Houston*. Urban Institute. https://www.urban.org/sites/default/files/publication/28671/412100-Life-after-Prison-Tracking-the-Experiences-of-Male-Prisoners-Returning-to-Chicago-Cleveland-and-Houston.PDF

Visher, C. A., & Mallik-Kane, K. (2007). Reentry experiences of men with health problems. In R. B. Greifinger (Ed.), *Public Health Behind Bars* (pp. 434–460). Springer. doi:10.1007/978-0-387-71695-4_25

Volkow, N. D. (2018). Preface. In *Principles of drug addiction treatment: A research-based guide* (3rd ed.). National Institute on Drug Abuse. https://www.drugabuse.gov/publications/principles-drug-addiction-treatment-research-based-guide-third-edition/preface

Wagner, P., & Sawyer, W. (2018). *Mass incarceration: The whole pie 2018*. Prison Policy Initiative. https://www.prisonpolicy.org/factsheets/pie2018_allimages.pdf

Waites, C. (2009). Building on strengths: Intergenerational practice with African American families. *Social Work*, *54*(3), 278–287. doi:10.1093w/54.3.278 PMID:19530575

Waites, C. (Ed.). (2008). *Social work practice with African Americans: An intergenerational perspective*. Routledge.

Wakefield, S., Lee, H., & Wildeman, C. (2016). Tough on crime, tough on families? Criminal justice and family life in American. *The Annals of the American Academy of Political and Social Science*, *665*(1), 8–21. doi.org/10.1177/0002716216637048

Wakefield, S., & Wildeman, C. (2014). *Children of the prison boom: Mass incarceration and the future of American inequality*. Oxford University Press.

Walkley, M., & Cox, T. L. (2013). Building trauma-informed schools and Communities. *Children & Schools*, *35*(2), 123–126. doi:10.1093/cs/cdt007

Wallace, D., Fahmy, C., Cotton, L., Jimmons, C., McKay, R., Stoffer, S., & Syed, S. (2016). Examining the role of familial support during prison and after release on post-incarceration mental health. *International Journal of Offender and Comparative Criminology*, *60*(1), 3–20. doi:10.1177/0306624X14548023

Walmsley, R. (2011). *World prison population list* (9th ed.). International Centre for Prison Studies. https://www.prisonstudies.org/sites/default/files/resources/downloads/wppl_9.pdf

Wang, E. A., Hong, C. S., Shavit, S., Sanders, R., Kessell, E., & Kushel, M. B. (2012). Engaging individuals recently released from prison into primary care: A randomized trial. *American Journal of Public Health*, *102*(9), 22–29. doi:10.2105/AJPH.2012.300894 PMID:22813476

Wang, E. A., Pletcher, M., Lin, F., Vittinghoff, E., Kertesz, S. G., Kiefe, C. I., & Bibbins-Domingo, K. (2009). Incarceration, incident hypertension, and access to health care: Findings from the coronary artery risk development in young adults (CARDIA) study. *Archives of Internal Medicine*, *169*(7), 687–693. doi:10.1001/archinternmed.2009.26 PMID:19364998

Wang, M., & Sheikh-Khalil, S. (2014). Does parental involvement matter for student achievement and mental health in high school? *Child Development*, *85*(2), 610–625. doi:10.1111/cdev.12153 PMID:24033259

Wang, M.-T., & Huguley, J. P. (2012). Parental racial socialization as a moderator of the effects of racial discrimination on educational success among African American adolescents. *Child Development*, *83*(5), 1716–1731. doi:10.1111/j.1467-8624.2012.01808.x PMID:22717004

Warren, J. G., Coker, G. L., & Collins, M. L. (2019). Children of Incarcerated Parents: Considerations for Professional School Counselors. *The Professional Counselor (Greensboro, N.C.)*, *9*(3), 185–199. doi:10.15241/jmw.9.3.185

Washington State Department of Social and Health Services. (2009). *Beyond the walls: A guide to services for families affected by incarceration.* https://snohomishcountywa.gov/DocumentCenter/View/6011/Beyond-the-Walls?bidId=

Washington, A. R. (2015). "It's like he'll be there for you": Middle School African American Males' Stories of Effective Professional School Counselors. *Journal of African American Males in Education*, *6*(2), 1–16.

Washington, H. M., Juan, S. C., & Haskins, A. R. (2018). Incapacitated involvement: Incarceration and fatherhood in fragile families at age 9. *Journal of Family Issues*, *39*(13), 3463–3486. doi:10.1177/0192513X18783225

Wasserman, G. A. (2003). *Risk and protective factors of child delinquency*. U.S. Dept. of Justice, Office of Justice Programs, Office of Juvenile Justice and Delinquency Prevention. doi:10.1037/e501772006-001

Weisburd, D., Hinkle, J. C., Famega, C., & Ready, J. (2011). The possible "backfire" effects of hot spots policing: An experimental assessment of impacts on legitimacy, fear and collective efficacy. *Journal of Experimental Criminology*, *7*(4), 297–320. doi:10.100711292-011-9130-z

Welton, A. D., & Harris, T. O. (2022). Youth of Color Social Movements for Racial Justice: The Politics of Interrogating the School-to-Prison Pipeline. *Educational Policy (Los Altos, Calif.)*, *36*(1), 57–99. doi:10.1177/08959048211059728

Western, B. (2018). *Homeward: Life in the year after prison.* Russell Sage Foundation. doi:10.7758/9781610448710

Western, B., Braga, A., Davis, J., & Sirois, C. (2015). Stress and hardship after prison. *American Journal of Sociology*, *120*(5), 1512–1547. doi:10.1086/681301

Western, B., & Pettit, B. (2010). Incarceration and social inequality. *Daedalus*, *139*(3), 8–19. doi.org/10.1162/DAED_a_00019

Western, B., & Wildeman, C. (2009). The black family and mass incarceration. *Annals*, *621*, 221–242.

Westervelt, E. (2019). *County jails struggle with a new role as america's prime centers for opioid detox.* https://www.npr.org/2019/04/24/716398909/county-jails-struggle-with-a-new-role-as-americas-prime-centers-for-opioid-detox

Wheelock, D., & Hartmann, D. (2007). Midnight basketball and the 1994 crime bill debates: The operation of a racial code. *The Sociological Quarterly*, *48*(2), 315–342. doi:10.1111/j.1533-8525.2007.00080.x

White Swan Foundation. (2016). *Peer counseling in an academic setting*. https://www.whiteswanfoundation.org/education/peer-counselling-in-academic-setting

White, J. M., Li, S., Ashby, C. E., Ferri, B., Wang, Q., Bern, P., & Cosier, M. (2019). Same as it ever was: The nexus of race, ability, and place in one urban school district. *Educational Studies*, *55*(4), 453–472. doi:10.1080/00131946.2019.1630130

White, T. (2016). Teach for America's paradoxical diversity initiative: Race, policy, and Black teacher displacement in urban schools. *Education Policy Analysis Archives*, *24*(16), 16. Advance online publication. doi:10.14507/epaa.24.2100

Whitford, D. K., Gage, N. A., Katsiyannis, A., Counts, J., Rapa, L. J., & McWhorter, A. (2019). The exclusionary discipline of American Indian and Alaska native (AI/an) students with and without disabilities: A civil rights data collection (CRDC) national analysis. *Journal of Child and Family Studies*, *28*(12), 3327–3337. doi:10.100710826-019-01511-8

Whitman, J. (2003). Harsh Justice: Criminal Punishment and the Widening Divide Between America and Europe. Oxford.

Wiatrowski, M. D., Griswold, D. B., & Roberts, M. K. (1981). Social control theory and delinquency. *American Sociological Review*, *46*(5), 525–341. doi:10.2307/2094936

Wildeman, C. (2014). Parental incarceration, child homelessness, and the invisible consequences of mass imprisonment. *The Annals of the American Academy of Political and Social Science*, *651*(1), 74–96. doi:10.1177/0002716213502921

Wildeman, C., Edwards, F. R., & Wakefield, S. (2020). The cumulative prevalence of termination of parental rights for U.S. children 2000 – 2016. *Child Maltreatment*, *25*(1), 32–42. doi:10.1177/1077559519848499 PMID:31113210

Wildeman, C., Scardamalia, K., Walsh, E. G., O'Brien, R. L., & Brew, B. (2017). Paternal incarceration and teachers' expectations of students. *Socius: Sociological Research for a Dynamic World*, *3*, 1–14. doi:10.1177/2378023117726610

Wildeman, C., & Wang, E. (2017). Mass incarceration, public health, and widening inequality in the USA. *Lancet*, *389*, 1464–1474. doi:10.1016/S0140-6736(17)30259-3

Wildeman, C., & Western, B. (2010). Incarceration in fragile families. *The Future of Children*, *20*(2), 157–177. doi:10.1353/foc.2010.0006

Williams, B. (2017). *The Impact on Reunification for Families with Incarcerated Parents: A Policy Analysis of the Adoption and Safe Families Act of 1997*. Available from ProQuest Central. (1964285542). http://nclive.org.ezproxy.nccu.edu/cgi-bin/nclsm?url=http://search.proquest.com.ezproxy.nccu.edu/dissertations-theses/impact-on-reunification-families-with/docview/1964285542/se-2?accountid=12713

Williams, D. R., & Mohammed, S. A. (2008). Discrimination and racial disparities in health: Evidence and needed research. *Journal of Behavioral Medicine*, *32*(1), 20–47. doi:10.100710865-008-9185-0 PMID:19030981

Williams, M. (2020). *Racial trauma: Assessment and treatment techniques for trauma rooted in racism* [Training, PowerPoint slides]. Pesi.

Williams, M. T., Printz, D. M. B., & DeLapp, R. C. T. (2018). Assessing racial trauma with the trauma symptoms of discrimination scale. *Psychology of Violence*, *8*(6), 735–747. Advance online publication. doi:10.1037/vio0000212

Williams-Mbengue, N. (n.d.) *The social and emotional well-being of children in foster care.* National Conference of State Legislatures. Retrieved from: https://www.ncsl.org/Portals/1/Documents/cyf/Social_Emotional_WellBeing_Newsletter.pdf

Williams, R. G., Baker, S. B., & Williams-DeVane, C. R. (2018). Effects of customized Counseling Interventions on Career and College Readiness Self-Efficacy of Three Female Foster Care Youth. *The Professional Counselor*, *8*(2), 159–174. doi:10.15241/rgw.8.2.159

Williams, T. M., Printz, D., Ching, T., & Wetterneck, T. C. (2018). Assessing PTSD in ethnic and racial minorities: Trauma and racial trauma. *Directions in Psychiatry*, *38*(3), 179–196.

Wilson, D. B., Gallagher, C. A., & MacKenzie, D. L. (2000). A meta-analysis of corrections-based education, vocation, and work programs for adult offenders. *Journal of Research in Crime and Delinquency*, *37*(4), 347–368. doi:10.1177/0022427800037004001

Wofford, J., & Ohrt, J. (2018). An integrated approach to counseling children diagnosed with ADHD, ODD, and chronic stressors. *The Family Journal (Alexandria, Va.)*, *26*(1), 105–109. doi:10.1177/1066480718756594

Wolff, N., Aizpurua, E., Caravaca Sanchez, F., & Peng, D. (2020). Childhood abuse classes for incarcerated men and women: Are there unique gender patterns in abuse classes? *Journal of Interpersonal Violence*, *§§§*, 1–29. doi:0.1177/0886260520965974

Wolff, N., Shi, J., & Siegel, J. (2009). Patterns of victimization among male and female inmates: Evidence of an enduring legacy. *Violence and Victims*, *24*(4), 469–484.

Wolf, K. C. (2014). Arrest decision making by school resource officers. *Youth Violence and Juvenile Justice*, *12*(2), 137–151. doi:10.1177/1541204013491294

Wolford, B. I. (2000). Youth education in the juvenile justice system. *Corrections Today*, *62*, 128–130.

Wolpow, R., Johnson, M. M., Hertel, R., & Kincaid, S. (2009). *The heart of learning and teaching: Compassion, resiliency, and academic success*. Office of Superintendent of Public Instruction (OSPI) Compassionate Schools.

Wolpow, R., Johnson, M. M., Hertel, R., & Kincaid, S. (2016). *The heart of learning and teaching: Compassion, resiliency, and academic success*. Office of Superintendent of Public Instruction (OSPI) Compassionate Schools.

Women's Prison Association. (1996). *When a mother is arrested: How the criminal justice and child welfare systems can work together more effectively: A needs assessment initiated by the Maryland department of human resources* (NCJ 174111). U.S. Department of Justice Office of Justice Programs. https://www.ojp.gov/ncjrs/virtual-library/abstracts/when-mother-arrested-how-criminal-justice-and-child-welfare-systems

Wong, C. A., Eccles, J. S., & Sameroff, A. (2003). The influence of ethnic discrimination and ethnic identification on African American adolescents' School and Socioemotional Adjustment. *Journal of Personality*, *71*(6), 1197–1232. doi:10.1111/1467-6494.7106012 PMID:14633063

Woodfield, M. J., & Cartwright, C. (2020). Parent-Child Interaction Therapy from the Parents' Perspective. *Journal of Child and Family Studies*, *29*(3), 632–647. http://dx.doi.org.ezproxy.nccu.edu/10.1007/s10826-019-01611-5. doi:10.100710826-019-01611-5

Workshop, S. (n.d.). *Coping with incarceration*. https://sesamestreetincommunities.org/topics/incarceration/

World Health Organization. (n.d.). *Mental health and prisons*. https://www.who.int/mental_health/policy/mh_in_prison.pdf

World Prison Brief, Institute for Crime & Justice Policy Research. (2020). *Highest to lowest - prison population total*. Highest to Lowest - Prison Population Total | World Prison Brief. https://www.prisonstudies.org/highest-to-lowest/prison-population-total?field_region_taxonomy_tid=All

Wright, M. O. D., & Masten, A. S. (2005). Resilience processes in development. In *Handbook of resilience in children* (pp. 17–37). Springer.

Yavorsky, J. E., Qian, Y., & Sargent, A. C. (2021). The gendered pandemic: The implications of COVID-19 for work and family. *Sociology Compass*, *15*. doi:10.1111oc4.12881

Yi, Y., Edwards, F. R., & Wildeman, C. (2020). Cumulative prevalence of confirmed maltreatment and foster care placements for U.S. children by race/ethnicity, 2011 – 2016. *American Journal of Public Health*, *110*(5), 704–709. doi:10.2105/AJPH.2019.305554 PMID:32191517

Young, D. (2017). *Transforming trauma seeking recovery for those in corrections*. https://www.pacesconnection.com/fileSendAction/fcType/0/fcOid/505446391196077409/filePointer/505446391196077421/fodoid/505446391196077416/Corrections%20Today%20Young%20Transforming%20Trauma%20CCP%20March%20April%202017.pdf

Zabern, A., & Bouteyre, E. (2017). Leading protective factors for children living out of home: A literature review. *Child & Family Social Work*, *23*(2), 324–335. doi-org.proxy.libraries.uc.edu/10.111/cfs.12398

Zakszeski, B. N., Ventresco, N. E., & Jaffe, A. R. (2017). Promoting resilience through trauma-focused practices: A critical review of school-based implementation. *School Mental Health*, *9*(4), 310–321. doi:10.100712310-017-9228-1

Zarse, E. M., Neff, M. R., Yoder, R., Hulvershorn, L., Chambers, J. E., & Chambers, R. A. (2019). The adverse childhood experiences questionnaire: Two decades of research on childhood trauma as a primary cause of adult mental illness, addiction, and medical diseases. *Cogent Medicine*, *6*(1), 1581447. doi:10.1080/2331205X.2019.1581447

Zeng, S., Corr, C. P., O'Grady, C., & Guan, Y. (2019). Adverse childhood experiences and preschool suspension expulsion: A population study. *Child Abuse & Neglect*, *97*, 104–149.

Zhang, Y., Maxwell, C. D., & Vaughn, M. S. (2009). The impact of state sentencing policies on the U.S. prison population. *Journal of Criminal Justice*, *37*(2), 190–199. doi:10.1016/j.jcrimjus.2009.02.012

Zimmerman, P. R., & Flaherty, S. M. (2007). Location monopolies and prison phone rates. *The Quarterly Review of Economics and Finance*, *47*(2), 261–278. doi:10.1016/j.qref.2006.12.002

Zlotnick, C., Tammy, T. W., & Soman, L. A. (2012). Life course outcomes on mental 104 and physical health: The impact of foster care on adulthood. *American Journal of Public Health*, *102*(3), 534–541. doi:10.2105/AJPH.2011.300285 PMID:22390519

About the Contributors

Kenya Johns, LPC, NCC, CAADC, CCTP, ACS, is a well-known advocate and community engager that focuses on creating communities and environments that foster collaboration, strengthens diversity equity and inclusion initiatives and further enhances communication and collaboration across all sectors. Dr. Johns is the current Mayor of the city of Beaver Falls, PA where she is committed to economic growth, communication engagement and sustainable growth. In addition to her current role of Mayor, Dr. Johns currently is a project manager on several concurrent projects, licensed professional counselor, diversity equity and inclusion presenter, national professional presenter, professional consultant, published author, researcher and a full-time faculty member in the Master of Counseling program where she serves as the School Counseling Program Director. In addition to her professional pursuits, Dr. Johns serves on several boards including local and national affiliations and is an avid mentor promoting emotional wellness and educational assistance. Dr. Johns is active in providing pro bono support within communities, schools, non-profits, and the reintegration population. Dr. Johns has been committed to helping create and sustain equitable communities through engagement with various sectors and engagement initiatives.

* * *

Jennifer Barrow is a Licensed Clinical Mental Health Counselor Supervisor, a National Certified Counselor, and veteran professional school counselor. Dr. Barrow serves as Associate Professor in the Department of Counseling and Higher Education at North Carolina Central University, where she directs the School Counseling and Testing Programs. Dr. Barrow's research and practice interests focus on depression, anxiety, counseling children and adolescents, and the enhancement of school counseling, in particular professional development and role advancement.

R. Erin W. Berzins is a licensed mental health counselor and counselor educator. Dr. Berzins has a background working with children of incarcerated parents and has spent most of her clinical counseling career working with children, adolescents, and families.

Hannah Bland is a licensed professional counselor and nationally certified counselor. She is an Assistant Professor in the Clinical Mental Health Counseling program at Spalding University. She is passionate about her teaching and enjoys teaching counselors-in-training. Prior to being an educator, Dr. Bland spent several years working full-time in male correctional settings. There, she provided crisis, assessment, and individual counseling services. She has professional interests in forensic populations, marginalized religious groups, Appalachian culture, and counseling ethics.

My'Kayla Bowser is a Masters student in the Counselor Education and Supervision program at the University of Arkansas. She has a clinical interest in working with incarcerated families.

Corrin N. Brown, Ed.S., is a practicing mental health counselor in pursuit of her LPC-MHSP license with the State of Tennessee. Corrin graduated with her Master of Arts degree in Counseling & Psychology, Clinical Mental Health Counseling from Tennessee Technological University (TTU) in May 2020 and has returned to TTU to complete her Ph.D. in Counseling & Supervision with an expected graduation date of Spring 2024. Research interests include a heavy emphasis on adverse childhood experiences (ACEs), interpersonal trauma, attachment, antisocial behavior, and personality development.

Liliana Burciaga is an assistant professor in the Clinical Mental Health Program at Lewis University with over 15 years of experience in the mental health field. She collaborates and partners with a local school district for trauma-engaged initiatives. Her research interests include trauma, mindfulness, social justice, and parenting. Lili is editorial board member of the International Association for Resilience and Trauma Counseling, Journal for Social Action in Counseling and Psychology, and The Journal of Counseling Research and Practice. She is a member of the Reentry Guide Initiative at the Education Justice Project and Co-Chair of the Counselors for Social Justice membership committee.

Lindsey Donald, BS, MS, is a doctoral student at Mississippi State University. Her research interest includes trauma, substance use, and working with survivors of childhood sexual abuse.

Christina Dukes, M.A., LPC-MHSP, NCC, is currently a second-year doctoral student in the Counseling and Supervision Program at Tennessee Tech University. She is a Licensed Professional Counselor/Mental Health Service Provider in the state of Tennessee and a National Certified Counselor through the National Board for Certified Counselors. She offers a diversity of work experience including her previous work in an adult inpatient acute care facility for the treatment of moderate to severe dual-diagnosis mental health and chemical dependency illnesses. Previous experience also includes providing mental health support to children and parents in support programs for low socioeconomic families and in local school systems. She continues to provide mental health services in her private practice to residents in the Upper Cumberland area. In addition, she volunteers with local, national, and international organizations to increase mental health and equity awareness for underrepresented populations.

Abel Enokela is a doctoral student of Guidance and Counselling Department, Faculty of Education, Ambrose Alli University, Edo State, Nigeria. He is a professional member of the Nigerian Institute of Management, MNIM (chartered); Counselling Association of Nigeria (CASSON); Association of Professional Counsellors in Nigeria (APROCON); and International Society of Policy Research and Evaluation in School-based Counselling (ISPRESC). His research interest focuses on mental health, abnormal psychology, domestic violence, and impacts of digitalization in the educational sector. He is involved in many multidisciplinary and interdisciplinary researches cutting across a wide range of issues. He has published many works on issues of mental health and psychological disruptions both in international and local publications. He has over 20 years of teaching experiences; and has headed international schools where he worked closely with adolescents. The author hopes to finish his PhD program with his external defense soon.

Joy Gray, M.Ed., LPC (PA), NCC, is a licensed professional counselor and doctoral candidate in Counselor Education and Supervision at the Pennsylvania State University, where she previously received a Master of Education in Clinical Rehabilitation and Mental Health Counseling. She has clinical experience as a Mental Health Professional in a School and Community Behavioral Health program as a team supervisor, providing individual and family counseling, case management, consultation, and crisis intervention. As a researcher, clinician, scholar, mentor, and instructor, her focus is on addressing structural inequity, criminalization and pathologization, trauma, and sociocultural factors in mental health and in the mental health field.

Lilia Farmanara Kneidel, Program Specialist for Elementary School Counseling in a large school district in Florida. A Maryland native, Lilia earned her B.S. in Sociology & Anthropology with a concentration in Criminal Justice from Towson University and her Master of Education in School Counseling from Loyola University Maryland. She has experience as a Professional School Counselor in traditional, virtual, and alternative school settings. Before moving to a district-based position, her most recent school counseling position was at a regional juvenile detention center. Dr. Kneidel's professional areas of expertise include counseling LGBTQ+ youth, social-emotional learning, crisis counseling, and trauma informed care.

Katherine M. Hermann-Turner, Ph.D., is an Associate Professor in the Department of Counseling & Psychology at Tennessee Technological University. As a faculty member, Katherine integrates her experiences as a family counselor, mother, and researcher into her courses for masters and doctoral level counseling students. Her current research interests include creativity in counseling, family systems, and the unique roles and stressors on women through a qualitative lenses and Relational Cultural Theory perspective. She is a Nationally Certified Counselor (NCC) and holds a License Professional Counselor – Mental Health Service Provider temporary (LPC-MHSP Temp.) license in Tennessee.

Chiquita Long Holmes, BS, MS, is currently a doctoral student at Mississippi State University pursuing a terminal degree in Counselor Education and Supervision. Chiquita has over 15 years of clinical, supervision, and administrative expertise in mental health. She has worked in several settings including inpatient/outpatient mental health, crisis intervention, trauma, and substance disorders. She also has instructional experience in clinical supervision, crisis intervention, multicultural counseling, and group facilitation. She is a member of several professional organizations and serves as Treasurer for Counselors for Social Justice and President of the Mississippi State University Student Chapter of Counselors for Social Justice.

Jessica Howland became a special education teacher in 1999. She taught in out of district schools and then moved to Plumsted Township School District. There, Dr. Howland became the Director of Special Services until 2019, when she accepted her current Director position with Freehold Regional High School District. Dr. Howland earned her Bachelors from Rutgers University, her Masters in Special Education from The College of New Jersey, and then returned to Rutgers earning her doctorate in Educational Administration and Supervision in 2014 and becoming the recipient of the Angelo L. Tomaso award for Excellence in Dissertation in 2015.

Pao-Yin Huang received her M.Ed. in Counseling and Counselor Education from the Pennsylvania State University. Pao-Yin is a current student at the University of Florida in her Ph.D. in Counseling and Counselor Education program. Pao-Yin has a diverse set of experiences including obtaining clinical experiences from working in an international school in Taiwan, a public middle school, the Herr clinic at PSU, and the Counseling and Wellness Center at the University of Florida in the USA. Research-wise, she has done studies on power issues within intimate partner violence, bias-based bullying in school, ACEs, using IAT to measure people's attitude towards social justice, social justice, and multicultural issues in Taiwanese counselor education. All these studies go along with her research interest in social justice, multicultural counseling, counselor education, gender and power issues, supervision, and issues related to international students. It is her dream and calling to stand with marginalized populations and advocate for a better future.

Stephanie Karlosky, M.A., LPC-MHSP-QS, is a Licensed Professional Counselor with the State of Tennessee and has the following designations: Approved Supervisor and Mental Health Service Provider. She has numerous experiences working with the public in community mental health agencies, universities, and in private clinical settings. Ms. Karlosky is actively engaged in the advancement of the counseling profession and has presented at national and world conferences on topics related to counseling practice, identity, and mentorship. In addition to these, Ms. Karlosky is currently a second-year doctoral student in the Counseling and Supervision Program at Tennessee Tech University. Her research interests include trauma, addiction, and neuroscience.

Tremaine N. Leslie is an Assistant professor of Counseling in the College of Professional Studies and Advancement at the National Louis University, Tampa campus. Her clinical work is focused on reducing stereotypes concerning mental health care and help seeking in minority populations, especially people of African descent. Multiculturalism forms the underpinning of her work and her scholarship is focused on the impact of incarceration on African American families, neuroscience informed counseling, and multicultural counseling supervision.

Tinmuk Li, BA, MA, is currently a dually enrolled Ph.D. student at Mississippi State University pursuing a terminal degree in Counselor Education and Supervision. Her research interests include diversity, spirituality, trauma, underserved populations, and social justice. She is a member of several professional organizations.

Sarah Littlebear, PhD, LPC, CPCS is counseling faculty at the University of the Cumberlands. She completed her PhD in Counselor Education at Auburn University and master's at Columbus State University. Dr. Littlebear has provided counseling to the criminal justice population and their families for years. She has presented on and is passionate about cultural competency in working with those who have a criminal background. Dr. Littlebear practices in Georgia.

E. Joan Looby, Ph.D., LPC, NCC, ACS, is a Professor of Counseling and Graduate and Program Coordinator of the clinical mental health counseling program in the Department of Counseling, Educational Psychology and Foundations at Mississippi State University. She also served as Assistant Dean in the College of Education. Dr. Looby's publication record includes a textbook on multicultural counseling, articles in refereed journals, book chapters, research reports training manuals, and conference proceedings. She has numerous international, national, state, and local presentations. Her research interests include diversity, eating disorders, spirituality, trauma, and sexual abuse. She has served on several editorial boards including Counseling and Values, Journal of Counseling and Development, Journal of Humanistic Education and Development and Counselor Education and Supervision, and is a member of several divisions of ACA.

Jordan McCoy is a current doctoral student in the Counselor Education & Supervision program. She received her master's degree in mental health counseling from the University of Cincinnati. She is originally from the Chicagoland area but has lived in Cincinnati/ NKY for 4 years. Previous clinical settings include agencies, jails, halfway houses and private practices. She has conducted assessments and provided individual and group counseling throughout her clinical tenure. She has worked with clients surrounding addiction, jail/prison-based issues and adjustment, anger management, diversion programs and others. Her research interest includes inmate and offender populations struggling with mental health and recidivism, substance abuse and suicide awareness and prevention.

Tony Michael is an Associate Professor of Counseling and Psychology at Tennessee Tech University. His research areas include attachment, Adverse Childhood Experiences, pedagogic theory, and mental health counseling. Dr. Michael is a Licensed Professional Counselor-Mental Health Service Provider, Registered Play Therapist-Supervisor, National Certified Counselor, and Approved Clinical Supervisor.

Tricia M. Mikolon, PhD, CRC, LPC, BC-TMH, earned her PhD in Counselor Education and Supervision from Regent University. Her Master's degree is in Rehabilitation Counseling from the University of Scranton, and her Bachelor of Science degree is in Psychology from Elizabethtown College. She is a Certified Rehabilitation Counselor and holds an LPC in Pennsylvania and is a Board Certified Telebehavioral Health Provider. Dr. Mikolon's interests include correctional fatigue, the impact of self-definition and coping skills on holistic recovery, and the use of art therapy techniques in counseling. She is employed in the Counseling Department at the University of the Cumberlands as an assistant professor and a contribution faculty member at Walden University and The Chicago School of Professional Psychology and has been on numerous dissertation committees. Additionally, she retired from the Pennsylvania Department of Corrections as a Psychological Services Specialist after 20 years. While there she served on the Critical Incident Stress Management Team (CISM) and provided instruction to staff on various training topics including mental health issues, suicide prevention, reinforcing positive behaviors and cognitive behavioral interventions on both the student and instructor training levels. She has authored works on rehabilitation counseling, online counseling and supervision, online education, multicultural and social justice considerations for telebehavioral health, the dissertation process, and corrections fatigue and has presented on the topics of corrections fatigue, motivational interviewing, gatekeeping in graduate admissions, self-care and supervision, and co-occurring disorders. She is an active member of Chi Sigma Iota, the American Counseling Association, and Psi Chi.

Debra Perez has been treating trauma in minority populations and rural communities in New Mexico as a licensed counselor for over 18 years. She began her career at a community mental health agency working with children through adults, utilizing community supports to assist clients on their path to wellness, self-acceptance, and healing. She then worked in a day treatment program with adolescents transitioning out of treatment foster care or residential treatment, and reintegrating back into their families and navigating probation and the juvenile judicial system. She then opened her own private practice, serving children, teens, adults, and seniors, providing individual, family, and couples therapy. She now provides telebehavioral health services online in a private practice serving rural New Mexico. Dr. Perez is a Board Certified Telebehavioral Health Provider, level two, and holds a special credential in problem gambling treatment and a certification in aromatherapy. She is a coeditor on a telebehavioral health book for counselors and has written chapters on working with children of same gendered parents and transitioning classrooms to the online platform. Dr. Perez is Core Faculty at Liberty University and serves on NM Counselors for Advocacy and Social Justice as president-elect and on the Diversity, Equity, Inclusion, and Social Justice Committee for the International Association of Resiliency and Trauma Counseling.

Sara Pickett is a doctoral candidate at the University of Cincinnati in the Counselor Education and Supervision program. She has a MA in Interdisciplinary Studies from New York University and a M.Ed. in Mental Health Counseling from the University of Louisville. She has worked as an adjunct instructor in psychology for several semesters and a mental health counselor since 2014. In terms of clinical settings, she previously worked with teenage boys in a residential facility, folks in recovery from opioids and other drugs, children with acute mental health struggles, and currently adults struggling with depression and anxiety frequently related to COVID- 19. Her research is mainly focused on incarceration and mental health, and her dissertation will include an original qualitative research study which examines how long-term committed relationship are potentially a mediating factor in the development of mental health symptoms while the male was incarcerated and has since been released.

Erin Kern Popejoy is an Associate Professor with the Counselor Education and Supervision program at the University of Arkansas. She has research and clinical expertise in trauma and attachment.

Erin Sappio, PhD, NCSP, is an Assistant Professor of Counseling at Stockton University, in New Jersey, USA. She received her PhD in School Psychology from Temple University and is a Nationally Certified School Psychologist and NJ Licensed Psychologist. She teaches courses in the Counseling program on Legal and Ethical Issues, Theories of Counseling, Assessment, and Research Methodology. She has an extensive background in cognitive behavior therapy, applied positive psychology, and mindful meditation. Dr. Sappio has a small private practice in New Jersey assisting clients through feelings of anxiety and depression and helping to elevate them to a higher level of personal flourishing.

Tabitha Schlatter, Ed.S., LPC-MHSP, PSC, is currently a second-year doctoral student in the Counseling and Supervision Program at Tennessee Tech University. She has been a licensed professional counselor with mental health service provider designation since 2015 and a licensed professional school counselor since 1995. She has served schools and their stakeholders as a school counselor in Kentucky and in Tennessee. She has completed first-level training in EMDR for treatment of trauma and is currently working toward the next level of EMDIRA Certification. She operates a private clinical practice and has experience as a staff therapist for an acute dual diagnosis inpatient setting as well as a behavioral health consultant in a family medical practice. She provided volunteer services for a three-year term to launch a faith-based recovery program, trained group facilitators serving in the program, and provided mental health consultation. She has engaged in advocacy since 2018 for professional counselors in the Upper Cumberland region as a Regional Representative with the TLPCA.

Valandra is associate professor with a joint appointment in the School of Social Work and the African & African American Studies program at the University of Arkansas. Her scholarship focus is on community engagement and the life experiences of African American families with intergenerational resilience, risks, and trauma related to sex trafficking, interpersonal violence, mass incarceration, and intersectional racism.

Regina Gavin Williams, Ph.D., NCC, LCMHC is an Assistant Professor in the Department of Counseling and Higher Education at North Carolina Central University. She is a foster youth advocate with research focusing on the adult self-sufficiency and college and career readiness of adolescents aging out of the foster care system, and support for foster caregivers. Dr. Williams' practice and research interests also focus on assisting adolescents with post-secondary education and career decision-making. Her teaching interests include career counseling, multicultural and gender issues in counseling, and supervised practicum in counseling.

Index

T

U

V

W

Y

Z

www.ingramcontent.com/pod-product-compliance
Lightning Source LLC
LaVergne TN
LVHW080535300926
849162LV00007B/1612
* 9 7 8 1 7 9 9 8 9 2 0 9 0 *